PERENNIAL PHILOSOPHICAL ISSUES

Edited by

VICTOR GRASSIAN

Harbor College
Wilmington, California

. . . all our dignity lies in thought.
Let us strive, then, to think well.
Pascal

PRENTICE-HALL, INC., Englewood Cliffs, New Jersey 07632

Library of Congress Cataloging in Publication Data
Main entry under title:

Perennial philosophical issues.

Includes bibliographies and index.
1. Philosophy—Addresses, essays, lectures.
2. Religion—Philosophy—Addresses, essays, lectures.
3. Ethics—Addresses, essays, lectures. I. Grassian, Victor.
BD41.P34 1984 100 83-16019
ISBN 0-13-656769-X

Editorial/production supervision and interior design: F. Hubert
Cover design: Wanda Lubelska
Manufacturing buyer: Harry P. Baisley

TO ESTHER, DAVID, AND DANIEL,
WHO SUFFERED THE INATTENTIVENESS OF THE AUTHOR
AS HE WORKED AWAY AT THIS MANUSCRIPT. AS ALWAYS, THEIR
LOVE SUSTAINED ME WHEN MY WORK COULD NOT.

Printed in the United States of America

10 9 8 7 6 5 4 3 2 1

ISBN 0-13-656769-X

PRENTICE-HALL INTERNATIONAL, INC., *London*
PRENTICE-HALL OF AUSTRALIA PTY. LIMITED, *Sydney*
EDITORA PRENTICE-HALL DO BRASIL, LTDA., *Rio de Janeiro*
PRENTICE-HALL CANADA INC., *Toronto*
PRENTICE-HALL OF INDIA PRIVATE LIMITED, *New Delhi*
PRENTICE-HALL OF JAPAN, INC., *Tokyo*
PRENTICE-HALL OF SOUTHEAST ASIA PTE. LTD., *Singapore*
WHITEHALL BOOKS LIMITED, *Wellington, New Zealand*

CONTENTS

Other Grounds for God's Existence

The Problem of Evil

Faith

Religion Without God (Humanistic Religion)

Chapter III THE MIND-BODY RELATIONSHIP, PERSONAL IDENTITY, AND THE AFTERLIFE 167

The Afterlife

The Concept of the Self and Personal Identity

The Mind-Body Relationship

Chapter VI DETERMINISM, FREE WILL, AND MORAL RESPONSIBILITY 416

Chapter VII POLITICAL PHILOSOPHY: GOVERNMENTAL AUTHORITY AND INDIVIDUAL AUTONOMY 471

PREFACE

In preparing this anthology, I have attempted to compile a selection of philosophical readings which will be stimulating to the beginning student with relatively undeveloped analytic skills, without being superficial to the more sophisticated reader who is at home in abstract thought. In attempting to lead students into an appreciation of philosophy, I have drawn upon the philosophical writings of nonphilosophers, writings which demonstrate how traditional philosophical issues grow out of the concerns we all have as human beings and the concerns of specialized fields of study. My hope is that these selections, as well as my own editorial contributions, will help dispel the common notion that the dialectic of philosophy is nothing more than an interminable verbal chess game that has nothing of value to offer to nonphilosophers.

In addition to my desire to encourage students of varying academic interests to see that "philosophy matters" and to *feel* the perplexity that often is a precursor to philosophical reflection, I have attempted to choose readings which will draw students themselves into the process of philosophical reflection and awaken them to the need to clarify and defend their own fundamental beliefs and general world view. It is my hope that this will in turn engender a more critical general analytic ability.

Although my predominant aim has been to cultivate critical thinking in beginning students, I have tried to present philosophical issues in their complexity, without sacrificing accuracy and philosophical sophistication for readability and wider access, as anthologies that stress relevance often do. If one believes, as I firmly do, that the main purpose of introducing students to philosophy is to encourage them to *think philosophically*—that is, deeply and rationally—about issues, it is essential that competing arguments and points of view on a given issue be presented so that students can get a sense of the considerations that make various philosophical positions attractive and, in the process, jar themselves from a complacent acceptance of their own underlying beliefs. This requires a depth of treatment lacking in so many of today's introductory philosophy texts that attempt to pique student interest. In addition, such books do not provide the editorial guidance that students need. One cannot realistically hope to make philosophy understandable to beginning college students simply by inserting some contemporary (and often quickly dated) material among the traditional philosophical excerpts. The students for whom these anthologies were intended need editorial guidance in understanding and connecting together the excerpts presented. In particular, all the introductory philosophy anthologies of which I am aware contain excerpts that presuppose an understanding of technical philosophical terms and perspectives that is not provided by the editor.

In order to remedy this deficiency, editors of introductory philosophy anthologies must do several things. First, they need to edit selections, especially the philosophical classics, more extensively to make them more readable and understandable to the philosophical novice. Careful editorial deletions of redundancies and of sections that are either too difficult or presuppose a background knowledge can often be accomplished *without sacrificing the richness of content.* Second, introductory philosophy anthologies require more comprehensive general chapter introductions and more complete introductions to specific selections than are usually provided. The chapter introductions should provide a general map of the philosophical terrain—a sense of the major issues and the relative stances that famous philosophers have taken—which serves to place the selections in some comprehensive perspective. The introductions to specific selections should, in turn, seek to place the writer and point of view expressed within a broader historical and philosophical perspective, while clarifying any technical philosophical terms that are employed. Third, editors of introductory philosophy anthologies should provide exciting, thought-provoking questions at the ends of excerpts that not only tie things together but also help the student reader focus on the weak points of arguments; such questions should encourage awareness of alternative answers and the need for supporting reasons, and should foster a general awareness of what constitutes responsible criticism. Fourth, it is useful that the editor provide relatively long *annotated* bibliographies which discuss the level of difficulty as well as content of further readings for students who are interested in pursuing a topic in greater detail or are interested in a topic not covered in the anthology.

It is with these considerations in mind that I have prepared this anthology, attempting to speak to the beginning student who needs to be enticed into philosophy, while at the same time stimulating the more advanced student who already has an interest and experience in reading abstract philosophy. I have tried to prepare an anthology that philosophy instructors will be neither afraid nor embarassed to use for a class of beginning college students of diverse abilities and interests—an anthology that seeks to make philosophy relevant, without sacrificing the substantial treatment of perennial philosophical issues and the classic readings that introductory philosophy students used to be exposed to when more was expected of them. I hope that the reader finds that the result lives up to the promise.

I am grateful for the helpful comments of Thomas E. Hill, Jr., Herbert Morris, Robert Yost, Kevin Galvin, Lorenz Mundstock, and Howard R. Cell. Charles E. Hornbeck deserves special thanks for his quite helpful detailed suggestions for stylistic improvements of the manuscript throughout the stages of its preparation, as well as for his suggestions as to philosophical substance. Special thanks also to my favorite librarian and most devoted proofreader—my wife, Esther.

Victor Grassian

Chapter I

THE NATURE OF PHILOSOPHY

The philosopher is the spectator of all time and of all existence.

Plato

Philosophy is a battle against the bewitchment of our intelligence by means of language.

Ludwig Wittgenstein

Philosophy is the attempt to understand the nature of the world and our place and destiny in it.

Maurice Cornford

Philosophy is the logic of the sciences.

Rudolf Carnap

We philosophize to attain a conception of the frame of things which shall on the whole be more rational than the somewhat chaotic view which everyone by nature carries about with him under his hat.

William James

Philosophy is the attempt to think clearly and methodically about certain notions (concepts) which are always turning up in our thinking and which seem necessary to our thinking but which the special sciences do not tell us about.

William James

Philosophy is the attempt to see life steadily and see it whole.

Matthew Arnold

There is nothing so strange and so unbelievable that it has not been said by one philosopher or another.

René Descartes

Philosophy . . . is something intermediate between theology and science. Like theology, it consists of speculations on matters as to which definite knowledge has, so far, been unascertainable; but like science, it appeals to human reason rather than to authority, whether that of tradition or revelation. All **definite** *knowledge . . . belongs to science, all* **dogma** *as to what surpasses definite knowledge belongs to theology. But between theology and science there is a No Man's Land, exposed to attack from both sides; this No Man's Land is philosophy. Almost all the questions of most interest to speculative minds are such as science cannot answer, and the confident answers of theologians no* *longer seem so convincing as they did in former centuries. . . . The studying of these questions, if not the answering of them, is the business of philosophy.*

Bertrand Russell

Surely philosophy is no other than sophisticated poetry.

Montaigne

Philosophy begins in wonder.

Aristotle

What is it to be a philospher? Of the varied images that come to mind, perhaps the most common is that of the *deep thinker*. But considering the amount of mental effort required in other fields of study, this appears a bit presumptuous, especially as a description of one's own field of study. At any rate, such an answer invites the further questions, "Think deeply about what?" and "What does one mean by the *depth* of a philosopher's thinking?" The answer to the first question is "most anything" and the answer to the second question brings us right back to the original question, "What is it to be a philosopher?" If we attempt to give a more specific definition of philosophy, such as one of those used to introduce this chapter, we immediately invite controversy, for such definitions reflect debatable viewpoints as to the *proper* or *most important* task of philosophy. Philosophy, you see, is a difficult subject to pin down.

Philosophers disagree sharply, as anyone who takes a philosophy course soon comes to realize. They do not even agree on what makes a question *philosophical*. Disagreement, it would appear, is at the very heart of the enterprise of philosophy. If an issue is described as a philosophical one in a particular field of study, it leads one to expect that the issue is a divisive one concerning some very general or fundamental presupposition of that field of study. It also suggests that the disagreement involves the very standards to be used in judging the adequacy of these presuppositions. When agreement is obtained on these standards, questions that were previously "philosophical" are often chipped away from the domain of philosophy and become part of a new branch of science. Yet it would be a mistake to suggest, as some have, that *all* of philosophy is a tentative, prescientific grappling with issues that ultimately will be resolved through the methods of science, for philosophy includes much more than this.

The word "philosophy" derives from the Greek words "philos" (loving or desiring) and "sophia" (wisdom). Consequently, at its birth in ancient Greece, philosophy was understood to be the love of wisdom, and philosophers were conceived to be the lovers (or seekers) of wisdom. But what is the quest for wisdom? Originally, this quest was understood broadly to include all reasoned attempts to satisfy intellectual curiosity about the world and the place of human beings within it. Today, philosophers distinguish philosophy from science, but this distinction did not exist for the ancient Greeks. The branches of what today would be called science—for example, physics, biology, psychology, anthropology, and sociology—were once part of philosophy. Since the various sciences of today attempt to understand the world and the place of human beings within it, one can no longer equate philosophy with such a broad quest for wisdom. Philosophers even disagree today about the possibility of obtaining a philosophical knowledge that transcends and unifies the knowledge obtainable by the special sciences. For some, the quest for philosophical wisdom is the quest for answers to such questions as "Why is there a physical world?" What is the meaning or purpose of human life?" "What is really right and worth seeking?" Others, who reject the view that philosophy provides a special access to *knowledge* dismiss the preceding questions as meaningless or noncognitive (i.e., incapable of true or false answers) and banish them from the field of *legitimate* philosophy.

Despite such disagreements, all would agree with the American philosopher William James (1842–1910) that philosophy is "an unusually persistent attempt to think things through," in the course of which one comes to grips with concepts and beliefs that underlie our understanding of things. For example, philosophers have come to grips with the meaning and justification of concepts and beliefs presupposed by scientists who work within diverse areas. Among these concepts are those of "cause," "explanation," and "substance." Among these beliefs are the beliefs that every event has a cause and that the laws of nature that operate today will operate tomorrow. Philosophers have also questioned the meanings and justifications of the more specific concepts and beliefs that are fundamental to particular sciences. Such concepts include "unconscious mental events," "self-deception," and "repression," concepts that play an important role in psychoanalysis. Such beliefs include the belief held by many physiologically oriented psychologists that every mental event has a physical cause.

When scientists begin to inquire into the meanings and interrelationships of the basic concepts of their science and the justifications of that science's most fundamental assumptions, they are doing *philosophy* of that science. For example, when psychologists argue over questions like, "Is psychology simply the study of behavior?" and "Can human behavior be adequately understood without inquiring into the structure of the human mind?" they are engaged in philosophy. Practicing psychologists conduct their research within an accepted *theoretical framework* of concepts and beliefs. Such a framework poses the problems, provides the methodology for solving them, and generates expectations about their solutions. If a practicing psychologist stands back from his practice, however, and inquires into the coherence and justifiability of the theoretical framework that it presupposes, he is engaged in the philosophy of psychology.

Nonscientific frameworks of concepts and beliefs can also be subjected to philosophical inquiry. For example, the framework of concepts and beliefs comprised by the Judeo-Christian religious tradition has been examined by philosophers, who ponder such questions as "What does the concept of 'God' mean?" and "Is there any justification for belief in God?" The concepts and beliefs which underlie ordinary thinking, too, can attract the attention of philosophers. They have examined the meanings of such concepts as "physical object," "mind," "freedom," "right," and "good," as well as the justification of common beliefs like:

> Physical objects exist when no one perceives them.
>
> The mind is distinct from the body.
>
> It is possible to conceive of a disembodied life-after-death.
>
> People often act freely and are morally responsible for what they do.
>
> Morality is not simply a matter of taste.

Questioning the meanings and justifications of such beliefs, which form the bedrock of our understanding of the world we inhabit and our place within it, has always been central to philosophy. What unites philosophers is not a particular subject matter or a particular set of shared assumptions, but a persistent inquisitive attitude of mind that probes deeply into the tangle of concepts and assumptions used to make sense of our experience. As the contemporary philosopher Sidney Hook put it, "Philosophy is not so much an activity that offers definite answers to questions as one that questions answers."

Whether philosophers see their task as restricted to the clarification and systematization of concepts and beliefs that underlie established ways of organizing our experience or see their task more ambitiously as one of providing a new and more coherent way of looking at things, they will always attempt to *justify* the positions they take. Such justification cannot be tested by experiment, but, like justification in mathematics, only by reasoning. Like a student attempting to solve a geometry problem, the philosopher typically has all the information needed; the task is rather one of *grasping* and *demonstrating* the logical interrelationships of the information. Accordingly, *logic*—the study of the principles and methods for distinguishing correct from incorrect reasoning—is such an essential tool of philosophy and is usually taught in philosophy departments. Not satisfied simply to be right, philosophers want to have *grounds* for being right.

Philosophy often begins in perplexity. As the philosopher Ludwig Wittgenstein (1889–1951) put it, "a philosophical problem typically gives us the impression that, though we know all that might be relevent to it, yet we cannot see clearly. We see all the pieces of a puzzle, but not how they fit together." This perplexity takes many forms. First, there is perplexity over the meaning of a word commonly used. For example, what does "love" mean? How does *loving* someone differ from *liking* him? Indeed, what does it mean to *like* someone? Does it mean to be concerned about him? But is it not possible for a benevolent person to be concerned about the welfare of those whom he does not like? Or does it mean to enjoy being in that person's presence? But is it not possible to like someone and be uncomfortable around him? . . . When we begin to think like this, we are in the grips of a very common type of philosophical perplexity. On the one hand, we believe that we must understand what a concept means since we use it so readily. Yet, we find the concept slipping through our fingers when we try to define it in relation to other concepts. Indeed, as in defining "love," our initial puzzlement over the meaning of a particular concept easily can become a broader puzzlement that encompasses a whole range of interrelated concepts.

Second, there is the common type of puzzlement that comes when deeply held beliefs appear to clash. Many philosophical problems have their roots in this type of puzzlement. For example, science appears to assume that every event is *caused* by some preceding event, that is, that every event is *determined.* From the viewpoint of science, this seems to be true of human behavior, thought, and feeling, no less than it is of other events. But then how can human beings rightly be said to act *freely* or to be *morally responsible* for what they do? If determinism is true, is it not inevitable that people behave as they do? And so is not free will an illusion? So is born the traditional philosophical problem of *free will and determinism.*

The clash of beliefs about the God of the Judeo-Christian tradition also generates puzzles. If God is all-powerful, all-knowing, and all-good, why is there so much undeserved suffering in this world? After all, if God is all-knowing and all-powerful, he must know that such suffering exists and must have the power to prevent it. But if he is all-good, he must disapprove of such suffering. Why then does he allow it? So is born the traditional *problem of evil,* which has puzzled both believers and nonbelievers in the God of the Judeo-Christian tradition.

The relationship of mind and body also generates deep puzzles. For the physiologist, all changes in the human body are due to previous physical changes. But this seems to conflict with the commonsense belief that our nonphysical thoughts and feelings can affect our body. Is this an illusion? How are we to understand the relationship of mind to body? What indeed do we mean by these terms? So is born the traditional *mind-body problem.*

In attempting to think such puzzles through, philosophers come to grips with our most basic ways of organizing experience. In order to make rational sense of the concepts and beliefs that underlie our understanding of things, they *analyze* these concepts and beliefs into their components to see if they can withstand rational scrutiny. This analytic spirit, which has always permeated philosophy, is best exemplified by the ancient Greek philosopher Socrates, who persistently analyzed the beliefs of his contemporaries. In the process, he challenged their complacent acceptance of the very foundations of their beliefs.

All great philosophers analyze concepts and beliefs. But *speculative* philosophers attempt much more. They attempt to construct a *world view*, a comprehensive picture of the whole of reality which allows the universe to be seen as a unified whole. In constructing world views, philosophers come to grips with fundamental philosophical questions relating to the nature and interrelationships of what "ultimately exists in reality," which is the concern of that branch of philosophy known as *metaphysics*. In arguing for their metaphysical answers, they come to grips with the nature, sources, and limits of knowledge, which is the concern of that branch of philosophy known as *epistemology* or *theory of knowledge*. In addition, they provide some general and comprehensive theory of the nature of the good life and of right conduct, which is the concern of that branch of philosophy known as *ethics*. For many people, this type of *systematic* or *speculative* thought *is* philosophy, and it is such philosophy that they associate with philosophical wisdom. This was the view of the speculative philosopher Alfred North Whitehead (1861–1947), who said "philosophy asks the simple question: What's it all about?"

Eventually all thinking people pose this very broad question to themselves and arrive at some world view, however tentative, unrefined, and uncertain. In the words of William James:

> The philosophy which is so important to each of us is not a technical matter; it is our more or less dumb sense of what life honestly and deeply means. It is only partly got from books; it is our individual way of just seeing and feeling the total push and pressure of the cosmos.

While the world views of most people are, as James claimed, more a matter of feeling than of thought (and, for that reason, one may refuse to follow James in calling them *philosophies*), philosophers do not present world views to be accepted or rejected according to individual temperament. Instead, they give arguments to rationally justify their world views. Still, the ultimate positions they arrive at, however more comprehensive and rationally coherent and defensible, are often comparable to the world views of nonphilosophers.

Philosophers, no less than others, differ in their beliefs as to whether or not there is a *supernatural* infinite and transcendent God who provides an ultimate explanation for the existence of the natural world and the place and purpose of human beings within it. *Theists* accept such an explanation, while *naturalists* reject it, often claiming that every aspect of the natural world, including human experiences, can be explained only through the methods of science and that human life has no other purpose than the purpose human beings *choose* to give it. Naturalists disagree, however, as to whether one can find adequate *meaning* for human life within a godless universe. Some, like the twentieth-century French philosophers Sartre and Camus, bemoan the meaninglessness of human life in a godless universe, but others accept a more optimistic viewpoint. Philosophers, just like other people, also disagree as to whether "mind" or "matter" is the most "fundamental stuff in the scheme of things." *Materialists* take matter as primary, while *idealists* take mind. The disagreement between naturalists and supernaturalists, such as theists, and the disagreement between materialists and idealists are perennial philosophical ones. In addition to such basic metaphysical disagreements, philosophers, no less than others, have disagreed as to whether morality depends entirely upon our desires or whether "objective reason" or some "intuitive insight," independent of subjective and variable human desires, enables us to discern what is right and good. This issue, too, is a perennial philosophical one, as is the issue of the grounds and limits of an individual's obligation to submit himself to some political authority.

From the 1930's through the 1950's, most English-speaking philosophers turned away from the construction of comprehensive world views and the apparently irresolvable disagreements they generate. Indeed, many of them dismissed some of the perennial concerns of systematic philosophers as "pseudoproblems" that were devoid of sense. Today, an increasing number of philosophers are turning their attention again to the formulation of some comprehensive world view and to the perennial philosophical questions such world views generate, but the present philosophical climate in the English-speaking world is still predominantly analytic and nonsystematic. The persistent message of Anglo-American philosophy in the twentieth century, a century which has aptly been described as "the age of analysis," is that philosophers' speculative reach should not exceed their analytic grasp. Aware of the lack of both clarity and justification of much previous speculative philosophy whose pretensions to "final truth" have slowly given way to the experimental and tentative methods of science, contemporary Anglo-American philosophers have largely confined their efforts to clarifying and criticizing particular narrowly defined issues. But the speculative impulse is too strong to be totally repressed. While the questioning and clarifying impulse of the analytic philosopher will always be central to philosophy, so too will be the unifying and visionary impulse of the systematic philosopher. The pendulum of prevailing philosophical interest perpetually moves between these two philosophical impulses.

1. PHILOSOPHY AND THE CRITIQUE OF COMMON SENSE

Bertrand Russell

BERTRAND RUSSELL (1872–1970) was the most widely known and one of the most influential of English-speaking twentieth-century philosophers. During his long life, Russell wrote prolifically on practically all the major areas of philosophy. Though as a young man his interests were primarily in logic, the foundations of mathematics, metaphysics, and epistemology, as he grew older he turned his attention more and more to practical questions of ethics and social philosophy. Unlike the popular image of the philosopher, Russell was quite concerned with controversial practical issues that generate popular debate. His clear, nontechnical, and witty writing style appealed to a very wide audience and earned him the Nobel Prize for literature in 1950. He was bitterly denounced by many for his unpopular positions, such as his advocacy of pacifism during World War I, his permissive beliefs about sexual morality before such beliefs were in vogue, and his outspoken criticisms of religion. In 1940, Russell was invited to lecture on logic and the philosophy of science at the City College of New York, but his appointment was judicially annulled on the grounds that he was likely to undermine the morals of his students. During the last years of his life, Russell was an outspoken critic of nuclear arms and American involvement in the Vietnam war.

The following excerpt comes from Russell's **The Problems of Philosophy** (1912), an introduction to some of the central problems of philosophy directed to beginners in philosophy. In the first part of this excerpt, Russell presents a view of philosophy as critical analysis. He points out that many common-sense beliefs turn out on deeper and more careful scrutiny to be not nearly so clear or obvious as most people think. As an example, Russell turns to common-sense beliefs concerning the nature of perception and thus introduces the traditional philosophical problem of distinguishing "appearance" from "reality." (We shall take up this problem in Chapter IV.) He challenges the tendency to accept the testimony of the senses by pointing out how colors, textures, shapes, and other properties of physical objects vary and depend upon the perspective of the perceiver. How, then, do we know which of an object's many conflicting appearances are its "real" properties? Indeed, how do we know that what we perceive is at all like these "real" properties? Finally, how do we even know there is a world of physical objects that exists independently of our minds?

While Russell claims that "the essential characteristic of philosophy . . . is criticism . . . of the principles employed in science and daily life," he goes on to claim that there is also a legitimate systematic and speculative element in philosophy. First, he sees philosophy as systematic in its attempt to give "unity and system" to the knowledge obtained through the diverse sciences. From this perspective, philosophy can be viewed as an attempt "to see the world as a whole." Second, he stresses the intellectually and emotionally liberating ability of speculative philosophy to open our minds to alternatives which mundane common sense conceals from us. Connected with this ability, Russell claims, is philosophy's concern with questions that are either permanently or temporarily incapable of definite answers. Those questions that are temporarily incapable of definite answer form the prescientific philosophical roots from which the branches of science grow.

Appearance and Reality

Is there any knowledge in the world which is so certain that no reasonable man could doubt it? This question, which at first sight might not seem difficult, is really one of the most difficult that can be asked. When we have realized the obstacles in the way of a straightforward and confident answer, we shall be well launched on the study of philosophy—for philosophy is merely the attempt to answer such ultimate questions, not carelessly and dogmatically, as we do in ordinary life and even in the sciences, but critically, after exploring all that makes such

Source: From *The Problems of Philosophy* by Bertrand Russell (1912), Chapters I, XIV, and XV. Reprinted by permission of Oxford University Press.

questions puzzling, and after realizing all the vagueness and confusion that underlie our ordinary ideas.

In daily life, we assume as certain many things which, on a closer scrutiny, are found to be so full of apparent contradictions that only a great amount of thought enables us to know what it is that we really may believe. In the search for certainty, it is natural to begin with our present experiences, and in some sense, no doubt, knowledge is to be derived from them. But any statement as to what it is that our immediate experiences make us know is very likely to be wrong. It seems to me that I am now sitting in a chair, at a table of a certain shape, on which I see sheets of paper with writing or print. By turning my head I see out of the window buildings and clouds and the sun. I believe that the sun is about ninety-three million miles from the earth; that it is a hot globe many times bigger than the earth; that, owing to the earth's rotation, it rises every morning, and will continue to do so for an indefinite time in the future. I believe that, if any other normal person comes into my room, he will see the same chairs and tables and books and papers as I see, and that the table which I see is the same as the table which I feel pressing against my arm. All this seems to be so evident as to be hardly worth stating, except in answer to a man who doubts whether I know anything. Yet all this may be reasonably doubted, and all of it requires much careful discussion before we can be sure that we have stated it in a form that is wholly true.

To make our difficulties plain, let us concentrate attention on the table. To the eye it is oblong, brown and shiny, to the touch it is smooth and cool and hard; when I tap it, it gives out a wooden sound. Any one else who sees and feels and hears the table will agree with this description, so that it might seem as if no difficulty would arise; but as soon as we try to be more precise our troubles begin. Although I believe that the table is 'really' of the same colour all over, the parts that reflect the light look much brighter than the other parts, and some parts look white because of reflected light. I know that, if I move, the parts that reflect the light will be different, so that the apparent distribution of colours on the table will change. It follows that if several people are looking at the table at the same moment, no two of them will see exactly the same distribution of colours, because no two can see it from exactly the same point of view, and any change in the point of view makes some change in the way the light is reflected. . . .

. . . It is evident . . . that there is no colour which preeminently appears to be *the* colour of the table, or even of any one particular part of the table—it appears to be of different colours from different points of view, and there is no reason for regarding some of these as more really its colour than others. And we know that even from a given point of view the colour will seem different by artificial light, or to a colour-blind man, or to a man wearing blue spectacles, while in the dark there will be no colour at all, though to touch and hearing the table will be unchanged. This colour is not something which is inherent in the table, but something depending upon the table and the spectator and the way the light falls on the table. When, in ordinary life, we speak of *the* colour of the table, we only mean the sort of colour which it will seem to have to a normal spectator from an ordinary point of view under usual conditions of light. But the other colours which appear under other conditions have just as good a right to be considered real; and therefore, to avoid favouritism, we are compelled to deny that, in itself, the table has any one particular colour.

The same thing applies to the texture. With the naked eye one can see the grain, but otherwise the table looks smooth and even. If we looked at it through a microscope, we should see roughnesses and hills and valleys, and all sorts of differences that are imperceptible to the naked eye. Which of these is the 'real' table? We are naturally tempted to say that what we see through the microscope is more real, but that in turn would be changed by a still more powerful microscope. If, then, we cannot trust what we see with the naked eye, why should we trust what we see through a microscope? Thus, again, the confidence in our senses with which we began deserts us.

The *shape* of the table is no better. We are all in the habit of judging as to the 'real' shapes of things, and we do this so unreflectingly that we come to think we actually see the real shapes. But, in fact, as we all have to learn if we try to draw, a given thing looks different in shape from every different point of view. If our table is 'really' rectangular, it will look, from almost all points of view, as if it had two acute angles and two obtuse angles. If opposite sides are parallel, they will look as if they converged to a point away from the spectator; if they are of equal length, they will look as if the nearer side were longer. All these things are not commonly noticed in looking at a table, because experience has taught us to construct the 'real' shape from the apparent shape, and the 'real' shape is what interests us as practical men. But the 'real' shape is not what we see; it is something inferred from what we see. And what we see is constantly changing in shape as we move about the room; so that here again the senses seem not to give us the truth about the table itself, but only about the appearance of the table.

Similar difficulties arise when we consider the sense of touch. It is true that the table always gives us a sensation of hardness, and we feel that it resists pressure. But the sensation we obtain depends upon how hard we press the table and also upon what part of the body we press with; thus the various sensations due to various pressures or various parts of the body cannot be supposed to reveal *directly* any definite property of the table, but at most to be *signs* of some property which perhaps *causes* all the sensations, but is not actually apparent in any of them. And the same applies still more obviously to the sounds which can be elicited by rapping the table.

Thus it becomes evident that the real table, if there is one, is not the same as what we immediately experience by sight or touch or hearing. The real table, if there is one, is not *immediately* known to us at all, but must be an inference from what is immediately known. . . .

Before we go further it will be well to consider for a moment what it is that we have discovered so far. It has appeared that, if we take any common object of the sort that is supposed to be known by the senses, what the senses *immediately* tell us is not the truth about the object as it is apart from us, but only the truth about certain sense-data[1] which, so far as we can see, depend upon the relations between us and the object. Thus what we directly see and feel is merely 'appearance', which we believe to be a sign of some 'reality' behind. But if the reality is not what appears, have we any means of knowing whether there is any reality at all? And if so, have we any means of finding out what it is like?

Such questions are bewildering, and it is difficult to know that even the strangest hypotheses may not be true. Thus our familiar table, which has roused but the slightest thoughts in us hitherto, has become a problem full of surprising possibilities. The one thing we know about it is that it is not what it seems. Beyond this modest result, so far, we have the most complete liberty of conjecture. Leibniz tells us it is a community of souls: Berkeley tells us it is an idea in the mind of God; sober science, scarcely less wonderful, tells us it is a vast collection of electric charges in violent motion.

Among these surprising possibilities, doubt suggests that perhaps there is no table at all. Philosophy, if it cannot *answer* so many ques-

[1]That is, sense impressions. EDITOR'S NOTE.

tions as we could wish, has at least the power of *asking* questions which increase the interest of the world, and show the strangeness and wonder lying just below the surface even in the commonest things of daily life. . . .

Philosophy as Criticism

. . . The essential characteristic of philosophy, which makes it a study distinct from science, is *criticism*. It examines critically the principles employed in science and in daily life; it searches out any inconsistencies there may be in these principles, and it only accepts them when, as the result of a critical inquiry, no reason for rejecting them has appeared. . . .

When, however, we speak of philosophy as a *criticism* of knowledge, it is necessary to impose a certain limitation. If we adopt the attitude of the complete sceptic, placing ourselves wholly outside all knowledge, and asking, from this outside position, to be compelled to return within the circle of knowledge, we are demanding what is impossible, and our scepticism can never be refuted. For all refutation must begin with some piece of knowledge which the disputants share; from blank doubt, no argument can begin. Hence the criticism of knowledge which philosophy employs must not be of this destructive kind, if any result is to be achieved. Against this absolute scepticism, no *logical* argument can be advanced. But it is not difficult to see that scepticism of this kind is unreasonable. Descartes' 'methodical doubt', with which modern philosophy began, is not of this kind, but is rather the kind of criticism which we are asserting to be the essence of philosophy. His 'methodical doubt' consisted in doubting whatever seemed doubtful; in pausing, with each apparent piece of knowledge, to ask himself whether, on reflection, he could feel certain that he really knew it. This is the kind of criticism which constitutes philosophy. Some knowledge . . . appears quite indubitable, however calmly and thoroughly we reflect upon it. In regard to such knowledge, philosophical criticism does not require that we should abstain from belief. But there are beliefs . . . which are entertained until we begin to reflect, but are found to melt away when subjected to a close inquiry. Such beliefs philosophy will bid us reject, unless some new line of argument is found to support them. But to reject the beliefs which do not appear open to any objections, however closely we examine them, is not reasonable, and is not what philosophy advocates. . . .

The Value of Philosophy

Having now come to the end of our brief and very incomplete review of the problems of philosophy,[2] it will be well to consider, in conclusion, what is the value of philosophy and why it ought to be studied. It is the more necessary to consider this question, in view of the fact that many men, under the influence of science or of practical affairs, are inclined to doubt whether philosophy is anything better than innocent but useless trifling, hair-splitting distinctions, and controversies on matters concerning which knowledge is impossible. . . .

. . . if we are not to fail in our endeavour to determine the value of philosophy, we must first free our minds from the prejudices of what are wrongly called 'practical' men. The 'practical' man, as this word is often used, is one who recognizes only material needs, who realizes that men must have food for the body, but is oblivious of the necessity of providing food for the mind. If all men were well off, if poverty and disease had been reduced to their lowest possible point, there would still remain much to be done to produce a valuable society; and even in the existing world the goods of the mind are

[2]In the book from which this selection is excerpted, Russell restricts his attention to philosophical issues relating to the nature of knowledge and meaning. EDITOR'S NOTE.

at least as important as the goods of the body. It is exclusively among the goods of the mind that the value of philosophy is to be found; and only those who are not indifferent to these goods can be persuaded that the study of philosophy is not a waste of time.

Philosophy, like all other studies, aims primarily at knowledge. The knowledge it aims at is the kind of knowledge which gives unity and system to the body of the sciences, and the kind which results from a critical examination of the grounds of our convictions, prejudices, and beliefs. But it cannot be maintained that philosophy has had any very great measure of success in its attempts to provide definite answers to its questions. If you ask a mathematician, a mineralogist, a historian, or any other man of learning, what definite body of truths has been ascertained by his science, his answer will last as long as you are willing to listen. But if you put the same question to a philosopher, he will, if he is candid, have to confess that his study has not achieved positive results such as have been achieved by other sciences. It is true that this is partly accounted for by the fact that, as soon as definite knowledge concerning any subject becomes possible, this subject ceases to be called philosophy, and becomes a separate science. The whole study of the heavens, which now belongs to astronomy, was once included in philosophy; Newton's great work was called 'the mathematical principles of natural philosophy'. Similarly, the study of the human mind, which was a part of philosophy, has now been separated from philosophy and has become the science of psychology. Thus, to a great extent, the uncertainty of philosophy is more apparent than real: those questions which are already capable of definite answers are placed in the sciences, while those only to which, at present, no definite answer can be given, remain to form the residue which is called philosophy.

This is, however, only a part of the truth concerning the uncertainty of philosophy. There are many questions—and among them those that are of the profoundest interest to our spiritual life—which, so far as we can see, must remain insoluble to the human intellect unless its powers become of quite a different order from what they are now. Has the universe any unity of plan or purpose, or is it a fortuitous concourse of atoms? Is consciousness a permanent part of the universe, giving hope of indefinite growth in wisdom, or is it a transitory accident on a small planet on which life must ultimately become impossible? Are good and evil of importance to the universe or only to man? Such questions are asked by philosophy and variously answered by various philosophers. But it would seem that, whether answers be otherwise discoverable or not, the answers suggested by philosophy are none of them demonstrably true. Yet, however slight may be the hope of discovering an answer, it is part of the business of philosophy to continue the consideration of such questions, to make us aware of their importance, to examine all the approaches to them, and to keep alive that speculative interest in the universe which is apt to be killed by confining ourselves to definitely ascertainable knowledge.

Many philosophers, it is true, have held that philosophy could establish the truth of certain answers to such fundamental questions. They have supposed that what is of most importance in religious beliefs could be proved by strict demonstration to be true. In order to judge of such attempts, it is necessary to take a survey of human knowledge, and to form an opinion as to its methods and its limitations. On such a subject it would be unwise to pronounce dogmatically; but if the investigations of our previous chapters have not led us astray, we shall be compelled to renounce the hope of finding philosophical proofs of religious beliefs. We cannot, therefore, include as part of the value of philosophy any definite set of answers to such questions. Hence, once more, the value of philosophy must not depend upon any supposed body of definitely ascertainable knowledge to be acquired by those who study it.

The value of philosophy is, in fact, to be sought largely in its very uncertainty. The man who has no tincture of philosophy goes through life imprisoned in the prejudices derived from common sense, from the habitual beliefs of his age or his nation, and from convictions which have grown up in his mind without the co-operation or consent of his deliberate reason. To such a man the world tends to become definite, finite, obvious; common objects rouse no questions, and unfamiliar possibilities are contemptuously rejected. As soon as we begin to philosophize, on the contrary, we find, as we saw in our opening chapters, that even the most everyday things lead to problems to which only very incomplete answers can be given. Philosophy, though unable to tell us with certainty what is the true answer to the doubts which it raises, is able to suggest many possibilities which enlarge our thoughts and free them from the tyranny of custom. Thus, while diminishing our feeling of certainty as to what things are, it greatly increases our knowledge as to what they may be; it removes the somewhat arrogant dogmatism of those who have never travelled into the region of liberating doubt, and it keeps alive our sense of wonder by showing familiar things in an unfamiliar aspect.

Apart from its utility in showing unsuspected possibilities, philosophy has a value—perhaps its chief value—through the greatness of the objects which it contemplates, and the freedom from narrow and personal aims resulting from this contemplation. The life of the instinctive man is shut up within the circle of his private interests: family and friends may be included, but the outer world is not regarded except as it may help or hinder what comes within the circle of instinctive wishes. In such a life there is something feverish and confined, in comparison with which the philosophic life is calm and free. The private world of instinctive interests is a small one, set in the midst of a great and powerful world which must, sooner or later, lay our private world in ruins. Unless we can so enlarge our interests as to include the whole outer world, we remain like a garrison in a beleagured fortress, knowing that the enemy prevents escape and that ultimate surrender is inevitable. In such a life there is no peace, but a constant strife between the insistence of desire and the powerlessness of will. In one way or another, if our life is to be great and free we must escape this prison and this strife. . . .

. . . The free intellect will see as God might see, without a *here* and *now,* without hopes and fears, without the trammels of customary beliefs and traditional prejudices, calmly, dispassionately, in the sole and exclusive desire of knowledge—knowledge as impersonal, as purely contemplative, as it is possible for man to attain. Hence also the free intellect will value more the abstract and universal knowledge into which the accidents of private history do not enter, than the knowledge brought by the senses, and dependent, as such knowledge must be, upon an exclusive and personal point of view and a body whose sense-organs distort as much as they reveal.

The mind which has become accustomed to the freedom and impartiality of philosophic contemplation will preserve something of the same freedom and impartiality in the world of action and emotion. It will view its purposes and desires as parts of the whole, with the absence of insistence that results from seeing them as infinitesimal fragments in a world of which all the rest is unaffected by any one man's deeds. The impartiality which, in contemplation, is the unalloyed desire for truth, is the very same quality of mind which, in action, is justice, and in emotion is that universal love which can be given to all, and not only to those who are judged useful or admirable. Thus contemplation enlarges not only the objects of our thoughts, but also the objects of our actions and our affections: it makes us citizens of the universe, not only of one walled city at war with all the rest. In this citizenship of the universe consists man's true freedom, and his liberation from the thraldom of narrow hopes and fears.

Thus, to sum up our discussion of the value

of philosophy; Philosophy is to be studied, not for the sake of any definite answers to its questions, since no definite answers can, as a rule, be known to be true, but rather for the sake of the questions themselves; because these questions enlarge our conception of what is possible, enrich our intellectual imagination and diminish the dogmatic assurance which closes the mind against speculation; but above all because, through the greatness of the universe which philosophy contemplates, the mind also is rendered great, and becomes capable of that union with the universe which constitutes its highest good.

2. PHILOSOPHY AND ARGUMENT

Baruch Brody

BARUCH BRODY (1943–) received his Ph.D. in philosophy from Princeton University and is presently Chair of the Philosophy Department at Rice University (Houston), having taught previously at M.I.T. His main philosophical interests are ethics, legal philosophy, and the philosophy of religion. The following excerpt comes from Brody's introduction to his text **Beginning Philosophy**. In this introduction, Brody, like Russell, focuses on the analytic or critical function of philosophy. Unlike Russell, however, and like most of today's well-known English-speaking philosophers, Brody's approach to philosophy is purely analytic and nonspeculative. As Brody sees it, philosophical questions are generated when people, having become troubled over the foundations of whole spheres of knowledge or of human life, subject these foundations to rational scrutiny. He stresses that philosophers defend the positions they ultimately arrive at by appealing to arguments. Reflecting the central role of the careful logical analysis of arguments in contemporary Anglo-American philosophy, Brody presents a useful introduction to the nature and analysis of arguments.

The Nature of Philosophical Problems

Think of the community where you grew up. Let us suppose that it was relatively homogeneous. Most of the people in such a community share certain basic beliefs about the values one ought to be pursuing in life and about the ways to pursue those values. No one lives his or her life entirely by those views (people are, after all, only human). But most of the people at least make some effort to do so. As a young person, you too are trained in those views, and you still find them attractive in many ways. Now suppose that you have recently come to wonder about these views. Perhaps you encountered people who hold very different beliefs about the values you ought to pursue in life. Or perhaps you have recently encountered new situations, ones in which you felt uncomfortable following the views you grew up with.

Many young people have had this experience, in previous times and in our own. And often the experience has led them to ask difficult questions like these: What really is the difference between right and wrong? How can I tell

Source: Baruch A. Brody, *Beginning Philosophy*, © 1977, pp. 1–9. Reprinted by permission of Prentice-Hall, Inc., Englewood Cliffs, N.J.

the difference between the two? Will I gain or lose in life if I stick to trying to do what is right? When people ask such questions, they are asking philosophical questions. . . . They form the subject matter of that part of philosophy which is called ethics.

Every society has its own pattern of social organization. But, in these many different patterns, there are certain common features. For example, in any given society, the various goods are always distributed unequally. Some people have a lot more of what is thought of as desirable (wealth, power, prestige, leisure, etc.) than others. This pattern is normally accepted by all involved; it seems to them to be the natural way for things to be organized. But there are special situations in which this pattern comes to be challenged, either by those who have received less than what they consider to be their fair share and who want more or by those who have received more than they consider their fair share and who feel troubled about it. At such times, it is not unusual for people to consider such questions as: Should there be differentiations between people? If there should, which ones are just and which ones are unjust? At such times, people often recognize that the current legal system is devoted to protecting the interests of those who received the greatest gains. This leads them to ask still further questions like: Do I really have any obligation to obey the law? If I do, may I violate that obligation in the attempt to change the social order?

When people start asking questions like this, they are also asking philosophical questions. These questions form the subject matter of a second major area of philosophy: social and political philosophy. . . .

Most people are brought up with beliefs about religious questions. In some cases, the beliefs taught are very extensive and call upon the believer to engage in a wide variety of religious practices. In other cases, the beliefs are far less extensive and seem to require very little by way of religious practices. Some people are brought up with antireligious beliefs. However it is rare to find someone whose upbringing has had nothing at all to say about religion.

In earlier times, people in a given society usually shared the same religion. But, of course, our society is not homogeneous in that way. From early youth, we know of the wide variety of religious beliefs and practices that are common in our home communities, and as we grow older we encounter still other forms of belief and practice. Moreover, we encounter ways of thinking about the world—most notably the scientific standpoint—which leave out the religious element altogether. All of this leads us to wonder about our religious heritage. It is natural, then, for a person to ask such questions as: Is there any rational basis for holding my religious beliefs, or, for that matter, for holding any religious beliefs? If not, what should one believe about religion? What difference should religion make in life?

These questions are also philosophical questions, and they form the subject matter of a third part of philosophy: philosophy of religion. . . .

Few things concern people more than the attempt to make sense of themselves and their fellow human beings. We have a sense of ourselves as being somehow special, and yet we know at the same time that we are, in many ways, just another part of the natural order surrounding us. One of the classic attempts to make sense of the duality of human nature claims that human beings are composed of two parts. One is a material object like all others. This is our body. The other is a nonmaterial substance. This is our soul. The soul is what truly makes us special. It differs from objects of the material world in that at least some of its actions are free. And it is the possibility of its survival that holds out the hope that we may survive the death of our material body.

This traditional picture of man has come under renewed challenge in recent years. There has been a revitalization of an alternative view of man, one that places man squarely in the material realm. This seems in any case to be the view of man that is most compatible with the findings of such sciences as biology and psychology. The development of this scientific view of man has forced us to confront such questions as: Is there really any way in which man is special? Is there any hope for our survival after death? Is there any place for human freedom and human responsibility? These are also important philosophical questions. They form part of the subject matter of a different branch of philosophy: metaphysics. . . .

Much of the first third of our life is devoted to our education. We are taught some of what mankind knows to be true. Moreover, and most important, we are taught how to go out and discover new truths. But, if our teachers are honest, they also teach us how hard it is to discover the truth, and how often people have been wrong when they thought that they knew the truth. The history of mankind could be written as the history of how people discovered that what they thought to be so really wasn't true after all. This is the case even in our own scientific era. Indeed, many have pointed out that one of the great merits of the scientific approach is that it never takes anything as certain. It always leaves open the possibility of revising any of our beliefs. When one learns this honest message, however, one cannot help but be troubled by it. And it naturally leads one to ask certain questions: Is there really such a thing as the truth? If so, how do we know when we have discovered it? Indeed, can we ever know that we have discovered the truth?

To ask these questions is to ask some very basic philosophical questions. These questions comprise that part of philosophy known as epistemology, or the theory of knowledge. . . .

We have so far introduced a number of philosophical questions. . . . But we have not said anything about what makes them philosophical questions, or what they all have in common. I think that there are a number of important characteristics of these questions that should be noted, characteristics that help explain the importance of these questions.

1. Each of these questions concerns itself with the nature and validity of some sphere of human life. The first set of questions concern our moral life, the second set our political life, the third our religious life, the fourth set have to do with the way in which we think about ourselves, and the fifth set have to do with our knowledge-gathering activities. This feature might lead one to suspect that there is an area of philosophy devoted to understanding the nature and validity of each major aspect of human existence. This suspicion is more or less accurate. In addition to the areas already mentioned, there is also a philosophy of art, a philosophy of science, and even a philosophy of philosophy (although some philosophers might share with you the suspicion that this looks dangerously like the beginning of a problem).

Philosophers have always prided themselves on the wide scope of their discipline. Philosophy seems to relate to so many other disciplines and to so many parts of human life. The first feature of philosophical problems, then, that they relate to major aspects of human existence, makes the broad scope of philosophy perfectly understandable. Philosophy is, in this way, a universal discipline.

This first feature of philosophical problems also helps explain why so many workers in other disciplines have turned to philosophy. Many eminent scientists have worked in the philosophy of science, many eminent artists have worried about the philosophy of art, many eminent jurists have written about the philosophy of law. They too have been troubled about the nature and validity of the activities that normally engage them, and this leads to philosophy.

2. The interest in a particular area of philosophy is usually proportional to the extent to which people feel troubled about the corresponding human activity. When, for example, religious people are satisfied with their

religious life, they have very little real interest in philosophy of religion (except as a sort of abstract intellectual game). But during a period of religious turmoil and doubt, when even those who are religious are troubled about their religious lives and beliefs, interest in the philosophy of religion rises. The same thing is true about the philosophy of science. The development of whole new types of scientific theory (like the theory of relativity and quantum mechanics) has seemed very troubling to many working scientists. These new theories are often not of the kind scientists were looking for. And this has left many scientists troubled about their own work. This, in turn, has given rise to a considerable growth of interest in the philosophy of science. Examples like this can be multiplied for all the fields of human activity.

Philosophy has always been viewed with a certain amount of suspicion. Indeed, one of the first of the great philosophers, Socrates, was condemned and executed for his philosophical activities. There were many in his home city, Athens, who viewed him as a dangerous character, given to corrupting the young. In a way, this view of philosophy is perfectly understandable. As we have just seen, the philosopher is concerned with examining the nature and the validity of major human activities. This process often results in a negative evaluation. So those who are engaged in the activity in question may well be justified in viewing philosophy as a potential challenge to them.

Nevertheless, it would not be correct to view philosophy as intrinsically revolutionary. To begin with, not all philosophical argumentation ends up with a negative evaluation of some activity or practice. On many occasions, the result of the philosophical investigation is a reaffirmation. For example, while some philosophers of religion have been very critical of both religious belief and religious practice, there have been others whose work has reaffirmed these same aspects of religion. Two notable examples are the Jewish thinker Maimonides and the Christian philosopher St. Thomas Aquinas. Second, and perhaps even more important, it is not really the philosopher who raises the potentially challenging questions about the nature and validity of the practice in question. As we have seen, these questions are already felt by people engaged in the activity. All the philosopher does is to channel their questioning into a serious and rigorous discussion.

3. Philosophical investigation can make a great difference in the way we carry out these human activities and practices. Let us look at just a few examples of this.

Jeremy Bentham is one of the great figures in the history of ethics, social and political philosophy, and the philosophy of law. During his lifetime, he was engaged in a critical reexamination of the English legal system. He looked at the basic principles of that system, and found them wanting. He saw that the system failed to take into account the consequences of its own rules and practices. As a result, he called for a major revamping of the English legal system, including changes which would increase the general welfare of the people. As a matter of fact, the English legal system was never totally overhauled along the lines that Bentham suggested. But his ideas made a great difference in the long run, and the law was never the same because of his philosophical examination of its foundations.

St. Thomas Aquinas is one of the great figures in the history of the philosophy of religion. In his lifetime, traditional religious ideas were being challenged by many young people who had come under the influence of the newly discovered Greek philosophy. St. Thomas, as we pointed out above, was not a revolutionary religious thinker; his work was rather a defense of the basic validity of traditional religious beliefs. Still, in the course of his reexamination of the foundations of religious belief, he found it necessary to restate and reinterpret many traditional ideas about both religion and morality. Catholicism was without doubt significantly changed and enriched by his activities.

We have seen so far that the following can be said about philosophical questions and their importance. Philosophical questions probe the nature and validity of various human activities, beliefs, and institutions. They arise because the people who are engaged in these activities, who hold these beliefs, who are part of these institutions, are themselves troubled about the foundations of these activities, beliefs, and institutions. The result of the philosophical activity may be a challenge or a reaffirmation. But, whatever the result, these activities, beliefs, and institutions are never the same afterwards.

The Nature of Philosophical Answers

Is there a God? This is a typical philosophical question. It probes the validity of a belief that is fundamental to many religious traditions. Now there obviously are only two possible answers to this question: yes and no. One doesn't have to be much of a philosopher to come up with an answer. What then can the philosopher contribute?

What makes an action right? This is another typical philosophical question. It probes the nature of a distinction (the distinction between right and wrong actions) that is fundamental to our whole moral life. Here there is no short, complete list of answers. Still, it is not hard to think of many possible answers. An action is right if it is in accord with the will of God. An action is right if it promotes my own self-interest. An action is right if it promotes the interests of the oppressed. Many others could be suggested. It is not hard to come up with answers to these philosophical questions. What then does the philosopher contribute?

What the philosopher is concerned with is not merely finding an answer to his questions. He is concerned with finding an answer that he can rationally defend. In other words, the philosopher is concerned with finding reasons for thinking that one of the possible answers to the philosophical question is the correct one. Many people attempt to answer questions that we can recognize as philosophical. Some base their answers on tradition, some on revelation, some on personal feelings. What distinguishes the philosophical approach is that it attempts to answer these philosophical questions by an appeal to reason.

For example, St. Thomas Aquinas is not famous for his answer "yes" to the question of whether God exists. That answer had been given by many both before and after his time. What made St. Thomas such an important philosopher was that he attempted to provide reasons for accepting that answer, reasons that could be defended rationally. Again, Jeremy Bentham is not famous merely for saying that the English legal system required a major overhauling; that had been said very frequently. What made him so important were the reasons he gave in criticizing that system, reasons that he felt could be defended rationally.

This explains why much of philosophy is concerned with discussing *arguments*, and not just answers or positions. Although there certainly are cases in which people put forward strikingly new positions and answers to philosophical questions, what most philosophers contribute, and what becomes the basis for most philosophical discussions, are new rational arguments for or against traditional answers. . . .

What is an argument and how does one go about deciding whether or not it is a good one? The purpose of every argument is to prove that something is true. Let us call the statement whose truth we are trying to prove the *conclusion* of the argument. In trying to prove the conclusion, we have to appeal to something else. Those other statements whose truth we appeal to are the *premises* of the argument. To put this another way, when one offers an argument, one sets out to prove the truth of the conclusion on the basis of the truth of the premises.

Let us look at an example of an argument. "Socrates must be mortal because he is a man and all men are mortal." Now this argument is an attempt to prove the truth of the statement that Socrates is mortal. So that statement is the conclusion of the argument. In trying to prove the truth of our conclusion, we appeal to the truth of two other statements: that all men are mortal and that Socrates is a man. So those two statements are the premises of our argument. We can then represent our argument in the following form, writing our conclusion under our premises:

All men are mortal
<u>Socrates is a man</u>
Socrates is mortal

Now that we have some idea of what an argument is, let us turn to the question of what makes an argument a good argument. A short answer is that an argument is a good one if it proves the truth of the conclusion; that, after all, is the whole purpose of offering the argument in the first place. But that isn't much of an answer. It just raises the further question of when the argument proves the truth of the conclusion.

The logician says that an argument is a valid argument if there is no way in which the premises can be true while the conclusion is false. The above argument is valid: there is no way in which Socrates could be immortal (that is, there is no way our conclusion could be false) if all men are mortal and Socrates is a man (if our premises are true). On the other hand, the following argument is not a valid argument:

<u>All men are mortal</u>
All animals are mortal

This argument is invalid because it could be that the premise could be (and is) true while the conclusion is false (all that this would require is the existence of some immortal animals). Note by the way, that this argument is invalid even though, in fact, both its premise and conclusion are true. It is invalid because the premise does not *prove* the truth of the conclusion. Despite the truth of the premise, the conclusion might still be false.

Consider the following argument:

All men are immortal
<u>Socrates is a man</u>
Socrates is immortal

This is a valid argument. There is no way in which the premises could be true and the conclusion false. Still, this argument does not prove the truth of its conclusion. The conclusion is, in fact, false. So the mere fact that an argument is valid is not enough for it to prove the truth of its conclusion. Something else is required. The logician says that the argument must also be sound; its premises must also be true. Only when an argument is both valid and sound does it prove the truth of its conclusion.[1]

Let us see where we stand. We have seen that the philosopher does not merely attempt to provide answers to philosophical questions; the philosopher also tries to prove that his answers

[1]Brody's discussion of arguments is restricted to what logicians call *deductive* arguments, that is, arguments in which it is claimed that the premises offer conclusive support for the conclusion (i.e., it is claimed that if the premises are true, the conclusion *must* be true). *Inductive* arguments, on the other hand, are arguments in which the premises are claimed to offer less than conclusive support for the conclusion (i.e., the conclusion is claimed to be made *probable* by the premises). The terms "validity" and "soundness" that Brody introduces are used by logicians only in reference to deductive arguments. Inductive arguments are said to be "strong" or "weak," but not "valid" or "sound." While Brody does not make this clear, a sound deductive argument must be valid *as well as* having only true premises (i.e., soundness presupposes validity). Consequently, logicians will first ask of a deductive argument whether it is valid. If this question is answered in the affirmative, they will then inquire as to whether it is sound. Valid deductive arguments need not have true conclusions, but sound deductive arguments must. EDITOR'S NOTE.

are the correct answers. He succeeds in doing so only if his arguments for his conclusions are both valid and sound.

Let us apply all of this to a simple philosophical argument. This is a simplified version of one of the standard arguments to prove the existence of God. It runs as follows: There must be a God, since everything has to have a cause. On analysis, this turns out to be the following argument:

Everything has a cause
There must be a First Cause, God

Confronted with this argument, as with any other, one must ask two questions. First, is the argument valid (does its conclusion follow from its premises)? And, secondly, is the argument sound (are its premises true)? There are considerable doubts here on both of these scores. To begin with, isn't there a possibility of the premise being true while the conclusion is false? Suppose that the universe has existed for an infinitely long period of time and that everything in it has been caused by something that existed before. This would be a case in which the premise of the argument is true while the conclusion is false. We do not know whether the universe really is that way, but that's not the point. The mere possibility of its being that way shows that the argument is *invalid*. Secondly, those who offer this argument cannot accept the truth of its premise, that everything has a cause, since they believe in a First Cause, which would have to be an Uncaused Cause. Ironically enough, the very people who offer this argument would have to reject it as *unsound*. In short, then, this argument has failed both of our tests, and it does not prove the truth of its conclusion. . . .[2]

[2]We shall discuss the first cause argument for God's existence in the next chapter. Clearly in the form in which Brody presents this argument, it is unsound. Yet there are many philosophers who would say that this argument can be transformed into a more precise (and more complicated) argument which is sound. Arguments in philosophy are rarely neatly refuted. Instead, philosophers tend to respond to legitimate criticisms of their arguments by refining them (e.g., by adding or qualifying premises). EDITOR'S NOTE.

3. PHILOSOPHY AND LANGUAGE

Friedrich Waismann

FRIEDRICH WAISMANN (1896–1959) was trained in Vienna as a mathematician. In his early years, he was a member of **The Vienna Circle** of **logical positivists**, a group of scientifically and mathematically minded philosophers and philosophically minded scientists and mathematicians. The logical positivists thought that the frustrating lack of progress in philosophy, as opposed to science, results from attempting to solve philosophical questions as they are imprecisely formulated in ordinary language. They believed that philosophical questions required reformulation in a more precise and logical language (namely, the language of modern mathematical or symbolic logic). While teaching at Oxford during and after World War II, Waismann came under the sway of the profoundly influential philosopher Ludwig Wittgenstein (1889–1951), from whom Waismann acquired the view that philosophical problems are often due to linguistical confusion. As Wittgenstein saw it, the grammatical form of concepts or the images suggested by language often mislead philosophers to ask questions that are **without meaning**. Such philosophical questions, which arise when language begins to play tricks on us, cannot be "solved," but only "dissolved" by uncovering the source of the linguistic confusion.

The following selection is an edited version of Waismann's essay "How I See Philosophy." While Brody and Russell in the preceding selections focus on philosophical questions that probe the foundations of ordinary and scientific beliefs, Waismann focuses on the abstract metaphysical questions philosophers often ask. Following Wittgenstein, Waismann claims that many of these questions result from the bewitchment of language. In particular, the noun form of concepts often leads philosophers to assume wrongly that these concepts refer to specific "things." For example, philosophers ask "What is time?" and then become puzzled when they cannot find anything named "time." Bewitched by the noun-form of "time" and the images suggested by ordinary expressions about time, philosophers pose questions that are devoid of sense.

Waismann also stresses, however, the positive contributions of abstract philosophizing. Like Russell, he speaks of the ability of philosophers to uncover the many tacit assumptions about the nature of our experience we unthinkingly make, assumptions which are presupposed by the structure of our language. He relates how philosophers often consider possibilities which lie outside the domain of our normal experience and by so doing make us more aware of the permanent features of our experience that we so easily take for granted. Also like Russell, Waismann points out that the questions philosophers ask are often the forerunners of more precise scientific questions or of more precise linguistic distinctions.

I

. . . From Plato to Schopenhauer philosophers are agreed that the source of their philosophizing is wonder. What gives rise to it is nothing recondite and rare but precisely those things which stare us in the face: memory, motion, general ideas. (Plato: What does 'horse' mean? A single particular horse? No, for it may refer to *any* horse; *all* the horses, the total class? No, for we may speak of this or that horse. But if it means neither a single horse nor all horses, what *does* it mean?) The idealist is shaken in just the same way when he comes to reflect that he has, in Schopenhauer's words, 'no knowledge of the sun but only of an eye that sees a sun, and no knowledge of the earth but only of a hand that feels an earth'. Can it be, then, that nothing whatsoever is known to us except our own consciousness?

In looking at such questions, it seems as if the mind's eye were growing dim and as if everything, even that which ought to be absolutely clear, was becoming oddly puzzling and unlike its usual self. To bring out what seems to be peculiar to these questions one might say that they are not so much questions as tokens of a profound uneasiness of mind. Try for a moment to put yourself into the frame of mind of which Augustine was possessed when he asked: How is it possible to measure time? Time consists of past, present and future. The past can't be mea-

Source: From "How I See Philosophy" by Friedrich Waismann, in *Contemporary British Philosophy*, Third Series, edited by H. D. Lewis, New York: The Macmillan Company, 1956, London: George Allen & Unwin, Ltd., pp. 449–58, 461–67. Reprinted by permission of The Macmillan Company and George Allen and Unwin, Ltd.

sured, it is gone; the future can't be measured, it is not yet here; and the present can't be measured, it has no extension. Augustine knew of course how time is measured and this was not his concern. What puzzled him was how it is *possible* to measure time, seeing that the past hour cannot be lifted out and placed alongside the present hour for comparison. Or look at it this way: what is measured is in the past, the measuring in the present: how can that be?

The philosopher as he ponders over some such problem has the appearance of a man who is deeply disquieted. He seems to be straining to grasp something which is beyond his powers. The words in which such a question presents itself do not quite bring out into the open the real point—which may, perhaps more aptly, be described as the recoil from the incomprehensible. If, on a straight railway journey, you suddenly come in sight of the very station you have just left behind, there will be terror, accompanied perhaps by slight giddiness. That is exactly how the philosopher feels when he says to himself, 'Of course time can be measured; but how *can* it?' It is as though, up to now, he had been passing heedlessly over the difficulties, and now, all of a sudden, he notices them and asks himself in alarm, 'But how can that be?' That is a sort of question which we only ask when it is the very facts themselves which confound us, when something about them strikes us as preposterous. . . .

We all have our moments when something quite ordinary suddenly strikes us as queer—for instance, when time appears to us as a curious thing. Not that we are often in this frame of mind; but on some occasions, when we look at things in a certain way, unexpectedly they seem to change as though by magic: they stare at us with a puzzling expression, and we begin to wonder whether they can possibly be the things we have known all our lives.

'Time flows' we say—a natural and innocent expression, and yet one pregnant with danger. It flows 'equably', in Newton's phrase, at an even rate. What can this mean? When something moves, it moves with a definite speed (and speed means: rate of change in time). To ask with what speed time moves, i.e. to ask how quickly time changes in time, is to ask the unaskable. It also flows, again in Newton's phrase, 'without relation to anything external.' How are we to figure that? Does time flow on irrespective of what happens in the world? Would it flow on even if everything in heaven and on earth came to a sudden standstill as Schopenhauer believed? For if this were not so, he said, time would have to stop with the stopping of the clock and move with the clock's movement. How odd: time flows at the same rate and yet without speed; and perhaps even without anything to occur in it? The expression is puzzling in another way. 'I can never catch myself being in the past or in the future', someone might say; 'whenever I think or perceive or breathe the word ''now'', I am in the present; therefore I am *always* in the present.' In saying this, he may think of the present moment as a bridge as it were from which he is looking down at the 'river of time'. Time is gliding along underneath the bridge, but the 'now' does not take part in the motion. What was future passes into the present (is just below the bridge) and then into the past, while the onlooker, the 'self' or the 'I', is always in the present. 'Time flows *through* the ''now'' ', he may feel to be a quite expressive metaphor. Yes, it sounds all right—until he suddenly comes to his senses and, with a start, realizes, 'But surely the moment flies?' (Query: How to succeed in wasting time? Answer: In this way, for instance—by trying, with eyes closed or staring vacantly in front of oneself, to catch the present moment as it is flitting by.) He may come now to look at matters in a different way. He sees himself advancing through time towards the future, and with this goes a suggestion of being active, just as at other times he may see himself floating down the stream whether he likes it or not. 'What exactly is it that is moving—the events in time or the present moment?', he may wonder. In the first case, it looks to him as if time were moving while he stands still; in the second case as if he were moving through time. 'How exactly is it' he may say in a dubious voice, 'am I always in the present? Is the present always eluding me?' Both ring true in a way; but they contradict each other. Again, does it make sense to ask, 'At what time is the present moment?' Yes, no doubt; but how *can* it, if the 'now' is but the fixed point from which the dating of any event ultimately receives its sense?

So he is pulled to and fro: 'I am always in the present, yet it slips through my fingers; I am going forward in time—no, I am carried down the stream.' He is using different pictures, each in its way quite appropriate to the occasion; yet when he tries to apply them jointly they clash. 'What a queer thing time must be', he may say to himself with a puzzled look on his face, 'what after all *is* time?'—expecting, half-expecting perhaps, that the answer will reveal to him time's hidden essence. Ranged beyond the intellectual are deeper levels of uneasiness—terror of the inevitability of time's passage, with all the reflections upon life that this forces upon us. Now all these anxious doubts release themselves in the question. 'What is time?' (*En passant*[1] this is a hint that *one* answer will never do—will never remove all these doubts that break out afresh on different levels and yet are expressed in the same form of words.)

As we all know what time is and yet cannot say what it is it feels mystifying; and precisely because of its elusiveness it catches our imagination. The more we look at it the more we are puzzled: it seems charged with paradoxes. 'What is time? What is this being made up of movement only without anything that is moving?' (Schopenhauer). How funny to have it bottled up! 'I've got here in my hand the most potent, the most enigmatic, the most fleeting of all essences—Time.' (Logan Pearsall Smith of an hour-glass.) For Shelley it is an 'unfathomable sea! whose waves are years', a 'shoreless flood', for Proust—well, why not leave something to the reader?

But isn't the answer to this that what mystifies us lies in the *noun* form 'the time'? Having a notion embodied in the form of a noun almost irresistibly makes us turn round to look for what it is 'the name of'. We are trying to catch the shadows cast by the opacities of speech. . . .

Yet the answer is a prosaic one: don't ask what time is but how the *word* 'time' is being used. Easier said than done; for . . . ordinary language . . . renews its spell over the philosopher, luring him on into the shadow chase. It is perhaps only when we turn to languages of a widely different grammatical structure that the way towards such possibilities of interpretation is entirely barred. 'It is highly probable that philosophers within the domain of the Ural-Altaic languages (where the subject-concept is least developed) will look differently "into the world" and be found on paths of thought different from those of the Indo-Europeans . . . '(Nietzsche).

II

. . . In philosophy, the real problem is not to find the answer to a given question but to find a sense for it.

To see in what the 'solution' of such a 'problem' consists let us start with Achilles who, according to Zeno, is to this day chasing the tortoise. Suppose that Achilles runs twice as fast as the tortoise. If the tortoise's start is 1, Achilles will have to cover successively 1, ½, ¼, ⅛, . . .;

[1]By the way (literally—"in passing"). EDITOR'S NOTE.

this series is endless; so he can never catch the tortoise. 'Nonsense!' (a mathematician's voice), 'the sum of the infinite series is finite, namely 2, and that settles it.' Though perfectly true, his remark is not to the point. It does not remove the sting from the puzzle, the disconcerting idea, namely, that however far we go in the series there is always a next term, that the lead the tortoise has in the race, though naturally getting smaller and smaller, yet never ceases to be: there *can* be no moment when it is strictly zero. It is *this* feature of the case, I suggest, that we do not understand and which throws us into a state of confusion.

But look at it this way. Suppose that we apply the same sort of argument to a minute, then we shall have to argue in some such way as this. Before the minute can be over the first half of it must elapse, then one-quarter of it, then one-eighth of it, and so on *ad infinitum*. This being an endless process, the minute can never come to an end. Immediately we have the argument in this form, the blunder leaps to the eye: we have been confusing two senses of 'never', a temporal and a non-temporal one. While it is quite correct to say that the sequence 1, ½, ¼, ⅛, . . . never ends, this sense of the word 'never' has nothing whatever to do with time. All it means is that there is no last term in the series, or (what comes to the same) that to any term, no matter how far out in the sequence, a successor can be constructed according to the simple rule 'halve it': that is meant here by 'never'; whereas in saying, for instance, that man will never find out anything to avert death, 'never' is meant in the sense 'at no time'. It is clear that the mathematical assertion concerning the possibility of going on in the sequence by forming new terms according to the rule does not state anything about actual occurrences in time. The mistake should really be obvious; in saying that, since the start is getting progressively smaller and yet can never cease to be, Achilles can never catch the tortoise, we jump from the mathematical, *non*-temporal to the temporal sense. Had there been two different words in our language to mark these senses the confusion could never have arisen, and the world would be poorer for one of its most attractive paradoxes. But the same word is as a matter of course used with different meanings. Result: something like a conjuring trick. While our attention is diverted, while, 'in our mind's eye', we stare fixedly at Achilles as he is speeding along, with each big bound diminishing his distance from the tortoise, the one sense is so innocuously palmed off for the other as to escape notice.

This way of bringing out the fallacy also holds when the other key term is used for presenting the puzzle. As there will 'always' be a next term in the sequence, i.e. a next step in the scheme of subdividing the racecourse (the word 'always' looking just as spotless and innocent) we readily fall into the trap of concluding that the tortoise will 'always' be ahead of Achilles, eternally to be chased by his pursuer.

Many are the types of bewilderment: there is the obsessional doubt—can I ever know that other people have experiences, that they see, hear and feel as I do? Can I be sure that memory does not always deceive me? Are there really material objects and not only sense-impressions 'of' them? There is the doubtlike uneasiness—what sort of being is possessed by numbers? There is the anxiety-doubt—are we really free? . . .

. . . when a philosopher wants to dispose of a question the one thing he must not do is: to give an answer. A philosophic question is not solved: it *dis*solves. And in what does the 'dissolving' consist? In making the meaning of the words used in putting the question so clear to ourselves that we are released from the spell it casts on us. Confusion was removed by calling to mind the use of language or, so far as the use *can* be distilled into rules, the rules: it therefore *was* a confusion about the use of language, or a confusion about rules. It is here that philosophy and grammar meet . . . .

III

What, only criticism and no meat? The philosopher a fog dispeller? If that were all he was capable of I would be sorry for him and leave him to his devices. Fortunately, this is not so. For one thing, a philosophic question, if pursued far enough, may lead to something positive—for instance, to a more profound understanding of language. Take the sceptical doubts as to material objects, other minds, etc. The first reaction is perhaps to say: these doubts are idle. Ordinarily, when I doubt whether I shall finish this article, after a time my doubt comes to an end. I cannot go on doubting for ever. It's the destiny of doubt to die. But the doubts raised by the sceptic never die. Are they doubts? Are they pseudo-questions? They appear so only when judged by the twin standards of common sense and common speech. The real trouble lies deeper: it arises from the sceptic casting doubt on the very facts which underlie the use of language, those permanent features of experience which make concept formation possible, which in fact are precipitated in the use of our most common words. Suppose that you see an object in front of you quite clearly, say, a pipe, and when you are going to pick it up it melts into thin air, then you may feel, 'Lord, I'm going mad' or something of the sort (unless the whole situation is such that you have reason to suspect that it was some clever trick). But what, the sceptic may press now, if such experiences were quite frequent? Would you be prepared to *dis*solve the connection between different sense experiences which form the hard core of our idea of a solid object, to *un*do what language has done—to part with the category of thing-hood? . . . the sceptic struggles to express himself in a language which is not fit for this purpose. He expresses himself misleadingly when he says that he doubts such-and-such *facts*: his doubts cut so deep that they affect the fabric of language itself. For what he doubts is already embodied in the very forms of speech, e.g. in what is condensed in the use of thing-words. The moment he tries to penetrate those deep-sunken layers, he undermines the language in which he ventilates his qualms—with the result that he seems to be talking nonsense. He is not. But in order to make his doubts fully expressible, language would first have to go into the melting-pot. (We can get a glimmering of what is needed from modern science where all the long-established categories—thinghood, causality, position—had to be revolutionized. This required nothing less than the construction of some new language, not the expression of new facts with the old one.)

If we look at the matter in this way the attitude of the sceptic is seen in a new light. He considers possibilities which lie far outside the domain of our current experience. If his doubts are taken seriously, they turn into observations which cast a new and searching light on the subsoil of language, showing what possibilities are open to our thought (though not to ordinary language), and what paths might have been pursued if the texture of our experience were different from what it is. These problems are not spurious, they make us aware of the vast background in which any current experiences are embodied, and to which language has adapted itself; thus they bring out the unmeasured sum of experience stored up in the use of our words and syntactical forms.

For another thing, a question may decide to go in for another career than dissolving. It may pass into science. . . .

A whole chapter might be written on the fate of questions, their curious adventures and transformations—how they change into others and in the process remain, and yet do not remain, the same. The original question may split and multiply almost like a character in a dream play. . . . It is interesting to watch how from a question . . . not too precise, somewhat blurred, new and better defined questions detach themselves, the parent question . . . giving rise to a scientist's progeny.

Now something else must be noted—how these questions become, not only precise, but clear (which is not the same thing). To illustrate, can the infinity represented by all natural numbers be compared with the infinity represented by all points in space? That is, can the one be said to be less than, or equal to, the other? When it was first asked, the question had no clear sense—perhaps no sense at all. Yet it guided G. Cantor in his ingenious search. Before set theory was discovered—or should I rather say 'invented'?—the question acted as a sort of signpost pointing vaguely to some so far uncharted region of thought. It is perhaps best characterized by saying that it guides our imagination in a given direction, stimulates research along new lines. Such questions do not 'dissolve': they are solved, only not in the existing system of thought but rather by constructing a new conceptual system—such as set theory—where the intended and faintly anticipated sense finds its full realization. They are therefore of the nature of incitements to the building of such systems, they point from the not-yet-meaningful to the meaningful.

The question is the first groping step of the mind in its journeyings that lead towards new horizons. The genius of the philosopher shows itself nowhere more strikingly than in the new kind of question he brings into the world. What distinguishes him and gives him his place is the passion of questioning. That his questions are at times not so clear is perhaps of not so much moment as one makes of it. There is nothing like clear thinking to protect one from making discoveries. It is all very well to talk of clarity, but when it becomes an obsession it is liable to nip the living thought in the bud. . . .

4. PHILOSOPHY AND THE HUMAN CONDITION

William Barrett

WILLIAM BARRETT (1913–   ) has been a professor of philosophy at New York University since 1950. His main philosophical interests are in contemporary philosophical currents of thought and in philosophical themes in modern literature. Barrett's interest in literature is reflected in his editorship from 1945 to 1953 of the prestigious and influential **Partisan Review**, a political and literary periodical. Barrett's recent book **The Truants: Adventures among the Intellectuals** consists of memoirs of his long association with this magazine and its contributors. Barrett's vivid portrayals of Philip Rahv, Delmore Schwartz, Hannah Arendt, Mary McCarthy, Edmund Wilson, Sidney Hook, Paul Goodman, and others provide insight into the intellectual currents of twentieth century American thought.

The selection that follows comes from the first chapter of Barrett's introduction to existentialism, **Irrational Man**. In an engaging writing style, Barrett introduces us to some of the main themes and figures in the existential approach to philosophy. The thread that unites the important figures of existentialism—Kierkegaard, Nietzsche, Heidegger, Husserl, Jaspers, Sartre , and Camus—is not allegiance to a particular abstract philosophical doctrine, but rather a concern with the concrete individual's experience of what it is to be a human being. Contemporary existentialists are united too in their criticism of the technical analytic approach to philosophy which has so dominated twentieth century Anglo-American philosophy. Following in the existential tradition, Barrett contends that the price of the increasing specialization and technical nature of modern analytic philosophy "leads away from the ordinary and concrete acts of understanding in terms of which man actually lives his day-to-day life." As a consequence, much of contemporary analytic philosophy is irrelevant to the nonprofessional, who turns to philosophy "to find release or peace from the torments and perplexities of life." The proper image of the philosopher, Barrett claims, is not that of a detached scholar engaged in academic research but of a person who is psychologically engaged in finding the very meaning of his existence. From this perspective, philosophy becomes intertwined with psychology and naturally leads to expression in literary form.

Existential thought has also spawned an existentialist school of psychology. Rejecting the behaviorist's view that human beings are "learning machines" subject to deterministic laws of learning (conditioning) and the Freudian emphasis upon the causal influence of unconscious mental events **that act upon us**, the existential psychologist seeks understanding of human behavior solely in a person's present conscious perception of himself and the meaning of his existence. Reflecting a central theme of existential philosophy, the existential psychologist rejects the approach of the scientific rationalist, who reduces concrete human experience to abstract categories and as such robs those experiences of their psychological and personal meaning.

This emphasis upon the personal involvement of an individual with the quest for meaning permeates all existential thought. As Nietzsche once put it, "It makes all the difference in the world whether a thinker stands in personal relation to his problems, to his destiny, his need and highest happiness, or can only feel and grasp them impersonally, with the tentacles of cold, prying thought." Existentialists also emphasize the **freedom** of human beings to choose their way of life, a choice that cannot be left to experience, reason, or divine revelation. Existentialists proclaim that our freedom, the anguish that its exercise involves and our tendency to escape from it by seeing ourselves as objects determined by the roles that we play, is at the very essence of the human condition.

The story is told (by Kierkegaard) of the absent-minded man so abstracted from his own life that he hardly knows he exists until, one fine morning, he wakes up to find himself dead. It is a story that has a special point today, since this civilization of ours has at last got its hands on weapons with which it could easily bring upon itself the fate of Kierkegaard's hero: we could wake up tomorrow morning dead—and without ever having touched the roots of our own existence. There is by this time widespread anxiety and even panic over the dangers of the atomic age; but the public soul-searching and stocktaking rarely, if ever, go to the heart of the matter. We do not ask ourselves what the ultimate ideas behind our civilization are that have brought us into this danger; we do not search for the human face behind the bewildering array of instruments that man has forged; in a word, we do not dare to be philosophical. Uneasy as we are over the atomic age, on the crucial question of existence itself we choose to remain as absent-minded as the man in Kierkegaard's story. One reason we do so lies in the curiously remote position to which modern society has relegated philosophy, and which philosophers themselves have been content to accept.

If philosophers are really to deal with the problem of human existence—and no other professional group in society is likely to take over the job for them—they might very well begin by asking: How does philosophy itself exist at the present time? Or, more concretely: How do philosophers exist in the modern world? Nothing very high-flown, metaphysical, or even abstract is intended by this question; and our preliminary answer to it is equally concrete and prosy. Philosophers today exist in the Academy, as members of departments of philosophy in universities, as professional teachers of a more or less theoretical subject known as philosophy. This simple observation, baldly factual and almost statistical, does not seem to take us very deeply into the abstruse problem of existence; but every effort at understanding must take off from our actual situation, the point at which we stand. "Know thyself!" is the command Socrates issued to philosophers at the beginning (or very close to it) of all Western philosophy; and contemporary philosophers might start on the journey of self-knowledge by coming to terms with the somewhat grubby and uninspiring fact of the social status of philosophy as a profession. It is in any case a fact with some interesting ambiguities.

To profess, according to the dictionary, is to confess or declare openly, and therefore publicly; consequently, to acknowledge a calling before the world. So the word bears originally a religious connotation, as when we speak of a profession of faith. But in our present society, with its elaborate subdividing of human functions, a profession is the specialized social task—requiring expertness and know-how—that one performs for pay: it is a living, one's livelihood. Professional people are lawyers, doctors, dentists, engineers—and also professors of philosophy. The profession of the philosopher in the modern world is to be a professor of philosophy; and the realm of Being which the philosopher inhabits as a living individual is no more recondite than a corner within the university.

Not enough has been made of this academic existence of the philosopher, though some contemporary Existentialists have directed searching comment upon it. The price one pays for having a profession is a *déformation professionelle*, as the French put it—a professional deformation. Doctors and engineers tend to see things from the viewpoint of their own specialty, and usually show a very marked blind spot to whatever falls outside this particular province. The more specialized a vision the sharper its focus; but also the more nearly total the blind spot toward all things that lie on the periphery of this focus. As a human being, functioning professionally within the Academy, the philosopher can hardly be expected to escape his own professional deformation, especially since it has become a law of modern society that man is assimilated more and more completely to his social function. And it is just here that a troublesome and profound ambiguity resides for the philosopher today. The profession of philosophy did not always have the narrow and specialized meaning it now has. In ancient Greece it had the very opposite: instead of a specialized theoretical discipline philosophy there was a concrete way of life, a total vision of man and the cosmos in the light of which the individual's whole life was to be lived. . . . Even in Plato, where the thought has already become more differentiated and specialized and where the main lines of philosophy as a theoretical discipline are being laid down, the *motive* of philosophy is very different from the cool pursuit of the savant engaged in research. Philosophy is for Plato a passionate way of life; and the imperishable example of Socrates, who lived and died for the philosophic life, was the guiding line of Plato's career for five decades after his master's death. Philosophy is the soul's search for salvation, which means for Plato deliverance from the suffering and evils of the natural world. Even today the motive for an Oriental's taking up the study of philosophy is altogether different from that of a Western student: for the Oriental the only reason for bothering with philosophy is to find release or peace from the torments and perplexities of life. Philosophy can never quite divest itself of these aboriginal claims. They are part of the past, which is never lost, lurking under the veneer of even the most sophisticatedly rational of contemporary philosophies; and even those philosophers who have altogether forsworn the great vision are called upon, particularly by the layman who may not be aware of the historical fate of specialization that has fallen upon philosophy, to give answers to the great questions.

The ancient claims of philosophy are somewhat embarrassing to the contemporary philosopher, who has to justify his existence within the sober community of professional savants and scientists. The modern university is as much an expression of the specialization of the age as is the modern factory. Moreover, the philosopher knows that everything we prize about our modern knowledge, each thing in it that represents an immense stride in certainty and power over what the past called its knowledge, is the result of specialization. Modern science was made possible by the social organization of knowledge. The philosopher today is therefore pressed, and simply by reason of his objective social role in the community, into an imitation of the scientist: he too seeks to perfect the weapons of his knowledge through specialization. Hence the extraordinary preoccupation with technique among modern philosophers, with logical and linguistic analysis, syntax and semantics; and in general with the refining away of all content for the sake of formal subtlety. The movement known as Logical Positivism, in this country (the atmosphere of humanism is probably more dominant in the European universities than here in the United States), actually trafficked upon the *guilt* philosophers felt at not being scientists; that is, at not being researchers producing reliable knowledge in the mode of science. The natural insecurity of philosophers, which in any case lies at the core of their whole uncertain enterprise, was here aggravated beyond measure by the insistence that they transform themselves into scientists.

Specialization is the price we pay for the advancement of knowledge. A price, because the path of specialization leads away from the ordinary and concrete acts of understanding in terms of which man actually lives his day-to-day life. . . . In fact, if they were candid, philosophers today would recognize that they have less and less influence upon the minds around them. To the degree that their existence has become specialized and academic, their importance beyond the university cloisters has declined. Their disputes have become disputes among themselves; and far from gaining the enthusiastic support needed for a strong popular movement, they now have little contact with whatever general intellectual elite still remain here outside the Academy. John Dewey was the last American philosopher to have any widespread influence on non-academic life in this country.

Such was the general philosophic situation here when, after the Second World War, the news of Existentialism arrived. It was news, which is in itself an unusual thing for philosophy these days. True, the public interest was not altogether directed toward the philosophic matters in question. It was news from France, and therefore distinguished by the particular color and excitement that French intellectual life is able to generate. French Existentialism was a kind of Bohemian ferment in Paris; it had, as a garnish for the philosophy, the cult its younger devotees had made of night-club hangouts,

American jazz, special hairdos and style of dress. All this made news for American journalists trying to report on the life that had gone on in Paris during the war and the German Occupation. Moreover, Existentialism was a literary movement as well, and its leaders—Jean-Paul Sartre, Albert Camus, Simone de Beauvoir—were brilliant and engaging writers. Nevertheless, that the American public was curious about the philosophy itself cannot altogether be denied. Perhaps the curiosity consisted in large part of wanting to know what the name, the big word, meant; nothing stirs up popular interest so much as a slogan. But there was also a genuine philosophic curiosity, however inchoate, in all this, for here was a movement that seemed to convey a message and a meaning to a good many people abroad, and Americans wanted to know about it. The desire for meaning still slumbers, though submerged, beneath the extroversion of American life. . . .

The important thing, to repeat, was that here was a philosophy that was able to cross the frontier from the Academy into the world at large. This should have been a welcome sign to professional philosophers that ordinary mankind still could hunger and thirst after philosophy if what they were given to bite down on was something that seemed to have a connection with their lives. Instead, the reception given the new movement by philosophers was anything but cordial. Existentialism was rejected, often without very much scrutiny, as sensationalism or mere "psychologizing," a literary attitude, postwar despair, nihilism, or heaven knows what besides. The very themes of Existentialism were something of a scandal to the detached sobriety of Anglo-American philosophy. Such matters as anxiety, death, the conflict between the bogus and the genuine self, the faceless man of the masses, the experience of the death of God are scarcely the themes of analytic philosophy. Yet they are themes of life: People do die, people do struggle all their lives between the demands of real and counterfeit selves, and we do live in an age in which neurotic anxiety has mounted out of all proportion so that even minds inclined to believe that all human problems can be solved by physical techniques begin to label "mental health" as the first of our public problems. The reaction of professional philosophers to Existentialism was merely a symptom of their imprisonment in the narrowness of their own discipline. Never was the professional deformation more in evidence. The divorce of mind from life was something that had happened to philosophers simply in the pursuit of their own specialized problems. Since philosophers are only a tiny fraction of the general population, the matter would not be worth laboring were it not that this divorce of mind from life happens also to be taking place, catastrophically, in modern civilization everywhere. It happens too, as we shall see, to be one of the central themes of existential philosophy—for which we may in time owe it no small debt.

All of this has to be said even when we do concede a certain sensational and youthfully morbid side to French Existentialism. The genius of Sartre—and by this time there can scarcely be doubt that it is real genius—has an undeniably morbid side. But there is no human temperament that does not potentially reveal some truth, and Sartre's morbidity has its own unique and revelatory power. It is true also that a good deal in French Existentialism was the expression of an historical mood—the shambles of defeat after the "phony war" and the experience of utter dereliction under the German Occupation. But are moods of this kind so unimportant and trifling as to be unworthy of the philosopher's consideration? Would it not in fact be a serious and appropriate task for the philosopher to elaborate what is involved in certain basic human moods? We are living in an epoch that has produced two world wars, and these wars were not merely passing incidents but characterize the age down to its marrow; surely a philosophy that has experienced these wars may be said to have some connection with the life of its time. Philosophers who dismissed Existentialism as "merely a mood" or "a postwar mood" betrayed a curious blindness to the concerns of the human spirit, in taking the view that philosophic truth can be found only in those areas of experience in which human moods are *not* present.

Naturally enough, something very deeply American came to the surface in this initial response to Existentialism. Once again the old drama of America confronting Europe was being played out. Existentialism was so definitely a European expression that its very somberness went against the grain of our native youthfulness and optimism. The new philosophy was not a peculiarly French phenomenon, but a creation of the western European continent at the moment in history when all of its horizons—political as well as spiritual—were rapidly shrinking. The American has not yet assimilated psychologically the disappearance of his own geographical frontier, his spiritual horizon is still the limitless play of human possibilities, and as yet he has not lived through the crucial experience of human finitude. (This last is still only an abstract phrase to him.) The expression of themes like those of Existentialism was bound to strike the American as a symptom of despair and defeat, and, generally, of the declining vigor of a senescent[1] civilization. But America, spiritually speaking, is still tied to European civilization, even though the political power lines now run the other way; and these European expressions simply point out the path that America itself will have eventually to trend; when it does it will know at last what the European is talking about.

It is necessary thus to emphasize the European—rather than the specifically French—origins of Existentialism. . . . Jean-Paul Sartre is not Existentialism—it still seems necessary to make this point for American readers; he does not even represent, as we shall see later, the deepest impulse of this philosophy. Now that French Existentialism as a popular movement . . . is safely dead, having left a few new reputations surviving in its wake, we can see it much more clearly for what it is—a small branch of a very much larger tree. And the roots of this larger tree reach down into the remotest depths of the Western tradition. Even in the portions of the tree more immediately visible to our contemporary eyes, we have something which is the combined product of many European thinkers, some of them operating in radically different national traditions. Sartre's immediate sources, for example, are German: *Martin Heidegger* (1889–1976) and *Karl Jaspers* (1883–1969), and for his method the great German phenomenologist, *Edmund Husserl* (1859–1938). Heidegger and Jaspers are, strictly speaking, the creators of existential philosophy in this century; they have given it its decisive stamp, brought its problems to new and more precise expression, and in general formed the model around which the thinking of all the other Existentialists revolves. Neither Heidegger nor Jaspers created their philosophies out of whole cloth; the atmosphere of German philosophy during the first part of this century had become quickened by the search for a new "philosophical anthropology"—a new interpretation of man—made necessary by the extraordinary additions to knowledge in all of the special sciences that dealt with man. . . .

But what lifted Heidegger and Jaspers above the level of their contemporary philosophic atmosphere and impelled them to give a new voice to the intellectual consciousness of the age was their decisive relation to two older nineteenth-century thinkers: *Sören Kierkegaard* (1813–1855) and *Friedrich Nietzsche* (1844–1900). Jaspers has been the more outspoken in acknowledging this filial relationship: the philosopher, he says, who has really *experienced* the thought of Kierkegaard and Nietzsche can never again philosophize in the traditional mode of academic philosophy. Neither

[1]Aging. EDITOR'S NOTE.

Kierkegaard nor Nietzsche was an academic philosopher; Nietzsche, for seven years a professor of Greek at Basel in Switzerland, did his most radical philosophizing after he had fled from the world of the university and its sober community of scholars; Kierkegaard never held an academic chair. Neither developed a system; both in fact gibed at systematizers and even the possibilities of a philosophic system; and while they proliferated in ideas that were far in advance of their time and could be spelled out only by the following century, these ideas were not the stock themes of academic philosophy. Ideas are not even the real subject matter of these philosophers—and this in itself is something of a revolution in Western philosophy: their central subject is the unique experience of the single one, the individual, who chooses to place himself on trial before the gravest question of his civilization. For both Kierkegaard and Nietzsche this gravest question is Christianity, though they were driven to opposite positions in regard to it. Kierkegaard set himself the task of determining whether Christianity can still be lived or whether a civilization still nominally Christian must finally confess spiritual bankruptcy; and all his ideas were simply sparks thrown off in the fiery process of seeking to realize the truth of Christ in his own life. Nietzsche begins with the confession of bankruptcy: God is dead, says Nietzsche, and European man if he were more honest, courageous, and had keener eyes for what went on in the depths of his own soul would know that this death has taken place there, despite the lip service still paid to the old formulae and ideals of religion . . . More than thinkers, Kierkegaard and Nietzsche were witnesses—witnesses who suffered for their time what the time itself would not acknowledge as its own secret wound. No concept or system of concepts lies at the center of either of their philosophies, but rather the individual human personality itself struggling for self-realization. No wonder both are among the greatest of intuitive psychologists. . . .

. . . .Existentialism numbers among its most powerful representatives Jews, Catholics, Protestants—as well as atheists. Contrary to the first facile journalistic reactions, the seriousness of existential thought does not arise merely out of the despair of a world from which God has departed. Such a generalization was prompted largely by the identification of existential philosophy with the school of Sartre. . . . So far as the central impulses of existential thought are concerned, it does not altogether matter, at least in one sense, in what religious sect a man finally finds his home. Nor it is mere heterogenous lumping-together to put Catholics, Jews, Protestants, and atheists under the rubric of one philosophy. This philosophy, as a particular mode of human thought, is single even though its practitioners wind up in different religious camps. What is common, and central, to all these philosophers is that the meaning of religion, and religious faith, is recast in relation to the individual. Each has put religion itself radically in question, and it is only to be expected that the faith, or the denial of faith, that emerges in their thought should be somewhat disconcerting to those who have followed the more public and external paths into a church. . . .

Modern experience—an ambiguous enough term, to be sure, and one that will require subsequent definition—is the bond among these philosophers. . . . Existentialism is not a passing fad or a mere philosophic mood of the postwar period but a major movement of human history. Over the past hundred years the development of philosophy has shown a remarkable enlargement of content, a progressive orientation toward the immediate and qualitative, the existent and the actual—toward "concreteness and adequacy," to use the words that A. N. Whitehead borrowed from William James. Philosophers can no longer attempt, as the British empiricists Locke and Hume attempted, to construct human experience out of simple ideas and elementary sensations. The psychic life of man is not a mosaic of such mental atoms, and philosophers were able to cling to this belief so long only because they had put their own abstractions in place of concrete experience. . . .

Of all the non-European philosophers, William James probably best deserves to be labeled an Existentialist. Indeed, at this late date, we may very well wonder whether it would not be more accurate to call James an Existentialist than a Pragmatist. What remains of American Pragmatism today is forced to think of him as the black sheep of the movement. Pragmatists nowadays acknowledge James's genius but are embarrassed by his extremes: by the unashamedly personal tone of his philosophizing, his willingness to give psychology the final voice over logic where the two seem in conflict, and his belief in the revelatory value of religious experience. . . . It is not merely a matter of tone, but of principle, that places James among the Existentialists: he plumped for a world which contained contingency, discontinuity, and in which the centers of experience were irreducibly plural and personal, as against a "block" universe that could be enclosed in a single rational system.

Pragmatism meant something more and different for James than it did for Charles Sanders Peirce or John Dewey. The contrast between James and Dewey, particularly, sheds light on the precise point at which Pragmatism, in the strict sense, ends and Existentialism begins. A comparison between the earlier and the later writings of Dewey is almost equally illuminating on the same point. Dewey is moving in the general existential direction of modern philosophy with his insistence that the modern philosopher must break with the whole classical tradition of thought. He sees the "negative" and destructive side of philosophy (with which Existentialism has been so heavily taxed by its critics): every thinker, Dewey tells us, puts some portion of the stable world in danger as soon as he begins to think. The genial inspiration that lies behind his whole rather gangling and loose-jointed philosophy is the belief that in all departments of human experience things do not fall from heaven but grow up out of the earth. Thinking itself is only the halting and fumbling effort of a thoroughly biological creature to cope with his environment. The image of man as an earth-bound and time-bound creature permeates Dewey's writings as it does that of the Existentialists—up to a point. Beyond that point he moves in a direction that is the very opposite of Existentialism. What Dewey never calls into question is the thing he labels Intelligence, which in his last writings came to mean simply Scientific Method. Dewey places the human person securely within his biological and social context, but he never goes past this context into that deepest center of the human person where fear and trembling start. Any examination of inner experience—really inner experience—would have seemed to Dewey to take the philosopher too far away from nature in the direction of the theological. We have to remind ourselves here of the provincial and over-theologized atmosphere of the America in which Dewey started his work, and against which he had to struggle so hard to establish the validity of a secular intelligence. Given Dewey's emphasis upon the biological and sociological contexts as ultimate, however, together with his interpretation of human thought as basically an effort to transform the environment, we end with the picture of man as essentially *homo faber*, the technological animal. This belief in technique is still a supreme article of the American faith. Dewey grew up in a period in which America was still wrestling with its frontier, and the mood of his writings is unshaken optimism at the expansion of our technical mastery over nature. Ultimately, the difference between Dewey and the Existentialists is the difference between America and Europe. The philosopher cannot seriously put to himself questions that his civilization has not lived. . . .

The reader may very well ask why, in view of this broader existential trend within modern philosophy, Existentialism should first have been greeted by professional philosophers in this country as an eccentric and sensational kind of tempest in a teapot. We should point out that Anglo-American philosophy is dominated by an altogether different and alien mode of thought—variously called analytic philosophy, Logical Positivism, or sometimes merely "scientific philosophy." No doubt, Positivism has also good claims to being the philosophy of this time: it takes as its central fact what is undoubtedly the central fact distinguishing our civilization from all others—science; but it goes on from this to take science as the ultimate ruler of human life, which it never has been and psychologically never can be. Positivist man is a curious creature who dwells in the tiny island of light composed of what he finds scientifically "meaningful," while the whole surrounding area in which ordinary men live from day to day and have their dealings with other men is consigned to the outer darkness of the "meaningless." Positivism has simply accepted the fractured being of modern man and erected a philosophy to intensify it. Existentialism, whether successfully or not, has attempted instead to gather all the elements of human reality into a total picture of man. Positivist man and Existentialist man are no doubt offspring of the same parent epoch, but, somewhat as Cain and Abel were, the brothers are divided unalterably by temperament and the initial choice they make of their own being. Of course there is on the contemporary scene a more powerful claimant to philosophic mastery than either of them: Marxism. Marxist man is a creature of technics, a busy and ingenious animal, with secular religious faith in History, of which he is the chosen collaborator. . . . Both Marxism and Positivism are, intellectually speaking, relics of the nineteenth-century Englightenment that have not yet come to terms with the shadow side of human life as grasped even by some of the nineteenth-century thinkers themselves. The Marxist and Positivist picture of man, consequently, is thin and oversimplified. Existential philosophy, as a revolt against such oversimplification, attempts to grasp the image of the whole man, even where this involves bringing to consciousness all that is dark and questionable in his existence. And in just this respect it is a much more authentic expression of our own contemporary experience.

FURTHER READINGS

introductory approaches to the study of philosophy

Since philosophical problems tend to be complex and interdependent, there is no obvious place to begin the study of philosophy. Some find it best to approach the subject historically, while others find it best to approach it through specific philosophical problems (as we do in this anthology). Since philosophical problems arise when one begins to think deeply about anything, a good way to become familiar with philosophy is by pursuing specific philosophical questions that arise in other fields of study. No matter what the chosen area, the diligent pursuit of specific philosophical questions will almost inevitably lead to a confrontation with perennial general philosophical questions.

Those with an interest in psychology will find a good introduction to some of the problems of philosophy in Leslie Stevenson's *Seven Theories of Human Nature* (Oxford: Oxford University Press, 1974), which discusses the views of human nature held by Plato, Christianity, Freud, Lorenz, Sartre, Skinner, and Marx. Stevenson, a philosopher, ties these theories of human nature to more general philosophical world views and prefaces his consideration of these theories with a good general discussion of the nature of philosophical "theories" and the ways in which they can be criticized.

Those with an interest in political science might begin with *Marx and Engels: Basic Writings in Politics and Philosophy*, edited by Lewis Feuer (Garden City, N.Y.: Anchor, 1959) and Plato's, the *Republic*. Of the many editions of the *Republic* I would recommend the one translated by Francis MacDonald Cornford, which also contains Cornford's general introduction to the work and his running summary of it (New York: Oxford University Press, 1945). Other more recent good translations, with editorial interpretation, are those of Allan Bloom (New York: Basic Books, 1968) and Raymond Larson (Arlington Heights, Ill.: AHM Publications, 1979). The political philosophy of Plato and Marx can then be followed by Karl Popper's classic criticism of the totalitarianism of Plato and Marx in his *The Open Society and Its Enemies* (5th ed.), (Princeton, N.J.: Princeton University Press, 1966). This can then be followed by Robert Tucker's *Philosophy and Myth in Karl Marx*, a sympathetic exposition of the idealism of Marx's early writings (Cambridge: Cambridge University Press, 1969).

Those with an interest in theoretical science might begin by turning to Ernest Nagel's *The Structure of Science* (New York: Harcourt, Brace and World, 1962) and supplement it with Thomas S. Kuhn's *The Structure of Scientific Revolutions* (Chicago: University of Chicago Press, 1970, originally published in 1962). Those with an analytic frame of mind who are interested in epistemological questions could begin by reading A.J. Ayer's *Language, Truth and Logic* (New York: Dover Publications, 1952, originally published in 1935), the classic exposition of logical positivism. From there, one could progress to Ayer's later books, *The Foundations of Empirical Knowledge* (London: Macmillan, 1940), *The Problems of Philosophy* (London: Penguin, 1956), and *The Central Questions of Philosophy* (New York: Holt, Rinehart and Winston, 1973). If these books are read in sequence, one can get a good sense of the manner in which philosophical positions evolve, as they are sharpened or modified to meet challenges. In addition, in the course of reading these books, one will be exposed to the fundamental questions of metaphysics and epistemology by a philosopher who writes clearly and engagingly.

For those who would prefer to approach philosophy by way of a broad analytic (and not historical) exposure to major philosophical issues, there are many good philosophy textbooks. The one I would recommend for its clarity and engaging style is John Hosper's *An Introduction to Philosophical Analysis*, 2nd ed. (Englewood Cliffs, N.J.: Prentice-Hall, 1967). For those with an interest in the history of ideas, I have two strong preferences, John Herman Randall's *The Making of the Modern Mind* (Boston: Houghton Mifflin, 1926) and William Pepperell Montague's *Great Visions of Philosophy* (Illinois: Open Court Publishing Company, 1950). Both books are written by accomplished philosophers who clearly and engagingly present in broad strokes the central ideas of major philosophical world views. Randall's book in intellectual history is, as far as I am aware, unmatched in its ability to explain the role that philosophical ideas have played in the evolution of Western culture. (The book begins with Medieval Christendom and goes through the beginning of the twentieth century.) Montague's book is unmatched in its broad presentation of the philosophical world views of specific philosophers. Unlike other contemporary secondary sources that analytically dissect the *particular* aspects of a famous philosopher's world view, Montague neglects the analytic details, while presenting a panoramic map of the main interconnected features of philosophical world views that demonstrate the *breadth* of their imaginative and comprehensive visions of the cosmos. In so doing, Montague presents the beauty and unity of a philosophical vision that is often lost in the more analytic historical texts. For those who are interested in more detail (perhaps about a particular philosopher), I would recommend W.T. Jones' five-volume *A History of Western Philosophy* (New York: Harcourt, 1969), which is noted for its clarity, many direct quotes, and for its attention to the role that philosophy has played in Western culture. (The emphasis on this book, however, is in the exposition of specific ideas of important philosophers. Unlike the Randall book, which is interested primarily in intellectual currents, these currents are only a secondary concern in the Jones' book.) Those who would like a brief and easily readable general discussion of the ideas of a famous philosopher should read Bertrand Russell's *A History of Western Philosophy* (New York: Simon and Schuster, 1945). One should be aware, however, that Russell's interpretations and criticisms have been challenged by other philosophers.

Those interested in the history of recent philosophy have many very readable books to which they can turn. An excellent introduction to twentieth-century analytic philosophy and American pragmatism, intended for a novice in philosophy, is found in Abraham Kaplan's *The New World of Philosophy* (New York: Vintage, 1961), which also covers existentialism, Freud, Communism, Buddhism, and Chinese and Indian philosophy. A good book for those interested in an historical exposure to the main ideas of existentialism is William Barrett's *Irrational Man* (New York: Doubleday, 1962). Jean-Paul Sartre explains existentialism, and in particular his own version of it, in his famous essay "Existentialism," translated by Bernard Frechtman (New York: Philosophical Library, 1947). This essay first appeared under the title "Existentialism is a Humanism." Those who would prefer to approach Existentialism through literature can turn to Sartre's many novels and plays, in particular *Nausea*, as well as to Albert Camus' novels *The Stranger, The Plague,* and *The Fall* and his philosophical essays "The Myth of Sisyphus" and "The Rebel." A good introduction to Hindu, Buddhist and Chinese philosophies is found in John M. Koller's *Oriental Philosophies* (New York: Scribners, 1970). The best introduction to the background, philosophy, and techniques of Zen Buddhism is found in D.T. Suzuki's *Zen Buddhism*, edited by William Barrett (Garden City, N.Y.: Doubleday, 1956). An excellent introduction to the ideas of influential English twentieth-century analytic philosophers is found in G. J. Warnock's short and very readable *English Philosophy Since 1900* (New York: Oxford University Press, 1966), which concentrates on the ideas of G. E. Moore, Russell, Wittgenstein, Ryle, and Austin, as well as the logical positivists. A more comprehensive general history of recent philosophy is John Passmore's *A Hundred Years of Philosophy* (New York: Basic Books, 1966), which can either be read through or used as an excellent reference source. The best source material for comparing different contemporary Anglo-American viewpoints of the nature of philosophy is found in the anthology *The Owl of Minerva*, edited by J. Bontempo and S. Jack Odell (New York: McGraw-Hill, 1975). The long introduction by the editors is especially good in mapping out the various viewpoints expressed in the anthology.

basic reference sources

The Encyclopedia of Philosophy (New York: Macmillan, 1967) is the prime general reference source in philosophy. Its eight volumes contain articles on specific philosophical topics as well as on the ideas of famous philosophers. The articles are, however, of varying difficulty. While most of them are accessible to a philosophy novice, some are addressed to the philosophically sophisticated. All articles have bibliographies. There is a useful index at the end of volume eight. This source is always the place to begin in the preparation of a paper in philosophy.

The Dictionary of the History of Ideas (New York: Scribner's, 1973) is another excellent reference source for broad general surveys of philosophical ideas. Unlike *The Encyclopedia of Philosophy*, however, there are no entries on particular philosophers in this four-volume (with an index as the fifth volume) reference source. Those interested in the ideas of a particular philosopher should turn to the excellent index, which does have entries on particular philosophers and refers the reader to particular subjects. One should always begin with the index and its extensive cross-reference in researching a particular topic.

dictionaries of philosophy

There are several dictionaries of philosophy which consist of brief definitions of philosophical terminology and problems as well as biographies of important classical and contemporary philosophers, including their most important writings. In addition, there are brief bibliographies at the end of some of the entries and cross references from one entry to another. Since philosophical concepts are often used with different meanings, those interested in the meaning of a particular philosophical concept would be wise to check the definitions provided in more than one dictionary.

A Dictionary of Philosophy, ed. Anthony Flew (New York: St. Martin's, 1979).

A Dictionary of Philosophy, by A.R. Lacey (New York: Scribner's, 1976).

Dictionary of Philosophy, ed. D.D. Runes (Paterson, N.J.: Littlefield, Adams and Co., 1960).

A Concise Encyclopedia of Western Philosophy and Philosophers, ed. J.O. Urmson (London: Hutchinson, 1975).

World Philosophy, ed. Frank N. Magill (Englewood Cliffs, N.J.: Salem Press, 1982). This five volume set replaces Magill's one volume *Masterpieces of World Philosophy in Summary Form*, published in 1961. The set consists of 225 summaries and critical and historical reviews of the major works of 156 philosophers. The works are arranged chronologically, but indexes of the titles and authors are included. Reviews of pertinent secondary sources, annotated bibliographies, and a glossary of philosophical terms are also included. The essays are very clearly written and are intended for the general reader. Highly recommended.

Treasury of World Philosophy, ed. D.D. Runes (Paterson, N.J.: Littlefield, Adams and Co., 1959). This over 1200 page reference source provides brief introductions to the principal ideas of 375 major philosophers from antiquity to the present day. While there is some representation of Oriental philosophers, the book is devoted primarily to Western philosophers. Each entry begins with a biographical sketch of the philosopher, a list of major works, and a concise statement of the philosopher's place and importance in the history of philosophy. This is followed by one or more representative (self-contained) excerpts from the philosopher's works. Depending on the importance of the philosopher, each excerpt runs from a few paragraphs to several pages in length.

Marxism, Communism and Western Society: A Comparative Encyclopedia, ed. C.D. Kernig (New York: Herder and Herder, 1972–73), 8 vols. This is an excellent reference source for those interested in comparing Marxist and Western analyses of philosophical topics that range over the entire spectrum of philosophy. Indeed, those who have no special interest in Marxist philosophy can obtain greater insight into the presuppositions and perspectives of Anglo-American philosophers by comparing these presuppositions and perspectives to different ones. The articles are comprehensive and usually contain extensive bibliographic references.

Philosopher's Index (Philosophy Documentation Center, Bowling Green University, Ohio). This periodical index consists of alphabetic subject and author listings of articles that appear in philosophical periodicals and of philosophy books that are currently in publication. An abstract of the content of the work appears with the author listing. An index to book reviews is appended to each issue.

Chapter II

RELIGION AND THE EXISTENCE OF GOD

. . . and I have felt
A presence that disturbs me with the joy
Of elevated thoughts; a sense sublime
Of something far more deeply interfused,
Whose dwelling is the light of setting suns,
And the round ocean and the living air,
And the blue sky, and in the mind of man;
A motion and a spirit, that impels
All thinking things, all objects of all thought.
And rolls through all things . . .

William Wordsworth

That man is the product of causes which had no provision of the end they were achieving; that his origin, his growth, his hopes and fears, his loves and his beliefs, are but the outcome of accidental collocations of atoms; that . . . no intensity of thought and feeling can preserve an individual life beyond the grave; that all the labours of the ages . . . are destined to extinction in the vast death of the solar system . . . all these things . . . are . . . so nearly certain, that no philosophy which rejects them can hope to stand . . .

Bertrand Russell

It is clear from what has been said that there is a substance which is eternal and unmovable and separate from sensible things. It has been shown also that this substance cannot have any magnitude, but is without parts and indivisible . . .

Aristotle

I maintain that all attempts to employ reason in theology in any merely speculative manner are altogether fruitless . . .

Immanuel Kant

. . . can there be a future good so great as to render acceptable, in retrospect, the whole human experience, with all its wickedness and suffering as well as all its sanctity and happiness? I think that perhaps there can, and indeed perhaps there is . . .

John Hick

"Tell me yourself, I challenge you—answer. Imagine that you are creating a fabric of human destiny with the object of making men happy in the end, giving them peace and rest at last, but that it was essential and inevitable to torture to death only one tiny creature—that baby beating its breast with its fist, for instance—and to found that edifice on its unavenged tears, would you consent to be the architect on those conditions? Tell me, and tell the truth."

"No, I wouldn't consent," said Alyosha softly.

Fyodor Dostoevsky

. . . .And though I have never gone back to [the] theologic supernaturalism [of my youth], I have come to appreciate more than I once did the symbolism in which is celebrated the human need of trusting to the larger vision, according to which calamities come and go but the continuity of life and faith in its better possibilities survive.

Morris Raphael Cohen

For so many of us, the first stirring of philosophical wonder and puzzlement comes when, as children, we stare up at the sky and feel overwhelmed by the awesome vastness of what we see. As we gaze at the stars above us, we wonder how far they extend. Are there boundaries to the physical world we inhabit? If so, what lies beyond these boundaries? If not, we wonder what a boundless universe would be like, vainly struggling to visualize such a puzzling notion. The wonder and puzzlement we feel as to the physical extent of the universe leads naturally to a wider metaphysical wonder and puzzlement. "Where did the world come from?" "Why is it here?" "Why are we here?" "Will we cease to exist when death inevitably comes or is there some life beyond the grave?" As these puzzling and troubling questions crowd in upon our undeveloped minds, we turn to our parents who tell us that there is a loving God who created us and everything else in this world and that we will join him when we die. We are usually satisfied with such an answer and feel more at home in the vastness of the world around us. The religious training most of us receive reinforces this feeling and amplifies the religious world view learned from our parents. But at some time most of us wonder if this world view is really true. As we grow older, we realize that there are different and conflicting religions.

How then do we know that the religion we were taught is the correct one? Are all religions, perhaps, false and accepted only because of the psychological comfort they provide? These questions are too troubling for most of us and we attempt to put them out of our minds, turning our attention to the practical problems of life that surround us. Sometimes, however, when the vastness of the undeserved suffering of this world hits us in a personal way, such doubts cannot be cast aside easily and we seriously question the justification of our religious belief in a loving, all-powerful God and a morally purposeful universe. In such a state, we turn again to the old metaphysical questions that we found so puzzling as children.

The Concept of "Religion"

For those brought up in the Judeo-Christian tradition the question of God's existence is the central one in the philosophy of religion (i.e., that branch of philosophy which considers the meaning and justification of religious beliefs and practices). An even more basic question that philosophy of religion must face, however, is what is meant by a *religion*. Many would define "religion" as "belief in a supernatural god." While such a definition gets at the heart of contemporary *Western* religion—that is, Christianity, Judaism, and Islam—it does not get at the heart of those *Eastern* religions in which the belief in some type of god does not play a central role. Indeed, some Confucians do not believe in a supernatural god at all, and some have suggested that this was true of Confucius as well. Similarly, not all Buddhists believe in a god. Yet Buddhism and Confucianism, all would agree, should be classified as religions. Since most of us do not know much about religions other than our own, it is understandable that we should attempt to define "religion" with our particular religion in mind. As a result, our definitions tend to be narrow and biased ones that fail to include religions different from our own.

According to the influential late Protestant theologian Paul Tillich, the essence of a "religious life" is an unconditional surrender to something around which one centers one's life and in which one seeks supreme fulfillment and meaning. It is this attitude of "ultimate concern," as Tillich called it, which he identified with "religious faith." Such a conception of religious faith is broad enough to encompass all the generally recognized religious faiths. However, most of us will find it too broad to be useful. After all, patriotism, money, power, or even such things as food and golf have been "the ultimate concern" of some people. While the concept of "religion" is at times identified loosely in ordinary language as "the object of one's ultimate concern" (e.g., "money is his religion"), most of us would recognize this usage as an extension of a narrower definition of "religion" *in its full sense*.

Recognizing the need to restrict the possible scope of the objects of religions' ultimate concerns, some have offered definitions of "religion" in which moral concerns play a central role. While this is true of today's widely held religions, it clearly was not true in the past. Indeed, early Judaism distinguished itself from the "pagan religions" that existed alongside it precisely because it conceived of God as a *moral* being. The association we readily make today between the concepts of religion and morality has not always been made. For example, the gods of Greek mythology were not ideals of moral perfection, and yet we tend to unhesitantly classify the belief in such beings as a form of religion.

Like many commonly used notions, the notion of "religion" is a *vague* one—that is, it does not sharply distinguish those things which are religions from those which are not. There is no single characteristic that all commonly recognized religions share, whether it is a particular belief (e.g., in gods) or a particular concern (e.g., to provide a moral code). On the contrary, there is a cluster of features that is associated with the concept of "religion." When all of these features are present, there can be no doubt that we are dealing with a religion. As more and more features are found to be lacking, however, we find ourselves less and less apt to describe what we have before us as a religion. In making such decisions, individuals will be influenced by their own views of what is *most important* in their own religion. There is, however, vast disagreement on this highly subjective matter and consequently vast disagreement on how "religion" ought to be defined.

What then are the features that are associated with religion? First, religions typically contain a framework of *beliefs* (a world view), providing a picture of the ultimate nature of things and of the place of human beings within the scheme of things. Often, but not always, such a world view involves a belief in supernatural beings. On the basis of this world view religions typically provide views of human nature, of what is right and wrong with human beings, and of how to put things straight. These, in turn, lead to comprehensive moral codes which prescribe ways of life. Such beliefs and moral codes are not, however, merely assented to in a purely intellectual manner; they generate *emotional commitment* and feelings of reverence, often coupled with feelings of awe and a response to certain aspects of experience as sacred or holy. The emotional dimension of religion is, in turn, reinforced by socially shared rituals and other *practices*.

Since many people in Western culture associate religion with the belief in a supernatural god, in rejecting such a belief, they reject religion as well. For example, this was true of Sigmund Freud (1856–1939), the founder of psychoanalysis, who claimed that "religion is the universal neurosis of mankind," and it was true of Karl Marx (1818–83), who claimed that "religion is the opium of the people." It was true, too, of Bertrand Russell (1872–1970), who persistently attacked religion as "an obstacle to social progress." These individuals clearly meant to attack the Judeo-Christian religious tradition and its belief in God, not religion defined more broadly as involving a socially shared, strong emotional commitment to a world view and the moral attitudes and actions it generates. (Indeed, in this sense, a commitment to Marx' own communistic philosophy has been said to be a religion.)

Not all philosophers who reject the belief in a supernatural god also lack an interest in defending some other type of religious outlook. Included in the selections of this chapter are defenses of religion or of religious outlooks by three well-known twentieth-century naturalistic philosophers—John Dewey, George Santayana, and Morris R. Cohen—who reject the belief in a supernatural god. For Dewey, the essence of a religious outlook is an *individual* commitment to the achievement of moral ideals. Born a Protestant, Dewey sees no special value in the rituals, ceremonies, and symbolism of specific organized religions. But Santayana, born a Catholic, and Cohen, born a Jew, see great value in them. For many in Western culture, however, such defenses of religion without God are feeble substitutes for the comfort that comes from belief in God. But, can one supply some proof or evidence justifying the belief in such a being? And if not, ought one to cling to this belief on faith? Is one not better off with such faith than without it?

The Judeo-Christian Concept of God

Before considering the rationality of belief in the god of the Judeo-Christian religious tradition, we must understand what a person within this tradition *means* by "God." What, to begin with, are the properties a being must possess to be a "god" at all? Clearly, we think of "gods" as more powerful than human beings. We also think of them as conscious beings. Most important, however, we think of them as "supernatural beings"—that is, as beings that are not subject to the laws of nature of this universe. We would not say, for example, that "Superman" was a supernatural being since we assume that he too was subject to the same laws of nature to which human beings are subject. His power came, not from his "supernatural" status, but from his nonhuman nature.

The god of the Judeo-Christian tradition (i.e., God) is, however, much more than a powerful, supernatural, and conscious being. He is:

1. personal (i.e., he is not only conscious but has emotions which enable us to relate to him as a *person* and to speak of him as loving and caring for human beings)
2. purely spiritual (noncorporeal)
3. actively involved in the universe (immanent), but separate from it (transcendent)
4. creator of all else that exists
5. eternal (always has and always will exist)
6. omnipotent (all-powerful)
7. omniscient (all-knowing)
8. morally perfect

While this concept of God is widely shared by Christians, Jews, and Muslims, theologians within these religions have strong disagreements as to specific interpretations of each of these attributes. For example, they disagree about what it means to attribute "emotions" to God. They also disagree about whether God's omniscience entails that he knows beforehand what choices human beings will make when they utilize the "free will" which he has given them. Many theologians, following Saint Augustine (354–430), believe that although God does have foreknowledge of human actions, this does not conflict with the existence of free will since God does not *force* human beings to make the choices that they do. Other theologians disagree, claiming that free will logically precludes foreknowledge of human choices, even by God. According to this view, although God knows everything *that can be known*, the choices of free agents (logically) cannot be known beforehand. In addition, while Jews and Muslims, as well as Christians, would accept the preceding characterization of God, Jews and Muslims would deny such Christian doctrines as the "trinity" and "incarnation" (i.e., that God is "three persons in one substance" and that God became man in the form of Jesus), doctrines that are central to the Christian concept of God.

Those who affirm the existence of God are usually referred to as *theists*. As usually defined, *atheists* are those who deny the existence of God, while *agnostics* are those who claim that we do not have sufficient evidence to know whether or not God exists. This characterization is not, however, as clear as it appears. Bertrand Russell, for example, referred to himself as an agnostic, but many of his commentators referred to him as an atheist. This disagreement was not over what Russell believed or disbelieved, but rather over the meaning of these two terms. As Russell saw it, while it was *possible* for God to exist, it was *highly improbable*—no more probable than the existence of the fancies of science fiction writers. As Russell apparently used these terms, atheists are those who deny that there is any possibility that God exists, while agnostics are those nonbelievers in God who grant the possibility, however remote, of God's existence. It may be better, however, to define *atheism* more broadly to include those who (to put it loosely) contend that there is "no reasonable chance" that God exists; after all, those who believe in God, we would all agree, need not be absolutely convinced that God exists. Just as one can *affirm* the existence of God, while admitting doubt, one can *deny* the existence of God, while admitting that there is a remote possibility that he might exist. In addition, just as one can affirm the existence of God on pure faith, without any consideration of evidence, one can deny the existence of God on sheer faith. Since we speak of theistic faith, should we not also speak of atheistic faith, leaving the term *agnostic* for those who neither affirm nor deny God's existence? *Agnostics* would then refer to those exposed to the belief in God who are either unthinkingly indifferent to the probability of his existence or those who, after reflection, contend that there is insufficient justification to warrant either affirming or denying God's existence.

The distinction between atheism and agnosticism is further complicated by the fact that some philosophers have gone so far as to assert that the very concept of God (or some interpretation of it) is meaningless. According to this point of view, since the very concept of God is meaningless, it is as meaningless to assert that God does not exist as to assert that he does. Consequently, if one defines atheism as the denial of God's existence and takes this claim to be synonymous with the claim that it is false that God exists, those who deny the meaningfulness of the concept of God cannot be said to be atheists. Believing that it would be more enlightening to describe such people as atheists, some philosophers have chosen to define *atheism* more broadly as the *rejection* of God's existence as either false or meaningless.

The dismissal of talk of God as meaningless was an especially prevalent view from the 1930's through the 1960's when many philosophers, known as *logical positivists*, accepted *the verifiability theory of meaning*, which asserts that statements are meaningless when there are no specific experiences that can be taken to verify (or falsify) them. In particular, the positivists claimed, when a theist says that there is an all-knowing, all-powerful God who loves us as a father loves his children but then goes on to say that this is compatible with the existence of all types of undeserved suffering, there is nothing asserted by such a claim, since there is nothing ruled out by it. In response, some contemporary theologians (e.g., John Hick) have claimed that the belief in God is verifiable if *after death* we encounter God and discover his good reasons for allowing undeserved suffering to exist in this world. Nevertheless, one is still faced with the problem of specifying what is to count as "encountering God." How, for example, could one verify that one had encountered a being of *unlimited power*? How does one verify, too, that God's goodness and love are "infinite," as theologians assert? In addition, as we shall see in the next chapter, there are some contemporary philosophers who would challenge the very intelligibility of the notion of a person continuing to exist after death. (This issue involves the meaning of personal identity, an issue we shall discuss in the next chapter.)

Arguments for God's Existence

No doubt, most people who believe in God do so, not because they have been convinced by rational argument, but because from an early age they have been indoctrinated to believe and find it comforting to believe. For example, the Bible, the main source of most Christians' and Jews' knowledge of God, begins with the *assumption* that there is a God, an assumption that is nowhere subjected to rational scrutiny. When as children we are first exposed to the stories of the Bible, we tend unquestioningly to assume the truth of these stories. For example, we read in the Old Testament about how God tested Abraham's faith by commanding him to sacrifice his beloved son Isaac—a sacrifice which was prevented at the last moment by God's intervention. We rarely stop, however, to reflect how Abraham knew that it was God who had "spoken" to him. If someone were to tell us today that God asked him to sacrifice his child, we would think that he had taken leave of his senses. If, on the other hand, we assume that it was indeed "God" who spoke to Abraham, does not the manner in which Abraham's faith was tested bring into question God's moral perfection? (Does not the Biblical story of God's treatment of Job also bring into question God's moral perfection?) When we are instructed about Biblical stories, we are rarely encouraged to consider questions of consistency and justification like these. We rarely are encouraged to think, too, of the fact that there are conflicting versions of the Bible, and that other religions have their own sacred books that contradict the Bible in important respects. It is only when the authority of the Bible (or a particular version or interpretation of it) is challenged by others that people tend to become aware of the need to find a justification for that authority.

prophecy

For many believers, that justification comes from alleged Biblical prophecies. (But other books of holy writings have their prophecies too.) Yet this attempted justification will not convince those who are not already convinced. For example, an atheist will not assume that Christ's coming was prophesied but will claim that it was precisely because people believed in the prophecy of Christ's coming that they mistakenly identified Jesus as Christ. An atheist also will not be convinced by the indefinite prophecies which so many different events can be taken to verify (e.g., "a great war between nations"). But even if there are specific definite and verified prophecies in the Bible, it is possible for an atheist to see them not as coming from God but as a manifestation of a *natural* human power of precognizance (knowing the future). (As we shall see in the next chapter, there are many who believe in such a power.) If precognizance is accepted, one can see the prophets mentioned in the Bible as psychics of their time who mistakenly thought their power came from God. One can certainly understand why people who believe in God and find themselves possessed of a strange and frightening power would want to believe that this power comes from God. No doubt, the evidence for the belief in a natural human capacity for precognizance is far from conclusive. But is this belief less likely to be true than the belief that God is the source of prophecy? After all, many would claim that there is independent evidence for the belief in precognizance and not for the belief in God.

miracles

Just as nonbelievers in God are apt to attempt either to reject the existence of specific prophecies mentioned in the Bible or to provide some nonreligious explanation for them, so, too, nonbelievers are apt either to reject or offer nonreligious explanations for the alleged biblical miracles. Especially since there are no direct witnesses to these alleged miracles, nonbelievers are apt to believe that the events described either did not happen at all or did not happen as described.

On the other hand, if descriptions of alleged miraculous events in the Bible are accepted by the nonbeliever, he will most likely seek a scientific explanation of them. For example, one might attribute Jesus' alleged healing power to some *natural* psychic process and not to God. (Indeed, Jesus often attributed his healing powers to the faith of those whom he healed.) There are, indeed, many today who emphasize the untapped power of the mind in causing physical changes in the body. Perhaps in the future there will be scientific laws and theories that will explain how the mind can effect cures that are now scientifically unexplainable. Is it any more likely that these cures are miracles from God than that they are natural phenomena that can be accounted for by scientific laws not yet discovered? In addition, if one attributes inexplicable cures to the workings of a good god, has one not as much right logically to attribute inexplicable contractions of diseases to the works of "the devil?" What right has one to assume that while there is always a scientific explanation for why some individuals get a given disease, there is not always a scientific explanation for why some individuals recover from a given disease? (See Selection #13 for a more thorough discussion of the argument from miracles for God's existence.)

Classical Philosophical Arguments for God's Existence

From the Middle Ages to the nineteenth century, most Western philosophers believed that there were good arguments for the existence of God. In support of this belief, philosophers usually relied on versions of the classical triad of arguments for God's existence—the *ontological, cosmological*, and *teleological* arguments. The teleological argument (or argument from design) claims that the apparent purposeful nature of the universe provides strong, but not conclusive, evidence that it has a designer—namely God. There are various versions of the cosmological argument for God's existence, which claims that God *must* exist as the ultimate cause or explanation for the existence of the physical world. According to one version, known as *the first cause argument*, since every event in the universe must have a cause and since the backward progression of causes must ultimately come to an end, there must be a god who is the supernatural first cause of all that exists in the universe. According to another version, known as *the argument from contingency*, while the universe may have always existed, there must be some ultimate explanation for its existence, an explanation that itself requires no further explanation. Only the existence of God, it is claimed, can provide such an explanation. There are also various forms of the ontological argument, which claims that the very definition of God makes it impossible that he should not exist. In addition to these classical arguments for God's existence, philosophers have turned to alleged direct experiences of God or to the existence of the human capacity to make moral distinctions as justification for the belief in God.

the ontological argument

Unlike other arguments for God's existence, the ontological argument does not have a widespread intuitive appeal. The classic formulation of this argument was presented by St. Anselm (1033–1109), and the argument in various forms, was defended by several subsequent philosophers, in particular, Descartes. In its simplest version, the ontological argument begins by defining God as an all-perfect being, a being possessing all conceivable perfections. It claims that such a being must exist, since existence itself is a "perfection" (i.e., it is better to exist than not to exist). If God did not exist, he would not be all-perfect. Consequently, he must exist. According to this argument, then, just as one knows *by definition* that a rectangle must have four sides, one knows *by definition* that God must exist.

For most philosophers, as well as practically everyone else, the ontological argument seems transparently fallacious. Yet there are still some defenders of versions of this argument and, even among the majority of philosophers who reject it, there is no consensus on *exactly* what is wrong with it. For most, however, it would suffice to say that "one cannot define beings into existence" or to put it slightly differently, "it makes no sense to make existence a defining property of an object." It is one thing to define a given concept and something quite different to speak of that concept as having application to something. For example, it is one thing to define a "perfect husband or wife" as someone who is always considerate, always loving, always understanding, and so on; it is something quite different to say that this concept has application to some individual. It would be nice if we could say that a perfect husband or wife must also, by definition, exist, otherwise he or she would not be perfect, but we all realize that language alone cannot create our hearts' desires. For some philosophers, however, the case is somehow different with God.

the first cause argument

According to the first cause argument, we find that things and events in this world are always caused by preceding things and events which have their own preceding causes. But, it is claimed, such a series of causes must finally come to an end in a supernatural first cause which we call God. This argument, practically all philosophers would readily agree, falls apart under scrutiny. First, even if one accepts all the assumptions (premises) of the argument, it does not at all establish the existence of the Judeo-Christian God, that is, a god who is omnipotent, omniscient, and so on. Second, even if this argument can establish that the universe has a beginning, it cannot establish a *single* first cause—that is, it cannot establish that all the various causal chains that exist in this universe ultimately merge. For example, it leaves open the possibility that the universe was created by a good and an evil deity working at cross-purposes. Third, it does not establish that the first cause (or causes) of the universe presently exists (exist). Fourth, even if it could establish that there must be a single ultimate cause of the universe, it does not establish that the *immediate* cause of the world is this ultimate cause. For example, it does not exclude the possibility that the world was created by the devil, who in turn was created by God.

Each of the premises of the first cause argument can also be challenged. First, if all things in this universe must have a cause, why does God not require a cause, too? If, on the other hand, we can conceive of God existing without a cause, why can we not conceive of the universe existing without a cause? Similarly, if we can conceive of God's existing eternally, why can we not equally as well conceive of the universe existing eternally?

the argument from contingency

Faced with such criticisms, defenders of the first cause argument often transform it into the more abstract argument from contingency which, while admitting that the world might have existed eternally, argues that if this were the case, there would still have to be an explanation for why the world existed eternally. A modern formulation of this argument is offered by the contemporary philosopher Richard Taylor (Selection #10). As Taylor sees it, all events in this universe and indeed the universe itself are *contingent*—that is, they require as an explanation for their existence something outside themselves. But one has not really *explained* the events in this universe nor the fact that there is a universe at all, until one has traced back one's explanations to some being that does not need to be explained by reference to something else—i.e., to a *necessary being* that *exists by its own nature*. As other philosophers see it, however, the notion of a "necessary being" is unintelligible. From their point of view, the quest for some ultimate explanation that is self-explanatory is a quest for something that is logically unintelligible.

the argument from design (teleological argument)

The argument from design has always been the most popular of arguments for God's existence among sophisticated and unsophisticated believers alike. Indeed, prior to the widespread acceptance of naturalistic theories of evolutionary development, most intellectuals took it for granted that the only reasonable explanation for the vast complexity of our world and especially for the purposeful activity of the living creatures that inhabit it was the hypothesis that it was designed by a supernatural being. Underlying this argument is the awe that practically all of us have felt, at one time or another, when we are struck by the remarkable complexity and order that surrounds us. How can something as complex as the world be an accident, we wonder. Does not the order which science continually discovers underlying the behavior of things suggest design? In particular, we stare awe-struck at the marvels of biological organisms and especially at the marvels of the human body. How is it possible that such an intricate mechanism as the human body has occurred simply by chance? How, too, we tend to wonder, could it be due simply to chance that our environment, which could so easily have been vastly different, is so well adapted to support life? Does not the mutual adjustment of things in this world strongly point to an intelligent designer—that is, to God? In Selection #6, A. Cressy Morrison, a scientist, presents a contemporary defense of the argument from design which reflects these common sentiments.

The definitive critique of the argument from design is found in David Hume's (1711–76) masterpiece, *Dialogues Concerning Natural Religion* (Selection #8). Hume presents three broad criticisms against this argument. First, he challenges our justification for comparing the world to man-made mechanisms or machines that are purposefully designed. Anticipating the nineteenth-century philosopher Feuerbach and the twentieth-century psychiatrist Freud, Hume suggests that by looking at God as an intelligent designer, we are unjustifiably projecting our own human attributes on the ultimate source of order in this universe. (It is not, as Feuerbach put it, that God created us in his image, but rather that we create God in our image.) Many hypotheses as to the ultimate origin of the world, Hume claims, are suggested by our experience and are equally arbitrary. Second, echoing the main criticism of the first cause argument, Hume claims that, for all we know, the principle of order in the universe may not have an external cause but be inherent in the very nature of the universe itself. We gain nothing intellectually, Hume claims, by inferring that the complex universe was designed by a complex God, for this hypothesis leads to the unanswerable question of how the complexity of God is to be explained. If we say as learned believers do that such is simply the nature of God and is not a result of any external cause, we can equally as well say the same of the universe. We obtain no satisfactory explanation of things, Hume claims, by explaining the universe in terms of a God at least equally in need of explanation as the universe he is meant to explain.

Third, Hume argues that even if we had sufficient basis for inferring a designer of this universe, we have no basis for inferring that this designer is God. If the world requires a designer, there is no reason to believe that he is, for example, all-powerful. For all we know, he may have been a "bungling deity," relative to standards of world-building known to deities, but not to us. Similarly, the world need not have been designed by only one deity but instead may have been designed by two or more deities working together or at cross-purposes. There is no evidence, furthermore, to suggest that the world was designed by a morally perfect deity or by a deity that is especially concerned about human beings.

While Hume's philosophical criticisms have greatly influenced philosophers, Darwin's theory of evolution through natural selection has done the most to weaken the argument from design by offering a purely naturalistic explanation for the adaptation of living creatures to their environment and the emergence of more complex organisms from simpler ones. A naturalistic explanation for the existence of very primitive organisms has in turn been sought in our current knowledge of chemistry, which has led to the laboratory synthesis of organic compounds from inorganic ones. This has provided evidence, it is claimed, for the chance emergence of simple organic compounds and then organisms under the physical conditions that existed in the oceans of this planet many ages ago. The likelihood of chance emergence of simple organisms from inorganic material and of Darwin's theory of evolution through natural selection has recently been called into question by "scientific creationists" who reject evolutionary theory and adhere to the story of creation outlined in the Bible. Adherents of this viewpoint defend their position by pointing out significant gaps in the evidence for and explanatory power of Darwin's theory of evolution. Darwinism has also been called into question by scientists who take evolution as a "fact," but challenge Darwin's theory of natural selection as the process by which evolution takes place. (See the editorial comments on pp. 165–66 of the suggestions for Further Reading.)

religious experience

As confidence in the cogency of the ontological, cosmological, and teleological arguments for God's existence waned in the nineteenth and twentieth centuries, many theologians turned away from appeals to abstract reason and to the nature of the world outside us as support for the belief in the existence of God, turning their attention instead to subjective human religious or moral experience.

As those who base belief in God on religious experience see it, one may have the most direct knowledge possible of God's existence, the knowledge that comes from *directly experiencing God's presence*. In spite of much diversity in the description of such alleged direct encounters with God, it is often claimed that while in the grips of this experience one feels oneself losing one's self-identity and "merging with God," feeling enveloped within the warmth and concern of a moral being. Nevertheless, those who have had such mystical experiences are united in claiming that words cannot adequately convey their content. However inadequate words may be to express to others the nature of a direct encounter with God, many of those who claim to have had such experiences contend that they know beyond the shadow of any doubt that such experiences are indeed encounters with God. The grounds they have for such a claim are rarely made clear.

One must recognize that a person who claims to be "experiencing God" is doing more than *neutrally describing the content of his experience* (e.g., I *felt* that . . .) but is attempting to give an explanation of the *cause of that experience*. While one should grant the sincerity of the very strong *beliefs* people have had that they are "in the presence of God," the mere strength of one's conviction is no guarantee of its truth. Clearly, some people who are convinced that they are experiencing God are deluded. Is it not *possible* then that all who think they are experiencing God are deluded? The answer must be yes. Indeed, many philosophers have claimed that this is not only possible, but *likely*. For example, Bertrand Russell once wrote that "From a scientific point of view, we can make no distinction between the man who eats little and sees heaven and the man who drinks much and sees snakes. Each is in an abnormal physical condition, and therefore has abnormal perceptions." Following Freud, others would stress that unfulfilled inner psychological needs are often the source of these perceptual illusions.

On the other hand, even if it were true that those who claim to be "experiencing God" were at that time in an "abnormal physical condition" or were "psychologically abnormal," this would not guarantee that they were victims of delusions. As the philosopher C.D. Broad (1887–1971) put it:

> Suppose, for the sake of argument, that there is an aspect of the world which remains altogether outside the ken of ordinary persons in their daily life. Then it seems very likely that some degree of mental or physical abnormality would be a necessary condition for getting sufficiently loosened from the objects of ordinary sense-perception to come into cognitive contact with this aspect of reality. Therefore the fact that those persons who claim to have this peculiar kind of cognition generally exhibit certain mental and physical abnormalities is rather what might be antici-

pated if their claims were true. One might need to be slightly ''cracked'' in order to have some peepholes into the super-sensible world.

But is there good reason to believe that alleged religious experiences of God are ''peepholes into the super-sensible world,'' and even if this were the case, is there good reason to believe that such experiences are experiences of God? Indeed, Broad himself, while accepting the view that religious experiences are probably often revelations of ''an aspect of [external] reality,'' also believed that this ''aspect of reality'' was most probably misdescribed as experiences of God. Clearly if there is some ''aspect of reality'' that is quite different from that part of reality that is open to normal perception, we would be at a loss to adequately describe it. Those who claim to have direct experiences of God emphasize this point, claiming that words that relate to ordinary experience cannot capture the character of these experiences. Yet they utilize the words of traditional theology to describe these experiences when they say they are experiencing God—that is, a transcendent, all-powerful, all-knowing, all-good creator of all else that exists. But how do they know they are experiencing such a being? (Indeed, many religious mystics, such as Saint Teresa, while convinced that an external reality was the cause of their mystical states, were concerned that it might be ''the devil'' attempting to deceive them.)

What good reasons then can people have for claiming to have experienced God or, indeed, any external reality? The profound effects of such experiences in giving individuals moral strength and a sense of purpose or in causing radical character transformation is not evidence of the nondelusional character of such experiences, for such effects can be attributed to the *strength of one's belief* in the nondelusional character of one's experience and not to the truth of that belief. Nor does the large number of people who have had such experiences support the view that such experiences are nondelusional, for delusions, too, can be widespread.

On the other hand, is it perhaps unfair for those who have never had such experiences to assume so readily that they are all delusions? (In Selection #11, William James, who was himself quite sympathetic to religious experiences, takes this position). Are naturalists such as Russell and Freud any more capable of providing evidence for their belief that religious experiences are all delusions than religious believers are capable of providing evidence for their belief that they are not? This is the central question. But even if one answers this question in the negative (as James would), those who have never had religious experiences will not have good reason to accept the testimony of others unless they are already inclined to believe in some reality hidden from normal perception. (James would agree.)

moral arguments for god's existence

According to some theologians, the key to establishing God's existence lies not in evidence gathered from the world outside of us, but in moral evidence from within. According to one version of this argument (defended by C.S. Lewis in Selection #12), since the demands of morality are experienced as objective external demands that are binding upon us independently of our own feelings or inclinations, there must be some moral lawgiver who is the external source of these moral demands—that is, God. Central to this argument is the assumption, challenged by others, that moral values are incapable of full explanation in terms of human psychological needs and desires and the demands of social life.

Another version of a moral argument for God's existence is found in the writings of the philosopher Immanuel Kant (1724–1804). As Kant saw it, the ''highest good'' of the moral life is that ''happiness be proportioned to moral virtue.'' Yet it is quite clear that this is often not the case in this world. Consequently, if morality is ultimately to make sense, there must be an afterlife in which virtue is rewarded and vice punished. For this reason, Kant claimed, the existence of an afterlife where reward is proportioned to desert, and of God to assure such an afterlife is a postulate (i.e., assumption) of the moral life. But even if it is true that the moral life would ultimately be senseless and life itself ultimately absurd or meaningless if God did not exist, does this provide a rational reason for assuming God's existence? If no conclusive proof or good evidence of God's existence can be given, would not rationality demand that we either reject the view that life would be meaningless without God or squarely face the fact that life most likely is meaningless?

the atheist's challenge: the problem of evil

Those who believe in God but who find themselves incapable of giving adequate arguments to defend that belief commonly retort at the end, "Well you show me that God doesn't exist. If you can't, then there is no more reason for not believing in God than there is for believing." Implicit in such a reply is the assumption that if there is no definite evidence for or against the existence of God, then the existence of God is as probable as his nonexistence. This is a mistake. Since there is an indefinitely large number of possible hypotheses concerning the ultimate origin of the universe (e.g., the universe has no external creator, or two creators working at cross-purposes), the burden of proof should be on those who choose one of these innumerable hypotheses, such as the belief in God. If no reason can be given why the belief in God is more likely to be true than any other hypothesis, an atheist is on solid ground if he rejects this belief as highly unlikely, while committing himself to no other specific hypothesis.

Nevertheless, atheists are not content simply to criticize the arguments theologians offer for God's existence. They also attempt to provide positive grounds for rejecting his existence. By far the strongest of these grounds is the problem of evil—that is, the problem of why an all-powerful, all-knowing, and perfectly good god would allow so much evil to exist in this world. For some atheists, the vast amount of evil in this world conclusively (deductively) establishes the nonexistence of God. They see no conceivable reason why a perfectly good being, knowing that this evil exists and having the power to prevent it, should choose not to use that power. Others while allowing that God might have a good reason for allowing evil to exist, believe that the immense amount of undeserved and apparently senseless suffering in this world makes such an hypothesis highly unlikely. Among those who contend that the problem of evil makes it unreasonable to believe in the Judeo-Christian God, some argue for a good god of limited power. (The problem of evil is discussed in Selectons #14–17.)

faith

Assuming that there is no proof or evidence for the existence of God and that the problem of evil does not make it irrational to believe in God, would it be rational, nevertheless, to believe in God simply on faith? Many laypersons and philosophers have thought so, including William James in his classic defense of faith, "The Will to Believe" (Selection #18). As James sees it, atheists and agnostics both neglect the fact that religious belief has profound *practical significance* and is not a matter for detached intellectual curiosity. So he argues that belief in God, even if based on no evidence whatsoever, can be *rational* belief. As the seventeenth-century philosopher Pascal, who offered a similar argument, put it, "the heart has its reasons that reason knows not of." James' essay has generated much philosophical criticism by philosophers who are morally fearful of the undesirable consequences they see lurking in the license to believe that James advocates. Yet James has had his defenders too.

5. AN ATHEIST'S SATIRICAL COMMENTARY ON THE JUDEO-CHRISTIAN GOD

Mark Twain

MARK TWAIN (1835–1910) was the pen name of Samuel Clemens, who is generally considered the greatest humorist in American literature. Although practically everyone as a youngster has had the delight of reading such classics as **The Adventures of Tom Sawyer** and **The Adventures of Huckleberry Finn**, most people are unaware that Twain was a caustic and earthy social critic of his day who wrote many essays in popular social criticism. Despite his extraordinary sense of humor, Twain had a strong depressive and melancholic streak in his personality. Depressed by financial misfortune, the deaths of his wife and youngest daughter from painful illnesses, and his own declining health, Twain became especially bitter in his later years. Nowhere is this bitterness greater than in Twain's many antireligious writings. Twain's unrelenting sarcastic attack on the belief in God is shown in his "Letters From Earth," which, given its highly unconventional viewpoint, was not published until after his death.

The following selection, which consists of excerpts from this work, attacks a literal interpretation of the Bible and the goodness of God. The setting Twain imagines for this work is itself diabolical. Satan has been banished from heaven for rebelling against God and decides to visit the Earth. He writes letters back to some of the angels about what he has found. In a nutshell, what he claims to have found is that in regard to religion, people unthinkably attribute to God actions which would be seen as the most atrocious of crimes were they committed by ordinary people. (Twain's view of the problem of evil is very amusingly and sarcastically presented in "Little Bessie," an abridged version of which is included along with other selections on the problems of evil in a later part of this chapter.)

While believers in God may be offended by the sacrilegious manner in which Twain discusses the Bible and God, a rational believer cannot help but be affected by what Twain says. Unlike more abstract philosophers, Twain writes for the average person. His ability to get at the heart of an issue with great clarity makes one think about the religious beliefs people tend to accept so uncritically. For this reason, the selections on religion begin with this caustic excerpt from vintage Twain.

Satan's Letter

This is a strange place, an extraordinary place, and interesting. There is nothing resembling it at home. The people are all insane, the other animals are all insane, the earth is insane, Nature itself is insane. Man is a marvelous curiosity. When he is at his very very best he is a sort of low grade nickel-plated angel; at his worst he is unspeakable, unimaginable; and first and last and all the time he is a sarcasm. Yet he blandly and in all sincerity calls himself the "noblest work of God." This is the truth I am telling you. And this is not a new idea with him,

Source: From *What Is Man? And Other Philosophical Writings*, Paul Baender (ed.), University of California Press, 1973.

he has talked it through all the ages, and believed it. Believed it, and found nobody among all his race to laugh at it.

Moreover—if I may put another strain upon you—he thinks he is the Creator's pet. He believes the Creator is proud of him; he even believes the Creator loves him; has a passion for him; sits up nights to admire him; yes, and watch over him and keep him out of trouble. He prays to Him, and thinks He listens. Isn't it a quaint idea? Fills his prayers with crude and bald and florid flatteries of Him, and thinks He sits and purrs over these extravagancies and enjoys them. He prays for help, and favor, and protection, every day; and does it with hopefulness and confidence, too, although no prayer of his has ever been answered. The daily affront, the daily defeat, do not discourage him, he goes on praying just the same. There is something almost fine about this perseverance. I must put one more strain upon you: he thinks he is going to heaven!

He has salaried teachers who tell him that. They also tell him there is a hell, of everlasting fire, and that he will go to it if he doesn't keep the Commandments. What are the Commandments? They are a curiosity. I will tell you about them by and by. . . .

Letter III

You have noticed that the human being is a curiosity. In times past he has had (and worn out and flung away) hundreds and hundreds of religions; today he has hundreds and hundreds of religions, and launches not fewer than three new ones every year. I could enlarge that number and still be within the facts.

One of his principal religions is called the Christian. A sketch of it will interest you. It is set forth in detail in a book containing two million words, called the Old and New Testaments. Also it has another name—The Word of God. For the Christian thinks every word of it was dictated by God—the one I have been speaking of.

It is full of interest. It has noble poetry in it; and some clever fables; and some blood-drenched history; and some good morals; and a wealth of obscenity; and upwards of a thousand lies.

This Bible is built mainly out of the fragments of older Bibles that had their day and crumbled to ruin. So it noticeably lacks in originality, necessarily. Its three or four most imposing and impressive events all happened in earlier Bibles; all its best precepts and rules of conduct came also from those Bibles . . .

That innocent Bible tells about the Creation. Of what—the universe? Yes, the universe. In six days!

God did it. He did not call it the universe—that name is modern. His whole attention was upon this world. He constructed it in five days—and then? It took him only one day to make twenty million suns and eighty million planets!

What were they for—according to his idea? To furnish light for this little toy-world. That was his whole purpose; he had no other. One of the twenty million suns . . . was to light it in the daytime, the rest were to help one of the universe's countless moons modify the darkness of its nights.

It is quite manifest that he believed his fresh-made skies were diamond-sown with those myriads of twinkling stars the moment his first-day's sun sank below the horizon; whereas, in fact, not a single star winked in that black vault until three years and a half after that memorable week's formidable industries had been completed.* Then one star appeared, all solitary and alone, and began to blink. Three years later another one appeared. The two blinked together

*It takes the light of the nearest star (61 Cygni) three and a half years to come to the earth, traveling at the rate of 186,000 miles per second. Arcturus had been shining 200 years before it was visible from the earth. Remoter stars gradually became visible after thousands and thousands of years—THE EDITOR [M. T.]

for more than four years before a third joined them. At the end of the first hundred years there were not yet twenty-five stars twinkling in the wide wastes of those gloomy skies. At the end of a thousand years not enough stars were yet visible to make a show. At the end of a million years only half of the present array had sent their light over the telescopic frontiers, and it took another million for the rest to follow suit, as the vulgar phrase goes. There being at that time no telescope, their advent was not observed.

For three hundred years, now, the Christian astronomer has known that his Deity didn't make the stars in those tremendous six days; but the Christian astronomer does not enlarge upon that detail. Neither does the priest.

In his Book, God . . . made those millions of prodigious suns to light this wee little orb, instead of appointing this orb's little sun to dance attendance upon them. He mentions Arcturus in his Book—you remember Arcturus; we went there once. It is one of this earth's night lamps!—that giant globe which is fifty thousand times as large as this earth's sun, and compares with it as a melon compares with a cathedral.

However, the Sunday school still teaches the child that Arcturus was created to help light this earth, and the child grows up and continues to believe it long after he has found out that the probabilities are against its being so.

According to the Book and its servants the universe is only six thousand years old. It is only within the last hundred years that studious, inquiring minds have found out that it is nearer a hundred million.

During the Six Days, God created man and the other animals.

He made a man and a woman and placed them in a pleasant garden, along with the other creatures. They all lived together there in harmony and contentment and blooming youth for some time; then trouble came. God had warned the man and the woman that they must not eat of the fruit of a certain tree. And he added a most strange remark: he said that if they ate of it they should surely die. Strange, for the reason that inasmuch as they had never seen a sample of death they could not possibly know what he meant. Neither would he nor any other god have been able to make those ignorant children understand what was meant, without furnishing a sample. The mere word could have no meaning for them, any more than it would have for an infant of days.

Presently a serpent sought them out privately, and came to them walking upright, which was the way of serpents in those days. The serpent said the forbidden fruit would store their vacant minds with knowledge. So they ate it, which was quite natural, for man is so made that he eagerly wants to know; whereas the priest, like God, whose imitator and representative he is, has made it his business from the beginning to keep him *from* knowing any useful thing.

Adam and Eve ate the forbidden fruit, and at once a great light streamed into their dim heads. They had acquired knowledge. What knowledge—useful knowledge? No—merely knowledge that there was such a thing as good, and such a thing as evil, and how to do evil. They couldn't do it before. Therefore all their acts up to this time had been without stain, without blame, without offense.

But now they could do evil—and suffer for it; now they had acquired what the Church calls an invaluable possession, the Moral Sense; that sense which differentiates man from the beast and sets him above the beast. Instead of below the beast—where one would suppose his proper place would be, since he is always foul-minded and guilty and the beast always clean-minded and innocent. It is like valuing a watch that must go wrong, above a watch that can't.

The Church still prizes the Moral Sense as man's noblest asset today, although the Church knows God had a distinctly poor opinion of it and did what he could in his clumsy way to keep his happy Children of the Garden from acquiring it.

Very well, Adam and Eve now knew what evil was, and how to do it. They knew how to do various kinds of wrong things, and among them one principal one—the one God had his mind on principally. That one was the art and mystery of sexual intercourse. To them it was a magnificent discovery, and they stopped idling around and turned their entire attention to it, poor exultant young things!

In the midst of one of these celebrations they heard God walking among the bushes, which was an afternoon custom of his, and they were smitten with fright. Why? Because they were naked. They had not known it before. They had not minded it before; neither had God.

In that memorable moment immodesty was born; and some people have valued it ever since, though it would certainly puzzle them to explain why.

Adam and Eve entered the world naked and unashamed—naked and pure-minded; and no descendant of theirs has ever entered it otherwise. All have entered it naked, unashamed, and clean in mind. They have entered it modest. They had to acquire immodesty and the soiled mind; there was no other way to get it. A Christian mother's first duty is to soil her child's mind, and she does not neglect it. Her lad grows up to be a missionary, and goes to the innocent savage and to the civilized Japanese, and soils their minds. Whereupon they adopt immodesty, they conceal their bodies, they stop bathing naked together.

The convention miscalled modesty has no standard, and cannot have one, because it is opposed to nature and reason, and is therefore an artificiality and subject to anybody's whim, anybody's diseased caprice. And so, in India the refined lady covers her face and breasts and leaves her legs naked from the hips down, while the refined European lady covers her legs and exposes her face and her breasts. . . .

To proceed with the Biblical curiosities. Naturally you will think the threat to punish Adam and Eve for disobeying was of course not carried out, since they did not create themselves, nor their natures nor their impulses nor their weaknesses, and hence were not properly subject to anyone's commands, and not responsible to anybody for their acts. It will surprise you to know that the threat *was* carried out. Adam and Eve were punished, and that crime finds apologists unto this day. . . .

As you perceive, the only person responsible for the couple's offense escaped; and not only escaped but became the executioner of the innocent.

In your country and mine we should have the privilege of making fun of this kind of morality, but it would be unkind to do it here. Many of these people have the reasoning faculty, but no one uses it in religious matters.

The best minds will tell you that when a man has begotten a child he is morally bound to tenderly care for it, protect it from hurt, shield it from disease, clothe it, feed it, bear with its waywardness, lay no hand upon it save in kindness and for its own good, and never in any case inflict upon it a wanton cruelty. God's treatment of his earthly children, every day and every night, is the exact opposite of all that, yet those best minds warmly justify these crimes, condone them, excuse them, and indignantly refuse to regard them as crimes at all, when *he* commits them. Your country and mine is an interesting one, but there is nothing there that is half so interesting as the human mind.

Very well, God banished Adam and Eve from the Garden, and eventually assassinated them. All for disobeying a command which he had no right to utter. But he did not stop there, as you will see. He has one code of morals for himself, and quite another for his children. He requires his children to deal justly—and gently—with offenders, and forgive them seventy-and-seven times; whereas he deals neither justly nor gently with anyone, and he did not forgive the ignorant and thoughtless first pair of juveniles even their first small offense and say, "You may go free this time, I will give you another chance."

On the contrary! He elected to punish *their* children, all through the ages to the end of time, for a trifling offense committed by others before they were born. He is punishing them yet. In mild ways? No, in atrocious ones.

You would not suppose that this kind of a Being gets many compliments. Undeceive yourself: the world calls him the All-Just, the All-Righteous, the All-Good, the All-Merciful, the All-Forgiving, the All-Truthful, the All-Loving, the Source of All Morality. These sarcasms are uttered daily, all over the world. But not as conscious sarcasms. No, they are meant seriously: they are uttered without a smile. . . .

Letter VI

It is most difficult to understand the disposition of the Bible God, it is such a confusion of contradictions; of watery instabilities and iron firmnesses; of goody-goody abstract morals made out of words, and concreted hell-born ones made out of acts; of fleeting kindnesses repented of in permanent malignities.

However, when after much puzzling you get at the key to his disposition, you do at last arrive at a sort of understanding of it. With a most quaint and juvenile and astonishing frankness he has furnished that key himself. It is jealousy!

I expect that to take your breath away. You are aware—for I have already told you in an earlier letter—that among human beings jealousy ranks distinctly as a weakness; a trademark of small minds. . . .

Jealousy. Do not forget it, keep it in mind. It is the key. With it you will come to partly understand God as we go along; without it nobody can understand him. As I have said, he has openly held up this treasonous key himself, for all to see. He says, naively, outspokenly, and without suggestion of embarrassment: "I the Lord thy God am a jealous God."

You see, it is only another way of saying, "I the Lord thy God am a small God; a small God, and fretful about small things."

He was giving a warning: he could not bear the thought of any other God getting some of the Sunday compliments of this comical little human race—he wanted all of them for himself. He valued them. To him they were riches; just as tin money is to a Zulu.

But wait—I am not fair; I am misrepresenting him; prejudice is beguiling me into saying what is not true. He did not say he wanted all of the adulations; he said nothing about not being willing to share them with his fellow gods; what he said was, "Thou shalt have no other gods *before* me."

It is a quite different thing, and puts him in a much better light—I confess it. There was an abundance of gods, the woods were full of them, as the saying is, and all he demanded was that he should be ranked as high as the others—not above any of them, but not below any of them. He was willing that they should fertilize earthly virgins, but not on any better terms than he could have for himself in his turn. He wanted to be held their equal. This he insisted upon, in the clearest language: he would have no other gods *before* him. They could march abreast with him, but none of them could head the procession, and he did not claim the right to head it himself.

Do you think he was able to stick to that upright and creditable position? No. He could keep to a bad resolution forever, but he couldn't keep to a good one a month. By and by he threw this one aside and calmly claimed to be the only God in the entire universe.

As I was saying, jealousy is the key; all through his history it is present and prominent. It is the blood and bone of his disposition, it is the basis of his character. How small a thing can wreck his composure and disorder his judgment if it touches the raw of his jealousy! And nothing warms up this trait so quickly and so surely and so exaggeratedly as a suspicion that some competition with the god-Trust is impending. The fear that if Adam and Eve ate of the fruit of the Tree of Knowledge they would "be as gods" so fired his jealousy that his reason was affected, and he could not treat those poor creatures either fairly or charitably, or even refrain from dealing cruelly and criminally with their blameless posterity.

To this day his reason has never recovered from that shock; a wild nightmare of vengefulness has possessed him ever since, and he has almost bankrupted his native ingenuities in inventing pains and miseries and humiliations and heartbreaks wherewith to embitter the brief lives of Adam's descendants. Think of the diseases he has contrived for them! They are multitudinous; no book can name them all. And each one is a trap, set for an innocent victim.

The human being is a machine. An automatic machine. It is composed of thousands of complex and delicate mechanisms, which perform their functions harmoniously and perfectly, in accordance with laws devised for their governance, and over which the man himself has no authority, no mastership, no control. For each one of these thousands of mechanisms the Creator has planned an enemy, whose office is to harass it, pester it, persecute it, damage it, afflict it with pains, and miseries, and ultimate destruction. Not one has been overlooked.

From cradle to grave these enemies are always at work; they know no rest, night or day. . . .

Disease! That is the main force, the diligent force, the devastating force! It attacks the infant the moment it is born; it furnishes it one malady after another; croup, measles, mumps, bowel troubles, teething pains, scarlet fever, and other childhood specialties. It chases the child into youth and furnishes it some specialties for that time of life. It chases the youth into maturity, maturity into age, and age into the grave.

With these facts before you will you now try to guess man's chiefest pet name for this ferocious Commander-in-Chief? I will save you the trouble—but you must not laugh. It is Our Father in Heaven! . . .

Letter VIII

Man is without any doubt the most interesting fool there is. Also the most eccentric. . . .

He can seldom take a plain fact and get any but a wrong meaning out of it. He cannot help this; it is the way the confusion he calls his mind is constructed. Consider the things he concedes, and the curious conclusions he draws from them.

For instance, he concedes that God made man. Made him without man's desire or privity.

This seems to plainly and indisputably make God, and God alone, responsible for man's acts. But man denies this.

He concedes that God has made angels perfect, without blemish, and immune from pain and death, and that he could have been similarly kind to man if he had wanted to, but denies that he was under any moral obligation to do it.

He concedes that man has no moral right to visit the child of his begetting with wanton cruelties, painful diseases and death, but refuses to limit God's privileges in this sort with the children of his begetting.

The Bible and man's statutes forbid murder, adultery, fornication, lying, treachery, robbery, oppression and other crimes, but contend that God is free of these laws and has a right to break them when he will.

He concedes that God gives to each man his temperament, his disposition, at birth; he concedes that man cannot by any process change this temperament, but must remain always under its dominion. Yet if it be full of dreadful passions, in one man's case, and barren of them in another man's, it is right and rational to punish the one for his crimes, and reward the other for abstaining from crime. . . .

Letter IX

. . .

It is claimed that from the beginning of time [God] foresaw everything that would happen in the world. If that is true, he foresaw that Adam and Eve would eat the apple; that their posterity would be unendurable and have to be drowned; that Noah's posterity would in their turn be unendurable, and that by and by he would have to leave his throne in heaven and come down and be crucified to save that same tiresome human race again. The whole of it? A part of it? Yes. How much of it? In each generation, for hundreds and hundreds of generations, a billion would die and all go to perdition except perhaps ten thousand out of the billion. The ten thousand would have to come from the little body of Christians, and only one in the hundred of that little body would stand any chance. None of them at all except such Roman Catholics as should have the luck to have a priest handy to sandpaper their souls at the last gasp, and here and there a Presbyterian. No others savable. All the others damned. By the million.

Shall you grant that he foresaw all this? The pulpit grants it. It is the same as granting that in the matter of intellect the Deity is the Head Pauper of the Universe, and that in the matter of morals and character he is away down on the level of David.

Letter X

The two Testaments are interesting, each in its own way. The Old one gives us a picture of these people's Deity as he was before he got religion, the other one gives us a picture of him as he appeared afterward. The Old Testament is interested mainly in blood and sensuality. The New one in Salvation. Salvation by fire.

The first time the Deity came down to earth, he brought life and death; when he came the second time, he brought hell.

Life was not a valuable gift, but death was. Life was a fever-dream made up of joys embittered by sorrows, pleasure poisoned by pain; a dream that was a nightmare-confusion of spasmodic and fleeting delights, ecstasies, exultations, happiness, interspersed with long-drawn miseries, griefs, perils, horrors, disappointments, defeats, humiliations, and despairs—the heaviest curse devisable by divine ingenuity; but death was sweet, death was gentle, death was kind; death healed the bruised spirit and the broken heart, and gave them rest and forgetfulness; death was man's best friend; when man could endure life no longer, death came and set him free.

In time, the Deity perceived that death was a mistake; a mistake, in that it was insufficient; insufficient, for the reason that while it was an admirable agent for the inflicting of misery upon the survivor, it allowed the dead person himself to escape from all further persecution in the blessed refuge of the grave. This was not satisfactory. A way must be contrived to pursue the dead beyond the tomb.

The Deity pondered this matter during four thousand years unsuccessfully, but as soon as he came down to earth and became a Christian his mind cleared and he knew what to do. He invented hell, and proclaimed it.

Now here is a curious thing. It is believed by everybody that while he was in heaven he was stern, hard, resentful, jealous, and cruel; but that when he came down to earth and assumed the name Jesus Christ, he became the opposite of what he was before: that is to say, he became sweet, and gentle, merciful, forgiving, and all harshness disappeared from his nature and a deep and yearning love for his poor human children took its place. Whereas it was as Jesus Christ that he devised hell and proclaimed it!

Which is to say, that as the meek and gentle Savior he was a thousand billion times crueler than ever he was in the Old Testament—oh, incomparably more atrocious than ever he was when he was at his very worst in those old days!

Meek and gentle? By and by we will examine this popular sarcasm by the light of the hell which he invented. . . .

DISCUSSION QUESTIONS

1. In the preceding excerpt from "Letters From Earth," Twain pokes fun at those who take the Bible literally. If you believe in God, how literally do you take the Bible? In particular, how would you reply to Twain's claims that:

a. It is inconsistent with astronomical knowledge to claim that the universe was created in six days and that stars were visible from the earth from the moment of its creation.

b. The astronomical insignificance of our planet and sun is inconsistent with the great importance religion places upon them.

c. The Judeo-Christian claim that human beings derive their dignity from their capacity to distinguish right from wrong is inconsistent with the Genesis story of God's prohibiting Adam and Eve to eat of "The Tree of Knowledge."

d. It would have been wrong for God to punish Adam and Eve since God created them with their impulses and weaknesses. (Consider, too, how God could rightfully hold Adam and Eve morally responsible and justly punishable for their act of disobedience since, according to Genesis, they had no moral sense at the time they disobeyed.)

e. A morally perfect being would never punish children for their parents' crimes, as God is supposed to punish us for Adam and Eve's sin.

f. The presence of diseases and other sources of human pain are incompatible with the goodness of God.

2. Many theologians take the Genesis story of Adam and Eve in the Garden of Eden allegorically, and not literally. To them, the story is not a report of some historical happening, but is symbolic of the human condition. What do you think of this approach? If this approach were accepted, what would be the symbolic meaning of the Garden of Eden story? If some stories in the Bible are to be taken allegorically, and not literally, how can we determine which ones and what meaning to attribute to a given story?

3. a. If you were Adam and Eve, what arguments would you use to convince God that you should be allowed to stay in the Garden of Eden?

b. If you were God, what arguments would you use to rebut the preceding arguments?

4. If you were debating Mark Twain, what would you seize upon as the weakest points in his various arguments against belief in the traditional Judeo-Christian God?

5. Does the picture of God seem to change from one part of the Bible to another? If so, how can we determine which description of God is most accurate? In particular, what do you think of the characterization of God as a "jealous" god? Is Twain right that a morally perfect deity would not have such a personality characteristic?

6. Do you believe in hell? What do you imagine it would be like? Would a morally perfect deity want anyone to suffer eternally, with no possibility of redemption? If not, what are we to make of the belief in hell? Do you agree with Twain that only a sadistic being would have invented such a place?

6. A SCIENTIST'S DEFENSE OF THE ARGUMENT FROM DESIGN

A. Cressy Morrison

A. CRESSY MORRISON (1884–1951), a chemist, was an executive for Union Carbide and Carbon Corporation and president of the New York Academy of Sciences. He was also a member of various governmental advisory groups dealing with science and commerce. Besides writing several books on scientific topics, Morrison wrote widely on religious topics and compiled the three-volume **Encyclopedia of Superstition**.

The following selection consists of excerpts from Morrison's book **Man Does Not Stand Alone** (1944), a modern defense of the argument from design. This argument was a very popular one in the seventeenth and eighteenth centuries with the rise of modern science. As most thinkers of that period saw it, the mathematical order of the universe pointed irresistibly toward a divine designer. This was the view of Isaac Newton, the most prominent scientist of that era. The most popular version of the argument from design was presented in the writings of William Paley (1743–1805) who was both a philosopher and minister in the Church of England. The argument from design was widely accepted by philosophers and scientists until Darwin's theory of evolution, which offered a purely naturalistic explanation of the adaptation of living creatures to their environment, gained wide acceptance in the late nineteenth and twentieth centuries. As many thinkers now saw it, the theory of evolution tended to undercut the force of the argument from design, and with it the belief in God. This was the contention of the famous biologist Julian Huxley (1887–1975) in **Man Stands Alone**. Morrison had Julian Huxley particularly in mind in titling his book **Man Does Not Stand Alone**. (Julian Huxley was the grandson of Thomas Huxley, a contemporary of Darwin, who was a very influential defender and popularizer of Darwin's theory of evolution.) Morrison's objective in this book is to show that the theory of evolution does not undercut the belief in a divine designer, as Huxley and others have argued. Drawing upon his knowledge as a scientist, Morrison argues that it is simply incredible to attribute to chance the exacting astronomical, chemical and biological conditions that are required for sustaining life on this planet. When we turn to living creatures, the evidence for God's existence becomes overwhelming, Morrison argues. Morrison's point of view is echoed today by proponents of "scientific creationism," who question the ability of Darwin's theory of evolution to account for the remarkable complexity of living creatures and their adaptation to their environment.

The Reason Why

The Golden Age of the natural philosopher reached its climax between 1820 and 1850. He sought evidence of the existence of definite design in creation by demonstrating the wonders of nature. He called attention to the ingenuity of the construction of the human eye with its telescopic and microscopic adjustments. He noted the wonderful flexibility and adjustability of the human joints. He marveled at the mysteries of reproduction and all the refinements and precision of the instrumentalities

Source: From *Man Does Not Stand Alone* by A. Cressy Morrison copyright © 1944, 1972 by Fleming H. Revell Company. Used by permission.

through which man and every living thing carried forward its life. He pointed out the unique chemical processes of living things, such as digestion and assimilation of food. Indeed, all the activities of nature were reviewed. Seen through the eye of his pious philosophy, these facts were to him conclusive evidences of the existence of design in nature, and, consequently, of a Designer. Paley used as an illustration the effect upon him of finding a watch in a pathway. Its mechanism was far less wonderful than many other evidences of design in nature. This led him to call attention to the fact that such an object would, however, convince the most skeptical of the evidences of an intellectual process applied to mechanics. He added that were this watch endowed with the power to bring into existence other watches, it would be a no greater marvel than the reproduction of man and animals. So far-reaching and so convincing was this process of reasoning that the sum of $48,000 was left to the Royal Society of Great Britain for an investigation in the various fields of science which would conclusively demonstrate the existence of God. The result was some twelve volumes written by members of the Royal Society and others. These studies brought forward with apparent conclusiveness the evidence of design, and demonstrated to the philosophers of that period the existence of a Supreme Being.

With the advent of Darwin, there entered into the thoughts of mankind a new conception—"the survival of the fittest" and the evolution of man. Darwin's comprehensive study and the vast number of sustaining facts which he brought to support his thesis carried conviction. To this day, his massing of evidence and the subsequent facts developed by his successors have sustained the theory of evolution and carried it far beyond Darwin's demonstrations. It is over eighty years since Darwin, and knowledge has developed enormously. While Darwin's theories stand as a rock of incredible strength, there is now being disclosed to the philosophic world a large number of demonstrable facts which carry us to other possible final conclusions. The modern science of genetics raises questions it is difficult to answer, and other new discoveries leave his work as only a great step in the advance of philosophic thought. . . .

Some of the followers of Darwin carried his deductions to the extreme of materialistic atheism. Those who felt the inspiration of belief in a Supreme Intelligence and a purpose in all things took the other extreme, and while attacking the atheistic attitude, also denied the facts of evolution. Today no such vigorous position need be taken by either the evolutionist or the religious minded, for science now has brought to light facts which go far to remove the apparent differences and enlighten both.

Curiously enough, the new discoveries and wider opportunities for investigation are bringing to life the conclusions of the natural philosophers which were completely eclipsed by the advent of Darwin's work. The sound arguments which showed the adaptation of man to nature should now be followed by a renewed investigation of the evidences of the adaptation of nature to man, which during the past eighty years has been relatively neglected. It is my purpose to bring to the attention of thinking people the facts now demonstrable which tend to sustain a belief in this adaptation and indicate its purpose.

The existence of a Supreme Being is demonstrated by infinite adjustments, without which life itself would be impossible. Man's presence on earth and the magnificent demonstrations of his intellect are a part of a program being carried out by the Supreme Intelligence. . . .

Our Unique World

Suppose you take ten pennies and mark them from 1 to 10. Put them in your pocket and give them a good shake. Now try to draw them out in sequence from 1 to 10, putting each coin back in your pocket after each draw.

Your chance of drawing No. 1 is 1 to 10. Your

chance of drawing 1 and 2 in succession would be 1 in 100. Your chance of drawing 1, 2, and 3 in succession would be one in a thousand. Your chance of drawing 1, 2, 3, and 4 in succession would be one in 10,000 and so on, until your chance of drawing from No. 1 to No. 10 in succession would reach the unbelievable figure of one chance in 10 billion.

The object in dealing with so simple a problem is to show how enormously figures multiply against chance.

So many essential conditions are necessary for life to exist on our earth that it is mathematically impossible that all of them could exist in proper relationship by chance on any one earth at one time. Therefore, there must be in nature some form of intelligent direction. If this be true, then there must be a purpose. . . .

The astronomers tell us that the chance of two stars passing sufficiently near to each other to develop a pulsating and destructive tide is in the order of millions and that a collision would be so rare that it is beyond calculation. Nevertheless, one of the astronomical theories is that at some time, let us say two billion years ago, a star did pass near enough to our sun to raise terrific tides and throw out into space those objects we know as the planets, which appear vast to us but are insignificant astronomically. Among those masses drawn out was that wisp of cosmos which became what we call the earth. It is a body of no importance astronomically, yet it may be demonstrated that it is the *most* important body so far known to us.

We must presume that the earth is composed of some of the elements which are to be found in the sun and none other. These elements are apportioned on earth in certain percentages, which, so far as the surface is concerned, have been fairly well ascertained. The bulk of the earth is now reduced to very permanent dimensions and its mass has been determined. Its speed in its orbit around the sun is extremely constant. Its rotation on its axis is determined so accurately that a variation of a second in a century would upset astronomical calculations. It is accompanied by a satellite known as the moon, whose motions are determined and whose sequence of variations repeat themselves every 18⅓ years. Had the bulk of the earth been greater or less, or had its speed been different, it would have been farther from or nearer to the sun, and this different condition would have profoundly affected life of all kinds, including man. So profoundly indeed, that had this earth varied in either respect to any marked degree, life as we know it could not have existed. Of all the planets, the earth is, so far as we now know, the only one whose relation to the sun makes our sort of life possible. . . .

The earth rotates on its axis in twenty-four hours or at the rate of about one thousand miles an hour. Suppose it turned at the rate of a hundred miles an hour. Why not? Our days and nights would then be ten times as long as now. The hot sun of summer would then burn up our vegetation each long day and every sprout would freeze in such a night. The sun, the source of all life, has a surface temperature of 12,000 degrees Fahrenheit, and our earth is just far enough away so that this "eternal fire" warms us just enough and not too much. It is marvelously stable, and during millions of years has varied so little that life as we know it has survived. If the temperature on earth had changed so much as fifty degrees on the average for a single year, all vegetation would be dead and man with it, roasted or frozen. The earth travels around the sun at the rate of eighteen miles each second. If the rate of revolution had been, say, six miles or forty miles each second, we would be too far from or too close to the sun for our form of life to exist.

Stars vary in size, as we all know. One is so large that if it were our sun, the orbit of the earth would be millions of miles inside its surface. Stars vary in the type of radiation. Many of their rays would be deadly to every known form of life. The intensity and volume of this radiation is anywhere from less than that of our sun to ten thousand times as great. If our sun gave off only one-half of its present radiation, we would freeze, and if it gave half as much more, we would have been reduced to dust long ago if we had ever been born as a protoplasmic spark of life. So our sun is about right for our life among millions of others which are not.

The earth is tilted at an angle of twenty-three degrees. This gives us our seasons. If it had not been tilted, the poles would be in eternal twilight. The water vapor from the ocean would move north and south, piling up continents of ice and leaving possibly a belt of green from the equator to the glaciers. Yes, we could live perhaps, unless the lowering of the ocean and the weight of the unbelievably vast mass of ice had depressed the poles causing our equator to bulge or erupt or at least show the need of a new waistline belt. The lowering of the ocean would expose vast new land areas and diminish the rainfall in all parts of the world, with fearful results. . . .

The moon is 240,000 miles away, and the tides twice a day are usually a gentle reminder of its presence. Tides of the ocean run as high as sixty feet in some places, and even the crust of the earth is twice a day bent outward several inches by the moon's attraction. All seems so regular that we do not grasp to any degree the vast power that lifts the whole area of the ocean several feet and bends the crust of the earth, seemingly so solid. Mars has a moon—a little one—only six thousand miles away from it. If our moon was, say, fifty thousand miles away instead of its present respectable distance, our tides would be so enormous that twice a day all the lowland of all the continents would be submerged by a rush of water so enormous that even the mountains would soon be eroded away, and probably no continent could have risen from the depths fast enough to exist today. The earth would crack with the turmoil and the tides in the air would create daily hurricanes.

If the continents were washed away, the average depth of water over the whole earth would be about a mile and a half and life could not exist except perhaps in the abysmal depth of the ocean, where it would feed upon itself till extinct. Science seems to sustain the theory that this condition did exist during the general chaos before the earth solidified. By well recognized laws, the very tides pushed the moon further and further away and at the same time slowed the rotation of the earth from less than a six-hour day to one of twenty-four. So the gentle moon has now become the lover's delight and is in splendid adjustment, which promises to remain safe for a billion years or so. . . .

Out of a chaotic mixture of the elements torn from the sun at twelve thousand degrees temperature, and thrown at every conceivable velocity into limitless space, has come our solar system. To chaos has come order so exact that the place any part will occupy at any time can be predicted to the second. The balance is so perfect that it has not varied in a billion years and points to eternity. All this through the reign of law. By this same law the established order as we see it in the solar system is repeated elsewhere. . . .

Animal Instincts

. . . The young salmon spends years at sea, then comes back to his own river, and, what is more, he travels up the side of the river into which flows the tributary in which he was born. . . . What brings them back so definitely? If a salmon going up a river is transferred to another tributary he will at once realize he is not in the right tributary and will fight his way down to the main stream and then turn up against the current to finish his destiny. . . . Eels migrate at maturity from all the ponds and rivers everywhere—those from Europe across thousands of miles of ocean—and go to the abysmal deeps south of Bermuda. There they breed and die. The little ones, with no apparent means of knowing anything except that they are in a wilderness of water, start back and find their way to the shore from which their parents came and thence to every river, lake and little pond, so that each body of water is always populated with eels. They have braved the mighty currents, storms, and tides, and have conquered the beating waves on every shore. They can now grow and when they are mature, they will, by some mysterious law, go back through it all to complete the cycle. Where does the directing impulse originate? No American eel has ever been caught in European waters and no European eel has ever been caught in American waters. Nature has also delayed the maturity of the European eel by a year or more to make up for its much greater journey. Do atoms and molecules when combined in an eel have a sense of direction and will power to exercise it? . . .

The Development of Mind

. . . In the mêlée of creation many creatures have come to exhibit a high degree of certain forms of instinct. . . . The wasp catches the grasshopper, digs a hole in the earth, stings the grasshopper in exactly the right place so that he becomes unconscious but lives as a form of preserved meat. The wasp lays her eggs exactly in the right place, perhaps not knowing that when they hatch, her children can eat without killing the insect on which they feed, which would be fatal to them. The wasp must have done all this right the first and every time, or there would be no wasps. Science cannot explain this mystery, and yet it cannot be attributed to chance. The wasp covers a hole in the earth, departs cheerfully, and dies. Neither she nor her ancestors have reasoned out the process, nor does she know what happens to her offspring or that there are such things as offspring. She doesn't even know that she has worked and lived her life for the preservation of the race. Bees and ants seem to understand how to organize and govern themselves. They have their soldiers and workers and slaves and drones. If you should pick up a piece of amber on the shore of the Baltic Sea, it might contain an ant imprisoned untold ages ago. You will find it is an almost exact replica of an ant existing today. Did evolution cease when the ant was adjusted to its surroundings in nature? Was the little brain of the ant too small an instrument to meet a higher purpose? Certainly, the ant as a socialized insect had learned much. It seems to apply the wonderful theory of "the greatest good for the greatest number" in a grim way. . . . In some species, the workers bring in little seeds to feed the other ants through the winter. The ants establish what is known as the grinding room, in which those which have developed gigantic jaws especially built for grinding prepare the food for the colony. This is their sole occupation. When the fall comes and the seeds are all ground, "the greatest good for the greatest number" requires that the food supply be conserved, and as there will be plenty of grinders in the new generation, the soldier ants kill off the grinders. . . .

How do the inanimate atoms and molecules of matter composing an ant set these complicated processes in motion? There must be intelligence somewhere. . . .

DISCUSSION QUESTIONS

1. How would a person who believes in evolution, but not divine creation, respond to Morrison's claim that "so many essential conditions are necessary for life to exist on our earth that it is mathematically impossible that all of them could exist in proper relationship by chance on any one earth at one time." Is there some fallacy in Morrison's argument?

2. Does the purposeful activity of animals point to some intelligent designer, as Morrison claims? Do the examples of animal instincts that Morrison relates support a belief in an all-powerful and all-good creator?

3. Does the evidence of purpose that Morrison relies upon to argue for the existence of God support the central role of human beings in God's pur-

poseful creation, as Judeo-Christian tradition claims.

4. A debate is presently being waged between evolutionists and creationists over the appropriateness of presenting the theistic view of divine creation in biology classes. As some creationists see it, there is **more scientific evidence** for the view that life forms did not develop in a single continuous evolutionary chain, but were the result of a purposeful and discontinuous act of divine creation. Other creationists claim that the scientific data is neutral between a creationist and evolutionary view of biological development. From this point of view, the creationist view is as sound a **theory** of biological development as is the evolutionary theory of natural selection and for that reason deserves equal attention in biology classes. Evolutionary theory, such creationists contend, is no less a doctrine of **faith** than divine creation theory. As things stand today, the creationists claim, the atheistic secular humanistic philosophy implicit in evolutionary theory is unfairly indoctrinated in the minds of young students of biology at the expense of the theistic creationist view. This claim is rejected by evolutionists, who contend that scientific evidence can be marshalled in support of evolutionary theory, but not in support of creationist theory. Creationism is simply **religion masquerading as science,** they claim, and for this reason should be kept out of **science** classes. What would Morrison say? What do you think?

7. A PANTHEIST'S REJECTION OF THE IDEA OF DIVINE PURPOSE

Benedict (Baruch) Spinoza

BENEDICT (BARUCH) SPINOZA (1632–77) was a very influential philosopher who was born a Dutch Jew. He was excommunicated from his synogogue for his unorthodox views. While earning his living as a lens maker, Spinoza turned his sharp intellect to philosophical problems. As knowledge of his philosophical originality spread, Spinoza was offered a university position in philosophy, but refused it for fear that it would cost him his philosophical independence. He died of tuberculosis, aggravated by the dust from lens grinding. His greatest work, **Ethics**, was not published until after his death. Spinoza's writings had a great influence upon the development of German Idealism, especially the philosophy of Friedrich Schelling (1775–1854). He also influenced writers in Germany and England, in particular, Johann Goethe (1749–1832) and the English romantic nature poets William Wordsworth (1770–1850) and Samuel Coleridge (1772–1834).

The following excerpt comes from the Appendix to Book I of Spinoza's **Ethics**. Greatly influenced by the deductive mathematical method (exemplified by Euclidean plane geometry), Spinoza attempts to derive philosophical "theorems" from certain self-evident "axioms" of reason. In the process, he attempts to achieve complete deductive metaphysical unity. While the **Ethics** itself is too technical for beginning philosophy students, the Appendix to Book I (which departs from the deductive model of the body of the **Ethics**) is admirably clear and free of technical philosophical vocabulary. Spinoza begins this Appendix by speaking of "God"; he is not, however, speaking of a personal being who stands outside of the universe (a transcendent being). On the contrary, for Spinoza, God **is** the universe and not something apart from it. The identification of God with the universe is called **pantheism**, and Spinoza is the foremost exponent of this view. When Albert Einstein was once asked if he believed in God, he replied, "I believe in the God of Spinoza." While Einstein did not expand upon this answer, he meant that he had an attitude of reverence for the mathematical beauty and unity of the universe, an attitude which played a role in his life similar to the role that the belief in a transcendental personal god plays in the lives of others. Like Spinoza, Einstein did not believe that the universe had any purpose or any external creator. Like Spinoza, he saw all the events and things in the universe as part of a single unified and deterministic whole.

In our selection, Spinoza criticizes the view that the universe has a purpose, attempting to uncover the psychological roots of this belief, which he sees as a fundamental misperception. He ridicules the view that the events and things of this universe were created for human beings. He then goes on to criticize the traditional religious view of the "objectivity of values" (i.e., that what is right or good does not depend on the psychological nature or "tastes" of human beings), expressing a "subjectivistic" view that moral beliefs are based on varying human feelings toward things and not on any principle of reason. The world view Spinoza expresses in this excerpt has had a great influence on subsequent thought. While Spinoza's nonpurposeful world view is a prevalent one among present day philosophers, it was a revolutionary one in his day. At that time, there was a widespread acceptance of the Aristotelian view, incorporated into Judeo-Christian religious metaphysics, that every animate and inanimate object in the universe had been made with a purpose either by God or by "Nature." From this point of view, to understand something was to understand what it was for. Cutting against this deeply embedded way of thinking, Spinoza claimed that to understand something is not to fit it into a purposeful order, but to adequately describe it and to discover the laws which govern it. Spinoza believed that while there is no reason why the pattern of laws that impose order upon our experience exist as they do, they are subject to comprehension by human beings and are worthy objects of human awe, no less than the purposeful God of the Judeo-Christian religious tradition.

In the foregoing I have explained the nature and properties of God. . . . Yet there still remain misconceptions not a few, which might and may prove very grave hindrances to the understanding of the concatenation[1] of things, as I have explained it above. I have therefore thought it worth while to bring these misconceptions before the bar of reason.

All such opinions spring from the notion commonly entertained, that all things in nature act as men themselves act, namely, with an end in view. It is accepted as certain, that God himself directs all things to a definite goal (for it is said that God made all things for man, and man that he might worship him). I will, therefore, consider this opinion, asking first, why it obtains general credence, and why all men are naturally so prone to adopt it? Secondly, I will point out its falsity; and, lastly, I will show how it has given rise to prejudices about good and bad, right and wrong, praise and blame, order and confusion, beauty and ugliness, and the like. However, this is not the place to deduce

Source: From *Ethics* by Benedict Spinoza (New York: Tudor Publishing Company, n.d.).

[1]Connection. EDITOR'S NOTE.

these misconceptions from the nature of the human mind: it will be sufficient here, if I assume as a starting point, what ought to be universally admitted, namely, that all men are born ignorant of the causes of things, that all have the desire to seek for what is useful to them, and that they are conscious of such desire. Herefrom it follows first, that men think themselves free, inasmuch as they are conscious of their volitions and desires, and never even dream, in their ignorance, of the causes which have disposed them to wish and desire. Secondly, that men do all things for an end, namely, for that which is useful to them, and which they seek. Thus it comes to pass that they only look for a knowledge of the purposes of events, and when these are learned, they are content, as having no cause for further doubt. If they cannot learn such causes from external sources, they are compelled to turn to considering themselves, and reflecting what end would have induced them personally to bring about the given event, and thus they necessarily judge other natures by their own. Further,as they find in themselves and outside themselves many means which assist them not a little in their search for what is useful, for instance, eyes for seeing, teeth for chewing, herbs and animals for yielding food, the sun for giving light, the sea for breeding fish, etc., they come to look on the whole of nature as a means for obtaining such conveniences. Now as they are aware that they found these conveniences and did not make them, they think they have cause for believing that some other being has made them for their use. As they look upon things as means, they cannot believe them to be self-created; but, judging from the means which they are accustomed to prepare for themselves, they are bound to believe in some ruler or rulers of the universe endowed with human freedom, who have arranged and adapted everything for human use. They are bound to estimate the nature of such rulers (having no information on the subject) in accordance with their own nature, and therefore they assert that the gods ordained everything for the use of man, in order to bind man to themselves and obtain from him the highest honors. . . . Thus the prejudice developed into superstition, and took deep root in the human mind; and for this reason everyone strove most zealously to understand and explain the purposes[2] of things; but in their endeavor to show that nature does nothing in vain, i.e., nothing which is useless to man, they only seem to have demonstrated that nature, the gods, and men are all mad together. Consider, I pray you, the result; among the many helps of nature they were bound to find some hindrances, such as storms, earthquakes, diseases, etc.: so they declared that such things happen, because the gods are angry at some wrong done them by men, or at some fault committed in their worship. Experience day by day protested and showed by infinite examples, that good and evil fortunes fall to the lot of pious and impious alike; still they would not abandon their inveterate prejudice, for it was more easy for them to class such contradictions among other unknown things of whose use they were ignorant, and thus to retain their actual and innate condition of ignorance, than to destroy the whole fabric of their reasoning and start afresh. They therefore laid down as an axiom, that God's judgments far transcend human understanding. Such a doctrine might well have sufficed to conceal the truth from the human race for all eternity, if mathematics had not furnished another standard of verity in considering solely the essence and properties of figures without regard to their purposes. . .

I have now sufficiently explained my first point. There is no need to show at length, that nature has no particular goal in view, and that purposes are mere human figments.

Further, this doctrine does away with the perfection of God: for, if God acts for an object, he necessarily desires something which he lacks. . . .

[2] "Final causes" in the original. EDITOR'S NOTE.

We must not omit to notice that the followers of this doctrine, anxious to display their talent in assigning purposes, have imported a new method of argument in proof of their theory—namely, a reduction, not to the impossible, but to ignorance; thus showing that they have no other method of exhibiting their doctrine. For example, if a stone falls from a roof on to some one's head and kills him, they will demonstrate by their new method, that the stone fell in order to kill the man; for, if it had not by God's will fallen with that object, how could so many circumstances (and there are often many concurrent circumstances) have all happened together by chance? Perhaps you will answer that the event is due to the facts that the wind was blowing, and the man was walking that way. "But why," they will insist, "was the wind blowing, and why was the man at that very time walking that way?" If you again answer, that the wind had then sprung up because the sea had begun to be agitated the day before, the weather being previously calm, and that the man had been invited by a friend, they will again insist: "But why was the sea agitated, and why was the man invited at that time?" So they will pursue their questions from cause to cause, till at last you take refuge in the will of God—in other words, the sanctuary of ignorance. So, again, when they survey the frame of the human body, they are amazed; and being ignorant of the causes of so great a work of art conclude that it has been fashioned, not mechanically, but by divine and supernatural skill, and has been so put together that one part shall not hurt another.

Hence anyone who seeks for the true causes of miracles, and strives to understand natural phenomena as an intelligent being, and not to gaze at them like a fool, is set down and denounced as an impious heretic by those, whom the masses adore as the interpreters of nature and the gods. Such persons know that, with the removal of ignorance, the wonder which forms their only available means for proving and preserving their authority would vanish also. But I now quit this subject, and pass on to my third point.

After men persuaded themselves, that everything which is created is created for their sake, they were bound to consider as the chief quality in everything that which is most useful to themselves, and to account those things the best of all which have the most beneficial effect on mankind. Further, they were bound to form abstract notions for the explanation of the nature of things, such as GOODNESS, BADNESS, ORDER, CONFUSION, WARMTH, COLD, BEAUTY, DEFORMITY, and so on; and from the belief that they are free agents arose the further notions PRAISE and BLAME, SIN and MERIT. . . .

. . . [These] abstract notions are nothing but modes of imagining . . . though they are considered by the ignorant as the chief attributes of things, inasmuch as they believe that everything was created for the sake of themselves; and, according as they are affected by it, style it good or bad, healthy or rotten and corrupt. For instance, if the motion whose objects we see communicate to our nerves be conducive to health, the objects causing it are styled BEAUTIFUL; if a contrary motion be excited, they are styled UGLY.

Things which are perceived through our sense of smell are styled fragrant or fetid; if through our taste, sweet or bitter, full-flavored or insipid, if through our touch, hard or soft, rough or smooth, etc.

Whatsoever affects our ears is said to give rise to noise, sound, or harmony. In this last case, there are men lunatic enough to believe that even God himself takes pleasure in harmony; and philosophers are not lacking who have persuaded themselves, that the motion of the heavenly bodies gives rise to harmony—all of which instances sufficiently show that everyone judges of things according to the state of his brain, or rather mistakes for things the forms of his imagination. We need no longer wonder that there have arisen all the controversies we have witnessed and finally scepticism: for, although human bodies in many respects agree, yet in very many others they differ; so that what seems good to one seems bad to another; what seems well ordered to one seems confused to another; what is pleasing to one displeases another, and so on. I need not further enumerate, because this is not the place to treat the subject at length, and also because the fact is sufficiently well known. It is commonly said: "So many men, so many minds; everyone is wise in his own way; brains differ as completely as palates." All of which proverbs show, that men judge of things according to their mental disposition, and rather imagine than understand; for, if they understood phenomena, they would, as mathematics attest, be convinced, if not attracted, by what I have urged. . . .

Many argue in this way. If all things follow from a necessity of the absolutely perfect nature of God, why are there so many imperfections in nature? such, for instance, as things corrupt to the point of putridity, loathsome deformity, confusion, evil, sin, etc. But these reasoners are, as I have said, easily confuted, for the perfection of things is to be reckoned only from their own nature and power; things are not more or less perfect, according as they delight or offend human senses, or according as they are serviceable or repugnant to mankind. . . .

DISCUSSION QUESTIONS

1. How would Spinoza reply to Morrison's argument for the existence of a divine intelligence? What do you think?

2. Why does Spinoza claim that a transcendent being who created the world for a purpose must necessarily be less than a perfect being? Would believers in the Judeo-Christian God accept Spinoza's conception of "a perfect being"? If not, how would they define this notion?

3. Why does Spinoza claim that attempts to explain things by appealing to the will of God are appeals to "the sanctuary of ignorance"? Do you agree? Why?

4. How would you reply to Spinoza's claim that the contrasts we make between good and bad, beautiful and ugly, and order and confusion are purely subjective notions that exist only in our minds and not in external objects and events? What bearing, if any, does this issue have on whether the universe is purposefully directed by a transcendent divine intelligence?

8. THE CLASSIC CRITICISM OF THE ARGUMENT FROM DESIGN

David Hume

DAVID HUME (1711–76), Scottish philosopher, historian, and political economist, was a profoundly influential philosopher who is noted for his extreme scepticism. Educated as a lawyer at the University of Edinburgh in Scotland, Hume abandoned his brief career in law to seek literary fame in France. His first literary endeavor, **A Treatise of Human Nature** (1739), later to be recognized as a philosophical masterpiece, was not well received when first published. (As Hume later lamented, the work "fell deadborn from the press.") Years later, Hume reformulated the ideas expressed in the **Treatise** into the shorter and more polished form of **An Enquiry Concerning Human Understanding** (1748) and **An Enquiry Concerning the Principles of Morals** (1751). These works, as well as Hume's other philosophical writings, were too sceptical for his day and, to Hume's disappointment, were largely ignored during his lifetime. It was only after his death that Hume's philosophical originality was recognized and his philosophical ideas began to exert a widespread influence that continues to this day. While Hume did not gain the literary fame he desired through his philosophical writings, he did gain that fame through his other literary endeavors. For example, his six-volume **History of England** (1754–62) earned him a reputation as a major historian. Hume also earned a reputation in economics which rivaled that of his good friend Adam Smith. Unable to find desirable employment as a professor of philosophy, Hume spent most of his life as a librarian to the Edinburgh Faculty of Law. He also had a brief career in government, including a post as England's chief representative to Paris and a post as Undersecretary of State for Colonial Affairs. A sociable, witty, kind, and even-tempered man of moderation, he was known to his many French friends as "le bon David" (the good David) and in Scotland as "Saint David."

Hume was the most important figure in the development of the school of philosophical thought known as **empiricism**. While **rationalists**, such as Spinoza, believed that the human mind was capable of discerning rational truths about matters of fact that would be true **regardless of the content of our experience**, the empiricists denied this possibility. As John Locke (1632–1706), the first influential empiricist put it, "The mind is a blank tablet upon which experience writes." In the technical vocabulary of philosophy, the empiricists claimed that all knowledge of matters of fact was **a posteriori**—that is, based on experience. Rationalists, on the other hand, denied this, claiming that some knowledge of matters of fact was **a priori**—that is, not based on (or prior to) experience. The philosophical power of Hume is that, unlike his predecessors in the empiricist tradition, he did not hesitate to accept the full logical consequences of the empiricist doctrine. The result was a devastating scepticism about the possibility of metaphysical knowledge. This scepticism anticipated and had a great influence upon the twentieth-century philosophical movement known as logical positivism. Immanuel Kant (1724–1804) who, along with Hume, has had a profound impact on contemporary philosophy, was, by his own report, wakened out of his "dogmatic slumber" by Hume's scepticism. Since Hume's logic could not be faulted, Kant attempted to overcome Hume's scepticism by challenging his basic empiricist assumption of the impossibility of **a priori** knowledge of matters of fact.

Nowhere is Hume's scepticism sharper than in his **Dialogues Concerning Natural Religion**,[1] which, upon the advice of friends such as the famous economist Adam Smith, was not published until after his death for fear of a hostile public reaction. As the title indicates, the work is written in dialogue form; the three participants of this dialogue are Demea, Cleanthes, and Philo, each of whom reflects a different philosophical approach to the possibility of religious knowledge. Demea is the typical rationalist of Hume's day who maintains that knowledge of God's existence can be derived (deductively) from principles of abstract reason, without any appeal to experience. Cleanthes and Philo, as empiricists, are united in attacking the validity

[1]In the terminology of Hume's day, *natural religion* was religion which was based solely on empirical evidence and/or rational argument. This type of religion was contrasted to *revealed religion*, which is religion based on divine revelation.

of rationalistic arguments for God's existence. They both agree that any justification for God's existence would have to be based on an (inductive) argument from experience, which would make the existence of God only probable, not absolutely certain. Cleanthes believes that the argument from design provides such a justification, and he offers a classic formulation of it. This argument is then subjected to devastating criticism by the sceptic Philo.

The following selection, consisting of excerpts from Hume's **Dialogues Concerning Natural Religion**, centers on the argument from design (as the bulk of the **Dialogues** do). It begins with Cleanthes' formulation of the argument to which Demea immediately objects on the general grounds that arguments that do not conclusively establish God's existence are unsatisfactory. Philo then takes up the criticism of the argument from design for the remainder of our selection. He challenges Cleanthes' argument that since the universe is like a machine, which experience teaches us is always a result of intelligent design, a divine intelligence is most likely the cause of the universe.

A full appreciation of Philo's criticism requires that one understand Hume's view of causation—a view which has had a profound impact on subsequent philosophy. As Hume saw it, the only justification that we have for claiming that "A (some event) causes B (another event)" is that experience has taught us that whenever A has occurred, B has occurred. Causal connections are not, Hume argued, uncovered by pure rational reflection but only by our experience of the "constant conjunctions" of events. Sceptical of causal inferences in general, Hume was especially sceptical of the causal inference involved in the argument from design. Most causal inferences proceed from one sort of event that we have observed in the past (e.g., the heating of water) to other events that we have also observed in the past (e.g., the boiling of water). On the basis of our experience of the constant conjunctions of events (e.g., the heating of water has always been followed by its boiling), we infer that the prior event **causes** the latter one (e.g., the heating of water **causes** it to boil)—i.e., that the prior event will always be followed by the latter one. However, since our observations are restricted to only one universe and do not go beyond phenomena within that one universe, no one has observed any constant conjunctions of specific events preceding the birth of universes. Consequently, one does not have sufficient basis for attributing any cause to the universe as a whole, Hume believed. At best, one is forced to resort to arguments from analogy which compare the universe to things we have experienced. But, Hume believed, no such analogies do justice to the uniqueness and diversity of the universe.

Accepting this view of causation, Philo argues that we have no justification for comparing the universe to anything within it. For all we know, the universe can be more like a vegetable or an animal than like a machine. If we accept such an analogy, we can see the origin of the universe as a purely blind biological process instead of as a result of intelligent planning. As far as the evidence goes, such explanations, however less psychologically satisfying to human beings, are no less logically possible. We reject such explanations and accept the traditional belief in a divine designer not on the basis of logic but because of our natural tendency to project human attributes upon nonhuman things. (This is called **anthropomorphism**.) While such a tendency is psychologically understandable, it is incapable of intellectual justification, Philo claims.

Furthermore, Philo argues, even if we assume that the world is like a machine and accept the inference that, as a result, the world was most likely a product of intelligent design, there is no way we can justify attributing the specific properties (e.g., omnipotence and moral perfection) of the Judeo-Christian God to this designer. Indeed, we have less basis for inferring a single designer than a plurality of them, Philo claims. In addition, Philo suggests that the hypothesis that God created the universe does not make things more comprehensible than they were before, as believers seem to think. This is so, since the belief in God leads naturally to the question "Who caused God?" If we simply say, as believers do, that God has no cause, but has always existed, why can we not say the same of the world? If one can say that the complexity of God is, in some sense, self-explanatory, one can equally as well say the same of the universe, Philo claims. Yet such a claim, Philo suggests, is in reality no explanation at all but rather an elaborate way of "confessing our ignorance."

In spite of his devastating criticisms in the earlier parts of the **Dialogues**, Philo takes a much more sympathetic view of the argument from design at the end of the **Dialogues**, claiming that the "cause or causes of order in the universe probably bear some remote analogy to human intelligence." (This part of the **Dialogues** is not included in our selection.) Hume's own position as to the force of the argument from design has been a subject of controversy among Humean scholars. (One should not lose sight of the fact that Hume was writing about one hundred years before Darwin's theory of evolution, even though the general philosophical idea of gradual evolution through natural selection goes back to the ancient pre-Socratic Greek philosophy of atomism and was offered as one of many speculative possibilities by Hume himself in the **Dialogues**.) Whatever force Hume may have attributed to the argument from design, he clearly believed that even if it provides sufficient evidence for the belief in an intelligent designer of the universe, it does not provide any adequate basis for inferring any of the traditional properties of God—in particular, his omnipotence, omniscience, and moral perfection. He also clearly believed that there was no good evidence for the belief in miracles and an afterlife. In addition, he believed that the doctrines that form the core of specific religions were all superstitions (e.g., the doctrine of "the fall of man" and the doctrines of "the divinity" and "resurrection" of Christ). Whatever ambivalences Hume might have felt on the matter of God's existence, it is certainly his sceptical attitudes which predominate in his writings and which have influenced subsequent philosophers. This sceptical attitude toward religion made Hume notorious among the Scottish clergy, who referred to him as "the great infidel."

[A Statement of the Argument from Design]

Not to lose any time in circumlocutions, said Cleanthes, . . . I shall briefly explain how I conceive this matter. Look round the world: Contemplate the whole and every part of it: You will find it to be nothing but one great machine, subdivided into an infinite number of lesser machines, which again admit of subdivisions to a degree beyond what human senses and faculties can trace and explain. All these various machines, and even their most minute parts, are adjusted to each other with an accuracy which ravishes into admiration all men who have ever contemplated them. The curious adapting of means to ends, throughout all nature, resembles exactly, though it much exceeds, the

Source: From *The Dialogues Concerning Natural Religion* by David Hume, published in London in 1779.

productions of human contrivance—of human design, thought, wisdom, and intelligence. Since therefore the effects resemble each other, we are led to infer, by all the rules of analogy, that the causes also resemble, and that the Author of Nature is somewhat similar to the mind of man, though possessed of much larger faculties, proportioned to the grandeur of the work which he has executed. By this argument *a posteriori*, and by this argument alone, do we prove at once the existence of a Deity and his similarity to human mind and intelligence.

[Demea's Objection]

I shall be so free, Cleanthes, said Demea, as to tell you that from the beginning I could not approve of your conclusion concerning the similarity of the Deity to men, still less can I approve of the mediums by which you endeavor to establish it. What! No demonstration of the Being of God! No abstract arguments! No proofs *a priori!* Are these which have hitherto been so much insisted on by philosophers all fallacy, all sophism? Can we reach no farther in this subject than experience and probability? . . .

[How Strong Is the Analogy?]

What I chiefly scruple in this subject, said Philo, is not so much that all religious arguments are by Cleanthes reduced to experience, as that they appear not to be even the most certain and irrefragable[2] of that inferior kind. That a stone will fall, that fire will burn, that the earth has solidity, we have observed a thousand and a thousand times; and when any new instance of this nature is presented, we draw without hesitation the accustomed inference. The exact similarity of the cases gives us a perfect assurance of a similar event, and a stronger evidence is never desired nor sought after. But wherever you depart, in the least, from the similarity of the cases, you diminish proportionably the evidence; and may at last bring it to a very weak *analogy*, which is confessedly liable to error and uncertainty. After having experienced the circulation of the blood in human creatures, we make no doubt that it takes place in Titius and Maevius; but from its circulation in frogs and fishes it is only a presumption, though a strong one, from analogy that it takes place in men and other animals. The analogical reasoning is much weaker when we infer the circulation of the sap in vegetables from our experience that the blood circulates in animals; and those who hastily followed that imperfect analogy are found, by more accurate experiments, to have been mistaken.

If we see a house, Cleanthes, we conclude, with the greatest certainty, that it had an architect or builder because this is precisely that species of effect which we have experienced to proceed from that species of cause. But surely you will not affirm that the universe bears such a resemblance to a house that we can with the same certainty infer a similar cause, or that the analogy is here entire and perfect. The dissimilitude is so striking that the utmost you can here pretend to is a guess, a conjecture, a presumption concerning a similar cause. . . .

. . . [Cleanthes replied] I should be deservedly blamed and detested did I allow that the proofs of a Deity amounted to no more than a guess or a conjecture. But is the whole adjustment of means to ends in a house and in the universe so slight a resemblance? . . . Steps of a stair are plainly contrived that human legs may use them in mounting; and this inference is certain and infallible. Human legs are also contrived for walking and mounting, and this inference, I allow, is not altogether so certain because of the dissimilarity which you remark, but does it, therefore, deserve the name only of presumption or conjecture?

Good God! cried Demea, interrupting him,

[2]Indisputable. EDITOR'S NOTE.

where are we? Zealous defenders of religion allow that the proofs of a Deity fall short of perfect evidence! And you, Philo, on whose assistance I depended in proving the adorable mysteriousness of the Divine Nature, do you assent to all these extravagant opinions of Cleanthes? . . .

You seem not to apprehend, replied Philo, that I argue with Cleanthes in his own way, and, by showing him the dangerous consequences of his tenets, hope at last to reduce him to our opinion. . . . Now, however much I may dissent, in other respects, from the dangerous principle of Cleanthes, I must allow that he has fairly represented that argument, and I shall endeavor so to state the matter to you that you will entertain no further scruples with regard to it.

Were a man to abstract from everything which he knows or has seen, he would be altogether incapable, merely from his own ideas, to determine what kind of scene the universe must be, or to give the preference to one state or situation of things above another. For as nothing which he clearly conceives could be esteemed impossible or implying a contradiction, every . . . fancy would be upon an equal footing; nor could he assign any just reason why he adheres to one idea or system, and rejects the others which are equally possible.

Again, after he opens his eyes and contemplates the world as it really is, it would be impossible for him at first to assign the cause of any one event, much less of the whole of things, or of the universe. He might set his fancy a rambling, and she might bring him in an infinite variety of reports and representations. These would all be possible; but, being all equally possible, he would never of himself give a satisfactory account for his preferring one of them to the rest. Experience alone can point out to him the true cause of any phenomenon.

Now, according to this method of reasoning, Demea, it follows (and is, indeed, tacitly allowed by Cleanthes himself) that order, arrangement, or the adjustment of final causes,[3] is not of itself any proof of design, but only so far as it has been experienced to proceed from that principle. For aught we can know *a priori*, matter may contain the source or spring of order originally within itself, as well as mind does; and there is no more difficulty in conceiving that the several elements, from an internal unknown cause, may fall into the most exquisite arrangement, than to conceive that their ideas, in the great universal mind, from a like internal unknown cause, fall into that arrangement. The equal possibility of both these suppositions is allowed. But, by experience, we find (according to Cleanthes) that there is a difference between them. Throw several pieces of steel together, without shape or form, they will never arrange themselves so as to compose a watch. Stone and mortar and wood, without an architect, never erect a house. But the ideas in a human mind, we see, by an unknown, inexplicable economy, arrange themselves so as to form the plan of a watch or house. Experience, therefore, proves that there is an original principle of order in mind, not in matter. From similar effects we infer similar causes. The adjustment of means to ends is alike in the universe, as in a machine of human contrivance. The causes, therefore, must be resembling.

I was from the beginning scandalized, I must own, with this resemblance which is asserted between the Deity and human creatures, and must conceive it to imply such a degradation of the Supreme Being as no sound theist could endure. With your assistance, therefore, Demea, I shall endeavor to defend what you justly call the adorable mysteriousness of the Divine Nature, and shall refute this reasoning of Cleanthes, provided he allows that I have made a fair representation of it.

[3]i.e., purposes. EDITOR'S NOTE.

When Cleanthes had assented, Philo, after a short pause, proceeded in the following manner.

That all inferences, Cleanthes, concerning fact are founded on experience, and that all experimental reasonings are founded on the supposition that similar causes prove similar effects, and similar effects similar causes, I shall not at present much dispute with you. But observe, I entreat you, with what extreme caution all just reasoners proceed in the transferring of experiments to similar cases. Unless the cases be exactly similar, they repose no perfect confidence in applying their past observation to any particular phenomenon. Every alteration of circumstances occasions a doubt concerning the event; and it requires new experiments to prove certainly that the new circumstances are of no moment or importance. A change in bulk, situation, arrangement, age, disposition of the air, or surrounding bodies—any of these particulars may be attended with the most unexpected consequences. And unless the objects be quite familiar to us, it is the highest temerity[4] to expect with assurance, after any of these changes, an event similar to that which before fell under our observation. . . .

But can you think, Cleanthes, that . . . [you are justified] in so wide a step as you have taken when you compared to the universe houses, ships, furniture, machines; and, from their similarity in some circumstances, inferred a similarity in their causes? Thought, design, intelligence, such as we discover in men and other animals, is no more than one of the springs and principles of the universe, as well as heat or cold, attraction or repulsion, and a hundred others which fall under daily observation. It is an active cause by which some particular parts of nature, we find, produce alterations on other parts. But can a conclusion, with any propriety, be transferred from parts to the whole? Does not the great disproportion bar all comparison and inference? From observing the growth of a hair, can we learn anything concerning the generation of a man? . . .

But allowing that we were to take the *operations* of one part of nature upon another for the foundation of our judgment concerning the *origin* of the whole (which never can be admitted), yet why select so minute, so weak, so bounded a principle as the reason and design of animals is found to be upon this planet? What peculiar privilege has this little agitation of the brain which we call *thought*, that we must thus make it the model of the whole universe? Our partiality in our own favor does indeed present it on all occasions, but sound philosophy ought carefully to guard against so natural an illusion. . . .

. . . Nature, we find, even from our limited experience, possesses an infinite number of springs and principles which incessantly discover themselves on every change of her position and situation. And what new and unknown principles would actuate her in so new and unknown a situation as that of the formation of a universe, we cannot, without the utmost temerity, pretend to determine.

A very small part of this great system, during a very short time, is very imperfectly discovered to us; and do we thence pronounce decisively concerning the origin of the whole?

Admirable conclusion! Stone, wood, brick, iron, brass, have not, at this time, in this minute globe of earth, an order or arrangement without human art and contrivance; therefore, the universe could not originally attain its order and arrangement without something similar to human art. But is a part of nature a rule for another part very wide of the former? Is it a rule for the whole? Is a very small part a rule for the universe? Is nature in one situation a certain rule for nature in another situation vastly different from the former?

[4]Boldness. EDITOR'S NOTE.

And can you blame me, Cleanthes, if I here imitate the prudent reserve of Simonides, who, according to the noted story, being asked by Hiero, *What God was?* desired a day to think of it, and then two days more; and after that manner continually prolonged the term, without ever bringing in his definition or description? Could you even blame me if I had answered, at first, *that I did not know*, and was sensible that this subject lay vastly beyond the reach of my faculties? . . . [H]aving found in so many other subjects much more familiar the imperfections and even contradictions of human reason, I never should expect any success from its feeble conjectures in a subject so sublime and so remote from the sphere of our observation. When two *species* of objects have always been observed to be conjoined together, I can *infer*, by custom, the existence of one wherever I *see* the existence of the other; and this I call an argument from experience. But how this argument can have place where the objects, as in the present case, are single, individual, without parallel or specific resemblance, may be difficult to explain. And will any man tell me with a serious countenance that an orderly universe must arise from some thought and art like the human because we have experience of it? To ascertain this reasoning it were requisite that we had experience of the origin of worlds; and it is not sufficient, surely, that we have seen ships and cities arise from human art and contrivance. . . .

[What Is the Cause of God?]

I shall endeavor to show you, a little more distinctly, the inconveniences of that anthropomorphism which you have embraced, and shall prove that there is no ground to suppose a plan of the world to be formed in the Divine mind, consisting of distinct ideas, differently arranged, in the same manner as an architect forms in his head the plan of a house which he intends to execute.

It is not easy, I own, to see what is gained by this supposition, whether we judge of the matter by *reason* or by *experience*. We are still obliged to mount higher in order to find the cause of this cause which you had assigned as satisfactory and conclusive. . . .

How, therefore, shall we satisfy ourselves concerning the cause of that Being whom you suppose the Author of Nature, or, according to your system of anthropomorphism, the ideal world into which you trace the material? Have we not the same reason to trace that ideal world into another ideal world or new intelligent principle? But if we stop and go no further, why go so far—why not stop at the material world? How can we satisfy ourselves without going on *in infinitum?* And, after all, what satisfaction is there in that infinite progression? Let us remember the story of the Indian philosopher and his elephant.[5] It was never more applicable than to the present subject. If the material world rests upon a similar ideal world, this ideal world must rest upon some other, and so on without end. It were better, therefore, never to look beyond the present material world. By supposing it to contain the principle of its order within itself, we really assert it to be God; and the sooner we arrive at that Divine Being, so much the better. When you go one step beyond the mundane system, you only excite an inquisitive humor which it is impossible ever to satisfy.

To say that the different ideas which compose the reason of the Supreme Being fall into order of themselves and by their own nature is really to talk without any precise meaning. If it has a meaning, I would fain know why it is not as good sense to say that the parts of the material world fall into order of themselves and by their

[5]The reference here is to an ancient Hindu belief that the (flat) world—which, it was claimed, would "fall" without some support underneath it—rested upon a gigantic elephant which in turn rested upon a gigantic tortoise. The tortoise's own source of support was either left unexplained or was shifted to yet another animal, *ad infinitum*. EDITOR'S NOTE.

own nature. Can the one opinion be intelligible, while the other is not so?

We have, indeed, experience of ideas which fall into order of themselves and without any *known* cause. But, I am sure, we have a much larger experience of matter which does the same, as in all instances of generation and vegetation where the accurate analysis of the cause exceeds all human comprehension. We have also experience of particular systems of thought and of matter which have no order; of the first in madness, of the second in corruption. Why, then, should we think that order is more essential to one than the other? And if it requires a cause in both, what do we gain by your system, in tracing the universe of objects into a similar universe of ideas? The first step which we make leads us on forever. It were, therefore, wise in us to limit all our inquiries to the present world, without looking farther. No satisfaction can ever be attained by these speculations which so far exceed the narrow bounds of human understanding. . . .

. . . In like manner, when it is asked, what cause produces order in the ideas of the Supreme Being, can any other reason be assigned by you, anthropomorphites, than that it is a *rational* faculty, and that such is the nature of the Deity? But why a similar answer will not be equally satisfactory in accounting for the order of the world, without having recourse to any such intelligent creator as you insist on, may be difficult to determine. It is only to say that *such* is the nature of material objects, and that they are all originally possessed of a *faculty* of order and proportion. These are only more learned and elaborate ways of confessing our ignorance; nor has the one hypothesis any real advantage above the other, except in its greater conformity to vulgar prejudices.

You have displayed this argument with great emphasis, replied Cleanthes: You seem not sensible how easy it is to answer it. Even in common life, if I assign a cause for any event, is it any objection, Philo, that I cannot assign the cause of that cause, and answer every new question which may incessantly be started? And what philosophers could possibly submit to so rigid a rule?—philosophers who confess ultimate causes to be totally unknown, and are sensible that the most refined principles into which they trace the phenomena are still to them as inexplicable as these phenomena themselves are to the vulgar. The order and arrangement of nature, the curious adjustment of final causes, the plain use and intention of every part and organ—all these bespeak in the clearest language an intelligent cause or author. The heavens and the earth join in the same testimony: The whole chorus of nature raises one hymn to the praises of its Creator. You alone, or almost alone, disturb this general harmony. You start abstruse doubts, cavils, and objections; you ask me what is the cause of this cause? I know not; I care not; that concerns not me. I have found a Deity; and here I stop my inquiry. Let those go farther who are wiser or more enterprising.

I pretend to be neither, replied Philo; and for that very reason I should never, perhaps, have attempted to go so far, especially when I am sensible that I must at last be contented to sit down with the same answer which, without further trouble, might have satisfied me from the beginning. . . .

[The Argument from Design Does Not Establish the Existence of the Judeo-Christian God.]

But to show you still more inconveniences, continued Philo, in your anthropomorphism, please to take a new survey of your principles. *Like effects prove like causes*. This is the experimental argument; and this, you say too, is the sole theological argument. Now it is certain that the liker the effects are which are seen and the liker the causes which are inferred, the stronger is the argument. Every departure on either side diminishes the probability and renders the experiment less conclusive. You cannot doubt of [this method of reasoning]; neither ought you to reject its consequences. . . .

. . . *First*, by this method of reasoning you renounce all claim to infinity in any of the attributes of the Deity. For, as the cause ought only to be proportioned to the effect, and the effect, so far as it falls under our cognizance, is not infinite, what pretension have we, upon your suppositions, to ascribe that attribute to the divine Being? You will still insist that, by removing him so much from all similarity to human creatures, we give in to the most arbitrary hypothesis, and at the same time weaken all proofs of his existence.

Secondly, you have no reason, on your theory, for ascribing perfection to the Deity, even in his finite capacity; or for supposing him free from every error, mistake, or incoherence, in his undertakings. There are many inexplicable difficulties in the works of nature which, if we allow a perfect author to be proved *a priori*, are easily solved, and become only seeming difficulties from the narrow capacity of man, who cannot trace infinite relations. But according to your method of reasoning, these difficulties become all real. . . . At least, you must acknowledge that it is impossible for us to tell, from our limited views, whether this system contains any great faults or deserves any considerable praise if compared to other possible and even real systems. . . .

But were this world ever so perfect a production, it must still remain uncertain whether all the excellences of the work can justly be ascribed to the workman. If we survey a ship, what an exalted idea must we form of the ingenuity of the carpenter who framed so complicated, useful, and beautiful a machine? And what surprise must we feel when we find him a stupid mechanic who imitated others, and copied an art which, through a long succession of ages, after multiplied trials, mistakes, corrections, deliberations, and controversies, had been gradually improving? Many worlds might have been botched and bungled, throughout an eternity, ere this system was struck out; much labor lost; many fruitless trials made; and a slow but continued improvement carried on during infinite ages in the art of world-making. In such subjects, who can determine where the truth, nay, who can conjecture where the probability lies, amidst a great number of hypotheses which may be proposed, and a still greater which may be imagined?

And what shadow of an argument, continued Philo, can you produce from your hypothesis to prove the unity of the Deity? A great number of men join in building a house or ship, in rearing a city, in framing a commonwealth; why may not several deities combine in contriving and framing a world? This is only so much greater similarity to human affairs. By sharing the work among several, we may so much further limit the attributes of each, and get rid of that extensive power and knowledge which must be supposed in one deity, and which, according to you, can only serve to weaken the proof of his existence. And if such foolish, such vicious creatures as man can yet often unite in framing and executing one plan, how much more those deities . . . whom we may suppose several degrees more perfect? . . . .

And why not become a perfect anthropomorphite? Why not assert the deity or deities to be corporeal, and to have eyes, a nose, mouth, ears, etc.? Epicurus maintained that no man had ever seen reason but in a human figure; therefore, the gods must have a human figure. And this argument, which is deservedly so much ridiculed by Cicero, becomes, according to you, solid and philosophical.

In a word, Cleanthes, a man who follows your hypothesis is able, perhaps, to assert or conjecture that the universe sometime arose from something like design; but beyond that position he cannot ascertain one single circumstance, and is left afterwards to fix every point of his theology by the utmost license of fancy and hypothesis. This world, for aught he knows, is very faulty and imperfect, compared to a superior standard; and was only the first rude essay of some infant deity who afterwards abandoned it, ashamed of his lame performance; it is the work only of some dependent, inferior deity, and is the object of derision to his superiors. . . .

[The Arbitrariness of All Hypotheses Concerning the Origin of the Universe]

Our friend Cleanthes, replied Philo, as you have heard, asserts that since no question of fact can be proved otherwise than by experience, the existence of a Deity admits not of proof from any other medium. The world, says he, resembles the works of human contrivance; therefore its cause must also resemble that of the other. Here we may remark that the operation of one very small part of nature, to wit, man, upon another very small part, to wit, that inanimate matter lying within his reach, is the rule by which Cleanthes judges of the origin of the whole; and he measures objects, so widely disproportioned, by the same individual standard. But to waive all objections drawn from this topic, I affirm that there are other parts of the universe (besides the machines of human invention) which bear still a greater resemblance to the fabric of the world, and which, therefore, afford a better conjecture concerning the universal origin of this system. These parts are animals and vegetables. The world plainly resembles more an animal or a vegetable than it does a watch or a knitting-loom. Its cause, therefore, it is more probable, resembles the cause of the former. The cause of the former is generation or vegetation. The cause, therefore, of the world we may infer to be something similar or analogous to generation or vegetation.

But how is it conceivable, said Demea, that the world can arise from anything similar to vegetation or generation?

Very easily, replied Philo. In like manner as a tree sheds its seed into the neighboring fields and produces other trees; so the great vegetable, the world, or this planetary system, produces within itself certain seeds which, being scattered into the surrounding chaos, vegetate into new worlds. A comet, for instance, is the seed of a world; and after it has been fully ripened, by passing from sun to sun, and star to star, it is at last tossed into the unformed elements which everywhere surround this universe, and immediately sprouts up into a new system.

Or if, for the sake of variety (for I see no other advantage) we should suppose this world to be an animal; a comet is the egg of this animal; and in like manner as an ostrich lays its egg in the sand, which, without any further care, hatches the egg and produces a new animal, so . . . I understand you, says Demea: But what wild, arbitrary suppositions are these? What *data* have you for such extraordinary conclusions? And is the slight, imaginary resemblance of the world to a vegetable or an animal sufficient to establish the same inference with regard to both? Objects which are in general so widely different; ought they to be a standard for each other?

Right, cries Philo: This is the topic on which I have all along insisted. I have still asserted that we have no *data* to establish any system of cosmogony.[6] Our experience, so imperfect in itself and so limited both in extent and duration, can afford us no probable conjecture concerning the whole of things. But if we must needs fix on some hypothesis, by what rule, pray, ought we to determine our choice? Is there any other rule than the great similarity of the ob-

[6]The theory of the origin of the universe. EDITOR'S NOTE.

jects compared? And does not a plant or an animal, which springs from vegetation or generation, bear a stronger resemblance to the world than does any artificial machine, which arises from reason and design? . . .

The Brahmins assert that the world arose from an infinite spider, who spun this whole complicated mass from his bowels, and annihilates afterwards the whole or any part of it, by absorbing it again and resolving it into his own essence. Here is a species of cosmogony which appears to us ridiculous because a spider is a little contemptible animal whose operations we are never likely to take for a model of the whole universe. But still here is a new species of analogy, even in our globe. And were there a planet wholly inhabited by spiders (which is very possible), this inference would there appear as natural and irrefragable as that which in our planet ascribes the origin of all things to design and intelligence, as explained by Cleanthes. Why an orderly system may not be spun from the belly as well as from the brain, it will be difficult for him to give a satisfactory reason.

I must confess, Philo, replied Cleanthes, that, of all men living, the task which you have undertaken, of raising doubts and objections, suits you best and seems, in a manner, natural and unavoidable to you. So great is your fertility of invention that I am not ashamed to acknowledge myself unable, on a sudden, to solve regularly such out-of-the-way difficulties as you incessantly start upon me; though I clearly see, in general, their fallacy and error. . . .

. . . What you ascribe to the fertility of my invention, replied Philo, is entirely owing to the nature of the subject. . . . [I]n such questions as the present, a hundred contradictory views may preserve a kind of imperfect analogy, and invention has here full scope to exert itself. Without any great effort of thought, I believe that I could, in an instant, propose other systems of cosmogony which would have some faint appearance of truth; though it is a thousand, a million to one if either yours or any one of mine be the true system. . . .

DISCUSSION QUESTIONS

1. Why does Philo think that Cleanthes' argument that the world was (most likely) designed by a deity is a weak one? How forceful do you think Philo's criticisms are?

2. In reply to Philo's objection that the hypothesis that God created the world leads naturally to the question "Who created God?" Demea replies "I know not, I care not. . . . I have found a Deity; and here I stop my inquiry." What is Philo's objection to this reply? Is it adequate? Why, or why not?

3. Is Philo right that even if we had evidence from experience for the existence of a designer, we have absolutely no evidence from experience for identifying that designer with God, and no evidence from experience for our monotheistic belief in a single creator?

4. Is Philo right to reject any attempt to explain the origin of the universe? If Philo were alive today would he object to astronomers who offer theories of the origin of the universe? If not, how, if at all, would he modify his claim that ". . . we have no **data** to establish any system of cosmogony"? (See p. 77.)

9. THE CLASSIC DEFENSE OF THE ONTOLOGICAL ARGUMENT

Saint Anselm

SAINT ANSELM (1033–1109), the most influential Christian theologian of the eleventh century, was Archbishop of Canterbury. He is remembered today primarily for his defense of the ontological argument for God's existence. Anselm's famous presentation of this argument comes from his **Proslogium**, which is usually translated as **Discourse**, but given the special nature of the discourse, it might be more appropriately called **Prayer**. In the Preface to the **Proslogium**, Anselm makes it clear that his aim in writing it is devotional, rather than abstractly speculative and that it is written for "someone trying to raise his mind to the contemplation of God and seeking to understand what he believes." Anselm's view that faith and love in God must precede philosophical reflection about God is central to his theological perspective, a perspective which follows in the tradition of Saint Augustine (354–430). From this perspective, theological discourses on the nature of God and the grounds for believing in him are a form of prayer to God which couples a profession of one's complete devotion with a plea for understanding. As Anselm himself puts it in the **Proslogium**, "I do not attempt, O Lord, to penetrate Thy profundity, for I deem my intellect in no way sufficient thereunto, but I desire to understand in some degree Thy truth, which my heart believes and loves. For I do not seek to understand in order that I may believe; but I believe, that I may understand. For I believe this too, that unless I believed, I should not understand." As the following brief selection indicates, Anselm's prayers to God for understanding took the form of logical dialectic (i.e., argumentation).

In our selection, Anselm begins by defining God as "a being than which nothing greater can be conceived" (i.e., "the greatest conceivable being"). Assuming that this concept makes sense (i.e., that one can understand what it means or, as Anselm puts it, that "it is in the understanding"), Anselm uses the method of **indirect proof** to establish that this concept must actually refer to something. An indirect proof of some statement, S, consists of deducing some contradiction from the assumption that S is false. Once this contradiction is deduced, one then deduces that the assumption that led to it (namely that S is false) is itself false (i.e., S must be true). Using this method, Anselm assumes, for the sake of argument, that the concept of "the greatest conceivable being" does not refer to an existent being but is only a concept in the mind or, to use his language, he assumes that "it exists in the understanding alone and not in reality." This, says Anselm, leads to the contradiction that the greatest conceivable being is not the greatest conceivable being, since it is greater to exist both in reality and in the understanding rather than in the understanding alone. Consequently, the greatest conceivable being—namely, God—exists in reality as well as in the understanding. After so establishing to his satisfaction God's existence, Anselm then goes on (again through an indirect proof) to establish God's **necessary** existence—that is, that God "cannot even be thought of as not existing."

God Truly Is

And so, O Lord, since thou givest understanding to faith, give me to understand—as far as thou knowest it to be good for me—that thou dost exist, as we believe, and that thou art what we believe thee to be. Now we believe that thou art a being than which none greater can be thought. Or can it be that there is no such being, since "the fool hath said in his heart, 'There is no God' "? But when this same fool hears what I am saying—"A being than which none greater can be thought"—he understands what he hears, and what he understands is in his understanding, even if he does not understand that it exists. . . . Even the fool, then, must be convinced that a being than which none greater can be thought exists at least in his understanding, since when he hears this he understands it, and whatever is understood is in the understanding. But clearly that than which a greater cannot be thought cannot exist in the understanding alone. For if it is actually in the understanding alone, it can be thought of as existing also in reality, and this is greater. Therefore, if that than which a greater cannot be thought is in the understanding alone, this same thing than which a greater cannot be thought is that than which a greater can be thought. But obviously this is impossible. Without doubt, therefore, there exists, both in the understanding and in reality, something than which a greater cannot be thought.

God Cannot Be Thought of as Nonexistent

And certainly it exists so truly that it cannot be thought of as nonexistent. For something can be thought of as existing, which cannot be thought of as not existing, and this is greater than that which *can* be thought of as not existing. Thus, if that than which a greater cannot be thought can be thought of as not existing, this very thing than which a greater cannot be thought is *not* that than which a greater cannot be thought. But this is contradictory. So, then, there truly is a being than which a greater cannot be thought—so truly that it cannot even be thought of as not existing.

And *thou* art this being, O Lord our God. Thou so truly art, then, O Lord my God, that thou canst not even be thought of as not existing. . . . And indeed whatever is, except thyself alone, can be thought of as not existing. Thou alone, therefore, of all beings, hast being in the truest and highest sense, since no other being so truly exists, and thus every other being has less being. Why, then, has "the fool said in his heart, 'There is no God,' " when it is so obvious to the rational mind that, of all beings, thou dost exist supremely? Why indeed, unless it is that he is a stupid fool?

Source: From *Scholastic Miscellany*, edited and translated by Eugene R. Fairweather (Volume X: The Library of Christian Classics). Published simultaneously in Great Britain and the United States of America by the S.C.M. Press Ltd., London, and The Westminster Press, Philadelphia in 1956. Used by permission.

DISCUSSION QUESTIONS

1. Do you find any plausibility in Anselm's claim that God "cannot even be thought of as not existing"? Argue as carefully as you can for your position.

2. Is it possible to prove that something exists just by considering its definition? Is it possible to prove that something doesn't exist by considering its definition?

3. In reply to Anselm, a monk by the name of Gaunilo claimed that Anselm's method must be mistaken, for with it one could prove the existence of "the greatest conceivable" anything. To use his specific example, "the greatest conceivable island" must exist for if it did not exist, one could think of "a greater island," namely one just like it in all respects, except that it exists. Anselm claimed in reply that only God cannot be conceived as not existing. Does this seem reasonable?

4. Can one utilize an ontological type argument to prove the existence of "the worst conceivable being"?

10. A CONTEMPORARY PHILOSOPHER'S DEFENSE OF THE ARGUMENT FROM CONTINGENCY

Richard Taylor

RICHARD TAYLOR (1919–) is a well known contemporary American philosopher who has written widely on diverse philosophical topics. The best known of his published works is his short book **Metaphysics**, an introduction to traditional metaphysical problems for philosophical novices. Taylor's defense of metaphysical positions not currently in vogue among contemporary Anglo-American philosophers makes **Metaphysics** an especially stimulating book.

The following selection comes from the chapter on God in Taylor's **Metaphysics**. The selection is a modern formulation of the argument from contingency, the classical formulation of which can be found in the **Summa Theologica** of Saint Thomas Aquinas (1225–74). Taylor begins by introducing and assuming "the principle of sufficient reason," which claims that every fact that is true (or thing that exists) must have an explanation. Taylor claims that this principle is so basic that it is "almost a part of reason itself." After introducing the principle of sufficient reason, Taylor next introduces the distinction between **contingent truths** and **necessary truths**. Contingent truths, he claims, are true statements whose explanations "depend on something else," while necessary truths are true statements whose explanations "depend only upon themselves." The examples Taylor gives of necessary truths are what philosophers call **analytic truths**—that is, definitional truths which say nothing about the world but only about the conventions of our language (e.g., "All bachelors are unmarried"). This is not controversial. What is controversial is Taylor's utilization of the notion of a **necessary being**—that is, of a being "whose reason for existence lies within itself," which Taylor takes to be equivalent to the notion of a "being that we cannot conceive not existing" (as opposed to a **contingent being**, whose "reason for existence exists outside of itself" and which we "can conceive not existing").

According to the principle of sufficient reason, there must be a reason why the world exists. Now, as Taylor sees it, this would be true even if the world always existed, for, in such a case, one could still ask, "Why did the world always exist?" Now, while it is logically possible for the world to be a necessary being itself, Taylor finds this implausible and consequently maintains that the world is a "contingent being" whose explanation must be sought outside of itself. Next, Taylor claims that since it is impossible that "the world depends for its existence upon something else, which in turn depends on still another thing, this depending upon still another, **ad infinitum**," it must follow "that the world derives its existence from something that exists by its own nature and which is accordingly eternal and imperishable"—namely, God.

The Principle of Sufficient Reason

Suppose you were strolling in the woods and, in addition to the sticks, stones, and other accustomed litter of the forest floor, you one day came upon some quite unaccustomed object, something not quite like what you had ever seen before and would never expect to find in such a place. Suppose, for example, that it is a large ball, about your own height, perfectly smooth and translucent. You would deem this puzzling and mysterious, certainly, but if one considers the matter, it is no more inherently mysterious that such a thing should exist than that anything else should exist. If you were quite accustomed to finding such objects of various sizes around you most of the time, but had never seen an ordinary rock, then upon finding a large rock in the woods one day you would be just as puzzled and mystified. This illustrates the fact that something that is mysterious ceases to seem so simply by its accustomed presence. It is strange indeed, for example, that a world such as ours should exist; yet few men are very often struck by this strangeness, but simply take it for granted.

Suppose, then, that you have found this translucent ball and are mystified by it. Now whatever else you might wonder about it, there is one thing you would hardly question; namely, that it did not appear there all by itself, that it owes its existence to something. You might not have the remotest idea whence and how it came to be there, but you would hardly doubt that there was an explanation. The idea that it might have come from nothing at all, that it might exist without there being any explanation of its existence, is one that few people would consider worthy of entertaining.

This illustrates a metaphysical belief that seems to be almost a part of reason itself, even though few men ever think upon it; the belief, namely, that there is some explanation for the existence of anything whatever, some reason why it should exist rather than not. The sheer nonexistence of anything, which is not to be confused with the passing out of existence of something, never requires a reason; but existence does. That there should never have been any such ball in the forest does not require any explanation or reason, but that there should ever be such a ball does. . . . That anything should not exist, then, and that, for instance, no such ball should exist in the forest, or that there should be no forest for it to occupy, or no continent containing a forest, or no earth, nor any world at all, do not seem to be things for which there needs to be any explanation or reason; but that such things should be, does seem to require a reason.

The principle involved here has been called the principle of sufficient reason. Actually, it is a very general principle, and is best expressed by saying that, in the case of any positive truth, there is some sufficient reason for it, something which, in this sense, makes it true—in short, that there is some sort of explanation, known or unknown, for everything.

Now some truths depend on something else, and are accordingly called *contingent*, while others depend only upon themselves, that is, are true by their very natures and are accordingly called *necessary*. There is, for example, a reason why the stone on my window sill is warm; namely, that the sun is shining upon it. This happens to be true, but not by its very nature. Hence, it is contingent, and depends upon something other than itself. It is also true that all the points of a circle are equidistant from the center, but this truth depends upon nothing but itself. No matter what happens, nothing can make it false. Similarly, it is a truth, and a necessary one, that if the stone on my window sill is a body, as it is, then it has a form, since this fact depends upon nothing but itself for its confirmation. Untruths are also, of course, either contingent or necessary, it being contingently

Source: Richard Taylor, *Metaphysics*, 2nd ed., © 1974, pp. 103–12. Reprinted by permission of Prentice-Hall, Inc., Englewood Cliffs, N.J.

false, for example, that the stone on my window sill is cold, and necessarily false that it is both a body and formless, since this is by its very nature impossible.

The principle of sufficient reason can be illustrated in various ways, as we have done, and if one thinks about it, he is apt to find that he presupposes it in his thinking about reality, but it cannot be proved. It does not appear to be itself a necessary truth, and at the same time it would be most odd to say it is contingent. If one were to try proving it, he would sooner or later have to appeal to considerations that are less plausible than the principle itself. Indeed, it is hard to see how one could even make an argument for it, without already assuming it. For this reason it might properly be called a presupposition of reason itself. One can deny that it is true, without embarrassment or fear of refutation, but one is then apt to find that what he is denying is not really what the principle asserts. We shall, then, treat it here as a datum—not something that is provably true, but as something which all men, whether they ever reflect upon it or not, seem more or less to presuppose.

The Existence of a World

It happens to be true that something exists, that there is, for example, a world, and while no one ever seriously supposes that this might not be so, that there might exist nothing at all, there still seems to be nothing the least necessary in this, considering it just by itself. That no world should ever exist at all is perfectly comprehensible and seems to express not the slightest absurdity. Considering any particular item in the world it seems not at all necessary in itself that it should ever have existed, nor does it appear any more necessary that the totality of these things, or any totality of things, should ever exist.

From the principle of sufficient reason it follows, of course, that there must be a reason, not only for the existence of everything in the world but for the world itself, meaning by "the world" simply everything that ever does exist, except God, in case there is a god. This principle does not imply that there must be some purpose or goal for everything, or for the totality of all things; for explanations need not, and in fact seldom are, teleological or purposeful. . . .

Consider again the strange ball that we imagine has been found in the forest. Now we can hardly doubt that there must be an explanation for the existence of such a thing, though we may have no notion what that explanation is. It is not, moreover, the fact of its having been found in the forest rather than elsewhere that renders an explanation necessary. It matters not in the least where it happens to be, for our question is not how it happens to be *there* but how it happens to exist at all. If we in our imagination annihilate the forest, leaving only this ball in an open field, our conviction that it is a contingent thing and owes its existence to something other than itself is not reduced in the least. If we now imagine the field to be annihilated, and in fact everything else as well to vanish into nothingness, leaving only this ball to constitute the entire physical universe, then we cannot for a moment suppose that its existence has thereby been explained, or the need of any explanation eliminated, or that its existence is suddenly rendered self-explanatory. If we now carry this thought one step further and suppose that no other reality ever has existed or ever will exist, that this ball forever constitutes the entire physical universe, then we must still insist on there being some reason independent of itself why it should exist rather than not. If there must be a reason for the existence of any particular thing, then the necessity of such a reason is not eliminated by the mere supposition that certain other things do *not* exist. And again, it matters not at all what the thing in question is, whether it be large and complex, such as the world we actually find ourselves in, or whether it be something small, simple and insignificant, such as a ball, a bacterium, or the merest grain of sand.

We do not avoid the necessity of a reason for the evidence of something merely by describing it in this way or that. . . .

Beginningless Existence

It should now be noted that it is no answer to the question, why a thing exists, to state *how long* it has existed. A geologist does not suppose that he has explained why there should be rivers and mountains merely by pointing out that they are old. Similarly, if one were to ask, concerning the ball of which we have spoken, for some sufficient reason for its being, he would not receive any answer upon being told that it had been there since yesterday. Nor would it be any better answer to say that it had existed since before anyone could remember, or even that it had always existed; for the question was not one concerning its age but its existence. If, to be sure, one were to ask where a given thing came from, or how it came into being, then upon learning that it had always existed he would learn that it never really *came* into being at all; but he could still reasonably wonder why it should exist at all. If, accordingly, the world—that is, the totality of all things excepting God, in case there is a god—had really no beginning at all, but has always existed in some form or other, then there is clearly no answer to the question, where it came from and when; it did not, on this supposition, *come* from anything at all, at any time. But still, it can be asked why there is a world, why indeed there is a beginningless world, why there should have perhaps always been something rather than nothing. And, if the principle of sufficient reason is a good principle, there must be an answer to that question, an answer that is by no means supplied by giving the world an age, or even an infinite age.

Creation

This brings out an important point with respect to the concept of creation that is often misunderstood, particularly by those whose thinking has been influenced by Christian ideas. People tend to think that creation—for example, the creation of the world by God—*means* creation *in time*, from which it of course logically follows that if the world had no beginning in time, then it cannot be the creation of God. This, however, is erroneous, for creation means essentially *dependence*, even in Christian theology. If one thing is the creation of another, then it depends for its existence on that other, and this is perfectly consistent with saying that both are eternal, that neither ever came into being, and hence, that neither was ever created at any point of time. Perhaps an analogy will help convey this point. Consider, then, a flame that is casting beams of light. Now there seems to be a clear sense in which the beams of light are dependent for their existence upon the flame, which is their source, while the flame, on the other hand, is not similarly dependent for its existence upon them. The beams of light arise from the flame, but the flame does not arise from them. In this sense, they are the creation of the flame; they derive their existence from it. And none of this has any reference to time; the relationship of dependence in such a case would not be altered in the slightest if we supposed that the flame, and with it the beams of light, had always existed, that neither had ever *come* into being.

Now if the world is the creation of God, its relationship to God should be thought of in this fashion; namely, that the world depends for its existence upon God, and could not exist independently of God. If God is eternal, as those who believe in God generally assume, then the world may (though it need not) be eternal too, without that altering in the least its dependence upon God for its existence, and hence without altering its being the creation of God. The supposition of God's eternality, on the other hand, does not by itself imply that the world is eternal too; for there is not the least reason why something of finite duration might not depend for its existence upon something of infinite duration—though the reverse is, of course, impossible.

God

If we think of God as "the creator of heaven and earth," and if we consider heaven and earth to include everything that exists except God, then we appear to have, in the foregoing considerations, fairly strong reasons for asserting that God, as so conceived, exists. Now of course most people have much more in mind than this when they think of God, for religions have ascribed to God ever so many attributes that are not at all implied by describing him merely as the creator of the world; but that is not relevant here. Most religious persons do, in any case, think of God as being at least the creator, as that being upon which everything ultimately depends, no matter what else they may say about him in addition. . . .

If, as seems clearly implied by the principle of sufficient reason, there must be a reason for the existence of heaven and earth—i.e., for the world—then that reason must be found either in the world itself, or outside it, in something that is literally supranatural, or outside heaven and earth. Now if we suppose that the world—i.e., the totality of all things except God—contains within itself the reason for its existence, we are supposing that it exists by its very nature, that is, that it is a necessary being. In that case there would, of course, be no reason for saying that it must depend upon God or anything else for its existence; for if it exists by its very nature, then it depends upon nothing but itself, much as the sun depends upon nothing but itself for its heat. This, however, is implausible, for we find nothing about the world or anything in it to suggest that it exists by its own nature, and we do find on the contrary, ever so many things to suggest that it does not. For in the first place, anything which exists by its very nature must necessarily be eternal and indestructible. It would be a self-contradiction to say of anything that it exists by its own nature, or is a necessarily existing thing, and at the same time to say that it comes into being or passes away, or that it ever could come into being or pass away. Nothing about the world seems at all like this, for concerning anything in the world, we can perfectly easily think of it as being annihilated, or as never having existed in the first place, without there being the slightest hint of any absurdity in such a supposition. Some of the things in the universe are, to be sure, very old; the moon, for example, or the stars and the planets. It is even possible to imagine that they have always existed. Yet it seems quite impossible to suppose that they owe their existence to nothing but themselves, that they bestow existence upon themselves by their very natures, or that they are in themselves things of such nature that it would be impossible for them not to exist. . . .

There seems to be nothing in the world, then, concerning which it is at all plausible to suppose that it exists by its own nature, or contains within itself the reason for its existence. In fact, everything in the world appears to be quite plainly the opposite, namely, something that not only need not exist, but at some time or other, past or future or both, does not in fact exist. Everything in the world seems to have a finite duration, whether long or short. Most things, such as ourselves, exist only for a short while; they come into being, then soon cease. Other things, like the heavenly bodies, last longer, but they are still corruptible, and from all that we can gather about them, they too seem destined eventually to perish. We arrive at the conclusion, then, that while the world may contain some things which have always existed and are destined never to perish, it is nevertheless doubtful that it contains any such thing and, in any case, everything in the world is capable of perishing, and nothing in it, however long it may already have existed and however long it may yet remain, exists by its own nature, but depends instead upon something else.

While this might be true of everything in the world, is it necessarily true of the world itself? That is, if we grant, as we seem forced to, that nothing in the world exists by its own nature, that everything in the world is contingent and perishable, must we also say that the world itself, or the totality of all these perishable things, is also contingent and perishable? Logically, we are not forced to, for it is logically possible that the totality of all perishable things might itself be imperishable, and hence, that the world might exist by its own nature, even though it is comprised exclusively of things which are contingent. It is not logically necessary that a totality should share the defects of its members. For example, even though every man is mortal, it does not follow from this that the human race, or the totality of all men, is also mortal; for it is possible that there will always be human beings, even though there are no human beings which will always exist. Similarly, it is possible that the world is in itself a necessary thing, even though it is comprised entirely of things that are contingent.

This is logically possible, but it is not plausible. For we find nothing whatever about the world, any more than in its parts, to suggest that it exists by its own nature. Concerning anything in the world, we have not the slightest difficulty in supposing that it should perish, or even, that it should never have existed in the first place. We have almost as little difficulty in supposing this of the world itself. It might be somewhat hard to think of everything as utterly perishing and leaving no trace whatever of its ever having been, but there seems to be not the slightest difficulty in imagining that the world should never have existed in the first place. We can, for instance, perfectly easily suppose that nothing in the world had ever existed except, let us suppose, a single grain of sand, and we can thus suppose that this grain of sand has forever constituted the whole universe. Now if we consider just this grain of sand, it is quite impossible for us to suppose that it exists by its very nature, and could never have failed to exist. It clearly depends for its existence upon something other than itself, if it depends on anything at all. The same will be true if we consider the world to consist, not of one grain of sand, but of two, or of a million, or, as we in fact find, of a vast number of stars and planets and all their minuter parts.

It would seem, then, that the world, in case it happens to exist at all—and this is quite beyond doubt—is contingent and thus dependent upon something other than itself for its existence, if it depends upon anything at all. And it must depend upon something, for otherwise there could be no reason why it exists in the first place. Now that upon which the world depends must be something that either exists by its own nature or does not. If it does not exist by its own nature, then it, in turn, depends for its existence upon something else, and so on. Now then, we can say either of two things; namely, (1) that the world depends for its existence upon something else, which in turn depends on still another thing, this depending upon still another, *ad infinitum*; or (2) that the world derives its existence from something that exists by its own nature and which is accordingly eternal and imperishable, and is the creator of heaven and earth. The first of these alternatives, however, is impossible, for it does not render a sufficient reason why anything should exist in the first place. Instead of supplying a reason why any world should exist, it repeatedly begs off giving a reason. It explains what is dependent and perishable in terms of what is itself dependent and perishable, leaving us still without a reason why perishable things should exist at all, which is what we are seeking. Ultimately, then, it would seem that the world, or the totality of contingent or perishable things, in case it exists at all, must depend upon something that is necessary and imperishable, and which accordingly exists, not in dependence upon something else, but by its own nature.

"Self-Caused"

What has been said thus far gives some intimation of what meaning should be attached to the concept of a self-caused being, a concept that it quite generally misunderstood, sometimes even by scholars. To say that something—God, for example—is self-caused, or is the cause of its own existence, does not mean that this being brings itself into existence, which is a perfectly absurd idea. Nothing can *bring* itself into existence. To say that something is self-caused means only that it exists, not contingently or in dependence upon something else, but by its own nature, which is only to say that it is a being which is such that it can neither come into being nor perish. Now whether such a being in fact exists or not, there is in any case no absurdity in the idea. We have found, in fact, that the principle of sufficient reason seems to point to the existence of such a being, as that upon which the world, with everything in it, must ultimately depend for its existence.

"Necessary Being"

A being that depends for its existence upon nothing but itself, and is in this sense self-caused, can equally be described as a necessary being; that is to say, a being that is not contingent, and hence not perishable. For in the case of anything which exists by its own nature, and is dependent upon nothing else, it is impossible that it should not exist, which is equivalent to saying that it is necessary. Many persons have professed to find the gravest difficulties in this concept, too, but that is partly because it has been confused with other notions. If it makes sense to speak of anything as an *impossible* being, or something which by its very nature does not exist, then it is hard to see why the idea of a necessary being, or something which in its very nature exists, should not be just as comprehensible. And of course, we have not the slightest difficulty in speaking of something, such as a square circle or a formless body, as an impossible being. And if it makes sense to speak of something as being perishable, contingent, and dependent upon something other than itself for its existence, as it surely does, then there seems to be no difficulty in thinking of something as imperishable and dependent upon nothing other than itself for its existence.

"First Cause"

From these considerations we can see also what is properly meant by a first cause, an appellative that has often been applied to God by theologians, and which many persons have deemed an absurdity. It is a common criticism of this notion to say that there need not be any first cause, since the series of causes and effects which constitute the history of the universe might be infinite or beginningless and must, in fact, be infinite in case the universe itself had no beginning in time. This criticism, however, reflects a total misconception of what is meant by a first cause. *First* here does not mean first in time, and when God is spoken of as a first cause, he is not being described as a being which, at some time in the remote past, *started* everything. To describe God as a first cause is only to say that he is literally a *primary* rather than a secondary cause, an *ultimate* rather than a derived cause, or a being upon which all other things, heaven and earth, ultimately depend for their existence. It is, in short, only to say that God is the creator, in the sense of creation explained above. Now this, of course, is perfectly consistent with saying that the world is eternal or beginningless. As we have seen, one gives no reason for the existence of a world merely by giving it an age, even if it is supposed to have an infinite age. To use a helpful analogy, we can say that the sun is the first cause of daylight and, for that matter, of the moonlight of the night as well, which means only that daylight and moonlight ultimately depend upon the sun for their existence. The moon, on the other hand, is only a secondary or derivative cause of its light. This light would be no less dependent upon the sun if we affirmed that it had no beginning, for an ageless and beginningless light requires a source no less than an ephemeral one. If we supposed that the sun has always existed, and with it its light, then we would have to say that the sun has always been the first—i.e., the primary or ultimate—cause of its light. Such is precisely the manner in which God should be thought of, and is by theologians often thought of, as the first cause of heaven and earth.

DISCUSSION QUESTIONS

1. If one concludes, as Taylor does, that God exists, what explanation, if any can be given as to why God exists or as to why he created the world at all or at the particular time that he did? Must one not, in the end, accept some brute facts (i.e., facts without explanations)? Must one not say, in the end, "That's the way it is?" If so, must we not reject the principle of sufficient reason? Why, or why not? Consider in this regard the following criticism (composed by the editor):

> Supporters of the argument from contingency claim that there must be a reason why the universe exists, that it cannot simply be accepted as "a brute fact." They fail to realize, however, that if there is a God who provides a reason for the existence of the universe, he, then, would have to be accepted as a brute fact. No doubt, the belief that there is a personal god behind the universe is more psychologically comforting than the belief that the universe "just happened," but the less psychologically comforting belief appears to be no less rational. Whether the universe existed eternally without any external cause or whether God provides a reason for its existence, we still cannot explain everything, though the argument from contingency claims that we should be able to.

How do you think Taylor would reply? What do you think?

2. What does Taylor mean by a "necessary being"? Does this notion make sense to you? Why, or why not? Is Taylor right that the notion of a "necessary being" is no more difficult to understand than the notion of an "impossible being"?

3. It has been suggested that the argument from contingency commits the same fallacy as the ontological argument. Critically discuss.

4. What reasons does Taylor give for rejecting the view that the world is a necessary being? Do you find Taylor's reasons convincing? Why, or why not?

5. Consider the following claim:

> Since it is conceivable that the world always existed, it is possible that it had no creator. Consequently, Taylor's argument must be fallacious.

What fundamental misunderstanding of Taylor's argument does this objection assume?

6. Does Taylor's argument logically rule out the possibility that the immediate explanation of the world is contingent, even though its ultimate explanation is necessary. For example, does he logically rule out the possibility that the world was created by the devil (a contingent being) who in turn was created by God (a necessary being)?

7. Does Taylor's argument logically rule out the possibility of more than one necessary being who created the world?

8. Even if one grants both that the notion of a "necessary being" is meaningful and that explanations are in some sense incomplete unless phenomena can ultimately be traced back to a necessary being, does this establish that there **are**

complete explanations? What would Taylor say? What do you think?

9. Do you see anything unintelligible with the hypothesis that the universe came into existence at some point in time, without any cause? If not, is this hypothesis less intellectually satisfying than the hypothesis that the universe always existed? Is the hypothesis that the universe always existed (with or without God), in turn, less intellectually satisfying than the hypothesis that God created it "out of nothing" as the Genesis story proclaims?

10. Some philosophers have contended that it makes no sense to speak of the explanation of a series of events as distinct from the explanations of the individual members of that series.[1] As these philosophers see it, while it is possible to seek explanations for any event that exists in this world in terms of preceding events and general scientific laws and theories, it makes no sense to ask for the explanation of the totality of events that comprise the world taken as a whole. Is this true?

[1]In particular, see Paul Edwards, "The Cosmological Argument" in *The Rationalist Annual*, 1959. The article is reprinted in *Readings in the Philosophy of Religion*, ed. Baruch Brody (Englewood Cliffs, N.J.: Prentice-Hall, 1974) and an abridged version of it (which contains the point mentioned in question 10) was incorporated by Edwards into his introduction to the chapter on the existence of God (Chapter V) in *A Modern Introduction to Philosophy*, 3rd ed., ed. Paul Edwards and Arthur Pap (New York: Macmillan, 1973).

11. A DEFENSE OF THE VIEW THAT MYSTICAL EXPERIENCE PROVIDES A BASIS FOR RELIGIOUS BELIEF

William James

WILLIAM JAMES (1842–1910), son of the philosophical theologian Henry James and the younger brother of the novelist Henry James, was a graduate of Harvard Medical School. Upon graduation, he taught anatomy and physiology at Harvard College. His interests then shifted primarily to psychology and philosophy, and he began teaching these subjects. His book **The Principles of Psychology** (1890) was a pioneering contribution to the understanding of psychological phenomena. In his later years his academic attention was almost exclusively focused on philosophy. Along with Charles Sanders Peirce (1839–1914) and John Dewey (1859–1952), James had a central role in the development of the American philosophical school of thinking called **pragmatism**, which identified the meaning or truth of statements with their observable consequences (or effects upon our experience). His predominant philosophical interest was the development of a pragmatic point of view which could integrate his empiricistic scientific temper with the claims of moral and religious experience.

The following selection comes from James' detailed study of religious psychology, **The Varieties of Religious Experience** (1902), which was originally presented by James as a series of lectures. It consists of excerpts from two of these lectures which deal with mystical experience. The selection begins with James' definition of a mystical experience as an alleged intuitive insight into some truth that defies linguistic expression. James then goes on to describe other features usually present in mystical experiences and mentions the similarity of mystical experiences to the states of consciousness produced by such mind-altering substances as alcohol and nitrous oxide ("laughing gas"). After describing altered states of consciousness that do not have religious significance, James turns his attention to descriptions of religious mystical states. (Many of the examples James gives of mystical experiences in the lectures from which this selection is excerpted have been deleted.) Having sketched the characteristics of mystical experiences, James draws three conclusions about them. First, he claims that the mystic has the right to see his experience as a nondelusional revelation of some external reality. Second, James claims (anticipating Freud) that since mystical experiences may be capable of purely psychological explanations ("they are in the mind") non-mystics need not acknowledge that mystical experiences are revelations of some external reality. Third, James concludes that while non-mystics need not accept the claims of mystics to truth, "the existence of mystical states absolutely overthrows the pretension of non-mystical states to be the sole and ultimate dictators of what we may believe."

. . . One may say truly, I think, that personal religious experience has its root and centre in mystical states of consciousness. . . . Whether my treatment of mystical states will shed more light or darkness, I do not know, for my own constitution shuts me out from their enjoyment almost entirely, and I can speak of them only at second hand. But though forced to look upon the subject so externally, I will be as objective and receptive as I can; and I think I shall at least succeed in convincing you of the reality of the states in question, and of the paramount importance of their function.

First of all, then, I ask, What does the expression ''mystical states of consciousness'' mean? How do we part off mystical states from other states?

The words ''mysticism'' and ''mystical'' are often used as terms of mere reproach, to throw at any opinion which we regard as vague and vast and sentimental, and without a base in either facts or logic. For some writers a ''mystic'' is any person who believes in thought-transference, or spirit-return. Employed in this way the word has little value: there are too many less ambiguous synonyms. So, to keep it useful by restricting it, I will simply propose to you four marks which, when an experience has them, may justify us in calling it mystical for the purpose of the present lectures. . . .

Source: William James, *The Varieties of Religious Experience* (New York: Longmans, Green and Company, 1902), Lectures XVI and VII. Permission to reprint granted by Paul R. Reynolds and Son.

1. Ineffability. The handiest of the marks by which I classify a state of mind as mystical is negative. The subject of it immediately says that it defies expression, that no adequate report of its contents can be given in words. It follows from this that its quality must be directly experienced; it cannot be imparted or transferred to others. In this peculiarity mystical states are more like states of feeling than like states of intellect. No one can make clear to another who has never had a certain feeling, in what the quality or worth of it consists. One must have musical ears to know the value of a symphony; one must have been in love one's self to understand a lover's state of mind. Lacking the heart or ear, we cannot interpret the musician or the lover justly, and are even likely to consider him weak-minded or absurd. The mystic finds that most of us accord to his experiences an equally incompetent treatment.

2. Noetic Quality. Although so similar to states of feeling, mystical states seem to those who experience them to be also states of knowledge. They are states of insight into depths of truth unplumbed by the discursive intellect.[1] They are illuminations, revelations, full of significance and importance, all inarticulate though they remain; and as a rule they carry with them a curious sense of authority for after-time.

These two characters will entitle any state to be called mystical, in the sense in which I use the word. Two other qualities are less sharply marked, but are usually found. These are:—

3. Transiency. Mystical states cannot be sustained for long. Except in rare instances, half an hour, or at most an hour or two, seems to be the limit beyond which they fade into the light of common day. Often, when faded, their quality can but imperfectly be reproduced in memory; but when they recur it is recognized; and from one recurrence to another it is susceptible of continuous development in what is felt as inner richness and importance.

4. Passivity. Although the oncoming of mystical states may be facilitated by preliminary voluntary operations, as by fixing the attention, or going through certain bodily performances, or in other ways which manuals of mysticism prescribe; yet when the characteristic sort of consciousness once has set in, the mystic feels as if his own will were in abeyance, and indeed sometimes as if he were grasped and held by a superior power. This latter peculiarity connects mystical states with certain definite phenomena of secondary or alternative personality, such as prophetic speech, automatic writing, or the mediumistic trance. When these latter conditions are well pronounced, however, there may be no recollection whatever of the phenomenon, and it may have no significance for the subject's usual inner life to which as it were, it makes a mere interruption. Mystical states, strictly so-called, are never merely interruptive. Some memory of their content always remains, and a profound sense of their importance. They modify the inner life of the subject between the times of their recurrence. Sharp divisions in this region are, however, difficult to make, and we find all sorts of gradations and mixtures.

These four characteristics are sufficient to mark out a group of states of consciousness peculiar enough to deserve a special name and to call for careful study. Let it then be called the mystical group.

Our next step should be to gain acquaintance with some typical examples. . . . I will begin . . . with phenomena which claim no special religious significance, and end with those of which the religious pretensions are extreme.

The simplest rudiment of mystical experience would seem to be that deepened sense of the significance of a maxim or formula which occasionally sweeps over me. "I've heard that said all my life," we exclaim, "but I never realized its full meaning until now." "When a fellow-monk," said Luther, "one day repeated the words of the Creed: 'I believe in the forgiveness of sins,' I saw the Scripture in an entirely new light; and straightway I felt as if I were born anew. It was as if I had found the door of paradise thrown wide open." This sense of deeper significance is not confined to rational propositions. Single words, and conjunctions of words, effects of light on land and sea, odors and musical sounds, all bring it when the mind is tuned aright. Most of us can remember the strangely moving power of passages in certain poems read when we were young, irrational doorways as they were through which the mystery of fact, the wildness and the pang of life, stole into our hearts and thrilled them. The words have now perhaps become mere polished surfaces for us; but lyric poetry and music are alive and significant only in proportion as they fetch these vague vistas of a life continuous with our own, beckoning and inviting, yet ever eluding our pursuit. We are alive or dead to the eternal inner message of the arts according as we have kept or lost this mystical susceptibility. . . .

[1]Proceeding to a conclusion through reason rather than intuition. EDITOR'S NOTE.

Somewhat deeper plunges into mystical consciousness are met with in yet other dreamy states. Such feelings as these which Charles Kingsley describes are surely far from being uncommon, especially in youth:—

"When I walk the fields, I am oppressed now and then with an innate feeling that everything I see has a meaning, if I could but understand it. And this feeling of being surrounded with truths which I cannot grasp amounts to indescribable awe sometimes. . . . Have you not felt that your real soul was imperceptible to your mental vision, except in a few hallowed moments?" . . .

The next step into mystical states carries us into a realm that public opinion and ethical philosophy have long since branded as pathological, though private practice and certain lyric strains of poetry seem still to bear witness to its ideality. I refer to the consciousness produced by intoxicants and anaesthetics, especially by alcohol. The sway of alcohol over mankind is unquestionably due to its power to stimulate the mystical faculties of human nature, usually crushed to earth by the cold facts and dry criticisms of the sober hour. . . .

Nitrous oxide and ether, especially nitrous oxide, when sufficiently diluted with air, stimulate the mystical consciousness in an extraordinary degree. Depth beyond depth of truth seems revealed to the inhaler. This truth fades out, however, or escapes, at the moment of coming to; and if any words remain over in which it seemed to clothe itself, they prove to be the veriest nonsense. Nevertheless, the sense of a profound meaning having been there persists; and I know more than one person is persuaded that in the nitrous oxide trance we have a genuine metaphysical revelation.

Some years ago I myself made some observations on this aspect of nitrous oxide intoxication, and reported them in print. One conclusion was forced upon my mind at that time, and my impression of its truth has ever since remained unshaken. It is that our normal waking consciousness, rational consciousness as we call it, is but one special type of consciousness, whilst all about it, parted from it by the filmiest of screens, there lie potential forms of consciousness entirely different. . . . No account of the universe in its totality can be final which leaves these other forms of consciousness quite disregarded. How to regard them is the question—for they are so discontinuous with ordinary consciousness. Yet they may determine attitudes though they cannot furnish formulas, and open a region though they fail to give a map. At any rate, they forbid a premature closing of our accounts with reality. Looking back on my own experiences, they all converge towards a kind of insight to which I cannot help ascribing some metaphysical significance. The keynote of it is invariably a reconciliation. It is as if the opposites of the world, whose contradictoriness and conflict make all our difficulties and troubles, were melted into unity. . . .

J. A. Symonds . . . records a mystical experience with chloroform, as follows:—

"After the choking and stifling had passed away, I seemed at first in a state of utter blankness; then came flashes of intense light, alternating with blackness, and with a keen vision of what was going on in the room around me, but no sensation of touch. I thought that I was near death; when, suddenly, my soul became aware of God, who was manifestly dealing with me, handling me, so to speak, in an intense personal present reality. I felt him streaming in like light upon me. . . . I cannot describe the ecstasy I felt. Then, as I gradually awoke from the influence of the anaesthetics, the old sense of my relation to the world began to return, the new sense of my relation to God began to fade. . . .

"Yet, this question remains, Is it possible that the inner sense of reality which succeeded, when my flesh was dead to impressions from without, to the ordinary sense of physical relations, was not a delusion but an actual experience? Is it possible that I, in that moment, felt what some of the saints have said they always felt, the undemonstrable but irrefragable[2] certainty of God?''

With this we make connection with religious mysticism pure and simple. . . .

In India, training in mystical insight has been known from time immemorial under the name of yoga. Yoga means the experimental union of the individual with the divine. It is based on persevering exercise; and the diet, posture, breathing, intellectual concentration, and moral discipline vary slightly in the different systems which teach it. The yogi, or disciple, who has by these means overcome the obscurations of his lower nature sufficiently, enters into the condition termed *samâdhi*, ''and comes face to face with facts which no instinct or reason can ever know.'' . . .

In the Christian church there have always been mystics. Although many of them have been viewed with suspicion, some have gained favor in the eyes of the authorities. The experiences of these have been treated as precedents, and a codified system of mystical theology has been based upon them, in which everything legitimate finds its place. The basis of the system is ''orison'' or meditation, the methodical elevation of the soul towards God. Through the practice of orison the higher levels of mystical experience may be attained. . . .

The first thing to be aimed at in orison is the mind's detachment from outer sensations, for these interfere with its concentration upon ideal things. Such manuals as Saint Ignatius's Spiritual Exercises recommend the disciple to expel sensation by a gradual series of efforts to imagine holy scenes . . . .

. . . Saint Teresa is the expert of experts in describing [mystical experiences], so I will turn immediately to what she says of one of the highest of them, the ''orison of union.''

[2]Indisputable. EDITOR'S NOTE.

''In the orison of union,'' says Saint Teresa, ''the soul is fully awake as regards God, but wholly asleep as regards things of this world and in respect of herself. During the short time the union lasts, she is as it were deprived of every feeling, and even if she would, she could not think of any single thing. Thus she needs to employ no artifice in order to arrest the use of her understanding: it remains so stricken with inactivity that she neither knows what she loves, nor in what manner she loves, nor what she wills. In short, she is utterly dead to the things of the world and lives solely in God. . . .

''Thus does God, when he raises a soul to union with himself, suspend the natural action of all her faculties. She neither sees, hears, nor understands, so long as she is united with God. But this time is always short, and it seems even shorter than it is. God establishes himself in the interior of this soul in such a way, that when she returns to herself, it is wholly impossible for her to doubt that she has been in God, and God in her. This truth remains so strongly impressed on her that, even though many years should pass without the condition returning, she can neither forget the favor she received, nor doubt of its reality. If you, nevertheless, ask how it is possible that the soul can see and understand that she has been in God, since during the union she has neither sight nor understanding, I reply that she does not see it then, but that she sees it clearly later, after she has returned to herself, not by any vision, but by a certitude which abides with her and which God alone can give her.

''But how, you will repeat, *can* one have such certainty in respect to what one does not see? This question, I am powerless to answer. These are secrets of God's omnipotence which it does not appertain to me to penetrate. All that I know is that I tell the truth; and I shall never believe that any soul who does not possess this certainty has ever been really united to God.''

. . . In spite of their repudiation of articulate self-description, mystical states in general assert a pretty distinct theoretic drift. It is possible to give the outcome of the majority of them in terms that point in definite philosophical directions. One of these directions is optimism, and the other is monism.[3] We pass into mystical states from out of ordinary consciousness as from a less into a more, as from a smallness into a vastness, and at the same time as from an unrest to a rest. We feel them as reconciling, unifying states. . . .

. . . In Paul's language, I live, yet not I, but Christ liveth in me. Only when I become as nothing can God enter in and no difference between his life and mine remain outstanding.

This overcoming of all the usual barriers between the individual and the Absolute is the great mystic achievement. In mystic states we both become one with the Absolute and we become aware of our oneness. This is the everlasting and triumphant mystical tradition, hardly altered by differences of clime[4] or creed. In Hinduism, in Neoplatonism, in Sufism, in Christian mysticism, in Whitmanism, we find the same recurring note, so that there is about mystical utterances an eternal unanimity which ought to make a critic stop and think, and which brings it about that the mystical classics have, as has been said, neither birthday nor native land. Perpetually telling of the unity of man with God, their speech antedates languages, and they do not grow old. . . .

I have now sketched with extreme brevity and insufficiency, but as fairly as I am able in the time allowed, the general traits of the mystic range of consciousness. *It is on the whole pantheistic*[5] *and optimistic, or at least the opposite of pessimistic. It is anti-naturalistic, and harmonizes best with twice-bornness and so-called other-worldly states of mind.*

My next task is to inquire whether we can invoke it as authoritative. Does it furnish any *warrant for the truth* of the twice-bornness and supernaturality and pantheism which it favors? I must give my answer to this question as concisely as I can.

In brief my answer is this—and I will divide it into three parts:—

1. Mystical states, when well developed, usually are, and have the right to be, absolutely authoritative over the individuals to whom they come.

2. No authority emanates from them which should make it a duty for those who stand outside of them to accept their revelations uncritically.

3. They break down the authority of the non-mystical or rationalistic consciousness, based upon the understanding and the senses alone. They show it to be only one kind of consciousness. They open out the possibility of other orders of truth, in which, so far as anything in us vitally responds to them, we may freely continue to have faith.

I will take up these points one by one.

Mystical States Are Self-Verifying for the Mystic

As a matter of psychological fact, mystical states of a well-pronounced and emphatic sort *are* usually authoritative over those who have them. They have been "there," and know. It is vain for rationalism to grumble about this. If the mystical truth that comes to a man proves to be a force that he can live by, what mandate have we of the majority to order him to live in another way? We can throw him into a prison or a madhouse, but we cannot change his mind—we commonly attach it only the more stubbornly to its beliefs. It mocks our utmost efforts, as a matter of fact, and in point of logic it absolutely escapes our jurisdiction. Our own more "rational" beliefs are based on evidence exactly similar in nature to that which mystics quote for theirs. Our senses, namely, have assured us of certain states of fact; but mystical

[3]A metaphysical view that stresses the oneness or unity of reality. EDITOR'S NOTE.

[4]Region. EDITOR'S NOTE.

[5]Pantheistic in the sense of "unifying," not in the sense of denying a supernatural God (as in the pantheism of Spinoza and Einstein—see p. 64). EDITOR'S NOTE.

experiences are as direct perceptions of fact for those who have them as any sensations ever were for us . . . .

The mystic is, in short, *invulnerable*, and must be left, whether we relish it or not, in undisturbed enjoyment of his creed . . . .

Non-Mystics Need Not Accept the Testimony of Mystics

But I now proceed to add that mystics have no right to claim that we ought to accept the deliverance of their peculiar experiences, if we are ourselves outsiders and feel no private call thereto. The utmost they can ever ask of us in this life is to admit that they establish a presumption. They form a consensus and have an unequivocal outcome; and it would be odd, mystics might say, if such a unanimous type of experience should prove to be altogether wrong. At bottom, however, this would only be an appeal to numbers, like the appeal to rationalism the other way; and the appeal to numbers has no logical force. If we acknowledge it, it is for "suggestive," not for logical reasons: we follow the majority because to do so suits our life.

But even this presumption from the unanimity of mystics is far from being strong. In characterizing mystic states as pantheistic, optimistic, etc., I am afraid I over-simplified the truth. I did so for expository reasons, and to keep us closer to the classic mystical tradition. The classic religious mysticism, it now must be confessed, is only a "privileged case." It is an *extract*, kept true to type by the selection of the fittest specimens and their preservation in "schools." It is carved out from a much larger mass; and if we take the larger mass as seriously as religious mysticism has historically taken itself, we find that the supposed unanimity largely disappears. . . . The fact is that the mystical feeling of enlargement, union, and emancipation has no specific intellectual content whatever of its own. It is capable of forming matrimonial alliances with material furnished by the most diverse philosophies and theologies, provided only they can find a place in their framework for its peculiar emotional mood. We have no right, therefore, to invoke its prestige as distinctively in favor of any special belief. . . .

So much for religious mysticism proper. But more remains to be told, for religious mysticism is only one half of mysticism. The other half has no accumulated traditions except those which the text-books on insanity supply. Open any one of these, and you will find abundant cases in which "mystical ideas" are cited as characteristic symptoms of enfeebled or deluded states of mind. In delusional insanity, paranoia, as they sometimes call it, we may have a *diabolical* mysticism, a sort of religious mysticism turned upside down. The same sense of ineffable importance in the smallest events, the same texts and words coming with new meanings, the same voices and visions and leadings and missions, the same controlling by extraneous powers; only this time the emotion is pessimistic: instead of consolations we have desolations; the meanings are dreadful; and the powers are enemies of life. It is evident that from the point of view of their psychological mechanism, the classic mysticism and these lower mysticisms spring from the same mental level, from that great subliminal or transmarginal region of which science is beginning to admit the existence but of which so little is really known. . . . To come from thence is no infallible credential. What comes must be sifted and tested, and run the gauntlet of confrontation with the total context of experience, just like what comes from the outer world of sense. Its value must be ascertained by empirical methods, so long as we are not mystics ourselves.

Once more, then, I repeat that non-mystics are under no obligation to acknowledge in mystical states a superior authority conferred on them by their intrinsic nature.

Mystical States May Possibly Be Windows to a Wider Reality

Yet, I repeat once more, the existence of mystical states absolutely overthrows the pretension of non-mystical states to be the sole and ultimate dictators of what we may believe. As a rule, mystical states merely add a supersensuous meaning to the ordinary outward data of consciousness. They are excitements like the emotions of love or ambition, gifts to our spirit by means of which facts already objectively before us fall into a new expressiveness and make a new connection with our active life. They do not contradict these facts as such, or deny anything that our senses have immediately seized. It is the rationalistic critic rather who plays the part of denier in the controversy, and his denials have no strength, for there never can be a state of facts to which new meaning may not truthfully be added, provided the mind ascend to a more enveloping point of view. It must always remain an open question whether mystical states may not possibly be such superior points of view, windows through which the mind looks out upon a more extensive and inclusive world. The difference of the views seen from the different mystical windows need not prevent us from entertaining this supposition. The wider world would in that case prove to have a mixed constitution like that of this world, that is all. It would have its celestial and its infernal regions, its tempting and its saving moments, its valid experiences and its counterfeit ones, just as our world has them; but it would be a wider world all the same . . . . yet the counting in of that wider world of meanings, and the serious dealing with it, might, in spite of all the perplexity, be indispensable stages in our approach to the final fullness of the truth.

DISCUSSION QUESTIONS

1. James claims that a mystical experience is not just a strong feeling that cannot be said to be "true" or "false," but a claim to knowledge. Yet he also says that mystical experiences defy expression. Is it possible to have **knowledge** that one cannot even express? Defend your position.

2. Assuming that there is a basic similarity in the content of mystical experiences, is this good evidence for the belief that such experiences are revelations of some external reality?

3. Does it make any sense to suggest, as James does, that although a non-mystic need not take the reports of a mystic as true descriptions of an external reality since they may be delusional experiences caused by unconscious psychological processes, mystical states, nevertheless, "have the right to be absolutely authoritative over the individuals to whom they come"?

4. Many mystics claim that they are like sighted people in the land of the blind. In what respects, if any, are mystical experiences different from the experience of sight?

5. Is the fact that mystical experiences can be drug-induced evidence for their illusory nature? Why, or why not?

6. Do you agree with James that "the existence of mystical states absolutely overthrows the pretension of non-mystical states to be the sole and ultimate dictators of what we may believe."

7. James claims that mystical states may be "windows through which the mind looks upon a more extensive and inclusive world." Do you think, however, that James would grant that some mystical states provide evidence for the existence of **God**? Should he? What possible evidence can be given for the nondelusional character of an alleged direct encounter with God? How strong could such evidence be? Has such evidence ever been given?

8. Unlike **arguments** for the existence of God which proceed from premises to conclusion, Judeo-Christian mystics often claim that their experiences provide **direct** (that is, noninferential) evidence for the existence of God. Is this possible or must Judeo-Christian mystics ultimately resort to arguments to rationally convince themselves, as well as others, that they are not deluded? Is this true, as well, for mystics who assert no more than that their experiences are direct evidence for the existence of a super-sensible reality? Can mystics rationally claim that they have **conclusive** direct evidence for the existence of a super-sensible reality?

12. A DEFENSE OF THE MORAL ARGUMENT FOR GOD'S EXISTENCE

C.S. Lewis

C.S. LEWIS (1898–1963) was a professor of Medieval and Renaissance English literature at Cambridge University, England. As well as being a distinguished scholar, Lewis was also the author of many popular children's books, including the famous multi-volumed fantasy, **The Chronicles of Narnia**. In addition, he authored many popular science fiction novels. His most widely known book is the classic **The Screwtape Letters** (1942), which consists of a series of letters of advice from the devil, Screwtape, to his nephew, Wormwood, on the best way to tempt a young Christian convert.

C.S. Lewis' philosophical reputation rests on his many books on religion. Reared as an Anglican Christian, he became an atheist in his teens and did not return to Christianity until his early thirties. (This conversion is related in Lewis' autobiography, **Surprised by Joy**.) He then became a popular defender of the faith. His famous BBC (British Broadcasting Corporation) radio broadcast talks on religion were published in his book **Mere Christianity** (1952). These talks provide Lewis' most basic exposition of his religious beliefs and his justification for them. This book as well as Lewis' other books on religion are directed primarily to persons who are uncertain of their religious beliefs.

The following selection comes from the first few chapters of **Mere Christianity**. Assuming that individuals, regardless of place or time, recognize the existence of certain objective, externally imposed, moral principles which provide constraints upon their behavior, Lewis argues that this points to a divine moral law-giver who directs the universe.

The Law of Human Nature

Every one has heard people quarrelling. Sometimes it sounds funny and sometimes it sounds merely unpleasant; but however it sounds, I believe we can learn something very important from listening to the kind of things they say. They say things like this: "How'd you like it if anyone did the same to you?"—"That's my seat, I was there first"—"Leave him alone, he isn't doing you any harm"—"Why should you shove in first?"—"Give me a bit of your orange, I gave you a bit of mine"—"Come on, you promised." People say things like that every day, educated people as well as uneducated, and children as well as grown-ups.

Now what interests me about all these remarks is that the man who makes them is not merely saying that the other man's behaviour does not happen to please him. He is appealing to some kind of standard of behaviour which he expects the other man to know about. And the other man very seldom replies: "To hell with your standard." Nearly always he tries to make out what he has been doing does not really go against the standard, or that if it does there is some special excuse. He pretends there is some special reason in this particular case why the person who took the seat first should not keep it, or that things were quite different when he was given the bit of orange, or that something has turned up which lets him off keeping his promise. It looks, in fact, very much as if both parties had in mind some kind of Law or Rule of fair play or decent behaviour or morality or whatever you like to call it, about which they really agreed. And they have. If they had not, they might, of course, fight like animals, but they could not quarrel in the human sense of the word. Quarrelling means trying to show that the other man is in the wrong. And there would be no sense in trying to do that unless you and he had some sort of agreement as to what Right and Wrong are; just as there would be no sense in saying that a footballer had committed a foul unless there was some agreement about the rules of football.

Now this Law or Rule about Right and Wrong used to be called the Law of Nature. Nowadays, when we talk of the "laws of nature" we usually mean things like gravitation, or heredity, or the laws of chemistry. But when the older thinkers called the Law of Right and Wrong "the Law of Nature," they really meant the Law of Human Nature. The idea was that, just as all bodies are governed by the law of gravitation, and organisms by biological laws, so the creature called man also had his law—with this great difference, that a body could not choose whether it obeyed the law of gravitation or not, but a man could choose either to obey the Law of Human Nature or to disobey it.

We may put this in another way. Each man is at every moment subjected to several different sets of law but there is only one of these which he is free to disobey. As a body, he is subjected to gravitation and cannot disobey it; if you leave him unsupported in mid-air, he has no more choice about falling than a stone has. As an organism, he is subjected to various biological laws which he cannot disobey any more than an animal can. That is, he cannot disobey those laws which he shares with other things; but the law which is peculiar to his human nature, the law he does not share with animals or vegetables or inorganic things, is the one he can disobey if he chooses.

This law was called the Law of Nature because people thought that every one knew it by nature and did not need to be taught it. They did not mean, of course, that you might not find an odd individual here and there who did not know it, just as you find a few people who are colour-blind or have no ear for a tune. But taking the race as a whole, they thought that the human idea of decent behavior was obvious to every one. And I believe they were right. If they were not, then all the things we said about the war[1] were nonsense. What was the sense in saying the enemy were in the wrong unless Right is a real thing which the Nazis at bottom knew as well as we did and ought to have practised? If they had had no notion of what we mean by right, then, though we might still have had to fight them, we could no more have blamed them for that than for the colour of their hair.

I know that some people say the idea of a Law of Nature or decent behaviour known to all men is unsound, because different civilisations and different ages have had quite different moralities.

But this is not true. There have been differences between their moralities, but these have never amounted to anything like a total difference. If anyone will take the trouble to compare the moral teaching of, say, the ancient Egyptians, Babylonians, Hindus, Chinese, Greeks and Romans, what will really strike him will be how very like they are to each other and to our own. . . . I need only ask the reader to think what a totally different morality would mean. Think of a country where people were admired for running away in battle, or where

[1]World War II. EDITOR'S NOTE.

a man felt proud of double-crossing all the people who had been kindest to him. You might just as well try to imagine a country where two and two made five. Men have differed as regards what people you ought to be unselfish to—whether it was only your own family, or your fellow countrymen, or everyone. But they always agreed that you ought not to put yourself first. Selfishness has never been admired. Men have differed as to whether you should have one wife or four. But they have always agreed that you must not simply have any woman you liked. . . .

The Reality of the Law

I now go back to what I said [before] . . . , that there were two odd things about the human race. First, that they were haunted by the idea of a sort of behaviour they ought to practise, what you might call fair play, or decency, or morality, or the Law of Nature. Second, that they did not in fact do so. Now some of you may wonder why I called this odd. It may seem to you the most natural thing in the world. In particular, you may have thought I was rather hard on the human race. After all, you may say, what I call breaking the Law of Right and Wrong or of Nature, only means that people are not perfect. And why on earth should I expect them to be? That would be a good answer if what I was trying to do was to fix the exact amount of blame which is due to us for not behaving as we expect others to behave. But that is not my job at all. I am not concerned at present with blame; I am trying to find out truth. And from that point of view the very idea of something being imperfect, of its not being what it ought to be, has certain consequences.

If you take a thing like a stone or a tree, it is what it is and there seems no sense in saying it ought to have been otherwise. Of course you may say a stone is "the wrong shape" if you want to use it for a rockery, or that a tree is a bad tree because it does not give you as much shade as you expected. But all you mean is that the stone or the tree does not happen to be convenient for some purpose of your own. You are not, except as a joke, blaming them for that. You really know, that, given the weather and the soil, the tree could not have been any different. What we, from our point of view, call a "bad" tree is obeying the laws of its nature just as much as a "good" one.

Now have you noticed what follows? It follows that what we usually call the laws of nature—the way weather works on a tree for example—may not really be *laws* in the strict sense, but only in a manner of speaking. When you say that falling stones always obey the law of gravitation, is not this much the same as saying that the law only means "what stones always do"? You do not really think that when a stone is let go, it suddenly remembers that it is under orders to fall to the ground. You only mean that, in fact, it does fall. In other words, you cannot be sure that there is anything over and above the facts themselves, any law about what ought to happen, as distinct from what does happen. The laws of nature, as applied to stones or trees, may only mean "what Nature, in fact, does." But if you turn to the Law of Human Nature, the Law of Decent Behaviour, it is a different matter. That law certainly does not mean "what human beings, in fact, do"; for as I said before, many of them do not obey this law at all, and none of them obey it completely. The law of gravity tells you what stones do if you drop them; but the Law of Human Nature tells you what human beings ought to do and do not. In other words, when you are dealing with humans, something else comes in above and beyond the actual facts. You have the facts (how men do behave) and you also have something else (how they ought to behave). In the rest of the universe there need not be anything but the facts. . . .

Now this is really so peculiar that one is tempted to try to explain it away. For instance, we might try to make out that when you say a man ought not to act as he does, you only mean the same as when you say that a stone is the wrong shape; namely, that what he is doing happens to be inconvenient to you. But that is simply untrue. A man occupying the corner seat in the train because he got there first, and a man who slipped into it while my back was turned and removed my bag, are both equally inconvenient. But I blame the second man and do not blame the first. I am not angry—except perhaps for a moment before I come to my senses—with a man who trips me up by accident; I am angry with a man who tries to trip me up even if he does not succeed. Yet the first has hurt me and the second has not. Sometimes the behaviour which I call bad is not inconvenient to me at all, but the very opposite. In war, each side may find a traitor on the other side very useful. But though they use him and pay him they regard him as human vermin. So you cannot say that what we call decent behaviour in others is simply the behaviour that happens to be useful to us. And as for decent behaviour in ourselves, I suppose it is pretty obvious that it does not mean the behaviour that pays. It means things like . . . doing school work honestly when it would be easy to cheat, leaving a girl alone when you would like to make love to her . . . keeping promises you would rather not keep, and telling the truth even when it makes you look a fool.

Some people say that though decent conduct does not mean what pays each particular person at a particular moment, still, it means what pays the human race as a whole; and that consequently there is no mystery about it. Human beings, after all, have some sense; they see that you cannot have any real safety or happiness except in a society where every one plays fair, and it is because they see this that they try to behave decently. Now, of course, it is perfectly true that safety and happiness can only come from individuals, classes, and nations being honest and fair and kind to each other. It is one of the most important truths in the world. But as an explanation of why we feel as we do about Right and Wrong it just misses the point. If we ask: "Why ought I to be unselfish?" and you reply "Because it is good for society," we may then ask, "Why should I care what's good for society except when it happens to pay *me* personally?" and then you will have to say, "Because you ought to be unselfish"—which simply brings us back to where we started. . . .

. . . Men ought to be unselfish, ought to be fair. Not that men are unselfish, nor that they like being unselfish, but that they ought to be. The Moral Law, or Law of Human Nature, is not simply a fact about human behaviour in the same way as the Law of Gravitation is, or may be, simply a fact about how heavy objects behave. On the other hand, it is not a mere fancy, for we cannot get rid of the idea, and most of the things we say and think about men would be reduced to nonsense if we did. And it is not simply a statement about how we should like men to behave for our own convenience; for the behaviour we call bad or unfair is not exactly the same as the behaviour we find inconvenient, and may even be the opposite. Consequently, this Rule of Right and Wrong, or Law of Human Nature, or whatever you call it, must somehow or other be a real thing—a thing that is really there, not made up by ourselves. And yet it is not a fact in the ordinary sense, in the same way as our actual behaviour is a fact. It begins to look as if we shall have to admit that there is more than one kind of reality; that, in this particular case, there is something above and beyond the ordinary facts of men's behaviour, and yet quite definitely real—a real law, which none of us made, but which we find pressing on us.

What Lies Behind the Law

Let us sum up what we have reached so far. In the case of stones and trees and things of that sort, what we call the Laws of Nature may not be anything except a way of speaking. When you say that nature is governed by certain laws, this may only mean that nature does, in fact, behave in a certain way. . . . But in the case of Man, we saw that this will not do. The Law of Human Nature, or of Right and Wrong, must be something above and beyond the actual facts of human behaviour. In this case, besides the actual facts, you have something else—a real law which we did not invent and which we know we ought to obey.

I now want to consider what this tells us about the universe we live in. Ever since men were able to think, they have been wondering what this universe really is and how it came to be there. And, very roughly, two views have been held. First, there is what is called the materialist view. People who take that view think that matter and space just happen to exist, and always have existed, nobody knows why; and that the matter, behaving in certain fixed ways, has just happened, by a sort of fluke, to produce creatures like ourselves who are able to think. By one chance in a thousand something hit our sun and made it produce the planets; and by another thousandth chance the chemicals necessary for life, and the right temperature, occurred on one of these planets, and so some of the matter on this earth came alive; and then, by a very long series of chances, the living creatures developed into things like us. The other view is the religious view. According to it, what is behind the universe is more like a mind than it is like anything else we know. That is to say, it is conscious, and has purposes, and prefers one thing to another. And on this view it made the universe, partly for purposes we do not know, but partly, at any rate, in order to produce creatures like itself—I mean, like itself to the extent of having minds. Please do not think that one of these views was held a long time ago and that that other has gradually taken its place. Wherever there have been thinking men both views turn up. And note this too. You cannot find out which view is the right one by science in the ordinary sense. Science works by experiments. It watches how things behave. . . . But why anything comes to be there at all, and whether there is anything behind the things science observes—something of a different kind—this is not a scientific question. If there is "Something Behind," then either it will have to remain altogether unknown to men or else make itself known in some different way. The statement that there is any such thing, and the statement that there is no such thing, are neither of them statements that science can make. . . . Supposing science ever became complete so that it knew every single thing in the whole universe. Is it not plain that the questions, "Why is there a universe?" "Why does it go on as it does?" "Has it any meaning?" would remain just as they were?

Now the position would be quite hopeless but for this. There is one thing, and only one, in the whole universe which we know more about than we could learn from external observation. That one thing is Man. We do not merely observe men, we *are* men. In this case we have, so to speak, inside information; we are in the know. And because of that, we know that men find themselves under a moral law, which they did not make, and cannot quite forget even when they try, and which they know they ought to obey. Notice the following point. Anyone studying Man from the outside as we study electricity or cabbages, not knowing our language and consequently not able to get any inside knowledge from us, but merely observing what we did, would never get the slightest evidence that we had this moral law. How could he? for his observations would only show what we did, and the moral law is about what we ought to do. In the same way, if there were anything above or behind the observed facts in the case of stones or the weather, we, by studying them from outside, could never hope to discover it.

The position of the question, then, is like this. We want to know whether the universe simply happens to be what it is for no reason or whether there is a power behind it that makes it what it is. Since that power, if it exists, would be not one of the observed facts but a reality which makes them, no mere observation of the facts can find it. There is only one case in which we can know whether there is anything more, namely our own case. And in that one case we find there is. Or put it the other way round. If there was a controlling power outside the universe, it could not show itself to us as one of the facts inside the universe—no more than the architect of a house could actually be a wall or staircase or fireplace in that house. The only way in which we could expect it to show itself would be inside ourselves as an influence or a command trying to get us to behave in a certain way. And that is just what we do find inside ourselves. . . . Suppose someone asked me, when I see a man in blue uniform going down the street leaving little paper packets at each house, why I suppose that they contain letters? I should reply, "Because whenever he leaves a similar little packet for me I find it does contain a letter." And if he then objected—"But you've never seen all these letters which you think the other people are getting," I should say, "Of course not, and I shouldn't expect to, because they're not addressed to me. I'm explaining the packets I'm not allowed to open by the ones I am allowed to open." It is the same about this question. The only packet I am allowed to open is Man. When I do, especially when I open that particular man called Myself, I find that I do not exist on my own, that I am under a law; that somebody or something wants me to behave in a certain way. . . .

Do not think I am going faster than I really am. I am not yet within a hundred miles of the God of Christian theology. All I have got to is a Something which is directing the universe, and which appears in me as a law urging me to do right and making me feel responsible and uncomfortable when I do wrong. I think we have to assume it is more like a mind than it is like anything else we know—because after all the only other thing we know is matter and you can hardly imagine a bit of matter giving instructions. But, of course, it need not be very like a mind, still less like a person. . . .

DISCUSSION QUESTIONS

1. According to Lewis, what is the distinction between laws of nature that scientists attempt to uncover and the law of human nature? Do you find Lewis' distinction adequate?

2 a. Do you agree with Lewis that morality cannot be defined in terms of what people find useful?

b. If morality cannot be defined in terms of what people find useful, does this entail that morality "is not made up by ourselves"?

3. How variable are the moral standards of different societies? Does this variability weaken the view that God is the ultimate source of moral standards and principles?

4. Are there some moral standards or principles that all societies accept as correct? If so, how do you account for this universal acceptance?

5. If a person asked "Why should I be unselfish?" how would you answer?

6. How do you think the atheistic founder of psychoanalysis, Sigmund Freud, would have replied to Lewis' claim that:

> . . .I find that. . .I am under a law; that somebody or something wants me to behave in a certain way. . . . [There] is a Something which is directing the universe, and which appears in me as a law urging me to do right and making me feel responsible and uncomfortable when I do wrong.

What do you think?

13. A CRITICISM OF THE ARGUMENT FROM MIRACLES

Editorial Comment

A widely popular argument for the existence of God is the "argument from miracles." This expression is misleading, however, for it suggests that there are events called miracles and that one can argue from the existence of these events to the existence of God as their cause. Yet, according to its most common definition, a "miracle" is "a violation of a law of nature caused by God." (Since God is, by definition, all-good, this violation must be for some good purpose.) When "miracles" are so defined, the question is not whether the existence of miracles can be used to justify belief in God, but rather whether miracles actually occur.

There is, however, no universal agreement on the definition of a "miracle." Indeed, at one time, there was heated theological debate as to whether or not other supernatural beings (i.e., the devil and the angels) could also violate the laws of nature of this world, and if so, whether such interventions should be described as miracles too. Nowadays, most Judeo-Christian believers do not entertain this possibility and assume that if there is any purposeful intervention in the laws of nature of this world, it must be attributed to God.

In addition, it has been claimed that a miracle need not involve a violation of a law of nature. In defense of this claim, the philosopher R. F. Holland relates the following story:

> A child riding his toy motor-car strays on to an unguarded railway crossing near his house and a wheel of his car gets stuck down the side of one of the rails. An express train is due to pass with the signals in its favor and a curve in the track makes it impossible for the driver to stop his train in time to avoid any obstruction he might encounter on the crossing. The mother coming out of the house to look for her child sees him on the crossing and hears the train approaching. She runs forward shouting and waving. The little boy remains seated in his car, looking downward, engrossed in the task of pedaling it free. The brakes of the train are applied and it comes to a rest a few feet from the child. The mother thanks God for a miracle; which she never ceases to think of as such, although, as she in due course learns, there was nothing supernatural about the manner in which the brakes of the train came to be applied. The driver had fainted, for a reason which had nothing to do with the presence of the child on the line, and the brakes were applied automatically as his hand ceased to exert pressure on the control lever. He fainted on this particular afternoon because his blood pressure had risen after an exceptionally heavy lunch during which he had quarrelled with a colleague, and the change in blood pressure caused a clot of blood to be dislodged and circulate. He fainted at the time when he did on the afternoon in question because this was the time at which the coagulation in his blood stream reached the brain.[1]

While nonbelievers in God will tend to see the case that Holland describes as a lucky coincidence of natural processes that was due to chance, many believers in God, like the boy's mother, will see such a coincidence of events as a sign of divine purposeful involvement in nature. For such individuals, even though the stopping of the train at the precise moment that it did may be fully capable of scientific or natural explanation, the *significance* of this event points to some purposeful agent behind

[1]R.F. Holland, "The Miraculous," *American Philosophical Quarterly*, 2 (1965), pp. 43–51.

it—namely, to God. From this point of view, God can reveal his purposeful intentions through the very workings of the laws of nature that he has ordained for governing events in this world as well as through the violation of these laws.

With the preceding discussion as a backdrop, how ought we to define a "miracle"? First, it is best to define a "miracle" broadly as some remarkable event caused by some supernatural being for some specific purpose which is either incapable of scientific explanation (i.e., a violation of a law of nature) or is a result of an amazing coincidence of events, all of which are capable of scientific explanation. If we accept this broad definition, we will be much less apt to uncritically assume, as many who argue for God's existence on the basis of miracles do, that if some significant but unexpected events in this world point to some purposeful supernatural power beyond this world, then that power must be the traditional Judeo-Christian God (i.e., all-powerful, eternal, the sole creator of all else that exists, etc.). It is for this reason, above all, that we ought not to define a "miracle" as something that is caused by God. Clearly, if it turns out that there is some supernatural god behind this world who does not have all the properties traditionally attributed to God (e.g., he is not omnipotent) but does have the power to intervene in the specific course of nature, we would quite naturally describe such interventions as "miraculous." As well as having the virtue of leaving open the conceptual possibility of miracles that are not caused by (the Judeo-Christian) God, our definition is broad enough to encompass miracles which involve violations of laws of nature (violation-miracles) and those described by Holland which do not (coincidence-miracles).

Now that we have briefly discussed the concept of a miracle, let us consider the question of whether we have any basis for believing in miracles and in attributing them to God, turning our attention first to alleged coincidence-miracles. No doubt, there have been many cases of horrible disasters being averted by amazing coincidences of events. Do we have any good reason, however, for calling them coincidence-miracles? Given the great number of events that occur every moment in this world, why should it be at all surprising that every once in a while some amazing beneficial coincidences occur purely by chance? If this were the case, one would expect many amazing harmful coincidences as well. Is this not the case? Clearly, when a horrible disaster occurs as a result of some incredible coincidence of events, we do not (at least at this time) turn to the devil as an explanation, but attribute it to an "unlucky break." Does not consistency demand, then, that we should attribute beneficial incredible coincidences of events to "lucky breaks"? No doubt, one can well understand why people *psychologically* prefer to believe that harmful coincidences are due to chance, while beneficial ones are not, but one is clearly begging the question (i.e., assuming precisely what is at issue) if one points towards beneficial coincidences as evidence for God's existence (or for some good supernatural power), while conveniently disregarding harmful coincidences.

Consider, for example, an airplane crash where hundreds die and only a few survive. Inevitably, some of the survivors will say, "It was a miracle." In saying this, they focus on the improbability of their survival in the face of so many casualities. Yet it may not at all have been improbable that *some* individuals would be lucky enough to survive purely by chance. The fact that there are survivors would not then be incredible; what would be incredible would be to accurately *pick out beforehand* who the survivors will be. If we are to see some divine hand that chooses to save some, while allowing others to perish, we must ask ourselves why God chose those that he did. While it is understandable that the survivors and their loved ones will want to see their survival as purposeful and significant rather than as a result of "blind chance," the loved ones of those who perished will not easily accept such an explanation. Similarly, when only a few people die in an airplane mishap, while hundreds survive, we do not tend to attribute the coincidental factors that caused their death to purposeful intervention, but are quite content to attribute it to "blind chance." Clearly, it would appear, people believe in coincidence-miracles not because they have *evidence* for them, but because *they find it comforting to so believe*.

While only those who already believe in God will be inclined to attribute amazing beneficial coincidences to God, surely the same cannot be said of the various violation-miracles referred to in the Bible. In the Old Testament, for example, we read of such amazing "unnatural" events as Lot's wife being turned into a "pillar of salt," "the parting of the Red Sea" and "manna from heaven," while in the New Testament, we read of the many alleged miracles performed by Christ such as his walking on water, turning water into wine, and feeding thousands with only a few loaves of bread and fish. No doubt, if such events occurred in the situations described in the Bible, one would have a powerful reason for believing in God. The question, however, is whether one has good reason for believing that such amazing events actually did happen. Nonbelievers in God unanimously claim that this question must be answered in the negative.

The classical argument for this position was stated by David Hume.[2] As Hume saw it, since an established law of nature is, by definition, one for which we have overwhelming direct evidence, while the only evidence we have for the alleged miracles reported in the Bible is the indirect evidence of the testimony of others, it is always more rational to place one's faith in the law of nature, rather than in the human testimony offered in support of an alleged miracle. As Hume put it, "No testimony is sufficient to establish a miracle unless the testimony be of such a kind that its falsehood would be more miraculous than the fact it endeavors to establish." This, Hume claimed, can never be the case, in view of the mass of evidence in support of natural laws and the notorious unreliability of human testimony. Given the strong motives for believing in miracles, the powerful human tendencies towards self-deception and deceit, and the ignorance of the witnesses, it is simply unreasonable to accept the indirect testimony offered for miracles, Hume concludes. While Hume stressed the ignorance, gullibility, and deceit of human beings, current psychological experiments and theories would emphasize instead the power for honest self-deception of even the most intelligent of human beings. For example, at the beginning of World War I, scores of English men and women reported seeing 80,000 Russian soldiers passing through England. In spite of the honest reports of so many people, in reality nothing of the sort had happened. The story evidently originated from a person's reading a telegram from a Russian to an English egg merchant. The words were "80,000 Russians are coming." The "Russians" referred to, however, were not soldiers but eggs![3]

As we move away from the alleged violation-miracles reported in the Bible, it is difficult to find examples of events which, if they occurred, would appear to be violation-miracles. The most recent famous alleged violation-miracle is one that occurred at Fatima, Portugal in 1917 when 70,000 people allegedly saw the sun plunge toward the ground and then return to its proper place in the sky. What is one to make of such testimony? Was this a mass hallucination? After all, since no one else in the world saw the sun move, it would be unreason-

[2]David Hume, "Of Miracles," in *An Inquiry Concerning Human Understanding* (Indianapolis: Bobbs-Merrill Company, Inc., 1955, originally published in 1748), pp. 117–41.

[3]C.D. Broad (1887–1971) relates this incident in his article "Hume's Theory of the Credibility of Miracles" in the *Proceedings of the Aristotelian Society, New Series* XVII (1916–17), 77–94.

able to say that God actually moved the sun (miraculously making sure, however, to counteract all the natural effects of such a feat—e.g., the most drastic of changes in temperature and gravitational force). What then did God do? Create the hallucination that the sun moved, an hallucination which was restricted to the witnesses at Fatima? If so, is it not possible that such a mass hallucination could be created quite naturally, perhaps due to the overwhelming desire to believe of the witnesses who were there precisely to witness a miracle?[4] Is it not possible that hallucinations can be transmitted through some type of "telepathic communication"? Most fundamentally, should one so readily accept the claim that there were 70,000 witnesses to the event previously described? Who, after all, counted? Is it not possible, furthermore, that at the time, very few thought they saw such a dramatic thing but, as the story spread, many more *imagined* that they too had seen much more than they really had. Clearly, one should not neglect the extreme emotionalism surrounding this event and the fact that the witnesses were uneducated devout believers who were expecting some type of miracle. Also, it is quite understandable that the most dramatic and amazing descriptions of the witnesses would be those that are later remembered and recounted to others, while those who saw nothing or something quite less dramatic kept their silence, perhaps in shame that there must be some unflattering reason why God chose to exclude them from the miraculous event. As we focus on such possible explanations of the alleged miracle at Fatima, it becomes clear that people who do not already believe in miracles are not apt to place much credence on the indirect testimony of others that a miracle occurred at Fatima.

Nonbelievers are also not apt to be convinced by alleged miracles for which it is claimed that we have direct evidence. While believers often point to alleged miraculous cures or to the famous Shroud of Turin, these examples do not seem to *contradict* well-established laws of nature as the alleged miracles in the Bible do, but are rather examples of things for which *there is no obvious scientific explanation at the present time*. Let us consider the Shroud of Turin. This is a mysterious 13½ ft. by 4¼ ft. linen cloth in which, it is claimed, the body of Jesus Christ was wrapped in his tomb. Impressed distinctly upon this cloth is a human form with clear facial features. Scientific studies carried out on this cloth, most notably in the 1970's, seem to suggest that the shroud image was not painted on by human hand, that the image is one of a corpse that most likely died of crucifixion, that the cloth was manufactured in the Middle East and was at one time in Palestine. It also appears that the image on the shroud is a "negative" (i.e., the photographic negative offers a much more recognizable picture of a human body—especially the face—than the cloth itself or any positive print). Some claim, furthermore that there is strong Gospel evidence for identifying the corpse whose image is impressed on the shroud with Jesus Christ.[5]

Even if we assume, for the sake of argument, that this shroud was indeed Jesus' burial cloth and that in some way Jesus' body made that imprint, one can still deny that this imprint was miraculously caused and seek some scientific explanation for it. For example, some scientists have suggested that the imprint was caused by a chemical reaction that occurred when am-

[4]The miracle had been promised to three children who are alleged to have had several religious experiences of a lady dressed in a white gown and veil who eventually claimed to be the Virgin Mary and promised some sign on the date in question.

[5]This evidence is related in Ian Wilson's interesting book *The Shroud of Turin* (Garden City, N.Y.: Doubleday & Company, 1978), which also traces the history of the shroud. Wilson, a newspaperman by profession, is a graduate of Oxford University and, at the time he wrote the book, was chairman of the British Society for the Turin Shroud.

monia vapors generated by a dead traumatized body reacted with the burial cloth which was impregnated with a combination of oil and spices that were applied to the body in an ancient burial rite. Other scientists who have studied the shroud have suggested that the imprint was caused by a mysterious type of "radiation" that probably emanated from the body wrapped in the shroud. Some have suggested, furthermore, that this radiation may be connected with the so-called "aura" that parapsychologists have claimed surrounds the body, especially those of psychics, and can be observed through Kirlian photography. Perhaps, it has been suggested, Jesus, while not supernatural, was a psychic. The Gospels, for example, are quite explicit that Jesus was believed to be a man with some special "power." Perhaps that power was a psychic power which was correlated with a special type of "radiation" that was released at his death or soon after it. Is this explanation not at least as rationally plausible and supported by the evidence as the belief that Jesus was divine and miraculously caused the imprint at the moment he was resurrected as believers have asserted? The evidence provided by the Shroud of Turin, even devout believers have lamented, seems frustratingly ambiguous.

As our discussion of the Shroud of Turin indicates, just as believers in God will seek religious explanations for inexplicable significant events, those of a purely scientific frame of mind will seek scientific explanations for the same events. It is important that we realize that faith in science can be as strong, and indeed as obstinate, as faith in God. It is always possible to seek scientific explanations for events, however extraordinary. This is no less true of events which appear to contradict *presently accepted* laws of nature than it is of presently inexplicable events. Since scientific laws of nature and the underlying theories that explain them have been revised to accomodate "anomalous" events (i.e., apparently "impossible" or "odd" or "disturbing" events),[6] today's scientifically inexplicable or impossible events can become the cornerstone of tomorrow's new science. For example, certain events which apparently contradicted Newton's laws of nature provided the impetus for the development and acceptance of Einstein's theory of relativity.

While the Shroud of Turin may be a puzzling mystery according to today's science, the same cannot be said of alleged miraculous cures. As any doctor or nurse will testify, there are many patients who are diagnosed as terminally ill who get well inexplicably. While a religious person may see the hand of God in some of these cures, a scientist will seek, and often eventually find, some scientific explanation. Even if it were true that those who pray to God or attend religious healing sessions or go to immerse themselves in the allegedly miraculous healing waters of Lourdes recover from ailments in greater percentages than those who do not, it is quite possible that it is the very *belief* that they will be cured that does the curing and not God. After all, science is learning more and more about the power of "mind over matter." Just as Freud's unorthodox view that repressed ideas could cause extreme physical symptoms such as paralysis and blindness ("hysterical conversion") became the orthodoxy of analytic psychiatry, so the current unorthodox research on the power of "psychic self-healing" may become the orthodoxy of tomorrow's medicine. There is clearly no need to turn to God for an explanation

[6]Thomas S. Kuhn's *The Structure of Scientific Revolutions* (Chicago: Univ. of Chicago Press, 1970, 2nd ed.) provides an excellent account of the nature of scientific revolutions (i.e., drastic changes in scientific ways of looking at events). As Kuhn's many examples demonstrate, a scientific world view, just like a theistic one, can be very resistant to anomalous events. Scientists will tend to cling to their scientific theories, attempting as best they can to "explain away" apparent anomalies, even if this requires ad hoc assumptions, until they find a new theory to cling to which seems to them better capable of explaining the same phenomena.

of the "cures" that are paraded in front of us by alleged healers.

Why, one may well ask, if God performs miraculous cures, does he not perform more dramatic ones? For example, imagine the dramatic impact of a healer on his knees praying to God to restore the lost arm of an amputee who kneels beside him. Before our very eyes, a limb "materializes" on what was just before a stump. While diehard scientists may scratch their heads looking for a scientific explanation of what they may decide to call "the human earthworm factor" (earthworms can regenerate lost tissue), this clearly would be dramatic evidence at least pointing to God or some personal supernatural being. Why then doesn't God perform such dramatic feats? Clearly, if beneficial inexplicable or apparently scientifically impossible events consistently occurred only to those who believed in God, one would have very good reason to believe in God. While many secular philosophers, following Hume, seem to think that there never could be sufficient evidence rationally justifying belief in miracles, this is wrong. One can well imagine dramatic evidence that would incline a fully open-minded person to believe in miracles. Why then does God not provide that evidence? If, as some theologians have suggested,[7] God has good reason for refraining from clearly revealing his hand and purposely performs only those miracles which are ambiguous enough to be interpreted scientifically as well as religiously, then belief in miracles does not justify faith in God, but presupposes that faith.

[7]John Hick takes this line in his account of the problem of evil in his book *Evil and the God of Love* (New York: Harper & Row, 1966).

DISCUSSION QUESTIONS

1. Do you believe that any miracle has, as a matter of fact, ever occurred? If so, is this belief based simply on faith or on rational evidence or argument? If so, is the evidence sufficiently strong that it should be able to convince an open-minded rational person that, at the very least, it is more probable than not that the miracle you believe in did indeed occur? Is the evidence sufficient to make it probable that the miracle was caused by God?

2. Even if you do not believe that there is, as a matter of fact, sufficient evidence to make it more probable than not that a miracle has occurred in the past, do you think that it is possible to imagine such evidence? If so, what conceivable event would provide the strongest evidence you can imagine for the belief in a miracle? Is there evidence that could make it more probable than not that the miracle was caused by God rather than by some other supernatural being or that while the event you imagine was indeed caused by some "invisible hand," that hand was not a supernatural being at all, but some very intelligent extra-terrestrial being whose knowledge of science far surpassed our own?

3. If God exists and performs miracles occasionally, what good reason do you think he might have for performing only ambiguous miracles today, while refraining from the more dramatic ones? If God does exist, do you think he would perform miracles at all? This French literary figure Voltaire (1694–1778), for example, once suggested that the belief in miracles is really blasphemous, for it suggests that God is not a perfect designer and has to intervene occasionally to make corrections in his creation. Critically comment.

14. THE UNDESERVED SUFFERINGS OF LITTLE CHILDREN: A POIGNANT LITERARY CHALLENGE TO BELIEF IN THE JUDEO-CHRISTIAN GOD

Fyodor Dostoevsky

FYODOR DOSTOEVSKY (1821–81) was one of the greatest novelists Russia has ever produced. As a young man, Dostoevsky was a utopian socialist. As a result of his very liberal views, he was charged with political conspiracy and sentenced to death. When he was on the scaffold, facing a firing squad, an official came forward with a reprieve from the Czar. Dostoevsky was then sentenced to four years of hard labor in Siberia and another four years of punishment as a common soldier. These years of punishment had a profound impact on Dostoevsky's thinking. Now believing that "evil is buried more deeply in humanity than the cure-all socialists think, that evil cannot be avoided in any organization of society," Dostoevsky abandoned the optimistic liberalism of his youth and became instead a passionate defender of the human need to submit to tradition.

Though he leaned toward atheism as a young man, Dostoevsky turned to Christian orthodoxy in his later years. He was, however, by his own admission, a man tormented by the psychological need to believe coupled with gnawing intellectual doubts that made such belief difficult. This torment within Dostoevsky himself is very movingly portrayed in the following selection from **The Brothers Karamazov** (1880), Dostoevsky's last novel. The novel centers around the murder of the evil Fyodor Karamazov and its effeccts on his four sons—Dimitri, a sensual soldier; Ivan, a sceptical and cynical intellectual; Alyosha, a kind and idealistic religious mystic, studying to become a monk; and Smerdyakov, the murderer. The intense psychological and moral conflicts of these characters dramatize Dostoevsky's own interest in psychological and moral problems.

In our selection, Ivan attempts to challenge the faith of Alyosha by poignantly presenting the problem of evil. As is true of all great literature, Dostoevsky's writing is likely to profoundly move you and is certain to bring home to you the grave intellectual challenge that undeserved suffering poses to belief in God. As Ivan suggests to Alyosha at the end of our selection, even if we have faith that the evil in this world is necessary for some greater good, the moral question is whether any end can justify certain very evil means. If Alyosha, as a kind human being, could not feel justified in allowing a small innocent child to be tortured, **regardless of the consequences**, can God be justified in allowing this?

. . . "I meant to speak of the suffering of mankind generally but we had better confine ourselves to the sufferings of the children. . . . Are you fond of children, Alyosha? I know you are, and you will understand why I prefer to speak of them. If they, too, suffer horribly on earth, they must suffer for their fathers' sins, they must be punished for their fathers, who have eaten the apple; but that reasoning is of the other world and is incomprehensible for the heart of man here on earth. The innocent must not suffer for another's sins, and especially such innocents! . . ."

"You speak with a strange air," observed Alyosha uneasily, "as though you were not quite yourself."

"By the way, a Bulgarian I met lately in Moscow," Ivan went on, seeming not to hear his brother's words, "told me about the crimes committed by Turks and Circassians in all parts of Bulgaria through fear of a general rising of the Slavs. They burn villages, murder, outrage women and children, they nail their prisoners by the ears to the fences, leave them so till morning. . . . People talk sometimes of bestial cruelty, but that's a great injustice and insult to the beasts; a beast can never be so cruel as a man, so artistically cruel. The tiger only tears and gnaws, that's all he can do. He would never think of nailing people by the ears, even if he were able to do it. These Turks took a pleasure in torturing children, too; cutting the unborn child from the mother's womb, and tossing babies up in the air and catching them on the points of their bayonets before their mother's eyes. Doing it before the mother's eyes was what gave zest to the amusement. Here is another scene that I thought very interesting. Imagine a trembling mother with her baby in her arms, a circle of invading Turks around her. They've planned a diversion; they pet the baby, laugh to make it laugh. They succeed, the baby laughs. At that moment a Turk points a pistol four inches from the baby's face. The baby laughs with glee, holds out its little hands to the pistol, and he pulls the trigger in the baby's face and blows out its brains. Artistic, wasn't it? By the way, Turks are particularly fond of sweet things, they say. . . ."

"Brother, what are you driving at?" asked Alyosha.

"I think if the devil doesn't exist, but man has created him, he has created him in his own image and likeness."

"Just as he did God, then?" observed Alyosha.

" 'It's wonderful how you can turn words,' as Polonius says in *Hamlet*," laughed Ivan. "You can turn my words against me. Well, I am glad. Yours must be a fine God, if man created Him in His image and likeness. . . .

"But I've still better things about children. I've collected a great great deal about Russian children, Alyosha. There was a little girl of five who was hated by her father and mother, 'most worthy and respectable people, of good education and breeding.' You see, I must repeat again, it is a peculiar characteristic of many people, this love of torturing children, and children only. To all other types of humanity these torturers behave mildly and benevolently. . . . It's just their defenselessness that tempts the tormentor, just the angelic confidence of the child who has no refuge and no appeal that sets his vile blood on fire.

"This poor child of five was subjected to every possible torture by those cultivated parents. They beat her, thrashed her, kicked her for no reason till her body was one bruise. Then, they went to greater refinements of cruelty—shut her up all night in the cold and frost in a privy, and because she didn't ask to be taken up at night

Source: From *The Brothers Karamazov* by Fyodor Dostoevsky, published in Russian in 1880 and translated into English by Constance Garnett (London: Heinemann, 1912).

(as though a child of five sleeping its angelic, sound sleep could be trained to wake and ask), they smeared her face and filled her mouth with excrement, and it was her mother, her mother did this. And that mother could sleep, hearing the poor child's groans! Can you understand why a little creature, who can't even understand what's done to her, should beat her little aching heart with her tiny fist in the dark and the cold, and weep her meek unresentful tears to dear kind God to protect her? Do you understand that, friend and brother, you pious and humble novice? Do you understand why this infamy must be and is permitted? Without it, I am told, man could not have existed on earth, for he could not have known good and evil. Why should he know that diabolical good and evil when it costs so much? Why, the whole world of knowledge is not worth that child's prayer to 'dear, kind God'! I say nothing of the sufferings of grown-up people, they have eaten the apple, damn them, and the devil take them all! But these little ones! I am making you suffer, Alyosha; I'll leave off it if you like.''

''Never mind. I want to suffer too,'' muttered Alyosha.

''One picture, only one more, because it's so curious, so characteristic, and I have only just read it in some collection of Russian antiquities. I've forgotten the name. I must look it up. It was in the darkest days of serfdom at the beginning of the century. There was in those days a general of aristocratic connections, the owner of great estates, one of those men—somewhat exceptional, I believe, even then—who, retiring from the service into a life of leisure, are convinced that they've earned absolute power over the lives of the subjects. There were such men then. So our general, settled on his property of two thousand souls, lives in pomp, and domineers over his poor neighbors as though they were dependents and buffoons. He has kennels of hundreds of hounds and nearly a hundred dog-boys—all mounted, and in uniform. One day a serf boy, a little child of eight, threw a stone in play and hurt the paw of the general's favorite hound. 'Why is my favorite dog lame?' He is told that the boy threw a stone that hurt the dog's paw. 'So you did it.' The general looked the child up and down. 'Take him.' He was taken—taken from his mother and kept shut up all night. Early that morning the general comes out on horseback, with the hounds, his dependents, dog-boys, and huntsmen, all mounted around him in full hunting parade. The servants are summoned for their edification, and in front of them all stands the mother of the child. The child is brought from the lock-up. It's a gloomy, cold foggy autumn day, a capital day for hunting. The general orders the child to be undressed; the child is stripped naked. He shivers, numb with terror, not daring to cry . . . 'Make him run,' commands the general. 'Run! run!' shout the dog-boys. The boy runs . . . 'At him!' yells the general, and he sets the whole pack of hounds on the child. The hounds catch him, and tear him to pieces before his mother's eyes! . . . I believe the general was afterwards declared incapable of administering his estates. Well—what did he deserve? To be shot? To be shot for the satisfaction of our moral feelings? Speak, Alyosha!''

''To be shot,'' murmured Alyosha, lifting his eyes to Ivan with a pale, twisted smile.

''Bravo!'' cried Ivan delighted. ''If even you say so . . . You're a pretty monk! So there is a little devil sitting in your heart, Alyosha Karamazov!''

''What I said was absurd, but—''

''That's just the point that 'but'!'' cried Ivan. ''Let me tell you novice, that the absurd is only too necessary on earth. The world stands on absurdities, and perhaps nothing would have come to pass in it without them. We know what we know!''

'What do you know?''

''I understand nothing,'' Ivan went on, as though in delirium. ''I don't want to understand anything now. I want to stick to the fact. I made up my mind long ago not to understand. If I try to understand anything, I shall be false to the fact and I have determined to stick to the fact."

"Why are you trying me?" Alyosha cried with sudden distress. "Will you say what you mean at last?"

"Of course, I will; that's what I've been leading up to. You are dear to me; I don't want to let you go, and I won't give you up to your Zossima."[1]

Ivan for a minute was silent, his face became all at once very sad.

"Listen! I took the case of children only to make my case clearer. Of the other tears of humanity with which the earth is soaked from its crust to its center, I will say nothing. I have narrowed my subject on purpose, I am a bug, and I recognize in all humility that I cannot understand why the world is arranged as it is. Men are themselves to blame, I suppose; they were given paradise, they wanted freedom, and stole fire from heaven, though they knew they would become unhappy, so there is no need to pity them. With my pitiful, earthly, Euclidean understanding, all I know is that there is suffering and that there are none guilty; I know that, and I can't consent to live by it! I must have justice, or I will destroy myself. And not justice in some remote infinite time and space, but here on earth, and that I could see myself. I have believed in it. I want to see it, and if I am dead by then, let me rise again, for if it all happens without me, it will be too unfair. Surely, I haven't suffered, simply that I, my crimes and my sufferings, may manure the soil of the future harmony for somebody else. I want to see with my own eyes the hind lie down with the lion and the victim rise up and embrace his murderer. I want to be there when everyone suddenly understands what it has all been for. All the religions of the world are built on this longing, and I am a believer. But there are the children, and what am I to do about them? That's a question I can't answer. For the hundredth time I repeat, there are numbers of questions, but I've only taken the children, because in their case what I mean is so unanswerably clear. Listen! If all must suffer to pay for the eternal harmony, what have children to do with it, tell me, please? It's beyond all comprehension why they should suffer, and why they should pay for the harmony. Why should they, too, furnish material to enrich the soil for the harmony of the future? I understand solidarity in sin among men. I understand solidarity in retribution, too; but there can be no such solidarity with children. And if it is really true that they must share responsibility for all their fathers' crimes, such a truth is not of this world and is beyond my comprehension. Some jester will say, perhaps, that the child would have grown up and have sinned, but you see he didn't grow up, he was torn to pieces by the dogs, at eight years old. Oh, Alyosha, I am not blaspheming! I understand, of course, what an upheaval of the universe it will be, when everything in heaven and earth blends in one hymn of praise and everything that lives and has lived cries aloud: 'Thou art just, O Lord, for Thy ways are revealed.' When the mother embraces the fiend who threw her child to the dogs, and all three cry aloud with tears, 'Thou are just, O Lord!' then, of course, the crown of knowledge will be reached and all will be made clear. But what pulls me up here is that I can't accept that harmony. And while I am on earth, I make haste to take my own measures. You see, Alyosha, perhaps it really may happen that if I live to that moment, or rise again to see it, I, too, perhaps, may cry aloud with the rest, looking at the mother embracing the child's torturer, 'Thou are just, O Lord!' but I don't want to cry aloud then. While there is still time, I hasten to protect myself and so I renounce the higher harmony altogether. It's not worth the tears of that one tortured child

[1]Zossima is the name of the monk under whom Alyosha is studying for the priesthood. EDITOR'S NOTE.

who beat itself on the breast with its little fist and prayed in its stinking outhouse with an unexpiated tear to 'dear, kind God'! It's not worth it, because those tears are unatoned for. They must be atoned for, or there can be no harmony. But how? How are you going to atone for them? Is it possible? By their being avenged? But what do I care for avenging them? What do I care for a hell for oppressors? What good can hell do, since those children have already been tortured? And what becomes of harmony, if there is hell? I want to forgive. I want to embrace. I don't want more suffering. And if the sufferings of children go to swell the sum of sufferings which was necessary to pay for truth, then I protest that the truth is not worth such a price. I don't want the mother to embrace the oppressor who threw her son to the dogs! She dare not forgive him! Let her forgive him for herself, if she will, let her forgive the torturer for the immeasurable suffering of her mother's heart. But the sufferings of her tortured child she has no right to forgive; she dare not forgive the torturer, even if the child were to forgive him! And if that is so, if they dare not forgive, what becomes of harmony? Is there in the whole world a being who would have the right to forgive and could forgive? I don't want harmony. From love of humanity I don't want it. I would rather be left with the unavenged suffering. I would rather remain with my unavenged suffering and unsatisfied indignation, *even if I were wrong*. Besides, too high a price is asked for harmony; it's beyond our means to pay so much to enter on it. And so I hasten to give back my entrance ticket, and if I am an honest man I am bound to give it back as soon as possible. And that I am doing. It's not God that I don't accept, Alyosha, only I most respectfully return Him the ticket."

"That's rebellion," murmured Alyosha, looking down.

"Rebellion? I am sorry you call it that," said Ivan earnestly. "One can hardly live in rebellion, and I want to live. Tell me yourself, I challenge you—answer. Imagine that you are creating a fabric of human destiny with the object of making men happy in the end, giving them peace and rest at last, but that it was essential and inevitable to torture to death only one tiny creature—that baby beating its breast with its fist, for instance—and to found that edifice on its unavenged tears, would you consent to be the architect on those conditions? Tell me, and tell the truth."

"No, I wouldn't consent," said Alyosha softly. . . .

"And you can admit the idea [Ivan continued] that men for whom you are building it would agree to accept their happiness on the foundation of the unexpiated blood of a little victim? And accepting it would remain happy for ever?"

"No I can't admit it. Brother," said Alyosha suddenly, with flashing eyes, "you said just now, is there a being in the whole world who would have the right to forgive and could forgive? But there is a Being and He can forgive everything, all and for all, because He gave His innocent blood for all and everything. You have forgotten Him, and on Him is built the edifice, and it is to Him they cry aloud, 'Thou are just, O Lord, for Thy ways are revealed!' " . . .

DISCUSSION QUESTIONS

1a. What is the most plausible reason a believer in God could give for why God did not prevent the undeserved suffering of children that Ivan so poignantly describes?

b. Is this reason sufficient to morally justify God's non-interference with such evil? Why?

2. Does Alyosha's invocation of Christ's crucifixion serve to justify, or make more acceptable, the sort of undeserved suffering that Ivan describes? Why?

3a. What is meant by the claim "the end does not justify the means"?

b. Do you accept this claim? Why? If you reject it, when does the end justify the means?

c. Is the view that "the end does not justify the means" inconsistent with Christian theology?

15. "LITTLE BESSIE": A MOCKING LITERARY CHALLENGE

Mark Twain

(For a biographical sketch of Mark Twain, see Selection #5.)

The problem of evil is the central issue in Mark Twain's satirical essay "Little Bessie." While Dostoevsky in the preceding selection was deeply troubled by the problem of evil, Twain pokes fun at what he sees as the total irrationality of the attempts religious people make to explain away the great undeserved suffering in this world. Twain believes that even a little child like Bessie can see through these vain attempts at justification. While Hume and Hick in the selections that follow tackle the problem of evil with much greater detail and philosophical sophistication, Twain gets quickly and simply to the heart of the central questions that the problem of evil generates. Some readers will be greatly amused by what Twain writes, others offended, but all will understand and perhaps will stop to think.

1. Little Bessie Would Assist Providence

Little Bessie was . . . a good child, and not shallow, not frivolous, but meditative and thoughtful, and much given to thinking out the reasons of things and trying to make them harmonise with results. One day she said—

"Mamma, why is there so much pain and sorrow and suffering? What is it all for?"

It was an easy question, and mamma had no difficulty in answering it:

"It is for our good, my child. In His wisdom and mercy the Lord sends us these afflictions to discipline us and make us better."

"Is it *He* that sends them?"

"Yes."

"Does He send *all* of them, mamma?"

"Yes, dear, all of them. None of them comes by accident; He alone sends them, and always out of love for us, and to make us better."

Source: Chapters 1–3 of "Little Bessie" in Mark Twain's *Fables of Man*, edited with an introduction by John S. Tuckey (1972). © 1972 by the Mark Twain Company, reprinted by permission of the University of California Press.

"Isn't it strange!"

"Strange? Why, no, I have never thought of it in that way. I have not heard any one call it strange before. It has always seemed natural and right to me, and wise and most kindly and merciful."

"Who first thought of it like that, mamma? Was it you?"

"Oh, no child, I was taught it."

"Who taught you so, mamma?"

"Why, really, I don't know—I can't remember. My mother, I suppose; or the preacher. But it's a thing that everybody knows."

"Well, anyway, it does seem strange. Did He give Billy Norris the typhus?"

"Yes."

"What for?"

"Why, to discipline him and make him good."

"But he died, mamma, and so it *couldn't* make him good."

"Well, then, I suppose it was for some other reason. We know it was a *good* reason, whatever it was."

"What do you think it was, mamma?"

"Oh, you ask so many questions! I think it was to discipline his parents."

"Well, then, it wasn't fair, mamma. Why should *his* life be taken away for their sake, when he wasn't doing anything?"

"Oh, *I* don't know! I only know it was for a good and wise and merciful reason."

"What reason, mamma?"

"I think—I think—well, it was a judgment; it was to punish them for some sin they had committed."

"But *he* was the one that was punished, mamma. Was that right?"

"Certainly, certainly. He does nothing that isn't right and wise and merciful. You can't understand these things now, dear, but when you are grown up you will understand them, and then you will see that they are just and wise."

After a pause:

"Did He make the roof fall in on the stranger that was trying to save the crippled old woman from the fire, mamma?"

"Yes, my child. *Wait!* Don't ask me why, because I don't know. I only know it was to discipline some one, or be a judgment upon somebody, or to show His power."

"That drunken man that stuck a pitchfork into Mrs. Welch's baby when—"

"Never mind about it, you needn't go into particulars; it was to discipline the child—*that* much is certain, anyway."

"Mamma, Mr. Burgess said in his sermon that billions of little creatures are sent into us to give us cholera, and typhoid, and lockjaw, and more than a thousand other sicknesses and—mamma, does He send them?"

"Oh, certainly, child, certainly. Of course."

"What for?"

"Oh, to *dis*cipline us! haven't I told you so, over and over again?"

"It's awful cruel, mamma! And silly! and if I—"

"Hush, oh *hush*! do you want to bring the lightning?"

"You know the lightning *did* come last week, mamma, and struck the new church, and burnt it down. Was it to discipline the church?"

(Wearily). "Oh, I suppose so."

"But it killed a hog that wasn't doing anything. Was it to discipline the hog, mamma?"

"Dear child, don't you want to run out and play a while? If you would like to—"

"Mamma, only think! Mr. Hollister says there isn't a bird or fish or reptile or any other animal that hasn't got an enemy that Providence has sent to bite it and chase it and pester it, and kill it, and suck its blood and discipline it and make it good and religious. Is that true, mother—because if it is true, why did Mr. Hollister laugh at it?"

"That Hollister is a scandalous person, and I don't want you to listen to anything he says."

"Why, mamma, he is very interesting, and *I* think he tries to be good. He says the wasps catch spiders and cram them down into their nests in the ground—*alive*, mamma!—and there they live and suffer days and days and days, and the hungry little wasps chewing their legs and gnawing into their bellies all the time, to make them good and religious and praise God for His infinite mercies. *I* think Mr. Hollister is just lovely, and ever so kind; for when I asked him if *he* would treat a spider like that, he said he hoped to be damned if he would; and then he—"

"My child! oh, do for goodness' sake—"

"And mamma, he says the spider is appointed to catch the fly, and drive her fangs into his bowels, and suck and suck and suck his blood, to discipline him and make him a Christian; and whenever the fly buzzes his wings with the pain and misery of it, you can see by the spider's grateful eye that she is thanking the Giver of All Good for—well, she's saying grace, as *he* says; and also, he—"

"Oh, aren't you *ever* going to get tired chattering! If you want to go out and play—"

"Mamma, he says himself that all troubles and pains and miseries and rotten diseases and horrors and villainies are sent to us in mercy and kindness to discipline us; and he says it is the duty of every father and mother to *help* Providence, every way they can; and says they can't do it by just scolding and whipping, for that won't answer, it is weak and no good—Providence's way is best, and it is every parent's duty and every *person's* duty to help discipline everybody, and cripple them and kill them, and starve them, and freeze them, and rot them with diseases, and lead them into murder and theft and dishonor and disgrace; and he says Providence's invention for disciplining us and the animals is the very brightest idea that ever was, and not even an idiot could get up anything shinier. Mamma, brother Eddie needs disciplining, right away; and I know where you can get the smallpox for him, and the itch, and the diphtheria, and bone-rot, and heart disease, and consumption, and—*Dear* mamma, have you fainted! I will run and bring help! Now *this* comes of staying in town this hot weather.''

2. Creation of Man

Mamma. You disobedient child, have you been associating with that irreligious Hollister again?

Bessie. Well, mamma, he is interesting, anyway, although wicked, and I can't help loving interesting people. Here is the conversation we had:

Hollister. Bessie, suppose you should take some meat and bones and fur, and make a cat out of it, and should tell the cat, Now you are not to be unkind to any creature, on pain of punishment and death. And suppose the cat should disobey, and catch a mouse and torture it and kill it. What would you do to the cat?

Bessie. Nothing.

H. Why?

B. Because I know what the cat would say. She would say. *It's my* nature, I couldn't help it; I didn't make my nature, *you* made it. And so you are responsible for what I've done—I'm not. I couldn't answer that, Mr. Hollister.

H. It's just the case of Frankenstein and his Monster over again.

B. What is that?

H. Frankenstein took some flesh and bones and blood and made a man out of them; the man ran away and fell to raping and robbing and murdering everywhere, and Frankenstein was horrified and in despair, and said, *I* made him, without asking his consent, and it makes me responsible for every crime he commits. *I* am the criminal, he is innocent.

B. Of course he was right.

H. I judge so. It's just the case of God and man and you and the cat over again.

B. How is that?

H. God made man, without man's consent, and made his nature, too; made it vicious instead of angelic, and then said, Be angelic, or I will punish you and destroy you. But no matter, God is responsible for everything man does, all the same; He can't get around that fact. There is only one Criminal, and it is not man.

Mamma. This is atrocious! it is wicked, blasphemous, irreverent, horrible!

Bessie. Yes'm, but it's true. And I'm not going to make a cat. I would be above making a cat if I couldn't make a good one.

3

Mamma, if a person by the name of Jones kills a person by the name of Smith just for amusement, it's murder, isn't it, and Jones is a murderer?

Yes, my child.

And Jones is punishable for it?

Yes, my child.

Why, mamma?

Why? Because God has forbidden homicide in the Ten Commandments, and therefore whoever kills a person commits a crime and must suffer for it.

But mamma, suppose Jones has by birth such

a violent temper that he can't control himself?

He *must* control himself. God requires it.

But he doesn't make his own temper, mamma, he is born with it, like the rabbit and the tiger; and so, why should he be held responsible?

Because God *says* he is responsible and *must* control his temper.

But he *can't*, mamma; and so, don't you think it is God that does the killing and is responsible, because it was *He* that gave him the temper which he couldn't control?

Peace, my child! He *must* control it, for God requires it, and that ends the matter. It settles it, and there is no room for argument.

(*After a thoughtful pause.*) It doesn't seem to me to settle it. Mamma, murder is murder, isn't it? and whoever commits it is a murderer? That is the plain simple fact, isn't it?

(*Suspiciously.*) What are you arriving at now, my child?

Mamma, when God designed Jones He could have given him a rabbit's temper if He had wanted to, couldn't He?

Yes.

Then Jones would not kill anybody and have to be hanged?

True.

But He chose to give Jones a temper that would *make* him kill Smith. Why, then, isn't *He* responsible?

Because He also gave Jones a Bible. The Bible gives Jones ample warning not to commit murder; and so if Jones commits it he alone is responsible.

(*Another pause.*) Mamma, did God make the house-fly?

Certainly, my darling.

What for?

For some great and good purpose, and to display His power.

What is the great and good purpose, mamma?

We do not know, my child. We only know that He makes *all* things for a great and good purpose. But this is too large a subject for a dear little Bessie like you. . . .

Possibly, mamma, yet it profoundly interests me. I have been reading about the fly, in the newest science-book. In that book he is called "the most dangerous animal and the most murderous that exists upon the earth, killing hundreds of thousands of men, women and children every year, by distributing deadly diseases among them." Think of it, mamma, the *most* fatal of all the animals! by all odds the most murderous of all the living things created by God. Listen to this, from the book:

> Now, the house fly has a very keen scent for filth of any kind. Whenever there is any within a hundred yards or so, the fly goes for it to smear its mouth and all the sticky hairs of its six legs with dirt and disease germs. A second or two suffices to gather up many thousands of these disease germs, and then off goes the fly to the nearest kitchen or dining room. There the fly crawls over the meat, butter, bread, cake, anything it can find in fact, and often gets into the milk pitcher, depositing large numbers of disease germs at every step. The house fly is as disgusting as it is dangerous.

Isn't it horrible, mamma! One fly produces fifty-two billions of descendants in 60 days in June and July, and they go and crawl over sick people and wade through pus, and sputa, and foul matter exuding from sores, and gaum themselves with every kind of disease-germ, then they go to everybody's dinner-table and wipe themselves off on the butter and the other food, and many and many a painful illness and ultimate death results from this loathsome industry. Mamma, they murder seven thousand persons in New York City alone, every year—people against whom they have no quarrel. To kill without cause is murder—nobody denies that. Mamma?

Well?

Have the flies a Bible?

Of course not.

You have said it is the Bible that makes man responsible. If God didn't give him a Bible to circumvent the nature that He deliberately gave him, God would be responsible. He gave the fly his murderous nature, and sent him forth unobstructed by a Bible or any other restraint to commit murder by wholesale. And so, therefore, God is Himself responsible. God is a murderer. Mr. Hollister says so. Mr. Hollister says God can't make one moral law for man and another for Himself. He says it would be laughable.

Do shut up! I wish that that tiresome Hollister was in H—amburg! He is an ignorant, unreasoning, illogical ass, and I have told you over and over again to keep out of his poisonous company. . . .

DISCUSSION QUESTIONS

1. If you shared Twain's attitude toward the belief in God, what would you say to the following attempts to explain why God allows suffering that is inherent in the very constitution of human beings and the world they inhabit (e.g., diseases, dangerous animals of prey, fires, floods, volcanoes, earthquakes, droughts, and famines)?

   a. They are God's punishment for sin.

   b. They are God's warning to human beings to mend their ways before it is too late.

   c. They are the inevitable results of the operation of laws of nature.

   d. They make it possible for us to appreciate the good things of life. If our world were devoid of pain or suffering, we wouldn't even understand that we are experiencing "pleasure," because we wouldn't have anything to compare it to.

   e. Things are evil only when looked at in isolation. However, when things are seen as a whole, as God sees things, evil is seen to be a necessary component of a good whole. Just as the human artist has in view the beauty of his composition taken as a whole, so it is with God.

   f. The existence of evil comes from the fact that God wants us to **merit** the supreme happiness of heaven and not simply give it to us as a gift. We could not merit the reward of heaven unless we were faced with personal struggles and were exposed to the possibility of defeat. This, in turn, requires that we inhabit a world in which people suffer.

2. What would be the best answer a believer in God could give to Bessie's questions as to why God allowed Billy Norris to suffer from and die of typhus and why he allows animals to suffer and prey upon each other?

3. Bessie claims that just as Frankenstein must ultimately accept responsibility for the actions of the monster he created, God must ultimately accept responsibility for the actions of the human beings he has created. Is this true? What, if any, are the important differences in these two cases that should affect our judgment of where responsibility ultimately lies?

4. It seems to Bessie that if we suppose that a person "has by birth such a violent temper that he can't control himself," there is no way that God could escape responsibility for any evil action he commits while angry. Is this true? What, if anything, is the most plausible reply a believer in the Judeo-Christian God could give as to why God does not see to it that people always have the power to control themselves?

16. A CLASSIC PHILOSOPHICAL CHALLENGE

David Hume

(For a biographical sketch of David Hume and discussion of his **Dialogues,** see Selection #8.)

The following selection is excerpted from David Hume's discussion of the problem of evil in Parts X and XI of his **Dialogues Concerning Natural Religion.** As the selection begins, Demea and Philo are emphasizing the sorrows of life. With the pessimistic picture of human life that he and Demea have painted as a backdrop, Philo raises the problem of evil, claiming that the existence of evil in this world is logically incompatible with the existence of an all-powerful, all-wise, and all-good creator.

Demea, the **a priori** rationalist, replies that one must have faith that our perception of unjustified evil comes from our limited perspective and consequent incapacity to see the moral necessity of evil in the total scheme of things. Cleanthes, the empiricist, interrupts, challenging the lack of empirical foundations for Demea's "arbitrary suppositions." He then goes on to challenge Demea's and Philo's pessimistic view of human life, claiming that there is more good than evil in the world.

Philo then objects that the existence of any evil, however small, is still incompatible with the existence of an infinitely powerful, wise, and good deity. But even if the existence of some evil is compatible with the existence of God, Philo reminds Cleanthes that, as an empiricist, he has the burden of providing evidence for the existence of such a deity, evidence which, Philo claims, does not exist. At this point, Cleanthes suggests the hypothesis of a finite god whose power, wisdom, and goodness are very great, but limited.

The sceptic Philo then takes up the argument for the remainder of our selection. As he sees it, there are four causes of evil in this world, all of which seem to serve no good purpose. While it is quite possible, he grants, that these causes are **compatible** with the existence of a finite but very powerful, wise, and good deity, there is no evidence to show that this possibility is at all **probable.** If this world were designed by some deity, Philo suggests, he is most likely an amoral deity, indifferent to the moral distinctions that mean so much to us.

[Demea and Philo: The Sorrows of Life Outweigh Its Joys]

It is my opinion, . . . replied Demea, that each man feels, in a manner, the truth of religion within his own breast; and, from a consciousness of his imbecility and misery rather than from any reasoning, is led to seek protection from that Being on whom he and all nature are dependent. So anxious or so tedious are even the best scenes of life that futurity is still the object of all our hopes and fears. We incessantly look forward and endeavor, by prayers, adoration, and sacrifice, to appease those unknown powers whom we find, by experience, so able to afflict and oppress us. Wretched creatures that we are! What resource for us amidst the innumerable ills of life did not religion suggest some methods of atonement, and appease those

Source: From *The Dialogues Concerning Natural Religion* by David Hume. Published in London in 1779.

terrors with which we are incessantly agitated and tormented?

I am indeed persuaded, said Philo, that the best and indeed the only method of bringing everyone to a due sense of religion is by just representations of the misery and wickedness of men. And for that purpose a talent of eloquence and strong imagery is more requisite than that of reasoning and argument. For is it necessary to prove what everyone feels within himself? It is only necessary to make us feel it, more intimately and sensibly.

The people, indeed, replied Demea, are sufficiently convinced of this great and melancholy truth. The miseries of life, the unhappiness of man, the general corruptions of our nature, the unsatisfactory enjoyment of pleasures, riches, honors—these phrases have become almost proverbial in all languages. And who can doubt of what all men declare from their own immediate feeling and experience?

. . . The whole earth, believe me, Philo, is cursed and polluted. A perpetual war is kindled amongst all living creatures. Necessity, hunger, want stimulate the strong and courageous; fear, anxiety, terror agitate the weak and infirm. The first entrance into life gives anguish to the newborn infant and to its wretched parent; weakness, impotence, distress attend each stage of that life, and it is, at last, finished in agony and horror.

Observe, too, says Philo, the curious artifices of nature in order to embitter the life of every living being. The stronger prey upon the weaker and keep them in perpetual terror and anxiety. The weaker, too, in their turn, often prey upon the stronger, and vex and molest them without relaxation. Consider that innumerable race of insects, which either are bred on the body of each animal or, flying about, infix their stings in him. These insects have others still less than themselves which torment them. And thus on each hand, before and behind, above and below, every animal is surrounded with enemies which incessantly seek his misery and destruction.

Man alone, said Demea, seems to be, in part, an exception to this rule. For by combination in society he can easily master lions, tigers, and bears, whose greater strength and agility naturally enable them to prey upon him.

On the contrary, it is here chiefly, cried Philo, that the uniform and equal maxims of nature are most apparent. Man, it is true, can, by combination, surmount all his *real* enemies and become master of the whole animal creation; but does he not immediately raise up to himself *imaginary* enemies, the demons of his fancy, who haunt him with superstitious terrors and blast every enjoyment of life?. . .

Besides, consider, Demea: This very society by which we surmount those wild beasts, our natural enemies, what new enemies does it not raise to us? What woe and misery does it not occasion? Man is the greatest enemy of man. Oppression, injustice, contempt, contumely,[1] violence, sedition, war, calumny,[2] treachery, fraud—by these they mutually torment each other, and they would soon dissolve that society which they had formed were it not for the dread of still greater ills which must attend their separation.

But though these external insults, said Demea, from animals, from men, from all the elements, which assault us form a frightful catalogue of woes, they are nothing in comparison of those which arise within ourselves, from the distempered condition of our mind and body. How many lie under the lingering torment of diseases? Hear the pathetic enumeration of the great poet.

Intestine stone and ulcer, colic-pangs,
Demoniac frenzy, moping melancholy,
And moon-struck madness, pining atrophy,
Marasmus, and wide-wasting pestilence.
Dire was the tossing, deep the groans: *Despair*
Tended the sick, busiest from couch to couch.
And over them triumphant *Death* his dart

[1]Insulting rudeness. EDITOR'S NOTE.

[2]Slander. EDITOR'S NOTE.

Shook: but delay'd to strike, though oft invok'd
With vows, as their chief good and final hope.[3]

The disorders of the mind, continued Demea, though more secret, are not perhaps less dismal and vexatious. Remorse, shame, anguish, rage, disappointment, anxiety, fear, dejection, despair—who has ever passed through life without cruel inroads from these tormentors? How many have scarcely ever felt any better sensations? Labor and poverty, so abhorred by everyone, are the certain lot of the far greater number; and those few privileged persons who enjoy ease and opulence never reach contentment or true felicity. All the goods of life united would not make a very happy man, but all the ills united would make a wretch indeed; and any one of them almost (and who can be free from every one), nay, often the absence of one good (and who can possess all) is sufficient to render life ineligible.

Were a stranger to drop on a sudden into this world, I would show him, as a specimen of its ills, a hospital full of diseases, a prison crowded with malefactors and debtors, a field of battle strewed with carcases, a fleet foundering in the ocean, a nation languishing under tyranny, famine, or pestilence. To turn the gay side of life to him and give him a notion of its pleasures—whither should I conduct him? To a ball, to an opera, to court? He might justly think that I was only showing him a diversity of distress and sorrow. . . .

[Philo: The Existence of the Judeo-Christian God Is Incompatible with the Existence of Evil]

And is it possible, Cleanthes, said Philo, that after all these reflections, and infinitely more which might be suggested, you can still persevere in your anthropomorphism, and assert the moral attributes of the Deity, his justice, benevolence, mercy, and rectitude, to be of the same nature with these virtues in human creatures? His power, we allow, is infinite; whatever he wills is executed; but neither man nor any other animal is happy; therefore, he does not will their happiness. His wisdom is infinite; he is never mistaken in choosing the means to any end; but the course of nature tends not to human or animal felicity; therefore, it is not established for that purpose. Through the whole compass of human knowledge there are no inferences more certain and infallible than these. In what respect, then, do his benevolence and mercy resemble the benevolence and mercy of men?

Epicurus' old questions are yet unanswered.

Is he willing to prevent evil, but not able? then is he impotent. Is he able, but not willing? then is he malevolent. Is he both able and willing? whence then is evil?. . .

And have you, at last, said Cleanthes smiling, betrayed your intentions, Philo? Your long agreement with Demea did indeed a little surprise me, but I find you were all the while erecting a concealed battery against me. And I must confess that you have now fallen upon a subject worthy of your noble spirit of opposition and controversy. If you can make out the present point, and prove mankind to be unhappy or corrupted, there is an end at once of all religion. For to what purpose establish the natural attributes of the Deity, while the moral are still doubtful and uncertain?

[Demea: Evil Is a Necessary Part of a Presently Imperceptible Greater Good]

You take umbrage very easily, replied Demea, at opinions the most innocent and the most generally received, even amongst the religious and devout themselves; and nothing can be more surprising than to find a topic like this—concerning the wickedness and misery of

[3]John Milton, *Paradise Lost,* Book XI. EDITOR'S NOTE.

man—charged with no less than atheism and profaneness. Have not all pious divines and preachers who have indulged their rhetoric on so fertile a subject; have they not easily, I say, given a solution of any difficulties which may attend it? This world is but a point in comparison of the universe; this life but a moment in comparison of eternity. The present evil phenomena, therefore, are rectified in other regions, and in some future period of existence. And the eyes of men, being then opened to larger views of things, see the whole connection of general laws, and trace, with adoration, the benevolence and rectitude of the Deity through all the mazes and intricacies of his providence.

[Cleanthes: Arbitrary Hypotheses Will Not Do; There Is More Good than Evil in the World]

No! replied Cleanthes, no! These arbitrary suppositions can never be admitted, contrary to matter of fact, visible and uncontroverted. Whence can any cause be known but from its known effects? Whence can any hypothesis be proved but from the apparent phenomena? To establish one hypothesis upon another is building entirely in the air; and the utmost we ever attain by these conjectures and fictions is to ascertain the bare possibility of our opinion, but never can we, upon such terms, establish its reality.

The only method of supporting divine benevolence—and it is what I willingly embrace—is to deny absolutely the misery and wickedness of man. Your representations are exaggerated; your melancholy views mostly fictitious; your inferences contrary to fact and experience. Health is more common than sickness; pleasure than pain; happiness than misery. And for one vexation which we meet with, we attain, upon computation, a hundred enjoyments.

[Philo: The Existence of Evil Makes It Impossible to Infer the Existence of the Judeo-Christian God]

Admitting your position, replied Philo, which yet is extremely doubtful, you must at the same time allow that, if pain be less frequent than pleasure, it is infinitely more violent and durable. One hour of it is often able to outweigh a day, a week, a month of our common insipid enjoyments; and how many days, weeks, and months are passed by several in the most acute torments? Pleasure, scarcely in one instance, is ever able to reach ecstasy and rapture; and in no one instance can it continue for any time at its highest pitch and altitude. . . But pain often, good God, how often! rises to torture and agony; and the longer it continues, it becomes still more genuine agony and torture. . . .

But not to insist upon these topics, continued Philo, though most obvious, certain, and important, I must use the freedom to admonish you, Cleanthes, that you have put the controversy upon a most dangerous issue, and are unawares introducing a total scepticism into the most essential articles of natural and revealed theology. What! no method of fixing a just foundation for religion unless we [claim that there is more happiness in life than unhappiness]. . . . But this is contrary to everyone's feeling and experience; it is contrary to an authority so established as nothing can subvert. No decisive proofs can ever be produced against this authority; nor is it possible for you to compute, estimate, and compare all the pains and all the pleasures in the lives of all men and of all animals; and thus, by your resting the whole system of religion on a point which, from its very nature, must forever be uncertain, you tacitly confess that that system is equally uncertain.

But allowing you what never will be believed, at least, what you never possibly can prove, that animal or, at least, human happiness in this life exceeds its misery, you have yet done nothing; for this is not, by any means, what we expect from infinite power, infinite wisdom, and infinite goodness. Why is there any misery at all in the world? Not by chance, surely. From some cause then. Is it from the intention of the Deity? But he is perfectly benevolent. Is it contrary to his intention? But he is almighty. Nothing can shake the solidity of this reasoning, so short, so clear, so decisive, except we assert that these subjects exceed all human capacity, and that our common measures of truth and falsehood are not applicable to them—a topic which I have all along insisted on, but which you have, from the beginning, rejected with scorn and indignation.

But I will be contented to retire still from this intrenchment, for I deny that you can ever force me in it. I will allow that pain or misery in man is *compatible* with infinite power and goodness in the Deity, even in your sense of these attributes: what are you advanced by all these concessions? A mere possible compatibility is not sufficient. You must *prove* these . . . attributes from the present mixed and confused phenomena, and from these alone. A hopeful undertaking! Were the phenomena ever so pure and unmixed, yet, being finite, they would be insufficient for that purpose. How much more, where they are also so jarring and discordant!

Here, Cleanthes, I find myself at ease in my argument. Here I triumph. Formerly, when we argued concerning the natural attributes of intelligence and design, I needed all my sceptical and metaphysical subtilty to elude your grasp. In many views of the universe and of its parts, particularly the latter, the beauty and fitness of final causes strike us with such irresistible force that all objections appear (what I believe they really are) mere cavils and sophisms; nor can we then imagine how it was ever possible for us to repose any weight on them. But there is no view of human life or of the condition of mankind from which, without the greatest violence, we can infer the moral attributes or learn that infinite wisdom, which we must discover by the eyes of faith alone. It is your turn now to tug the laboring oar, and to support your philosophical subtilties against the dictates of plain reason and experience.

[Cleanthes: A Finite God]

I scruple not to allow, said Cleanthes, that I have been apt to suspect the frequent repetition of the word *infinite,* which we meet with in all theological writers, to savor more of panegyric[4] than of philosophy, and that any purposes of reasoning, and even of religion, would be better served were we to rest contented with more accurate and more moderate expressions. The terms *admirable, excellent, superlatively great, wise,* and *holy*—these sufficiently fill the imaginations of men, and anything beyond, besides that it leads into absurdities, has no influence on the affections or sentiments. Thus, in the present subject, if we abandon all human analogy, as seems your intention, Demea, I am afraid we abandon all religion and retain no conception of the great object of our adoration. If we preserve human analogy, we must forever find it impossible to reconcile any mixture of evil in the universe with infinite attributes; much less can we ever prove the latter from the former. But supposing the Author of Nature to be finitely perfect, though far exceeding mankind, a satisfactory account may then be given of natural and moral evil, and every untoward phenomenon be explained and adjusted. A less evil may then be chosen in order to reach a desirable end; and, in a word, benevolence, regulated by wisdom and limited by necessity, may

[4]Eulogy. EDITOR'S NOTE.

produce just such a world as the present. You, Philo, who are so prompt at starting views and reflections and analogies, I would gladly hear, at length, without interruption, your opinion of this new theory. . . .

[Philo: There Is No Basis for Inferring a Very Powerful, Wise, and Benevolent Creator of Our World]

My sentiments, replied Philo, are not worth being made a mystery of; and, therefore, without any ceremony, I shall deliver what occurs to me with regard to the present subject. It must, I think, be allowed that, if a very limited intelligence whom we shall suppose utterly unacquainted with the universe were assured that it were the production of a very good, wise, and powerful being, however finite, he would, from his conjectures, form *beforehand* a different notion of it from what we find it to be by experience; nor would he ever imagine, merely from these attributes of the cause of which he is informed, that the effect could be so full of vice and misery and disorder, as it appears in this life. Supposing now that this person were brought into the world, still assured that it was the workmanship of such a sublime and benevolent being, he might, perhaps, be surprised at the disappointment, but would never retract his former belief if founded on any very solid argument, since such a limited intelligence must be sensible of his own blindness and ignorance, and must allow that there may be many solutions of those phenomena which will forever escape his comprehension. But supposing, which is the real case with regard to man, that this creature is not antecedently convinced of a supreme intelligence, benevolent, and powerful, but is left to gather such a belief from the appearance of things—this entirely alters the case, nor will he ever find any reason for such a conclusion. He may be fully convinced of the narrow limits of his understanding, but this will not help him in forming an inference concerning the goodness of superior powers, since he must form that inference from what he knows, not from what he is ignorant of. . . .

In short, I repeat the question: Is the world, considered in general and as it appears to us in this life, different from what a man or such a limited being would, *beforehand,* expect from a very powerful, wise, and benevolent Deity? It must be strange prejudice to assert the contrary. And from thence I conclude that, however consistent the world may be, allowing certain suppositions and conjectures with the idea of such a Deity, it can never afford us an inference concerning his existence. The consistency is not absolutely denied, only the inference. Conjectures, especially where infinity is excluded from the divine attributes, may perhaps be sufficient to prove a consistency, but can never be foundations for any inference.

[Philo: There Are Four Causes of Natural Evil, None of Which Seem Necessary]

There seem to be *four* circumstances on which depend all or the greatest part of the ills that molest sensible creatures; and it is not impossible but all these circumstances may be necessary and unavoidable. We know so little beyond common life, or even of common life, that, with regard to the economy of a universe, there is no conjecture, however wild, which may not be just; nor any one, however plausible, which may not be erroneous. All that belongs to human understanding, in this deep ignorance and obscurity, is to be sceptical or at least cautious, and not to admit of any hypothesis whatever, much less of any which is supported by no appearance of probability. Now this I assert to be the case with regard to all the causes of evil and the circumstances on which it depends. None of them appear to human reason in the least degree necessary or unavoidable, nor can we suppose them such, without the utmost license of imagination.

The *first* circumstance which introduces evil is that contrivance or economy of the animal creation by which pains, as well as pleasures, are employed to excite all creatures to action, and make them vigilant in the great work of self-preservation. Now pleasure alone, in its various degrees, seems to human understanding sufficient for this purpose. All animals might be constantly in a state of enjoyment; but when urged by any of the necessities of nature, such as thirst, hunger, weariness; instead of pain, they might feel a diminution of pleasure by which they might be prompted to seek that object which is necessary to their subsistence. Men pursue pleasure as eagerly as they avoid pain; at least, they might have been so constituted. It seems, therefore, plainly possible to carry on the business of life without any pain. Why then is any animal ever rendered susceptible of such a sensation. . .

But a capacity of pain would not alone produce pain were it not for the *second* circumstance, viz., the conducting of the world by general laws; and this seems nowise necessary to a very perfect being. It is true, if everything were conducted by particular volitions, the course of nature would be perpetually broken, and no man could employ his reason in the conduct of life. But might not other particular volitions remedy this inconvenience? In short, might not the Deity exterminate all ill, wherever it were to be found, and produce all good, without any preparation or long progress of causes and effects?

Besides, we must consider that, according to the present economy of the world, the course of nature, though supposed exactly regular, yet to us appears not so, and many events are uncertain, and many disappoint our expectations. Health and sickness, calm and tempest, with an infinite number of other accidents whose causes are unknown and variable, have a great influence both on the fortunes of particular persons and on the prosperity of public societies; and indeed all human life, in a manner, depends on such accidents. A being, therefore, who knows the secret springs of the universe might easily, by particular volitions, turn all these accidents to the good of mankind and render the whole world happy, without discovering himself in any operation. A fleet whose purposes were salutary to society might always meet with a fair wind; good princes enjoy sound health and long life; persons born to power and authority be framed with good tempers and virtuous dispositions. A few such events as these, regularly and wisely conducted, would change the face of the world; and yet would no more seem to disturb the course of nature or confound human conduct than the present economy of things where the causes are secret and variable and compounded. Some small touches given to Caligula's brain in his infancy might have converted him into a Trajan.[5] One wave, a little higher than the rest, by burying Caesar and his fortune in the bottom of the ocean, might have restored liberty to a considerable part of mankind. There may, for aught we know, be good reasons why Providence interposes not in this manner, but they are unknown to us; and, though the mere supposition that such reasons exist may be sufficient to *save* the conclusion concerning the divine attributes, yet surely it can never be sufficient to *establish* that conclusion.

If everything in the universe be conducted by general laws, and if animals be rendered susceptible of pain, it scarcely seems possible but some ill must arise in the various shocks of matter and the various concurrence and opposition of general laws; but this ill would be very rare were it not for the *third* circumstance which I proposed to mention, viz., the great frugality with which all powers and faculties are distributed to every particular being. . . . Every animal has the requisite endowments [to keep them-

[5]A much better Roman emperor. EDITOR'S NOTE.

selves alive]; but these endowments are bestowed with so scrupulous an economy that any considerable diminution must entirely destroy the creature. Wherever one power is increased, there is a proportional abatement in the others. Animals which excel in swiftness are commonly defective in force. Those which possess both are either imperfect in some of their senses or are oppressed with the most craving wants. The human species, whose chief excellence is reason and sagacity, is . . . the most deficient in bodily advantages. . . . In short, nature seems to have formed an exact calculation of the necessities of her creatures; and, like a *rigid master,* has afforded them little more powers or endowments than what are strictly sufficient to supply those necessities. An *indulgent parent* would have bestowed a large stock in order to guard against accidents, and secure the happiness and welfare of the creature in the most unfortunate concurrence of circumstances. Every course of life would not have been so surrounded with precipices that the least departure from the true path, by mistake or necessity, must involve us in misery and ruin. Some reserve, some fund, would have been provided to ensure happiness, nor would the powers and the necessities have been adjusted with so rigid an economy. The Author of Nature is inconceivably powerful; his force is supposed great, if not altogether inexhaustible; nor is there any reason, as far as we can judge, to make him observe this strict frugality in his dealings with his creatures. It would have been better, were his power extremely limited, to have created fewer animals, and to have endowed these with more faculties for their happiness and preservation. A builder is never esteemed prudent who undertakes a plan beyond what his stock will enable him to finish. . . .

The *fourth* circumstance whence arises the misery and ill of the universe is the inaccurate workmanship of all the springs and principles of the great machine of nature. It must be acknowledged that there are few parts of the universe which seem not to serve some purpose, and whose removal would not produce a visible defect and disorder in the whole. The parts hang all together, nor can one be touched without affecting the rest, in a greater or less degree. But at the same time, it must be observed that none of these parts or principles, however useful, are so accurately adjusted as to keep precisely within those bounds in which their utility consists; but they are, all of them, apt, on every occasion, to run into the one extreme or the other. One would imagine that this grand production had not received the last hand of the maker—so little finished is every part, and so coarse are the strokes with which it is executed. Thus the winds are requisite to convey the vapors along the surface of the globe, and to assist men in navigation; but how often, rising up to tempests and hurricanes, do they become pernicious? Rains are necessary to nourish all the plants and animals of the earth; but how often are they defective? how often excessive? Heat is requisite to all life and vegetation, but is not always found in the due proportion. . . . There is nothing so advantageous in the universe but what frequently becomes pernicious, by its excess or defect; nor has nature guarded, with the requisite accuracy, against all disorder or confusion. The irregularity is never perhaps so great as to destroy any species, but is often sufficient to involve the individuals in ruin and misery.

On the concurrence, then, of these *four* circumstances does all or the greatest part of natural evil[6] depend. Were all living creatures incapable of pain, or were the world administered by particular volitions, evil never could have found access into the universe; and were animals endowed with a large stock of powers and faculties, beyond what strict necessity requires, or were the several springs and principles of the universe so accurately framed as to preserve always the just temperament and medium, there must have been very little ill in compari-

[6]Natural evils are those evils that are inherent in nature, as opposed to *moral evils* which result from the immorality of human beings. EDITOR'S NOTE.

son of what we feel at present. What then shall we pronounce on this occasion? Shall we say that these circumstances are not necessary, and that they might easily have been altered in the contrivance of the universe? This decision seems too presumptuous for creatures so blind and ignorant. Let us be more modest in our conclusions. Let us allow that, if the goodness of the Deity (I mean a goodness like the human) could be established on any tolerable reasons *a priori,* these phenomena, however untoward, would not be sufficient to subvert that principle, but might easily, in some unknown manner, be reconcilable to it. But let us still assert that, as this goodness is not antecedently established but must be inferred from the phenomena, there can be no grounds for such an inference while there are so many ills in the universe, and while these ills might so easily have been remedied, as far as human understanding can be allowed to judge on such a subject. I am sceptic enough to allow that the bad appearances, notwithstanding all my reasonings, may be compatible with such attributes as you suppose, but surely they can never prove these attributes. . . .

Look round this universe. What an immense profusion of beings, animated and organized, sensible and active! You admire this prodigious variety and fecundity. But inspect a little more narrowly these living existences, the only beings worth regarding. How hostile and destructive to each other! How insufficient all of them for their own happiness! How contemptible or odious to the spectator! The whole presents nothing but the idea of a blind nature, impregnated by a great vivifying principle, and pouring forth from her lap, without discernment or parental care, her maimed and abortive children!

Here the Manichaean[7] system occurs as a proper hypothesis to solve the difficulty . . . by giving a plausible account of the strange mixture of good and ill which appears in life. But if we consider, on the other hand, the perfect uniformity and agreement of the parts of the universe, we shall not discover in it any marks of the combat of a malevolent with a benevolent being. There is indeed an opposition of pains and pleasures in the feelings of sensible creatures; but are not all the operations of nature carried on by an opposition of principles, of hot and cold, moist and dry, light and heavy? The true conclusion is that the original source of all things is entirely indifferent to all these principles, and has no more regard to good above ill than to heat above cold, or to drought above moisture, or to light above heavy.

There may *four* hypotheses be framed concerning the first causes of the universe: that they are endowed with perfect goodness; that they have perfect malice; that they are opposite and have both goodness and malice; that they have neither goodness nor malice. Mixed phenomena can never prove the two former unmixed principles; and the uniformity and steadiness of general laws seem to oppose the third. The fourth, therefore, seems by far the most probable.

[Philo: The Existence of Moral Evil also Counts Against the Goodness of the Creator]

What I have said concerning natural evil will apply to moral with little or no variation; and we have no more reason to infer that the rectitude of the Supreme Being resembles human rectitude than that his benevolence resembles the human. Nay, it will be thought that we have still greater cause to exclude from him moral sentiments, such as we feel them, since moral evil, in the opinion of many, is much more predominant above moral good than natural evil above natural good.

But even though this should not be allowed, and though the virtue which is in mankind should be acknowledged much superior to the vice; yet, so long as there is any vice at all in

[7]A religious philosophy that held that the nature of the world is to be attributed to two finite forces, one good and the other evil. EDITOR'S NOTE.

the universe, it will very much puzzle you anthropomorphites how to account for it. You must assign a cause for it, without having recourse to the first cause. But as every effect must have a cause, and that cause another, you must either carry on the progression *in infinitum* or rest on that original principle, who is the ultimate cause of all things. . . .

Hold! hold! cried Demea: Whither does your imagination hurry you? I joined in alliance with you in order to prove the incomprehensible nature of the Divine Being, and refute the principles of Cleanthes, who would measure everything by human rule and standard. But I now find you running into all the topics of the greatest libertines and infidels, and betraying that holy cause which you seemingly espoused. Are you secretly, then, a more dangerous enemy than Cleanthes himself?

And are you so late in perceiving it? replied Cleanthes. Believe me, Demea, your friend Philo, from the beginning, has been amusing himself at both our expense; and it must be confessed that the injudicious reasoning of our vulgar theology has given him but too just a handle of ridicule. The total infirmity of human reason, the absolute incomprehensibility of the Divine Nature, the great and universal misery, and still greater wickedness of men—these are strange topics, surely, to be so fondly cherished by orthodox divines and doctors. In ages of stupidity and ignorance, indeed, these principles may safely be espoused; and perhaps no views of things are more proper to promote superstition than such as encourage the blind amazement, the diffidence, and melancholy of mankind. But at present . . .

Blame not so much, interposed Philo, the ignorance of these reverend gentlemen. They know how to change their style with the times. Formerly, it was a most popular theological topic to maintain that human life was vanity and misery, and to exaggerate all the ills and pains which are incident to men. But of late years, divines, we find, begin to retract this position and maintain, though still with some hesitation, that there are more goods than evils, more pleasures than pains, even in this life. When religion stood entirely upon temper and education, it was thought proper to encourage melancholy; as, indeed, mankind never have recourse to superior powers so readily as in that disposition. But as men have now learned to form principles and to draw consequences, it is necessary to change the batteries, and to make use of such arguments as will endure at least some scrutiny and examination. . . .

Thus Philo continued to the last his spirit of opposition, and his censure of established opinions. But I could observe that Demea did not at all relish the latter part of the discourse; and he took occasion soon after, on some pretence or other, to leave the company.[8]

DISCUSSION QUESTIONS

1. According to the contemporary philosopher Nelson Pike,[9] the existence of evil raises a problem for the belief in the existence of God only if one supposes that it is **logically impossible** to reconcile the existence of evil with the existence of God. Since a nonbeliever cannot show this, he cannot argue against the belief in God on the basis of the problem of evil, Pike argues. How do you think Hume would have replied to such a claim? How would you reply?

2. Consider the following claim (composed by the editor):

> While it is possible that all the evil that exists in this world is necessary for some greater good, it is equally possible that all the good that exists in this world is necessary for some greater evil. We tend to believe the first hypothesis rather than the second, not because it is more likely to be true, but because it is more comforting.

Critically discuss.

3. Which of the following positions on the problem of evil do you hold?

a. The existence of an all-powerful, all-knowing,

[8]This remark is made by Pamphilus, the narrator of the *Dialogues*. EDITOR'S NOTE.

[9]Nelson Pike, "Hume on Evil," *The Philosophical Review*, 72 (1963), 180-97.

and all-good deity is logically incompatible with the evil that exists in this world.

b. While it is possible that an all-powerful, all-knowing, and all-good deity has a good reason for allowing evil to exist, the magnitude of the evil that exists in this world makes this improbable.

c. There is some explanation for the evil that exists in this world that makes it compatible with the existence of an all-powerful, all-knowing, and all-good deity. Furthermore, such an explanation does not make the existence of such a deity unlikely. (What is this explanation?)

4. Do you think it is more likely that the world was created by a deity (or deities) of finite power, wisdom, and goodness than that it was created by an all-powerful, all-knowing, and all-good deity?

5. Is Hume correct that pain is not a necessary motive for action since conscious creatures could be motivated by a diminution of pleasure instead of driven by pain to actions that are necessary for their well-being. If what we now call "pain" were eliminated, would the diminution of pleasure then be considered a pain? If the intense pains that presently exist were eliminated, would the pleasures that remain be as pleasurable as they were before? Can experiences be described as pleasurable or painful in isolation or are these concepts comparative in nature? If they are comparative, is Hume's suggestion incoherent?

6. In reply to Hume's suggestion that God could intervene secretly and on special occasions to prevent exceptional and excessive evils, the theologian John Hick writes:

> . . . evils are exceptional only in relation to other evils which are routine. And therefore unless God eliminated all evils whatsoever there would always be relatively outstanding ones of which it would be said that He should have secretly prevented them. If, for example, divine providence had eliminated Hitler in his infancy we might now point instead to Mussolini as an example of a human monster whom God ought secretly to have excised from the human race; and if there were no Mussolini we should point to someone else. . .[10]

Critically comment.

7. If human beings were endowed with more industry and perseverance, as Hume's third complaint suggests, would this make the world any **better** or simply make people **more efficient** in achieving their good or bad ends?

8. Do you agree with Philo that, given the nature of our world, if it has a designer, he is most likely morally indifferent to us? If you disagree, how would you criticize his reasoning?

9. What point is Philo making when he claims of the evil that exists in this world:

> You must assign a cause for it, without having recourse to the first cause. But as every effect must have a cause, and that cause another; you must either carry on the progression **in infinitum** or rest on that original principle, who is the ultimate cause of all things.

How would you reply?

[10]John Hick, *Evil and the God of Love* (New York: Harper & Row, 1966), p. 328.

17. THEOLOGICAL ANSWERS TO THE PROBLEM OF EVIL

John Hick

JOHN HICK (1922–) is a well-known contemporary theologian who began his career as a Presbyterian minister in rural England. He has taught at Cornell University in New York, at Princeton Theological Seminary in New Jersey, as well as at Cambridge University and the University of

Birmingham in England. He presently teaches at the Claremont Graduate School in California. Unlike many defenders of the Christian faith, Hick has been very much influenced by contemporary analytic philosophy. In his many writings on philosophical issues relating to Christianity, Hick has tried to offer some rational account of Christian belief that can withstand contemporary philosophical canons of intelligibility and rationality.

In the following selection, which comes from the third edition (1983) of his **Philosophy of Religion**, Hick discusses the three main Christian responses to the problem of evil. According to one response, which is suggested by a literal reading of the Bible, evil is a result of the fall of human beings from an original state of blissful harmony. Another response, favored by a school of contemporary theologians, hinges on the denial of God's omnipotence.

According to the third response, which Hick embraces, moral evil (evil for which human beings are responsible) is due to the misuse of human free will. Such evil could be eliminated by God, Hick claims, only by turning us into puppets who do not have the free choice of going astray. The existence of non-moral[1] evil (evil for which human beings are not responsible), Hick claims, must be understood in terms of the Christian conception of the purpose of this world—"soul-building" (i.e., the development of moral character). God's purpose in the creation of the world was not "to construct a paradise whose inhabitants would experience a maximum of pleasure and a minimum of pain," but rather to construct a place of challenges and dangers in which human beings would be forced to grapple with difficult moral struggles and moral choices which are necessary for moral growth. A logically necessary condition for such a world, Hick argues, is the existence of non-moral evil. For example, it is non-moral evil which makes it possible for human beings to develop such moral qualities as sympathy, unselfishness and courage. As Hick sees it, the value of soul-building outweighs the non-moral evil that makes it possible. (Hick's view of the problem of evil is developed in detail in his book **Evil and the God of Love**, a book devoted entirely to the problem of evil.)

The Problem

For many people it is, more than anything else, the appalling depth and extent of human suffering, together with the selfishness and greed which produce so much of this, that makes the idea of a loving Creator seem implausible. . . .

Rather than attempt to define "evil" in terms of some theological theory (for example, as "that which is contrary to God's will"), it seems better to define it ostensively, by indicating that to which the word refers. It refers to physical pain, mental suffering, and moral wickedness. The last is one of the causes of the first two, for an enormous amount of human pain arises from mankind's inhumanity. This pain includes such major scourges as poverty, oppression and persecution, war, and all the injustice, indignity, and inequity that occur in human societies. Even disease is fostered, to an extent that has not yet been precisely determined by psychosomatic medicine, by emotional and moral factors seated both in the individual and in his or her social environment. However, although a great deal of pain and suffering are caused by human action, there is much more that arises from such

[1] Also called natural or physical evil in the literature. EDITOR'S NOTE.

natural causes as bacteria and earthquakes, storm, fire, lightning, flood, and drought.

As a challenge to theism, the problem of evil has traditionally been posed in the form of a dilemma: if God is perfectly loving, God must wish to abolish all evil; and if God is all-powerful, God must be able to abolish all evil. But evil exists; therefore God cannot be both omnipotent and perfectly loving.

One possible solution (offered, for example, by contemporary Christian Science) can be ruled out immediately so far as the traditional Judaic-Christian faith is concerned. To say that evil is an illusion of the human mind is impossible within a religion based upon the stark realism of the Bible. Its pages faithfully reflect the characteristic mixture of good and evil in human experience. They record every kind of sorrow and suffering, every mode of "man's inhumanity to man" and of our painfully insecure existence in the world. There is no attempt to regard evil as anything but dark, menacingly ugly, heart-rending, and crushing. There can be no doubt, then, that for biblical faith evil is entirely real and in no sense an illusion.

There are three main Christian responses to the problem of evil: the Augustinian response, hinging upon the concept of the fall of man from an original state of righteousness; the Irenaean response, hinging upon the idea of the gradual creation of a perfected humanity through life in a highly imperfect world; and the response of modern process theology, hinging upon the idea of a God who is not all-powerful and not in fact able to prevent the evils arising either in human beings or in the processes of nature.

Before examining each of these three responses, or theodicies,[2] we will discuss a position that is common to all of them.

The common ground is some form of what has come to be called the free-will defense, at least so far as the moral evil of human wickedness is concerned; for Christian thought has always seen moral evil as related to human freedom and responsibility. To be a person is to be a finite center of freedom, a (relatively) self-directing agent responsible for one's own decisions. This involves being free to act wrongly as well as rightly. There can therefore be no certainty in advance that a genuinely free moral agent will never choose amiss. Consequently, according to the strong form of free-will defense, the possibility of wrongdoing is logically inseparable from the creation of finite persons, and to say that God should not have created beings who might sin amounts to saying that God should not have created people.

This thesis has been challenged in some recent philosophical discussions of the problem of evil, in which it is claimed that no contradiction is involved in saying that God might have made people who would be genuinely free but who could at the same time be guaranteed always to act rightly. To quote from one of these discussions:

> If there is no logical impossibility in a man's freely choosing the good on one, or on several occasions, there cannot be a logical impossibility in his freely choosing the good on every occasion. God was not, then, faced with a choice between making innocent automata and making beings who, in acting freely, would sometimes go wrong: there was open to him the obviously better possibility of making beings who would act freely but always go right. Clearly, his failure to avail himself of this possibility is inconsistent with his being both omnipotent and wholly good.

This argument has considerable power. A modified form of free-will defense has, however, been suggested in response to it. If by free actions we mean actions that are not externally compelled but flow from the nature of agents as they react to the circumstances in which they find themselves, then there is indeed no contradiction between our being free and our actions' being "caused" (by our own God-given

[2]"Theodicy," formed (by Leibniz) from the Greek *theos*, god, and *dike*, righteous, is a technical term for attempts to solve the theological problem of evil. AUTHOR'S NOTE.

nature) and thus being in principle predictable. However, it is suggested, there is a contradiction in saying that *God* is the cause of our acting as we do *and* that we are free beings specifically in relation to God. The contradiction is between holding that God has so made us that we shall of necessity act in a certain way, and that we are genuinely independent persons *in relation to God*. If all our thoughts and actions are divinely predestined, then however free and responsible we may seem to ourselves to be, we are not free and responsible in the sight of God but must instead be God's puppets. Such "freedom" would be comparable to that of patients acting out a series of posthypnotic suggestions: they appear to themselves to be free, but their volitions have actually been predetermined by the will of the hypnotist, in relation to whom the patients are therefore not genuinely free agents. Thus, it is suggested, while God *could* have created such beings, there would have been no point in doing so—at least not if God is seeking to create sons and daughters rather than human puppets.

The Augustinian Theodicy

The main traditional Christian response to the problem of evil was first formulated by St. Augustine (354–430 A.D.) and has constituted the majority report of the Christian mind through the centuries, although it has been much criticized in recent times. It includes both philosophical and theological strands. The main philosophical position is the idea of the negative or privative nature of evil. Augustine holds firmly to the Hebrew-Christian conviction that the universe is *good*—that is to say, it is the creation of a good God for a good purpose. There are, according to Augustine, higher and lower, greater and lesser goods in immense abundance and variety; however, everything that has being is good in its own way and degree, except insofar as it has become spoiled or corrupted. Evil—whether it be an evil will, an instance of pain, or some disorder or decay in nature—has therefore not been set there by God but represents the going wrong of something that is inherently good. Augustine points to blindness as an example. Blindness is not a "thing." The only thing involved is the eye, which is in itself good; the evil of blindness consists of the lack of a proper functioning of the eye. Generalizing the principle, Augustine holds that evil always consists of the malfunctioning of something that is in itself good.

As it originally came forth from the hand of God, then, the universe was a perfect harmony expressing the creative divine intention. It was a graded hierarchy of higher and lower forms of being, each good in its own place. How, then, did evil come about? It came about initially in those levels of the universe that involve free will: the levels of the angels and of human beings. Some of the angels turned from the supreme Good, which is God, to lesser goods, thereby rebelling against their creator; they in turn tempted the first man and woman to fall. This fall of angelic and human beings was the origin of moral evil or sin. The natural evils of disease, of "nature red in tooth and claw," and of earthquake, storm, and so on are the penal consequences of sin, for humanity was intended to be lord of the earth, and this human defection has set all nature awry. Thus Augustine could say, "All evil is either sin or the punishment for sin."

The Augustinian theodicy adds that at the end of history there will come the judgment, when many will enter into eternal life and many others (who in their freedom have rejected God's offer of salvation) into eternal torment. . . .

The Augustinian theodicy fulfills the intention lying behind it, which is to clear the creator of any responsibility for the existence of evil by loading that responsibility without remainder upon the creature. Evil stems from the culpable misuse of creaturely freedom in a tragic act, of cosmic significance, in the prehistory of the human race—an act that was prefigured in the heavenly realms by the incomprehensible fall of some of the angels, the chief of whom is now Satan, God's Enemy. . . .

The basic criticism [of this view] is directed at the idea that a universe which God has created with absolute power, so as to be exactly as God wishes it to be, containing no evil of any kind, has nevertheless gone wrong. It is true that the free creatures who are part of it are free to fall. However, since they are finitely perfect, without any taint or trace of evil in them, and since they dwell in a finitely perfect environment, they will never in fact fall into sin. Thus, it is said, the very idea of a perfect creation's going wrong spontaneously and without cause is a self-contradiction. . . .

The basic criticism, then, is that a flawless creation would never go wrong and that if the creation does in fact go wrong the ultimate responsibility for this must be with its creator: for "This is where the buck stops"!

This criticism agrees with . . . [the] contention that it was logically possible for God to have created free beings who would never in fact fall. As we shall see in the next section, the alternative Irenaean theodicy takes up the further thought that although God *could* have created beings who were from the beginning finitely perfect, God has not in fact done so because such beings would never be able to become free and responsible sons and daughters of God.

A second criticism, made in the light of modern knowledge, is that we cannot today realistically think of the human species as having been once morally and spiritually perfect and then falling from that state into the chronic self-centeredness which is the human condition as we now know it. All the evidence suggests that humanity gradually emerged out of lower forms of life with a very limited moral awareness and with very crude religious conceptions. Again, it is no longer possible to regard the natural evils of disease, earthquakes, and the like as consequences of the fall of humanity, for we now know that they existed long before human beings came upon the scene. Life preyed upon life, and there were storms and earthquakes as well as disease (signs of arthritis have been found in the bones of some prehistoric animals) during the hundreds of millions of years before *homo sapiens* emerged. . . .

The Irenaean Theodicy

Even from before the time of Augustine another response to the problem of evil had already been present within the developing Christian tradition. This has its basis in the thought of the early Greek-speaking Fathers of the Church, perhaps the most important of whom was St. Irenaeus (*c.* 130–*c.* 202 A.D.). He distinguished two stages of the creation of the human race. In the first stage human beings were brought into existence as intelligent animals endowed with the capacity for immense moral and spiritual development. They were not the perfect pre-fallen Adam and Eve of the Augustinian tradition, but immature creatures, at the beginning of a long process of growth. In the second stage of their creation, which is now taking place, they are gradually being transformed through their own free responses from human animals into "children of God". . . .

If, going beyond Irenaeus himself, we ask why humans should have been initially created as immature and imperfect beings rather than as a race of perfect creatures, the answer centers upon the positive value of human freedom. Two mutually supporting considerations are suggested. One depends upon the intuitive judgment that a human goodness that has come about through the making of free and responsible moral choices, in situations of real difficulty and temptation, is intrinisically more valuable . . . than a goodness that has been created ready-made, without the free participation of the human agent. This intuition points to the creation of the human race, not in a state of perfection, but in a state of imperfection from which it is nevertheless possible to move through moral struggle toward eventual completed humanization.

The other consideration is that if men and women had been initially created in the direct presence of God, who is infinite in life and power, goodness and knowledge, they would have had no genuine freedom in relation to their Maker. In order to be fully personal and therefore morally free beings, they have accordingly (it is suggested) been created at a distance from God—not a spatial but an epistemic distance, a distance in the dimension of knowledge. They are formed within and as part of an autonomous universe within which God is not overwhelmingly evident but in which God may become known by the free interpretative response of faith. . . . Thus the human situation is one of tension between the natural selfishness arising from our instinct for survival, and the calls of both morality and religion to transcend our self-centeredness. Whereas the Augustinian theology sees our perfection as lying in the distant past, in an original state long since forfeited by the primordial calamity of the fall, the Irenaean type of theology sees our perfection as lying before us in the future, at the end of a lengthy and arduous process of further creation through time.

Thus the answer of the Irenaean theodicy to the question of the origin of moral evil is that it is a necessary condition of the creation of humanity at an epistemic distance from God, in a state in which one has a genuine freedom in relation to one's Maker and can freely develop, in response to God's noncoercive presence, toward one's own fulfillment as a child of God.

We may now turn to the problem of pain and suffering. Even though the bulk of actual human pain is traceable, as a sole or part cause, to misused human freedom, there remain other sources of pain that are entirely independent of the human will—for example, bacteria, earthquake, hurricane, storm, flood, drought, and blight. In practice it is often impossible to trace a boundary between the suffering that results from human wickedness and folly and that which befalls humanity from without; both are inextricably mingled in human experience. For our present purpose, however, it is important to note that the latter category does exist and that it seems to be built into the very structure of our world. In response to it, theodicy, if it is wisely conducted, follows a negative path. It is not possible to show positively that each item of human pain serves God's purpose of good; on the other hand, it does seem possible to show that the divine purpose, at least as it is understood in the Irenaean theology, could not be forwarded in a world that was designed as a permanent hedonistic paradise.[3]

An essential premise of this argument concerns the nature of the divine purpose in creating the world. The skeptic's normal assumption is that humanity is to be viewed as a completed creation and that God's purpose in making the world was to provide a suitable dwelling place for this fully formed creature. Since God is good and loving, the environment that God creates for human life will naturally be as pleasant and as comfortable as possible. The problem is essentially similar to that of someone who builds a cage for a pet animal. Since our world in fact contains sources of pain, hardship, and danger of innumerable kinds, the conclusion follows that this world cannot have been created by a perfectly benevolent and all-powerful deity.

According to the Irenaean theodicy, however, God's purpose was not to construct a paradise whose inhabitants would experience a maximum of pleasure and a minimum of pain. The world is seen, instead, as a place of "soul-making" or person-making in which free beings, grappling with the tasks and challenges of their existence in a common environment, may become

[3]From the Greek *hedone*, pleasure. AUTHOR'S NOTE.

"children of God" and "heirs of eternal life." Our world, with all its rough edges, is the sphere in which this second and harder state of the creative process is taking place.

This conception of the world (whether or not set in Irenaeus's theological framework) can be supported by the method of "counterfactual hypothesis." Suppose that, contrary to fact, this world were a paradise from which all possibility of pain and suffering were excluded. The consequences would be very far-reaching. For example, no one could ever injure anyone else: the murderer's knife would turn to paper or the bullets to thin air; the bank safe, robbed of a million dollars, would miraculously become filled with another million dollars; fraud, deceit, conspiracy, and treason would somehow leave the fabric of society undamaged. No one would ever be injured by accident: the mountain climber, steeplejack, or playing child falling from a height would float unharmed to the ground; the reckless driver would never meet with disaster. There would be no need to work, since no harm could result from avoiding work; there would be no call to be concerned for others in time of need or danger, for in such a world there could be no real needs or dangers.

To make possible this continual series of individual adjustments, nature would have to work by "special providences" instead of running according to general laws that we must learn to respect on penalty of pain or death. The laws of nature would have to be extremely flexible: sometimes gravity would operate, sometimes not; sometimes an object would be hard and solid, sometimes soft. There could be no sciences, for there would be no enduring world structure to investigate. In eliminating the problems and hardships of an objective environment with its own laws, life would become like a dream in which, delightfully but aimlessly, we would float and drift at ease.

One can at least begin to imagine such a world—and it is evident that in it our present ethical concepts would have no meaning. If, for example, the notion of harming someone is an essential element in the concept of a wrong action, in a hedonistic paradise there could be no wrong actions—nor therefore any right actions in distinction from wrong. Courage and fortitude would have no point in an environment in which there is, by definition, no danger or difficulty. Generosity, kindness, the *agape*[4] aspect of love, prudence, unselfishness, and other ethical notions that presuppose life in an objective environment could not even be formed. Consequently, such a world, however well it might promote pleasure, would be very ill adapted for the development of the moral qualities of human personality. In relation to this purpose it might well be the worst of all possible worlds!

It would seem, then, that an environment intended to make possible the growth in free beings of the finest characteristics of personal life must have a good deal in common with our present world. It must operate according to general and dependable laws, and it must present real dangers, difficulties, problems, obstacles, and possibilities of pain, failure, sorrow, frustration, and defeat. If it did not contain the particular trials and perils that—subtracting the considerable human contribution—our world contains, it would have to contain others instead.

To realize this fact is not, by any means, to be in possession of a detailed theodicy. However, it is to understand that this world, with all its "heartaches and the thousand natural shocks that flesh is heir to," an environment so manifestly not designed for the maximization of human pleasure and the minimization of human pain, may nevertheless be rather well adapted to the quite different purpose of "soul making."

And so the Irenaean answer to the question, Why natural evil? is that only a world that has this general character could constitute an effec-

[4]Altruistic love. EDITOR'S NOTE.

tive environment for the second stage (or the beginning of the second stage) of God's creative work, whereby human animals are being gradually transformed through their own free responses into "children of God."

At this point, the Irenaean theodicy points forward in three ways to the subject of life after death. . . .

First, although there are many striking instances of good being triumphantly brought out of evil through a person's reaction to it, there are many other cases in which the opposite has happened. Sometimes obstacles breed strength of character, dangers evoke courage and unselfishness, and calamities produce patience and moral steadfastness. On the other hand, sometimes they lead to resentment, fear, grasping selfishness, and disintegration of character. Therefore, it would seem that any divine purpose of soul making that is at work in earthly history must continue beyond this life if it is ever to achieve more than a partial and fragmentary success.

Second, if we ask the ultimate question—whether the business of person making is worth all the toil and sorrow of human life—the answer must be in terms of a future good great enough to justify all that has happened on the way to it. Its claim is that the endless enjoyment of that fullness of life and joy, beyond our present imaginations, which is the eventual fulfillment of God's love toward us, will render manifestly worthwhile all the pain and travail of the long journey of human life toward it, both in this world and perhaps in other worlds as well.

Third, not only does a theodicy of the Irenaean type require a positive doctrine of life after death but, insofar as the theodicy is to be complete, it also requires that *all* human beings shall in the end attain the heavenly state. . . .

[EDITOR'S NOTE: Hick elaborates his own version of the Irenaean theodicy in his book *Evil and the God of Love*. In this book, Hick is greatly troubled by the apparently excessive suffering in this world, suffering that seems to serve no useful purpose. Accepting the hypothesis of a divine purpose of soul-making, which cannot be achieved in a purely hedonistic paradise, Hick questions the need for the extreme and crushing evils that this world contains. For example, he poignantly asks:

> When a child dies of cerebral meningitis, his little personality undeveloped and his life unfulfilled, leaving only an unquenchable aching void in his parents' lives; or when a charming, lively, and intelligent woman suffers from a shrinking of the brain which destroys her personality and leaves her in an asylum, barely able to recognize her nearest relatives, until death comes in middle life as a baneful blessing . . . when such things happen we can see no gain to the soul, whether of the victim or of others, but on the contrary only a ruthless destructive process which is inimical to human values. It seems as though "As flies to wanton boys, are we to the gods, They kill us for their sport." (p. 330)

The intractable problem, as Hick sees it, is to find a justification for the immense amount of apparently *pointless* and *undeserved* suffering. Unable to find a satisfactory explanation for this fact, Hick, like the voice from the whirlwind in the Biblical Book of Job, turns to the notion of mystery, claiming that, perhaps, "the very mysteriousness of this life is an important aspect of its character as a sphere of soul-making." (p. 331) Hick tests this possibility by imagining a world which, although not entirely free from pain and suffering, does not contain the haphazard and apparently pointless pain and suffering of this world. Instead, human suffering would always be perceived to be justly deserved or else to serve the constructive purpose of soul-making. In such a world, Hick writes:

> . . . human misery would not evoke deep personal sympathy or call forth organized relief and sacrificial help and service. For it is presupposed in these compassionate reactions both that the suffering is not deserved and that it is *bad* for the sufferer. . . . It seems, then, that in a world that is to be the scene of compassionate love and self-giving for others, suffering must fall upon mankind with something of the haphazardness and inequity that we now experience. (p. 332)

In addition, Hick contends that if there were a clear

apportioning of pleasure and pain with desert, people would no longer have the opportunity to do the right, simply because it is right, without any expectation of reward. Nevertheless, as Hick's appeal to mystery indicates, such considerations do not eradicate the stark irrationality and lack of moral meaning of so much of the suffering that exists in this world. Acutely aware of this fact, Hick looks to an afterlife which transforms evil into good. It is only if such an afterlife exists, Hick claims, that a satisfactory justification can be given for the misery of this world. Unlike the traditional Augustinian theodicy which envisions an eternal hell for sinners, Hick affirms in faith that "there will in the final accounting be no personal life that is unperfected and no suffering that has not eventually become a phase in the fulfillment of God's good purpose."

The vision of the ultimate end of life that Hick presents is that of the enjoyment of an unending common good which will be seen by its participants as justifying all that has been endured to achieve it. As Hick sees it, such a view is the only one compatible with a belief in a morally perfect and omnipotent deity. In particular, he claims that the idea of hell is incompatible with the existence of such a deity. Hick also rejects the view, accepted by some theologians, of the divine annihilation of the unredeemed, for this too would suggest that God has failed in the case of all those souls whose fate is extinction. Can we believe, then, that God will motivate (persuade) all the free creatures that he has created to respond to him, without robbing any of them of their free will? This is the key question, as Hick sees it. Believing that human freedom precludes foreknowledge (even by God) of human actions, Hick has faith that given God's unceasing desire to actively work for the salvation of all human beings, he will never abandon any as irredeemably evil. Even though human freedom makes it impossible to know for sure that God will ultimately win over all, it seems "a practical certainty," Hick contends, that the infinite love and resourcefulness of God will achieve this objective.]

Process Theodicy

Process theology is a modern development in which a number of Christian theologians have adopted as their metaphysical framework the philosophy of A. N. Whitehead (1861–1947). For a number of reasons, including the fact of evil in the world, process theology holds that God cannot be unlimited in power but interacts with the process of the universe, which God has not created but is nevertheless able to influence. . . .

. . . God is subject to the limitations imposed by the basic laws of the universe, for God has not created the universe *ex nihilo*,[5] thereby establishing its structure, but rather the universe is an uncreated process which includes the deity. . . . [The universe operates according to principles that] fall outside the scope even of the divine will. . . . [As one process theologian puts it,] "God does not refrain from controlling the creatures simply because it is better for God to use persuasion, but because it is necessarily the case that God cannot completely control the creatures." . . .[6]

Such a theodicy appeals in two main ways. One is that it avoids the traditional problem arising from the belief in divine omnipotence. God is not the all-powerful creator of the universe, responsible for its character, but is a part—though a uniquely basic part—of the universe itself, unable either to vary its fundamental structure or to intervene directly in its changing details. Thus God does not need to be justified for permitting evil, since it is not within God's power to prevent it. . . . The other appeal consists of the stirring summons to engage on God's side in the never-ending struggle against the evils of an intractable world. This was the moral appeal of earlier forms of belief in a finite God who claims our support in the ongoing battle of light against darkness—as in

[5]Out of nothing. EDITOR'S NOTE.

[6]Hick goes on to summarize the metaphysics of process theology, which sees evil as an inherent part of a universal creative process. According to this view, God, within the limitations of his power, acts to maximize the harmony and intensity of experience within the universe—accepting the evil that this process requires, an evil that is justified by the greater good that it brings into existence. EDITOR'S NOTE.

ancient Zoroastrianism and Manichaeism, or (as a tentative hypothesis) in the thought of John Stuart Mill, who wrote:

> A creed like this . . . allows it to be believed that all the mass of evil which exists was undesigned by, and exists not by the appointment of, but in spite of the Being whom we are called upon to worship. A virtuous human being assumes in this theory the exalted character of a fellow-labourer with the Highest, a fellow combatant in the great strife. . . .

However, despite its appeal, the process theodicy has been severely criticized.

One basic claim is that it involves a morally and religiously unacceptable elitism. In all ages the majority of people have lived in hunger or the threat and fear of hunger—often severely undernourished, subject to crippling injuries and debilitating diseases, so that only the fittest could survive infancy—and they have dwelt under conditions of oppression or slavery and in a constant state of insecurity and anxiety. . . . The process theodicy does not suggest that it is their own individual fault that hundreds of millions of human beings have been born into and have had to endure this situation. The high intensity of physical and mental suffering that is possible at the human level of experience is just part of the actual process of the universe. What makes it acceptable to God, according to the process theodicy, is the fact that the same complex process that has produced all this suffering has also produced the cream of the human species. For each one such "marvelous human being," perhaps tens of thousands of others have existed without any significant degree of personal freedom and without any opportunity for intellectual, moral, aesthetic, or spiritual development, their lives spent in a desperate and degrading struggle to survive. But God is apparently content that this great mass of human suffering has been endured and this great mass of human potentiality has been undeveloped because, as part of the same world process, the elite have fulfilled in themselves some of the finer possibilities of human existence. . . .

Clearly, it can be questioned whether such a God is to be equated with the God of the New Testament, understood as the Creator who values all human creatures with a universal and impartial love. Clearly, again, this is far from being the God of contemporary liberation theology, who is the God of the poor and the oppressed, the enslaved and all against whom the structures of human society discriminate. These individuals are deprived of the opportunity of developing the moral and spiritual, intellectual and aesthetic potentialities of their nature. The God of the process theodicy is the God of the elite, of the great and successful among mankind. He is apparently the God of saints rather than of sinners; of geniuses rather than of the dull and retarded and mentally defective; of the cream of humanity rather than of the anonymous millions who have been driven to self-seeking, violence, greed, and deceit, in a desperate struggle to survive, or of those millions who have been crippled by malnutrition and have suffered and died under oppression and exploitation, plague and famine, flood and earthquake, or again of those—perhaps numbering about half the sum of human births—who have perished in infancy. . . .

. . . God may indeed . . . find the total spectacle of human life through the ages to be good on balance; for in the total divine experience the sufferings of those who suffer, and the inadequacies of those whose human potential remains undeveloped, are overbalanced by the happiness and achievements of the fortunate. However, the starving and the oppressed, the victims of Auschwitz, the human wrecks who are irreparably brain-damaged or mind-damaged, and those others who have loved and agonized over them, can hardly be expected to share the process God's point of view or to regard such a God as worthy of their worship and praise. It is not they but others who benefit from the bracing doctrine, reminiscent of nineteenth-century *laissez faire* capitalist theory, that though the weak may go to the wall, the system as a whole is good because it also produces those who are spiritually and culturally rich.

The situation would, of course, be transformed if a process theodicy were able to affirm [which it does not] the eventual successful completion of the creative process in a future heavenly fulfillment in which all are eventually to participate. Then the tragedy of human life, though real, would not be ultimate. . . .

DISCUSSION QUESTIONS

1. What is the Augustinian answer to the problem of evil? Why does Hick find this answer inadequate? Do you agree?

2. What answer do process theologians give to the problem of evil? Why does Hick find this answer inadequate? Do you agree? Why?

3. What is the reason Hick gives for the logical impossibility of God's creating free human beings, while knowing that not one of them will ever choose to misuse that freedom? Does such a view entail that it is impossible for God to know beforehand what a free being will choose? If so, must we reject the possibility of prophecy? Do you believe that human free will is incompatible with God's foreknowledge of human actions? Why?

4. Even if God did not know beforehand what Hitler would do, why did he not intervene to stop Hitler **after** he embarked on his program of mass genocidal extermination and it became obvious that there was no reasonable likelihood that he would repent?

5. Assuming that God knows beforehand what free creatures will choose, consider the following claim made by Bertrand Russell:

> If I were going to beget a child knowing that the child was going to be a homicidal maniac, I should be responsible for his crimes. If God knew in advance the sins of which man would be guilty, he was clearly responsible for all the consequences of those sins when he decided to create man.

Do you agree with Russell? If God does know beforehand that some free creatures he creates, whether human beings or angels, will choose to misuse their free will, why does he choose to create them instead of using his omnipotent power to create other human beings or angels who will not misuse their free will? (Consider, in particular, Satan, the alleged fallen angel.)

6. Some Christian theologians have contended that those who obtain the supreme happiness of heaven exercise freedom of choice in their heavenly condition but, given the conditions that obtain in heaven, choose never to misuse it? If this is possible in heaven, why is it not possible here on earth?

7. Assuming that "angels" exist, do you think Hick would say that they have free will? If not, what is wrong with human beings not having free will? Are we better than the angels? If, on the other hand, angels do have free will, would Hick have to be committed to the view that it is possible that they too could misuse their free will **as much as** human beings do? If not, why? If so, is there a good reason for saying that this is, nevertheless, improbable? If so, could God make it less probable that human beings would misuse their free will as much as they do now? If so, should he? Defend your position.

8. Since human free will is limited in many respects (e.g., we cannot fly on our own accord or make ourselves disappear and reappear at another place in the world at will), would it not be better if human beings were created without the power to kill other human beings, and, consequently, without the power to prematurely cut short the soul building of other free creatures? How do you think Hick would reply? What do you think?

9. If God is all-powerful, could he have created us with the moral traits that he desires without making us go through any suffering? If he had this power, why did he not use it? How do you think Hick would reply? What do you think?

10. Do you think that Hick believes that there are laws of nature in heaven? If so, will there be suffering in heaven? If not, would life in heaven "become like a dream in which, delightfully but aimlessly, we would float and drift at ease"? In what

respect, if any, does Hick believe that suffering in this world is, at least in part, entailed by the existence of laws of nature? Do you agree? Why, or why not?

11. If such moral traits as unselfishness and courage have place only in a world where there is non-moral evil, will there be non-moral evil in heaven? If not, what is the point of developing moral traits that will have no use in heaven? And if they have no use in heaven, can we be sure that they will not disappear eventually from lack of use?

12. Even if the value of soul-building outweighs the disvalue of the evil necessary for its realization, does "the end (morally) justify the means" in this case? (Recall Ivan's question to Alyosha at the end of our selection from Dostoevsky's **The Brothers Karamazov.**)

13. If, as Hick suggests (in **Evil and the God of Love**), there is a need for unmerited suffering to call forth feelings of compassion and self-sacrifice, would not moral evil suffice? Does it seem plausible to say that non-moral evil is also required?

14. Consider the following alleged paradox, offered by the atheistic philosopher H.J. McCloskey, in the view that physical evil is necessary for the creation of the moral virtues:

> We either have obligations to lessen physical evil or we have not. If we have obligations to lessen physical evil then we are thereby reducing the total good in the universe. If, on the other hand, our obligation is to increase the total good in the universe it is our duty to prevent the reduction of physical evil and possibly even to increase the total amount of physical evil. Theists usually hold that we are obliged to reduce the physical evil in the universe; but in maintaining this, the theist is . . . maintaining that it is his duty to reduce the total amount of real good in the universe, and thereby to make the universe worse. Conversely, if by eliminating the physical evil he is not making the universe worse, then that amount of evil which he eliminates was unnecessary. . . .
>
> . . . [the theist's claim that physical evil plus the moral good it produces is better than physical good and its moral goods] is seen to imply that war plus courage plus the many other moral virtues war brings into play are better than peace and its virtues; that famine and its moral virtues are better than plenty; that disease and its moral virtues are better than health. Some Christians in the past, in consistency with this mode of reasoning, opposed the use of anesthetics to leave scope for the virtues of endurance and courage, and they opposed state aid to the sick and needy to leave scope for the virtues of charity and sympathy. . . .[7]

In your own words, what is McCloskey's point? What do you think Hick would say in reply? What do you think?

15. What do you think of Hick's appeal (in **Evil and the God of Love**) to mystery and his endorsement of the view that it may be "fit that there should be . . . a doubtful and cloudy state of things, for the better exercise of virtue and faith"?

16. If, as Hick claims (in **Evil and the God of Love**) God will "never cease to desire and actively work for the salvation of each created person," would it not be best for God to show his hand more directly to nonbelievers (e.g., through miracles and special revelations)?

17. Hick's account of the problem of evil is confined to the problem of human suffering. What plausible reason, if any, can a believer in God give for the suffering of animals?

18. Could a believer in an all-powerful, all-knowing, and all-evil deity give as plausible an account of good as Hick gives of evil?

[7]H.J. McCloskey, "God and Evil," in *God and Evil,* ed. Nelson Pike (Englewood Cliffs, N.J.: Prentice-Hall, 1964), p. 75.

18. A DEFENSE OF FAITH IN GOD WITHOUT EVIDENCE

William James

(For a biographical sketch of William James, see Selection #11.)

The following selection is an edited version of William James' classic defense of religious faith, "The Will to Believe." Assuming that the existence of God cannot be conclusively proved or made probable, James argues that it is reasonable, nevertheless, to accept the existence of God on faith. As James sees it, since belief in God has a great practical impact upon the meaning of one's life and the way one lives, one ought to consider these practical consequences in determining the reasonableness of such a belief.

In focusing upon the practical benefits of belief in God, James follows in the footsteps of the famous seventeenth-century mathematician and philosopher Blaise Pascal. Yet there are important differences in their positions. As Pascal saw it, given the intellectual uncertainty of God's existence, we cannot appeal to reason to decide whether to believe or to disbelieve. Nevertheless, we must do one or the other. Consider this choice then as a gamble. Do we gamble on God or against him? If we gamble on him and he exists, we obtain the eternal and incomparable bliss of heaven. If we gamble on him and he does not exist, at most we lose the much more limited good of the satisfaction of human desires that our religion condemns. On the other hand, if we gamble against him, we risk the possibility of eternal damnation in hell, should our gamble turn out to be mistaken; and all we stand to gain, should our gamble turn out to be right, is the limited good of the satisfaction of certain human desires. Clearly then, it would be the height of foolishness not to gamble on God. This argument is known as "Pascal's Wager."

James' defense of faith is, however, not at all anchored, as Pascal's is, to the belief that God would exclude nonbelievers from heaven. Such a belief had no plausibility at all for James. The reward that awaits those who believe in God, as James saw it, is the reward of a more meaningful life here on earth and, perhaps, the chance of "encountering God" here on earth. Also unlike Pascal (who saw Catholicism as the only religious choice), James' defense of religious faith is not anchored to any specific religion nor even to belief in the Judeo-Christian God. As the reader will note, James' defense of faith in what he calls "the religious hypothesis" is broader than a defense of faith in God. Clearly, however, "the religious hypothesis" James focuses upon in "The Will to Believe" is the belief in God. But, like his father, James sees such a belief as a **personal** commitment that does not have to be embedded within the dogmas and rituals of a specific religion. (James' father studied for the Presbyterian ministry at Princeton Theological Seminary but left, dissatisfied with "the lack of spirituality in professional religion.")

The Will to Believe

. . . I have brought with me to-night something like a sermon on justification by faith to read to you,—I mean an essay in justification *of* faith, a defence of our right to adopt a believing attitude in religious matters, in spite of the fact that our merely logical intellect may not have been coerced. 'The Will to Believe,' accordingly, is the title of my paper.

I have long defended to my own students the lawfulness of voluntary adopted faith; but as soon as they have got well imbued with the logical spirit, they have as a rule refused to admit my contention to be lawful philosophically, even though in point of fact they were personally all the time chock-full of some faith or other themselves. I am all the while, however, so profoundly convinced that my own position is correct, that your invitation has seemed to me a good occasion to make my statements more clear. Perhaps your minds will be more open than those with which I have hitherto had to deal. I will be as little technical as I can, though I must begin by setting up some technical distinctions that will help us in the end.

[The Notion of a "Genuine Option"]

Let us give the name of *hypothesis* to anything that may be proposed to our belief; and just as the electricians speak of live and dead wires, let us speak of any hypothesis as either *live* or *dead*. A live hypothesis is one which appeals as a real possibility to him to whom it is proposed. If I ask you to believe in the Mahdi,[1] the notion makes no electric connection with your nature,—it refuses to scintillate with any credibility at all. As an hypothesis it is completely dead. To an Arab, however (even if he be not one of the Mahdi's followers), the hypothesis is among the mind's possibilities: it is alive. This shows that deadness and liveness in an hypothesis are not intrinsic properties, but relations to the individual thinker. They are measured by his willingness to act. The maximum of liveness in an hypothesis means willingness to act irrevocably. Practically, that means belief; but there is some believing tendency wherever there is willingness to act at all.

Next, let us call the decision between two hypotheses an *option*. Options may be of several kinds. They may be—1, *living* or *dead*; 2, *forced* or *avoidable*; 3, *momentous* or *trivial*; and for our purposes we may call an option a *genuine* option when it is of the forced, living, and momentous kind.

1. A living option is one in which both hypotheses are live ones. If I say to you: "Be a theosophist[2] or be a Mohammedan," it is probably a dead option, because for you neither hypothesis is likely to be alive. But if I say: "Be an agnostic or be a Christian," it is otherwise: trained as you are, each hypothesis makes some appeal, however small, to your belief.

2. Next, if I say to you: "Choose between going out with your umbrella or without it," I do not offer you a genuine option, for it is not forced. You can easily avoid it by not going out at all. Similarly, if I say, "Either love me or hate me," "Either call my theory true or call it false," your option is avoidable. You may remain indifferent to me, neither loving nor hating, and you may decline to offer any judgment as to my theory. But if I say "Either accept this truth or go without it," I put on you a forced option, for there is no standing place outside of the alternative. Every dilemma based on a complete logical disjunction, with no possibility of not choosing, is an option of this forced kind.

3. Finally, if I were Dr. Nansen and proposed to

Source: From *The Will to Believe.* Published in *The New World,* June, 1896. Originally an address to the Philosophical Clubs of Yale and Brown Universities.

[1] "The guided one," a title taken by Mohammed Ahmed, who captured Khartoum in 1885. EDITOR'S NOTE.

[2] Various religious systems which center upon the belief in a direct mystical encounter with God. EDITOR'S NOTE.

you to join my North Pole expedition, your option would be momentous; for this would probably be your only similar opportunity, and your choice now would either exclude you from the North Pole sort of immortality altogether or put at least the chance of it into your hands. He who refuses to embrace a unique opportunity loses the prize as surely as if he tried and failed. *Per contra*, the option is trivial when the opportunity is not unique, when the stake is insignificant, or when the decision is reversible if it later prove unwise. Such trivial options abound in the scientific life. A chemist finds an hypothesis live enough to spend a year in its verification; he believes in it to that extent. But if his experiments prove inconclusive either way, he is quit for his loss of time, no vital harm being done.

It will facilitate our discussion if we keep all these distinctions well in mind. . . .

In Pascal's *Thoughts* there is a celebrated passage known in literature as Pascal's wager. In it he tries to force us into Christianity by reasoning as if our concern with truth resembled our concern with the stakes in a game of chance. Translated freely his words are these; You must either believe or not believe that God is—which will you do? Your human reason cannot say. A game is going on between you and the nature of things which at the day of judgment will bring out either heads or tails. Weigh what your gains and your losses would be if you should stake all you have on heads, or God's existence; if you win in such case, you gain eternal beatitude; if you lose, you lose nothing at all. If there were an infinity of chances, and only one for God in this wager, still you ought to stake your all on God for though you surely risk a finite loss by this procedure, any finite loss is reasonable, even a certain one is reasonable, if there is but the possibility of infinite gain. Go then, and take holy water, and have masses said; belief will come and stupefy your scruples. . . .

The thesis I defend is, briefly stated, this: *Our passional nature not only lawfully may, but must, decide an option between propositions, whenever it is a genuine option that cannot by its nature be decided on intellectual grounds; for to say, under such circumstances, "Do not decide, but leave the question open," is itself a passional decision,—just like deciding yes or no,—and is attended with the same risk of losing the truth.* The thesis thus abstractly expressed will, I trust, soon become quite clear. . . .

[The Will to Believe and Factual Questions]

And now, let us go straight at our question. I have said, and now repeat it, that not only as a matter of fact do we find our passional nature influencing us in our opinions, but that there are some options between opinions in which this influence must be regarded both as an inevitable and as a lawful determinant of our choice.

I fear here that some of you my hearers will begin to scent danger, and lend an inhospitable ear. Two first steps of passion you have indeed had to admit as necessary—we must think so as to avoid dupery, and we must think so as to gain truth; but the surest path to those ideal consummations, you will probably consider, is from now onwards to take no further passional step.

Well, of course, I agree as far as the facts will allow. Wherever the option between losing truth and gaining it is not momentous, we can throw the chance of *gaining truth* away, and at any rate save ourselves from any chance of *believing falsehood*, by not making up our minds at all till objective evidence has come. In scientific questions, this is almost always the case; and even in human affairs in general, the need of acting is seldom so urgent that a false belief to act on is better than no belief at all. Law courts, indeed, have to decide on the best evidence attainable for the moment, because a judge's duty is to make law as well as to ascertain it. . . . But in our dealings with objective nature we obviously are recorders, not makers, of the truth; and decisions for the mere sake of deciding promptly and getting on to the next business would be wholly out of place. Throughout the breadth of physical nature facts are what they are quite independently of us, and seldom is there any such hurry about them that the risks of being duped by believing a premature theory need be faced. The questions here are always trivial options, the hypotheses are hardly living (at any rate not living for us spectators), the choice between believing truth or falsehood is seldom forced. The attitude of sceptical balance is therefore the absolutely wise one if we would escape mistakes. . . .

I speak, of course, here of the purely judging mind. For purposes of discovery such difference is to be less highly recommended, and science would be far less advanced than she is if the passionate desires of individuals to get their own faiths confirmed had been kept out of the game. . . . The most useful investigator, because the most sensitive observer, is always he whose eager interest in one side of the question is balanced by an equally keen nervousness lest he become deceived. Science has organized this nervousness into a regular *technique*, her so-called method of verification; and she has fallen so deeply in love with the method that one may even say she has ceased to care for truth by itself at all. It is only truth as technically verified that interests her. The truth of truths might come in merely affirmative form, and she would decline to touch it. . . . Human passions, however, are stronger than technical rules. "Le coeur a ses raisons," as Pascal says, "que la raison ne connait pas;"[3] and however indifferent to all but the bare rules of the game the umpire, the abstract intellect, may be, the concrete players who furnish him the materials to judge of are usually, each one of them, in love with some pet 'live hypothesis' of his own. Let us agree, however, that wherever there is no forced option, the dispassionately judicial intellect with no pet hypothesis, saving us, as it does, from dupery at any rate, ought to be our ideal.

The question next arises: Are there not somewhere forced options in our speculative questions, and can we (as men who may be interested at least as much in positively gaining truth as in merely escaping dupery) always wait with impunity till the coercive evidence shall have arrived? It seems . . . improbable that the truth should be so nicely adjusted to our needs and powers as that. . . .

[The Will to Believe and Questions Relating to Morality or Dependent on Personal Action]

Moral questions immediately present themselves as questions whose solution cannot wait for sensible proof. A moral question is a question not of what sensibly exists, but of what is good, or would be good if it did exist. Science can tell us what exists; but to compare the *worths*, both of what exists and of what does not exist, we must consult not science, but what Pascal calls our heart. Science herself consults her heart when she lays it down that the infinite ascertainment of fact and correction of false belief are the supreme goods for man. Challenge the statement, and science can only repeat it oracularly, or else prove it by showing that such ascertainment and correction bring man all sorts of other goods which man's heart in turn declares. The question of having moral beliefs at all or not having them is decided by our will. Are our moral preferences true or false, or are they only odd biological phenomena, making things good or bad for *us*, but in themselves indifferent? How can your pure intellect decide? If your heart does not *want* a world of moral reality, your head will assuredly never make you believe in one. . . .

Turn now from these wide questions of good to a certain class of questions of fact, questions

[3] "The heart has its reasons, which reason does not know." EDITOR'S NOTE.

concerning personal relations, states of mind between one man and another. *Do you like me or not?*—for example. Whether you do or not depends, in countless instances, on whether I meet you half-way, am willing to assume that you must like me, and show you trust and expectation. The previous faith on my part in your liking's existence is in such cases what makes your liking come. But if I stand aloof, and refuse to budge an inch until I have objective evidence, until you shall have done something apt . . . ten to one your liking never comes. How many women's hearts are vanquished by the mere sanguine insistence of some man that they *must* love him! he will not consent to the hypothesis that they cannot. The desire for a certain kind of truth here brings about that special truth's existence; and so it is in innumerable cases of other sorts. Who gains promotions, boons, appointments, but the man in whose life they are seen to play the part of live hypotheses, who discounts them, sacrifices other things for their sake before they have come, and takes risks for them in advance? His faith acts on the powers above him as a claim, and creates its own verification.

A social organism of any sort whatever, large or small, is what it is because each member proceeds to his own duty with a trust that the other members will simultaneously do theirs. Wherever a desired result is achieved by the co-operation of many independent persons, its existence as a fact is a pure consequence of the precursive faith in one another of those immediately concerned. A government, an army, a commercial system, a ship, a college, an athletic team, all exist on this condition, without which not only is nothing achieved, but nothing is even attempted. A whole train of passengers (individually brave enough) will be looted by a few highwaymen, simply because the latter can count on one another, while each passenger fears that if he makes a movement of resistance, he will be shot before any one else backs him up. If we believed that the whole car-full would rise at once with us, we should each severally rise, and train-robbing would never even be attempted. There are, then, cases where a fact cannot come at all unless a preliminary faith exists in its coming. *And where faith in a fact can help create the fact*, that would be an insane logic which should say that faith running ahead of scientific evidence is the 'lowest kind of immorality' into which a thinking being can fall. Yet such is the logic by which our scientific absolutists pretend to regulate our lives!

[The Will to Believe and Religious Faith]

In truths dependent on our personal action, then, faith based on desire is certainly a lawful and possibly an indispensable thing.

But now, it will be said, these are all childish human cases, and have nothing to do with great cosmical matters, like the question of religious faith. Let us then pass on to that. Religions differ so much in their accidents that in discussing the religious question we must make it very generic and broad. What then do we now mean by the religious hypothesis? Science says things are; morality says some things are better than other things; and religion says essentially two things.

First, she says that the best things are the more eternal things, the overlapping things, the things in the universe that throw the last stone, so to speak, and say the final word. ''Perfection is eternal,''—this phrase of Charles Secretan seems a good way of putting this first affirmation of religion, an affirmation which obviously cannot yet be verified scientifically at all.

The second affirmation of religion is that we are better off even now if we believe her first affirmation to be true.

Now, let us consider what the logical elements of this situation are *in case the religious hypothesis in both its branches be really true.*

(Of course, we must admit that possibility at the outset. If we are to discuss the question at all, it must involve a living option. If for any of you religion be a hypothesis that cannot, by any living possibility be true, then you need go no further. I speak to the 'saving remnant' alone.) So proceeding, we see, first, that religion offers itself as a *momentous* option. We are supposed to gain, even now, by our belief, and to lose by our non-belief, a certain vital good. Secondly, religion is a *forced* option, so far as that good goes. We cannot escape the issue by remaining sceptical and waiting for more light, because, although we do avoid error in that way *if religion be untrue*, we lose the good, *if it be true*, just as certainly as if we positively chose to disbelieve. It is as if a man should hesitate indefinitely to ask a certain woman to marry him because he was not perfectly sure that she would prove an angel after he brought her home. Would he not cut himself off from that particular angel-possibility as decisively as if he went and married some one else? Scepticism, then, is not avoidance of option; it is option of a certain particular kind of risk. *Better risk loss of truth than chance of error*,—that is your faith-vetoer's exact position. He is actively playing his stake as much as the believer is; he is backing the field, against the religious hypothesis, just as the believer is backing the religious hypothesis against the field. To preach scepticism to us as a duty until 'sufficient evidence' for religion be found, is tantamount therefore to telling us, when in presence of the religious hypothesis, that to yield to our fear of its being error is wiser and better than to yield to our hope that it may be true. It is not intellect against all passions, then; it is only intellect with one passion laying down its law. And by what, forsooth, is the supreme wisdom of this passion warranted? Dupery for dupery, what proof is there that dupery through hope is so much worse than dupery through fear? I, for one, can see no proof; and I simply refuse obedience to the scientist's command to imitate his kind of option, in a case where my own stake is important enough to give me the right to choose my own form of risk. If religion be true and the evidence for it be still insufficient, I do not wish . . . to forfeit my sole chance in life of getting upon the winning side,—that chance depending, of course, on my willingness to run the risk of acting as if my passional need of taking the world religiously might be prophetic and right.

All this is on the supposition that it really may be prophetic and right, and that, even to us who are discussing the matter, religion is a live hypothesis which may be true. Now, to most of us religion comes in a still further way that makes a veto on our active faith even more illogical. The more perfect and more eternal aspect of the universe is represented in our religions as having personal form. The universe is no longer a mere *It* to us, but a *Thou*. . . . We feel, too, as if the appeal of religion to us were made to our own active good-will, as if evidence might be forever withheld from us unless we met the hypothesis half-way. To take a trivial illustration: just as a man who in a company of gentlemen made no advances, asked a warrant for every concession, and believed no one's word without proof, would cut himself off by such churlishness from all the social rewards that a more trusting spirit would earn,—so here, one who should shut himself up in snarling logicality and try to make the gods extort his recognition willy-nilly, or not get it at all, might cut himself off forever from his only opportunity of making the gods' acquaintance. This feeling, forced on us we know not whence, that by obstinately believing that there are gods (although not to do so would be so easy both for our logic and our life) we are doing the universe the deepest service we can, seems part of the living essence of the religious hypothesis. If the hypothesis *were* true in all its parts, including this one, then pure intellectualism, with its veto on our making willing advances, would be an absurdity; and some participation of our sympathetic nature would be logically required. I, therefore, for one, cannot see my way to accepting the agnostic rules for truth-seeking, or wilfully agree to keep my willing nature out of the game. I cannot do so for this plain reason, that *a rule of thinking which would absolutely prevent me from acknowledging certain kinds of truth if those kinds of truth were really there, would be an irrational rule*. That for me is the long and short of the formal logic of the situation, no matter what the kinds of truth might materially be.

I confess I do not see how this logic can be escaped. But sad experience makes me fear that some of you may still shrink from radically saying with me, *in abstracto*, that we have the right to believe at our own risk any hypothesis that is live enough to tempt our will. I suspect, however, that if this is so, it is because you have got away from the abstract logical point of view altogether, and are thinking (perhaps without realizing it) of some particular religious hypothesis which for you is dead. The freedom to 'believe what we will' you apply to the case of some patent superstition; and the faith you think of is the faith defined by the schoolboy when he said, "Faith is when you believe something that you know ain't true." I can only repeat that this is misapprehension. *In concreto*, the freedom to believe can only cover living options which the intellect of the individual cannot by itself resolve; and living options never seem absurdities to him who has them to consider. When I look at the religious question as it really puts itself to concrete men, and when I think of all the possibilities which both practically and theoretically it involves, then this command that we shall put a stopper on our heart, instincts, and courage, and *wait*—acting of course meanwhile more or less as if religion were *not* true[4]—till doomsday, or till such time as our intellect and senses working together may have raked in evidence enough,—this command, I say, seems to me the queerest idol ever manufactured in the philosophic cave. . . .

DISCUSSION QUESTIONS

1a. What does James mean by "the religious hypothesis"?

b. Why does he think that this hypothesis is a "genuine option"? Do you agree? Why, or why not? (In particular, focus on why James thinks that the religious hypothesis is "momentous.")

c. According to James, why should those who find the religious hypothesis to be a genuine option accept that hypothesis as true? Do you agree?

2. James' argument in "The Will to Believe" is restricted to those beliefs that "cannot . . . be decided on intellectual grounds." Do you think that this is true of "the religious hypothesis"? Is it true of the belief in God? Is there no evidence making such beliefs either probable or improbable? If so, how does this affect James' argument?

3. Consider the following claim (composed by the editor):

I agree with James that I would be better off if I believed in God than if I did not. I cannot, however, choose to believe; all I can do is choose to want to believe. If one admits, as James does, that there is not sufficient evidence to make

[4]Since belief is measured by action, he who forbids us to believe religion to be true, necessarily also forbids us to act as we should if we did believe it to be true. The whole defence of religious faith hinges upon action. If the action required or inspired by the religious hypothesis is in no way different from that dictated by the naturalistic hypothesis, then religious faith is a pure superfluity, better pruned away, and controversy about its legitimacy is a piece of idle trifling, unworthy of serious minds. I myself believe, of course, that the religious hypothesis gives to the world an expression which specifically determines our reactions, and makes them in a large part unlike what they might be on a purely naturalistic scheme of belief. AUTHOR'S NOTE.

God's existence more probable than not, one cannot, at least while focusing on this lack of evidence, really "believe"; all one can do is "hope." Is James advocating, then, that we shut our minds to the lack of evidence? If so, I for one, cannot do this.

Critically discuss.

4. Consider the following quotation from William Clifford's "The Ethics of Belief," to which James wrote his essay as a reply:

> Every time we let ourselves believe for unworthy reasons, we weaken our powers of self-control, of doubting, of judicially and fairly weighing evidence. We all suffer severely enough from the maintenance and support of false beliefs. . . . But a greater . . . evil arises when the credulous character is maintained and supported, when a habit of believing for unworthy reasons is fostered. . . . If I let myself believe anything on insufficient evidence, there may be no great harm done by the mere belief. . . . But I cannot help doing this great wrong to Man, that I make myself credulous. The danger to society is not merely that it should believe wrong things, though this is great enough; but that it should become credulous and lose the habit of testing things and inquiring into them; for then it must sink back into savagery.

Does James have an effective reply? What do you think?

5. Consider the following claim (composed by the editor):

> In "The Will to Believe," James does not advocate conversion to any particular religion but just to a very amorphous religious conception of the nature of things. I suspect, however, that such an amorphous, undifferentiated, theism could not have the practical consequences in one's life that James focuses upon in his argument. On the other hand, if one turns to specific religions, like Christianity, it is wrong to assume that belief and disbelief are on a par intellectually. Specific metaphysical religious beliefs are more like fairy tales than open scientific questions. As James defines it, the "liveness" of a belief has nothing to do with the evidence that can be marshalled in support of it, but is entirely a matter of what one is psychologically capable of accepting. Yet people notoriously are often capable of accepting all sorts of unjustified prejudices whose chances of being true are close to nil. The anti-intellectualism underlying James' position can be used to justify the most pernicious wishful thinking.

Critically comment.

6. If a person is better off as a result of religious faith, as James suggests, should that person resist thinking about arguments that serve to undercut that faith? After all, however much religious belief is due to our passionate, nonintellectual natures, people do change their opinions about a particular religion as a result of arguments. Does an acceptance of James' position lead consequently to the view that one ought not to think critically about one's religious beliefs?

19. THE VALUE OF RELIGIOUS IMAGINATION

George Santayana

GEORGE SANTAYANA (1863–1952) was born in Spain but educated in the United States, receiving both his Bachelors and Ph.D. degrees from Harvard. He taught philosophy at Harvard from 1889 until 1912, when the luxury of an inheritance allowed him to resign. He then returned to Europe, eventually settling in Italy, where from the outbreak of World War II until his death he secluded himself in a convent, devoting himself to his writing and detaching himself from the turmoil of the outside world. Santayana's most famous philosophical writings are his multi-volumed **Life of Reason** and **Realms of Being**, in which Santayana expresses his idiosyncratic naturalistic and materialistic philosophy. With his flair for language, Santayana was a distinguished novelist, essayist, and poet, as well as philosopher.

As a naturalist, Santayana rejects the belief in a supernatural god. Nevertheless, he sees religion as having a profound significance for human beings. Religion, he claims, should not be seen as an attempt to arrive at some superscientific truth. Instead of being judged by the standard of literal truth, it should be judged on the basis of its imaginative richness and ability to provide a comprehensive organization for our moral experience. As such, he claims, religion should be seen as a type of comprehensive poetry which imaginatively and symbolically expresses human ideals and transmits the lessons of experience.

. . . Like my parents, I have always set myself down officially as a Catholic: but this is a matter of sympathy and traditional allegiance, not of philosophy. In my adolescence, religion on its doctrinal and emotional side occupied me much more than it does now. I was more unhappy and unsettled; but I have never had any unquestioning faith in any dogma, and have never been what is called a practising Catholic. Indeed, it would hardly have been possible. My mother, like her father before her, was a Deist: she was sure there was a God, for who else could have made the world? But God was too great to take special thought for man: sacrifices, prayers, churches, and tales of immortality were invented by rascally priests in order to dominate the foolish. My father, except for the Deism, was emphatically of the same opinion. Thus, although I learned my prayers and catechism by rote, as was then inevitable in Spain, I knew that my parents regarded all religion as a work of human imagination. And I agreed, and still agree, with them there. But this carried an implication in their minds against which every instinct in me rebelled, namely that the works of human imagination are bad. No, said I to myself even as a boy; they are good, they alone are good; and the rest—the whole real world—is ashes in the mouth. My sympathies were entirely with those other members of my family who were devout believers. I loved the Christian epic, and all those doctrines and observances which bring it down into daily life. . . . For my own part, I was quite sure that life was not worth living; for if religion was false everything was worthless, and almost everything, if religion was true. . . .

Since those early years my feelings on this subject have become less strident. Does not modern philosophy teach that our idea of the so-called real world is also a work of imagination? A religion—for there are other religions than the Christian—simply offers a system of faith different from the vulgar one, or extending beyond it. The question is which imaginative system you will trust. My matured conclusion has been that no system is to be trusted, not even that of science in any literal or pictorial sense; but all systems may be used and, up to a certain point, trusted as symbols. Science expresses in human terms our dynamic relation to surrounding reality. Philosophies and religions, where they do not misrepresent these same dynamic relations and do not contradict science, express destiny in moral dimensions, in obviously mythical and

Source: From George Santayana, "Brief History of My Opinions," in *Contemporary American Philosophy*, Vol. II, eds. G. P. Adams and W. P. Montague. Reprinted with the permission of Russell & Russell and George Allen & Unwin and from George Santayana, *Reason in Religion*, Volume 3 of *The Life of Reason* (New York: Charles Scribner's Sons, 1905).

poetical images: but how else should these moral truths be expressed at all in a traditional or popular fashion? Religions are the great fairy-tales of the conscience. . . .[1]

Experience has repeatedly confirmed that well-known maxim of Bacon's, that "a little philosophy inclineth man's mind to atheism, but depth in philosophy bringeth men's minds about to religion." In every age the most comprehensive thinkers have found in the religion of their time and country something they could accept, interpreting and illustrating that religion so as to give it depth and universal application. Even the heretics and atheists, if they have had profundity, turn out after a while to be forerunners of some new orthodoxy. What they rebel against is a religion alien to their nature; they are atheists only by accident, and relatively to a convention which inwardly offends them, but they yearn mightily in their own souls after the religious acceptance of a world interpreted in their own fashion. . . .

At the same time, when Bacon penned the sage epigram we have quoted he forgot to add that the God to whom depth in philosophy brings back men's minds is far from being the same from whom a little philosophy estranges them. It would be pitiful indeed if mature reflection bred no better conceptions than those which have drifted down the muddy stream of time, where tradition and passion have jumbled everything together. . . . Each religion, so dear to those whose life it sanctifies, and fulfilling so necessary a function in the society that has adopted it, necessarily contradicts every other religion, and probably contradicts itself. What religion a man shall have is a historical accident, quite as much as what language he shall speak. In the rare circumstances where a choice is possible, he may, with some difficulty, make an exchange; but even then he is only adopting a new convention which may be more agreeable to his personal temper but which is essentially as arbitrary as the old. . . .

. . . every living and healthy religion has a marked idiosyncrasy. Its power consists in its special and surprising message and in the bias which that revelation gives to life. The vistas it opens and the mysteries it propounds are another world to live in; and another world to live in—whether we expect ever to pass wholly into it or no—is what we mean by having a religion. . . .

Thus religion has the same original relation to life that poetry has; only poetry, which never pretends to literal validity, adds a pure value to existence, the value of a liberal imaginative exercise. The poetic value of religion would initially be greater than that of poetry itself, because religion deals with higher and more practical themes, with sides of life which are in greater need of some imaginative touch and ideal interpretation than are those pleasant or pompous things which ordinary poetry dwells upon. But this initial advantage is neutralised in part by the abuse to which religion is subject, whenever its symbolic rightness is taken for scientific truth. Like poetry, it improves the world only by imagining it improved, but not content with making this addition to the mind's furniture—an addition which might be useful and ennobling—it thinks to confer a more radical benefit by persuading mankind that, in spite of appearances, the world is really such as that rather arbitrary idealisation has painted it. This spurious satisfaction is naturally the prelude to many a disappointment. . . . The value of religion becomes equivocal. Religion remains an imaginative achievement, a symbolic representation of moral reality which may have a most important function in vitalising the mind and in transmitting, by way of parables, the lessons of experience. But it becomes at the same time a continuous incidental deception; and this deception, in proportion as it is strenuously denied to be such, can work indefinite harm in the world and in the conscience.

On the whole, however, religion should not

[1]The selection from *Contemporary American Philosophy* ends here. The next excerpt is Chapter I, pp. 3–13, of *Reason in Religion*. EDITOR'S NOTE.

be conceived as having taken the place of anything better, but rather as having come to relieve situations which, but for its presence, would have been infinitely worse. In the thick of active life, or in the monotony of practical slavery, there is more need to stimulate fancy than to control it. Natural instinct is not much disturbed in the human brain by what may happen in that thin superstratum of ideas which commonly overlays it. We must not blame religion for preventing the development of a moral and natural science which at any rate would seldom have appeared; we must rather thank it for the sensibility, the reverence, the speculative insight which it has introduced into the world. . . .[2]

Herein lies the chief difference between those in whom religion is spontaneous and primary—a very few—and those in whom it is imitative and secondary. To the former, divine things are inward values, projected by chance into images furnished by poetic tradition or by external nature, while to the latter, divine things are in the first instance objective factors of nature or of social tradition, although they have come, perhaps, to possess some point of contact with the interests of the inner life on account of the supposed physical influence which those superhuman entities have over human fortunes. In a word, theology, for those whose religion is secondary, is simply a false physics, a doctrine about eventual experience not founded on the experience of the past. Such a false physics, however, is soon discredited by events; it does not require much experience or much shrewdness to discover that supernatural beings and laws are without the empirical efficacy which was attributed to them. True physics and true history must always tend, in enlightened minds, to supplant those misinterpreted religious traditions. Therefore, those whose reflection or sentiment does not furnish them with a key to the moral symbolism and poetic validity underlying theological ideas, if they apply their intelligence to the subject at all, and care to be sincere, will very soon come to regard religion as a delusion. Where religion is primary, however, all that worldly dread of fraud and illusion becomes irrelevant, as it is irrelevant to an artist's pleasure to be warned that the beauty he expresses has no objective existence. . . .

[2]End of Chapter I, *Reason in Religion*. The next excerpt is from Chapter IX, pp. 156–58, of the same work. EDITOR'S NOTE.

DISCUSSION QUESTION

1. According to Santayana, what is the value of religion? What does he find wrong with it? What do you think of Santayana's view of religion?

20. THE VALUE OF RELIGIOUS RITUAL

Morris Raphael Cohen

MORRIS RAPHAEL COHEN (1880–1947) was born in Russia and immigrated to the United States with his family when he was twelve years old. Like most Jewish immigrants, Cohen settled into the tenements of lower Manhattan ("the East Side") in New York City. He received his bachelor's degree from The College of the City of New York (City College) and his Ph.D. in philosophy from Harvard, where he studied under William James. After teaching mathematics for six years at City College, Cohen moved over to the philosophy department in 1912 and remained there until 1938, when he moved to the University of Chicago, from which he retired in 1942.

Cohen had a reputation as an outstanding teacher and practitioner of the Socratic method of questioning. He wrote on many aspects of philosophy, but his main interests and contributions were in the philosophy of law and the philosophy of science. Although brought up an Orthodox Jew, Cohen abandoned the supernaturalism of his youth and became firmly committed to a naturalistic world view. Like Santayana, Cohen saw great value, nevertheless, in the rituals of organized religion, as the following selection indicates.

In the winter of 1890 there had been some question as to whether my mother, my sister and myself should go to join the rest of the family in America, and I wrote a letter to my father expressing my fear of the irreligious surroundings to which I should thus be subject and my hope that he would allow me to continue my pious studies where I was. But my father's efforts to establish a livelihood for himself and his family in the following months in Minsk were doomed to failure. And when my mother, my sister and I traveled to America two years later, my youthful fears of what would happen to my religion in the irreligious atmosphere of America were borne out by events. It was only a few months after we had arrived that my childhood faith was broken on the sharp edge of Mr. Tunick's skepticism. The questions our old neighbor asked of my father and my father's inability to give a rational answer shocked me to the quick. The angels that guard us, recited in every prayer, had been very real to me. I had lived in strict conformity to the tenets of Jewish Orthodoxy. But I could not forget Mr. Tunick's questions: "What proof have you that there is a God and that he told anything to Moses? And why should I believe that Jews are the only ones that have the truth? And are there not other people just as intelligent as we, and can we prove the Jewish religion is superior to all others?"

After some soul-searching I came to the conclusion that I had no evidence that could efficiently answer these questions. I have not since that day ever seen any reason to change that conclusion.

The loss of the religion of my childhood brought no suffering in its train. It seemed to me that the restraints from which I was freed out-balanced the consolations that were lost. Perhaps that is because not all of the consolations were lost. Rational argument could never wholly efface a natural clinging to the joys of Friday night. Much less could it efface the larger spiritual patterns and values of my childhood religion. Indeed, in my youthful rejection of the Orthodox Jewish observances, I did not feel that I was cutting myself off from religion. I knew that the rejection of ritual is itself deeply rooted in the Hebraic tradition. I could not forget that the Hebrew Prophets, from Amos to Jeremiah, the founders of spiritual monotheism, all made Jahveh despise the ritual with which Israel believed it served Him. . . .

If I was a heretic, at least I felt that I was erring in good company. As with ritual, so, I felt, with creed. The essence of religion, it seemed to me, was not in the words uttered with the lips but rather in the faith which shows itself in our moral life. I could not bring myself to think that a just God would condemn the upright and spiritual-minded men I knew in all churches, and outside of all churches, merely because they did not pronounce the right for-

Source: Excerpted with permission of Macmillan Publishing Co., Inc. from *A Dreamer's Journey* by Morris Raphael Cohen.

mulas. Beyond any divinity of creed, it seemed to me, there was a God of morality. . . .

I remember as a boy having a talk with the late Joseph Jacobs. He asked, "Why do your young people on the East Side keep away from the synagogue? Don't they believe in religion?" I replied, "Going to synagogue or not going is a minor matter, Mr. Jacobs. We take religion more seriously than you do." I think that was the truth. True religion must be an expression of the inner soul and cannot be forced on anyone merely because he happens to have been born of a certain ancestry. It seemed to me that in the friction between the older generation and the younger generation which the religious question brought to the fore in the days of my youth, both sides were at fault. The older generation was at fault in not distinguishing between ritual forms and true religious faith. It was lacking in human sympathy with the honest views of the younger generation. It could not learn that the real vitality of a religion does not show itself in the power to resist the advance of new truth but rather in the capacity to adapt itself to whatever new light it can get.

On the other hand there was a certain superficiality in the attitude that many of my generation took towards religion. We used to read accounts of conflict between science and religion in which, we were told, science had gradually conquered. This, however, seemed to me to leave out of consideration the realm where science cannot rule, where neither the telescope nor the microscope can penetrate, the realm of ideal expression. Appropriation or rejection of science thus did not solve the problem of religion. Those who called themselves atheists seemed to be singularly blind, as a rule, to the limitations of our knowledge and to the infinite possibilities beyond us. And those who call themselves materialists appeared to me to be shutting themselves off from philosophy, wisdom, and the life of the spirit, which are certainly not material things. Those of my circle who rejected religion *in toto* seemed to me to be casting away the ideals that had sustained our people through so many generations before we had fashioned guideposts to our own lives that could stand up against the sort of buffeting that the old guideposts had withstood. In this some of us lost sight of the larger view . . . that we have no right to break away from the past until we have appropriated all its experience and wisdom. . . .

The ideal of intellectual integrity compelled me and many others of my generation to reject superstitions that had been bound up with the practices of our Orthodox parents, but it did not prevent us from cherishing the spiritual values which they had found in those practices. . . . The struggle between Orthodoxy and active opposition to all religion seemed to me, like so many of the passionate struggles of life, to overlook possibilities and values which a more tolerant and rational outlook could find.

Indeed I marveled then, and have never ceased to marvel, at the fact that on matters where knowledge is readily demonstrable—such as cooking or chemistry—discussions show little of the heated mood of the zealot and fanatic, whereas, in matters on which it is much more difficult to arrive at the truth, such as questions of religion, we are inclined to be very sure of ourselves. Perhaps we try to make up by our vehemence for the lack of demonstrative evidence.

Of course, if you claim to be in possession of a special revelation, then you have a mortgage on the truth of the universe, the other fellow can have nothing true to tell you, and the thing to do is to hold on to your revealed truth with all the ardor that is in you. But then the other fellow is just as certain that he alone has all the truth and there is no use in any argumentation. But if you take your stand on human history and human reason, and recognize, for example, that the claim to the possession of a special revelation of the Jew is, as such, not a bit better than that of the Christian or the Mohammedan, or any of the ten thousand other claims, then, it seemed to me, you must grant that each possesses both truth and error. . . .

In the days of my first youthful revolt against the Jewish observances, I was inclined to regard cults, prayer and ritual as of little importance in comparison with belief or faith. This was certainly the view that my teacher William James took of the matter. . . . My own studies of the great historic religions led me, however, to see that ritual, what men do on certain occasions, is a primary fact in human religious experience, and that the beliefs and emotions associated with ritual are more variable than ritual itself, as is shown by the diverse explanations and justifications of the Hebrew Sabbath and the Easter ceremonies. . . .

Men cling to sanctified phrases not only because of the insights they contain but even more because, through ritual and repetition, they have become redolent with the wine of human experience. For each of us the symbolism of our childhood offers paths to peace and understanding that can never be wholly replaced by other symbolisms. For me the ancient ceremonies that celebrate the coming and going of life, the wedding ceremony, the *b'rith*,[1] and the funeral service, give an expression to the continuity of the spiritual tradition that is more eloquent than any phrases of my own creation. The ritual may be diluted by English and by modernisms, but the Hebraic God is still a potent symbol of the continuous life of which we individuals are waves. So it is, too, with the celebration of the eternal struggle for freedom, in the family service of the Passover.

Like vivid illustrations in the book of my life are the prayers of my parents, the services at their graves, the memory of an old man chanting funeral songs at the *Jahrzeit*[2] of my dear friend, Dr. Himwich, the unveiling of the monument to the beloved comrade of my life's journeys, and the celebration of the continuity of generations in the Passover services in the home of my parents and in the homes of my children. And though I have never gone back to theologic supernaturalism, I have come to appreciate more than I once did the symbolism in which is celebrated the human need of trusting to the larger vision, according to which calamities come and go but the continuity of life and faith in its better possibilities survive.

DISCUSSION QUESTION

1. According to Cohen, what is the value of religion? What is the source of this value? How important is it? Do you agree with Cohen that religion can maintain this value for people once they reject the metaphysical beliefs of their religion?

[1]The circumcision ceremony of newborn Jewish males, signifying a covenant with God (see *Genesis* 17). EDITOR'S NOTE.

[2]Jewish memorial prayers at the anniversary of a person's death. EDITOR'S NOTE.

21. THE RELIGIOUS ATTITUDE TOWARD LIFE AS A COMMITMENT TO MORAL IDEALS

John Dewey

JOHN DEWEY (1859–1952) was the most influential American philosopher of the twentieth century. He taught philosophy at the University of Michigan from 1884 to 1894 and then moved on to teach at the University of Chicago until 1904, when he received an appointment to teach at Columbia University in New York City; he remained there until his retirement in 1930. Dewey wrote prolifically not only in philosophy but also in education, psychology, and public affairs. His educational theories had a great impact upon the progressive movement in American education. Committed throughout his life to the experimental method and to narrowing the gap between thought and action, Dewey advocated experimental teaching methods and believed that education should be concerned with the development of manual skills as well as with the development of the intellect. Learning, he stressed, must be related to the interests of students and connected with contemporary problems. As a social philosopher, Dewey conceived of democracy as a primary moral value and attempted to translate this abstract commitment into practical working principles for twentieth-century society. Dewey's general philosophy is called **instrumentalism**. According to this philosophy, human thoughts should be seen as instruments or tools developed by human beings to solve their multiple individual and social problems. Since these problems are constantly changing, there is no final truth but rather a constant experimental and evolutionary movement toward the resolution of the changing troubling situations that stir human thought.

Dewey's instrumentalism was a specific version of the more general approach to philosophy known as **pragmatism**. The pragmatic viewpoint was first developed by Charles Sanders Peirce in the 1870's and later reformulated and popularized by William James. Through the writings of James, Dewey, Peirce, and others, pragmatism flourished in the United States during the early part of the twentieth century. United by their common emphasis upon the bearing of **practical consequences** on the meaning and truth of statements, the pragmatists differed in their conception of practical consequences. For Dewey, like Peirce, the emphasis was upon those practical consequences which are capable of public experimental verification. For James, however, the practical consequences of a belief were identified with the significance of that belief in the life of the individual—that is, with its ability to satisfy human needs and interests. Peirce and Dewey strongly dissented from James' view that truth is what brings satisfaction. In reaction, Peirce renamed his own philosophy **pragmaticism** (a word ugly enough, he commented, that no one would be likely to steal it) and Dewey named his view **instrumentalism**. Both Peirce and Dewey were highly critical of James' defense of the rationality of religious beliefs in his "The Will to Believe." Both believed that by intertwining the question of the **psychological value** of religious beliefs with the **meaning and rational grounds** for religious beliefs, James had abandoned their central philosophical commitment to the public experimental verification of beliefs.

Like Santayana and Cohen, Dewey (raised a Protestant) was a committed naturalist who rejected the belief in a supernatural god. Like them, he also rejected traditional religious claims to super-scientific truth. Unlike them, however, he saw little value in organized religions and their ritualistic observances. Seeing the value of religion in its ability to engender emotional commitment to very general unifying moral ideals, Dewey broadly defined a "religious attitude" as the state of mind accompanying "any activity pursued in behalf of an ideal and against obstacles and in spite of threat of personal loss because of a conviction of its general and enduring value." Dewey argues that the religious attitude should be freed from supernaturalism and from a commitment to any particular institutionalized religion with its cults and creeds. Utilizing the language of traditional theology in an unorthodox way, Dewey goes on to define "God" as this never ending striving for ideal values or, as he puts it, the "active relation between ideal and actual."

Religion Versus the Religious

Never before in history has mankind been so much of two minds, so divided into two camps, as it is today. Religions have traditionally been allied with ideas of the supernatural, and often have been based upon explicit beliefs about it. Today there are many who hold that nothing worthy of being called religious is possible apart from the supernatural. . . .

The opposed group consists of those who think the advance of culture and science has completely discredited the supernatural and with it all religions that were allied with belief in it. But they go beyond this point. The extremists in this group believe that with elimination of the supernatural not only must historic religions be dismissed but with them everything of a religious nature. . . .

There is one idea held in common by these two opposite groups: identification of the religious with the supernatural. The question I shall raise . . . concerns the ground for and the consequences of this identification: its reasons and its value. In the discussion I shall develop another conception of the nature of the religious phase of experience, one that separates it from the supernatural and the things that have grown up about it. I shall try to show that these derivations are encumbrances and that what is genuinely religious will undergo an emancipation when it is relieved from them. . . .

The heart of my point . . . is that there is a difference between religion, *a* religion, and the religious; between anything that may be denoted by a noun substantive and the quality of experience that is designated by an adjective. It is not easy to find a definition of religion in the substantive sense that wins general acceptance. However, in the *Oxford Dictionary* I find the following: "Recognition on the part of man of some unseen higher power as having control of his destiny and as being entitled to obedience, reverence and worship."

This particular definition is less explicit in assertion of the supernatural character of the higher unseen power than are others that might be cited. It is, however, surcharged with implications having their source in ideas connected with the belief in the supernatural, characteristic of historic religions. Let us suppose that one familiar with the history of religions, including those called primitive, compares the definition with the variety of known facts and by means of the comparison sets out to determine just what the definition means. I think he will be struck by three facts that reduce the terms of the definition in such a low common denominator that little meaning is left.

He will note that the "unseen powers" referred to have been conceived in a multitude of incompatible ways. Eliminating the differences, nothing is left beyond the bare reference to something unseen and powerful. . . .

There is no greater similarity in the ways in which obedience and reverence have been expressed. There has been worship of animals, of ghosts, of ancestors, phallic worship, as well as of a Being of dread power and of love and wisdom. Reverence has been expressed in the human sacrifices of the Peruvians and Aztecs; the sexual orgies of some Oriental religions; exorcisms and ablutions; the offering of the humble and contrite mind of the Hebrew prophet, the elaborate rituals of the Greek and Roman Churches. . . .

Finally, there is no discernible unity in the moral motivations appealed to and utilized. They have been as far apart as fear of lasting torture, hope of enduring bliss in which sexual enjoyment has sometimes been a conspicuous element; mortification of the flesh and extreme asceticism; prostitution and chastity; wars to extirpate the unbeliever; persecution to convert or punish the unbeliever, and philanthropic zeal;

Source: From *A Common Faith,* Chapters I and II, by John Dewey (New Haven, Conn.: Yale University Press, 1934). Reprinted by permission of Yale University Press.

servile acceptance of imposed dogma, along with brotherly love and aspiration for a reign of justice among men.

I have, of course, mentioned only a sparse number of the facts which fill volumes in any well-stocked library. It may be asked by those who do not like to look upon the darker side of the history of religions why the darker facts should be brought up. We all know that civilized man has a background of bestiality and superstition and that these elements are still with us. Indeed, have not some religions, including the most influential forms of Christianity, taught that the heart of man is totally corrupt? How could the course of religion in its entire sweep not be marked by practices that are shameful in their cruelty and lustfulness, and by beliefs that are degraded and intellectually incredible? What else than what we find could be expected, in the case of people having little knowledge and no secure method of knowing; with primitive institutions, and with so little control of natural forces that they lived in a constant state of fear?

I gladly admit that historic religions have been relative to the conditions of social culture in which peoples lived. Indeed, what I am concerned with is to press home the logic of this method of disposal of outgrown traits of past religions. Beliefs and practices in a religion that now prevails are by this logic relative to the present state of culture. If so much flexibility has obtained in the past regarding an unseen power, the way it affects human destiny, and the attitudes we are to take toward it, why should it be assumed that change in conception and action has now come to an end? The logic involved in getting rid of inconvenient aspects of past religions compels us to inquire how much in religions now accepted are survivals from outgrown cultures. It compels us to ask what conception of unseen powers and our relations to them would be consonant with the best achievements and aspirations of the present. It demands that in imagination we wipe the slate clean and start afresh by asking what would be the idea of the unseen, of the manner of its control over us and the ways in which reverence and obedience would be manifested, if whatever is basically religious in experience had the opportunity to express itself free from all historic encumbrances.

So we return to the elements of the definition that has been given. What boots it to accept, in defense of the universality of religion, a definition that applies equally to the most savage and degraded beliefs and practices that have related to unseen powers and to noble ideals of a religion having the greatest share of moral content? There are two points involved. One of them is that there is nothing left worth preserving in the notions of unseen powers, controlling human destiny to which obedience, reverence and worship are due, if we glide silently over the nature that has been attributed to the powers, the radically diverse ways in which they have been supposed to control human destiny, and in which submission and awe have been manifested. The other point is that when we begin to select, to choose, and say that some present ways of thinking about the unseen powers are better than others; that the reverence shown by a free and self-respecting human being is better than the servile obedience rendered to an arbitrary power by frightened men; that we should believe that control of human destiny is exercised by a wise and loving spirit rather than by madcap ghosts or sheer force—when I say, we begin to choose, we have entered upon a road that has not yet come to an end. We have reached a point that invites us to proceed farther.

For we are forced to acknowledge that concretely there is no such thing as religion in the singular. There is only a multitude of religions. . . . It is probable that religions have been universal in the sense that all the peoples we know anything about have had *a* religion. But the differences among them are so great and so shocking that any common element that can be extracted is meaningless. . . . Choice among religions is imperative, and the necessity for choice leaves nothing of any force in the argument from universality. Moreover, when once we enter upon the road of choice, there is at once presented a possibility not yet generally realized.

For the historic increase of the ethical and ideal content of religions suggests that the process of purification may be carried further. It indicates that further choice is imminent in which certain values and functions in experience may be selected. This possibility is what I had in mind in speaking of the difference between the religious and a religion. I am not proposing a religion, but rather the emancipation of elements and outlooks that may be called religious. For the moment we have a religion, whether that of the Sioux Indian or of Judaism or of Christianity, that moment the ideal factors in experience that may be called religious take on a load that is not inherent in them, a load of current beliefs and of institutional practices that are irrelevant to them. . . .

To be somewhat more explicit, a religion (and as I have just said there is no such thing as religion in general) always signifies a special body of beliefs and practices having some kind of institutional organization, loose or tight. In contrast, the adjective "religious" denotes nothing in the way of a specifiable entity, either institutional or as a system of beliefs. It does not denote anything to which one can specifically point as one can point to this and that historic religion or existing church. For it does not denote anything that can exist by itself or that can be organized into a particular and distinctive form of existence. It denotes attitudes that may be taken toward every object and every proposed end or ideal. . . .

What has been said does not imply that all moral faith in ideal ends is by virtue of that fact religious in quality. The religious is "morality touched by emotion" only when the ends of moral conviction arouse emotions that are not only intense but are actuated and supported by ends so inclusive that they unify the self. . . .

If we apply the conception set forth to the terms of the definition [of religion] earlier quoted, these terms take on a new significance. An unseen power controlling our destiny becomes the power of an ideal. . . .

Any activity pursued in behalf of an ideal end against obstacles and in spite of threats of personal loss because of conviction of its general and enduring value is religious in quality. Many a person, inquirer, artist, philanthropist, citizen, men and women in the humblest walks of life, have achieved, without presumption and without display, such unification of themselves and of their relations to the conditions of existence. It remains to extend their spirit and inspiration to ever wider numbers. If I have said anything about religions and religion that seems harsh, I have said those things because of a firm belief that the claim on the part of religions to possess a monopoly of ideals and of the supernatural means by which alone, it is alleged, they can be furthered, stands in the way of the realization of distinctively religious values inherent in natural experience. . . . The opposition between religious values as I conceive them and religions is not to be bridged. Just because the release of these values is so important, their identification with the creeds and cults of religions must be dissolved.

Faith and Its Object

All religions, as I pointed out . . . involve specific intellectual beliefs, and they attach—some greater, some less—importance to assent to these doctrines as true, true in the intellectual sense. They have literatures held especially sacred, containing historical material with which the validity of the religions is connected. They have developed a doctrinal apparatus it is incumbent upon "believers" (with varying degrees of strictness in different religions) to accept. They also insist that there is some special and isolated channel of access to the truths they hold.

No one will deny, I suppose, that the present crisis in religion is intimately bound up with these claims. . . .

It is no part of my intention to rehearse in any detail the weighty facts that collectively go by the name of the conflict of science and religion. . . .

The significant bearing for my purpose . . . is that new methods of inquiry and reflection have become for the educated man today the final arbiter of all questions of fact. . . . Nothing less than a revolution in the "seat of intellectual authority" has taken place. . . .

The scope of the change is well illustrated by the fact that whenever a particular outpost is surrendered it is usually met by the remark from a liberal theologian that the particular doctrine or supposed historic or literary tenet surrendered was never, after all, an intrinsic part of religious belief, and that without it the true nature of religion stands out more clearly than before. Equally significant is the growing gulf between fundamentalists and liberals in the churches. What is not realized—although perhaps it is more definitely seen by fundamentalists than by liberals—is that the issues does not concern this and that piecemeal *item* of belief, but centers in the question of the method by which any and every item of intellectual belief is to be arrived at and justified.

The positive lesson is that religious qualities and values if they are real at all are not bound up with any single item of intellectual assent, not even that of the existence of the God of theism; and that, under existing conditions, the religious function in experience can be emancipated only through surrender of the whole notion of special truths that are religious by their own nature, together with the idea of peculiar avenues of access to such truths. For were we to admit that there is but one method for ascertaining fact and truth—that conveyed by the word "scientific" in its most general and generous sense—no discovery in any branch of knowledge and inquiry could then disturb the faith that is religious. I should describe this faith as the unification of the self through allegiance to inclusive ideal ends, which imagination presents to us and to which the human will responds as worthy of controlling our desires and choices. . . .

These considerations may be applied to the idea of God, or, to avoid misleading conceptions, to the idea of the divine. This idea is, as I have said, one of ideal possibilities unified through imaginative realization and projection. . . . We are in the presence neither of ideals completely embodied in existence nor yet of ideals that are mere rootless ideals, fantasies, utopias. For there are forces in nature and society that generate and support the ideals. They are further unified by the action that gives them coherence and solidity. It is this *active* relation between ideal and actual to which I would give the name "God." I would not insist that the name *must* be given. There are those who hold that the associations of the term with the supernatural are so numerous and close that any use of the word "God" is sure to give rise to misconception and be taken as a concession to traditional ideas.

They may be correct in this view. But the facts to which I have referred are there, and they need to be brought out with all possible clearness and force. . . .

. . . Whether one gives the name "God" to this union, operative in thought and action, is a matter for individual decision. But the *function* of such a working union of the ideal and actual seems to me to be identical with the force that has in fact been attached to the conception of God in all the religions that have a spiritual content; and a clear idea of that function seems to me urgently needed at the present time. . .

DISCUSSION QUESTIONS

1. Consider the following criticism of Dewey's religious philosophy by Morris Raphael Cohen:

> One of the effective ways of avoiding any real discussion of religion or discrimination of its darker from its brighter side is to define or identify it as "our highest aspiration." . . .
>
> . . . In the interests of intellectual honesty we must also reject the identification of religion with . . . altruistic conduct. . . .
>
> . . . to identify all religion with vague altruism rules out not only all the historic tribal and national religions, Hinduism, and most of the Old Testament, but also Christianity of the Orthodox, Catholic, and Fundamentalist-Protestant type . . . . This "liberal" . . . view is logically bound to apply the term "religious" to philanthropic atheists and Communists who, in the interests of humanity and to stop the exploitation of the masses by the clergy, are the avowed enemies of all religion. And indeed there are many who do speak of Communism as a religion. But this is surely to cause hopeless confusion . . . . Consider the vast varieties of religions ancient and modern. Are they all expressions of our highest aspirations? . . .
>
> Instead, then, of darkening counsel by beginning with arbitrary and confusing definitions of religion, let us recognize that the term "religion" is generally used and understood to apply to Christianity, Judaism, Islam, Hinduism, etc., and that these represent certain forms of organized life. . . . Religion is first of all something that makes people do something when children are born, when they become mature, when they marry, and when they die. It makes people go to church, sacrifice, fast, feast or pray. A religion that does not get so organized or embodied in life is a mere ghost, the creature of a cultivated imagination. . . .[1]

How do you think Dewey would reply? What do you think?

[1] Morris R. Cohen, *The Faith of a Liberal* (New York: Henry Holt and Company, 1946), pp. 339–40.

FURTHER READINGS

general reference sources

The Encyclopedia of Philosophy. New York: Macmillan, 1967. Contains many articles relating to the philosophy of religion, including: Agnosticism; Atheism; Cosmological Arguments for the Existence of God; Creation, Religious Doctrine of; Evil, Problem of; Faith; Fideism; God, Concepts of; Moral Arguments for the Existence of God; Pantheism; Philosophy of Religion, Problems of; Religion, Psychological Explanations of; Religion and Morality; Religion and Science; Religious Experience, Argument for the Existence of God; Religious Language; and Teleological Argument for the Existence of God.

The Dictionary of the History of Ideas. New York: Scribners, 1973. Contains the following articles relating to the philosophy of religion: Agnosticism; Atheism; Cosmology—God; Creation; Evil—Religion; Faith; God—Existence of; Ontology—God; Religion—Experience; Religion—Language; Religion—Philosophy; Religion—Psychology; Religion—Morality; and Religion—Science.

anthologies

Alston, William P., ed., *Religious Belief and Philosophical Thought.* New York: Harcourt, Brace and World, 1963. This anthology contains a wide spectrum of classical and contemporary selections on the philosophy of religion. Each section begins with a very clear, detailed, and nontechnical editorial introduction to the section's topic, which would be quite useful to the beginning philosophy student. The topics covered (in order) are: Arguments for the Existence of God; Religious Experience; Criticisms of Theism; Immortality; Revelation; Faith; Religion and Science; and Religious Alternatives to Theism.

Brody, Baruch A., ed., *Readings in the Philosophy of Religion.* Englewood Cliffs, N.J.: Prentice-Hall 1974. This anthology is geared to the more advanced philosophy student who has had some exposure to technical linguistic analysis. (A few of the articles utilize logical symbolism.) The articles and excerpts are predominantly by contemporary analytic philosophers, but sections begin with excerpts from historically influential philosophers and theologians. The chapters begin with short and clear introductions to the topics covered. The book ends with a very good bibliographic essay for students interested in further readings on the topics covered. These topics are (in order): The Existence of God; Talking About God; The Divine Attributes; God's Relation to the World (creation, time, and miracles); Man's Relation to God (religious experience, prayer and ritual, morality and religion); and The End of Things (immortality and resurrection.)

Bronstein, Daniel J. and Harold M. Schulweis, eds., *Approaches to the Philosophy of Religion.* Englewood Cliffs, N.J.: Prentice-Hall, 1954. This older anthology consists of classic source material and the writings of philosophers who were active in the first half of the twentieth century. It contains a section on God and Human Freedom and a section on Church and State which are not covered in any of the other anthologies. In addition to these topics, the anthology has sections on: What is Religion?; The Existence of God; God and Evil; and Immortality.

Burill, Donald, ed., *The Cosmological Argument.* New York: Doubleday, 1967. An anthology of classical and contemporary material on cosmological arguments for God's existence.

Cahn, Steven, ed., *Philosophy of Religion.* New York: Harper & Row, 1970. All the excerpts in this anthology are by contemporary analytic philosophers. Like the Brody anthology, it is geared to the philosophically sophisticated. The topics covered (in order) are: The Attributes of God; The Language of Religious Discourse; Religious Experience; and Faith and Reason.

Edwards, Paul, and Arthur Pap, eds., *A Modern Introduction to Philosophy,* 3rd ed., Chapter V. New York: Macmillan, 1973. This comprehensive anthology of articles for introductory philosophy would serve as an excellent supplement to our anthology for the serious student seeking a broader exposure to the problems of the philosophy of religion. The last eleven pages of Edwards' long introduction to the philosophy of religion consist of a very clear and detailed discussion of the rationality of belief in God on faith (''fideism'') and of the verifiability and meaningfulness of religious statements, a topic not covered in our anthology. There are also several articles in the Edwards and Pap anthology on these topics. In addition, there is a clear and informative debate between the Jesuit theologian F.C. Copleston and the philosopher Bertrand Russell which was originally broadcast over the British radio in 1948. Students interested in classic defenses of arguments for God's existence would also be interested in Copleston's commentary on Thomas Aquinas' Five Ways and William Paley's defense of the argument from design (where he compares the world to a watch and God to a watchmaker). Following the articles is a comprehensive nineteen page bibliographic essay on material in the philosophy of religion which would prove very useful to the student doing research on a specific topic in the philosophy of religion.

Flew, Anthony, and Alasdair MacIntyre, eds., *New Essays in Philosophical Theology.* New York: Macmillan, 1955. An anthology of articles and excerpts by contemporary analytic philosophers on the meaning of religious statements. Like the Brody and Cahn anthologies, this book presupposes some philosophic sophistication.

Hick, John, ed., *Classical and Contemporary Readings in the Philosophy of Religion.* Englewood Cliffs, N.J.: Prentice-Hall, 1964. Like Alston's, this anthology provides a well-rounded collection of classical and contemporary material on the philosophy of religion. Hick's anthology is, however, more historically oriented than Alston's, which is more problem oriented. While the readings are arranged historically and not topicially, there is a useful topical table of contents. Given the method of organization, Hick's topical introductory comments are gathered together at the very end of the book. These comments will be very useful to those seeking an historical overview of approaches to problems in the philosophy of religion. (Those seeking clear and nontechnical analytic introductions should see Alston.) The topics covered are: Arguments for the Existence of God; Revelation and Faith; The Problem of Evil; Religion and Theology; and Religious Language.

Hick, John, ed., *The Existence of God.* New York: Macmillan, 1964. An anthology of selections on traditional arguments for the existence of God and the logical possibility and religious desirability of such proofs. Part I, "The Theistic Arguments," contains selections on the ontological, cosmological, teleological, and moral arguments for God's existence. Part II, "Discussions and Questions," consists of the Russell-Copleston radio debate on the existence of God, and an excerpt from the nineteenth-century atheistic philosopher Ludwig Feuerbach, who (anticipating Freud) claims that the belief in God is a "projection" of human attributes and human needs. This is followed by excerpts from the twentieth-century theologian John Baillie and the nineteenth-century philosopher Søren Kierkegaard, who sees proofs as irrelevant and impossible substitutes for a living religious faith and commitment. Part III, "Contemporary Problems," is concerned with the meaning and verifiability of religious statements.

Hick, John, and Arthur C. McGill, eds., *The Many-Faced Argument.* New York: Macmillan, 1967. An anthology of classical and contemporary sources on the ontological argument for God's existence.

Pike, Nelson, ed., *God and Evil.* Englewood Cliffs, N.J.: Prentice-Hall, 1964. An anthology of classical and contemporary selections on the problem of evil.

Plantinga, Alvin, ed., *The Ontological Argument.* New York: Doubleday, 1965. An anthology of classical and contemporary selections on the ontological argument.

Stewart, David, ed., *Exploring the Philosophy of Religion.* Englewood Cliffs, N.J.: Prentice-Hall, 1980. This anthology contains selections from both classical and contemporary sources organized into the following seven sections; Religious Experience; Arguments for God's Existence; Faith and Reason; Religious Language; The Problem of Evil; Death and Human Destiny; and Religion and Ethics.

books and articles

Clifford, W.K, "The Ethics of Belief" in his *Lectures and Essays,* Vol. II. London: Macmillan, 1879. Also included in the Brody and Bronstein-Schulweis anthologies. Clifford (1845–79), a mathematician and scientifically oriented philosopher, is remembered today primarily for this essay in which he argues that people should never believe things without sufficient evidence. James' famous essay "The Will to Believe" was written as a critical response to Clifford's essay.

Dewey, John, *A Common Faith.* New Haven. Conn.: Yale University Press, 1934. This short (86-page) book, an excerpt of which appears in our anthology, was based on a series of lectures Dewey presented at Yale University. Dewey argues for "the emancipation of the religious quality of experience" from what he sees as "the heritage of dogmatism and supernaturalism that characterize historical religions."

Durkheim, Emile, *The Elementary Forms of the Religious Life.* New York: Free Press, 1965 (originally published in 1915). In this classic study of primitive religion, Durkheim, one of the founders of modern sociology, considers the definition and origin of religion. He sees such notions as animism, naturism, totemism, myth, and ritual as essential forms of religious thought and practice. He also sees religion (as well as philosophy and morals) as a product of the social conditions of human beings and not, as Freud did, as inherent in the isolated minds of individuals seeking to find individual security. Its length (507 pages) and dry style make this a book one is apt to want to skim rather than to read cover to cover. However, the detailed table of contents and index make it an excellent reference source.

Freud, Sigmund, *The Future of an Illusion.* Garden City, N.Y.: Doubleday, 1964 (originally published in German in 1927). This is the authorized English translation. Freud wrote *The Future of an Illusion* late in his career, when his interest in psychoanalysis had expanded beyond his earlier clinical concerns. At this time in his life, general problems of civilization occupied much of Freud's attention. In this influential short work (about 100 pages), the atheist Freud argues that religion is an illusion or "crutch" human beings manufacture to make more tolerable their helplessness before the forces of nature.

Griffins, David Ray, *God, Power and Evil: A Process Theology.* Philadelphia: Westminster Press, 1976. A process theologian's defense of a limited god. In his *Philosophy of Religion* (3rd ed.), John Hick criticizes Griffin's view in particular in his discussion of process theology's approach to the problem of evil. This discussion is not included in the selection from Hick that is included in this chapter.

Hick, John, *Evil and the God of Love.* New York: Harper & Row, 1966. A detailed historical and analytic treatment of various theological attempts to tackle the problem of evil. Hick, a believer, presents his own solution and attempts to meet criticisms.

Hick, John, *Faith and Knowledge.* Ithaca, N.Y.: Cornell University Press, 1957. A detailed historical and analytic treatment of the rationality of faith by a believer. This book is more technical than the two other books by Hick mentioned in this bibliography.

Hick, John, *Philosophy of Religion* (3rd ed.). Englewood Cliffs, N.J.: Prentice-Hall, 1983. This excellent, clearly written introduction to the problems of the philosophy of religion as seen by today's analytically oriented philosophers is geared to the beginning student. The topics covered are: Definition of Religion; The Judeo-Christian Concept of God; Grounds for Belief and Disbelief in God; The Problem of Evil; Revelation and Faith; Problems of Religious Language; The Problem of Verification; The Conflicting Truth Claims of Different Religions; Human Destiny: Immortality and Resurrection; Human Destiny; Karma and Reincarnation.

Hume, David, *Dialogues Concerning Natural Religion.* Indianapolis: Bobbs-Merrill, 1947 and 1970. The 1970 edition of Hume's classic *Dialogues Concerning Natural Religion* (excerpts of which appear in this anthology) was edited by Nelson Pike, a professor of philosophy at the University of California at Irvine, while the 1947 edition was edited by the late Norman Kemp Smith, professor of philosophy at the University of Edinburgh, Great Britain. The text of the dialogues is easier to read in Pike's edition since the Kemp Smith edition has detailed footnotes and marks in the body indicating changes Hume made in the manuscript—information that will interest a Humean scholar but not the average reader. Nevertheless, the Kemp Smith edition contains a section by section summary and analysis of the *Dialogues,* which is lacking in the Pike edition. In addition, Kemp Smith's introductory essay is much more extensive, providing the reader with a general background of Hume's views regarding religion and his own religious background, which is lacking in the Pike edition. Both Kemp Smith and Pike present editorial analyses of the *Dialogues* as a whole. Their points of view, however, as to Hume's own position on the issues debated by Philo, Cleanthes, and Demea are very different. For this reason, students who are interested in this question should read both editorial essays. Such students should also turn to Richard H. Popkin's editorial introduction to the Hackett Publishing Company's printing of Hume's *Dialogues Concerning Natural Religion, The Immortality of the Soul,* and *Of Suicide* (Indianapolis: Hackett Publishing Company, 1980). As Popkin sees it, it is a mistake to identify Hume with Philo (as Kemp Smith does) for "as Cleanthes moderated his claims and Philo enlarged his [in the later dialogues], in a serious sense Cleanthes comes to represent a portion of what Hume really believed." Popkin also mentions the influence that Hume has had on such Christians as Kierkegaard, who accept the existence of God on faith, a discussion lacking in the other two editions of the *Dialogues.* In addition, the other two essays in Popkin's edition provide an excellent reflection of Hume's rejection of the specific dogmas of Christianity. While presenting an excellent and lucid introduction to Hume's views on religion and a broad summary of the content of the *Dialogues,* Popkin does not provide the analysis found in Kemp Smith and Pike and the summary provided by Kemp Smith.

Kierkegaard, Søren, *Concluding Unscientific Postscript,* Book I—Chapter I and Book II—Chapters I and II. Princeton, N.J.: Princeton University Press, 1941 (originally published in Copenhagen in 1846). Also included in the Edwards-Pap, Bronstein-Schulweis, Alston, and Hick (*Classical and Contemporary . . .*) anthologies. This is a classic defense of the right to believe in God, not simply without evidence, but *in spite of* evidence which makes this belief appear irrational.

Kaufmann, Walter, *Critique of Religion and Philosophy.* New York: Doubleday, 1961. A witty and lucid unsympathetic critique of ideas in Western religious tradition. While Kaufmann does not attempt to provide a "balanced" treatment of the various sides of the issues he discusses, he does bring a wide knowledge of his subject to his writings and his remarks are thought-provoking.

Kushner, Harold S., *When Bad Things Happen to Good People.* New York: Schocken Books, 1981. In this best-seller, Kushner, a rabbi, tackles the problem of evil and opts for a finite benevolent god. Kushner wrote the book after his son died at the age of fourteen of progeria, the rapid aging disease. Troubled deeply by the injustice of his son's death and the personal agony that this death caused him, Kushner abandoned his previous orthodox belief in an omnipotent deity. His reflections led him to write this very poignant book. Kushner brings out what he sees as the inadequacies of common Judeo-Christian responses to the problem of evil. The very clear and nontechnical discussion is directed to a wide lay audience who believe or want to believe in God, but are troubled by the problem of evil and seek reassurance. Such readers should find this book very stimulating.

Lewis, C.S., *Mere Christianity.* London: Geoffrey Bles, 1952. This very simply expressed defense of basic Christian beliefs was presented by Lewis (who was an atheist as a young man) in a series of British radio broadcasts. (A short excerpt from this book is included in this chapter.)

Lewis, C.S., *The Problem of Pain.* New York: Macmillan, 1959. A very clear and nontechnical attempt by a Christian believer to answer the challenge posed by the problem of evil. Unlike the more "liberal" theological view of Hick, which departs significantly from standard Christian doctrine (e.g., Hick does not believe in "hell"), Lewis' views are quite orthodox.

Martin, C.B., *Religious Belief.* Ithaca, N.Y.: Cornell University Press, 1959. Martin attempts to set out as clearly as possible what he sees as the difficulties and confusions in religious assertions and arguments relating to God. While very clearly written, the careful analytic dissection of religious claims and arguments is apt to prove difficult for philosophical novices. Martin considers such issues as "Seeing God," "Life-after-death," "Faith," and "Why is there anything at all."

Matson, Wallace I., *The Existence of God.* Ithaca, N.Y.: Cornell University Press, 1965. A consideration of ontological, cosmological, and teleological arguments for God's existence, the problem of evil, James' "Will to Believe," and the connection between morality and belief in God. The book is analytically oriented, but is clear and nontechnical and is written from the point of view of a nonbeliever. Of special interest is Matson's criticism of the arguments from probability (pp. 102–11) and entropy (pp. 111–19) that are utilized by many contemporary "creationists."

Mill, John Stuart, *Theism.* Indianapolis: Bobbs Merrill, 1951 (originally published in 1874 as *Three Essays on Religion). Theism* is the last major work completed by Mill. It was published a year after his death, along with two considerably shorter, earlier essays on religion. In *Theism,* Mill considers various arguments for the existence of God, the attributes of God, immortality, and revelation. Mill accepts the argument from design as providing probable evidence for the existence of a *finite* deity whose moral attributes are uncertain. This edition of Mill's writings on religion contains a clear, twelve-page introduction by Richard Taylor. A more recent edition of Mill's writings on religion is *Three Essays on Religion.* New York: Greenwood Press, 1969.

Plantinga, Alvin, *God, Freedom and Evil.* New York: Harper and Row, 1974. This book is geared to the sophisticated reader of philosophy, but most of it would be understandable and stimulating to a beginning student. It consists of an intricate analytic dissection of the ontological argument for God's existence and the problem of evil, in addition to a very brief discussion of the cosmological and teleological arguments for God's existence.

Russell, Bertrand, *Why I Am Not a Christian.* New York: Simon & Schuster, 1957. This book contains many of Russell's articles deeply critical of religion. The main article is "Why I Am Not a Christian," which was used as the title of the book. In this very readable and nontechnical article, Russell considers and rejects several arguments for the existence of God and then goes on to defend the claim that "Christ was not the best and wisest of men." Also of special interest is Russell's earlier essay "A Free Man's Worship," in which Russell expresses, in very literary form, a rather pessimistic view of the human condition and of the place of human beings in the scheme of things. The excerpt from Russell at the beginning of this chapter comes from this work. It occurs at the beginning of the essay, right after Russell's imaginative and stimulating version of a creation story which he puts in the mouth of Mephistopheles (the devil in the Faust legend to whom Faust sold his soul). As one would expect, this creation story is quite different from the version in the Bible.

Scriven, Michael, *Primary Philosophy.* New York: McGraw Hill, 1966. In chapter 4 of this introductory text, Scriven presents a detailed defense of atheism. While the writing style is perhaps too concise and choppy, Scriven clearly considers and criticizes many arguments for the existence of God (considerably more than is usually considered), and considers and defends arguments against the existence of God. He also considers the relevance of reason and faith to the belief in God. The detailed subdivisions in the table of contents makes the text a good reference source for students seeking a short analytic treatment of particular arguments for the existence of God.

Stace, W.T., *Mysticism and Philosophy.* Philadelphia: Lippincott, 1960. This book contains a sympathetic discussion of religious mysticism.

Taylor, Richard, *Metaphysics,* (3rd ed.), Chapter 7. Englewood Cliffs, N.J.: Prentice-Hall, 1983. As well as presenting a defense of the argument from contingency (which is included in our anthology), Taylor considers and defends a version of the argument from design in his chapter on God in this general introduction to metaphysics. The writing style is very clear.

Teresa of Avila, Saint, *The Life of St. Teresa of Avila.* Westminister, Maryland: The Newman Press, 1962. In Chapters 25–29 of this autobiography, translated from the original Spanish, St. Teresa discusses her mystical experiences and how she was reassured that these visions were the work of God and not the devil.

Twain, Mark, *Letters From Earth.* New York: Harper & Row, 1938. A selection of Twain's essays, many of which consist of sarcastic criticism of religion and, in particular, of those who take the Bible literally. In addition, these essays reveal Twain's cynical and pessimistic view of human nature. As one reviewer put it, "Twain in the raw, jeering, brilliant, pulverizing . . ." The first and main article is "Letters From Earth," which was used for the title of the book. (Only a small part of this essay was included in this chapter.)

Wisdom, John, "Gods" in *Philosophy and Psychoanalysis.* Oxford: Blackwell, 1953. A very influential and sympathetic discussion of the unverifiability of the belief of God's existence. Unlike some other analytic philosophers, Wisdom is unwilling to say that unverifiable statements are meaningless.

editorial note and suggested readings on the current creationism versus evolution controversy

For many years after the 1859 publication of Darwin's *The Origin of Species,* there was great opposition to the teaching of evolution in public school science classes. With the increasing support of evolutionary theory among scientists, the teaching of evolutionary theory in science classes has today become a matter of course. From the perspective of the majority of today's scientifically oriented biology teachers, the Biblical story of creation is a myth that has no place in the teaching of biological science. Recently, however, there has been great controversy over the appropriateness of teaching the Biblical version of creation alongside evolutionary theory. Individuals with degrees in science and fundamentalist religious leanings proclaim that the empirical evidence supports the Biblical story of creation at least as much as—many would say more than—it supports evolutionary theory. While the "creationists," as they are called, call "creationism" a science, most biologists disagree. The creationist view has been given added credence by the fact that biologists have come to question the empirical support for Darwin's theory of evolution *through natural selection.* While the belief in evolution itself is not a subject of controversy among experts in biology, the false impression is often created that it is. What is a subject of controversy among the experts is the specific mechanism by which evolution occurs. According to the influential contemporary theory of "punctuated equilibrium," contrary to Darwin's view that species evolve slowly and continuously from generation to generation, the creation of new species occurs rapidly during specific periods characterized by drastic environmental changes. This view of evolution is taken by its supporters to explain the gaps in transitional forms that has plagued fossil-hunters and given such delight to anti-evolutionists, and it is also taken to explain why some animals whose remains span millions of years in the fossil record give no evidence of evolutionary change.

This new view of evolution, which emphasizes the role of environmental catastrophes in evolutionary development, is explained in the feature article "Enigmas of Evolution" which appeared in the March 29, 1982 issue of *Newsweek* magazine (pp. 44–49), an article which centers on the views of America's most popular writer and lecturer on evolution, Stephen Gould, a professor at Harvard University. It was Gould, along with Niles Eldredge—a paleontologist at the American Museum of Natural History—who first proposed the punctuated equilibrium theory of evolution. Detailed support for this theory can be found in Steven M. Stanley's *The New Evolutionary Timetable* (New York: Basic Books, 1981). Another informative book on this topic is Francis Hitching's *The Neck of the Giraffe: Where Darwin Went Wrong* (New Haven, Conn.: Ticknor and Fields, 1982), which relates the difficulties with Darwinian natural selection and sketches alternative views of evolution; Chapter 5, Creation vs. Evolution, presents the main issues of controversy between creationists and evolutionists and also provides references to literature on both sides of this issue.

Chapter III

THE MIND-BODY RELATIONSHIP, PERSONAL IDENTITY, AND THE AFTERLIFE

. . . so long as we have the body . . .we shall never attain completely what we desire . . .

Plato

All that exists is body. All that occurs is motion.

Thomas Hobbes

Now I know that I exist, and at the same time I observe absolutely nothing else as belonging to my nature or essence except the mere fact that I am a conscious being; and just from this I can validly infer that my essence consists simply in the fact that I am a conscious being.

René Descartes

Our mental conditions are simply the symbols in consciousness of the changes which take place automatically in the organism . . . . [T]he feeling we call volition is not the cause of a voluntary act, but the symbol of that state of the brain which is the immediate cause of that act. We are conscious automata . . . .

T.H. Huxley

In saying that a person is not to be described as a mind coupled with a body, I am not saying . . . that people are just machines . . . . In ordinary life . . . we seldom use the noun "mind" . . . at all. What we do is to talk of people, of people calculating, conjuring, hoping, resolving . . . and so on.

Gilbert Ryle

The statement that "consciousness is a process in the brain" . . . is a reasonable scientific hypothesis . . .

U.T. Place

. . . there is nothing in the world over and above those entities which are postulated by physics.

J.J.C. Smart

Next to the error of those who deny God . . . there is none more effectual in leading feeble spirits from the straight path than to imagine that . . . after this life we have nothing to fear or to hope for, any more than the flies or the ants . . . Our soul is in its nature entirely independent of the body, and in consequence . . . it is not liable to die with it.

René Descartes

All the evidence goes to show that what we regard as our mental life is bound up with brain structure and organized bodily energy. Therefore it is rational to suppose that mental life ceases when bodily life ceases. The argument is only one of probability, but it is as strong as those upon which most scientific conclusions are based.

Bertrand Russell

. . . to find wherein personal identity consists, we must consider what **person** *stands for—which is a thinking intelligent being, that has reason and reflection, and can consider itself as itself, the same thinking thing, in different times and places.*

John Locke

Sensuous experiences are possible only in connexion with a living [embodied] organism.

P.T. Geach

The Puzzle of Personal Identity and the Concept of an Afterlife

No less than questions concerning the ultimate nature of the universe and our place in the scheme of things, the perennial philosophical question of the relationship of mind and body has its roots in the stirrings of childhood philosophical wonder, in this case, the wonder that we experience when we contemplate our own deaths. Do we cease to exist with the death of our physical bodies or can we survive their ultimate destruction? Are we simply to be equated with our bodies or are we something else? If we are more than our bodies, what are we? If our parents believe in God, they assure us of our immortality but rarely go into details. Indeed as we grow older and can better articulate questions concerning the nature of our own existence, we may be surprised to find that while many profess faith in an afterlife, most do not have a clear conception of the nature of that afterlife. Among those who offer some specific belief, some speak of a disembodied existence, while others speak of "the resurrection of the body" or of an ethereal, ghost-like "astral body" that escapes unnoticed from the physical body that is destined to be destroyed. Yet, others speak of some type of "reincarnation of the soul." Still others speak vaguely of "life's ultimate merging with the flow of being." What all these concepts mean, however, we are rarely told. Certainly, for example, no one will deny that our bodies will "merge with being" in the sense that the chemicals that compose our bodies ultimately will be "recycled" by nature into the nutrients that feed other organisms. Yet this is certainly not what we want when we seek solace from the gnawing thought of the possible end of our existence. What those of us who have been imbued with the ideas of Western religion want is the preservation of our personal identity, of that unity of consciousness that we call ourselves. But what is that unity of consciousness that we call ourselves? Certainly, it would not appear to be connected with a particular body, for we seem easily to be able to imagine the possibility of existing with an entirely different body.

For example, can you not easily imagine yourself waking up one morning, feeling strangely different body sensations and not recognizing the room that you are in. You stretch and move your arms into your field of vision and are startled to see something that you don't recognize as your arm. You run to a mirror in the room, feeling strangely taller than you have felt before; then you find yourself staring panic-stricken and befuddled at a strange image that greets you in the mirror. You scream in horror and someone comes in and calls you by a strange name. Meanwhile in the place that you seem to remember as your home, the person whose name you are being called is waking up and undergoing an experience similar to yours. Many philosophers from John Locke (1632–1704) to the present as well as many science fiction writers have been fascinated by the possibility of such "body transferences." But does what seems so easily imaginable really make sense? Is it not possible for us to redescribe the same case of alleged bodily transference in an entirely different way. You wake up one morning, not remembering who you really are. You think you're someone else and you seem indeed to remember things that happened to that person. But everyone around you assures you that you are not that person; you only seem to think you are. In some inexplicable way, you seem to remember accurately things that happened to that other person, but have suffered amnesia as to your own past. Equally inexplicably, you have assumed many of that person's personality traits. Similarly, the person you mistakenly think you are also has suffered amnesia and seems to have picked up some of your personality traits and memories. It is suggested that the two of you have been victims of a mysterious process of telepathic thought-transference with accompanying amnesia. This is maddening. Are you the person you seem to remember yourself as being who has undergone a drastic body change or are you the person whose body you possess who has undergone a drastic personality and apparent memory change? This question cannot be answered, of course, until we come to grips with the question of what constitutes personal identity.

According to many philosophers, most notably Locke, personal identity must be defined in terms of memory. According to this view, to be able to remember the thoughts and feelings of a person who was conscious in the past is just what it means to be that person. But this seems inadequate, for we seem easily able to imagine ourselves either continuing to exist in a state of amnesia as to our past or *mistakenly seeming to remember events* that never happened to us. To say that someone "really" remembers rather than just delusively "seems" to remember, *presupposes* that that person really is the same person he seems to remember himself as being. Consequently, those who attempt to define personal identity in terms of memory are compelled to resort to the notion of personal identity to distinguish real from apparent memories. We are, as logicians would put it, begging the question or arguing in a circle—that is, assuming precisely what is at issue. If memory cannot provide the underlying unity of consciousness that we call ourselves, what then can provide it?

Many philosophers have claimed that one must postulate the existence of a "soul" to provide that unity. But what a soul is and how it provides that unity we are never told. Since a soul is supposed to be unobservable, how can we know when a given body is occupied by the "same" soul? How do we know that a given body is not "occupied" by several different souls (for example, in cases of "multiple personality") or that the single soul that supposedly occupies a given body does not change from day to day or second to second, replaced each time by another soul psychologically similar to it? If one claims, as so many of us will, that one knows in one's own case that one's soul remains the same, what is it that one knows? Does the notion of a soul in any way *explain* our sense of personal identity or does it simply give us the specious sense of an explanation, leaving us as much in the dark as we were before?

Nevertheless, many of us associate our personal identity with the continued existence of an immaterial soul and conceive of the afterlife as the "freeing" of this soul from its "occupancy" of a particular body. Such a view of personal identity was popular in the ancient world and had an influence on the ancient Greek philosopher Plato (427?–347 B.C.). As Plato depicts it, a person *is* an immaterial mind or soul that "possesses" or "uses" a particular body. It is the soul that feels, senses, thinks and chooses—that is, is conscious. While Nature has so disposed matters that souls have conscious desires that correspond to the physical needs of the bodies they possess, the soul is capable of existing and can go on being conscious after the destruction of the body. Indeed, Plato likens the soul to a bird and the body to a cage. The body, in Plato's view, is "the prison of the soul," from which the soul, like a bird in its cage, longs to be free. With death comes the possibility of this freedom. (In practice, however, Plato believed that most souls when liberated from the body retain the carnal desires that they experienced when they possessed a body and continue to "haunt this earth.")

The Platonic identification of one's self with an immaterial soul whose essential characteristic is its consciousness can also be found in the writings of René Descartes (1596–1650), who had a profound impact upon subsequent philosophers' conceptions of the relationship of mind and body. An accomplished scientist and mathematician, Descartes naturally accepted the prevalent scientific view of his day that the world of physical objects is subject to the deterministic[1] laws of mechanics. Yet the Christian religion to which he was deeply committed led him to reject the view that human decisions and actions are completely mechanically determined, a view which he believed would entail that human actions were unfree. Descartes' solution was to draw a radical metaphysical distinction between completely mechanically determined unconscious physical objects and immaterial, indestructible, and consequently immortal, conscious souls, which are capable of interfering with the deterministic order of the physical world.

In Descartes' view a person's "essence"—that is, that which cannot be taken away from one without destroying one's personal identity—is one's consciousness. The states of consciousness that are essential to one's existence, Descartes claimed, are properties of the soul, not the body. Believing that only creatures with souls could be conscious and apparently accepting the Christian view that animals do not have souls, Descartes was willing to accept the logical consequence that animals are totally determined "machines" or "automatons" devoid of feelings and other states of consciousness. Among the biological creatures of this world, only human beings are conscious; only human beings have the "freedom of will" to interfere with the deterministic order of physical causes and effects, Descartes believed. Like Plato, Descartes identified persons with souls and not physical bodies and assumed that souls can go on being conscious in a disembodied state eternally after the destruction of their physical bodies. While in this world conscious experiences are dependent upon physical bodies (e.g., sight is dependent upon the eye, optic nerve, and brain), there is no necessity for this dependence. One can conceive, for example, of someone who has no eyes having the experience called sight as in a dream.

Even if it makes sense, as Descartes believed, to imagine ourselves in a disembodied existence having conscious experiences similar to those that are in this world dependent upon a body, is it plausible to believe, as Descartes did, that

[1]Determinism is the philosophical doctrine that any event (E) has a scientific cause (C)—i.e., that it falls under a scientific law that asserts that whenever C occurs, E will occur—and, as such, is in principle predictable, given a knowledge of the scientific law involved and the events that preceded it. We shall discuss this view and its bearing on human free will and moral responsibility in a subsequent chapter.

such experiences would continue without a body? Many have thought not. Besides, how could we recognize loved ones if the afterlife consists of some sort of disembodied existence? Through telepathic communication? But how would we know that we are not simply imagining this, alone in the boundless solitude of our own disembodied existence? Do we not want a more substantial type of afterlife? Perhaps because of this need, the belief in some type of bodily afterlife is so prevalent today.

Many people familiar with the literature on parapsychological experiences have turned to the notion of an "astral body," a ghostlike duplicate of one's earthly body which it occupies. On this view, a person is to be identified with a particular astral body which is the true subject of one's states of consciousness. Others turn to the notions of reincarnation or resurrection. But again the question of personal identity remains unsettled. For example, does it make sense to speak, as some do, of a person being reincarnated into the body of an animal such as a dog, or even a fish? Is such a thing conceivable? Certainly we cannot impose a human personality, desires, emotions, and memories upon such creatures. But if we subtract such qualities from ourselves, with what are we left? Similarly, how are we to imagine resurrection? What sort of a body will the resurrected body be? The body we had at death? Will the resurrected body have the deformities that it possessed in this life? No, say Christian theologians, it will be "a perfected body." But what that means, we are not told. Indeed, some theologians, following St. Paul, suggest that the resurrected body may be quite unlike the physical body. But if that is the case, will not the problem of identification still remain? When I think, as I sometimes do, of my dead father and longingly hope to see "him" again, it is the face of my father as I knew him in his later years that I see before me, not some strange body that contains my father's memories. If I shall "meet my father again" after death, as Judeo-Christian religious tradition says I will, how will I know that it is he? How can we distinguish a world of *newly* created beings who appear to have the memories of beings that no longer exist from a world of resurrected beings who are *the same as* beings that existed in a different world?

The Mind-Body Relationship

However we choose to conceive the nature of the afterlife and the notion of personal identity that we in Western culture assume it presupposes, we imagine that, in some sense, "our" consciousness will continue beyond the grave. Like Plato and Descartes, we tend to associate ourselves not with our physical bodies but with the various states of consciousness that, at least in this world, seem to depend upon physical occurrences within our brains. For example, our visual sensations are dependent upon electrochemical nerve impulses generated by our optic nerves, which are stimulated by the light waves that reach the retinas of our eyes. These nerve impulses travel very rapidly to a particular part of our brains (the visual cortex), where they in some mysterious way give rise to states of consciousness that we call sight. While one can turn to a physiologist to learn *how* light affects the retina and *how* it causes a nerve impulse, it seems that no one can tell us *how* a purely physical process can give rise to states of consciousness.

For many philosophers, it has seemed incomprehensible that a purely physical process could ever give rise to—that is, "cause"—a state of consciousness that is so unlike it. Such philosophers have been struck by the fact that states of consciousness, unlike physical processes, are *private* events. While a physiologist knows much more than I do about the nature of the physical processes that give rise to my visual sensations, the physiologist is incapable of having direct access to my visual sensations as I do.

The actual visual sensations that I experience when I see, say a red apple, seem to be directly available only to me. How then, some philosophers have wondered, can I be sure that you are seeing "the same" color as I am when you look at the same red apple? You may call it "red," but is it not possible that the way you see red is quite different from the way I see it?

Like Descartes, many philosophers have been fascinated and puzzled by the apparent utter privacy of our states of consciousness. There is, for example, a fundamental difference between the manner in which I "know" that I am in pain—that is, simply by *feeling* it—and the manner in which I know that someone else is in pain. While I *infer* the existence of other people's pain from their behavior (e.g., they groan or say they are in pain), this is not true of myself. However uncertain one may be of the states of consciousness of others, one seems to have *infallible* knowledge of the nature of one's own states of consciousness. Accepting this point of view, many philosophers, like Descartes, have assumed that mental and physical events are radically different sorts of events and have been puzzled by their relationship.

Dualist Theories

The view of the mind-body relationship that most people find initially most plausible is *interactionism*, the view held by Descartes. According to this view, physical events are capable of causing mental events while mental events in turn are capable of causing physical events. For example, the complex physical event that begins with light entering one's eye and ends with a nervĕ impulse in the visual cortex causes a visual sensation (mental event). Similarily, thoughts of frightening things (mental events) can cause physical events like the more rapid beating of one's heart. While many philosophers have seen mind-body interactionism as self-evident, others have seen this interactionism as incomprehensible, given the radical difference of mental and physical events and our inability to *explain* how mental and physical events can cause each other. Such a view does not, however, have the force it once had among philosophers, due in large measure to David Hume's classical analysis of causation (see p. 69).

Under the influence of Hume, many contemporary philosophers would claim that all *fundamental* modes of causation are brute facts of experience that are incapable of explanation. With Hume, they would claim that causal "connections" neither can be intuitively "seen" nor logically deduced from certain self-evident truths, but must be based on the brute facts of the "constant conjunctions" of events that we happen to observe in this world—that is, our observations that certain types of events regularly lead to other types of events. While Hume himself did not mention this, we can reduce the mystery of the innumerable constant conjunctions we happen to find in this world by attempting to explain many of them in terms of a limited number of primitive constant conjunctions *that we happen to find in this world*. In this manner, science can reduce the mystery of *how* some events "cause" other events by seeking to analyze complex constant conjunctions into a series of these primitive constant conjunctions of events (i.e., "X causes Y" can be broken up into X causes A_1 causes A_2 causes A_3 . . . causes Y) or by devising theories that assume laws that reflect these primitive constant conjunctions. For example, the kinetic theory of gases assumes that the unobservable molecules it postulates to explain various laws (constant conjunctions of events) relating to the behavior of gases obey the laws of Newtonian mechanics that observable objects do.

From this point of view, explanation consists in analyzing complicated causal connections in such a way that we recognize in the complicated system the interplay of very familiar constant conjunctions that we often take as not needing explanation (e.g., billiard balls are moved when they are hit by other billiard balls). Indeed, defenders of this point of view would stress that our quest for explanations not only come to a natural *psychological* halt at these primitive familiar constant conjunctions, but also that the quest for explanations must *logically* come to a halt at this point. Explanations of the causal "mechanism" by which a given event "causes" another event must ultimately be based on the acceptance of primitive constant conjunctions which are themselves incapable of explanation and are simply a reflection of the brute fact that the events of this world occur in a particular repeatable order. From this point of view, the "how" of causation simply does not make sense when one speaks of primitive, as opposed to complex, causal relationships. The causal connection between body and mind, it has been suggested, is one of these inexplicable primitive causal connections.

Since prior to Hume most philosophers thought that all causal relationships must be capable of some type of logical or intuitive explanation, many philosophers who were greatly influenced by Descartes' mind-body dualism rejected Descartes' hypothesis of mind-body interactionism. For example, the French philosopher Nicolas Malebranche (1638–1715) claimed that physical and mental events are in themselves incapable of causing anything and that God is the only true cause of change in the universe. As Malebranche saw it, the apparent causal interaction between physical and mental events is actually caused by God's constant intervention in the scheme of events in this world. For example, the cavity in my tooth does not really cause my pain, but is rather an occasion for God to cause me to feel pain. Similarly, the fear I feel is an occasion for God to cause my heart to beat faster. Malebranche's view that there is no causal connection, but only regular correlation, between mental and physical events is called *parallelism;* and his belief that his correlation is caused by God's constant intervention is called *occasionalism.*

Accepting Malebranche's parallelism, the German philosopher Gottfried Leibniz (1646–1716) rejected Malebranche's occasionalism, seeing such a view as inconsistent with the perfect wisdom of God. As Leibinz saw it, all physical events in this world are caused only by preceding physical events while mental events are caused only by preceding mental events. Nevertheless, God created the stream of physical causes and independent stream of mental causes in this world with a *preestablished harmony* that makes it falsely appear that physical and mental events interact. Believing that mental events must be caused by preceding mental events, parallelists like Leibniz were forced to hypothesize "unconscious mental events" as the true causes of many conscious mental events since conscious mental events are not uniformly preceded by other conscious mental events.

With the continuing discovery of underlying physical determinants for states of consciousness, another theory of the relationship of mental and physical events became popular in the nineteenth and twentieth centuries. According to this theory, called *epiphenomenalism*, mental events are always caused by preceding physical (neurological) events, but are themselves powerless to affect these physical events—that is, mental events are merely "by-products" (or epiphenomena) of physical events. In the poetic words of the epiphenomenalistic philosopher George Santayana, states of consciousness are nothing but a "lyric cry in the midst of business."

The Denial of Mental Substance (Souls): The Bundle Theory and the Double Aspect Theory

While the epiphenomenalist admits the metaphysical difference between mental and physical *events*, most epiphenomenalists would claim that both mental and physical processes are properties of physical *substances.* This is not, however, the only view that epiphenomenalists have taken. Like David Hume, some epiphenomenalists have denied that there is any underlying substance that is the subject of mental states. (A *substance* is that which has properties and undergoes changes, but remains the same through change.) As Hume saw it, the states of consciousness that we identify with ourselves do not ''belong'' to any substance at all. On the Humean view, a person is not a soul that has states of consciousness, as Descartes claimed, nor a physical body that has states of consciousness, as many epiphenomenalists have claimed. A person is instead nothing more than an aggregate or ''bundle'' of momentary states of consciousness which possess whatever unity they do by virtue of their mutual interrelationships, and not by virtue of being properties of some underlying simple continuing substance. Such a view, however, has seemed unsatisfactory to most philosophers. (Indeed, Hume found it unsatisfying, but felt compelled logically to accept it.)

Most philosophers have taken it as self-evident that mental and physical properties must be properties of either mental or immaterial substances. This view was, however, rejected by Baruch Spinoza (1632–77), who claimed that mental and physical properties are two different ''aspects'' of the same underlying substance that is necessarily neither purely mental nor physical. Indeed, Spinoza believed that all things in this world have both physical and mental attributes, just as a coin must always have two sides. Spinoza's view that physical and mental attributes are attributes of the same (''neutral'') substance is called *the double aspect theory* and his view that apparently purely physical objects have a mental aspect (which may not be intense enough to be described as ''consciousness'') is called *panpsychism*, a view which was held by many other philosophers, including Leibniz.

An influential contemporary ''double aspect'' theory of the mind-body relationship is the *person theory* of Peter Strawson. Rejecting Descartes' view that states of consciousness are states of mental substances (minds or souls) as well as the view that states of consciousness are states of purely physical bodies, Strawson argues that states of consciousness must be attributed to substances that contain both physical and mental aspects. Strawson calls such substances *persons*. Strawson, consequently, rejects as unintelligible the notion of the disembodied existence of a purely mental substance.

The Denial of a Duality of Physical and Mental Events as well as of Physical and Mental Substances: Idealism and Materialism

Seeking fundamental metaphysical unity, some philosophers have rejected the dualism of mental and physical events as well as the dualism of mental and physical substances. For example, the English philosopher George Berkeley (1685–1753) accepted the philosophical doctrine known as *idealism* (which we shall discuss in the next chapter), which asserts that ultimate reality consists of spirits (souls) and their mental states. Physical objects, Berkeley claimed, are simply ideas in the mind of God. While idealists like Berkeley claim that everything that exists is ''really'' mental, some philosophers like Thomas Hobbes (1588–1679) claim that everything that exists is ''really'' physical. It is this view that is often defined as *materialism*. According to this usage, a materialist is a person who believes that reality consists of physical bodies and physical processes. *Materialism* is however, sometimes defined more broadly as the view that mental substances do not exist and that physical processes are more fundamental than mental processes. According to this broader definition, epiphenomenalism can be classified as a materialistic view even though it is usually classified as a dualistic view (because of its acceptance of a duality of physical and mental events, even though it denies a duality of physical and mental substances). According to this usage, materialists are those who believe that all events that exist in this world can be explained on the basis of laws of nature which do not refer to private mental entities or processes but only to publicly observable physical entities or processes.

Behaviorism

Behaviorism, which is widely held among contemporary psychologists, is another form of materialism, broadly defined. While behaviorists are united in the belief that human "behavior" is the most important element in the study of human psychology, there are several different versions of this viewpoint. Historically, the term "behaviorism" can be traced to the influential psychologist J.B. Watson (1878–1958), who wanted to establish psychology as a science. As Watson saw it, the proper aim of any science is predictability and control, which require that its subject matter be open to public verification. Since states of consciousness are private and consequently unverifiable, psychologists should turn their attention exclusively toward publicly verifiable physical behavior, Watson claimed. This view of behaviorism is often called *methodolgical behaviorism.* It is not a metaphysical theory of the ultimate nature of reality, but a scientific viewpoint as to the proper subject matter of the science of psychology. While methodological behaviorists may accept the ultimate metaphysical difference between private unverifiable states of consciousness and observable verifiable physical behavior, they will nevertheless assert that psychology should be concerned only with the latter. If a methodological behaviorist goes on to assert, as Watson did in some of his writings, that states of consciousness are in reality nothing more than physical processes, he is also a *metaphysical behaviorist.*

Methodological behaviorists also differ in their concept of behavior. While Watson used this concept very broadly to encompass microscopic molecular behavior unobservable to the naked eye, this is not true of the highly influential contemporary methodological behaviorist B.F. Skinner, who restricts his use of the term "behavior" to external bodily behavior such as walking and talking. As Skinner sees it, the proper purpose of psychology is to formulate laws of learning which tell us that if such and such is done to an organism, then one can expect the organism to respond in such and such a publicly observable way. There is no need, Skinner believes, to hypothesize inner mental (or physical) processes to explain the connection between these stimuli and responses, as, for example, Freudians do.

Among philosophers, the most widely held type of behaviorism is best called conceptual behaviorism but is usually referred to as *logical behaviorism.* Unlike the metaphysical behaviorist, who professes to be offering a theory as to what "really exists," the logical behaviorist sees his task more modestly as that of unraveling the meaning of mentalistic concepts. As the logical behaviorist sees it, these concepts are, at least in part, definable in terms of publicly observable behavior. The most philosophically influential defense of this point of view can be found in Gilbert Ryle's *The Concept of Mind* (1949), a book which has generated much discussion among contemporary philosophers. As Ryle sees it, most mentalistic terms do not refer to private, hidden events that occur in a mysterious place called "the mind," but rather refer to the dispositions or tendencies people have to behave in particular ways. A person's "mind" is not some type of substance or thing, as philosophers under the influence of Descartes like to think of it, but rather is a way of broadly and misleadingly referring to a person's tendencies and abilities to do various sorts of things, Ryle claims.

For example, Ryle claims, dualists under the sway of Descartes, mistakenly assume that emotions such as vanity, love, and anger are inner mental events that occur "in persons' minds" and that *cause* persons to behave as they do. For example, when we say that a person boasts from vanity, the dualist falsely interprets this to mean that there occurs in that person's mind a particular private feeling of vanity which causes that person's publicly observable boasting. This is all wrong, Ryle passionately argues. To say that a person boasts from vanity is not to attribute a hidden ghostly occurrence to that person but to relate his boasting to his behavior as a whole—(e.g., he is the sort of person who will behave in such and such a way in such and such circumstances). Similarly, when we say that "Jack loves Alice," the dualist falsely tends to assume that Jack experiences a specific "feeling of love" that causes him to behave in the way that he does to Alice. Again, this is all wrong, Ryle would say. By definition, a feeling becomes a *feeling of love* only when it is accompanied by specific behavior or, at the least, the tendency towards specific behavior. (Imagine Jack claiming that he loves Alice, but never behaving toward her or having any inclination to behave toward her in a manner that expresses that love. Can this be "love"?) We are all aware of the fact that alleged feelings of love can often be redescribed in different ways (e.g., as feelings of physical attraction or infatuation) when related to the general pattern of a person's behavior. The important and certainly correct point that Ryle makes is that the mentalistic words we use to describe our feelings and emotions are often used not simply to name particular subjectively observed states of consciousness, but rather to *interpret* these states of consciousness by relating them to publicly observable behavior and to social context. For example, there is no specific discernable feeling called anger. First of all, it is possible to be angry without feeling angry. For example, imagine a person who is deeply insulted by someone else. Without thinking and without feeling angry he rushes over to the insulter, face flushed, and hits him. Clearly, such a person may later admit that he must have been very angry to do such a thing. Secondly, even though being angry usually involves feeling angry (e.g., feeling one's face flush, one's heart beating faster), these feelings become "feelings of anger" only when accompanied by beliefs (e.g., one's awareness that he was insulted) and/or behavior. (There have been psychological experiments in which the sorts of feelings that people have when angry are produced by means of electrodes and hormone injection. Participants in these experiments do not know how to describe their feelings. They do not describe them as feelings of anger since their feelings are not directed toward anything, as anger is.)

The Identity Theory

In spite of Ryle's convincing behavioristic analyses of many mentalistic concepts, he does not deny the existence of private feelings, which he makes no attempt to define in behavioristic terms. Consequently, Ryle leaves himself open to the dualist who will say that since feelings, as well as thoughts and other states of consciousness, cannot be reduced to behavior, they must have a special nonphysical status. Even if these private mental events do not do much to explain behavior, they still exist, the dualist will say, and still create the puzzle of their relationship to physical processes. Most contemporary materialists would accept the dualist's contention that states of consciousness cannot be defined or made to refer to an organism's overt behavior, while rejecting the dualist's conclusion that they are nonphysical occurences. As many of them see it, while a sensation of pain, for example, is not *definable* in terms of external behavior or neurological activity within the brain, it is reasonable from a scientific point of view to assume that the term "pain" *refers* to some brain process. This very influential and controversial contemporary materialistic viewpoint is called the *identity theory*. As identity theorists see it, just as it is possible for the same thing to be known under two descriptions with different meanings (e.g., the terms "the morning star" and "the evening star" both refer to the same object, namely the planet Venus), it is scientifically reasonable to believe that the processes picked out by mentalistic terms which refer to states of consciousness will turn out to be the same as processes picked out by physical terms. Identity theorists claim that these processes are neurological ones that occur in the brain.

In claiming the identity of mental states and brain states, the modern materialistic identity theory is in agreement with Spinoza's double aspect theory. For Spinoza, however, the world consisted of a single substance (which he called "God") that has both a physical and a mental aspect. Consequently, for Spinoza the mental and the physical were equally real. Modern materialistic identity theorists, however, claim that only the physical really exists. Human beings, they claim are nothing more than physical substances and their physical processes. Like epiphenomenalists, identity theorists make the scientific assumption that no state of consciousness can occur without an underlying neurological process, but while epiphenomenalists see the underlying neurological process as "different from" the state of consciousness that it causes, identity theorists see them as one and "the same" event.

In order to see this better, let us consider the statement "Jack's thought of Alice caused his heart to beat faster" and analyze this statement from the interactionist's, epiphenomenalist's, and identity theorist's points of view. The interactionist will take this statement literally, seeing Jack's thought of Alice as a state of consciousness that, without any intervention by some underlying neurological process, *causes* Jack's heart to beat faster. On the other hand, both the epiphenomenalist and the identity theorist will seek some underlying neurological process to account for Jack's heart beating faster. As the epiphenomenalist will see it, however, Jack's thought is something quite different from the neurological event which causes Jack's heart to beat faster. On his view, the state of consciousness which consists of Jack's thought of Alice was *caused* by either the very same neurological event that caused Jack's heart to beat faster or by some other neurological event causally related to it. The identity theorist, like the epiphenomenalist, will seek some neurological event as the true cause of Jack's heart beating faster and will assume, again like the epiphenomenalist, that this neurological event or some neurological event causally related to it will be found to account for Jack's thought of Alice. Unlike the epiphenomenalist, however, the identity theorist will identify Jack's thought of Alice with the neurological event which the epiphenomenalist will see as its cause.

The reader should notice that the debate between interactionists on the one hand and epiphenomenalists and identity theorists on the other is at least in part of a scientific (empirical) nature since it hinges on the question of whether or not states of consciousness can *as a matter of fact* occur without underlying neurological accompaniments. Believers in parapsychological phenomena such as telepathy and clairvoyance will often strongly dispute the claim that states of consciousness cannot exist without neurological accompaniments. The debate between epiphenomenalists and identity theorists, however, is purely conceptual or philosophical in nature since it concerns the question of the difference in *meaning* between the claim that states of consciousness and brain states refer to *the same event* and the claim that they are *different events* that are *casually related* to each other. Contemporary philosophers hotly debate this issue today. The identity theory's defenders often compare the identity theory to scientific theoretical identities such as "Water is (really) H_2O" or "Light is (really) an electromagnetic radiation" and claim that the statement that states of consciousness are (really) brain states should be seen in the same light. Their philosophical opponents, however, think that even if states of consciousness are capable of explanation in terms of brain states, as the properties of water are capable of explanation in terms of chemical theory and the laws of optics are capable of explanation in terms of electromagnetic theory, it is still illegitimate to equate the two as identity theorists do. Perhaps, too, as some philosophers would be the first to suggest, much of the problem arises from the fact that the mind-body relationship is unique and cannot be assimilated to the categories we employ in understanding other things. Furthermore, if we say that states of consciousness are brain states, will we not begin to speak of the "privileged access" people have to certain physical events—namely, certain of their brain states? Is it not the case, as some philosophers have suggested, that as we begin to think of states of consciousness in a more physical way, we will begin at the same time to think of certain physical events in a more mentalistic way, in the last analysis leaving ourselves no less puzzled by the unique relationship of mind and body?

22. THE MYTH OF IMMORTALITY

Clarence Darrow

CLARENCE DARROW (1857–1938) was a criminal trial lawyer who was very well-known in his day for his defense of controversial issues and his flamboyant style. He appeared as defense attorney in support of early union organizers, including the socialist Eugene V. Debs. In a well-known trial in 1925, he defended John Scopes' right to teach evolution in a Tennessee school, while pitted against William Jennings Bryan, the orator and previous nominee for President of the United States, for the prosecution. Darrow also defended the infamous Leopold and Loeb in their widely publicized 1924 trial for the kidnapping and murder of a boy, successfully saving them from the death penalty. Darrow wrote and fought for the more humane treatment of prisoners and was a leader of the movement to abolish the death penalty. In a day when few public figures wrote or spoke out against the belief in God, Darrow relished defending the atheistic point of view.

In the following selection, Darrow ridicules belief in immortality. While not explicitly providing an analysis of the concept of personal identity, Darrow considers and rejects three views of immortality which presuppose different views of personal identity. First, he considers the view that persons are spiritual substances that continue to exist after the destruction of the physical bodies they occupy. Second, he considers the view that persons are identifiable with their states of consciousness, in particular their memories, which are capable of existing after the destruction of their physical bodies. Third, he considers the traditional Christian view of immortality that presupposes "the resurrection of the body."

There is, perhaps, no more striking example of the credulity of man than the widespread belief in immortality. This idea includes not only the belief that death is not the end of what we call life, but that personal identity involving memory persists beyond the grave. So determined is the ordinary individual to hold fast to this belief that, as a rule, he refuses to read or to think upon the subject lest it cast doubt upon his cherished dream. Of those who may chance to look at this contribution, many will do so with the determination not to be convinced, and will refuse even to consider the manifold reasons that might weaken their faith. I know that this is true, for I know the reluctance with which I long approached the subject and my firm determination not to give up my hope. Thus the myth will stand in the way of a sensible adjustment to facts.

Even many of those who claim to believe in immortality still tell themselves and others that neither side of the question is susceptible of proof. Just what can these hopeful ones believe that the word "proof" involves? The evidence against the persistence of personal consciousness is as strong as the evidence of gravitation, and much more obvious. It is as convincing and unassailable as the proof of the destruction of wood or coal by fire. If it is not certain that death ends personal identity and memory, then almost nothing that man accepts as true is susceptible of proof . . .

It is customary to speak of a "belief in immortality." First, then, let us see what is meant by the word "belief." If I take a train in Chicago at noon, bound for New York, I believe I will reach that city the next morning. I believe it because I have been to New York. I have read about the city, I have known many other people who have been there, and their stories are not inconsistent with any known facts in my own experience. I have even examined the timetables, and I know just how I will go and how long the trip will take. In other words, when I board the train for New York, I believe I will reach that city because I have *reason* to believe it.

But if I am told that next week I shall start on a trip to Goofville; that I shall not take my body with me; that I shall stay for all eternity: can I find a single fact connected with my journey—the way I shall go, the part of me that is to go, the time of the journey, the country I shall reach, its location in space, the way I shall live there—or anything that would lead to a rational belief that I shall really make the trip? Have I ever known anyone who has made the journey and returned? If I am really to believe, I must try to get some information about all these important facts.

But people hesitate to ask questions about life after death. They do not ask, for they know that only silence comes out of the eternal darkness of endless space. If people really believed in a beautiful, happy, glorious land waiting to receive them when they died; if they believed that their friends would be waiting to meet them; if they believed that all pain and suffering would be left behind: why should they live through weeks, months, and even years of pain and torture while a cancer eats its way to the vital parts of the body? Why should one fight off death? Because he does *not* believe in any real sense: he only hopes. Everyone knows that there is no real evidence of any such state of bliss; so we are told not to search for proof. We are to accept through faith alone. But every thinking person knows that faith can only come through belief. Belief implies a condition of mind that accepts a certain idea. This condition can be brought about only by evidence. True, the evidence may be simply the unsupported statement of your grandmother; it may be wholly insufficient for reasoning men; but, good or

Source: Clarence Darrow, "The Myth of the Soul." This article first appeared in *The Forum,* Oct. 1928 (Vol. 80). It was reprinted in Clarence Darrow, *Verdicts Out of Court,* edited by Arthur and Lila Weinberg (New York: Quadrangle Books, 1963). Reprinted with the permission of Arthur and Lila Weinberg.

bad, it must be enough for the believer or he could not believe.

Upon what evidence, then, are we asked to believe in immortality? There is no evidence. One is told to rely on faith, and no doubt this serves the purpose so long as one can believe blindly whatever he is told. But if there is no evidence upon which to build a positive belief in immortality, let us examine the other side of the question. Perhaps evidence can be found to support a positive conviction that immortality is a delusion.

The Soul

The belief in immortality expresses itself in two different forms. On the one hand, there is a belief in the immortality of the "soul." This is sometimes interpreted to mean simply that the identity, the consciousness, the memory of the individual persists after death. On the other hand, many religious creeds have formulated a belief in "the resurrection of the body"—which is something else again. It will be necessary to examine both forms of this belief in turn.

The idea of continued life after death is very old. It doubtless had its roots back in the childhood of the race. In view of the limited knowledge of primitive man, it was not unreasonable. His dead friends and relatives visited him in dreams and visions and were present in his feeling and imagination until they were forgotten. Therefore the lifeless body did not raise the question of dissolution, but rather of duality. It was thought that man was a dual being possessing a body and a soul as separate entities, and that when a man died, his soul was released from his body to continue its life apart. Consequently, food and drink were placed upon the graves of the dead to be used in the long journey into the unknown. In modified forms, this belief in the duality of man persists to the present day.

But primitive man had no conception of life as having a beginning and an end. In this he was like the rest of the animals. Today, everyone of ordinary intelligence knows how life begins, and to examine the beginnings of life leads to inevitable conclusions about the way life ends. If a man has a soul, it must creep in somewhere during the period of gestation and growth.

All the higher forms of animal life grow from a single cell. Before the individual life can begin its development, it must be fertilized by union with another cell; then the cell divides and multiplies until it takes the form and pattern of its kind. At a certain regular time the being emerges into the world. During its term of life millions of cells in its body are born, die, and are replaced until, through age, disease, or some catastrophe, the cells fall apart and the individual life is ended.

It is obvious that but for the fertilization of the cell under right conditions, the being would not have lived. It is idle to say that the initial cell has a soul. In one sense it has life; but even that is precarious and depends for its continued life upon union with another cell of the proper kind. The human mother is the bearer of probably ten thousand of one kind of cell, and the human father of countless billions of the other kind. Only a very small fraction of these result in human life. If the unfertilized cells of the female and the unused cells of the male are human beings possessed of souls, then the population of the world is infinitely greater than has ever been dreamed. Of course no such idea as belief in the immortality of the germ cells could satisfy the yearnings of the individual for a survival of life after death.

If that which is called a "soul" is a separate entity apart from the body, when, then, and where and how was this soul placed in the human structure? The individual began with the union of two cells, neither of which had a soul. How could these two soulless cells produce a soul? I must leave this search to the metaphysicians. When they have found the answer,

I hope they will tell me, for I should really like to know.

We know that a baby may live and fully develop in its mother's womb and then, through some shock at birth, may be born without life. In the past, these babies were promptly buried. But now we know that in many cases, where the bodily structure is complete, the machine may be set to work by artificial respiration or electricity. Then it will run like any other human body through its allotted term of years. We also know that in many cases of drowning, or when some mishap virtually destroys life without hopelessly impairing the body, artificial means may set it in motion once more, so that it will complete its term of existence until the final catastrophe comes. Are we to believe that somewhere around the stillborn child and somewhere in the vicinity of the drowned man there hovers a detached soul waiting to be summoned back into the body by a pulmotor? This, too, must be left to the metaphysicians.

The beginnings of life yield no evidence of the beginnings of a soul. It is idle to say that the something in the human being which we call "life" is the soul itself, for the soul is generally taken to distinguish human beings from other forms of life. There is life in all animals and plants, and at least potential life in inorganic matter. This potential life is simply unreleased force and matter—the great storehouse from which all forms of life emerge and are constantly replenished. It is impossible to draw the line between inorganic matter and the simpler forms of plant life, and equally impossible to draw the line between plant life and animal life, or between other forms of animal life and what we human beings are pleased to call the highest form. If the thing which we call "life" is itself the soul, then cows have souls; and, in the very nature of things, we must allow souls to all forms of life and to inorganic matter as well.

Life itself is something very real, as distinguished from the soul. Every man knows that his life had a beginning. Can one imagine an organism that has a beginning and no end? If I did not exist in the infinite past, why should I, or could I, exist in the infinite future? "But," says some, "your consciousness, your memory may exist even after you are dead. This is what we mean by the soul." Let us examine this point a little.

I have no remembrance of the months that I lay in my mother's womb. I cannot recall the day of my birth nor the time when I first opened my eyes to the light of the sun. I cannot remember when I was an infant, or when I began to creep on the floor, or when I was taught to walk, or anything before I was five or six years old. Still, all of these events were important, wonderful, and strange in a new life. What I call my "consciousness," for lack of a better word and a better understanding, developed with my growth and the crowding experiences I met at every turn. I have a hazy recollection of the burial of a boy soldier who was shot toward the end of the Civil War. He was buried near the schoolhouse when I was seven years old. But I have no remembrance of the assassination of Abraham Lincoln, although I must then have been eight years old. I must have known about it at the time, for my family and my community idolized Lincoln, and all America was in mourning at his death. Why do I remember the dead boy soldier who was buried a year before? Perhaps because I knew him well. Perhaps because his family was close to my childish life. Possibly because it came to me as my first knowledge of death. At all events, it made so deep an impression that I recall it now.

"Ah, yes," say the believers in the soul, "what you say confirms our own belief. You certainly existed when these early experiences took place. You were conscious of them at the time, even though you are not aware of it now. In the same way, may not your consciousness persist after you die, even though you are not aware of the fact?"

On the contrary, my fading memory of the

events that filled the early years of my life lead me to the opposite conclusion. So far as these incidents are concerned, the mind and consciousness of the boy are already dead. Even now, am I fully alive? I am seventy-one years old. I often fail to recollect the names of some of those I knew full well. Many events do not make the lasting impression that they once did. I know that it will be only a few years, even if my body still survives decay, when few important matters will even register in my mind. I know how it is with the old. I know that physical life can persist beyond the time when the mind can fully function. I know that if I live to an extreme old age, my mind will fail. I shall eat and drink and go to my bed in an automatic way. Memory—which is all that binds me to the past—will already be dead. All that will remain will be a vegetative existence; I shall sit and doze in the chimney corner, and my body will function in a measure even though the ego will already be practically dead. I am sure that if I die of what is called "old age," my consciousness will gradually slip away with my failing emotions; I shall no more be aware of the near approach of final dissolution than is the dying tree.

In primitive times, before men knew anything about the human body or the universe of which it is a part, it was not unreasonable to believe in spirits, ghosts, and the duality of man. For one thing, celestial geography was much simpler then. Just above the earth was a firmament in which the stars were set, and above the firmament was heaven. The place was easy of access, and in dreams the angels were seen going up and coming down on a ladder. But now we have a slightly more adequate conception of space and the infinite universe of which we are so small a part. Our great telescopes reveal countless worlds and planetary systems which make our own sink into utter insignificance in comparison. We have every reason to think that beyond our sight there is endless space filled with still more planets, so infinite in size and number that no brain has the smallest conception of their extent. Is there any reason to think that in this universe, with its myriads of worlds, there is no other life so important as our own? Is it possible that the inhabitants of the earth have been singled out for special favor and endowed with souls and immortal life? Is it at all reasonable to suppose that any special account is taken of the human atoms that forever come and go upon this planet?

If man has a soul that persists after death, that goes to a heaven of the blessed or to a hell of the damned, where are these places? It is not so easily imagined as it once was. How does the soul make its journey? What does immortal man find when he gets there, and how will he live after he reaches the end of endless space? We know that the atmosphere will be absent; that there will be no light, no heat—only the infinite reaches of darkness and frigidity. In view of modern knowledge, can anyone *really believe* in the persistence of individual life and memory?

The Resurrection of the Body

There are those who base their hope of a future life upon the resurrection of the body. This is a purely religious doctrine. It is safe to say that few intelligent men who are willing to look obvious facts in the face hold any such belief. Yet we are seriously told that Elijah was carried bodily to heaven in a chariot of fire, and that Jesus arose from the dead and ascended into heaven. The New Testament abounds in passages that support this doctrine. St. Paul states the tenet over and over again. In the fifteenth chapter of First Corinthians he says: "If Christ be preached that he arose from the dead, how say some among you that there is no resurrection of the dead? . . . And if Christ be not risen, then is our preaching vain . . . For if the dead rise not, then is not Christ raised," The Apostles' Creed says: "I believe in the resurrection of the body." This has been carried into substantially all the orthodox creeds; and while it is more or less minimized by neglect and omission, it is still a cardinal doctrine of the orthodox churches.

Two thousand years ago, in Palestine, little was known of man, of the earth, or of the universe. It was then currently believed that the earth was only four thousand years old, that life had begun anew after the deluge about two thousand years before, and that the entire earth was soon to be destroyed. Today it is fairly well established that man has been upon the earth for a million years. During that long stretch of time the world has changed many times; it is changing every moment. At least three or four ice ages have swept across continents, driving death before them, carrying human beings into the sea or burying them deep in the earth. Animals have fed on man and on each other. Every dead body, no matter whether consumed by fire or buried in the earth, has been resolved into its elements, so that the matter and energy that once formed human beings has fed animals and plants and other men . . . . Thus the body of every man now living is in part made from the bodies of those why have been dead for ages.

Yet we are still asked to believe in the resurrection of the body. By what alchemy, then, are the individual bodies that have successfully fed the generations of men to be separated and restored to their former identities? And if I am to be resurrected, what particular *I* shall be called from the grave, from the animals and plants and the bodies of other men who shall inherit this body I now call my own? My body has been made over and over, piece by piece, as the days went by, and will continue to be so made until the end. It has changed so slowly that each new cell is fitted into the living part, and will go on changing until the final crisis comes. Is it the child in the mother's womb or the tottering frame of the old man that shall be brought back? The mere thought of such a resurrection beggars reason, ignores facts, and enthrones blind faith, wild dreams, hopeless hopes, and cowardly fears as sovereign of the human mind.

The Indestructability of Matter and Force

Some of those who profess to believe in the immortality of man—whether it be of his soul or of his body—have drawn what comfort they could from the modern scientific doctrine of the indestructibility of matter and force. This doctrine, they say, only confirms in scientific language what they have always believed. This, however, is pure sophistry.[1] It is probably true that no matter or force has ever been or ever can be destroyed. But it is likewise true that there is no connection whatever between the notion that personal consciousness and memory persist after death and the scientific theory that matter and force are indestructible. For the scientific theory carries with it a corollary, that the forms of matter and energy are constantly changing through an endless cycle of new combinations. Of what possible use would it be, then, to have a consciousness that was immortal, but which, from the moment of death, was dispersed into new combinations so that no two parts of the original identity could ever be reunited again?

These natural processes of change, which in the human being take the forms of growth, disease, senility, death, and decay, are essentially the same as the processes by which a lump of coal is disintegrated in burning. One may watch the lump of coal burning in the grate until nothing but ashes remains. Part of the coal goes up the chimney in the form of smoke; part of it radiates through the house as heat; the resi-

[1]Logically unsound, but psychologically convincing, argumentation. EDITOR'S NOTE.

due lies in the ashes on the hearth. So it is with human life. In all forms of life nature is engaged in combining, breaking down, and recombining her store of energy and matter into new forms. The thing we call "life" is nothing other than a state of equilibrium which endures for a short span of years between the two opposing tendencies of nature—the one that builds up, and the one that tears down. In old age, the tearing-down process has already gained the ascendency, and when death intervenes, the equilibrium is finally upset by the complete stoppage of the building-up process, so that nothing remains but complete disintegration. The energy thus released may be converted into grass or trees or animal life; or it may lie dormant until caught up again in the crucible of nature's laboratory. But whatever happens, the man—the *You* and the *I*—like the lump of coal that has been burned, is gone, irrevocably dispersed. All the King's horses and all the King's men cannot restore it to its former unity.

The idea that man is a being set apart, distinct from all the rest of nature, is born of man's emotions, of his loves and hates, of his hopes and fears, and of the primitive conceptions of undeveloped minds. The *You* or the *I* which is known to our friends does not consist of an immaterial something called a "soul" which cannot be conceived. We know perfectly well what we mean when we talk about this *You* and this *Me:* and it is equally plain that the whole fabric that makes up our separate personalities is destroyed, dispersed, disintegrated beyond repair by what we call "death."

The Desire for Another Life

Those who refuse to give up the idea of immortality declare that nature never creates a desire without providing the means for its satisfaction. They likewise insist that all people, from the rudest to the most civilized, yearn for another life. As a matter of fact, nature creates many desires which she does not satisfy; most of the wishes of men meet no fruition. But nature does not create any emotion demanding a future life. The only yearning that the individual has is to keep on living—which is a very different thing. This urge is found in every animal, in every plant. It is simply the momentum of a living structure: or, as Schopenhauer[2] put it, "the will to live." What we long for is a continuation of our present state of existence, not an uncertain reincarnation in a mysterious world of which we know nothing.

The Believer's Last Resort

All men recognize the hopelessness of finding any evidence that the individual will persist beyond the grave. As a last resort, we are told that it is better that the doctrine be believed even if it is not true. We are assured that without this faith, life is only desolation and despair. However that may be, it remains that many of the conclusions of logic are not pleasant to contemplate; still, so long as men think and feel, at least some of them will use their faculties as best they can. For if we are to believe things that are not true, who is to write our creed? Is it safe to leave it to any man or organization to pick out the errors that we must accept? The whole history of the world has answered this question in a way that cannot be mistaken.

And after all, is the belief in immortality necessary or even desirable for man? Millions of

[2]Schopenhauer (1788–1860) was a German philosopher noted for his pessimistic metaphysical viewpoint, according to which ultimate reality should be seen as the purposeless striving of a nonrational force which he called "will"—a cosmic force that has its analog in the blind strivings of the human will. From Schopenhauer's bleak perspective, human beings are caught up in a meaningless struggle for existence in which all is stress, conflict, and tension. Influenced by the teachings of Eastern religions, Schopenhauer claimed that salvation from the miseries of life can come only through one's detachment from earthly things. EDITOR'S NOTE.

men and women have no such faith; they go on with their daily tasks and feel joy and sorrow without the lure of immortal life. The things that really affect the happiness of the individual are the matters of daily living. They are the companionship of friends, the games and contemplations. They are misunderstandings and cruel judgments, false friends and debts, poverty and disease. They are our joys in our living companions and our sorrows over those who die. Whatever our faith, we mainly live in the present—in the here and now. Those who hold the view that man is mortal are never troubled by metaphysical problems. At the end of the day's labor we are glad to lose our consciousness in sleep; and intellectually, at least, we look forward to the long rest from the stresses and storms that are always incidental to existence.

When we fully understand the brevity of life, its fleeting joys and unavoidable pains; when we accept the fact that all men and women are approaching an inevitable doom: the consciousness of it should make us more kindly and considerate of each other. This feeling should make men and women use their best efforts to help their fellow travellers on the road, to make the path brighter and easier as we journey on. It should bring a closer kinship, a better understanding, and a deeper sympathy for the wayfarers who must live a common life and die a common death.

DISCUSSION QUESTIONS

1. Darrow writes, "We know perfectly well what we mean when we talk about this **You** and this **Me**: and it is equally plain that the whole fabric that makes up our separate personalities is destroyed, dispersed, disintegrated beyond repair by what we call 'death.' " What evidence does Darrow give in support of this claim? Is it convincing? Does it establish or make highly probable that personal identity does not continue past bodily death? What conception of personal identity does Darrow seem to accept? Do you accept it also? (Reconsider this question after reading the selections by Hick, Locke, and Quinton that follow.)

2. What meaning(s) does Darrow attribute to the concept of "the soul"? What do you think most people who use this concept today mean by it? Is this concept, as commonly used, intelligible? If not, why?

3. Is it possible for a person's soul to be immortal and yet for personal identity to cease at the death of one's body? Why?

4. Do animals have immortal souls? Why? What of early forms of man such as the Neanderthals who engaged in ritualistic burial of their dead, along with tools and food, indicating that they expected their dead to have an afterlife? Is there any adequate basis for believing in an afterlife for homo sapiens, but not for the Neanderthal? Where is the line to be drawn?

5. Why does Darrow reject the belief in the resurrection of the body? Does he have adequate grounds for this rejection?

6. Why does Darrow claim that the belief in the indestructability of matter and force does not support the belief in immortality? Do you think that those who claim that the soul cannot be destroyed have the same view of personal identity in mind that Darrow seems to in his discussion of this issue? If not, does the belief in the indestructibility of the soul have more plausibility with this different concept of personal identity?

23. RESURRECTION

John Hick

(For a biographical sketch of John Hick, see Selection #17.)

In the following selection, John Hick defends the **conceptual possibility** (not the **factual truth**) of the notion of immortality involving "the resurrection of the body." In defending this possibility, Hick relies heavily on the view that the **evidence** (which need not be identified with the **meaning**) of personal identity is to be sought in the continuity of memory.

The conception of immortality involving the resurrection of the physical body is the orthodox Christian view of immortality. Nevertheless, with the exception of Thomas Aquinas, Christian philosophers have had surprisingly little to say about this notion. Attempting a synthesis of the Platonic and Aristotelian views of the mind-body relationship, Aquinas accepted the Platonic view that the **soul is a substance** that can, and will, exist after the destruction of the physical body it occupies, along with the Aristotelian view that **a person is a physical body** that has certain capabilities. Like many contemporary analytic philosophers, Aquinas was quite aware of the conceptual difficulties involved in the identification of disembodied souls and in the ascription of sensations and emotions to them. While he believed that souls survived the destruction of the physical bodies they occupied, he did not conceive the soul as capable of sensation and emotion, as many contemporary Christian believers do, but rather as capable only of thought and acts of will. Can such an impoverished notion of the soul be identified with a person that existed in embodied form? To this question, Aquinas answered "No." The preservation of personal identity, he believed, was to await the ulitmate union of the soul with "the resurrected body." Only resurrection, and not mere immortality of the soul, could fulfill the promise of the eternal happiness of heaven or the eternal agony of hell guaranteed by the Holy Scriptures, Aquinas believed.

The Immortality of the Soul

Some kind of distinction between physical body and immaterial or semi-material soul seems to be as old as human culture; the existence of such a distinction has been indicated by the manner of burial of the earliest human skeletons yet discovered. Anthropologists offer various conjectures about the origin of the distinction: perhaps it was first suggested by memories of dead persons, by dreams of them, by the sight of reflections of oneself in water and on other bright surfaces, or by meditation upon the significance of religious rites which grew up spontaneously in face of the fact of death.

It was Plato (428/7–348/7 B.C.), the philosopher who has most deeply and lastingly influenced western culture, who systematically developed the body-mind dichotomy and first attempted to prove the immortality of the soul.

Plato argues that although the body belongs to the sensible world and shares its changing

Source: John Hick, *Philosophy of Religion*, 3rd ed., © 1983, pp. 122–27. Adapted by permission of Prentice-Hall, Inc., Englewood Cliffs, N.J.

and impermanent nature, the intellect is related to the unchanging realities of which we are aware when we think not of particular good things but of Goodness itself, not of specific just acts but of Justice itself, and of the other "universals" or eternal Ideas by participation in which physical things and events have their own specific characteristics. Being related to this higher and abiding realm rather than to the evanescent world of sense, the soul is immortal. Hence, one who devotes one's life to the contemplation of eternal realities rather than to the gratification of the fleeting desires of the body will find at death that whereas one's body turns to dust, one's soul gravitates to the realm of the unchanging, there to live forever. Plato painted an awe-inspiring picture, of haunting beauty and persuasiveness, which has moved and elevated the minds of men and women in many different centuries and lands. Nevertheless, it is not today (as it was during the first centuries of the Christian era) the common philosophy of the west; and a demonstration of immortality which presupposes Plato's metaphysical system cannot claim to constitute a proof for a twentieth-century person.

Plato used the further argument that the only things that can suffer destruction are those which are composite, since to destroy something means to disintegrate it into its constituent parts. All material bodies are composite; the soul, however, is simple and therefore imperishable. This argument was adopted by Aquinas and became standard in Roman Catholic theology. . . .

This type of reasoning has been criticized on several grounds. Kant pointed out that although it is true that a simple substance cannot disintegrate, consciousness may nevertheless cease to exist through the diminution of its intensity to zero. Modern psychology has also questioned the basic premise that the mind is a simple entity. It seems instead to be a structure of only relative unity, normally fairly stable and tightly integrated but capable under stress of various degrees of division and dissolution. This comment from psychology makes it clear that the assumption that the soul is a simple substance is not an empirical observation but a metaphysical theory. As such, it cannot provide the basis for a general proof of immortality.

The body-soul distinction, first formulated as a philosophical doctrine in ancient Greece, was baptized into Christianity, ran through the medieval period, and entered the modern world with the public status of a self-evident truth when it was redefined in the seventeenth century by Descartes. Since World War II, however, Descartes' mind-matter dualism, having been taken for granted for many centuries, has been strongly criticized by philosophers of the contemporary analytical school.[1] It is argued that the words that describe mental characteristics and operations—such as "intelligent," "thoughtful," "carefree," "happy," "calculating," and the like—apply in practice to types of human behavior and to behavioral dispositions. They refer to the empirical individual, the observable human being who is born and grows and acts and feels and dies, and not to the shadowy proceedings of a mysterious "ghost in the machine." An individual is thus very much what he or she appears to be—a creature of flesh and blood, who behaves and is capable of behaving in a characteristic range of ways—rather than a nonphysical soul incomprehensibly interacting with a physical body.

As a result of this development, much mid-twentieth-century philosphy has come to see the human being as in the biblical writings, not as an eternal soul temporarily attached to a mortal body, but as a form of finite, mortal, psychophysical life. Thus, the Old Testament scholar J. Pedersen said of the Hebrews that for them "the body is the soul in its outward form." This way of thinking has led to quite a different conception of death from that found

[1]See Selection #30 from Gilbert Ryle's *The Concept of Mind.* EDITOR'S NOTE.

in Plato and the Neoplatonic strand in European thought.

The Re-Creation of the Psychophysical Person

Only toward the end of the Old Testament period did afterlife beliefs come to have any real importance within Judaism. Previously, Hebrew religious insight had focused so fully upon God's covenant with the nation, as an organism that continued through the centuries while successive generations lived and died, that the thought of a divine purpose for the individual, a purpose transcending this present life, developed only when the breakdown of the nation as a political entity threw into prominence the individual and the problem of the individual's destiny.

When a positive conviction arose of God's purpose holding each man and woman in being beyond the crisis of death, this conviction took the non-Platonic form of belief in the resurrection of the body. . . .

The religious difference between the Platonic belief in the immortality of the soul, and the Judaic-Christian belief in the resurrection of the body is that the latter postulates a special divine act of re-creation. This produces a sense of utter dependence upon God in the hour of death . . . . Hence, in the Jewish and Christian conception, death is something real and fearful. It is not thought to be like walking from one room to another, or like taking off an old coat and putting on a new one. It means sheer unqualified extinction—passing out from the lighted circle of life into "death's dateless night." Only through the sovereign creative love of God can there be a new existence beyond the grave.

What does "the resurrection of the dead" mean? Saint Paul's discussion provides the basic Christian answer to this question.[2] His conception of the general resurrection (distinguished from the unique resurrection of Jesus) has nothing to do with the resuscitation of corpses in a cemetery. It concerns God's re-creation or reconstitution of the human psychophysical individual, not as the organism that has died but as a *soma pneumatikon,* a "spiritual body," inhabiting a spiritual world as the physical body inhabits our present material world.

A major problem confronting any such doctrine is that of providing criteria of personal identity to link the earthly life and the resurrection life. Paul does not specifically consider this question, but one may perhaps develop his thought along lines such as the following.

Suppose, first, that someone—John Smith—living in the United States were suddenly and inexplicably to disappear before the eyes of his friends, and that at the same moment an exact replica of him were inexplicably to appear in India. The person who appears in India is exactly similar in both physical and mental characteristics to the person who disappeared in America. There is continuity of memory, complete similarity of bodily features including fingerprints, hair and eye coloration, and stomach contents, and also of beliefs, habits, emotions, and mental dispositions. Further, the "John Smith" replica thinks of himself as being the John Smith who disappeared in the United States. After all possible tests have been made and have proved positive, the factors leading his friends to accept "John Smith" as John Smith would surely prevail and would cause them to overlook even his mysterious transference from one continent to another, rather than treat "John Smith," with all of John Smith's memories and other characteristics, as someone other than John Smith.

[2]Corinthians 15. AUTHOR'S NOTE.

Suppose, second, that our John Smith, instead of inexplicably disappearing, dies, but that at the moment of his death a "John Smith" replica, again complete with memories and all other characteristics, appears in India. Even with the corpse on our hands, we would, I think, still have to accept this "John Smith" as the John Smith who had died. We would just have to say that he had been miraculously re-created in another place.

Now suppose, third, that on John Smith's death the "John Smith" replica appears, not in India, but as a resurrection replica in a different world altogether, a resurrection world inhabited only by resurrected persons. This world occupies its own space distinct from that with which we are now familiar. That is to say, an object in the resurrection world is not situated at any distance or in any direction from the objects in our present world, although each object in either world is spatially related to every other object in the same world.

This supposition provides a model by which one may begin to conceive of the divine re-creation of the embodied human personality. In this model, the element of the strange and mysterious has been reduced to a minimum by one's following the view of some of the early Church Fathers that the resurrection body has the same shape as the physical body, and ignoring Paul's own hint that it may be as unlike the physical body as a full grain of wheat differs from the wheat seed. . . .

What is the basis for this Judaic-Christian belief in the divine re-creation or reconstitution of the human personality after death? There is, of course, an argument from authority, in that life after death is taught throughout the New Testament (although very rarely in the Old Testament). More basically, though, belief in the resurrection arises as a corollary of faith in the sovereign purpose of God, which is not restricted by death and which holds us in being beyond our natural mortality. In a similar vein it is argued that if it be the divine plan to create finite persons to exist in fellowship with God, then it contradicts both that intention and God's love for the human creatures if God allows men and women to pass out of existence when the divine purpose for them still remains largely unfulfilled.

It is this promised fulfillment of God's purpose for the individual, in which the full possibilities of human nature will be realized, that constitutes the "heaven" symbolized in the New Testament as a joyous banquet in which all and sundry rejoice together. As we saw when discussing the problem of evil, it is questionable whether any theodicy can succeed without drawing into itself this . . . faith in an eternal, and therefore infinite, good which thus outweighs all the pains and sorrows that have been endured on the way to it.

Balancing the idea of heaven in Christian tradition is the idea of hell. This, too, is relevant to the problem of theodicy. Just as the reconciling of God's goodness and power with the fact of evil requires that out of the travail of history there shall come in the end an eternal good for humanity, so likewise it would seem to preclude eternal human misery. The only kind of evil that is finally incompatible with God's unlimited power and love would be utterly pointless and wasted suffering, pain which is never redeemed and worked into the fulfilling of God's good purpose. Unending torment would constitute precisely such suffering; for being eternal, it could never lead to a good end beyond itself. Thus, hell as conceived by its enthusiasts, such as Augustine or Calvin, is a major part of the problem of evil! If hell is construed as eternal torment, the theological motive behind the idea is directly at variance with the urge to seek a theodicy. However, it is by no means clear that the doctrine of eternal punishment can claim a secure New Testament basis.

If, on the other hand, "hell" means a continuation of the purgatorial suffering often experienced in this life, and leading eventually to the high good of heaven, it no longer stands in conflict with the needs of theodicy. Again, the idea of hell may be deliteralized and valued as a powerful and pregnant symbol of the grave responsibility inherent in our human freedom in relation to our Maker . . . .

DISCUSSION QUESTIONS

1. Do the examples Hick presents of alleged "bodily resurrection" conclusively establish the possibility of life-after-death? Can the evidence for personal identity be equated with its **definition?** What is its definition?

2. Is a totally disembodied life-after-death possible? Is it as plausible as resurrection? As desirable?

3. In discussing Hick's view of the basis for identifying a (hypothetical) resurrection-world person with a formerly existing earthly person, the philosopher Terrence Penelhum claims that while this identification is **logically possible,** it is not **logically required.** As Penelhum sees it, identification can only be automatic and unquestionable when there is bodily continuity, something that would be lacking in a case of resurrection. In such a case, Penelhum claims, it is a matter of **linguistic decision and not of the discovery of fact** whether a resurrected being is **the same person** as his or her earthly counterpart or a **different, but very similar person.**[3] Agreeing that the choice between these two conflicting descriptions is indeed a linguistic one and not a choice between two conflicting statements of fact, Hick in reply writes that "the decision to identify [the resurrected person as the same person as the earthly person] is much more reasonable, and is liable to create far fewer problems than would be the decision to regard them as different people."[4] Are Penelhum's claim and Hick's reply to it satisfactory? If you were told that upon death, a replica of your body would be created by God and that it was simply a matter of "linguistic decision" whether you would continue to exist, would it make any sense for you to **anticipate** your afterlife? Is the view that questions concerning the personal identity of resurrected beings are questions of language and not of fact inconsistent with the hopes and fears that we have concerning an afterlife? If so, must Penelhum's view and Hick's reply to it be rejected, or must we reconsider the idea of the rationality of one's anticipation of an afterlife?

4. If it is possible for God to create one resurrected replica of person X, complete with the set of memory traces of person X at the moment of death, then it would seem to be possible as well for him to create two (or any number of) replicas. But if this were to happen, we would seem to be logically compelled to say that the replicas were exactly like, but not identical to, the original person X. Since this is true when we imagine more than one replica, may it not also be true when we imagine a single replica? Aware of this problem, Hick claims that while the existence of more than one replica would make it logically impossible to identify the replicas with previously existing earthly beings, there would be no problem if there were only a single replica.[5] Is this true? Is the important issue the bare logical possibility of multiple replicas or their actuality? If one accepts Hick's view that it is actuality and not mere possibility that is important, would this not imply that if God first creates only a single replica of Mr. X, then we would be justified in describing the resurrected replica of Mr. X as the same person as the earthly Mr. X, but then if God should create another replica, we would have to abandon our original identification? Does the correctness of one's identification of oneself as someone who lived previously logically depend on the existence of competitors? If not, must we conclude that Hick's view of the preservation of personal identity through resurrection does not allow us to distinguish those resurrected beings who are identical to beings who have died and those who are exactly similar to them?

[3]Terrence Penelhum, *Survival and Disembodied Existence* (New York: Humanities Press, 1969), Chapter 15, "The Resurrection of the Person," pp. 278–95.

[4]John Hick, *Death and Eternal Life* (New York: Harper & Row, 1976), p. 288.

[5]Ibid, pp. 288–89.

24. A HUMAN BEING IS A UNION OF AN IMMATERIAL SOUL AND PHYSICAL BODY

René Descartes

RENÉ DESCARTES (1596–1650) is referred to as "the father of modern philosophy" because of his immense impact on the subsequent development of philosophy. Educated by Jesuits (members of a Roman Catholic religious order noted for its emphasis upon learning and rigorous analytic reasoning), Descartes was taught the predominant **Scholastic** (Medieval) philosophy of his day—a philosophy which combined Christian authority with Aristotelian metaphysics. Although he remained a devoted Catholic throughout his life, Descartes' philosophy (which is often referred to in its Latinized form as **Cartesian** philosophy) constituted a profound break with the Scholastic tradition. A renowned French mathematician and scientist himself (he invented analytic geometry), Descartes was greatly influenced by the spirit of experimental, mathematical, and nonauthoritarian inquiry, which constituted the scientific revolution of the sixteenth and seventeenth centuries, a spirit of inquiry which began with Copernicus (1473–1543), was continued by Galileo (1564–1642) and Kepler (1571–1630), and culminated in the mechanistic physics of Newton (1642–1727). As the mechanistic explanations of the new science gained influence, the purposive theological world view of the Middle Ages began to lose influence. In its stead, the new science resurrected the materialistic principles of the ancient Greek and Roman **atomists,** Democritus and Lucretius. According to these philosophers, **all** things are composed **in their entirety** of rapidly moving, minute bits of matter, called atoms, of particular shapes and mass. The materialistic world view of the Greek and Roman atomists, coupled with the determinism of the new science which saw the world as a mechanical system that ran according to various mathematically expressible laws of nature, challenged the traditional scholastic purposive and religious world view. While Descartes' contemporary, the English philosopher Thomas Hobbes (1588–1679), fully embraced the materialistic and deterministic world view of the new science which threatened the traditional Judeo-Christian world view, Descartes attempted a reconciliation between these two world views. The solution, as Descartes saw it, was to divide the world into two radically different realms of existence—mind and matter. Although a human body is subject to the deterministic laws of mechanics no less than the physical universe itself, superimposed upon the purely physical, unconscious human body is the immaterial and conscious substance of mind (or, interchangeably for Descartes, **soul**), which interacts with a particular human body, unrestrained by the mechanistic laws that exert control over this body. Consequently, it is in the realm of mind that Descartes found room for the notion of "freedom of the will," a notion which was central to the Judeo-Christian world view, but alien to the deterministic mechanistic world view of the new science. Descartes' attempt to reconcile religion and science, his mind-body interactionism, and his concern with epistemological questions (to be discussed in the next chapter) set the stage for subsequent philosophers who accepted Descartes' new formulation of the fundamental philosophical questions, while often disagreeing with his answers to them.

The following selection, which provides an outline of Descartes' view of the mind-body relationship, is from several of Descartes' philosophical writings. It begins with Descartes' resolution at the outset of his **Meditations** to doubt all that can be doubted, until he arrives at some self-evident truths which can provide the **foundation** from which he can **deductively** build a **structure** of knowledge. (It was this mathematical view of the structure of knowledge that influenced Spinoza—see Selection #7.) Rejecting the possibility of constructing a foundation of knowledge upon sense perceptions, which are capable of deceiving us as in dreams, Descartes observes that there can be no doubt that he exists, for in the very act of thinking that he exists, or indeed of being in any conscious state, it necessarily follows that there must be **something** that thinks or is conscious. What then, Descartes next asks, is the nature of this substance that is the subject of consciousness and whose existence is self-evidently revealed in any state of consciousness. It is—and so **he** is—Descartes claims, a conscious unextended substance which is distinct from the unconscious physical body with which, he believes, it interacts, but at this point cannot be sure. Beginning with the certainty of his existence as a conscious nonphysical being, Descartes next goes on (in a passage of the **Meditations** that is not included) to establish the certainty of God's existence. Having established this, Descartes proceeds to establish the reality of a physical mind-independent world, and, in particular, of his own physical body. He then reflects upon that "certain unity" of mind and body which results from their interaction. Cognizant of the prevailing scientific beliefs about the nature of human physiology, Descartes attributes a central role to the pineal gland (which is located at the very center of the brain) in the interaction of mind and body.

The selection ends with Descartes' answer to the question "What distinguishes human beings from animals and complex machines (robots)?" It is, he claims, the human capacities to use language in a spontaneous, non-parrot-like manner and to engage in conscious intellectual deliberation which can be utilized in diverse problem-solving activities. Apparently seeing intellectual perception as inseparable from all other states of consciousness, Descartes rejects the view that animals are conscious in the primitive sense of having sensations and feelings (e.g., experiencing pleasure and pain) but are not capable of intellectual perception—a view held by Aristotle, who speaks of "degrees of the soul." Consequently, animals were for Descartes mindless creatures devoid of consciousness—mere automatons whose behavior was totally determined by the mechanical states of their physical organs. Descartes then affirms that the human immaterial soul (mind), whose capacities distinguish human beings from animals and machines, is immortal.

[One Cannot Be Certain of the Existence of Physical Objects]

Some years ago now I observed the multitude of errors that I had accepted as true in my earliest years, and the dubiousness of the whole superstructure I had since then reared on them; and the consequent need of making a clean sweep for once in my life, and beginning again from the very foundations, if I would establish some secure and lasting result in science. But the task appeared enormous, and I put it off till I should reach such a mature age that no increased aptitude for learning anything was likely to follow. Thus I delayed so long that now it would be blameworthy to spend in deliberation what time I have left for action. Today is my chance; I have banished all care from my mind, I have secured myself peace, I have retired by myself; at length I shall be at leisure to make a clean sweep, in all seriousness and with full freedom, of all my opinions.

To this end I shall not have to show they are all false, which very likely I could never manage; but reason already convinces me that I must withhold assent no less carefully from what is not plainly certain and indubitable than from what is obviously false; so the discovery of some reason for doubt as regards each opinion will justify the rejection of all. This will not mean going over each of them—an unending task; when the foundation is undermined, the superstructure will collapse of itself; so I will proceed at once to attack the very principles on which all my former beliefs rested.

What I have so far accepted as true *par excellence,* I have got either from the senses or by means of the senses. Now I have sometimes caught the senses deceiving me; and a wise man never entirely trusts those who have once cheated him.

'But although the senses may sometimes deceive us about some minute or remote objects, yet there are many other facts as to which doubt is plainly impossible, although these are gathered from the same source: e.g. that I am here, sitting by the fire, wearing a winter cloak, holding this paper in my hands, and so on. Again, these hands, and my whole body—how can their existence be denied? Unless indeed I likened myself to some lunatics, whose brains are so upset by persistent melancholy vapours that they firmly assert they are kings, when really they are miserably poor; or that they are clad in purple, when really they are naked; or that they have a head of pottery, or are pumpkins, or are made of glass; but then they are madmen, and I should appear no less mad if I took them as a precedent for my own case.'

A fine argument! As though I were not a man who habitually sleeps at night and has the same impressions (or even wilder ones) in sleep as these men do when awake! How often, in the still of the night, I have the familiar conviction that I am here, wearing a cloak, sitting by the fire—when really I am undressed and lying in bed! 'But now at any rate I am looking at this paper with wide-awake eyes; the head I am now shaking is not asleep; I put out this hand deliberately and consciously; a sleeping man would have no such distinct experiences.' As though I did not recall having been formerly deceived by just such reflections during sleep! When I reflect more carefully on this, I am bewildered; and my very bewilderment confirms the idea of my being asleep. . . .

But it is not enough to have observed this; I must take care to bear it in mind. My ordinary opinions keep on coming back; and they take possession of my belief, on which they have a lien by long use and the right of custom, even against my will. . . . So I think it will be well

Source: Selections from Descartes' (1st, 2nd, & 6th) *Meditations, Principles of Philosophy* (Pt. IV: CXCVI), and *Discourse on Method* (Pt. V) are from *Descartes: Philosophical Writings,* trans. Elizabeth Anscombe & Peter Geach (Surrey, England: Thomas Nelson & Sons, 1966). Reprinted with the permission of the publisher and Professors Anscombe and Geach. The selection from *The Passions of the Soul* is from *The Philosophical Works of Descartes,* trans. E. Haldane & G.R.T. Ross (Cambridge: Cambridge University Press, 1931). Reprinted by permission.

to turn my will in the opposite direction; deceive myself, and pretend they are wholly false and imaginary; until in the end the influence of prejudice on either side is counterbalanced, and no bad habit can any longer deflect my judgment from a true perception of facts. . . .

I will suppose, then, not that there is a supremely good God, the source of truth; but that there is an evil spirit,[1] who is supremely powerful and intelligent, and does his utmost to deceive me. I will suppose that sky, air, earth, colours, shapes, sounds and all external objects are mere delusive dreams, by means of which he lays snares for my credulity. I will consider myself as having no hands, no eyes, no flesh, no blood, no senses, but just having false belief that I have all these things. I will remain firmly fixed in this meditation, and resolutely take care that, so far as in me lies, even if it is not in my power to know some truth, I may not assent to falsehood nor let myself be imposed upon by that deceiver, however powerful and intelligent he may be. . . .

[A Person Is a Conscious Indivisible Being that Has a Special Relationship to a Body]

Yesterday's meditation plunged me into doubts of such gravity that I cannot forget them, and yet do not see how to resolve them. I am bewildered, as though I had suddenly fallen into a deep sea, and could neither plant my foot on the bottom nor swim up to the top. But I will make an effort, and try once more the same path as I entered upon yesterday; I will reject, that is, whatever admits of the least doubt, just as if I had found it was wholly false; and I will go on until I know something for certain—if it is only this, that there is nothing certain. . . .

I suppose, therefore, that whatever things I see are illusions; I believe that none of the things my lying memory represents to have happened really did so; I have no senses: body, shape, extension, motion, place are merely fictions of my mind. What then is true? Perhaps only this one thing, that nothing is certain.

How do I know, however, that there is not something different from all the things I have mentioned, as to which there is not the least occasion of doubt?—Is there a God (or whatever I call him) who gives me these very thoughts? But why, on the other hand, should I think so? Perhaps I myself may be the author of them.—Well, am *I*, at any rate, something? But I have already said I have no senses[2] and no body. At this point I hesitate, what follows from this? Am I so bound to a body and its senses that without them I cannot exist?—'But I have convinced myself that nothing in the world exists—no sky, no earth, no minds, no bodies; so am not I likewise non-existent?' But if I did convince myself of anything, I must have existed. 'But there is some deceiver, supremely powerful, supremely intelligent, who purposely always deceives me.' If he deceives me, then again I undoubtedly exist; let him deceive me as much as he may, he will never bring it about that, at the time of thinking that I am something, I am in fact nothing. Thus I have now weighed all considerations enough and more than enough; and must at length conclude that this proposition 'I am', 'I exist,' whenever I utter it or conceive it in my mind, is necessarily true.

But I do not yet sufficiently understand what is this 'I' that necessarily exists. I must take care, then, that I do not rashly take something else for the 'I', and thus go wrong even in the knowledge that I am maintaining to be the most certain and evident of all. So I will consider afresh what I believe myself to be before I happened

[1]In some translations, the word "genius" is used, and, as a result, commentators often speak of Descartes' "evil genius." EDITOR'S NOTE.

[2]At this point in the *Meditations,* Descartes does not conceive of sensation as a species of consciousness, but as an activity of bodily sense organs, and consequently as something whose existence can be doubted along with that of the body. EDITOR'S NOTE.

upon my present way of thinking; from this conception I will subtract whatever can be in the least shaken by the arguments adduced, so that what at last remains shall be precisely the unshakably certain element.

What, then, did I formerly think I was? A man. But what is a man? Shall I say 'a rational animal'? No; in that case I should have to go on to ask what an animal is and what 'rational' is, and so from a single question I should fall into several of greater difficulty; and I have not now the leisure to waste on such subtleties. I will rather consider what used to occur to me spontaneously and naturally whenever I was considering the question 'what am I?' First came the thought that I had a face, hands, arms—in fact the whole structure of limbs that is observable also in a corpse, and that I called 'the body'. Further, that I am nourished, that I move, that I have sensations, that I am conscious, these acts I assigned to the soul. But as to the nature of this soul, either it did not attract my attention, or else I fancied something subtle like air . . . mingled among the grosser parts of my body. As regards 'body' I had no doubt, and I thought I distinctly understood its nature; if I had tried to describe my conception, I might have given this explanation: 'By *body* I mean whatever is capable of being bounded by some shape, and comprehended by some place, and of occupying space in such a way that all other bodies are excluded; moreover of being perceived by touch, sight, hearing, taste, or smell; and further, of being moved in various ways, not of itself but by some other body that touches it.' For the power of self-movement, and the further powers of sensation and consciousness, I judged not to belong in any way to the essence of body; indeed, I marvelled even that there were some bodies in which such faculties were found.

What am I to say now, when I am supposing that there is some all-powerful and . . . malignant deceiver, who has taken care to delude me about everything as much as he can? Can I, in the first place, say I have the least part of the characteristics that I said belonged to the essence of body? I concentrate, I think, I consider; nothing comes to mind; it would be wearisome and futile to repeat the reasons. Well, what of the properties I ascribed to the soul? Nutrition and locomotion? Since I have no body, these are mere delusions. Sensation? This cannot happen apart from a body; and in sleep I have seemed to have sensations that I have since realized never happened. Consciousness? At this point I come to the fact that there is consciousness; of this and this only I cannot be deprived. *I* am, *I* exist; that is certain. For how long? For as long as I am experiencing, maybe, if I wholly ceased from experiencing, I should at once wholly cease to be. For the present I am admitting only what is necessarily true; so 'I am' precisely taken refers only to a conscious being; that is a mind, a soul, an intellect, a reason—words whose meaning I did not previously know. I am a real being, and really exist; but what sort of being? As I said, a conscious being. . . .

. . . A conscious being. What is that? A being that doubts, understands, asserts, denies, is willing, is unwilling; further, that has sense and imagination. These are a good many properties—if only they all belong to me. But how can they fail to? Am *I* not the very person who is now 'doubting' almost everything; who 'understands' something and 'asserts' this one thing to be true, and 'denies' other things; who 'is willing' to know more, and 'is unwilling' to be deceived; who 'imagines' many things, even involuntarily, and perceives many things coming as it were from the 'senses'? Even if I am all the while asleep; even if my creator does all he can to deceive me; how can any of these things be less of a fact than my existence? Is any of these something distinct from my consciousness? Can any of them be called a separate thing from myself? It is so clear that it is I who doubt, understand, will, that I cannot think how to explain it more clearly. Further, it is I who imagine; for even if, as I supposed, no imagined object is real, yet the power of imagination really exists and goes to make up my experience. Finally, it is I who have sensations, or who perceive corporeal objects as it were by the senses. Thus, I am now seeing light, hearing a noise, feeling heat. These objects are unreal, for I am asleep; but at least I seem to see, to hear, to be warmed. This cannot be unreal; and this is what is properly called my sensation; further, sensation, precisely so regarded, is nothing but an act of consciousness. . . .[3]

[EDITOR'S NOTE. Descartes goes on in the *Meditations* to discuss the idea of corporeal substance whose essence, he observes, is "magnitude or extension in length, breadth and depth; shape, which arises from this extension's having boundaries; position, a relation between objects possessing shape; and motion or change of position." He then proceeds, through various arguments, to establish the certainty of God's existence. In particular, he claims that his idea of God as an infinite or perfect being must derive from the actual existence of an infinite or perfect being. He then goes on to observe that God "must be liable to no defects. From this it is clear enough that he cannot be deceitful; for it is obvious by the light of nature that any fraud or deceit depends on some defect." Having established God's existence as a nondeceitful being, Descartes claims that God "cannot have given me a faculty whose right employment could ever lead me astray." All his errors of judgment come not from God, but from the fact that his human will to believe often extends more widely than his understanding. As long as his will to believe" is confined to what the understanding shows it clearly and distinctly, I just cannot go wrong," Descartes concludes. Having arrived at this conclusion, Descartes reconsiders the question of God's existence and concludes by a version of the ontological argument that he has a clear and distinct idea of the inseparability of the idea of God and of God's actual existence. Our excerpt from the *Meditations* resumes at this point.]

. . . I know that whatever I clearly and distinctly understand can be made by God just as I understand it; so my ability to understand one thing clearly and distinctly apart from another is enough to assure me that they are distinct, because God at least can separate them. . . . Now I know that I exist, and at the same time I observe absolutely nothing else as belonging to my nature or essence except the mere fact that I am a conscious being; and just from this I can validly infer that my essence consists simply in the fact that I am a conscious being. It is indeed possible (or rather, as I shall say later on, it is certain)[4] that I have a body closely bound up with myself; but at the same time I have, on the one hand, a clear and distinct idea of myself taken simply as a conscious, not an extended, being; and, on the other hand, a distinct idea of body, taken simply as an extended, not a conscious, being; so it is certain that I am really distinct from my body, and could exist without it. . . .

Now there is no more explicit lesson of nature than that I have a body; that it is being injured when I feel pain; that it needs food, or drink, when I suffer from hunger, or thirst, and so on. So I must not doubt that there is some truth in this. Nature also teaches by these sensations of pain, hunger, thirst, etc., that I am not present in my body merely as a pilot is present in a ship; I am most tightly bound to it, and as it were mixed up with it, so that I and it form a unit. Otherwise, when the body is hurt, I, who am simply a conscious being, would not feel pain on that account, but would perceive the

[3]Notice the difference between this concept of sensation and the previous one. EDITOR'S NOTE.

[4]According to Descartes, this follows from the fact that he has a clear and distinct idea that the powers of extension (shape and motion) cannot be understood "apart from a substance to inhere in." This substance, he argues, cannot be himself. Consequently, "either this substance is a body—is of corporeal nature— . . . or else it is God, or some creature nobler than bodies. . . . But since God is not deceitful, it is quite obvious that he neither implants the ideas in me by his own direct action, nor yet by means of some creature. . . ." For, if either of these two hypotheses were true, Descartes would be incapable of *knowing* this, and since God has given him a strong inclination to believe in the existence of corporeal objects that cause his waking sensations, God would be deceitful, which is contrary to fact. EDITOR'S NOTE.

injury by a pure act of understanding, as the pilot perceives by sight any breakages there may be in the ship; and when the body needs food or drink, I should explicitly understand the fact, and not have confused sensations of hunger and thirst. For these sensations of thirst, hunger, pain, etc., are simply confused modes of consciousness that arise from the mind's being united to, and as it were mixed up with, the body. . . .

I must begin by observing the great difference between mind and body. Body is of its nature always divisible; mind is wholly indivisible. When I consider the mind—that is, myself, in so far as I am merely a conscious being—I can distinguish no parts within myself; I understand myself to be a single and complete thing. Although the whole mind seems to be united to the whole body, yet when a foot or an arm or any other part of the body is cut off I am not aware that any subtraction has been made from the mind. Nor can the faculties of will, feeling, understanding and so on be called its parts; for it is one and the same mind that wills, feels, and understands. On the other hand, I cannot think of any corporeal or extended object without being readily able to divide it in thought and therefore conceiving of it as divisible. This would be enough to show me the total difference between mind and body, even if I did not sufficiently know this already. . . .[5]

[The Soul Interacts with the Body Through the Brain's Pineal Gland]

It is likewise necessary to know that although the soul is joined to the whole body, there is yet in that a certain part in which it exercises its functions more particularly than in all the others; and it is usually believed that this part is the brain, or possibly the heart: the brain, because it is with it that the organs of sense are connected, and the heart because it is apparently in it that we experience the passions.[6] But, in examining the matter with care, it seems as though I had clearly ascertained that the part of the body in which the soul exercises its functions immediately is in nowise the heart, nor the whole of the brain, but merely the most inward of all its parts, to wit, a certain very small gland which is situated in the middle of its substance and so suspended above the duct whereby the animal spirits[7] in its anterior cavities have communication with those in the posterior, that the slightest movements which take place in it may alter very greatly the course of these spirits; and reciprocally that the smallest changes which occur in the course of the spirits may do much to change the movements of this gland.

The reason which persuades me that the soul cannot have any other seat in all the body than this gland wherein to exercise its functions immediately, is that I reflect that the other parts of our brain are all of them double, just as we have two eyes, two hands, two ears, and finally all the organs of our outside senses are double; and inasmuch as we have but one solitary and simple thought of one particular thing at one and the same moment, it must necessarily be the case that there must somewhere be a place where the two images which come to us by the two eyes, where the two other impressions which proceed from a single object by means of the double organs of the other senses, can unite before arriving at the soul, in order that they may not represent to it two objects instead of one. And it is easy to apprehend how these images or other impressions might unite in this gland by the intermission of the spirits which fill the cavities of the brain; but there is no other place in the body where they can be thus united unless they are so in this gland. . . .

[5]The excerpt from Descartes' *Meditations* ends at this point and the excerpt from Descartes' *Passions of the Soul* begins. EDITOR'S NOTE.

[6]In Descartes' day, it was believed that emotions (passions) were caused by activity in the heart. EDITOR'S NOTE.

[7]In Descartes' day, it was believed that the nerves were filled with a minute, rapidly moving liquid called "the animal spirits." EDITOR'S NOTE.

Let us then conceive here that the soul has its principal seat in the little gland which exists in the middle of the brain, from whence it radiates forth through all the remainder of the body by means of the animal spirits, nerves, and even the blood, which, participating in the impressions of the spirits, can carry them by the arteries into all the members. And recollecting what has been said above about the machine of our body, i.e. that the little filaments of our nerves are so distributed in all its parts, that on the occasion of the diverse movements which are there excited by sensible objects, they open in diverse ways the pores of the brain, which causes the animal spirits contained in these cavities to enter in diverse ways into the muscles, by which means they can move the members in all the different ways in which they are capable of being moved; and also that all the other causes which are capable of moving the spirits in diverse ways suffice to conduct them into diverse muscles; let us here add that the small gland which is the main seat of the soul is so suspended between the cavities which contain the spirits that it can be moved by them in as many different ways as there are sensible diversities in the object, but that it may also be moved in diverse ways by the soul, whose nature is such that it receives in itself as many diverse impressions, that is to say, that it possesses as many diverse perceptions as there are diverse movements in this gland. Reciprocally, likewise, the machine of the body is so formed that from the simple fact that this gland is diversely moved by the soul, or by such other cause, whatever it is, it thrusts the spirits which surround it towards the pores of the brain, which conduct them by the nerves into the muscles, by which means it causes them to move the limbs. . . .[8]

Now it is conclusively proved that the soul has sensations of what affects various members of the body, not by its presence in those members, but only by its presence in the brain. Various diseases affect only the brain, but destroy or disturb all sensation. Again, sleep occurs only in the brain; and every day we lose a great part of our sensory powers in sleep and regain them on awakening. Again, if the brain is intact, a mere obstruction of the paths by which the nerves reach it from the external parts is enough to destroy sensations in those parts. Finally, pain is sometimes felt in a limb when there is no cause of pain in it, but only in another part traversed by the nerves from that limb to the brain.

The last point may be shown by innumerable observations; it will be enough to mention one here. A girl with a seriously diseased hand used to have her eyes bandaged when the surgeon came, lest she should be afraid on seeing the surgical instruments. After some days her arm was amputated at the elbow because of a creeping gangrene; napkins were put in its place, so that she did not in the least know she had lost it. At this time she complained of feeling pains now in one, now in another finger of the amputated hand. The only possible reason is this: the nerves that formerly led down from the brain to the hand, and that now ended in the arm near the elbow, were undergoing the same disturbances as would formerly have had to arise in the hand, so as to produce in the soul, seated in the brain, the sensation of pain in this or that finger. . . .[9]

[The Difference Between Human Beings and Animals or Machines]

. . . If there were machines with the organs and appearance of a monkey, or some other irrational animal, we should have no means of telling that they were not altogether of the same nature as those animals; whereas if there were machines resembling our bodies, and imitating

[8]The excerpt from *The Passions of the Soul* ends at this point and the excerpt from *Principles of Philosophy* begins. EDITOR'S NOTE.

[9]The excerpt from *Principles of Philosophy* ends here and the excerpt from *Discourse on the Method* begins. EDITOR'S NOTE.

our actions as far as is morally possible, we should still have two means of telling that, all the same, they were not real men. First, they could never use words or other constructed signs, as we do to declare our thoughts to others. It is quite conceivable that a machine should be so made as to utter words, and even utter them in connexion with physical events that cause a change in one of its orgins; so that e.g. if it is touched in one part, it asks what you want to say to it, and if touched in another, it cries out that it is hurt; but not that it should be so made as to arrange words variously in response to the meaning of what is said in its presence, as even the dullest men can do. Secondly, while they might do many things as well as any of us or better, they would infallibly fail in others, revealing that they acted not from knowledge but only from the disposition of their organs. For while reason is a universal tool that may serve in all kinds of circumstances, these organs need a special arrangement for each special action; so it is morally impossible that a machine should contain so many varied arrangements as to act in all the events of life in the way reason enables us to act.

Now in just these two ways we can also recognize the difference between men and brutes. For it is a very remarkable thing that there are no men so dull and stupid, not even lunatics, that they cannot arrange various words and form a sentence to make their thoughts understood; but no other animal, however perfect or well bred, can do the like. This does not come from their lacking the organs; for magpies and parrots can utter words like ourselves, and yet they cannot talk like us, that is, with any sign of being aware of what they say. Whereas men born deaf-mutes, and thus devoid of the organs that others use for speech, as much as brutes are or more so, usually invent for themselves signs by which they make themselves understood to those who are normally with them, and who thus have a chance to learn their language. This is evidence that brutes not only have a smaller degree of reason than men, but are wholly lacking in it. For it may be seen that a very small degree of reason is needed in order to talk. . . . Nor must we think, like some of the ancients, that brutes talk but we cannot understand their language; for if that were true, since many of their organs are analogous to ours, they could make themselves understood to us, as well as to their fellows. It is another very remarkable thing that although several brutes exhibit more skill than we in some of their actions, they show none at all in many other circumstances; so their excelling us is no proof that they have a mind. . .; it rather shows that they have none, and that it is nature that acts in them according to the arrangements of their organs; just as we see how a clock, composed merely of wheels and springs, can reckon the hours and measure time more correctly than we can with all our wisdom.

. . . The rational soul cannot be extracted from the potentiality of matter, but must be specially created. . . . After the error of denying God, . . . there is none more likely to turn weak characters from the straight way of virtue than the supposition that the soul of brutes must be of the same nature as ours, so that after this life we have no more to hope or fear than flies or ants. Whereas, when we realise how much they really differ from us, we understand much better the arguments proving that our soul is of a nature entirely independent of the body, and thus not liable to die with it; and since we can discern no other causes that should destroy it, we are naturally led to decide that it is immortal.

DISCUSSION QUESTIONS

1. Does Descartes' attempt to build the edifice of certain knowledge upon the foundation of self-evident truths withstand the assumption of the existence of an evil genius who does everything possible to deceive Descartes? Can anyone ever be absolutely certain of anything? If so, what?

2. Descartes claims that it is logically impossible for an evil genius to deceive him into believing that he exists when he really does not. Could the evil genius, however, deceive Descartes into believing that other people exist, when they really do not?

3. Does Descartes believe that it is possible for a person to exist in a totally disembodied form? According to Descartes, what is essential to one's personal identity (i.e., that which cannot be taken away from a person without destroying that person)?

4. Does Descartes have any adequate basis for claiming that it is the mind and not the body which is the subject of states of consciousness? If it is difficult to imagine how physical bodies can be conscious, is it less difficult to imagine how a nonphysical substance can be conscious? Indeed, what basis, if any, is there for believing in nonphysical substances called "minds," as well as physical substances?

5. According to Descartes, how does the mind differ from the body?

6. Even if the mind (the soul) **can** exist apart from the body, does Descartes provide any good reason to believe that the soul **actually** will one day exist apart from the body, let alone that the soul is immortal?

7. How does Descartes see the causal connection between mind and body? Does he explain how mind and body interact? Does he attempt such an explanation?

8. What does Descartes mean when he claims ". . . I am not present in my body merely as a pilot is present in a ship; I am most tightly bound to it . . . so that I and it form a unit"?

9. According to Descartes, which of the following describes our relationship to our bodies and minds:

a. We are bodies which have minds.

b. We are minds which have bodies.

c. We are persons who have both bodies and minds.

d. We are persons who are both bodies and minds.

Which way would you put it? Why?

10. Do you agree with Descartes' view of what distinguishes human beings from other animals and complicated machines? Why?

11. In his short story "Robbie" (in **i, robot**), Isaac Asimov describes the sadness of a little girl, Gloria, whose parents have taken away her beloved robot, Robbie. Seeing Gloria's sadness as unjustified, her mother attempts to console her, but Gloria remains unconsoled. As Asimov writes:

> "Why do you cry, Gloria? Robbie was only a machine, just a nasty old machine. He wasn't alive at all."
>
> "He was **not** no machine!" screamed Gloria, fiercely and ungrammatically." He was a **person** just like you and me and he was my **friend.** I want him back. Oh, Mamma, I want him back."

How can the issue between Gloria and her mother be resolved? What do the key notions **person, machine,** and **alive** in the above passage mean?

12. If a robot were manufactured that behaved exactly like a human being and looked externally just like one, but instead of being constructed like a human being (i.e., of blood, muscles, bones, etc.) was constructed in a different way (e.g., of wires and electrical circuits), would this show that the robot did not have feelings, thoughts, and other states of consciousness? Would it make any difference if the internal structure of the robot were identical to the internal structure of human beings, but its chemical composition were different? (For example, while its brain, heart, lungs, and other internal organs would function exactly as human organs, they might be made of silicon compounds rather than of carbon compounds as the internal organs of human beings are.)

25. THE BUNDLE THEORY OF THE SELF

David Hume

(For a biographical sketch of David Hume, see Selection #8.)

The following selection is from Hume's **Treatise.** In this selection Hume employs his empiricist philosophy to reject the Cartesian idea of an immaterial substance (soul or mind) that is the "subject" or "owner" of states of consciousness. Believing, as an empiricist, that all knowledge derives from experience—that is, from states of consciousness (or in Hume's philosophical terminology, from **impressions**[1]—Hume contends that the existence of spiritual substance that Descartes took to be self-evident was not simply questionable, but actually meaningless. From Hume's perspective, if the Cartesian concept (idea) of an unchangeable immaterial substance which is the subject of experience were meaningful, it would have to be revealed in some state of consciousness. Yet introspection, Hume claims, reveals nothing but the states of consciousness themselves and no underlying core or subject to which they adhere. "What we call the self," Hume contends, is no single unchangeable thing but merely "a bundle or collection of different perceptions" which are misleadingly united together in our minds by a psychological process of association. (As we shall see in the next chapter, Hume employs a similar argument to deny the existence of an external physical world that causes our perceptions. In Hume's metaphysics, the world consists not of minds with their states of consciousness and physical bodies with their mass, shape, position, and motion, as it did for Descartes, but simply in various "bundles" of successive impermanent states of consciousness.)

There are some philosophers who imagine we are every moment intimately conscious of what we call our *self*; that we feel its existence and its continuance in existence; and are certain, beyond the evidence of a demonstration, both of its perfect identity and simplicity. The strongest sensation, the most violent passion, say they, instead of distracting us from this view, only fix it the more intensely, and make us consider their influence on *self* either by their pain or pleasure. To attempt a further proof of this were to weaken its evidence; since no proof can be derived from any fact of which we are so intimately conscious; nor is there anything of which we can be certain if we doubt of this.

Unluckily all these positive assertions are contrary to that very experience which is pleaded for them; nor have we any idea of *self*, after the manner it is here explained. For, from what impression could this idea be derived? This question it is impossible to answer without a manifest contradiction and absurdity; and yet it is a question which must necessarily be answered, if we would have the idea of self pass for clear

Source: Section 6, Part IV, Book I of David Hume's *A Treatise of Human Nature,* a work first published in 1739.

[1]Technically, Hume calls the mind's contents *perceptions* and claims that these perceptions consist either of impressions (sensations, feelings and emotions) or *ideas* (the "representations of imagination and memory" which derive from impressions). Conceiving of ideas as mental images of impressions, Hume conceived of thinking as mental imagery which, however complex or fanciful, are representations of previously experienced impressions.

and intelligible. It must be some one impression that gives rise to every real idea. But self or person is not any one impression, but that to which our several impressions and ideas are supposed to have a reference. If any impression gives rise to the idea of self, that impression must continue invariably the same, through the whole course of our lives; since self is supposed to exist after that manner. But there is no impression constant and invariable. Pain and pleasure, grief and joy, passions and sensations succeed each other, and never all exist at the same time. It cannot therefore be from any of these impressions, or from any other, that the idea of self is derived; and consequently there is no such idea.

But further, what must become of all our particular perceptions upon this hypothesis? All these are different, and distinguishable, and separable from each other, and may be separately considered, and may exist separately, and have no need of anything to support their existence. After what manner therefore do they belong to self, and how are they connected with it? For my part, when I enter most intimately into what I call *myself,* I always stumble on some particular perception or other, of heat or cold, light or shade, love or hatred, pain or pleasure. I never can catch *myself* at any time without a perception, and never can observe anything but the perception. When my perceptions are removed for any time, as by sound sleep, so long am I insensible of *myself,* and may truly be said not to exist. And were all my perceptions removed by death, and could I neither think, nor feel, nor see, nor love, nor hate, after the dissolution of my body, I should be entirely annihilated, nor do I conceive what is further requisite to make me a perfect nonentity. If any one, upon serious and unprejudiced reflection, thinks he has a different notion of *himself,* I must confess I can reason no longer with him. All I can allow him is, that he may be in the right as well as I, and that we are essentially different in this particular. He may, perhaps, perceive something simple and continued, which he calls *himself;* though I am certain there is no such principle in me.

But setting aside some metaphysicians of this kind, I may venture to affirm of the rest of mankind, that they are nothing but a bundle or collection of different perceptions, which succeed each other with an inconceivable rapidity, and are in a perpetual flux and movement. Our eyes cannot turn in their sockets without varying our perceptions. Our thought is still more variable than our sight; and all our other senses and faculties contribute to this change; nor is there any single power of the soul, which remains unalterably the same, perhaps for one moment. The mind is a kind of theater, where several perceptions successively make their appearance; pass, repass, glide away, and mingle in an infinite variety of postures and situations. There is properly no *simplicity* in it at one time, nor *identity* in different, whatever natural propension we may have to imagine that simplicity and identity. The comparison of the theater must not mislead us. They are the successive perceptions only, that constitute the mind; nor have we the most distant notion of the place where these scenes are represented, or of the materials of which it is composed.

[EDITOR'S NOTE. Hume then goes on to claim that it is the mind's imaginative propensity to confuse the close relation of discrete perceptions that exist in succession with the uninterrupted existence of a single perception that accounts for our ascription of identity to successive perceptions. The unity of a bundle of perceptions that constitutes our notion of the self is a unity that exists in our minds and does not reflect "any real connection among the perceptions themselves," Hume claims. Hume contends that this *feeling* of unity is caused by the perceptions of memory and the close causal relations that exist among our perceptions. These factors, he writes, give rise to a "fiction or imaginary principle of union" which makes us unite discrete perceptions by means of the fiction of a single uninterrupted substance that is mistakenly taken to account for our sense of identity through the shifting temporal flux of changing perceptions. Nevertheless, honestly admitting his own dissatisfaction with his inability to "explain the principles that unite our successive perceptions in our thought or consciousness" (that is, to explain what binds a bundle of perceptions together), Hume closes his account of personal identity with the confession that "I must plead the privilege of a sceptic, and confess that this difficulty is too hard for my understanding."]

DISCUSSION QUESTIONS

1. What does Hume mean when he says that the mind is "like a theatre"? Why does he also claim that this analogy could be misleading?

2. Some Eastern religions speak of a merging of individual consciousness at bodily death into some all-inclusive "cosmic consciousness." Is such a view consistent with Hume's view of the self? With Descartes'?

3. Do you agree with Hume that personal identity cannot be identified with the continued existence of a specific spiritual substance (the soul) which is the subject of experiences. In drawing your conclusion, consider the following criticism of Hume's view of personal identity by the philosopher Thomas Reid (1785):

> . . . identity supposes **an uninterrupted continuance of existence**. . . . All mankind place their personality in something that **cannot be divided, or consist of parts**. . . . My personal identity, therefore, implies the continued existence of that indivisible thing which I call **myself.** Whatever this self may be, it is something which thinks, and deliberates, and resolves, and acts, and suffers. I am not thought; I am not action; I am not feeling; I am something that thinks, and acts, and suffers. My thoughts, and actions, and feelings, change every moment; they have no continued, but a successive, existence; but that **self,** or I, to which they belong is permanent, and has the same relation to all the succeeding thoughts, actions, and feelings which I call mine. . . .The thoughts and feelings of which we are conscious are continually changing . . . but something which I call **myself** remains under this change of thought.[2]

4. According to Hume's view of personal identity, what binds "a bundle of perceptions" together? Is it logically possible to have a perception that is not a member of any bundle of perceptions? If not, is Hume's account of personal identity capable of accounting for this logical impossibility? Must Hume's account be rejected for this reason?

[2] *Essays on the Intellectual Powers of Man,* Chapter 4.

26. MEMORY IS THE CRITERION OF PERSONAL IDENTITY: A PIONEERING ANALYSIS

John Locke

JOHN LOCKE (1632–1704), the founder of the empiricist movement in philosophy, was educated in the classics and scholastic philosophy in England and lectured in the classics at Oxford as a young man. During these years, he became acquainted with Descartes' philosophical writings and became friendly with several scientists of his day, notably the chemist Robert Boyle, from whom he absorbed the new science of his day, with its corpuscular (atomic) theory and experimental method of inquiry. Dissatisfied with his life at Oxford, Locke turned to the study of medicine. A few years after completing his medical studies, he met Lord Ashley, who later was to become Earl of Shaftesbury. They became very good friends and Locke joined Ashley in the capacity of personal physician and political ally. From then on, Locke became enmeshed in the political scheming and controversy that surrounded the Earl of Schaftesbury. When Shaftesbury became Lord Chancellor of England in 1672, Locke was appointed to a governmental position. A few years later, Shaftesbury, an opponent of the then King of England and strong supporter of parliamentary power, was forced to flee from England to Holland when the royalist faction gained the upper hand. His close association with Shaftesbury brought Locke under suspicion and he too fled to Holland. In Holland, Locke wrote extensively on various subjects, while deeply engaged in the political plot to set William of Orange upon the English throne. With the plot accomplished (as a result of the Glorious Revolution of 1688), Locke returned to England in 1689. A year later, his two philosophical masterpiecces, **An Essay Concerning Human Understanding** and **The Two Treatises of Government,** were published, establishing Locke's fame as a great philosopher.

Greatly influenced by Descartes, Locke's purpose in **An Essay Concerning Human Understanding** was, in his own words, "to inquire into the origin, certainty and extent of human knowledge." In the **Essay,** Locke considers how the mind operates in learning about the world and in the process lays down the fundamental principles of the empiricist philosophy which would later be refined and developed by George Berkeley and David Hume. (Locke, Berkeley, and Hume are the triad of English philosophers referred to as **the British Empiricists.**) Highly critical of the rationalistic **a priori** foundations of Descartes' phiosophy (i.e., Descartes' belief that knowledge of matters of fact can be discerned by reason alone), Locke's central concern in the **Essay** was to refute the rationalist belief in **innate** (i.e., inborn) **ideas.** All knowledge, Locke argues, comes from experience. The mind, he contends, is at birth a **tabula rasa** (i.e., blank slate) upon which experience writes. This contention is the cornerstone of British Empiricism.

The selection that follows is from Locke's **Essay.** As the selections from Darrow and Hick which opened this chapter indicate, memory seems to play a central role in our concept of personal identity. While Darrow and Hick do not explicitly identify personal identity with continuity of memory, many philosophers have. Our excerpt consists of Locke's defense of this position. Locke was the first philosopher to delve deeply into the puzzling question, "What is it by virtue of which a person is **the same person** from one moment to the next?"

Parting with Descartes, who identified personal identity with the continuous existence of a spiritual substance (soul) that is the subject of experiences, Locke argues that it is continuity of memory and not of spiritual substance that defines personal identity and is the necessary condition of moral responsibility. In the section of the **Essay** that immediately precedes our excerpt, Locke carefully distinguishes the concepts of "same (spiritual) substance," "same man," and "same person." Accepting Descartes' view (later to be rejected by Hume) that experiences must be **experiences of** some underlying spiritual substance (the soul), Locke is puzzled by the possibility that different souls can, for all we know, occupy the same body at different times. Aware of the unverifiable nature of assertions about the soul, Locke turns his attention to observable matters. First, however, he contends that the notion of "the same man" cannot be identified with the notion of "the same soul." In defense of this contention, Locke, reflecting ordinary usage, observes that the former notion, unlike the latter one, implies the notion of having **a human body.** For example, if one believes in the transmigration of men's souls into those of animals (as some of Locke's contemporaries did,) although one might want to say that an animal, like a dog, has "the same soul" as someone that once lived, one would not want to say that a dog **is** a man. Because of considerations such as this, Locke concludes that ". . . I presume it is not the idea of a thinking or rational being [i.e., Descartes' view of the soul] alone that makes the idea of a man in most people's sense, but of a body, so and so shaped joined to it, and if that be the idea of a man, the same successive body not shifted all at once must, as well as the same immaterial spirit, go to the making of the same man." With this preliminary analytic clarification, Locke turns to the concept of personal identity and reveals the puzzling nature of a concept that previous philosophers took for granted.

. . . to find wherein personal identity consists, we must consider what *person* stands for;—which, I think, is a thinking intelligent being, that has reason and reflection, and can consider itself as itself, the same thinking thing, in different times and places; which it does only by that consciousness which is inseparable from thinking, and, as it seems to me, essential to it: it being impossible for any one to perceive without *perceiving* that he does perceive. When we see, hear, smell, taste, feel, meditate, or will anything, we know that we do so. Thus it is always as to our present sensations and perceptions: and by this every one is to himself that which he calls *self:*—it not being considered, in this case, whether the same self be continued in the same or divers substances. For, since consciousness always accompanies thinking, and it is that which makes every one to be what he calls self, and thereby distinguishes himself from all other thinking things, in this alone consists personal identity, i.e. the sameness of a rational being; and as far as this consciousness can be extended backwards to any past action or thought, so far reaches the identity of that person; it is the same self now it was then; and it is by the same self with this present one that now reflects on it, that that action was done.

But it is further inquired, whether it be the same identical substance. This few would think they had reason to doubt of, if these perceptions, with their consciousness, always remained present in the mind, whereby the same thinking thing would be always consciously present, and, as would be thought, evidently the same to itself. But that which seems to make the difficulty is this, that this consciousness being interrupted always by forgetfulness, there being no moment of our lives wherein we have the whole train of all our past actions before our eyes in one view, . . . and that the greatest part of our lives, not reflecting on our past selves, being intent on our present thoughts, and in sound sleep having no thoughts at all, . . . doubts are raised whether we are the same thinking thing, i.e., the same *substance* or no. Which, however reasonable or unreasonable, concerns not *personal* identity at all. The question being what makes the same person; and not whether it be the same identical substance, which always thinks in the same person, which, in this case, matters not at all. . . . For, it being the same consciousness that makes a man be himself to himself, personal identity depends on that on-

Source: Book 2, Chapter 27 of John Locke's *An Essay Concerning Human Understanding.*

ly, whether it be annexed solely to one individual substance, or can be continued in a succession of several substances. . . .

But the question is, Whether if the same substance which thinks be changed, it can be the same person; or, remaining the same, it can be different persons?

And to this I answer: First, This can be no question at all to those who place thought in a purely material animal constitution, void of an immaterial substance. For, whether their supposition be true or no, it is plain they conceive personal identity preserved in something else than identity of substance; as animal identity is preserved in identity of life, and not of substance. And therefore those who place thinking in an immaterial substance only, before they can come to deal with these men, must show why personal identity cannot be preserved in the change of immaterial substances, or variety of particular immaterial substances, as well as animal identity is preserved in the change of material substances, or variety of particular bodies: unless they will say, it is one immaterial spirit that makes the same life in brutes, as it is one immaterial spirit that makes the same person in men; which the Cartesians[1] at least will not admit, for fear of making brutes thinking things too.

But next, as to the first part of the question, Whether, if the same thinking substance (supposing immaterial substances only to think) be changed, it can be the same person? I answer, that cannot be resolved but by those who know what kind of substances they are that do think; and whether the consciousness of past actions can be transferred from one thinking substance to another . . . why it may not be possible . . . [to seem to remember something] which really never was . . . will by us, till we have clearer views of the nature of thinking substances, be best resolved in the goodness of God; who, as far as the happiness or misery of any of his sensible creatures is concerned in it, will not . . . transfer from one to another that consciousness which draws reward or punishment with it. . . . But yet, to return to the question before us, it must be allowed, that, if the same consciousness . . . can be transferred from one thinking substance to another, it will be possible that two thinking substances may make but one person. For the same consciousness being preserved, whether in the same or different substances, the personal identity is preserved.

As to the second part of the question, Whether the same immaterial substance remaining, there may be two distinct persons; which question seems to me to be built on this,—Whether the same immaterial being, being conscious of the action of its past duration, may be wholly stripped of all the consciousness of its past existence, and lose it beyond the power of ever retrieving it again: and so as it were beginning a new account from a new period, have a consciousness that *cannot* reach beyond this new state. All those who hold pre-existence are evidently of this mind; since they allow the soul to have no remaining consciousness of what it did in that pre-existent state either wholly separate from body, or informing any other body. . . . Suppose a Christian Platonist or a Pythagorean should, upon God's having ended all his works of creation the seventh day, think his soul hath existed ever since; and should imagine it has revolved in several human bodies; as I once met with one, who was persuaded his had been the *soul* of Socrates (how reasonably I will not dispute; this I know, that in the post he filled, which was no inconsiderable one, he passed for a very rational man, and the press has shown that he wanted not parts or learning;)—would any one say, that he, being not conscious of any of Socrates' actions or thoughts, could be the same *person* with Socrates? Let any one reflect upon himself, and conclude that he has in himself an immaterial spirit, which is that which thinks in him, and, in the constant change of his body keeps him the same: and is

[1]Followers of Descartes. EDITOR'S NOTE.

that which he calls *himself:* let him also suppose it to be the same soul that was in Nestor or Thersites, at the siege of Troy . . . but he now having no consciousness of any of the actions either of Nestor or Thersites, does or can he conceive himself the same person with either of them? Can he be concerned in either of their actions? attribute them to himself, or think them his own, more than the actions of any other men that ever existed? So that this consciousness, not reaching to any of the actions of either of those men, he is no more one *self* with either of them than if the soul or immaterial spirit that now informs him had been created, and began to exist, when it began to inform his present body; though it were never so true, that the same *spirit* that informed Nestor's or Thersites' body were numerically the same that now informs his. For this would no more make him the same person with Nestor, than if some of the particles of matter that were once a part of Nestor were now a part of this man; the same immaterial substance, without the same consciousness, no more making the same person, by being united to any body, than the same particle of matter, without consciousness, united to any body, makes the same person. But let him once find himself conscious of any of the actions of Nestor, he then finds himself the same person with Nestor.

And thus may we be able, without any difficulty, to conceive the same person at the resurrection, though in a body not exactly in make or parts the same which he had here,—the same consciousness going along with the soul that inhabits it. But yet the soul alone, in the change of bodies, would scarce to any one but to him that makes the soul the man, be enough to make the same man. For should the soul of a prince, carrying with it the consciousness of the prince's past life, enter and inform the body of a cobbler, as soon as deserted by his own soul, every one sees he would be the same *person* with the prince, accountable only for the prince's actions: but who would say it was the same *man?* The body too goes to the making the man, and would, I guess, to everybody determine the man in this case, wherein the soul, with all its princely thoughts about it, would not make another man: but he would be the same cobbler to every one besides himself. . . .

But though the same immaterial substance or soul does not alone, wherever it be, and in whatsoever state, make the same *man;* yet it is plain, consciousness, as far as ever it can be extended—should it be to ages past—unites existences and actions very remote in time into the same *person*, . . . so that whatever has the consciousness of present and past actions, is the same person to whom they both belong. Had I the same consciousness that I saw the ark and Noah's flood, as that I saw an overflowing of the Thames last winter, or as that I write now, I could no more doubt that I who write this now, that saw the Thames overflowed last winter, and that viewed the flood at the general deluge, was the same *self,*—place that self in what *substance* you please—than that I who write this am the same *myself* now whilst I write (whether I consist of all the same substance, material or immaterial, or no) that I was yesterday. For as to this point of being the same self, it matters not whether this present self be made up of the same or other substances—I being so much concerned, and as justly accountable for any action that was done a thousand years since, appropriated to me now by this self-consciousness, as I am for what I did the last moment. . . .

This may show us wherein personal identity consists: not in the identity of substance, but, as I have said, in the identity of consciousness, wherein if Socrates and the present mayor of Queensborough agree, they are the same person: if the same Socrates waking and sleeping do not partake of the same consciousness, Socrates waking and sleeping is not the same person. And to punish Socrates waking for what sleeping Socrates thought, and waking Socrates was never conscious of, would be no more of right, than to punish one twin for what his brother-twin did, where of he knew nothing, because their outsides were so like, that they could not be distinguished; for such twins have been seen.

But yet possibly it will still be objected,—Suppose I wholly lose the memory of some parts of my life, beyond a possibility of retrieving them, so that perhaps I shall never be conscious of them again; yet am I not the same person that did those actions, had those thoughts that I once was conscious of, though I have now forgot them? To which I answer, that we must here take notice what the word *I* is applied to; which, in this case, is the *man* only. And the same man being presumed to be the same person, I is easily here supposed to stand also for the same person. But if it be possible for the same man to have distinct incommunicable consciousness at different times, it is past doubt the same man would at different times make different persons; which, we see, is the sense of mankind in the solemnist declaration of their opinions, human laws not punishing the mad man for the sober man's actions, nor the sober man for what the mad man did,—thereby making them two persons: which is somewhat explained by our way of speaking in English when we say such an one is "not himself," or is "beside himself"; in which phrases it is insinuated, as if those who now, or at least first used them, thought that self was changed; the self-same person was no longer in that man. . . .

But is not a man drunk and sober the same person? why else is he punished for the act he commits when drunk, though he be never afterwards conscious of it? Just as much the same person as a man that walks, and does other things in his sleep, is the same person, and is answerable for any mischief he shall do in it. Human laws punish both, with a justice suitable to *their* way of knowledge;—because, in these cases, they cannot distinguish certainly what is real, what counterfeit: and so the ignorance in drunkenness or sleep is not admitted as a plea. For, though punishment be annexed to personality, and personality to consciousness, and the drunkard perhaps be not conscious of what he did, yet human judicatures justly punish him; because the fact is proved against him, but want of consciousness cannot be proved for him. But in the Great Day, wherein the secrets of all hearts shall be laid open, it may be reasonable to think, no one shall be made to answer for what he knows nothing of; but shall receive his doom, his conscience accusing or excusing him.

Nothing but consciousness can unite remote existences into the same person: the identity of substance will not do it; for whatever substance there is, however framed, without consciousness there is no person. . . .

Could we suppose two distinct incommunicable consciousnesses acting in the same body, the one constantly by day, the other by night; and, on the other side, the same consciousness, acting by intervals, in two distinct bodies: I ask, in the first case, whether the day- and the night-man would not be two as distinct persons as Socrates and Plato? And whether, in the second case, there would not be one person in two distinct bodies, as much as one man is the same in two distinct clothings? Nor is it at all material to say, that this same, and this distinct consciousness, in the cases above mentioned, is owing to the same and distinct immaterial substances, bringing it with them to those bodies; which, whether true or no, alters not the case: since it is evident the personal identity would equally be determined by the consciousness, whether that consciousness were annexed to some individual immaterial substance or no. For, granting that the thinking substance in man must be necessarily supposed immaterial, it is evident that immaterial thinking thing may sometimes part with its past consciousness, and be restored to it again: as appears in the forgetfulness men often have of their past actions; and the mind many times recovers the memory of a past consciousness, which it had lost for twenty years together. Make these intervals of memory and forgetfulness to take their turns regularly by day and night, and you have two persons with the same immaterial spirit, as much as in the former instance two persons with the same body. So that self is not determined by identity or diversity of substance, which it cannot be sure of, but only by identity of consciousness. . . .

DISCUSSION QUESTIONS

1. According to Locke, in what does personal identity consist? On this view, is it logically possible (i.e., does it make sense) to suppose that a person did something, but cannot remember doing it?

2. According to Locke, is it logically possible to suppose that a person can honestly seem to remember doing something or being someone without doing or being that something or someone? How does Locke try to handle this possibility? Why is he troubled by it? Should he be?

3. If memories are essential to personal identity, does this entail that we cease to exist when in a dreamless sleep or when unconscious? Is such a conclusion acceptable?

4. According to Locke, can a person rightfully be held responsible for a crime that he forgot he committed? What reason would Locke give for his conclusion? Do you agree? What if a person takes a drug with the intention of forgetting something he did?

5. What justification does Locke give for the legal practice of punishing a man for what he did when drunk, even though he does not remember his action at that time? Do you find this reason compelling? Is there a better one?

6. Assuming the existence of a soul that can be reincarnated into different bodies, would it be wrong, as Locke claims, to say that having the same soul makes one "the same person" as a previously existing person, even if one has no memories of what that previous person did or felt?

7. Critically consider Locke's discussion of the cobbler and the prince. Do you find any fault with Locke's analysis? Is the situation more complex than Locke makes it appear? For example, if the cobbler's body is to contain the prince's memories, will this body talk like the prince previously did? Will it have the same emotional reactions that the prince previously had? Is it possible that the cobbler's face may be incapable of expressing the prince's previous emotions?

8. Locke claims, "Had I the same consciousness that I saw the ark and Noah's flood, . . . as that I write now, I could no more doubt that I who write this now . . . and that viewed the flood at the general deluge, was the same **self.**" Critically comment.

9. Consider the following famous criticism of Locke's view of personal identity by Thomas Reid (1785):

> [On Locke's view of personal identity] **a man may be, and at the same time not be, the person that did a particular action.** Suppose a brave officer to have been flogged when a boy at school for robbing an orchard, to have taken a standard from the enemy in his first campaign, and to have been made a general in advanced life; suppose, also, which must be admitted to be possible, that when he took the standard, he was conscious of his having been flogged at school, and that, when made a general, he was conscious of his taking the standard, but had absolutely lost the consciousness of his flogging. These things being supposed, it follows, from Mr. Locke's doctrine, that he who was flogged at school is the same person who took the standard, and that he who took the standard is the same person who was made a general. Whence it follows, if there be any truth in logic, that the general is the same person with him who was flogged at school. But the general's consciousness does not reach so far back as his flogging; therefore, according to Mr. Locke's doctrine, he is not the person who was flogged. Therefore the general is, and at the same time is not, the same person with him who was flogged at school.[2]

Can Locke's view of personal identity be modified to avoid Reid's objection?

10. Assuming that you were told that you will be tortured tomorrow, but that at the moment of torture will have total amnesia as to your past and will have no memory of the torture afterwards, would you feel any less concerned about the torture than you would be if your memories were not to be af-

[2] *Essays on the Intellectual Powers of Man*, Chapter 6.

fected? According to Locke's analysis of personal identity, is it really **you** who will be tortured? Is Locke's view acceptable?

11. In the light of the selections from Descartes and Locke, what sense, if any, would you make of the following:

a. A person exists without a body.

b. One person has (or controls) two bodies.

c. One person has two minds (or souls).

d. One body is controlled (possessed) by two souls.

27. MEMORY IS THE CRITERION OF PERSONAL IDENTITY: A MORE REFINED ANALYSIS

Anthony Quinton

ANTHONY QUINTON (1925–) teaches philosophy at Oxford University, where he himself was educated. He also has been a visiting professor at many American universities. The author of many philosophical articles, his fields of special interest are ethical and political philosophy and the mind-body problem.

In the selection that follows, Quinton defends a more sophisticated analysis of personal identity as continuity of memory than that presented by Locke. (Quinton's analysis, for example, is not subject to Thomas Reid's famous "Gallant Officer" example which he used to refute Locke's analysis—see question 9 in the preceding selection.) By the use of certain imaginative cases of "bodily transference" (even into nonhuman forms), Quinton concludes that bodily identity or continuity is not necessary for personal identity. As Quinton sees it, Locke was right to equate personal identity with the connected sequence of a person's states of consciousness, logically distinct from that person's physical body, or any other physical body.

The Soul and Spiritual Substance

Philosophers in recent times have had very little to say about the soul. The word, perhaps, has uncomfortably ecclesiastical[1] associations, and the idea seems to be bound up with a number of discredited or at any rate generally disregarded theories. In the history of philosophy the soul has been used for two distinct purposes: first, as an explanation of the vitality that distinguishes human beings, and also animals and plants, from the broad mass of material objects, and, secondly, as the seat of consciousness. The first of these, which sees the soul as an ethereal but nonetheless physical entity, a volatile collection of fire-atoms or a stream of animal spirits, on some views dissipated with the dissolution of the body, on

Source: Anthony Quinton, "The Soul," *The Journal of Philosophy*, 59 (1962), 393–409. Reprinted with the permission of *The Journal of Philosophy* and Anthony Quinton.

[1]Religious. EDITOR'S NOTE.

others absorbed at death into the cosmic soul, and on others again as capable of independent existence, need not detain us. The second, however, the soul of Plato and Descartes, deserves a closer examination than it now usually receives. For it tends to be identified with the view that in each person there is to be found a spiritual substance which is the subject of his mental states and the bearer of his personal identity. But on its widest interpretation, as the nonphysical aspect of a person, its acceptance need not involve either the existence of a spiritual substance over and above the mental states that make up a person's inner, conscious life or the proposition that this spiritual substance is what ultimately determines a person's identity through time. When philosophers dismiss the soul it is usually because they reject one or both of these supposed consequences of belief in it . . . .

Spiritual substance cannot be the criterion of personal identity, and it may or may not be presupposed by the existence of conscious mental states . . . . Locke saw that spiritual substance could not account for personal identity and, although he believed in its existence, speculated whether it might not have been possible for God to endow a material substance with the power of thinking. Yet he clearly believed in the soul as the connected sequence of a person's conscious states, regarded this sequence as what a person essentially was, and held it to be capable of existing independently of the body. I want to consider whether an empirical concept of the soul, which, like Locke's, interprets it as a sequence of mental states logically distinct from the body and is neutral with regard to the problem of the subject, can be constructed.

The Empirical Concept of the Soul

It will be admitted that among all the facts that involve a person there is a class that can be described as mental in some sense or other. Is it enough to define the soul as the temporally extended totality of mental states and events that belong to a person? It will not be enough to provide a concept of the soul as something logically distinct from the body if the idea of the series of a person's mental states involves some reference to the particular human body that he possesses. In the first place, therefore a nonbodily criterion of personal identity must be produced. For if the soul were the series of mental states associated with a given body, in the sense of being publicly reported by it and being manifested by its behavior, two temporally separate mental states could belong to the history of the same soul only if they were in fact associated with one and the same human body. This notion of the soul could have no application to mental states that were not associated with bodies. The soul must, then, be a series of mental states that is identified through time in virtue of the properties and relations of these mental states themselves. Both the elements of the complex and the relations that make an identifiable persisting thing out of them must be mental. To establish the possibility of such a mental criterion of identity will be the hardest part of the undertaking.

Locke's criterion of memory has been much criticized, and it is certainly untenable in some of the interpretations it has been given. It will not do to say that two mental states belong to the same soul if and only if whoever has the later one can recollect the earlier one if the possibility of recollection involved is factual and not formal.[2] For people forget things, and the paradox of the gallant officer is generated in which he is revealed as identical with both his childish and his senile selves while these are not identical with each other. However, a more plausible criterion can be offered in terms of continuity of character and memory. Two soul-phases belong to the same soul, on this view,

[2] "Formal"—"a conceptual requirement" (i.e., entailed by the very meaning of the concept involved). EDITOR'S NOTE.

if they are connected by a continuous character and memory path. A soul-phase is a set of contemporaneous mental states belonging to the same momentary consciousness. Two soul-phases are directly continuous if they are temporally juxtaposed, if the character revealed by the constituents of each is closely similar, and if the later contains recollections of some elements of the earlier. Two soul-phases are indirectly continuous and connected by a continuous character and memory path if there is a series of soul-phases all of whose members are directly continuous with their immediate predecessors and successors in the series and if the original soul-phases are the two end points of the series . . . .

Now there is an objection to the idea that memory can be any sort of fundamental criterion of identity which rests on the view that a memory criterion presupposes a bodily criterion . . . .

At the outset it must be admitted that the theory of a bodily criterion has a number of virtues. It has, first, the theoretical attraction of simplicity, in that it requires only one mode of treatment for the identification through time of all enduring things, treating human beings as just one variety of concrete objects. Second, it has a practical appeal, in that its application yields uncontentiously correct answers in the very great majority of the actual cases of personal identification with which we are called upon to deal. Finally, it has the merit of realism, for it is, in fact, the procedure of identification that we do most commonly apply . . . .

It does seem strange, all the same, to say that all statements about disembodied or reincarnated persons are self-contradictory. Is it really at all plausible to say this about such familiar things as the simpler type of classical ghost story? . . . . To try to settle the case we had better consider some concrete instances. Suppose I am walking on the beach with my friend *A*. He walks off a fair distance, treads on a large mine that someone has forgotten to remove, and is physically demolished in front of my eyes. Others, attracted by the noise, draw near and help to collect the scattered remains of *A* for burial. That night, alone in my room, I hear *A*'s voice and see a luminous but intangible object, of very much the shape and size of *A*, standing in the corner. The remarks that come from it are in *A*'s characteristic style and refer to matters that only *A* could have known about. Suspecting a hallucination, I photograph it and call in witnesses who hear and see what I do. The apparition returns afterwards and tells of where it has been and what it has seen. It would be very peculiar to insist, in these circumstances, that *A* no longer existed, even though his body no longer exists except as stains on the rocks and in a small box in the mortuary. It is not essential for the argument that the luminous object look like *A* or that it speak in *A*'s voice. If it were a featureless cylinder and spoke like a talking weighing machine we should simply take longer becoming convinced that it really was *A*. But if continuity of character and memory were manifested with normal amplitude, we surely should be convinced.

Consider a slightly different case. I know two men *B* and *C*. *B* is a dark, tall, thin, puritanical Scotsman of sardonic temperament with whom I have gone on bird-watching expeditions. *C* is a fair, short, plump . . . Pole of indestructible enterprise and optimism with whom I have made a number of more urban outings. One day I come into a room where both appear to be, and the dark, tall, thin man suggests that he and I pursue tonight some acquaintances I made with *C*, though he says it was with him, a couple of nights ago. The short, fair, plump, cheerful-looking man reminds me in a strong Polish accent of a promise I had made to *B*, though he says it was to him, and which I had forgotten about, to go in search of owls on this very night. At first I suspect a conspiracy, but the thing continues far beyond any sort of joke, for good perhaps, and is accompanied by suitable amazement on their part at each other's appearance, their own reflections in the mirror, and so forth.

Now what would it be reasonable to say in these circumstances: that *B* and *C* have changed bodies (the consequence of a mental criterion), that they have switched character and memories (the consequence of a bodily criterion), or neither? It seems to me quite clear that we should not say that *B* and *C* had switched characters and memories. And if this is correct, it follows that bodily identity is not a logically complete criterion of personal identity; at best it could be a necessary condition of personal identity. Of the other alternatives, that of refusing to identify either of the psychophysical hybrids before us with *B* and *C* may seem the most scrupulous and proper. But the refusal might take a number of different forms. It might be a categorical denial that either of the hybrids is *B* or *C*. It might, more sophisticatedly be an assertion that the concept of personal identity had broken down and that there was no correct answer, affirmative or negative, to the question: which of these two is *B* and which *C*? It might, uninterestingly, be a state of amazed and inarticulate confusion.

What support is there for the conclusion required by the empirical concept of the soul, that *B* and *C* have substituted bodies? First of all, the rather weak evidence of imaginative literature. In F. Anstey's story *Vice Versa* the corpulent and repressive Mr. Bultitude and his athletic and impulsive schoolboy son are the victims of a similar rearrangement. The author shows not the smallest trace of hesitation in calling the thing with the father's character and memories the father and the thing with the father's body the son. (Cf. also Conan Doyle's *Keinplatz Experiment*.) A solider support is to be found by reflecting on the probable attitude after the switch of those who are most concerned with our original pair, *B* and *C*, as persons, those who have the greatest interest in answering the question of their personal identity: their parents, their wives, their children, their closest friends. Would they say that *B* and *C* had ceased to exist, that they had exchanged characters and memories or that they had exchanged bodies? It is surely plain that if the character and memories of *B* and *C* really survived intact in their new bodily surroundings those closely concerned with them would say that the two had exchanged bodies, that the original persons were where the characters and memories were. For why, after all, do we bother to identify people so carefully? What is unique about individual people that is important enough for us to call them by individual proper names? In our general relations with other human beings their bodies are for the most part intrinsically unimportant. We use them as convenient recognition devices enabling us to locate without difficulty the persisting character and memory complexes in which we are interested, which we love or like. It would be upsetting if a complex with which we were emotionally involved came to have a monstrous or repulsive physical appearance, it would be socially embarrassing if it kept shifting from body to body while most such complexes stayed put, and it would be confusing and tiresome if such shifting around were generally widespread, for it would be a laborious business finding out where one's friends and family were. But that our concern and affection would follow the character and memory complex and not its original bodily associate is surely clear. In the case of general shifting about we should be in the position of people trying to find their intimates in the dark. If the shifts were both frequent and spatially radical we should no doubt give up the attempt to identify individual people, the whole character of relations between people would change, and human life would be like an unending sequence of shortish ocean trips. But, as long as the transfers did not involve large movements in space, the character and memory complexes we are concerned with could be kept track of through their audible identification of themselves. And there is no reason to doubt that the victim of such a bodily transfer would regard himself as the person whom he seems to remember himself as being. I conclude, then, that although, as things stand, our concept of a person is not called upon to withstand these strains and, therefore, that in the face of a psychophysical transfer we might at first not know what to say, we should not identify the people in question as those who now have the bodies they used to have and that it would be the natural thing to extend our concept of a person, given the purposes for which it has been constructed, so as to identify anyone present to us now with whoever it was who used to have the same character and memories as he has. In other words the soul, defined as a series of mental states connected by continuity of character and memory, is the essential constituent of personality. The soul, therefore, is not only logically distinct from any particular human body with which it is associated; it is also what a person fundamentally is . . . .

Nothing that I have said so far has any direct bearing on the question whether the soul can exist in an entirely disembodied state. All I have tried to show is that there is no necessary connection between the soul as a series of mental states linked by character and memory and any particular continuing human body. The question now arises: must the soul be associated with some human body? The apparent intelligibility of my crude ghost story might seem to suggest that not even a body is required, let alone a human one. And the same point appears to be made by the intelligibility of stories in which trees, toadstools, pieces of furniture, and so on are endowed with personal characteristics. But a good deal of caution is needed here . . . . It is an essential part of the story that the soul in question have physical manifestations. Only in our own case does it seem that strictly disembodied existence is conceivable, in the sense that we can conceive circumstances in which there would be some good reason to claim that a soul existed in a disembodied state. Now how tenuous and nonhuman could these physical manifestations be? To take a fairly mild example, discussed by Professor Malcolm, could we regard a tree as another person? He maintains with great firmness that we could not, on the rather flimsy ground that trees haven't got mouths and, therefore, could not be said to speak or communicate with us or make memory claims. But if a knothole in a tree trunk physically emitted sounds in the form of speech, why should we not call it a mouth? We may presume that ventriloquism, hidden record-players and microphones, dwarfs concealed in the foliage, and so forth have all been ruled out. If the remarks of the tree were coherent and appropriate to its situation and exhibited the type of continuity that the remarks of persons normally do exhibit, why shouldn't we regard the tree as a person?

Whatever the logic of the matter, it might be argued, the causal facts of the situation make the whole inquiry into the possibility of a soul's humanly or totally disembodied existence an entirely fantastic one. That people have the memories and characters that they do, that they have memories and characters at all, has as its causally necessary condition the relatively undisturbed persistence of a particular bit of physiological apparatus. One can admit this without concluding that the inquiry is altogether without practical point. For the bit of physiological apparatus in question is not the human body as a whole, but the brain. Certainly lavish changes in the noncerebral parts of the human body often affect the character and perhaps even to some extent the memories of the person whose body it is. But there is no strict relationship here. Now it is sometimes said that the last bit of the body to wear out is the brain, that the brain takes the first and lion's share of the body's nourishment, and that the brains of people who have starved to death are often found in perfectly good structural order. It is already possible to graft bits of one human body on to another, corneas, fingers, and even, I believe, legs. Might it not be possible to remove the brain from an otherwise worn-out human body and replace it either in a manufactured human body or in a cerebrally untenanted one? In this case we should have a causally conceivable analogue of reincarnation. If this were to become possible and if the resultant creatures appeared in a coherent way to exhibit the character and memories previously associated with the brain that had been fitted into them, we could say that the original person was still in existence even though only a relatively minute part of its original mass and volume was present in the new physical whole. Yet if strict bodily identity is a necessary condition of personal identity, such a description of the outcome would be ruled out as self-contradictory. I conclude, therefore, not only that a logically adequate concept of the soul is constructible but that the construction has some possible utility even in the light of our knowledge of the causal conditions of human life.

DISCUSSION QUESTIONS

1. What reason does Quinton give for rejecting the view that bodily identity is necessary for personal identity? Do you agree? Why?

2. How does Quinton's analysis of personal identity overcome Reid's "gallant officer" objection to Locke's account of personal identity?

3. Consider the following two cases:
   a. X disappears and then Y appears who looks and behaves exactly like X, claims to be X, and correctly seems to remember doing what X did.
   b. X disappears, then Y and Z appear, both looking and behaving exactly like X, claiming to be X, and correctly seeming to remember doing what X did.

Is there any possible way to know in case b whether Y or Z is "the same person" as X and as such has the "true memories" of X. If there is no way to tell in this case, how can we be sure in case a whether X and Y are the same person, rather than two different, although similar, persons? Does Quinton give us a way of resolving this puzzle? Do you see any way to resolve it?

4. Consider the following case:
   John and Henry are brothers who know a great deal about one another's past. Something unfortunate happens: John gets the idea he is Henry, and Henry gets the idea he is John. John seems to remember doing what Henry did, and Henry seems to remember doing what John did. They are put away for treatment. Later a friend asks, "Is John all right now?" and if John has come out of his delusion under the treatment we can answer, "Yes." But now suppose John and Henry die before the treatment has had any effect and a friend asks, "I wonder if John is all right now?" If John and Henry are disembodied spirits, what possible criteria for their identity could be appealed to in order to answer the nightmare question? Yet divine judgment demands an answer.[2]

Critically comment.

5. Is the notion of a disembodied existence possible? If so, could we ever identify anyone in such an existence, and if we could not, how would we ever know that anyone else existed?

6. In his article "A Philosopher's Nightmare" (Selection #36), Jonathan Harrison imagines the transplantation of the brain of a person (Ludwig) into the body (minus brain) of another person (Marcus) who was suffering from a brain disease. Is Harrison right to assume, as he does, that the hybrid is Ludwig and not Marcus? If so, how would you reply to someone who said that the hybrid was Marcus who, because of his new brain, has the delusion that he is Ludwig?

7. If an exact duplicate of your brain could be developed and used to replace your brain, would you be the same person? What if two duplicates were created, one of which is used to replace your brain and the other transplanted into some other body?

[2]C.B. Martin, *Religious Belief* (Ithaca, N.Y.: Cornell Univ. Press, 1959), p. 107.

28. A DUALIST'S PERCEPTION OF THE PUZZLE OF THE MIND-BODY RELATIONSHIP

John Tyndall

JOHN TYNDALL (1820–93) was a highly respected English mathematician, physicist, and chemist of his day who wrote a great number of scientific papers on various topics, as well as several books. His scientific works have been translated into most European languages. In addition to his fame as a research scientist, Tyndall was a popular lecturer on scientific topics and on the philosophical implications of science. His 1874 Presidential Address to the British Association for the Advancement of Science was very critical of the Judeo-Christian world view and provoked much controversy. Tyndall's address, his replies to its critics, and his other philosophical writings are gathered together in his two-volume **Fragments of Science.**

In the following selection from his 1868 Presidential Address to the Mathematical and Physical Section of the British Association for the Advancement of Science, Tyndall expresses the puzzlement that so many scientists and philosophers have felt about the mind-body relationship. As a scientist, Tyndall cannot find any "real bond of union" capable of explaining the obvious correlation of mental and physical states. Although Tyndall does not specifically opt for a particular position on the mind-body relationship, he is inclined toward **parallelism**—seeing every mental event as having a physical correlate, but not vice versa. Unlike epiphenomenalists, Tyndall, struck by the impossibility of explaining "how" a physical event can "cause" a mental event, does not contend that there is any causal connection between the physical and mental realms. Although he does not say this, Tyndall probably believes that the notion of causation should be restricted to the physical realm, where it is possible to explain "the causal mechanisms" underlying causal connections.

You will notice that I am stating my truth strongly, as at the beginning we agreed it should be stated. But I must go still further, and affirm that in the eyes of science *the animal body* is just as much the product of molecular force as the stalk and ear of corn, or as the crystal of salt or sugar. Many of the parts of the body are obviously mechanical. Take the human heart, for example, with its system of valves, or take the exquisite mechanism of the eye or hand. . . . As regards matter, the animal body creates nothing; as regards force, it creates nothing. . . . All that has been said, then, regarding the plant may be restated with regard to the animal. Every particle that enters into the composition of a muscle, a nerve, or a bone, has been placed in its position by molecular force. And unless the existence of law in these matters be denied, and the element of caprice introduced, we must conclude that, given the relation of any molecule of the body to its environment, its position in the body might be determined mathematically. Our difficulty is not with the *quality* of the problem, but with its *complexity;* and this dif-

Source: This selection is part of Tyndall's Presidential Address, delivered in 1868, to the Mathematical and Physical Section of the British Association. The full text can be found under the title of "Scientific Materialism" in Volume II of Tyndall's *Fragments of Science.*

ficulty might be met by the simple expansion of the faculties which we now possess. Given this expansion, with the necessary molecular data, and the chick might be deduced as rigorously and as logically from the egg as the existence of Neptune from the disturbances of Uranus, or as conical refraction from the undulatory theory of light.

You see I am not mincing matters, but avowing nakedly what many scientific thinkers more or less distinctly believe. The formation of a crystal, a plant, or an animal, is in their eyes a purely mechanical problem, which differs from the problems of ordinary mechanics in the smallness of the masses and the complexity of the processes involved. Here you have one half of our dual truth; let us now glance at the other half. Associated with this wonderful mechanism of the animal body we have phenomena no less certain than those of physics, but between which and the mechanism we discern no necessary connection. A man, for example, can say, *I feel, I think, I love;* but how does *consciousness* infuse itself into the problem? The human brain is said to be the organ of thought and feeling; when we are hurt the brain feels it, when we ponder it is the brain that thinks, when our passions or affections are excited it is through the instrumentality of the brain. Let us endeavor to be a little more precise here. I hardly imagine there exists a profound scientific thinker, who has reflected upon the subject, unwilling to admit the extreme probability of the hypothesis that, for every fact of consciousness, whether in the domain of sense, of thought, or of emotion, a definite molecular condition of motion or structure is set up in the brain; or who would be disposed even to deny that if the motion or structure be induced by internal causes instead of external, the effect on consciousness will be the same? Let any nerve, for, example, be thrown by morbid action into the precise state of motion which would be communicated to it by the pulses of a heated body, surely that nerve will declare itself hot—the mind will accept the subjective intimation exactly as if it were objective. The retina may be excited by purely mechanical means. A blow on the eye causes a luminous flash, and the mere pressure of the finger on the external ball produces a star of light, which Newton compared to the circles on a peacock's tail. Disease makes people see visions and dream dreams; but, in all such cases, could we examine the organs implicated, we should, on philosophical grounds, expect to find them in that precise molecular condition which the real objects, if present, would superinduce.

The relation of physics to consciousness being thus invariable, it follows that, given the state of the brain, the corresponding thought or feeling, . . . might be inferred. But how inferred? It would be at bottom not a case of logical inference at all, but of empirical association. You may reply that many of the inferences of science are of this character; the inference, for example, that an electric current of a given direction will deflect a magnetic needle in a definite way; but the cases differ in this, that the passage from the current to the needle, if not demonstrable, is thinkable, and that we entertain no doubt as to the final mechanical solution of the problem. But the passage from the physics of the brain to the corresponding facts of consciousness is unthinkable. Granted that a definite thought, and a definite molecular action in the brain occur simultaneously; we do not possess the intellectual organ, nor apparently any rudiment of the organ, which would enable us to pass, by a process of reasoning, from the one to the other. They appear together, but we do not know why. Were our minds and senses so expanded, strengthened, and illuminated as to enable us to see and feel the very molecules of the brain; were we capable of following all their motions, all their groupings, all their electric discharges, if such there be; and were we intimately acquainted with the corresponding states of thought and feeling, we should be as far as ever from the solution of the problem, "How are these physical processes connected with the facts of consciousness?'' The chasm between the two classes of phenomena would still remain intellectually impassable. Let the consciousness of *love*, for example, be associated with a right-handed spiral motion of the molecules of the brain, and the consciousness of *hate* with a left-handed spiral motion. We should then know when we love that the motion is in one direction, and when we hate that the motion is in the other; but the ''WHY?'' would remain as unanswerable as before.

In affirming that the growth of the body is mechanical, and that thought, as exercised by us, has its correlative in the physics of the brain, I think the position of the ''Materialist'' is stated, as far as that position is a tenable one. I think the materialist will be able finally to maintain this position against all attacks; but I do not think, in the present condition of the human mind, that he can pass beyond this position. I do not think he is entitled to say that his molecular groupings and his molecular motions *explain* everything. In reality, they explain nothing. The utmost he can affirm is the association of two classes of phenomena, of whose real bond of union he is in absolute ignorance. . . .

DISCUSSION QUESTION

1. In what sense does Tyndall endorse the materialist viewpoint? What does he find inadequate about this viewpoint? What do you think?

29. EPIPHENOMENALISM

Thomas Huxley

THOMAS HUXLEY (1825–95) was born in the suburbs of London and trained as a surgeon. His many papers on biology and paleontology (the study of fossils and early life forms) established his reputation in these fields. From 1854 to 1885, he taught natural history at the Royal School of Mines. With his breadth of self-taught learning (including philosophy), Huxley was widely recognized in England as an intellectual leader. A devoted believer in Darwin's theory of evolution (which was advocated in Darwin's **Origin of Species,** published in 1859), Huxley was Darwin's chief advocate against his many (often religious) opponents. A strong supporter of scientific method and a religious sceptic, Huxley was the first to coin the term "agnostic," which he used to describe his own attitude toward belief in the Judeo-Christian god. In addition to championing Darwin's theory of evolution, Huxley worked for educational reform, held numerous public offices, and served on many royal commissions. He was noted for his ability as a writer and lecturer in clarifying abstruse subjects for lay audiences.

In the selection that follows, Huxley defends the epiphenomenalistic point of view, extending to human beings Descartes' idea that animals are machines (automatons). Huxley contends that there is good evidence that the human physical body is itself capable of the functions that Descartes attributed to the soul. Consequently, Huxley claims, the soul is a superfluous entity that should be rejected on scientific grounds. While Descartes' Catholicism motivated him to draw a radical dichotomy between animals as unconscious automatons and humans as unities of unconscious body and conscious soul, Huxley saw matter as the only substance that exists and consciousness as an attribute of organized matter. For that reason, he was able to see human beings as **conscious** automatons (which is self-contradictory in Cartesian metaphysics).

In our excerpt, Huxley begins by describing the scientfic evidence for Descartes' conclusion that animals are machines. He then goes on to give evidence for extending this conclusion to human beings. Next, he defends the epiphenomenalistic view that mental events are casually inactive byproducts of physical processes in the brain. In his analogy, "The mind stands related to the body as the bell of the clock to the works. . ." As to the manner in which the body affects the mind, he pleads ignorance, saying of this matter, "I really know nothing and never hope to know anything." At the end of our excerpt, he contends that the Cartesian belief that physical determinism is incompatible with human free will is mistaken, if "free will" is defined as it should be defined. (We shall return to this issue in Chapter VI.)

[Descartes' View that Animals Are Unconscious Machines]

There remains a doctrine to which Descartes attached great weight. . . . It is the doctrine that brute animals are mere machines or automata, devoid not only of reason, but of any kind of consciousness. . . .

The process of reasoning by which Descartes arrived at this startling conclusion is well shown in the following passage of the "Réponses:"

But as regards the souls of beasts, . . . it appears to me to be a very remarkable circumstance that no movement can take place, either in the bodies of beasts, or even in our own, if these bodies have not in themselves all the organs and instruments by means of which the very same movements would be accomplished in a machine. So that, even in us, the spirit, or the soul, does not directly move the limbs, but only determines the course of that very subtle liquid which is called the animal spirits, which, running continually from the heart by the brain into the muscles, is the cause of all the movements of our limbs, and often may cause many different motions, one as easily as the other.

And it does not even always exert this determination; for among the movements which take place in us, there are many which do not depend on the mind at all, such as the beating of the heart, the digestion of food, the nutrition, the respiration of those who sleep; and even in those who are awake, walking, singing, and other similar actions, when they are performed without the mind thinking about them. And, when one who falls from a height throws his hands forward to save his head, it is in virtue of no ratiocination[1] that he performs this action; it does not depend upon his mind, but takes place merely because his senses being affected by the present danger, some change arises in his brain which determines the animal spirits to pass thence into the nerves, in such a manner as is required to produce this motion, in the same way as in a machine, and without the mind being able to hinder it. Now since we observe this in ourselves, why should we be so much astonished if the light reflected from the body of a wolf into the eye of a sheep has the same force to excite in it the motion of flight?

After having observed this, if we wish to learn by reasoning, whether certain movements of beasts are comparable to those which are effected in us by the operation of the mind, or, on the contrary, to those which depend only on the animal spirits and the disposition of the organs, it is necessary to consider the

Source: This selection consists of the major parts of Huxley's article, "On the Hypothesis that Animals Are Automata and Its History," first published in 1874. The entire essay can be found in Huxley's volume *Methods and Results,* published in 1898 by Macmillan and Co., New York and London.

[1]Reasoning. EDITOR'S NOTE.

difference between the two . . . and then it will easily be seen, that all the actions of beasts are similar only to those which we perform without the help of our minds. For which reason we shall be forced to conclude, that we know of the existence in them of no other principle of motion than the disposition of their organs. . . .

[Reflex Action and Consciously Motivated Behavior]

Descartes' line of argument is perfectly clear. He starts from reflex action in man, from the unquestionable fact that, in ourselves, co-ordinate, purposive, actions may take place, without intervention of consciousness or volition, or even contrary to the latter. As actions of a certain degree of complexity are brought about by mere mechanism, why may not actions of still greater complexity be the result of a more refined mechanism? What proof is there that brutes are other than a superior race of marionettes, which eat without pleasure, cry without pain, desire nothing, know nothing, and only simulate intelligence as a bee simulates a mathematician?

The Port Royalists[2] adopted the hypothesis that brutes are machines, and are said to have carried its practical applications so far as to treat domestic animals with neglect, if not with actual cruelty. . . . Modern research has brought to light a great multitude of facts, which not only show that Descartes' view is defensible, but render it far more defensible than it was in his day.

It must be premised, that it is wholly impossible absolutely to prove the presence or absence of consciousness in anything but one's own brain, though, by analogy, we are justified in assuming its existence in other men. Now if, by some accident, a man's spinal cord is divided, his limbs are paralysed . . . below the point of injury; and he is incapable of experiencing all those states of consciousness which, in his uninjured state, would be excited by irritation of those nerves which come off below the injury. . . . However near the brain the spinal cord is injured, consciousness remains intact, except that the irritation of parts below the injury is no longer represented by sensation. On the other hand, pressure upon the anterior division of the brain, or extensive injuries to it, abolish consciousness. Hence, it is a highly probable conclusion, that consciousness in man depends upon the integrity of the anterior division of the brain, while the middle and hinder divisions of the brain, and the rest of the nervous centres, have nothing to do with it. And it is further highly probable, that what is true for man is true for other vertebrated animals.

We may assume, then, that in a living vertebrated animal, any segment of a cerebro-spinal axis (or spinal cord and brain) separated from that anterior division of the brain which is the organ of consciousness, is as completely incapable of giving rise to consciousness as we know it to be incapable of carrying out volitions. Nevertheless, this separated segment of the spinal cord is not passive and inert. On the contrary, it is the seat of extremely remarkable powers. In our imaginary case of injury, the man would, as we have seen, be devoid of sensation in his legs, and would have not the least power of moving them. But, if the soles of his feet were tickled, the legs would be drawn up just as vigorously as they would have been before the injury. We know exactly what happens when the soles of the feet are tickled; a molecular change takes place in the sensory nerves of the skin, and is propagated along them and through the posterior roots of the spinal nerves, which are constituted by them, to the grey matter of the spinal cord. Through that gray matter the molecular motion is reflected into the anterior roots of the same nerves, constituted by the filaments which supply the muscles of the legs, and

[2]A group of reform-minded Roman Catholics named after the Abbey, Port Royal, located in Paris, where they were centered. EDITOR'S NOTE.

travelling along these motor filaments, reaches the muscles, which at once contract, and cause the limbs to be drawn up.

In order to move the legs in this way, a definite co-ordination of muscular contractions is necessary; the muscles must contract in a certain order and with dully proportioned force; and moreover, as the feet are drawn away from the source of irritation, it may be said that the action has a final cause, or is purposive.

Thus, it follows, that the grey matter of the segment of the man's spinal cord, though it is devoid of consciousness, nevertheless responds to a simple stimulus by giving rise to a complex set of muscular contractions, co-ordinated towards a definite end, and serving an obvious purpose.

[Effect of Brain Damage in a Lower Animal]

If the spinal cord of a frog is cut across, so as to provide us with a segment separated from the brain, we shall have a subject parallel to the injured man, on which experiments can be made without remorse; as we have a right to conclude that a frog's spinal cord is not likely to be conscious, when a man's is not.

Now the frog behaves just as the man did. The legs utterly paralysed, so far as voluntary movement is concerned; but they are vigorously drawn up to the body when any irritant is applied to the foot. But let us study our frog a little farther. Touch the skin of the side of the body with a little acetic acid, which gives rise to all the signs of great pain in an uninjured frog. In this case, there can be no pain, because the application is made to a part of the skin supplied with nerves which come off from the cord below the point of section; nevertheless, the frog lifts up the limb of the same side, and applies the foot to rub off the acetic acid; and, what is still more remarkable, if the limb be held so that the frog cannot use it, it will, by and by, move the limb of the other side, turn it across the body, and use it for the same rubbing process. It is impossible that the frog, if it were in its entirety and could reason, should perform actions more purposive than these: and yet we have most complete assurance that, in this case, the frog is not acting from purpose, has no consciousness, and is a mere insensible machine.

But now suppose that, instead of making a section of the cord in the middle of the body, it had been made in such a manner as to separate the hindermost division of the brain from the rest of the organ, and suppose the foremost two-thirds of the brain entirely taken away. The frog is then absolutely devoid of any spontaneity; it sits upright in the attitude which a frog habitually assumes; and it will not stir unless it is touched; but it differs from the frog which I have just described in this, that, if it be thrown into the water, it begins to swim, and swims just as well as the perfect frog does. But swimming requires the combination and successive co-ordination of a great number of muscular actions. And we are forced to conclude, that the impression made upon the sensory nerves of the skin of the frog by the contact with the water into which it is thrown, causes the transmission to the central nervous apparatus of an impulse which sets going a certain machinery by which all the muscles of swimming are brought into play in due co-ordination. If the frog be stimulated by some irritating body, it jumps or walks as well as the complete frog can do. The simple sensory impression, acting through the machinery of the cord, gives rise to these complex combined movements.

It is possible to go a step farther. Suppose that only the anterior division of the brain . . . is removed. If that operation is performed quickly and skillfully, the frog may be kept in a state of full bodily vigour for months, or it may be for years; but it will sit unmoved. It sees nothing: it hears nothing. It will starve sooner than feed itself, although food put into its mouth is swallowed. On irritation, it jumps or walks; if thrown into the water it swims. If it be put on the hand, it sits there, crouched, perfectly quiet, and would sit there for ever. If the hand be inclined very gently and slowly, so that the frog would naturally tend to slip off, the creature's fore paws are shifted on to the edge of the hand, until he can just prevent himself from falling. If the turning of the hand be slowly continued, he mounts up with great care and deliberation, putting first one leg forward and then another, until he balances himself with perfect precision upon the edge; and if the turning of the hand is continued, he goes through the needful set of muscular operations, until he comes to be seated in security, upon the back of the hand. The doing of all this requires a delicacy of co-ordination, and a precision of adjustment of the muscular apparatus of the body, which are only comparable to those of a rope-dancer. To the ordinary influences of light, the frog, deprived of its cerebral hemispheres, appears to be blind. Nevertheless, if the animal be put upon a table, with a book at some little distance between it and the light, and the skin of the hinder part of its body is then irritated, it will jump forward, avoiding the book by passing to the right or left of it. Therefore, although the frog appears to have no sensation of light, visible objects act through its brain upon the motor mechanism of its body.

It is obvious, that had Descartes been acquainted with these remarkable results of modern research, they would have furnished him with far more powerful arguments than he possessed in favour of his view of the automatism of brutes. The habits of a frog, leading its natural life, involve such simple adaptations to surrounding conditions, that the machinery which is competent to do so much without the intervention of consciousness, might well do all. And this argument is vastly strengthened by what has been learned in recent times of the marvellously complex operations which are performed mechanically, and to all appearance without consciousness, by men, when, in consequence of injury or disease, they are reduced to a condition more or less comparable to that of a frog, in which the anterior part of the brain has been removed. A case has recently been published by an eminent French physician, Dr. Mesnet, which illustrates this condition so remarkably, that I make no apology for dwelling upon it at considerable length.

[The Case of Sergeant F.]

A sergeant of the French army, F——, twenty-seven years of age, was wounded during the battle of Bazeilles, by a ball which fractured his left parietal bone. He ran his bayonet through the Prussian soldier who wounded him, but almost immediately his right arm became paralyzed; after walking about two hundred yards, his right leg became similarly affected, and he lost his senses. When he recovered them, three weeks afterwards, in a hospital at Mayence, the right half of the body was completely paralysed, and remained in this condition for a year. At present, the only trace of the paralysis which remains is a slight weakness of the right half of the body. Three or four months after the wound was inflicted, periodical disturbances of the functions of the brain made their appearance, and have continued ever since. The disturbances last from fifteen to thirty hours; the intervals at which they occur being from fifteen to thirty days.

For four years, therefore, the life of this man has been divided into alternating phases—short abnormal states intervening between long normal states.

In the periods of normal life, the ex-sergeant's health is perfect; he is intelligent and kindly, and performs, satisfactorily, the duties of a hospital attendant. The commencement of the abnormal state is ushered in by uneasiness and a sense of weight about the forehead, which the patient compares to the constriction of a circle of iron; and, after its termination, he complains, for some hours, of dullness and heaviness of the head. But the transition from the normal to the abnormal state takes place in a few minutes, without convulsions or cries, and without anything to indicate the change to a bystander. His movements remain free and his expression calm, except for a contraction of the brow, an incessant movement of the eyeballs, and a chewing motion of the jaws. The eyes are wide open, and their pupils dilated. If the man happens to be in a place to which he is accustomed, he walks about as usual; but, if he is in a new place, or if obstacles are intentionally placed in his way, he stumbles gently against them, stops, and then, feeling over the objects with his hands, passes on one side of them. He offers no resistance to any change of direction which may be impressed upon him, or to the forcible acceleration or retardation of his movements. He eats, drinks, smokes, walks about, dresses and undresses himself, rises and goes to bed at the accustomed hours. Nevertheless, pins may be run into his body, or strong electric shocks may be sent through it, without causing the least indication of pain; no odorous substance, pleasant or unpleasant, makes the least impression; he eats and drinks with avidity whatever is offered, and takes . . . vinegar, or quinine, as readily as water; no noise affects him; and light influences him only under certain conditions. Dr. Mesnet remarks, that the sense of touch alone seems to persist, and indeed to be more acute and delicate than in the normal state: and it is by means of the nerves of touch, almost exclusively, that his organism is brought into relation with the external world. Here a difficulty arises. It is clear from the facts detailed, that the nervous apparatus by which, in the normal state, sensations of touch are excited, is that by which external influences determine the movements of the body, in the abnormal state. But does the state of consciousness, which we term a tactile sensation, accompany the operation of this nervous apparatus in the abnormal state? Or is consciousness utterly absent, the man being reduced to an insensible mechanism?

It is impossible to obtain direct evidence in favour of the one conclusion or the other; all that can be said is, that the case of the frog shows that the man may be devoid of any kind of consciousness.

A further difficult problem is this. The man is insensible to sensory impressions made through the ear, the nose, the tongue, and, to a great extent, the eye; nor is he susceptible of pain from causes operating during his abnormal state. Nevertheless, it is possible so to act upon his tactile apparatus, as to give rise to those molecular changes in his sensorium,[3] which are ordinarily the causes of associated trains of ideas. I give a striking example of this process in Dr. Mesnet's words:—

> He was taking a walk in the garden under a bunch of trees. We placed in his hand his walking stick which he had let fall a few minutes before. He feels it, passes his hand over the bent handle a few times, becomes attentive, seems to extend his ear, and suddenly calls out, "Henry," then, "Here they are. There are about twenty to our two! We have reached our end." And then, with his hand behind his back, as if about to leap, he prepares to attack with his weapon. He crouches in a level, green grass, his head concealed by a tree, in the position of a hunter, and follows all the short-distance movements of the enemy which he believes he sees, with accompanying movements of his hands and shoulders.

In a subsequent abnormal period, Dr. Mesnet caused the patient to repeat this scene by placing him in the same conditions. Now, in this case, the question arises whether the series of actions constituting this singular pantomime was accompanied by the ordinary states of consciousness, the appropriate train of ideas, or not? Did the man dream that he was skirmishing? Or was

[3]That part of the brain which receives nerve impulses from the various sensory areas of the body. EDITOR'S NOTE.

he in the condition of . . . a senseless mechanism worked by molecular changes in his nervous system? The analogy of the frog shows that the latter assumption is perfectly justifiable. . . .

Again, the manner in which the frog, though apparently insensible to light, is yet, under some circumstances, influenced by visual images, finds a singular parallel in the case of the ex-sergeant.

Sitting at a table, in one of his abnormal states, he took up a pen, felt for paper and ink, and began to write a letter to his general, in which he recommended himself for a medal, on account of his good conduct and courage. It occurred to Dr. Mesnet to ascertain experimentally how far vision was concerned in this act of writing. He therefore interposed a screen between the man's eyes and his hands; under these circumstances he went on writing for a short time, but the words became illegible, and he finally stopped, without manifesting any discontent. On the withdrawal of the screen, he began to write again where he had left off. The substitution of water for ink in the inkstand had a similar result. He stopped, looked at his pen, wiped it on his coat, dipped it in the water, and began again with the same effect.

On one occasion, he began to write upon the topmost of ten super-imposed sheets of paper. After he had written a line or two, this sheet was suddenly drawn away. There was a slight expression of surprise, but he continued his letter on the second sheet exactly as if it had been the first. This operation was repeated five times, so that the fifth sheet contained nothing but the writer's signature at the bottom of the page. Nevertheless, when the signature was finished, his eyes turned to the top of the blank sheet, and he went through the form of reading over what he had written, a movement of lips accompanying each word; moreover, with his pen, he put in such corrections as were needed, in that part of the blank page which corresponded with the position of the words which required correction, in the sheets which had been taken away. If the five sheets had been transparent, therefore, they would, when superposed, have formed a properly written and corrected letter.

Immediately after he had written his letter, F— got up, walked down to the garden, made himself a cigarette, lighted and smoked it. He was about to prepare another, but sought in vain for his tobacco-pouch, which had been purposely taken away. The pouch was now thrust before his eyes and put under his nose, but he neither saw nor smelt it; yet, when it was placed in his hand, he at once seized it, made a fresh cigarette, and ignited a match to light the latter. The match was blown out, and another lighted match placed close before his eyes, but he made no attempt to take it; and, if his cigarette was lighted for him, he made no attempt to smoke. All this time the eyes were vacant, and neither winked, nor exhibited any contraction of the pupils. From these and other experiments, Dr. Mesnet draws the conclusion that his patient sees some things and not others; that the sense of sight is accessible to all things which are brought into relation with him by the sense of touch, and, on the contrary, insensible to things which lie outside this relation. He sees the match he holds and does not see any other.

Just so the frog ''sees'' the book which is in the way of his jump, at the same time that isolated visual impressions take no effect upon him.

As I have pointed out, it is impossible to prove that F—— is absolutely unconscious in his abnormal state, but it is no less impossible to prove the contrary; and the case of the frog goes a long way to justify the assumption that, in the abnormal state, the man is a mere insensible machine. . . . And would Descartes not have been justified in asking why we need deny that animals are machines, when men, in a state of unconsciousness, perform, mechanically, actions as complicated and as seemingly rational as those of any animal?

[Animals Are Conscious Automata]

But though I do not think that Descartes' hypothesis can be positively refuted, I am not disposed to accept it. The doctrine of continuity is too well established for it to be permissible to me to suppose that any complex natural phenomenon comes into existence suddenly, and without being preceded by simpler modifications; and very strong arguments would be needed to prove that such complex phenomena as those of consciousness, first make their appearance in man. We know, that, in the individual man, consciousness grows from a dim glimmer to its full light, whether we consider the infant advancing in years or the adult emerging from slumber and swoon. We know, further, that the lower animals possess, though less developed, that part of the brain which we have every reason to believe to be the organ of consciousness in man; and as, in other cases, function and organ are proportional, so we have a right to conclude it is with the brain; and that the brutes, though they may not possess our intensity of consciousness, and though from the absence of language, they can have no trains of thoughts, but only trains of feelings, yet have a consciousness which, more or less distinctly, foreshadows our own.

I confess that, in view of the struggle for existence which goes on in the animal world, and of the frightful quantity of pain with which it must be accompanied, I should be glad if the probabilities were in favour of Descartes' hypothesis; but, on the other hand, considering the terrible practical consequences to domestic animals which might ensue from any error on our part, it is as well to err on the right side, if we err at all, and deal with them as weaker brethren, who are bound, like the rest of us, to pay their toll for living. . . .

But though we may see reason to disagree with Descartes' hypothesis that brutes are unconscious machines, it does not follow that he was wrong in regarding them as automata. They may be more or less conscious, sensitive, automata; and the view that they are such conscious machines is that which is implicitly, or explicitly adopted by most persons. When we speak of the actions of the lower animals being guided by instinct and not by reason, what we really mean is that, though they feel as we do, yet their actions are the results of their physical organisation. We believe, in short, that they are machines, one part of which (the nervous system) not only sets the rest in motion, and co-ordinates its movements in relation with changes in surrounding bodies, but is provided with special apparatus, the function of which is the calling into existence of those states of consciousness which are termed sensations, emotions, and ideas. I believe that this generally accepted view is the best expression of the facts at present known.

It is experimentally demonstrable—any one who cares to run a pin into himself may perform a sufficient demonstration of the fact—that a mode of motion of the nervous system is the immediate antecedent of a state of consciousness. All but the adherents of "Occasionalism," or of the doctrine of "Pre-established Harmony" (if any such now exist), must admit that we have as much reason for regarding the mode of motion of the nervous system as the cause of the state of consciousness, as we have for regarding any event as the cause of another. How the one phenomenon causes the other we know, as much or as little, as in any other case of causation; but we have as much right to believe that the sensation is an effect of the molecular change, as we have to believe that motion is an effect of impact. . . .

As I have endeavored to show, we are justified in supposing that something analogous to what happens in ourselves takes place in the brutes, and that the affections of their sensory nerves give rise to molecular changes in the brain, which again give rise to . . . the corresponding states of consciousness. Nor can there be any reasonable doubt that the emotions of brutes, and such ideas as they possess, are similarly dependent upon molecular brain changes. Each sensory impression leaves behind a record in the structure of the brain . . . which is competent, under certain conditions, to reproduce, in a fainter condition, the state of consciousness which corresponds with that sensory impression. . . . [This is] the physical basis of memory.

It may be assumed, then, that molecular changes in the brain are the causes of all the states of consciousness of brutes. Is there any evidence that these states of consciousness may, conversely, cause those molecular changes which give rise to muscular motion? I see no such evidence. The frog walks, hops, swims and goes through his gymnastic performances quite as well without consciousness, and consequently without volition, as with it; and, if a frog, in his natural state, possesses anything corresponding with what we call volition, there is no reason to think that it is anything but a concomitant of the molecular changes in the brain which form part of the series involved in the production of motion.

The consciousness of brutes would appear to be related to the mechanism of their body simply as a collateral product of its working, and to be as completely without any power of modifying that working as the steam-whistle which accompanies the work of a locomotive engine is without influence upon its machinery. Their volition, if they have any, is an emotion indicative of physical changes, not a cause of such changes.

This conception of the relations of states of consciousness with molecular changes in the brain . . . does not prevent us from ascribing free will to brutes. For an agent is free when there is nothing to prevent him from doing that which he desires to do. If a greyhound chases a hare, he is a free agent, because his action is in entire accordance with his strong desire to catch the hare; while so long as he is held back by the leash he is not free, being prevented by external force from following his inclination. And the ascription of freedom to the greyhound under the former circumstances is by no means inconsistent with the other aspect of the facts of the case—that he is a machine impelled to the chase, and caused, at the same time, to have the desire to catch the game by the impression which the rays of light proceeding from the hare make upon his eyes, and through them upon his brain.

Much ingenious argument has at various times been bestowed upon the question: How is it possible to imagine that volition, which is a state of consciousness, and, as such, has not the slightest community of nature with matter in motion, can act upon the moving matter of which the body is composed, as it is assumed to do in voluntary acts? But if, as is here suggested, the voluntary acts of brutes—or, in other words, the acts which they desire to perform—are as purely mechanical as the rest of their actions, and are simply accompanied by the state of consciousness called volition, the inquiry, so far as they are concerned, becomes superfluous. Their volitions do not enter into the chain of causation of their actions at all. . . .

[Human Beings Are Also Conscious Machines]

. . . to the best of my judgment, the argumentation which applies to brutes holds equally good of men; and, therefore, that all states of consciousness in us, as in them, are immediately caused by molecular changes of the brain-substance. It seems to me that in men, as in brutes, there is no proof that any state of consciousness is the cause of change in the motion of the matter of the organism. If these positions are well based, it follows that our mental conditions are simply the symbols in consciousness of the changes which takes place automatically in the organism; and that, to take an extreme illustration, the feeling we call volition is not the cause of a voluntary act, but the symbol of that state of the brain which is the immediate cause of that act. We are conscious automata, endowed with free will in the only intelligible sense of that much-abused term—inasmuch as in many respects we are able to do as we like—but none the less parts of the great series of causes and effects which, in unbroken continuity, composes that which is, and has been, and shall be—the sum of existence. . . .

DISCUSSION QUESTIONS

1. According to Huxley, on what grounds, if any, can a person infer that other human beings are conscious? Do we have similar justification for attributing consciousness to animals? Can we be certain that other human beings or animals are conscious?

2. Science fiction writers have often imagined robots of the future which are made to look and behave exactly like human beings. In such cases, could we ever have good reason to believe they were conscious? Why, or why not?

3. What reason does Huxley give in defense of his suggestion that Sergent F., in his abnormal states, acts as an unconscious machine? Do you think this is likely? Why, or why not?

4. Compare Huxley's and Descartes' views of the mind-body relationship in animals and in human beings. Which view is more plausible? Why? Are you satisfied with either view? If not, why not?

5. Why does Huxley believe that we have good reason to accept epiphenomenalism over interactionism? What advantage does Huxley attribute to epiphenomenalism over interactionism? How important is this advantage? Is the mind-body relationship any less puzzling if we accept epiphenomenalism over interactionism?

30. BEHAVIORISM

Gilbert Ryle

GILBERT RYLE (1900–76), Professor of Metaphysical Philosophy at Oxford University, was a prominent figure in the twentieth-century British school of analytic philosophy. His philosophical writings cover a wide range of topics and display a literary and informal style, often couched in striking metaphors, which soften for the general reader the intricacies of Ryle's analytic arguments. Like Wittgenstein at Cambridge University (see the introduction to Selection #3), Ryle believed that many philosophical problems are a result of the tendency of philosophers to be misled by the grammatical structure of concepts and statements.

The belief that the traditional mind-body problem can be dissolved by a closer attention to the use of language is central to Ryle's most influential and controversial work, **The Concept of Mind** (1949), from which the bulk of the following selection is excerpted. Ryle believes that the attractiveness of Cartesian dualism results primarily from the misleading grammatical fact that the word "mind" is a noun, leading us to mistake **the mind** for an immaterial **thing** that exists alongside and interacts with physical bodies. This belief, which Ryle ridicules as the belief in "the ghost in the machine," is devoid of explanatory power, he claims. The Cartesian attempts to explain how a human being does something by postulating a hidden ghostly being, "the mind" or "soul," that does it. This, however, Ryle claims, leaves us as much in the dark as to the process by which "the mind" accomplishes what it does as we originally were when we asked how a **human being** accomplishes what he does. (This is the point of the allegory of the ignorant peasants and their first experience with a modern railway train, which begins our selection from Ryle. This allegory is excerpted from a talk Ryle once gave on British radio.) A person's "mind," Ryle contends, is not a "thing," but is a broad way of characterizing a person's propensity (disposition) to behave in particular ways.

Descartes' Myth: The Official Doctrine of "The Ghost in the Machine"

The story is told of some peasants who were terrified at the sight of their first railway-train. Their pastor therefore gave them a lecture explaining how a steam-engine works. One of the peasants then said, "Yes, pastor, we quite understand what you say about the steam-engine. But there is really a horse inside, isn't there?" So used were they to horse-drawn carts that they could not take in the idea that some vehicles propel themselves.

We might invent a sequel. The peasants examined the engine and peeped into every crevice of it. They then said, "Certainly we cannot see, feel, or hear a horse there. We are foiled. But we know there is a horse there, so it must be a ghost-horse which, like the fairies, hides from mortal eyes."

The pastor objected, "But, after all, horses themselves are made of moving parts, just as the steam-engine is made of moving parts. You know what their muscles, joints, and blood-vessels do. So why is there a mystery in the self-propulsion of a steam-engine, if there is none in that of a horse? What do you think makes the horse's hooves go to and fro?" After a pause a peasant replied, "What makes the horse's hooves go is four extra little ghost-horses inside."

Poor simple-minded peasants! Yet just such a story has been the official theory of the mind for the last three very scientific centuries . . . .

. . . The legend that we have told and sold runs like this. A person consists of two theatres, one bodily and one non-bodily. In his Theatre A go on the incidents which we can explore by eye and instrument. But a person also incorporates a second theatre, Theatre B. Here there go on incidents which are totally unlike, though synchronized with those that go on in Theatre A. These Theatre B episodes are changes in the states, not of bits of flesh, but of something called "consciousness," which occupies no space. Only the proprietor of Theatre B has first-hand knowledge of what goes on in it. It is a secret theatre. The experimentalist tries to open its doors, but it has no doors. He tries to peep through its windows, but it has no windows. He is foiled.

We tend nowadays to treat it as obvious that a person, unlike a newt, lives the two lives, life A and life B, each completely unlike, though mysteriously geared to the other. Ingrained hypotheses do feel obvious, however redundant they may be. The peasants in my story correctly thought that a steam-engine was hugely different from a cart and automatically but incorrectly explained the difference by postulating a ghost-horse inside. So most of us, correctly thinking that there are huge differences between a clock and a person, automatically but incorrectly explain these differences by postulating an extra set of ghost-works inside. We correctly

Source: From Gilbert Ryle's lecture for the BBC series "The Physical Basis of Mind," later printed in *The Physical Basis of Mind,* ed. P. Laslett (Oxford: Basil Blackwell, 1950), and from Ryle, *The Concept of Mind* (New York: Barnes and Noble, 1949). Reprinted by permission of Barnes and Noble and Basil Blackwell.

say that people are not like clocks, since people meditate, calculate, and invent things; they make plans, dream dreams, and shirk their obligations; they get angry, feel depressed, scan the heavens, and have likes and dislikes; they work, play, and idle; they are sane, crazy, or imbecile; they are skilful at some things and bunglers at others. Where we go wrong is in explaining these familiar actions and conditions as the operations of a secondary set of secret works.

Everybody knows quite well when to describe someone as acting absent-mindedly or with heed, as babbling deliriously or reasoning coherently, as feeling angry but not showing it, as wanting one thing but pretending to want another, as being ambitious, patriotic, or miserly. We often get our accounts and estimates of other people and of ourselves wrong; but we more often get them right. We did not need to learn the legend of the two theatres before we were able to talk sense about people and to deal effectively with them. Nor has this fairly new-fangled legend helped us to do it better . . . .

In saying that a person is not to be described as a mind coupled with a body I am not saying . . . that people are just machines. Nor are engines just wagons or live bodies just corpses. What is wrong with the story of the two theatres is not that it reports differences which are not there but that it misrepresents differences which are there. It is a story with the right characters but the wrong plot. It is an attempt to explain a genuine difference—or rather a galaxy of differences—but its effect, like that of the peasant's theory, is merely to reduplicate the thing to be explained. It says, "The difference between a machine like a human body on the one hand and a human being on the other, is that in a human being, besides the organs which we do see, there is a counterpart set of organs which we do not see; besides the causes and effects which we can witness, there is a counterpart series of causes and effects which we cannot witness." So now we ask, "But what explains the differences between what goes on in the Theatre B of a sane man and what goes on in that of a lunatic? A third theatre, Theatre C?"

No, what prevents us from examining Theatre B is not that it has no doors or windows, but that there is no such theatre. What prevented the peasants from finding the horse, was not that it was a ghost-horse, but that there was no horse. None the less, the engine *was* different from a wagon and ordinary people *are* different not only from machines, but also from animals, imbeciles, infants, and corpses. They also differ in countless important ways from one another. I have not begun to show how we should grade these differences. I have only shown how we should not grade them.

One last word. In ordinary life (save when we want to sound knowing) we seldom use the noun "mind" or the adjective "mental" at all. What we do is to talk of people, of people calculating, conjuring, hoping, resolving, tasting, bluffing, fretting, and so on. Nor, in ordinary life, do we talk of "matter" or of things being "material." What we do is to talk of steel, granite, and water; of wood, moss, and grain; of flesh, bone, and sinew. The umbrella-titles "mind" and "matter" obliterate the very differences that ought to interest us. Theorists should drop both these words. "Mind" and "matter" are echoes from the hustings of philosophy, and prejudice the solutions of all problems posed in terms of them.[1]

There is a doctrine about the nature and place of minds which is so prevalent among theorists and even among laymen that it deserves to be described as the official theory. Most philosophers, psychologists and religious teachers subscribe, with minor reservations, to its main articles and, although they admit certain theoretical difficulties in it, they tend to assume that these can be overcome without serious modifications being made to the architecture of the theory. It will be argued here

[1]The excerpt from Ryle's talk on British radio ends here and the excerpt from Ryle's *The Concept of Mind* begins. EDITOR'S NOTE.

that the central principles of the doctrine are unsound and conflict with the whole body of what we know about minds when we are not speculating about them.

The official doctrine, which hails chiefly from Descartes, is something like this. With the doubtful exceptions of idiots and infants in arms every human being has both a body and a mind. Some would prefer to say that every human being is both a body and a mind. His body and his mind are ordinarily harnessed together, but after the death of the body his mind may continue to exist and function.

Human bodies are in space and are subject to the mechanical laws which govern all other bodies in space. Bodily processes and states can be inspected by external observers. So a man's bodily life is as much a public affair as are the lives of animals and reptiles and even as the careers of trees, crystals and planets.

But minds are not in space, nor are their operations subject to mechanical laws. The workings of one mind are not witnessable by other observers; its career is private. Only I can take direct cognisance of the states and processes of my own mind. A person therefore lives through two collateral histories, one consisting of what happens in and to his body, the other consisting of what happens in and to his mind. The first is public, the second private. The events in the first history are events in the physical world, those in the second are events in the mental world . . . .

It is customary to express this bifurcation of his two lives and of his two worlds by saying that the things and events which belong to the physical world, including his own body, are external, while the workings of his own mind are internal. This antithesis of outer and inner is of course meant to be construed as a metaphor, since minds, not being in space, could not be described as being spatially inside anything else, or as having things going on spatially inside themselves. But relapses from this good intention are common and theorists are found speculating how stimuli, the physical sources of which are yards or miles outside a person's skin, can generate mental responses inside his skull, or how decisions framed inside his cranium can set going movements of his extremities.

Even when 'inner' and 'outer' are construed as metaphors, the problem how a person's mind and body influence one another is notoriously charged with theoretical difficulties. What the mind wills, the legs, arms and the tongue execute; what affects the ear and the eye has something to do with what the mind perceives; grimaces and smiles betray the mind's moods and bodily castigations lead, it is hoped, to moral improvement. But the actual transactions between the episodes of the private history and those of the public history remain mysterious, since by definition they can belong to neither series . . . .

Underlying this partly metaphorical representation of the bifurcation of a person's two lives there is a seemingly more profound and philosophical assumption. It is assumed that there are two different kinds of existence or status. What exists or happens may have the status of physical existence, or it may have the status of mental existence. Somewhat as the faces of coins are either heads or tails, or somewhat as living creatures are either male or female, so, it is supposed, some existing is physical existing, other existing is mental existing. It is a necessary feature of what has physical existence that it is in space and time, it is a necessary feature of what has mental existence that it is in time but not in space. What has physical existence is composed of matter, or else is a function of matter; what has mental existence consists of consciousness, or else is a function of consciousness.

There is thus a polar opposition between mind and matter, an opposition which is often brought out as follows. Material objects are situated in a common field, known as 'space', and what happens to one body in one part of space is mechanically connected with what happens to other bodies in other parts of space. But mental happenings occur in insulated fields, known as 'minds', and there is, apart maybe from telepathy, no direct causal connection between what happens in one mind and what happens in another. Only through the medium of the public physical world can the mind of one person make a difference to the mind of another . . . .

What sort of knowledge can be secured of the workings of a mind? On the one side, according to the official theory, a person has direct knowledge of the best imaginable kind of the workings of his own mind. Mental states and processes are (or are normally) conscious states and processes, and the consciousness which irradiates them can engender no illusions and leaves the door open for no doubts. A person's present thinkings, feelings and willings, his perceivings, rememberings and imaginings are intrinsically 'phosphorescent'; their existence and their nature are inevitably betrayed to their owner. The inner life is a stream of consciousness of such a sort that it would be absurd to suggest that the mind whose life is that stream might be unaware of what is passing down it.

True, the evidence adduced recently by Freud seems to show that there exist channels tributary to this stream, which run hidden from their owner. People are actuated by impulses the existence of which they vigorously disavow; some of their thoughts differ from the thoughts which they acknowledge; and some of the actions which they think they will to perform they do not really will. They are thoroughly gulled by some of their own hypocrisies and they successfully ignore facts about their mental lives which on the official theory ought to be patent to them. Holders of the official theory tend, however, to maintain that anyhow in normal circumstances a person must be directly and authentically seized of the present state and workings of his own mind.

Besides being currently supplied with these alleged immediate data of consciousness, a person is also generally supposed to be able to exercise from time to time a special kind of perception, namely inner perception, or introspection. He can take a (non-optical) 'look' at what is passing in his mind. Not only can he view and scrutinize a flower through his sense of sight and listen to and discriminate the notes of a bell through his sense of hearing; he can also reflectively or introspectively watch, without any bodily organ of sense, the current episodes of his inner life. This self-observation is also commonly supposed to be immune from illusion, confusion or doubt. A mind's reports of its own affairs have a certainty superior to the best that is possessed by its reports of matters in the physical world . . . .

On the other side, one person has no direct access of any sort to the events of the inner life of another. He cannot do better than make problematic inferences from the observed behaviour of the other person's body to the states of mind which, by analogy from his own conduct, he supposes to be signalised by that behaviour. Direct access to the workings of a mind is the privilege of that mind itself; in default of such privileged access, the workings of one mind are inevitably occult to everyone else. For the supposed arguments from bodily movements similar to their own to mental workings similar to their own would lack any possibility of observational corroboration. Not unnaturally, therefore, an adherent of the official theory finds it difficult to resist this consequence of his premisses, that he has no good reason to believe that there do exist minds other than his own. Even if he prefers to believe that to other human bodies there are harnessed minds not unlike his own, he cannot claim to be able to discover their individual characteristics, or the particular things that they undergo and do. Absolute solitude is on this showing the ineluctable destiny of the soul. Only our bodies can meet.

As a necessary corollary of this general scheme there is implicitly prescribed a special way of construing our ordinary concepts of mental powers and operations. The verbs, nouns and adjectives, with which in ordinary life we describe the wits, characters and higher-grade performances of the people with whom we have do, are required to be construed as signifying special episodes in their secret histories, or else as signifying tendencies for such episodes to occur. When someone is described as knowing, believing or guessing something, as hoping, dreading, intending or shirking something, as designing this or being amused at that, these verbs are supposed to denote the occurrence of specific modifications in his (to us) occult stream of consciousness. Only his own privileged access to this stream in direct awareness and introspection could provide authentic testimony that these mental-conduct verbs were correctly or incorrectly applied . . . .

The Absurdity of the Official Doctrine

Such in outline is the official theory. I shall often speak of it, with deliberate abusiveness, as 'the dogma of the Ghost in the Machine'. I hope to prove that it is entirely false, and false not in detail but in principle. It is not merely an assemblage of particular mistakes. It is one big mistake and a mistake of a special kind. It is, namely, a category-mistake. It represents the facts of mental life as if they belonged to one logical type or category (or range of types or categories), when they actually belong to another. The dogma is therefore a philosopher's myth. In attempting to explode the myth I shall probably be taken to be denying well-known facts about the mental life of human beings, and my plea that I aim at doing nothing more than rectify the logic of mental-conduct concepts will probably be disallowed as mere subterfuge.

I must first indicate what is meant by the phrase 'Category-mistake'. This I do in a series of illustrations.

A foreigner visiting Oxford or Cambridge for the first time is shown a number of colleges, libraries, playing fields, museums, scientific departments and administrative offices. He then asks 'But where is the University? I have seen where the members of the Colleges live, where the Registrar works, where the scientists experiment and the rest. But I have not yet seen the University in which reside and work the members of your University.' It has then to be explained to him that the University is not another collateral institution, some ulterior counterpart to the colleges, laboratories and offices which he has seen. The University is just the way in which all that he has already seen is organized. When they are seen and when their co-ordination is understood, the University has been seen. His mistake lay in his innocent assumption that it was correct to speak of Christ Church, the Bodleian Library, the Ashmolean Museum *and* the University, to speak, that is, as if 'the University' stood for an extra member of the class of which these other units are members. He was mistakenly allocating the University to the same category as that to which the other institutions belong.

The same mistake would be made by a child witnessing the march-past of a division, who, having had pointed out to him such and such battalions, batteries, squadrons, etc., asked when the division was going to appear. He would be supposing that a division was a counterpart to the units already seen, partly similar to them and partly unlike them. He would be shown his mistake by being told that in watching the battalions, batteries and squadrons marching past he had been watching the division marching past. The march-past was not a parade of battalions, batteries, squadrons *and* a division; it was a parade of the battalions, batteries and squadrons *of* a division . . . .

The theoretically interesting category-mistakes are those made by people who are perfectly competent to apply concepts, at least in the situations with which they are familiar, but are still liable in their abstract thinking to allocate those concepts to logical types to which they do not belong . . . .

My destructive purpose is to show that a family of radical category-mistakes is the source of the double-life theory. The representation of a person as a ghost mysteriously ensconced in a machine derives from this argument. Because, as is true, a person's thinking, feeling and purposive doing cannot be described solely in the idioms of physics, chemistry and physiology, therefore they must be described in counterpart idioms. As the human body is a complex organised unit, so the human mind must be another complex organised unit, though one made of a different sort of stuff and with a different sort of structure. Or, again, as the human body, like any other parcel of matter, is a field of causes and effects, so the mind must be another field of causes and effects . . . .

The Origin of the Category-mistake

One of the chief intellectual origins of what I have yet to prove to be the Cartesian category-mistake seems to be this. When Galileo showed that his methods of scientific discovery were competent to provide a mechanical theory which should cover every occupant of space, Descartes found in himself two conflicting motives. As a man of scientific genius he could not but endorse the claims of mechanics, yet as a religious and moral man he could not accept, as Hobbes accepted, the discouraging rider to those claims, namely that human nature differs only in degree of complexity from clockwork. The mental could not be just a variety of the mechanical.

He and subsequent philosophers naturally but erroneously availed themselves of the following escape-route. Since mental-conduct words are not to be construed as signifying the occurrence of mechanical processes, they must be construed as signifying the occurrence of non-mechanical processes; since mechanical laws explain movements in space as the effects of other movements in space, other laws must explain some of the non-spatial workings of minds as the effects of other non-spatial workings of minds. The difference between the human behaviours which we describe as intelligent and those which we describe as unintelligent must be a difference in their causation; so, while some movements of human tongues and limbs are the effects of mechanical causes, others must be the effects of non-mechanical causes, i.e. some issue from movements of particles of matter, others from workings of the mind.

The differences between the physical and the mental were thus represented as differences inside the common framework of the categories of 'thing', 'stuff', 'attribute', 'state', 'process', 'change', 'cause' and 'effect'. Minds are things, but different sorts of things from bodies; mental processes are causes and effects, but different sorts of causes and effects from bodily movements. And so on. Somewhat as the foreigner expected the University to be an extra edifice, rather like a college but also considerably different, so the repudiators of mechanism represented minds as extra centres of causal processes, rather like machines but also considerably different from them. Their theory was a para-mechanical hypothesis.

That this assumption was at the heart of the doctrine is shown by the fact that there was from the beginning felt to be a major theoretical difficulty in explaining how minds can influence and be influenced by bodies. How can a mental process, such as willing, cause spatial movements like the movements of the tongue? How can a physical change in the optic nerve have among its effects a mind's perception of a flash of light? This notorious crux by itself shows the logical mould into which Descartes pressed his theory of the mind. It was the self-same mould into which he and Galileo set their mechanics. Still unwittingly adhering to the grammar of mechanics, he tried to avert disaster by describing minds in what was merely an obverse vocabulary. The working of minds had to be described by the mere negatives of the specific descriptions given to bodies; they are not in space, they are not motions, they are not modifications of matter, they are not accessible to public observation. . . .

As thus represented, minds are not merely ghosts harnessed to machines, they are themselves just spectral machines. Though the human body is an engine, it is not quite an ordinary engine, since some of its workings are governed by another engine inside it—this interior governor-engine being one of a very special sort. It is invisible, inaudible and it has no size or weight. It cannot be taken to bits and the laws it obeys are not those known to ordinary engineers. Nothing is known of how it governs the bodily engine. . . .

Emotion

In this chapter I discuss certain of the concepts of emotion and feeling.

This scrutiny is necessary because adherents of the dogma of the ghost in the machine can adduce in support of it the consent of most philosophers and psychologists to the view that emotions are internal or private experiences. Emotions are described as turbulences in the stream of consciousness, the owner of which cannot help directly registering them; to external witnesses they are, in consequence, necessarily occult. They are occurrences which take place not in the public, physical world but in your or my secret, mental world.

I shall argue that the word 'emotion' is used to designate at least three or four different kinds of things, which I shall call 'inclinations' (or 'motives'), 'moods', 'agitations' (or 'commotions') and 'feelings'. Inclinations and moods, including agitations, are not occurrences and do not therefore take place either publicly or privately. They are propensities, not acts or states. They are, however, propensities of different kinds, and their differences are important. Feelings, on the other hand, are occurrences, but the place that mention of them should take in descriptions of human behaviour is very different from that which the standard theories accord to it. Moods or frames of mind are, unlike motives, but like maladies and states of the weather, temporary conditions which in a certain way *collect* occurrences, but they are not themselves extra occurrences. . . .

. . . it is necessary to do justice to the crucial fact that we do report feelings in such idioms as 'qualms of apprehension' and 'glows of pride'; we do, that is, distinguish a glow of pride from a glow of warmth, and I shall have to try to bring out the force of such distinctions. I hope to show that though it is quite proper to describe someone as feeling a throb of compassion, his compassion is not be equated with a throb or a series of throbs, any more than his fatigue is his gasps; so no disillusioning consequences would follow from acknowledging that throbs, twinges and other feelings are bodily sensations.

In one sense, then, of 'emotion' the feelings are emotions. But there is quite another sense of 'emotion' in which theorists classify as emotions the motives by which people's higher-level behaviour is explained. When a man is described as vain, considerate, avaricious, patriotic or indolent, an explanation is being given of why he conducts his actions, daydreams and thoughts in the way he does, and according to the standard terminology, vanity, kindliness, avarice, patriotism and laziness rank as species of emotion; they come thence to be spoken of as feelings.

But there is a great verbal muddle here, associated with a great logical muddle. To begin with, when someone is described as a vain or indolent man, the words 'vain' and 'indolent' are used to signify more or less lasting traits in his character. In this use he might be said to have been vain since childhood, or indolent during his entire half-holiday. His vanity and indolence are dispositional properties, which could be unpacked in such expressions as 'Whenever situations of certain sorts have arisen, he has always or usually tried to make himself prominent' or 'Whenever he was faced by an option between doing something difficult and not doing it, he shirked doing the difficult thing'. Sentences beginning with 'Whenever' are not singular occurrence reports. Motive words used in this way signify tendencies or propensities and therefore cannot signify the occurrence of feelings. They are elliptical expressions of general hypothetical propositions of a certain sort, and cannot be construed as expressing categorical narratives of episodes.

It will however be objected that, besides this dispositional use of motive words, there must also be a corresponding active use of them. For a man to be punctual in the dispositional sense of the adjective, he must tend to be punctual on particular occasions; and the sense in which he is said to be punctual for a particular rendezvous is not the dispositional but the active sense of 'punctual'. 'He tends to be at his rendezvous on time' expresses a general hypothetical proposition, the truth of which requires that there should also be corresponding true categorical propositions of the pattern 'he was at today's rendezvous in good time'. So, it will be argued, for a man to be a vain or indolent man there must be particular exercises of vanity and indolence occurring at particular moments, and these will be actual emotions or feelings.

This argument certainly establishes something, but it does not establish the point desired. While it is true that to describe a man as vain is to say that he is subject to a specific tendency, it is not true that the particular exercises of this tendency consist in his registering particular thrills or twinges. On the contrary, on hearing that a man is vain we expect him, in the first instance, to behave in certain ways, namely to talk a lot about himself, to cleave to the society of the eminent, to reject criticisms, to seek the footlights and to disengage himself from conversations about the merits of others. We expect him also to indulge in roseate daydreams about his own successes, to avoid recalling past failures and to plan for his own advancement. To be vain is to tend to act in these and innumerable other kindred ways. Certainly we also expect the vain man to feel certain pangs and flutters in certain situations; we expect him to have an acute sinking feeling, when an eminent person forgets his name, and to feel bouyant of heart and light of toe on hearing of the misfortunes of his rivals. But feelings of pique and buoyancy are not more directly indicative of vanity than are public acts of boasting or private acts of daydreaming. Indeed they are less directly indicative, for reasons which will shortly appear.

Some theorists will object that to speak of an act of boasting as one of the direct exercises of vanity is to leave out the cardinal factor in the situation. When we explain why a man boasts by saying that it is because he is vain, we are forgetting that a disposition is not an event and so cannot be a cause. The cause of his boasting must be an event antecedent to his beginning to boast. He must be moved to boast by some actual 'impulse', namely an impulse of vanity. So the immediate or direct actualisations of vanity are particular vanity impulses, and these are feelings. The vain man is a man who tends to register particular feelings of vanity; these cause or impel him to boast, or perhaps to will to boast, and to do all the other things which we say are done from vanity.

It should be noticed that this argument takes it for granted that to explain an act as done from a certain motive, in this case from vanity, is to give a causal explanation. This means that it assumes that a mind, in this case the boaster's mind, is a field of special causes; that is why a vanity feeling has been called in to be the inner cause of the overt boasting. I shall shortly argue that to explain an act as done from a certain motive is not analogous to saying that the glass broke, because a stone hit it, but to the quite different type of statement that the glass broke, when the stone hit it, because the glass was brittle. Just as there are no other momentary actualisations of brittleness than, for example, flying into fragments when struck, so no other momentary actualisations of chronic vanity need to be postulated than such things as boasting, daydreaming about triumphs and avoiding conversations about the merits of others.

But before expanding this argument I want to show how intrinsically unplausible the view is that, on each occasion that a vain man behaves vaingloriously, he experiences a particular palpitation or pricking of vanity. To put it quite dogmatically, the vain man never feels vain. Certainly, when thwarted, he feels acute dudgeon and when unexpectedly successful, he feels buoyant. But there is no special thrill or pang which we call a 'feeling of vanity'. Indeed, if there were such a recognisable specific feeling, and the vain man was constantly experiencing it, he would be the first instead of the last person to recognize how vain he was. . . .

DISCUSSION QUESTIONS

1. According to Ryle, how does Descartes' view of the mind-body relationship resemble the story of the peasants and the steam engine?

2. What is "the official theory" of the mind-body relationship which Ryle criticizes?

3. What does Ryle mean by a "category mistake"? What sort of a category mistake does he attribute to the official theory?

4. According to Ryle, what is the proper analysis of "Jones acted from vanity"? What is the analysis that he criticizes as improper? Do you agree? Can the same be said, if "anger" or "fear" is substituted for "vanity"? Can a similar analysis be given of "Jones grimaced from pain." If not, how should this statement be analyzed? Does this analysis generate a philosophical puzzle about the nature of the mind-body relationship that Ryle sidesteps?

5. If robots of the future could be made to behave indistinguishably from human beings, would Ryle be committed to the view that they have "a mind"? Do you think this would totally decide the question?

6. Can the concept of "thinking" be analyzed behaviorally? Do you agree with the behaviorist Watson that "thought is nothing but talking to ourselves"?

31. MATERIALISM: THE IDENTITY THEORY

J.J.C. Smart

J.J.C. Smart (1920–) is a professor of philosophy at the University of Adelaide in Australia, noted for his defense of controversial philosophical opinions. His major philosophical concerns are in the philosophy of science, philosophy of mind, and ethics. He is perhaps the most well-known defender of the contemporary materialistic view known as "the identity theory," which asserts that sensations **are** brain processes.

While sympathetic to Ryle's attempt to circumvent Cartesian dualism through the use of behavioristic analyses of mentalistic terms, Smart believes that sensations cannot be so analyzed. Indeed, Ryle makes no attempt to provide behavioristic analyses of sensations. As the dualist will see it, these sensations must be nonphysical in nature. Smart rejects this view as contrary to the purely materialistic metaphysics that he believes is suggested by the advance of science. It seems incomprehensible to Smart that nonphysical entities or properties could arise in the course of the purely biophysical evolutionary process that scientists assume gave rise first to unconscious life forms and then to conscious ones. The rejection of an immaterial soul as the subject of states of consciousness and the identification of these states of consciousness (sensations) with brain processes is, as Smart sees it, the only way to avoid the theoretical anomaly of accepting the existence of nonphysical states that are alien to (or to use his term, that "dangle from") the purely materialistic theoretical framework suggested by science.

The identity Smart proposes between sensations and brain processes is not **definitional** (i.e., sensations cannot be defined in terms of brain processes) but empirical (i.e., a reflection of the facts as we find them). From Smart's perspective, the **meaning (sense)** of the concepts we use to report our sensations is itself neutral between materialism and Cartesian dualism. When we report a particular sensation, Smart claims, we report no more than that our immediate experience is like previous experiences we have had under standard physical conditions. While it is logically possible that the sensations we report in this manner may turn out to **refer to** nonphysical states of an immaterial soul, as Cartesian dualists assume, it is also logically possible that they **refer to** brain processes of purely physical organisms, as materialists contend. The true nature of the referents of sensation terms, Smart believes, is a question that can be resolved only by turning to the empirical facts and to the explanatory power of scientific laws and theories. Smart contends that the ever-increasing ability of the laws and theories of physics to explain diverse phenomena supports the acceptance of the materialistic view that sensations refer to complicated brain processes.

First of all let me try to explain what I mean by "materialism." I shall then go on to try to defend the doctrine. By "materialism" I mean the theory that there is nothing in the world over and above those entities which are postulated by physics (or, of course, those entities which will be postulated by future and more adequate physical theories). Thus I do not hold materialism to be wedded to the billiard-ball physics of the nineteenth century. The less visualizable particles of modern physics count as matter. Note that energy counts as matter for my purposes: indeed in modern physics energy and matter are not sharply distinguishable. . . .

Source: J.J.C. Smart, "Materialism," *The Journal of Philosophy,* 60 (1963). Reprinted with the permission of *The Journal of Philosophy* and J.J.C. Smart.

. . .I wish to lay down that it is incompatible with materialism that there should be any irreducibly "emergent" laws or properties, say in biology or psychology. According to the view I propose to defend, there are no irreducible laws or properties in biology, any more than there are in electronics. Given the "natural history" of a superheterodyne (its wiring diagram), a physicist is able to explain, using only laws of physics, its mode of behavior and its properties (for example, the property of being able to receive such and such a radio station which broadcasts on 25 megacycles). Just as electronics gives the physical explanation of the workings of superheterodynes, etc., so biology gives (or approximates to giving) physical and chemical explanations of the workings of organisms or parts of organisms. The biologist needs natural history just as the engineer needs wiring diagrams, but neither needs nonphysical laws.

It will now become clear why I define materialism in the way I have done above. I am concerned to deny that in the world there are nonphysical entities and nonphysical laws. In particular I wish to deny the doctrine of psychophysical dualism. (I also want to deny any theory of "emergent properties," since irreducibly nonphysical properties are just about as repugnant to me as are irreducibly nonphysical entities.)

Popular theologians sometimes argue against materialism by saying that "you can't put love in a test tube." Well you can't put a gravitational field in a test tube (except in some rather strained sense of these words), but there is nothing incompatible with materialism, as I have defined it, in the notion of a gravitational field.

Similarly, even though love may elude test tubes, it does not elude materialistic metaphysics, since it can be analyzed as a pattern of bodily behavior or, perhaps better, as the internal state of the human organism that accounts for this behavior. (A dualist who analyzes love as an internal state will perhaps say that it is a soul state, whereas the materialist will say that it is a brain state. It seems to me that much of our ordinary language about the mental is neither dualistic nor materialistic but is neutral between the two. Thus, to say that a locution is not materialistic is not to say that it is immaterialistic.)

But what about consciousness? Can we interpret the having of an after-image or of a painful sensation as something material, namely, a brain state or brain process? We seem to be immediately aware of pains and after-images, and we seem to be immediately aware of them as something different from a neurophysiological state or process. For example, the after-image may be green speckled with red, whereas the neurophysiologist looking into our brains would be unlikely to see something green speckled with red. However, if we object to materialism in this way we are victims of a confusion which U. T. Place has called "the phenomenological fallacy." To say that an image . . . is green is not to say that the conscious experience of having the image . . . is green. It is to say that it is the sort of experience we have when in normal conditions we look at a green apple, for example. Apples and unripe bananas can be green, but not the experiences of seeing them. . . .

When we report that a lemon is yellow we are reacting to the lemon. But when we report that the lemon looks yellow we are reacting to our own internal state. When I say "it looks to me that there is a yellow lemon" I am saying, roughly, that what is going on in me is like what goes on in me when there really is a yellow lemon in front of me, my eyes are open, the light is daylight, and so on. That is, our talk of immediate experience is derivative from our talk about the external world. Furthermore, since our talk of immediate experience is in terms of a typical stimulus situation (and in the case of some words for aches and pains and the like it may, as we shall see, be in terms of some typical *response* situation) we can see that our talk of immediate experience is itself neutral between materialism and dualism. It reports our internal goings on as like or unlike what internally goes on in typical situations, but the dualist would construe these goings on as goings on in an immaterial substance, whereas the materialist would construe these goings on as taking place inside our skulls.

Our talk about immediate experiences is derivative from our language of physical objects. This is so even with much of our language of bodily sensations and aches and pains. A stabbing pain is the sort of going on which is like what goes on when a pin is stuck into you. . . . However, some of our sensation words do not seem to work like 'stabbing pain'. Consider 'ache'. Perhaps here the reference to a typical stimulus situation should be replaced by a reference to a typical response situation. Instead of "what is going on in me is like what goes on in me when a yellow lemon is before me" we could have some such thing as "what is going on in me is like what goes on in me when I groan, yelp, etc." In any case it is not inconsistent with the present view to suppose that, when children have got the idea of referring to their own internal goings on as like or unlike what goes on in some typical situation, they can then in some cases go on simply to classify them as like or unlike one another. (All the aches are more like one another than any of them are to any of the itches, for example.) In other words, they may be able to report some of their internal goings on as like or unlike one another, and thus to report these goings on, even when their language is not tied closely to stimulus or response situations. Notice that I am still denying that we introspect any nonphysical property such as *achiness*. To say that a process is an ache is simply to classify it with other processes that are felt to be like it, and this class of processes constitutes the aches. . .

It is important to realize that, if the view that I wish to defend is correct, conscious experiences must be processes involving millions of neurons . . . . As P.K. Feyerabend[1] has pointed out, this shows how a sensation (or a brain process) can possess such properties as of being clear or confused (well-defined or ill-defined), as well as why a sensation seems to be a simple entity in a way in which the details of a brain process are not simple. Brain processes can well have . . . properties that cannot even meaningfully be asserted of individual neurons, still less of individual molecules or atoms. Feyerabend compares this case with that of the density of a fluid, the notion of which can be meaningfully applied only to a large statistically homogeneous ensemble of particles and which has no application in the case of a single particle or small group of particles. Notice also that the materialist hypothesis does not imply that there is anything like consciousness in a single atom, or even in a single neuron for that matter. A conscious experience is a very complex process involving vast numbers of neurons. It is a process, not a stuff. . . .

Consider this example. In some future state of physiological technology we might be able to keep a human brain alive *in vitro*.[2] Leaving the question of the morality of such an experiment to one side, let us suppose that the experiment is done. By suitable electrodes inserted into appropriate parts of this brain we get it to have the illusion of perceiving things and also to have pains, and feelings of moving its nonexistent limbs, and so one. (This brain might even be able to think verbally, for it might have learned a language before it was put *in vitro;* or else, by suitable signals from our electrodes, we might even give it the illusion of learning a language in the normal way.). . . . In the present case we have mental experiences, but no behavior. This brings out vividly that what is important in psychology is what goes on in the central nervous system, not what goes on in the face, larynx, and limbs. It can of course be agreed that what goes on in the face, larynx, and limbs provides observational data whereby the psychologist can postulate what goes on in the central nervous system. If experiences are postulated on the basis of behavior, instead of being grammatical fictions out of behavior, then we can deal with the case of the brain *in vitro*. For whereas grammatical fictions are nothing over and above what they are fictions out of, entities such as are postulated in an hypothesis could still exist even if there had been no possible evidence for them. There could be electrons even if there were no macroscopic bodies, and there could be processes in the central nervous

[1]A contemporary materialist who defends the identity theory. EDITOR'S NOTE.

[2]In an artificial environment outside of a living organism. EDITOR'S NOTE.

system even if there were no attached body and, hence, no bodily behavior. Of course I do not wish to deny that in the case of the brain *in vitro* we could have evidence other than that of bodily behavior: electroencephalographic evidence, for example. . . .

It may be asked why I should demand of a tenable philosophy of mind that it should be compatible with materialism, in the sense in which I have defined it. One reason is as follows. How could a nonphysical property or entity suddenly arise in the course of animal evolution? A change in a gene is a change in a complex molecule which causes a change in the biochemistry of the cell. This may lead to changes in the shape or organization of the developing embryo. But what sort of chemical process could lead to the springing into existence of something nonphysical? No enzyme can catalyze the production of a spook! Perhaps it will be said that the nonphysical extraphysical comes into existence as a by-product: that whenever there is a certain complex physical structure, then, by an irreducible extraphysical law, there is also a nonphysical entity. Such laws would be quite outside normal scientific conceptions and quite inexplicable . . . .To say the very least, we can vastly simplify our cosmological outlook if we can defend a materialistic philosophy of mind. . . .

DISCUSSION QUESTIONS

1. Do you agree with Smart that the statement "I have an ache," means "what is going on in me is like what goes on in me when I groan, yelp, etc." If not, what does it mean?

2. According to Smart, what is the general nature of what is going on in a person when he or she has an ache? What does he deny that it is? Do you agree? Why, or why not?

3. Can you imagine certain discoveries that would prove Smart wrong or would at least count against his position?

4. Some philosophers[3] have claimed that although sensations can be identified with brain processes, it is a mistake to assume, as Smart does, that these brain processes have only physical properties. According to these philosophers, the complex physical processes that are the referents of the terms that we use to describe sensations have psychological properties that are irreducibly nonphysical in nature. For example, when we describe a particular toothache as intense and throbbing, these properties of our toothache are not the same as those physical properties that physiologists ascribe to physical phenomena such as nerve impulses, it is claimed. Consequently, if sensations are to be identified with brain processes, they can be identified only with those brain processes that have both psychological and physical properties. From this point of view, the psychological properties of physical processes are "emergent" properties that come into being when physical processes obtain a certain level of organizational complexity. What would Smart say of such a view? What do you think?

[3]For example, see James W. Cornman and Keith Lehrer, *Philosophical Problems and Arguments: An Introduction*, 2nd ed. (New York: Macmillan, 1974), pp. 302–11.

32. PARAPSYCHOLOGY AND LIFE AFTER DEATH

Editorial Comment

The Basic Areas of Parapsychological Study: Some Preliminary Definitions

Parapsychology is the study of the *alleged* psychic phenomena of telepathy, clairvoyance, precognition, and psychokinesis that are presently incapable of scientific explanation. *Psi* is the general term used in parapsychology for phenomena considered to be parapsychological. Psi phenomena fall into two categories: *extrasensory perception* (ESP), or the cognitive forms of psi and *psychokinesis,* or the motor forms of psi—that is, the ability to influence the behavior of objects (e.g., moving them) through mental concentration. In ESP, the information that is obtained does not originate from sense perception or from cognitive inference (i.e., reasoning). ESP can further be subdivided into the two categories of telepathy and clairvoyance. *Telepathy* is commonly known as the ability "to read the minds" of others—that is, the ability to obtain information about the contents of another person's mind (or brain) which originates from that other person's mind.[1] *Clairvoyance* is the ability to obtain information about events or objects that does not originate telepathically from some other mind. Clairvoyance and telepathy encompass past and future occurrences, as well as present ones. *Precognition* is the term parapsychologists use to describe ESP of future thoughts (precognitive telepathy) and of future events (precognitive clairvoyance). *Psychometry* is a special form of clairvoyant ability which consists of the ability to divine knowledge about an object or about a person connected with it, through physical contact with that object.

Introduction: The Clash of World Views

As William James, the influential American philosopher and psychologist, emphasized, while philosophers do not like to admit this, it is often psychological temperament more than reason that leads them to espouse or reject particular philosophical theories. Philosophers tend by temperament to be either "tender-minded" or "tough-minded" in general philosophical attitude, James claimed. The tough-minded, who pride themselves on their scientific and

[1]Most, but not all, supporters of telepathy are dualists who accept the possibility of the direct interaction of two "minds," without the intervention of any physical process. Nevertheless, if one accepts the view that every mental event is correlated with a brain state, one can see the source of telepathic power as a brain state in the agent's brain which directly causes a corresponding brain state in the subject's brain. Indeed, such a view is held by some supporters of telepathy. Originally, it was thought that the source of telepathy might be some type of brain wave that could be picked up by physical receptors on the analogy of radio waves. However, unlike electrical and other types of physical radiation which are governed by the inverse square law (i.e., the power of the radiation varies inversely with the square of the distance from the source), experimental studies indicate that telepathic power does not depend on the subject's distance from the telepathic source and is not affected by any physical barrier. This has led materialistically inclined theorists to speculate as to other possible materialistic explanations of telepathy. According to one theory, the state of an agent's brain in telepathic transference affects the state of the subject's brain without any intervening events or transfer of physical energy. In order to give a general explanation of such a possible phenomenon, it is suggested that "any two substances exert an influence on each other that tends to make them become more alike" and that the strength of this influence increases with the complexity of the physical objects involved. This so called "resonance" between physical bodies, it is suggested, might be intense in structures as complicated as human brains.

open-minded attitude, usually are materialistic, deterministic, and irreligious in philosophical world view; while their tender-minded counterparts, who seek knowledge that goes beyond the confines of scientific method, tend to assume a religious, dualistic, and indeterministic philosophical world view. Members of the two groups, James wrote, "have a low opinion of each other. . . . The tough think of the tender as sentimentalists and soft-heads. The tender feel the tough to be unrefined. . . ."

In our day, tough-minded materialistic philosophers like J.J.C. Smart have no patience with their tender-minded counterparts who turn to the occult or to such parapsychological phenomena as telepathy and clairvoyance. As Smart and other tough-minded contemporary materialists see it, those who dabble in such subjects are sentimentalists who seek premises to support their tender-minded conclusions—in particular, mind-body dualism, the immortality of the soul, and the existence of God. Nevertheless, in spite of the pride that materialistic philosophers take in their open-minded scientific outlook, they tend to reject out of hand the claims made by supporters of parapsychological phenomena. Since such phenomena do not seem to fit into their materialistic world view, they are rejected as too "fantastic" to be seriously considered. The world simply cannot be inhabited by the nonmaterialistic "spooks" (to use Smart's own expression) to which parapsychologists seem so attracted. The world, it would appear, must be based on more "solid" stuff for materialists such as Smart. As Smart puts it, ". . . there is nothing in the world over and above those entities which are postulated by physics. . . ."

Yet if we turn to contemporary theoretical physics we find that the "entities" postulated by physicists are not nearly as "substantial" as they once were. The old physics of a world consisting of discrete substantial particles which have a distinctive mass and position in three dimensional space seems to have given way to a new physics where mass and energy are considered interchangeable. Indeed some contemporary theoretical physicists find themselves turning to the nonmaterialistic concepts of Eastern mysticism to understand "physical" reality; for example, the contemporary physicist Henry Stapp, echoing many a mystic, claims that the world appears "not as a structure built out of independently existing, unanalyzable entries, but rather as a web of relationships between elements whose meanings arise entirely from their relationship to the whole."[2] From this point of view, metaphysically inclined contemporary physicists have claimed that "fields or relationships alone are *real* and that objects and events are *really* patterns in a cosmic process." Some physicists go further, suggesting that physical reality, as seen by contemporary quantum mechanics, is essentially "mental." For example, echoing the idealistic philosopher Berkeley, the renowned British astronomer Sir Arthur Eddington claims that "the stuff of the world is mind-stuff."[3] A committment to the entities postulated by physics, it would appear, is a rather open-ended commitment. Scientific theories change and along with them their metaphysical underpinnings. A commitment to scientific method need not, one should realize, involve a commitment to a materialistic world view nor indeed to any contemporary world view. Paraphrasing Hamlet, there may indeed be more to this world than is dreamt of in any person's philosophy.

The Study of Parapsychological Phenomena: Some Recent Historical Background

Recalling Hume's thesis about human gullibility and the unreliability of testimony when "the love of wonder is excited,"[4] one is wise

[2] "Physics and Mysticism," *Newsweek*, July 23, 1979, p. 85.

[3] Ibid, p. 86.

[4] See p. 105.

initially to assume a sceptical attitude toward the claims made on behalf of the existence of parapsychological phenomena. Since much of the evidence that is presented in their support consists of specific *spontaneous cases* of alleged examples of such phenomena, most of us have to rely upon the indirect testimony of others that certain events occurred as described. No doubt, just as one should be suspicious of the accuracy of descriptions of alleged miraculous occurrences, one should also be suspicious of the accuracy of anecdotal descriptions of alleged parapsychological occurrences. Nevertheless, in this century a serious attempt has been made in various universities to go beyond this anecdotal evidence and to devise controlled experimental studies of parapsychological phenomena.

The most influential figure in the history of parapsychological research is Joseph Banks Rhine of Duke University, who conducted controlled experiments in the abilities of subjects to telepathically or clairvoyantly "guess" which card of a specially constructed deck of cards was either being observed or thought about by an aide (called an "agent"). Rhine published his results in *Extra-Sensory Perception* (1934), in which he claimed that the consistent accurate card guessing ability of some individuals could not reasonably be attributed to chance. Using sophisticated tests, Rhine attempted to isolate telepathic ability from clairvoyant ability. Given the possibility of precognition, this was not an easy matter. For example, in one of Rhine's early experiments, an agent was asked to think of a card and the subject was then asked to guess what card that was and to make a record of it. The agent was told not to record the card he was thinking of until a signal was transmitted to him, indicating that the subject had recorded his guess. With this procedure it would appear that if ESP were involved in a subject's correct guesses, it would have to be telepathy rather than clairvoyance. As Rhine realized, however, such an experiment could not rule out the possibility that the information about the agent's thought was obtained clairvoyantly, rather than telepathically, from a precognition of the agent's later written report. This led to more sophisticated experiments which were continued at Duke University by Rhine's associate J. Gaither Pratt.

With Rhine and Pratt's pioneering efforts, parapsychological laboratories were set up in other universities in the United States. In order to eliminate the possibility of human mistakes and cheating, random number generators and mechanical scoring machines have replaced the card shuffling and human scoring of the Rhine-Pratt experiments. As a result of these experiments, many researchers have claimed that telepathy and clairvoyance have been experimentally isolated and that the evidence is equally good (some would say, overwhelming) for both. They may, of course, be wrong; but certainly we are not dealing here with crackpots or charlatans who prey upon the gullibility of the masses.

In addition to the experimental evidence adduced for parapsychological phenomena by researchers in major universities, there is much support for such phenomena among members of the renowned British and American Societies for Psychical Research. The British Society was founded in 1882 and included as its charter members the influential philosopher Henry Sidgwick, the classical scholar Frederick Meyers, and several respected physicists. The American Society was formed three years later with the astronomer Simon Newcomb as president and the well-known philosopher William James as a charter member, and later president. In addition to James and Sidgwick, such respected philosophers as Henri Bergson, F. S. Schiller, C.D. Broad, and H. H. Price have held the office of president of one or the other of these two societies.

Explaining Away ESP

As members of the Societies for Psychical Research readily would admit, many alleged spontaneous cases of telepathic or clairvoyant abilities are capable of nonparapsychological explanations. Doubtlessly, many can be attributed to outright deception or to unintentional exaggerations of phenomena. For example, there are cases where the alleged possessor of telephatic or clairvoyant powers alters his information unintentionally, while making the report more appealing and dramatic. Consider the case of a mother worrying about her son who is fighting in a war. She thinks with apprehension of the danger he is in, and her anxiety results in a dream that indicates to her that her son is dying. If this does not happen, she forgets about it. If however, her son happens to die at a comparable time, the mother attributes a parapsychological significance to her dream and perhaps unknowingly embellishes her remembrance of it with details which make her dream appear to be more in accord with the specific circumstances surrounding her son's death. Falsely believing that the specific information surrounding her son's death, which has been imparted to her through normal channels, was contained in her dream, she tells her friends who are deeply impressed by her apparent precognitive ability. Also, a dream may arise as a manifestation of wishes and tendencies to action which are reinforced by the suggestive power of the dream. (For example, a person may have a dream that she will be living in a particular house. Her memory of this dream then influences her decision to buy a house that is similar to the one about which she dreamt.)

In addition, a dream may be a consequence of previous reasoning (perhaps on an unconscious level) about future events which are actually inferred on the basis of ordinarily observable data plus knowledge of certain general scientific laws. According to this point of view, although cases of alleged precognition appear to be noninferential, this is not really so. In support of this possibility, students of parapsychology have pointed to the well-known cases of the "calculating boys" who, never having studied the mathematical laws involved, were able to give immediate solutions to mathematical problems like determining the logarithms of large numbers. These solutions simply "popped into the boys' heads" without any conscious calculation. It has been suggested that the most plausible explanation for this strange power is that the boys actually performed an unconscious deductive inference based on an unconscious knowledge of a mathematical law. Perhaps, it has been suggested, individuals are equally capable of deducing future events from an unconscious knowledge of specific scientific laws and existing states of affairs. Similarly, a dream may arise as a consequence of an inference drawn from stimuli which affect us unconsciously. For example, a man may dream that he has an abscess on his leg which, as a matter of fact, he develops in a day or two. In this case we may assume that the dream was called forth by pathological changes in the tissues of the leg, which existed at the time of the dream, but were not consciously felt.

Instances in which different persons have similar mental processes or shared experiences may resemble telepathy. People living together for a long time, such as old married couples, often find themselves saying the same thing at the same time, or suddenly having the same idea. These events are explicable as identical unconscious associations of similar psyches to some jointly perceived stimulus. Such conformity in reactions can occur also among strangers. If we ask a child to name some color, he usually says "red"; when asked to name a one-digit number most people will name "three" or "seven"; when asked to name a geometric figure they will name a circle or a square. Such occurrences can misleadingly give the impression of a successful telephatic transference. It also is possible that a person can discover information about a person he is in close physical contact with (e.g., touching) by cues he receives from involuntary motor reactions (e.g., rapid pulses) in the manner of a lie detector.

While many cases of alleged spontaneous ESP

are capable of being explained away, many students of parapsychology strongly believe that this is not true of all cases. For example, the British and American Societies for Psychical Research maintain large files of documented case studies of alleged telepathic and clairvoyant experiences and alleged "encounters with spirits" which *seem* incapable of nonparapsychological explanations. Let us consider some of these cases[5] and then reflect upon them. After this, we shall go on to discuss the evidence for a belief in an afterlife based on so-called "death-bed experiences."

Alleged Cases of Telepathy

Mrs. B., when about ten years old, was taking a walk along a country lane. Suddenly, a vision appeared to her—she saw her mother lying as if dead on the floor of one of the rooms of her house. Before going home, she stopped to fetch the doctor. On arriving home, she led the doctor into the room that she had seen in her vision. They found her mother lying as she had seen her. The mother, whom she had left in perfect health, had had a sudden heart attack. Only the opportune arrival of the doctor saved her life.

A machinist on board a steamer, while reading a journal, had the vision of the face of his wife whom he had seen for the last time two years ago. At the same time, he heard her call several times: "It is not my fault!" Afterward, the image of an unknown man appeared to him, which he distinctly remembered. When returning home to his wife a ½ year later, he told her of his vision, and she confessed that precisely at that time she had had intimate relations with a man who looked exactly like the man in his vision. Later on, he corroborated the similarity himself.

The pianist Friedberg, as a young student, once called upon his teacher in order to submit for his judgment a composition that had come to his mind during the night. The surprised teacher showed him the manuscript of his composition which he had written the same night, the content of which was identical to Friedberg's.

Alleged Cases of Clairvoyance of the Present

swedenborg and the stockholm fire

Perhaps the most famous alleged possessor of psychic powers was the celebrated Swedish mystic, Emanuel Swedenborg (1688—1782), who attracted the attention of the philosopher Immanuel Kant. Having heard about Swedenborg's alleged psychic powers, Kant asked an English friend who was to visit Sweden to check out these stories. After interviewing many distinguished persons in Stockholm who had evidence of Swedenborg's psychic feats, the English friend reported several of these feats to Kant, most notably Swedenborg's alleged extraordinary description of the progress of a great fire in Stockholm on July 29, 1759. This took place at a party in Gottenburg which is about three hundred miles from Stockholm. Kant describes this incident in a book he wrote about Swedenborg:

> About six o'clock Swedenborg went out, and returned to the company quite pale and alarmed. He said that a dangerous fire had just broken out in Stockholm, at the Södermalm, and that it was spreading very fast. . . . He said that the house of one of his friends, whom he named, was already in ashes; and that his own was in danger. At eight o'clock, after he had

[5]For facility in reading, I will not preface my descriptions of these cases continually with the disclaimer, "it is alleged that"; nevertheless, the reader should realize that some of these cases may never have happened as described. The cases I have chosen, however, are either very famous ones for which the evidence *appears* overwhelming or are chosen as representatives of recurrent types of cases in the parapsychological literature.

been out again, he joyfully exclaimed, "Thank God! the fire is extinguished; the third door from my house!" This news occasioned great commotion throughout the whole city. . . . It was announced to the Governor the same evening. On Sunday morning Swedenborg was summoned to the Governor, who questioned him concerning the disaster. Swedenborg described the fire precisely; how it had begun and in what manner it had ceased, and how long it had continued. On the same day the news spread thorugh the city and as the Governor thought it worthy of attention, the consternation was considerably increased; because many were in trouble on account of their friends and property. . . . On Monday evening a messenger arrived at Gottenburg, who was dispatched by the Board of Trade during the time of the fire. In the letters brought by him, the fire was described precisely in the manner stated by Swedenborg. On Tuesday a Royal Courier arrived at the Governor's with the melancholy intelligence of the fire, of the losses which it had occasioned, and of the houses it had damaged and ruined, not in the least differing from that which Swedenborg had given at the very time when it happened; for the fire was extinguished at eight o'clock.[6]

walker and the railway accident

On June 27, 1928, Mr. Dudley F. Walker, of Stoughton, Great Britain, had a vivid dream in which he seemed to witness a terrible railway accident. At the commencement of his dream he seemed to be in a railway signal box at night, over a line that he had never seen before (Mr. Walker was not in any way connected with railways). A train was approaching, which in some way he knew to be an express excursion full of people returning from some function. He felt somehow that "the train was doomed," and then found himself "hovering in the air" and following the train, which was slowing as it approached a station. Then he was horrified to see another train coming in the opposite direction on the same line, and although they both seemed to be travelling fairly slowly there was a violent collision. He saw the express locomotive and its coaches "pitch and twist" in the air with a terrific noise.

Later, he seemed to be walking beside the wreckage in the light of dawn, "viewing with a feeling of terror the huge, overturned engine and smashed coaches." The scene was one of "indescribable horror"; bodies, most of them of women and girls, lying beside the track, and the body of a man in a ghastly state, on the side of an overturned coach.

Walker awoke early next morning feeling too upset to eat his breakfast, and recounted the dream to his mother, who in turn told his sister while he was dressing. On arriving at his place of business he told the managing director of his firm about the dream, and also noted it in his diary.

[6]Kant's description is quoted from his *Dreams of a Spirit-Seer,* trans. Goerwitz (London: Swann Sonnelschein & Co., 1900). The spirit-seer is Swedenborg. Kant also refers to the Stockholm fire in a letter written earlier. Unaccountably, however, while Kant's attitude to Swedenborg's alleged psychic powers is highly favorable in the letter, it is totally agnostic in the book. For example, Kant claims in the letter that the story of Swedenborg's clairvoyant vision of the Stockholm fire seems to him "to be free from all possible doubt." In this book, Kant is skeptical and is condescending and sneering in his general attitude toward Swedenborg. Did Kant change his mind about Swedenborg in the period between the letter and the book? If he did, he seems to have changed his mind again, for in a much later lecture on the subject of "rational psychology," Kant refers again quite favorably to Swedenborg. See C. D. Broad, "Kant and Psychical Research," in *Religion, Philosophy and Psychical Research* (New York: Harcourt, Brace and Company, 1953). Broad is himself skeptical of the reliablity of the testimony given by Kant's English friend which Kant relates, without mentioning its source. There are, however, other references to Swedenborg's alleged clairvoyant vision of the Stockholm fire which *differ in details.* Kant's description is often quoted in books in parapsychology without any mention of the ambiguity as to Kant's own attitude toward Swedenborg. In one book, for example, Kant's description is offered with no explanation as "the true account"; in another, it is misleadingly suggested that Kant was a direct witness to Swedenborg's feat. Again, a warning to the reader to take heed of Humes's thesis about the unreliability of testimony when "the love of wonder is excited"!

When leaving the office later in the day, he was astonished to see all the newspaper placards announcing a serious railway accident which had happened at Darlington, over two hundred and fifty miles away, on the previous night at about the same time as he had experienced his dream. He was even more amazed when, on reading the reports of the crash, he discovered that they corresponded in a number of details with the events in his dream.[7]

mrs. titus' clairvoyant vision of a dead girl

On Monday, October 31, 1898, a young girl disappeared from her home in Enfield, New Hampshire. She was last seen crossing a bridge over a lake. An intense search of the shore of the lake and some nearby woods was made, and for two days a diver searched vainly for her body.

On the day before the girl disappeared, Mrs. Titus, a nonprofessional "medium" living at Lebanon, some four miles from the girl's home, told her husband she had a presentiment that "something awful was going to happen," and on the Monday morning declared that it had happened. At midday her husband, who worked with the girl's sister at a mill, told Mrs. Titus that this sister had gone home, he imagined because her mother was ill. In the evening they heard that the girl, whom they did not know, was missing.

The following day, Mrs. Titus affirmed that the girl was in the lake and this, of course, was no more than a natural supposition. On Wednesday evening, however, she fell into a trance, and when awakened by her husband said that if he had left her she would have discovered the girl's whereabouts. Later that evening she went into another trance, during which she said that she could see the girl standing on a frost-covered log on the bridge, that her foot had slipped and she had fallen back into the lake. The body, she said, was lying in a certain place, which she described, by the bridge, between two logs and covered with mud. One foot, with a new rubber shoe on it, was projecting. The next morning, Mr. Titus related the facts of his wife's trance visions to some workmates, and his foreman gave him permission to taker Mrs. Titus to the bridge. She quickly identified the place seen during her trance, but no body was visible. On telling their story to a local mill-owner, a Mr. Whitney who had organized the search, he returned to the bridge with them, and instructed the diver to search at the spot pointed out by the medium. Sure enough, he found the body, lying exactly as she had "seen" it.

The water, the diver claimed, was so dark that he could see nothing and was able to find the body only by feeling for it.[8]

Alleged Cases of Clairvoyance of the Present Accompanied by "Out-of-Body" Experiences: The "Astral Body"

A man sailing from Liverpool to New York had a vision in which he saw his wife enter his cabin; she came up to his berth, kissed him, and after awhile went away. The figure was seen by his cabin-mate. When he arrived in N.Y., his wife asked him if he was aware of the fact that she had come to see him in his cabin during the voyage. She indicated the respective day and said that she had been anxious about him. Then she experienced the feeling that she walked over the stormy sea, found the boat on which he sailed, and that she went to his cabin and kissed him. She also correctly described the boat, which she had never seen before, as well as the furniture in his cabin.

A man, during a very difficult ascent on a

[7]Simeon Edmunds, *Miracles of the Mind:* An Introduction to Parapsychology (Springfield, Ill.: Charles C Thomas, 1965), pp. 38-40. Courtesy of Charles C Thomas, Publisher, Springfield, Illinois.

[8]Ibid., pp. 40–41. Courtesy of Charles C Thomas, Publisher, Springfield, Illinois.

mountain felt tired and decided to remain halfway up the mountain. His company continued the ascent. He sat down in a small recess, and for awhile felt very satisfied with the view of the surrounding peaks, but suddenly he was seized by a fit of stiffness along with a fear of dying. Soon he began to feel his body fading away, and at last he had the feeling that he was dead, and that he floated over the country like a light balloon. He was astonished at distinctly seeing the course of the further ascent of his friends. When they returned to him they brought him to consciousness and he could, according to the memory of his vision, describe exactly some events on their way to the summit.

A Swedish experimenter reported numerous successful experiments in which the subjects were able to describe distant scenes. In one remarkable case a girl, Alma Radberg, was asked to go in her imagination to the office of a company director in Stockholm, where she had never been before. She saw the director seated at his desk and minutely described the room in which he was sitting. Then Alma was instructed to grasp in her imagination a bunch of keys she saw lying on the table, to press the keys, to put her hand on the director's shoulder, thus arousing his attention. Alma declared that the director had noticed her. As a matter of fact, he had had no idea that an experiment was being conducted with him and declared at a later time that he had had a very peculiar feeling on that particular day, and at the same hour. He had sat absorbed in his work, when suddenly his sight was attracted to a bunch of keys, which were lying next to him on the desk; then he saw somewhat vaguely the figure of a woman. Thinking that it was the maid, he did not pay any attention at first. But since the apparition continued to reappear, he called out and stood up in order to see what was going on. It turned out that nobody had entered the room.[9]

[9]This case is related in Milan Ryzl, *Parapsychology: A Scientific Approach* (New York: Hawthorn Books, 1970), pp. 63-64.

Alleged Cases of Precognition

Dubois-Reymond, professor at the University of Berlin, often told his students of a doctor known to him who had attended a woman who was very seriously ill with an intestinal disease. Twice the doctor dreamed that he was reading some treatise on a certain page of a booklet about a medicine that could cure the woman. He made out a prescription and the woman recovered. One year later the doctor happened to get hold of a just-published booklet in which he actually found on the indicated page a recommendation of the medicine he prescribed.

Mr. H.'s wife dreamed several times of a house and its furniture, which she described perfectly but she did not know where it was. Sometime later, Mr. H. rented a house for several months. When discussing the terms in the absence of his wife, the landlady told him that one room was from time to time haunted by some female figure. When Mrs. H. arived, she recognized the house of her dreams, and the landlady recognized in her the person whose apparition used to appear in the house.

An agent of a shipping company, Morris, was sailing on a ship. The night before landing he had a dream that he would be fatally wounded by a splinter of a charge fired from a cannon. The dream frightened him and knowing that the landing of his ship was to be greeted by the firing of a cannon, he ordered the captain not to fire the shot of welcome this time. Later, he found that he had to allow the celebration firing, but he ordered that the shot be fired only when he, after reaching a safe place, gave the order to the captain, who in turn would give the signal for firing by holding his arm up. At a critical moment, a fly happened to rest on the captain's nose. The movement of his hand in repelling it was taken for the order to shoot. The splinter of the premature charge seriously wounded Morris, who died several days later.[10]

[10]Ibid., p. 172.

A woman woke her husband one night to describe a terrifying dream. She saw a large ornamental chandelier above their child's bed fall and crush the child to death. In her dream, the clock in the room read 4:35. Her husband laughed at her anxiety when she took the child into her own bed, but he did not laugh two hours later when a crash was heard from the child's room and the time was 4:35. The chandelier had fallen down onto the empty child's bed.[11]

Alleged Communication from the Dead

the apparition of the dead girl with a scratch

An apparition of a girl appeared to her brother nine years after her death, with a conspicuous scratch on her cheek. Troubled by this apparition, the young man took a train trip to his parents to tell them about it. His mother then revealed to him that she herself had made that scratch accidently while preparing her daughter's body for burial, but that she had then at once covered it with powder and never mentioned it to anyone. Unknown to the son, his trip to his parents' home came at an opportune moment for his mother was to die a short while later. If it were not for the apparition, he most likely would not have seen his mother before she died.[12]

swedenborg and the spirit of the dutch ambassador

The widow of the Dutch Ambassador in Stockholm, sometime after the death of her husband, was called upon by a goldsmith to pay for a silver service which her husband had purchased from him. The widow was convinced that her late husband had been much too orderly not to have paid this debt, yet she was unable to find the receipt. In her sorrow, and because the amount was considerable, she requested Swedenborg to call at her house. After apologizing to him for troubling him, she said that if, as all people say, he possessed the extraordinary gift of conversing with the souls of the departed, he would perhaps have the kindness to ask her husband how it was about the silver service. Swedenborg agreed. Three days afterwards, the said lady had company at her house for coffee. Swedenborg called and in his cool way informed her that he had conversed with her husband. The debt had been paid several months before his decease, and the receipt was in a bureau in the room upstairs. The lady replied that the bureau had been quite cleared out, and that the receipt was not found among all the papers. Swedenborg said that her husband had described to him how, after pulling out the left-hand drawer, a board would appear, which required to be drawn out, when a secret compartment would be disclosed, containing his private Dutch correspondence as well as the receipt. Upon hearing this description the whole company arose and accompanied the lady into the room upstairs. The bureau was opened: they did as they were directed; the compartment was found, of which no one had ever known before; and to the great astonishment of all, the papers were discovered there, in accordance with his description.[13]

mrs. garrett and the spirit of captain irwin

On the 2nd of October, 1930, a well known British investigator, Harry Price, at that time director of the "National Laboratory of Psychical Research," London, engaged Mrs. Garrett, a well-known medium, for a seance to be held on

[11]This case is related in S. Krippner, "The Paranormal and Man's Pliable Future," *Psychoanalytic Review,* 56 (1969), pp. 28–43.

[12]Related in Edmunds, op. cit., p. 113.

[13]Related in Kant's *Dreams of a Spirit-Seer,* op. cit.

the 7th of October. In the early hours of Sunday, the 5th of October, the great new airship, R. 101, crashed on a hillside in France with the loss of all but six of her passsengers and crew. The seance took place as arranged on the following Tuesday afternoon, its object being the attempt to establish communication with the late Sir Arthur Conan Doyle.

As soon as Mrs. Garrett had gone into a trance, her "control" announced that someone named Irving or Irwin was anxious to speak. The medium's voice changed, and in short, sharp phrases, as if laboring under great difficulties, announced that Flight Lieutenant Irwin, captain of the R. 101, was speaking. He went on to give a detailed, accurate, and highly technical account of the disaster and of the events preceding it, together with a description of the many faults of design and construction which were the cause of the crash. Among his many statements were the following:

> "Whole bulk of the dirigible was too much for her engine capacity." "Engines too heavy." "Oil pipe plugged." "Airscrews too small." "Severe tension on the fabric, which is chafing." "Cruising speed bad and ship swinging badly." "No one knew ship properly." "Added middle section entirely wrong." "Superstructure of envelope contained no resilience and far too much weight on envelope." "This exorbitant scheme of carbon and hydrogen is entirely and absolutely wrong." "We almost scraped the roofs of Achy." "Kept to railway."

At the subsequent enquiry into the circumstances of the crash practically all these statements were shown to be correct, although none of those who attended the seance, and emphatically not Mrs. Garrett, had the slightest knowledge of aviation. None of the remaining statements was proved incorrect, and all may well have been true; indeed, several were shown to be probably correct. The statement concerning the roofs of Achy is of special interest, for although it is such a small village that no ordinary maps show it and it is not named in guide books, it was shown on the special large scale flying maps used in the navigation of the airship. Evidence was given at the inquiry that the R. 101 passed over Achy at a height of not more than three hundred feet from the ground.[14]

mr. chaffin's will

Mr. Chaffin, a farmer in North Carolina, died in 1921. He left a will, dated 1905, in which all of his property was left to one of his four sons, Marshall Chaffin. Four years later, another son, James, began having vivid dreams (or half-awake "visions") in which his father appeared at his bedside and spoke to him. In one of these, his father was dressed in an old overcoat and said "You will find my will in my overcoat pocket." James found the overcoat and inside a pocket was a piece of paper on which was written "Read the 27th chapter of *Genesis* in my daddie's old Bible." James found the old Bible, and within the section mentioned, there was another will, dated 1919. In it, the writer said that after reading *Genesis* chapter 27 (which describes how Jacob delivered his father Isaac into blessing him rather than his brother Esau), he wished his property to be divided equally among his four sons. While the will was not witnessed, it was valid according to the law of North Carolina and its directive was carried out.[15]

the apparition of harry price

In October 1948, a Swedish textile worker suffering from emaciation, was admitted to a hospital at Lund. The patient said that he was persistently haunted by the ghost of an elderly Englishman. Although the patient understood very little English, he had managed to gather that his ghostly visitor, who had given his name as Price, had during his lifetime been very active in psychical research. Unknown to the patient's doctor, a psychical researcher who knew Harry Price, Harry Price had died in March of

[14]Edmunds, op. cit., p. 79.

[15]Ibid., pp. 118–23.

that year. It was at the ghost's instigation that the patient had registered at the hospital at Lund instead of in his own district.[16]

the cross-correspondences

Among the most fascinating of cases investigated by the Societies for Psychical Research was that of the so-called "cross-correspondences" in the first quarter of this century. Independently of each other, a number of automatic writers began to produce scripts containing many rather abstruse literary allusions, mostly to the Greek and Latin classics. While the meaning of these allusions could not be discerned by reading the scripts independently of each other, they did make sense when read together. As it turned out, what one automatist had written referred to something which another automatist had written. Indeed, sometimes directions were given in a script requesting that it be sent to another automatist. Nevertheless, none of the automatists knew each other. Finally, in the very scripts themselves, it was claimed that their author was Frederick Myers, a classical scholar, who had died shortly before the Cross-Correspondences began.[17]

Some Reflections on the Cases

What are we to say of these alleged cases of ESP? Did they all really happen as described? Probably not, but most likely some did. Can those that really did happen be explained away without recourse to parapsychological powers? Most serious students of parapsychology emphatically would say no. Can this be attributed merely to the initial bias of those who are attracted to parapsychological research? Most probably not. Assuming that some phenomena require parapsychological explanation, scientifically oriented parapsychologists have sought the simplest explanation for them. For example, if a given phenomenon can be explained equally as well as "a communication from a spirit from the dead" and by the assumption of telepathic communication among the living, then if we have independent evidence for the existence of telepathic powers but not for the existence of an afterlife, it would be simpler to attribute the phenomenon in question to telepathy. (The general philosopical principle that directs us to eliminate unnecessary hypotheses is called "Ockham's razor.")

Most parapsychologists, however, have found it necessary to assume clairvoyance as well as telepathy. The experimental evidence from parapsychological laboratories of the independence of clairvoyance from telepathy is supported by such spontaneous cases of ESP as that of Mrs. Titus and the drowned girl, which appear to impart information of which no other living human being has knowledge. (Some have fancifully suggested that apparent clairvoyant experiences are in reality telepathic communications from spirits or from "the mind of God.") In addition, even when the event in question is witnessed by others, the clairvoyant often witnesses the event from a unique perspective. For example, the mountain climber who had an alleged clairvoyant vision of the continued ascent of his companions seemed to witness the event as if he were hovering above them, seeing them as no one or combination of them could see each other. As our cases of alleged clairvoyance of the present indicate, a common accompaniment of such experience is the feeling of "leaving one's body" and "hovering in the air." It is such experiences that have led many to speak of "astral bodies."

It is the possible existence of precognitive ESP that many parapsychologists, as well as others, find especially psychologically and philosophically troubling. If people can "know" what will happen to them, regardless of what

[16]This case is related in C.D. Broad's review of John Bjorkhem, Det Ockulta Promlemet, *Journal of the Society for Psychical Research,* 37, no. 673 (1953), 35–38.

[17]This case is related in Edmunds, op. cit., pp. 127–30, as well as in many other books and articles on parapsychology.

they do to prevent it, it has been said, then the future is simply "fated" to occur and "free will" is an illusion. (Consider the case of Morris and the cannon, but also consider as well the quite different case of the chandelier and the child.) If one's vision of the future is "caused" by the future event, then must we revise our common sense notion that an event can only be caused by a preceding one? Given the troubling implications of the acceptance of precognition, alternative explanations have been offered for apparent precognitive experiences.

First, some have suggested that although cases of apparent precognition seem to be noninferential, this is not so. It is suggested that the psychic subject has in reality performed an unconscious inference based on premises acquired by nonprecognitive means. For example, let us imagine that Mrs. X has a clairvoyant vision of the death of Mr. X. Suppose that his death was already determined at the time of this vision by his physical condition. The apparent precognitive experience could then be explained by supposing that Mrs. X in some normal or psychic way ascertained the nature of her husband's physical condition and inferred that her husband would die from it.

According to another theory, a person's apparent precognition of a future event is itself in reality the cause (or partial cause) of the future event. As already mentioned, the simplest example of this would be those situations where a person's memory of a dream causes her to act in such a way as to fulfill the dream. Even in cases in which the future event depends upon the actions of others, it has been suggested that psychic subjects may exercise a telepathic influence on the actions of those people. Indeed, it has even been suggested that some events predicted by psychics are actually a result of the psychic's power of psychokinesis. For example, the apparent ability of some people to consistently accurately predict the cards that a machine utilizing a randomizing procedure displays could be attributed to the psychic's psychokinetic ability to influence the randomizing machine. Such an hypothesis, however (which introduces the sort of power that "witches" have been supposed to possess), strikes many scientifically oriented people as more fantastic than the acceptance of precognition.

Let us turn our attention now to the cases of alleged "communications from the dead." (Notice that even if one had good evidence for believing in the survival of a "person" or of her "soul" upon the death of her body on the basis of these alleged communications from the dead, this would be insufficient to establish *immortality*. It is, after all, possible that there is an afterlife, but only of a finite duration.) Most of our cases can be explained on the basis of telepathy alone. In the case of the apparition of the girl with the scratch, the simplest explanation, of course, would be that the brother actually saw his mother scratch his sister, but later forgot about it, only to remember it again and to embellish his remembrance with a "vision" of his sister. Similarly, the boy's mother may have been mistaken in claiming that she never told anyone about the scratch, and the boy might have overheard—the knowledge making, perhaps, an unconscious imprint in his mind. It is also possible that the mother unknowingly spoke her thoughts aloud or spoke up in a dream, again being overheard by her son. If these nonparapsychological explanations are inadequate, one can always resort to telepathy, claiming that the boy read his mother's mind either at the time of the alleged apparition or at a previous time. If the knowledge was acquired at a previous time, it probably was originally registered on an unconscious level and was brought up to consciousness at the time of the apparition and embellished with an imagined vision of his sister. Such an explanation can be applied equally as well to the case of Mr. Chaffin's will.

Similarly, Swedenborg and Garrett, might have read (on an unconscious level) the minds of their alleged spiritual contacts while they were alive, only to call up the information so obtained to consciousness at a later date. More probable, perhaps, is the possibility that most of us constantly pick up telepathic messages on an unconscious level which most of us are incapable of bringing to consciousness. The wife of the Dutch Ambassador, for example, might have read her husband's mind and Swedenborg unknowingly might have read the widow's mind and not that of her husband. On this hypothesis, "mediums" who see themselves as communicating with the dead are simply exercising telepathic powers which they unconsciously embellish with dramatic detail. Many students of parapsychological phenomena have accepted this point of view, seeing mediums as telepathic individuals who derive "spirits" from their own minds or from the minds of others. Such a view is supported by a number of cases of mediums conjuring alleged "spirits" who turned out to be either alive at the time or fictitious people conjured up by clients of the mediums (usually parapsychological researchers testing the telepathy hypothesis). Finally, it is conceivable that although there is no preservation of personal identity after bodily death, traces of one's thoughts continue to exist for some period of time after one's death and are capable of retrieval by psychics.

While telepathy suffices as an explanation of most alleged communications from the dead, it runs into problems in the cases of the apparition of Harry Price and the cross-correspondences. In the case of the cross-correspondences, for example, are we to assume that one of the automatists or some other living person who was knowledgeable of the classics concocted this elaborate scheme and then telepathically conveyed the partial scripts to each of the automatists? Did Frederick Myers (consciously or unconsciously) plan this before he died and telepathically communicate the scripts to the automatists before he died? Is this explanation more plausible than attributing it to a post-mortem design and post-mortem telepathic communication? If so, what are we to say in the case of apparition of Harry Price?

Near-Death Experiences

The experience is familiar to many who work in hospital emergency rooms. A patient who was on the verge of death—perhaps even pronounced dead—recovers later and describes the experience she had when her body exhibited very faint or no signs of life. According to one commonly repeated account, the patient feels herself rushing through a long dark tunnel, while noise rings in her ears. Suddenly, she finds herself "floating above her body," feeling as if she has taken on a vaporous "spiritual body" that retains the rough outlines of her earthly physical body. With the calm detachment of a spectator, she watches the medical team's frantic efforts to revive her. She sees and hears what is happening about her but is incapable of communicating with anyone. Soon other things begin to happen. The "spirits" of relatives or friends who have died come to meet and help her or a loving, warm "presence" or "being of light" causes her to evaluate her life and helps her along by showing her a panoramic playback of the major events of her life. Witnessing this playback, she is made to feel the *effect* her actions have had on others.[18] Drawn to the source of light, she feels that she is approaching the border between earthly life and some new realm

[18]As a person who had this experience described it:

I first was out of my body, above the building, and I could see my body lying there. Then I became aware of the light. . . . Then it seemed . . . everything in my life went by for review. . . . I was really very, very ashamed of a lot of the things that I experienced because it seemed that . . . the light was showing me what I did wrong. And it was very real.

. . . When . . . I would experience a past event, it was like I was seeing it through eyes with (I guess you would say) omnipotent knowledge, guiding me, and helping me to see.

That's the part that has stuck with me, because it showed me not only what I had done but *even how what I had done had affected other people.* And it wasn't like I was looking at a movie projector because I could *feel* these things . . . . I found out that not even your thoughts are lost . . . . [Moody, *Reflections on Life after Life,* (Atlanta: Mockingbird Books, 1975), pp. 34–35].

of being. Wanting very much to continue beyond the border, she is drawn back by a feeling of obligation to those left behind, and she recovers.

Once dismissed as nothing more than hallucinations, "near death" experiences such as this are now being seriously examined by several people with backgrounds in medicine and/or psychology, notably Raymond A. Moody and Elizabeth Kubler-Ross.[19]

Not surprising, those like Moody and Kubler-Ross who are interested enough in "near-death" experiences to devote considerable time to their study, tend to discount the possibility that these experiences are nothing more than hallucinations. Indeed, Kubler-Ross, on the basis of hundreds of interviews, goes so far as to assert that "I know beyond a shadow of a doubt that there is life after death" and is also convinced that the often reported beckoning light is God. Other researchers are more circumspect in drawing conclusions. Moody, for example, explicitly states that he does not think that his investigations "prove anything," even though he does argue against various proposed explanations of near-death experiences that do not involve the belief in an afterlife. Others who have studied near-death experiences are more sceptical. Many attempt to explain away these experiences as hallucinatory projections that the human brain produces in order to cope with the approach of death.

There are, however, several factors which suggest that more than mere hallucination is involved in such experiences. For example, as Moody and Kubler-Ross emphasize, subjects often report heightened mental abilities in their near-death out-of-body experiences which are often confirmed by attendant physicians and nurses. For example, Moody writes that "Several doctors have told me that they were utterly baffled about how patients with no medical knowledge could describe in such detail and correctly the procedure used in resuscitation attempts even though these events took place while the doctors knew the patients involved to be 'dead.' " Kubler-Ross confirms this. Most telling is that in some cases patients report details of the medical procedure performed on themselves or the unrelated activities of those close by that seem to require a vantage point above their bodies; precisely the vantage point they believe themselves to have had while "out-of-body." Such out-of-body experiences point, of course, to clairvoyance. Perhaps, as death approaches, clairvoyant power becomes heightened. The experience, for example, of separation between mind and body and of a speedy journey through a long tunnel has been confirmed by students of clairvoyance, as commonly preceding out-of-body clairvoyant experiences.

There are other features of near-death experiences, however, that many would claim point beyond clairvoyance to the existence of an afterlife. For example, it has often been claimed that the hypothesis of hallucinatory wish-fulfillment does not explain why an hallucinating sub-

[19] The present interest in near-death experiences is the result of the independent research of Dr. Raymond Moody and Dr. Elizabeth Kubler-Ross. Moody, who holds a Ph.D. in philosophy as well as an M.D., developed his interest in this area while a medical student intending to specialize in the philosophy of medicine. After interviewing many of those who reported having near-death experiences, Moody published the results of his investigations in *Life After Life* (1976) and in his subsequent *Reflections on Life After Life* (1977). Moody's discoveries were strongly reinforced by the independent observations of Kubler-Ross, a psychiatrist noted for her research into the psychological processes that the terminally ill go through when they become aware of their condition. Kubler-Ross' observations on near-death experiences became widely known as a result of various magazine interviews (see bibliography). The widespread interest in Moody's books and Kubler-Ross' interviews led others to conduct research into near-death experiences, continuing the investigative process begun by Moody and Kubler-Ross. For example, in his *Reflections of Death* (1981), Michael B. Sabom, a cardiologist, reports the statistical frequency of the various elementss of near-death experiences, something that was neglected by Moody and Kubler-Ross. According to Sabom, of those who have near-death experiences, which include elements described by Moody and Kubler-Ross, 33% *report* only out-of-body experience, 48% transcendental experiences, with 19% reporting both.

ject should restrict her near-death hallucinations of people to those who have already died. Indeed, it is claimed that there have been cases where the subject encounters relatives whom she did not know were dead. Similarly, it is claimed that the hallucination hypothesis does not explain why small children who are dying see dead relatives or religious figures but not their own parents, unless they are already dead.

No doubt, initial critical scepticism is required here, as it is required in the area of parapsychological research. One should, for example, assume some scepticism as to the reliability of the apparently impressive data collected by the researchers on near-death experiences, realizing that it is quite common for researchers to color their data with their own preconceived beliefs and "leading questions." A study of the growing literature in this area indicates a greater diversity in the elements surrounding near-death experiences than one finds in the well-known descriptions offered by Moody and Kubler-Ross. This diversity reduces to mere speculative fancy many of the "theories" that are rashly being offered for these experiences. Understandably, Christians tend to see God behind these experiences, while those with a predisposition toward the concepts of Eastern mysticism paint a different picture of the significance of the data. Nevertheless, the reader should be aware that many scientifically trained people who have studied the data of near-death experiences as well as the data of parapsychology believe that such data ought to lead us away from a materialistic world view and toward a dualistic one. Such a claim would generate heated debate among contemporary philosophers.

DISCUSSION QUESTIONS

1. Assuming that the alleged parapsychological events described in this selection really happened as described, what theory or theories do you think can best account for them? In particular, do you think that the cross-correspondence case and the case of the apparition of Harry Price can reasonably be accounted for only on the basis of a belief in an afterlife?

2. Discuss the philosophical implications of the belief in precognition.

3. Discuss the bearing that telepathy, clairvoyance, and communication with the dead have on the mind-body problem.

4. Consider the following claims:

   a. Jones **is** Smith, who lived 200 years ago. **(reincarnation)**

   b. Jones is **temporarily controlled by** the spirit of Smith, who lived 200 years ago. **(temporary medium possession)**

   c. Jones is a clairvoyant who has the ability to read the thoughts of people who no longer exist and to dramatically internalize their personalities. **(clairvoyance with dramatic embellishment)**

Is there any way these hypotheses can be distinguished?

5. Do you think that the death-bed experiences described by Kubler-Ross and Moody provide strong evidence for the belief in an afterlife? In God? Critically discuss.

FURTHER READINGS

introductory texts and anthologies on the mind-body problem for beginning students

Flew, Anthony, ed., *Body, Mind and Death.* New York: Macmillan, 1964. An excellent and well-edited anthology of classical sources on the mind-body problem (including the problem of personal identity). The selections are prefaced with an excellent twenty-eight-page introduction by Flew and there is a good bibliography.

Plato, *Phaedo, Republic,* and *Phaedrus.* There are numerous editions of these three separate works. Plato's conception of the mind-body relationship sketched in the introduction to this chapter can be found in Plato's early dialogue *Phaedo*, which centers around the last moments of Socrates' life as he converses about death and immortality with his friends prior to drinking the hemlock (the mode of capital punishment in ancient Athens). Plato's view of the mind-body relationship is quite different, however, in his *Republic* (Book IV) and *Phaedrus.* For example, whereas Plato is emphatic about the unity of the soul in the *Phaedo,* in the *Republic* and *Phaedrus* the soul is conceived as having "parts." Similarly, in the *Phaedo,* moral conflict is conceived as a conflict between the soul, which is considered wholly good and rational, and the irrational passions of the body, whereas in the *Republic* and *Phaedrus* such conflict is seen as a disharmony within the soul itself.

Shaffer, Jerome A., *Philosophy of Mind.* Englewood Cliffs, N.J.: Prentice-Hall, 1968. An excellent introductory text on the mind-body problem geared to the beginning student. In addition to a discussion of the traditional theories of the nature and relationship of mind and body, there is a discussion of the nature of and explanations for human *actions* (as opposed to *bodily movements),* a topic that has been in the forefront of contemporary discussions of the mind-body problem. (This topic involves the distinction between reasons and causes and the issue of free will.)

Skinner, B.F., *Science and Human Behavior.* New York: Macmillan, 1953. The famous contemporary behavioral psychologist's clearest and most complete defense of (methodological) behaviorism.

Taylor, Richard, *Metaphysics.* Englewood Cliffs, N.J.: Prentice-Hall, 1963. In the first three chapters of this book, Taylor very lucidly spells out for beginning philosophy students classical theories of the mind-body relationship and their various difficulties.

more advanced texts and anthologies on contemporary viewpoints on the mind-body problem

Armstrong, D.M., *A Materialist Theory of the Mind.* New York: Humanities Press, 1968. A comprehensive (366 pp.) defense of the identity theory and criticism of alternative views of the mind-body relationship for the more advanced student. The good index will prove useful to those interested in particular aspects of the mind-body problem.

Chappell, V.C., ed., *The Philosophy of Mind.* Englewood Cliffs, N.J.: Prentice-Hall, 1962. An anthology of selections by contemporary Anglo-American analytic philosophers expressing different viewpoints on the mind-body relationship. The book begins with an excellent introduction, mapping out contemporary concerns on aspects of the mind-body problem that is geared to a reader with some philosophical background.

Davis, Lawrence, *Theory of Action.* Englewood Cliffs, N.J.: Prentice-Hall, 1979. A clear exposition of contemporary concerns over the nature of human actions. Its chapters cover (in order): nature of action; actions and events; ability; intention; explanations of action; autonomy; and responsibility. While lucidly written, this text is geared to philosophically sophisticated readers.

Gustafson, D.F., ed., *Essays in Philosophical Psychology.* Garden City, N.Y.: Doubleday, 1964. An anthology of articles by contemporary Anglo-American analytic philosophers on conceptual problems associated with the mind-body problem, geared to those with prior exposure to analytic philosophy.

O'Connor, John, ed., *Modern Materialism: Readings on Mind-Body Identity.* New York: Harcourt, Brace and World, 1969. An anthology of sophisticated articles by contemporary philosophers evaluating the modern version of materialism known as the identity theory. While these technical articles are directed to scholars and advanced students, O'Connor provides a comprehensive and nontechnical introduction and summary of various approaches to the identity theory.

Ryle, Gilbert, *The Concept of Mind.* New York: Barnes and Noble, 1949. A very influential defense of logical behaviorism. While Ryle's book can be understood by beginning philosophy students, only those with a prior interest in theoretical psychology or analytic philosophy are apt to find it worthwhile to read the entire book. For most beginning students, brief excerpts, such as those in our anthology, will suffice. The detailed table of contents makes it easy to locate Ryle's treatment of specific topics. For a good critical review of *The Concept of Mind,* see Stuart Hampshire's review included in O.P. Wood and G. Pitcher, eds., *Ryle—A Collection of Critical Essays* (Garden City, N.Y.: Doubleday, 1970).

Smythies, John R., ed., *Brain and Mind.* London: Routledge & Kegan Paul, 1965 or New York: Humanities Press, 1965. An anthology of essays on the connection between mind and brain and comments upon these essays by four philosophers, and one neuroanatomist, one neurologist, one psychiatrist, one psychologist, and one cybernetician (those who study complex electronic computers in an attempt to explain the manner in which the human brain operates). The articles are all clearly written, but most are technical and geared to the more advanced philosophy student. Especially interesting (and less technical) are H.H. Price's "Survival and the Idea of 'Another World' " and John Belloff's "The Identity Hypothesis: A Critique." Both articles are commented upon by others.

Strawson, Peter, *Individuals,* Chapter 3. London: Methuen, 1959. In this influential book, Strawson, a contemporary English analytic philosopher argues that the concept of a person is a logically primitive one that cannot be reduced to either that of mind or that of body. This book is geared to the philosophically sophisticated. (A very clear and nontechnical discussion of Strawson's position can be found on pp. 52–55 of Jerome Shaffer's elementary text *Philosophy of Mind,* listed separately in this bibliography.) While claiming that the notion of disembodied existence is intelligible, Strawson contends that such an existence is a "strictly solitary" and "unattractive" one that is parasitic upon one's prior embodiment. The disembodied person, Strawson claims, "must always think of himself as *dis*embodied, as a former person." Such a being, Strawson contends, has "no personal life of his own to lead," but is restricted to reminiscences of his embodied previous life or to a vicarious interest in the affairs of those who are embodied.

Vesey, G.N.A., ed., *Mind and Body.* London: George Allen & Unwin, 1964. A comprehensive anthology of philosophical selections on the mind-body problem, organized chronologically from Descartes to the present day. There are many more philosophers represented in this book than in the more elementary anthology by Anthony Flew previously listed in this bibliography.

texts and anthologies on personal identity and the intelligibility of a disembodied afterlife

Martin, C.B., *Religious Belief.* Ithaca, N.Y.: Cornell University Press, 1959. In Chapter 6, Martin raises the question of the intelligibility of disembodied existence. Martin's use of imaginative examples should make his sophisticated analytic discussion interesting and understandable to beginning philosophy students.

Penelhum, Terrence, *Survival and Disembodied Existence.* New York: Humanities Press, 1969. A detailed criticism of dualism and survival after death. Penelhum challenges the very intelligibility of the notion of disembodied survival but allows that the doctrine of the survival of "astral bodies" may be intelligible.

Perry, John, *A Dialogue on Personal Identity.* Indianapolis: Hackett Publishing Company, 1978. A short and very readable dialogue which introduces, develops, and criticizes positions and arguments that have appeared in the philosophical literature. Highly recommended for the beginning student.

Perry, John, ed., *Personal Identity.* New York: Lieber-Atherton, 1975. A good anthology of classical and contemporary sources on the philosophical problem of personal identity. The majority of the articles are geared to the philosophically sophisticated. Perry's own introduction, while sophisticated, should, however, be understandable and useful to the beginning student.

Shoemaker, Sydney, *Self-Knowledge and Self-Identity.* Ithaca, N.Y.: Cornell University Press, 1963. A very influential and path-breaking contemporary analysis of the philosophical problem of personal identity, geared to the philosophically sophisticated. Shoemaker criticizes the substance, bundle, and memory views of personal identity and argues for materialism.

Williams, B.A.O., *Problems of the Self.* London: Cambridge University Press, 1973. Williams argues that a bodily criterion for personal identity is primary and memory is secondary.

parapsychology, reincarnation, and survival after death

Broad, C.D., *Lectures on Psychical Research.* London: Routledge and Kegan Paul, 1962. A collection of the well-known British philosopher C.D. Broad's lectures on psychical research, his special interest. The lectures are clearly written and directed to a lay audience.

Ducasse, C.J., *A Critical Examination of the Belief in a Life After Death.* Springfield, Ill.: Charles C Thomas, 1961. A very detailed discussion of the notion of life after death. Ducasse argues that material from psychical research makes survival after death probable. Ducasse prefaces his discussion with an analysis of the concepts of "mind" and "matter" and of the traditional mind-body relationship. He also discusses the idea of reincarnation. The excellent and detailed subheadings of this book makes it a good one through which to browse. The wealth of cases provided and provoking analyses at an elementary level make this an excellent book for beginning students.

Edmunds, Simeon, *Miracles of the Mind: An Introduction to Parapsychology.* Springfield, Ill.: Charles C Thomas, 1965. A good outline of the history and scope of parapsychological study and the theories offered as explanations. The book is notable for its abundance of examples of spontaneous cases, examples well-known to parapsychological researchers but previously scattered throughout an extensive literature.

Hansel, C.E.M., *ESP and Parapsychology: A Critical Reevaluation.* Buffalo, N.Y.: Prometheus Books, 1980. The most comprehensive sceptical treatment of parapsychology to date. Hansel scrutinizes and criticizes various experiments in support of parapsychological phenomena, including J.B. Rhine's well known work at Duke University.

Hick, John, *Death and Eternal Life.* New York: Harper & Row, 1976. A comprehensive descriptive and analytic discussion of conceptions of immortality which takes account of the teachings of Eastern as well as Western religious traditions and the data of parapsychology. Hick also presents his own view, which is a blend of Eastern and Western views. (Drawing from Eastern views, Hick accepts multiple lives, but suggests that it is more reasonable to believe that these take place "in different worlds." Hick also attempts to mediate between Eastern conceptions of the unreality of the self and its eventual "blending" with the selves of others and Western conceptions of the preservation of personal identity.)

Kubler-Ross, Elizabeth, interviews in *People,* Vol. 4, No. 21 (November 24, 1975). p. 66+ and in *Psychology Today,* 10 (September 1976), p. 48+. Kubler-Ross is a psychiatrist who is well known for her study of the psychological processes that the terminally ill experience when they learn of their condition. In these two interviews, Kubler-Ross relates deathbed experiences that have features which exactly parallel those described by Moody. Kubler-Ross, unlike Moody, sees these experiences as pointing, without any doubt, to the existence of an afterlife and to the existence of God.

Lamont, Corliss, *The Illusion of Immortality,* 4th ed.

New York: Ungar, 1965. Lamont considers various aspects of the problem of an afterlife, surveying arguments from historical, scientific, social, and philosophical angles. While he claims that the belief in immortality is an illusion and upon the whole a harmful one, he is sympathetic to the human longing for immortality. He is sharp in his criticism of conflicting Christian tendencies to speak of the resurrection of the body while at the same time to minimize the importance of the body and to maintain a radical separation between mind and body.

Ludwig, Jan. ed., *Philosophy and Parapsychology.* Buffalo, N.Y.: Prometheus Books, 1978. A comprehensive anthology of articles on parapsychology and its philosophical implications.

Moody, Raymond A., *Life After Life* and *Reflections on Life After Life.* Atlanta: Mockingbird Books, 1975 and 1977. The first book contains case studies of alleged "otherworldly" deathbed experiences and Moody's analysis of possible explanations. The second book consists of further reflections on the cases described in the first book and new case studies that bring out additional features of the experiences not mentioned in the first book. Moody, who has a Ph.D. in philosophy as well as an M.D., is currently a practicing physician. It was in his role as a physician that he obtained the data for his books.

Price, H.H., "Survival and the Idea of 'Another World' " in John Smythies ed., *Brain and Mind.* New York: Humanities Press, 1965. Price argues that the belief in survival after death is intelligible and reasonable. His article is criticized by A. Flew and J. Smythies in the same book.

Ring, Kenneth, *Life at Death.* New York: Coward, McCann and Geoghegan, 1980. Ring, a professor of psychology at the University of Connecticut, attempts to scientifically evaluate the deathbed experiences mentioned by Kubler-Ross and Moody. Dismissing other views as scientifically inadequate, Ring argues that such experiences provide strong evidence for an afterlife and support a mystical idealistic (i.e., nonmaterial) world view.

Ryzl, Milan, *Parapsychology: A Scientific Approach.* New York: Hawthorn Books, 1970. A discussion of spontaneous cases and experimental investigations of parapsychological phenomena and theories as to the nature of such phenomena.

Sabom, Michael B., *Recollections of Death.* New York: Harper & Row, 1981. Published after Moody's book, Sabom, an American cardiologist, supplements Moody's description of near death experiences with a statistical account of the incidence of the various elements of these experiences. Sabom, like Moody, takes these experiences as suggestive of the reality of an afterlife.

Siegel, Ronald, "Accounting for After-Life Experiences," *Psychology Today* Vol. 15 (January 1981), pp. 65–75; reprinted as "Life After Death" in George O. Abell and Barry Singer, eds., *Science and the Paranormal* (N.Y.: Scribner, 1981), pp. 159–84. Seigel, a pscyhologist at UCLA, criticizes the view that near-death experiences provide evidence for an afterlife. An expert on drug-induced hallucinations, Siegel claims that near-death experiences are identical to drug-induced experiences and are similarly hallucinatory. Siegel claims that these hallucinatory experiences are caused by neurological excitations triggered by physiological stimuli that affect those who are close to death.

The Skeptical Inquirer, journal of the Committe for the Scientific Investigation of the Paranormal. This journal, published quarterly, contains skeptical critical scientific investigations of paranormal and fringe-science claims.

Stevenson, Ian, *Twenty Cases Suggestive of Reincarnation.* New York: American Society for Psychical Research, 1966. In this fascinating book, Stevenson, an M.D. with an academic position in the Department of Neurology and Psychiatry at the University of Virginia's School of Medicine, describes cases *suggestive* of reincarnation. In these cases, young children appear to recollect things that happened to people who have died. Furthermore, these children assume behavioral and physical mannerisms of the deceased personality, and there are often physical resemblances as well (e.g., similar birth marks). After describing the cases, Stevenson discusses possible explanations for them. The discussion is thorough and analytic, but easily readable.

Wheatley, James M.O., and Hoyt L. Edge, *Philosophical Dimensions of Parapsychology.* Springfield, Ill.: Charles C. Thomas, 1976. An anthology of articles, primarily by philosophers but including psychologists and parapsychologists, on the philosophical implications of parapsychological phenomena.

Wilson, Ian. *All in the Mind.* Garden City, N.Y.: Doubleday, 1982. A critical discussion of alleged cases of reincarnation, hypnotic regression, multiple personality, stigmata, and other alleged mental powers. Wilson casts doubt on the evidence Stevenson presents in support of reincarnation in his book *Twenty Cases Suggestive of Reincarnation.* Reducing alleged cases of reincarnation to the psychiatric category of the dissociated states of consciousness of multiple personality, Wilson seeks a purely naturalistic explanation for such phenomena. He emphasizes the untapped powers of the mind and its suggestibility to the will of hypnotists and others.

minds and machines

Anderson, Alan Ross, ed., *Minds and Machines.* Englewood Cliffs, N.J.: Prentice-Hall, 1964. An anthology of various recent articles on the topic of mentality and machines (e.g., Can machines think?).

Gunderson, Keith, *Mentality and Machines.* New York: Anchor, 1971. A collection of Keith Gunderson's articles on mentality and machines and the bearing of this topic on the traditional mind-body problem. There is an extensive bibliography of classical and contemporary discussions on this topic.

encyclopedia of philosophy

Articles in *The Encyclopedia of Philosophy.* (New York: Macmillan, 1967): Behaviorism; Consciousness; Emotion and Feeling; ESP Phenomena, Philosophical Implications of; Immortality; Materialism; Mind-Body Problem; Other Minds; Panpsychism; Personal Identity; Precognition; Private Language Problem; Psychological Behaviorism; Psychology; Thinking; Unconscious; Unconscious, Psycholoanalytic Theories of.

dictionary of the history of ideas

Articles in *The Dictionary of the History of Ideas* (New York: Scribners, 1973): Behaviorism; Death and Immortality; Man-Machine from the Greeks to the Computor; Psychological Ideas in Antiquity; Psychological Schools in European Thought.

other bibliographies

A very complete annotated bibliography (seventeen *packed* pages) on the mind-body problem is found in Paul Edwards, and Arthur Pap's *A Modern Introduction to Philosophy,* 3rd ed. (New York: Macmillan, 1973). Shorter useful bibliographies can be found in W. Alston, and R. Brandt, *The Problems of Philosophy,* 3rd ed. (Boston: Allyn and Bacon, 1978); and A. Flew, *Body, Mind and Death* (New York: Macmillan, 1964). Those interested in classical sources should refer to Flew's bibliography.

Chapter IV

PERCEPTION AND OUR KNOWLEDGE OF AN EXTERNAL WORLD

One has no knowledge of the sun but only of an eye that sees a sun, and no knowledge of the earth but only of a hand that feels an earth.

Arthur Schopenhauer

I shall suppose . . . that . . . some evil genius not less powerful than deceitful, has employed his whole energies in deceiving me; I shall consider that the heavens, the earth . . . and all other external things are nought but the illusions and dreams of which this genius has availed himself in order to lay traps for my credulity; I shall consider myself as having no hands, no eyes, no flesh, no blood . . . yet falsely believing myself to possess all these things . . .

René Descartes

. . . if. . . anyone will be so sceptical as to distrust his senses, and to affirm that all we see and hear, feel and taste, think and do, during our whole being, is but the series and deluding appearances of a long dream . . . I must desire him to consider, that if all be a dream, then he doth but dream that he makes the question, and so it is not much matter that a waking man should answer him. But yet, if he pleases, he may dream that I make him this answer, that the certainty of things existing [outside the mind] . . . when we have the testimony of our senses for it, is not only as great as our frame can attain to, but as our condition needs.

John Locke

But, though we might possibly have all our sensations without them, yet perhaps it may be thought easier to conceive and explain the manner of their production, by supposing external bodies [that produce them]. . . . But neither can this be said. For, though we give the materialists their external bodies, they by their own confession are never the nearer knowing how our ideas are produced; since they own them-

The table I write on . . . exists; that is, I see and feel it. . . . There was an odour, that is, it was smelt; there was a sound, that is, it was heard. . . . This is all I can understand by these and the like expressions. For as to what is said of the **absolute** *existence of unthinking things, without any relation to their being perceived, that is to me perfectly unintelligible.*

George Berkeley

selves unable to comprehend in what manner body can act upon spirit. . . . [To believe that bodies exist without being perceived] is to suppose, without any reason at all, that God has created innumerable things that are entirely useless, and serve to no manner of purpose.

George Berkeley

Matter consists of groups of permanent possibilities of sensation.

John Stuart Mill

Strictly speaking, ***nothing exists except sensations*** *(and the minds which perceive them). The rest is . . . fiction. But this does not mean that the conception of a star or the conception of an electron is worthless or untrue. Their truth and value consist in their capacity for helping to organize our experience and predict our sensations.*

W. T. Stace

We think that grass is green, that stones are hard, and that snow is cold. But physics assures us that the greenness of grass, the hardness of stones, and the coldness of snow, are not the greenness, hardness and coldness that we know in our own experience, but something very different. The observer, when he seems to himself to be observing a stone, is really, if physics is to be believed, observing the effects of the stone upon himself.

Bertrand Russell

Let us then suppose the mind to be, as we say, white paper, void of all characters, without any ideas; how comes it to be furnished? . . . To this I answer, in one word, from ***experience.*** *In that all our knowledge is founded, and from that it ultimately derives itself.*

John Locke

If we really were plastic organisms, without an extensive preprogramming, then the state our minds achieved would simply be a reflection of the individual's environment, and would therefore be extraordinarily impoverished. Fortunately for us, we are preprogrammed with rich systems that are part of our biological endowment.

Noam Chomsky

In the late 1960s, as many young people decided to "drop out and tune in" to psychedelic drugs such as LSD, a debate ranged over the nature of drug-induced experiences. The critics dismissed such experiences as "hallucinatory," while the advocates praised them as "revelatory." For some proponents of psychedelic drugs, what such drugs revealed was not some objective truth about external reality, but rather some purely subjective truth about the workings of a particular drug user's own mind. For others, however, psychedelic drugs did, indeed, reveal some truth about the external world that lies beyond the confines of an individual human mind. It was, they claimed, as if a veil were lifted, revealing some aspect of the external world that lies hidden by the blinkers of ordinary perception. Their critics hotly disagreed. In the midst of this strongly passionate disagreement, few disputants paused to reflect on the meaning and standards that should be utilized in distinguishing "appearance" from "reality," a problem that has intrigued philosophers from the first stirrings of philosophical wonder.

That a distinction must often be made between appearance and reality, even the most philosophically unsophisticated soon come to realize. For example, the stick that appears crooked when half submerged in water is, we all realize, really straight. An object that appears one color under a particular light may really be another color under more appropriate or natural light. The lake we seem to see as we drive through a desert may really be a mirage caused, science tells us, by the bending (refraction) of light as it passes through layers of air of differing temperatures. No external source, however, need trigger the mind's power to play tricks upon us. While really asleep in bed, one may dream that one is awake and engaged in some activity somewhere else. As the philosopher Descartes was troubled to observe, since the experiences one has in a dream can be as vivid and coherent as those one has while awake, dream experiences may be indistinguishable in themselves from waking experiences. How then do we ever know for sure that our sensory experiences are caused by external physical objects, Descartes pondered. Even if this can be known, what is the relationship between our sensory experiences and the object itself when we see an external physical object such as a tree? The tree presents clear sensory impressions of color and shape as we look at it and clear tactile sensations as we feel its heavy solid trunk and soft willowy leaves. But is the tree as experienced by human beings like the tree as it exists without the human eyes that see it and the human hands that feel it? Clearly, it must look different to other creatures whose sensory organs are differently constructed from our own. The leaf we see with the naked human eye looks quite different under a microscope. How, one may wonder, does it look to a tiny insect who crawls upon it, lost in its relative immensity?

If we turn to science to tell us about the nature of the tree we perceive, the difference between appearance and reality seems even more striking. The tree, like all physical objects, we are told, is mostly empty space and is composed of collections of colorless particles called atoms which move rapidly thorugh the relative void of the tree's interior. The green and brown colors that we see as we look at the tree are caused, we are told, by the particular wavelengths of light waves that are generated by the sun and reflected off the tree. These light waves pass through the various parts of the eye, finally reaching the retina, where they produce a nerve impulse within the optic nerve. This nerve impulse is carried to the visual cortex of the brain, where it produces the experience of sight. Colors, according to this picture, do not exist in the objects we perceive, but only in the minds of those who see. The range of colors that objects appear to us to have results from the fact that we are receptive in a particular way to only a particular tiny range of electromagnetic waves. Were we sensitive in a different way or to different electromagnetic waves, as some animals are, the nature and range of the colors we perceive would be quite different. Furthermore, since it takes time for light to travel to our eyes from the objects we see, we can only see objects as they *were* rather than as they *are*. For example, when we look up at the sun, we see the sun as it was eight minutes ago for it takes light that much time to travel the ninety-three million miles that separate the sun from the earth. A star that we gaze upon on a starry night may have long ceased to exist before its light reaches our eyes. The picture science presents of the external world seems, consequently, to shatter our common-sense belief that we often directly perceive objects as they are when we perceive them.

Objects, it would appear, are not experienced directly, but only indirectly through the sensory experiences they cause. But what is the nature of these external objects that cause our sense experiences? Prior to the advent of quantum mechanics, we could visualize them as composed of minute atoms consisting of a nucleus of protons and neutrons with orbiting electrons. With the advent of quantum mechanics, however, this tidy picture has been demolished as many more subatomic particles have been discovered, ''particles,'' furthermore, that sometimes seem to be more like ''waves'' or ''energy'' than like discrete material substances that have a particular mass and shape and occupy a particular position in space. The ''solidity'' of matter seems to melt as we plumb the depths of the atom. No longer can we visualize the internal structure of the atom, which contemporary physicists tell us is occupied by such strange things as quarks, gluons, mesons, neutrinos, and gravitons. Even physicists themselves admit that they do not know quite what to make of such strange ''entities'' and their puzzling behaviors. Perhaps, it is claimed, they are not ''real'' objects at all, but only convenient myths or calculating devices that allow us to predict the order of our experience. As physicist John A. Wheeler of the University of Texas puts it, ''[one should] give up thinking of nature as a machine that goes on independent of the observer. What we conceive of as reality is a few iron posts of observation with papier-mâché construction between them that is but the elaborate work of our imagination.'' Such provocative claims bring modern physicists back to some of the central philosophical problems of epistemology (the theory of knowledge). What is the relationship of the human mind to the external world it supposedly perceives? What does it mean to say that we are perceiving an external object? How is such perception possible? What is it to say that we know that something exists or that some statement is true? How do we distinguish meaningful statements from nonsensical ones?

From the dawn of ''modern philosophy'' in the seventeenth century up until the present, epistemological questions have preoccupied professional philosophers. Prior to this time, metaphysical questions concerned with ''what ultimately exists'' were in the forefront of philosophical discussions. For example, influenced by Aristotle and Christian philosophy, the central philosophical concern throughout the Middle Ages was to determine what exists and to find ''the place'' of all that exists within a purposeful God-created universe. From such a perspective, philosophy, throughout the Middle Ages, was naturally seen as ''the handmaiden of theology.'' This view of philosophy came to be challenged however, as the experimental, mathematical, and nonauthoritarian spirit of inquiry of the sixteenth and seventeenth centuries (''the scientific revolution'') spread throughout the Western world. In the midst of this exciting period of intellectual rebirth lived the French mathematician, scientist, and philosopher René Descartes (1596–1650), '' the father of modern philosophy.'' It was Descartes' philosophical writings, above all else, that provided the impetus for the modern shift of philosophical attention from metaphysical to epistemological questions.

While previous philosophers constructed their elaborate metaphysical schemes without questioning the adequacy of their *method* of arriving at philosophical truth, Descartes, inflamed with the new spirit of inquiry, turned his acute analytic eye to precisely this question. In this famous *Meditations,* Descartes begins by questioning the legitimacy of claims to knowledge. Reflecting upon the many occasions in which deeply-held beliefs turn out to be false or rationally unjustified, Descartes resolves to cast aside all claims to knowledge that can be doubted, until he comes to some claim or claims that are certain, beyond the shadow of any doubt. Once these indubitable truths are discovered, he will, like Euclid, proceed deductively to build a *structure* of knowledge upon the foundations of these indubitable truths. Admitting that "All that up to the present time I have accepted as most true and certain I have learned either from the senses or through the senses," Descartes first considers whether sense experience can supply us with certain knowledge of the nature and existence of an external physical world. Considering the possibility of dreams, which are in themselves indistinguishable from waking experiences, Descartes finds himself forced to admit the logical possibility that any given experience of some physical reality may be hallucinatory. Indeed, it is even possible that the bodies we perceive ourselves to have are not as they appear to us to be or indeed may not even exist at all. Shaken by this realization. Descartes goes on to entertain the unsettling possibility that all of life is a dream, writing:

> . . . I have long had fixed in my mind the belief that an all-powerful God existed by whom I had been created as I am. But how do I know that He has not brought it to pass that there is no earth, no heaven, no extended body . . . and that nevertheless [I possess the perception of all these things and that] they seem to me to exist just exactly as I now see them?

It is only when Descartes proves to his satisfaction the existence of a benevolent God who would not permit him to be deceived in an indetectable way that he is willing to abandon the frightening hypothesis that all his perceptions of a physical world, including the existence of his own physical body, are hallucinatory.

The Legacy of Descartes: Rationalism Versus Empiricism

Descartes' central question, "How is knowledge possible?" and his quest for a *structure* of knowledge based on either self-evident truths of reason or the unquestionable testimony of the senses set the stage for subsequent philosophers. On the European continent, *rationalists* such as Spinoza (1632–77) and Leibniz (1646–1716) followed Descartes in rejecting the possibility of forming a bedrock of indubitable knowledge upon the fallible immediate testimony of the senses. As they saw it, sense experiences were not the self-evident starting points of knowledge but rather *unstructured data* that required restructuring within a mathematical deductive model of reality which intellectual insight could grasp. Just as Galileo (1564–1642), Kepler (1571–1630), and Newton (1642–1727) had deciphered the mathematical laws governing the behavior of physical bodies, the rationalists believed that a philosopher could decipher the structure of reality through the use of abstract concepts and mathematical models.[1]

While Descartes' attempt to uncover a mathematical structure of reality was at the forefront of the philosophies of the rationalists, at the forefront of the philosophies of the British empiricists such as Locke (1632–1704), Berkeley (1685–1753), and Hume (1711–66) was Descartes' subjectivistic standpoint and his emphasis upon the problem of bridging the gap between private sense experience and public knowledge of an external physical reality. Instead of providing metaphysical descriptions of

[1]It is often said that the rationalists sought conclusively to deduce (on the model of Euclidean geometry) all legitimate claims to knowledge from the base of certain self-evident *a priori* truths. While this is true of Spinoza, there is much in the writings of Descartes and Leibniz which indicate a belief that knowledge is dependent upon sense experience. For example, Descartes, in his extensive discussion of method, envisions a scientist as a theoretician who devises theoretical models to fit the content of sense experience and is willing to reject or revise these models in the face of recalcitrant sense experiences. Nevertheless, Descartes also seemed to believe that these experimental tentative models could eventually culminate in a final and complete deductive system built on the base of self-evident metaphysical truths. The conflict between these two models of knowledge is never clearly resolved by Descartes.

the world from the point of view of some external observer, the empiricists proceeded by turning first to what is subjectively most certain, as Descartes did. While both Locke and Berkeley (unlike Hume) accepted some self-evident *a priori* truths, the empiricists were united in their emphasis upon *private* sense experience as the ultimate provider of the materials for knowledge. Searching no less than the rationalists for certain knowledge, beyond the shadow of any rational doubt, the empiricists thought they found such knowledge in the immediate noninferential testimony of the senses. On their view, the mind is like a passive screen upon which sense experience is projected. The activity of the mind, on the empiricist view, consists in analyzing one's thoughts of these sense experiences into their atomic components, recombining these components into new combinations, and noticing the similarities and patterns of repeated occurrence of one's actual sense experiences ("the association of ideas"). As well as leading to a particular school of epistemology which sought to erect the foundations of knowledge upon the self-evident testimony of immediate sense experience, the epistemological viewpoint of Locke, Berkeley, and Hume also led to the development of the introspectionist psychology of the nineteenth and early twentieth centuries, which saw the task of the science of psychology to be the cataloging and analysis of the contents of the mind and the discovery of the principles of the association of ideas.

Attempting to reconcile the insights of the rationalists and the empiricists and to overcome the apparently insurmountable problems these philosophies faced, Immanuel Kant (1724–1804) accepted the empiricists' claim that human understanding can function properly only by way of its access to sense experience. Nevertheless, Kant argued, the rationalists were right that knowledge is not based, as the empiricists believed, in the mind's passive acceptance of the self-revealing and uninterpreted testimony of subjective experience. As Kant saw it, the mind imposes a *structure* upon sense experience which makes it impossible for the mind to know anything that cannot be accommodated to the conceptual grid of that structure, which shapes the form of our experiences. Kant claimed that the empiricists were wrong to assume that knowledge begins with attaching labels to bits of sense experience that require no interpretation. In Kant's view, our knowledge of the external world is not a knowledge of objects as they are in themselves, but the result of the way our minds inevitably *organize* our experience.

In spite of Kant's profound influence upon subsequent philosophy, the empiricist tradition continued to thrive along with the new Kantian synthesis throughout the nineteenth and twentieth centuries. Let us turn our attention first to a consideration of this empiricist tradition, which found its culmination in the *logical empiricism* of the twentieth century, and then to the contemporary, essentially Kantian, epistemological viewpoints, whose influences have grown in the second part of the twentieth century as the influence of logical empiricism has declined.

Empiricism and the Problem of Perception

In spite of their many philosophical differences, the British empiricists, were united in claiming that the fundamental building blocks of knowledge were the subjective states of consciousness of sentient organisms, that is, our sense impressions, which we usually see as "externally caused," and our inner feelings, emotions, memories, and thoughts, which we see as caused by "the operations of our own minds." It was these *ideas,*[2] as Locke and Berkeley called them,

[2]Locke's and Berkeley's concept of an *idea* was synonymous with *a state of consciousness* and as such was much broader than today's concept of an *idea.*

or *impressions and ideas*[3] as Hume called them, or *sense data,* as the logical empiricists called them, which the empiricists believed were the direct objects of perception. For example, when we look at a tree, what we actually perceive, the empiricists claimed, are our own sense experiences of the tree. Our claim that we see a tree, they asserted, goes beyond the direct testimony of our senses, either by postulating an external cause of our sense experiences of the tree or in making some hypothesis about other sense experiences we would have or others would have if they did certain things. (For example, if I am really seeing a tree, I should also be able to feel it and others should be able to see and feel it as well.) While a doubt can arise as to whether one is perceiving a physical object or hallucinating, one cannot, the empiricists believed, doubt that one has the sense experiences that are immediately before one's consciousness. This, they claimed, is the starting point of knowledge. While Locke and Berkeley were not themselves consistent empiricists and allowed for concepts which could not be ultimately reduced to the content of one's own consciousness, Hume and the logical empiricists attempted precisely such a reduction, holding that all our concepts must either originate directly in experience or else be compounded of ideas that originated in experience. In the process, they dismissed as meaningless the *a priori* concepts of rationalistic philosophers.

The central problem facing the empiricists was how one can justify inferring an "external world" from purely private sense experience. Since one's sense experiences are necessarily private and the only source of our knowledge of things, do we have a right to infer that there are physical objects that exist apart from the sense experiences that they are commonly taken to "cause"? In addition, if we are justified in believing in such objects, what is their relationship to and how, if at all, do they resemble the sense perceptions we have of them? Locke, Berkeley, and Hume gave different answers to these questions.

[3]See the footnote on p. 201 for Hume's distinction between *impressions* and *ideas.*

Locke: Critical (or Representative) Realism

Like Descartes, Locke was greatly influenced by the new science that flourished in his day. That science proclaimed that physical reality is composed of minute particles that occupied space and that moved about from one part of space to another. The mass and velocity of these particles were measurable and subject to mathematical laws, which enabled human beings to understand and predict the course of nature. Accepting this view of physical reality, Locke (as well as Descartes) embraced a *causal theory of perception* called *critical,* or *representative, realism* which reflected the teachings of the new science. According to this theory of perception, we do not directly perceive physical objects in themselves, but only the sense impressions (ideas) they cause. The sense impressions of color, odor, taste, and sound exist only "in the minds" of sentient creatures like ourselves and not "in the physical objects themselves." (For example, physical objects in themselves are really colorless.) While objects may be said to have the qualities of color, odor, taste, and sound, they do so, Locke claimed, only in the secondary sense of having the power to produce these sense impressions in the minds of sentient organisms. Locke distinguished these *secondary qualities* of physical objects from their *primary qualities*—namely, their shape, size, position, and motion—properties which the science of his day attributed to the ultimate constituents of matter, (in Locke's terminology, the "insensible particles" of which physical objects are composed). The ideas we have of primary qualities—that is, the sizes, shapes, positions, and motions we perceive—consequently, resemble qualities that objects really have, whereas the ideas that we have that correspond to secondary qualities do not resemble objects' secondary qualities, Locke claimed. Since, as Locke saw it, a person does not directly perceive physical objects but knows of them only indirectly through the sense impressions they cause, Locke was aware that these physical objects might not exist even though our sense impressions suggested that they did. Nevertheless, Locke claimed that the coherence of our sense impressions (while awake) and their independence of human will is best explained by the belief that they are caused by external physical objects.

Berkeley: Idealism

Locke's view of perception was subjected to penetrating criticism by Bishop George Berkeley. First, Berkeley attacked the arguments Locke used to support his distinction between primary and secondary qualities. For example, while Locke had pointed to the variability of our ideas of secondary qualities to support his belief that such ideas exist only in the mind, he had neglected the fact that the apparent shape, size, and position of objects also vary with conditions of perception. Furthermore, Berkeley claimed, since it is impossible to *imagine* something having a size and shape without also having some color, the notion of primary qualities existing without secondary qualities is unintelligible. Finally, Berkeley attacked the intelligibility of the notion of physical substance (or matter) which Locke, admittedly to his own dissatisfaction, could define only as "the supposed but unknown support of those qualities we find existing, which we imagine cannot subsist . . . without something to support them." Since Locke could in no way explain how matter "supports" primary qualities, Berkeley rejected the notion of matter not simply as unknowable, but as unintelligible. Unlike the later philosopher Kant, who would claim that all *knowledge* is restricted to the mind's sense impressions but also *assume* the existence of unknowable objects behind these sense impressions, Berkeley argued that it is actually meaningless to say that something exists apart from the mind.

What we call physical objects, Berkeley claimed, are simply coherent sets of sense impressions—they are, in fact, the sum total of the sense impressions associated with the idea of a given object and not, as Locke believed, some unknowable material substance that causes these impressions. As Berkeley saw it, Locke, in making this assumption, was misled by the grammatical structure of our language, which distinguishes the subject from the predicates we attribute to it. For example, the grammatical structure of the statement "Snow is white, soft, cold . . ." made Locke think that snow is more than the sum of the sense impressions that we misleadingly say snow *has,* thinking in the process that snow is one thing and its qualities another. It is as if one peeled away the various skins of an onion, waiting to find a core underneath, only to discover that there was nothing more to the onion than the skins we peeled away.

As Berkeley saw it, the universe consists simply of ideas and the minds that have them. While it is often claimed that Berkeley denied the existence of physical objects, he did not see himself as doing this at all. As he saw it, physical objects *are* simply collections of ideas. What he did deny was the existence of material substances supposed to exist independently of minds. In its most common usage, any theory of perception which makes such a denial is a form of *idealism.*

Like Locke, however, Berkeley believed that our sense experiences of physical objects (which appear to be beyond our control) have to be caused by something independent of our own minds. Since he rejected Locke's view that they are caused by insensible material substances and rejected as well the view that a given sense experience could cause another sense experience (the view of causation later to be adopted by Hume), he was left with God. As he saw it, physical objects (or better, the systematic collections of ideas that we call physical objects) do not cease to exist when they are not perceived by beings of this world, for God always perceives them and causes us to have "similar" perceptions. Berkeley's view is well-expressed in Ronald Knox' limerick:

There was a young man who said, "God
Must think it exceedingly odd
  if he finds that this tree
  Continues to be
When there's no one about in the Quad."

Reply

Dear Sir:
  Your astonishment's odd;
I am always about in the Quad.
  And that's why the tree
  Will continue to be.
Since observed by
Yours faithfully,
God.

Although Berkeley's view of perception has been described by some as a work of a madman, Berkeley saw his philosophy as a vindication of common sense and a clearing up of the obstructions to clear understanding that other philosophers had needlessly created. By viewing physical objects as systematic or coherent patterns of sense impressions, Berkeley also saw his theory as making it possible, as Locke's theory did not, to verify the distinction between hallucinations and reality. For example, Shakespeare's Macbeth knew that the dagger that he saw was hallucinatory because he knew that if he reached for the dagger he saw, he would not be able to feel it, and he knew as well that others would not be able to see and feel it. While Locke would have admitted that this was the only evidence Macbeth could have for the hallucinatory quality of his experience, he would have claimed, nevertheless, that what it *means* to say that Macbeth's experience was hallucinatory is that this experience was not *caused* by an external object. On Berkeley's view, however, the failure to have certain sense experiences is what is *meant* by having an hallucination. As Berkeley saw it, the reality of physical objects is determined by the systematic correlations of the ideas that constitute them and not by the correspondence of our sense impressions to certain properties of "matter," as Descartes and Locke believed. The latter view must lead to scepticism, Berkeley believed. Descartes attempted to escape this scepticism through the goodness of God, but only by claiming that God created "matter," which in some mysterious and unknowable (and apparently senseless) way causes ideas in our minds which God can cause directly. Such a view seemed absurd to Berkeley.

The Legacy of Hume: Scepticism and Phenomenalism

As we saw, in order to preserve the common-sense belief in the existence of physical objects which are unperceived by any sentient being of this world, Berkeley introduced a non-worldly always-perceiving being, God. If, as Berkeley claimed, an existing physical object must be perceived (and not merely perceivable) by some sentient creature, then, without God, physical objects would come into and go out of existence depending on whether there were sentient creatures around to perceive them. Seeing himself as a vindicator of common sense, Berkeley, understandably, could not easily accept such a radical conclusion. While one can well understand Berkeley's motives for introducing God into his theory of perception, Hume, the more consistent empiricist, challenged Berkeley's justification for this desperate maneuver. Indeed, as Hume saw it, Berkeley had no more justification for believing in the existence of spiritual (or mental) substances than

Locke had for believing in material substances. The very same sceptical argument that Berkeley so effectively used to challenge the very intelligibility of Locke's view of matter could be utilized to challenge the intelligibility of the notion of spiritual substance. Just as a physical object is no more than the collection of sense impressions we misleadingly attribute to that physical object, so too, Hume believed, a "mind" is nothing more than a collection of states of consciousness, including feelings and thoughts. (Recall our discussion of Hume's "bundle theory of the self" in Chapter III on the mind-body problem.) Locke's world of matter, minds, and states of consciousness, which was reduced by Berkeley to a world of minds and their states of consciousness, was even further reduced by Hume to a world of states of consciousness alone.

Having rejected Locke's and Berkeley's view that the orderliness of our sense perceptions is *caused* by material or mental substances, Hume was forced to take that orderliness as a brute, unexplainable fact of experience. For example, while we are inclined to think that a billard ball *must* move when it is struck by another billard ball, all we really know is that it always has, Hume claimed. This regularity in the past naturally gives rise to our *psychological habit* of assuming its continuation in the future. It is our habit of expecting the future to be like the past that is the foundation of our expectation of the future course of our experience and of our notion of causation, Hume claimed. For example, when we say that "gravity *causes* all unsupported heavier-than-air bodies which are close to the earth to fall," all we really are asserting is that this has always happened in the past and always will in the future (or, more precisely for Hume, that whenever we have had or will have an experience of an unsupported heavier-than-air body in the proximity of the surface of our planet, we have had, and will continue to have, an experience of its falling to the surface of our planet). But what rational grounds do we have, Hume asked, to assume, as we readily do, that the regularities that we have observed in the past will continue in the future? Certainly this belief cannot be deductively, and consequently conclusively, justified, for it is quite possible for the regularities of the past to cease in the future. What right then do we have for assuming that "the future will be like the past" or, to put it another way, "that the course of nature continues always uniformly the same"? The natural reply is, "because it always has." Implicit in such a reply, however, is our belief that the future *will continue* to be like the past because it always *has been.* But this is the very principle we are attempting to justify. Consequently, we are, Hume claimed, arguing "in a circle and taking for granted that which is the very point in question." Hume's sceptical conclusion was that in spite of the psychological confidence that we naturally place upon it, our habit of inferring that the future will be like the past *(the principle of induction)* is actually incapable of rational justification.

Uncomfortable with, but unable to logically refute his own sceptical arguments, Hume was willing to stand by the sceptical conclusions he was forced to draw. For example, returning to the problem of perception, Hume, unlike Berkeley, was willing to accept the conclusion that physical objects cease to exist when unperceived. Physical objects, as he saw it, are no more than coherent patterns of discrete and interrupted sense impressions. Nevertheless, the regularity of such sense impressions leads us imaginatively to "fill in the gaps" by falsely believing in continuously existing physical objects. Unsatisfied with such an approach, John Stuart Mill (1806–73) attempted to meet the problem of the continued existence of physical objects by enlarging the definition of a physical object to include possible as well as actual sense impressions.[4] For example, according to Mill, the belief that there is a table in an unoccupied room

[4]Such a view was suggested by Berkeley himself, but not developed.

simply means that *if* a person were to go into the room and look in the direction of the table, *then* he would have certain visual impressions and if he reached for it, *then* he would have certain tactile impressions, and so on. Berkeley's mistake, Mill believed, was to equate the existence of physical objects with actual sense impressions instead of equating them with possible sense impression. As Mill put it, physical objects are (by definition) "groups of permanent possibilities of sensations." The view that physical objects can be defined as (are "logical constructions" out of) possible sense impressions is called *phenomenalism.* Along with the strong influence of empiricism, the phenomenalistic view of perception was widely held among professional philosophers from 1930 until 1950, during the period in which the twentieth-century philosophical descendents of Hume, the logical empiricists (or logical positivists) had a strong influence upon philosophical thought. At the forefront of this movement was the *verificationist theory of meaning,* which, in its strongest form, held that "the meaning of a statement is its method of verification." Since verification, as the logical empiricists originally saw it, must in the last analysis refer to sense impressions, the logical empiricists seemed logically compelled to accept the phenomenalistic view of perception.

Enthusiasm for phenomenalism among philosophers during the heyday of logical empiricism turned to doubt and then to widespread rejection as attempts to reduce physical object statements to statements about sense impressions and the verification principle itself were subjected to forceful criticism. It soon became clear to most philosophers that physical object statements could not be defined in terms of a finite number of statements about the sense impressions individuals would have if they did such and such. First, regardless of the complexity of the analyses provided, it seemed clear that no finite set of sense impressions could ever logically entail the existence of a physical object (or to put it another way, exclude the possibility of hallucination). For example, it will not do simply to say that "A table exists in the next room" means that "If an observer were to go to the next room, he would have a certain visual experience, and if he reached out in the direction of this visual experience, he would have a certain tactile experience," for it could be possible for a person who is hallucinating to have these perceptions even though there is no table in the next room. Second, it seemed equally clear that the existence of a physical object does not in itself logically entail specific statements about the sense impressions individuals would have. For example, it will not do to say that if a table exists in the next room, a person will have certain visual and tactile sensations in its presence, for a person may not have such perceptions as a result of inattentiveness or because he has been hypnotized or anesthetized or in some other way rendered unconscious of the table's presence or perhaps because the table is blocked by some other object, and so on. . . . Some phenomenalists attempted to overcome this difficulty by referring to "normal" observers and "normal" conditions of observation. Such a maneuver, however, merely shifted the initial difficulty into the difficulty of specifying what was to count as "normal" conditions of observation (which in practice simply meant "those conditions that permit an observer to perceive things as they really are") and "normal" observers ("those who in such conditions perceive things as they really are"). Third, phenomenalistic analyses seemed incapable of being expressed purely in the language of sense impressions. For example, the claim that "A table exists in the next room" means that "a normal observer would have certain sense impressions if he went to the next room" makes reference to the notions of an "observer" and "the next room," which are not themselves sense impressions.

Given such difficulties, some philosophers now claimed that physical object statements should be seen as "theoretical" statements that organize and explain sense impression language. They disagreed, however, on how physical object statements organized and explained sense impressions. While some returned to a causal theory of perception which, like Locke's, infers the existence of "real" underlying physical entities that cause our sense perceptions and that provide for their coherence and predictability, others refused to make such an inference, seeing physical object statements as "instruments" or "calculating devices" which organize our sense perceptions and enable us to make predictions about them, but do not refer to anything beyond them. In arguing over such issues, philosophers have transformed the traditional problem of perception into the more general philosophical problem of "the cognitive status of theories" and the nature of language.

Influenced by Wittgenstein's view that many philosophical problems are a result of linguistic confusion and, consequently, should be "dissolved," rather than "solved," still other philosophers have dismissed the traditional philosophical problem of perception as a confusion. As they see it, the underlying confusion here is that we directly perceive only sense impressions and not physical objects—a confusion generated by Descartes and assumed by Locke, Berkeley, Hume, and the early logical empiricists. Once we reject this assumption, these philosophers claim, and return to the commonsense belief that we directly experience physical objects which present different appearances, the problem of perception dissolves. Their critics, however, claim that the problem does not dissolve at all but is merely covered up. And the debate continues.

The Contemporary Challenge to Empiricism

The decline in the second half of the twentieth century of philosophical support for phenomenalism and of interest in the traditional philosophical problem of perception, which played such a central role in the development of empiricism, is a sign of a deeper philosophical dissatisfaction with the basic tenets of empiricism. Influenced by Descartes' search for a foundation of knowledge built upon a bedrock of certainty and realizing that certainty could not be found in statements referring to the publicly observable physical world, the empiricists sought that bedrock in the immediate contents of one's private consciousness. While one could always be mistaken as to whether one was really observing a particular physical object, the empiricists believed that one could not doubt the contents of one's own states of consciousness—for example, that one has a particular feeling, emotion, or thought or that one has a sense impression of a particular color, sound, and so on. As the empiricists saw it, all knowledge and indeed, in the last analysis, all meaningful discourse must refer to the immediate noninferential contents of one's private states of consciousness. The simplest elements of language, on this view, consist of names of unanalyzable states of consciousness. For example, for each of us, the word "blue" is the name of a particular sense impression of color that we learned as children as our parents pointed to objects and said "blue" to us while we experienced a purely private and unanalyzable sense impression of color. As the classical empiricist saw it, language acquisition begins by attaching names to our experiences and then abstracting and compounding these experiences to form new combinations, the ultimate unanalyzable components of which originate directly from experience. Underlying such a view of language and knowledge is the belief that there are some words that refer to states of consciousness whose identification as states of consciousness of a particular type are immediate, free of any theoretical presuppositions, and certain. It is these unproblematic states of private consciousness that were seen as the foundation upon which the problematic, intersubjective structure of knowledge must ultimately rest.

According to a growing number of contemporary philosophers, this view of knowledge and language is quite wrong. Accepting Kant's view that human beings are not passive recipients of sense impressions but active agents that *interpret* these sense impressions in the light of background assumptions and conceptual categories, these philosophers echo Kant in claiming that, as the contemporary philosopher John Searle puts it:

> . . . what counts as reality . . . is a matter of the categories that we impose on the world. . . . [W]hen we experience the world we experience it *through* linguistic categories that help to shape the experiences themselves. The world doesn't come to us already sliced up into objects and experiences; what counts as an object is already a function of our system of representation. . . . The mistake is to suppose that the application of language to the world consists of attaching labels to objects that are, so to speak, self-identifying. On my view, the world divides the way we divide it, and our main way of dividing things up is language. Our concept of reality is a matter of our linguistic categories.[5]

As Searle and many other contemporary philosophers see it, the empiricists' fundamental mistake was their belief that the contents of one's state of consciousness could be stripped of their inferential or theoretical components so as to reveal the neutral sublinguistic building blocks of knowledge. This, the critics say, is quite wrong. All observation, however primitive, is necessarily interpretive and, consequently, in a broad sense, theoretical. How we see reality depends not only on what is out there, but also *what we see it as,* and what we see it as depends on the structure of our mind.

Borrowing from the ideas of Gestalt psychology, contemporary philosophers have come to emphasize the idea that perception is always of organized patterns and not of individual parts that are merely added together. For example, consider the following two pictures:

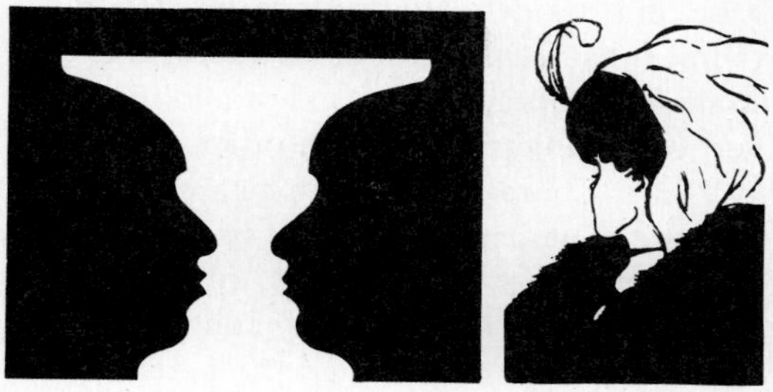

What do you see? Some people will see picture 1 as a white vase on a black background while others will see it as two black faces facing each other on a white background. Similarly, some will see picture 2 as a picture of a young girl, while others will see it as a picture of an old woman. While in a sense seeing the same thing (i.e., the same combinations of lines and colors), human beings can *observe* quite different things depending on how their minds structure what they see.

Following in the tradition of Kant, some philosophers have assumed that human beings are born with certain innate ways of structuring their experience. A famous defender of such a view is the renowned philosopher and linguist Noam Chomsky, who began to put his ideas forward in the late 1950's. Unlike the behavioral psychologists, who (like the empiricists) believed that the human mind comes into this world a "blank tablet" which passively receives the imprints of experience and then responds to them through a simple association process, Chomsky argued that the simple mechanism of association of ideas could not explain the phenomenal ability of human beings to master so easily the extraordinarily complicated task of acquiring a language. As he saw it, in order for this to be accomplished, human beings must be genetically programmed to do it. Believing that all human beings have the same genetic program as far as language acquisition is concerned, Chomsky attempted to uncover the basic lin-

[5]John Searle, interview in Brian Magee, *Men of Ideas* (New York: Viking Press, 1978), p. 184.

guistic structure that corresponds to this genetic program. Translating a fundamental belief of Kant into modern linguistic terms, Chomsky claimed that this structure puts inescapable constraints on our capacity to understand the world and communicate with each other.

While Chomsky has emphasized the invariance of human categories of linguistic interpretation, other philosophers, notably those with an interest in the history and philosophy of science, have emphasized the practical and variable nature of the theoretical concepts we utilize to organize the contents of our experiences. These philosophers claim that rival scientific theories provide us with rival conceptual frameworks which can never directly collide. We choose one theory over another not because the rejected one has been shown by neutral nontheoretical observation to be false, but because the one that we accept gives simpler and more economical explanations. From this point of view, sense experiences do not function as the foundations of knowledge but as stimuli provoking us to make revisions in our *system of beliefs* in the simplest and most economical fashion—revisions from which statements about immediate sense experiences are not themselves immune.

33. A DEFENSE OF A CAUSAL THEORY OF PERCEPTION

Bertrand Russell

(For a biographical sketch of Bertrand Russell, see Selection #1.)

In the selection that follows, Russell defends a causal theory of perception that has its origins in Descartes and Locke. Following in their tradition, Russell argues that physical objects are not the **direct objects of perception,** but are **inferred.** Since the content of one's sense experience when one perceives a physical object can be indistinguishable, in itself, from an illusory experience it seems clear to Russell, as it did to Descartes and Locke, that the direct objects of perception are private sense experiences and not physical objects. The belief in unobservable external physical objects that cause our sense experiences is a logical inference that explains the coherence of these experiences. The nature of these inferred external physical objects is a scientific question. Like Descartes and Locke before him, Russell is struck by the differences between our sense experiences of qualities, which we naively see as existing "in" external physical objects, and the true nature of physical objects, revealed to us by science. Since the distinction between private sense experiences and inferred external physical objects is central to the causal theory of perception, critical realists give a special name to the sense experiences which they see as the direct, noninferential content of perception. Russell calls these sense experiences **percepts.** (The most common term used to describe them by twentieth-century philosophers has been **sense data,** or in the singular, **sense datum.**)

When we consider perception—visual or auditory—of an external event, there are three different matters to be examined. There is first the process in the outside world, from the event to the percipient's body; there is next the process in his body, in so far as this can be known by an outside observer; lastly, there is the question, which must be faced sooner or later, whether the percipient can perceive something of the process in his body which no other observer could perceive. We will take these points in order.

If it is to be possible to "perceive" an event not in the percipient's body, there must be a physical process in the outer world such that, when a certain event occurs, it produces a stimulus of a certain kind at the surface of the percipient's body. Suppose, for example, that pictures of different animals are exhibited on a magic lantern to a class of children, and all the children are asked to say the name of each animal in turn. We may assume that the children are sufficiently familiar with animals to say "cat," "dog," "giraffe," "hippopotamus," etc., at the right moments. We must then suppose—taking the physical world for granted—that some process travels from each picture to the eyes of the various children, retaining throughout these journeys such peculiarities, that, when the process reaches their eyes, it can in one case stimulate the word "cat" and in another the word "dog." All this the physical theory of light provides for. But there is one interesting point . . . that should be noticed in this connection. If the usual physical theory of light is correct, the various children will receive stimuli which differ greatly according to their distance and direction from the picture, and according to the way the light falls. . . .

The fact that it is possible for a number of people to perceive the same noise or the same colored pattern obviously depends upon the fact that a physical process can travel outward from a center and retain certain of its characteristics unchanged, or very little changed. The most notable of such characteristics is frequency in a wave-motion. That, no doubt, affords a biological reason for the fact that our most delicate senses, sight and hearing, are sensitive to frequencies, which determine color in what we see and pitch in what we hear. If there were not, in the physical world, processes spreading out from centers and retaining certain characters practically unchanged, it would be impossible for different percipients to perceive the same object from different points of view, and we should not have been able to discover that we all live in a common world.

We come now to the process in the percipient's body, in so far as this can be perceived by an outside observer. This raises no new philosophical problems, because we are still concerned, as before, with the perception of events outside the observer's body. The observer, now, is supposed to be a physiologist, observing, say, what goes on in the eye when light falls upon it. His means of knowing are, in principle, exactly the same as the observation of dead matter. An event in an eye upon which light is falling causes light-waves to travel in a certain manner until they reach the eye of the physiologist. They there cause a process in the physiologist's eye and optic nerve and brain, which ends in what he calls "seeing what happens in the eye he is observing." But this event, which happens in the physiologist, is not what happened in the eye he was observing; it is only connected with this by a complicated causal chain. Thus our knowledge of physiology is no more direct or intimate than our knowledge of processes in dead matter; we do not know any more about

Source: From Chapter XII ("Physics and Perception") and Chapter XIII ("Physical and Perceptual Space") of *The Outline of Philosophy* published by George Allen and Unwin, 1927. The book was published in the United States by W. W. Norton and Co., under the title *Philosophy.*

our eyes than about the trees and fields and clouds that we see by means of them. The event which happens when a physiologist observes an eye is an event in him, not on the eye that he is observing.

. . . It may be said that we do not in fact proceed to *infer* the physical world from our perceptions, but that we begin at once with a rough-and-ready knowledge of the physical world, and only at a late stage of sophistication compel ourselves to regard our knowledge of the physical world as an inference. What is valid in this statement is the fact that our knowledge of the physical world is not at first inferential, but that is only because we take our percepts to *be* the physical world. Sophistication and philosophy come in at the stage at which we realize that the physical world cannot be identified with our percepts. When my boy was three years old, I showed him Jupiter, and told him that Jupiter was larger than earth. He insisted that I must be speaking of some other Jupiter, because, as he patiently explained, the one he was seeing was obviously quite small. After some efforts, I had to give it up and leave him unconvinced. In the case of the heavenly bodies, adults have got used to the idea that what is really there can only be *inferred* from what they see. . . .

. . . A lamp at the top of a tall building might produce the same visual stimulus as Jupiter, or at any rate one practically indistinguishable from that produced by Jupiter. A blow on the nose might make us "see stars." Theoretically, it should be possible to apply a stimulus direct to the optic nerve, which should give us a visual sensation. Thus when we think we see Jupiter, we may be mistaken. We are less likely to be mistaken if we say that the surface of the eye is being stimulated in a certain way, and still less likely to be mistaken if we say that the optic nerve is being stimulated in a certain way. We do not eliminate the risk of error completely unless we confine ourselves to saying that an event of a certain sort is happening in the brain; this statement may still be true if we see Jupiter in a dream. . . .

. . . The sun looks red in a London fog, grass looks blue through blue spectacles, everything looks yellow to a person suffering from jaundice. But suppose you ask: What color are you seeing? The person who answers, in these cases, red for the sun, blue for the grass, and yellow for the sickroom of the jaundiced patient, is answering quite truly. And in each of these cases he is stating something that he *knows*. What he knows in such cases is what I call a "percept." I shall contend later that, from the standpoint of physics, a percept is in the brain; for the present, I am only concerned to say that a percept is what is most indubitable in our knowledge of the world. . . .

. . . We are often misled as to what is happening, either by peculiarities of the medium between the object and our bodies, or by unusual states of our bodies, or by a temporary or permanent abnormality in the brain. But in all these cases *something* is really happening, as to which, if we turn our attention to it, we can obtain knowledge that is not misleading. At one time when, owing to illness, I had been taking a great deal of quinine, I became hypersensitive to noise, so that when the nurse rustled the newspaper I thought she was spilling a scuttle of coals on the floor. The interpretation was mistaken, but it was quite true that I heard a loud noise. It is commonplace that a man whose leg has been amputated can still feel pains in it; here again, he does really feel the pains, and is only mistaken in his belief that they come from his leg. A percept is an observable event, but its interpretation as knowledge of this or that event in the physical world is liable to be mistaken, for reasons which physics and physiology can make fairly clear. . . . [1]

Perhaps there is nothing so difficult for the imagination as to teach it to feel about space as modern science compels us to think. This is the task which must [now] be atempted. . . . The gist of the matter is that percepts . . . are

[1] The selection from Chapter XII ends here and the selection from Chapter XIII begins. EDITOR'S NOTE.

in our heads; that percepts are what we can know with most certainty. . . .

But when I say that my percepts are in my head, I am saying something which is ambiguous until the different kinds of space have been explained, for the statement is only true in connection with *physical* space. There is also a space in our percepts, and of this space the statement would not be true. When I say that there is space in our percepts, I mean nothing at all difficult to understand. I mean—to take the sense of sight, which is the most important in this connection—that in what we see at one time there is up and down, right and left, inside and outside. If we see, say, a circle on a blackboard, all these relations exist within what we see. The circle has a top half and a bottom half, a right-hand half and a left-hand half, an inside and an outside. Those relations alone are enough to make up a space of sorts. But the space of every-day life is filled out with what we derive from touch and movement—how a thing feels when we touch it, and what movements are necessary in order to grasp it. Other elements also come into the genesis of the space in which everybody believes who has not been troubled by philosophy; but it is unnecessary for our purposes to go into this question any more deeply. The point that concerns us is that a man's percepts are private to himself: what I see, no one else sees; what I hear, no one else hears; what I touch, no one else touches; and so on. True, others hear and see something very like what I hear and see, if they are suitably placed; but there are always differences. Sounds are less loud at a distance; objects change their visual appearance according to the laws of perspective. Therefore it is impossible for two persons at the same time to have exactly identical percepts. It follows that the space of percepts, like the percepts, must be private; there are as many perceptual spaces as there are percipients. My percept of a table is outside my percept of my head, in my perceptual space; but it does not follow that it is outside my head as a physical object in physical space. Physical space is neutral and public: in this space, all my percepts are in my head, even the most distant star *as I see it*. Physical and perceptual space have relations, but they are not identical, and failure to grasp the difference between them is a potent source of confusion.

To say that you see a star when you see the light that has come from it is no more correct than to say that you see New Zealand when you see a New Zealander in London. Your perception when (as we say) you see a star is causally connected, in the first instance, with what happens in the brain, the optic nerve, and the eye, then with a light-wave which, according to physics, can be traced back to the star as its source. Your sensations will be closely similar if the light comes from a lamp at the top of a mast. The physical space in which you believe the "real" star to be is an elaborate inference; what is given is the private space in which the speck of light you see is situated. It is still an open question whether the space of sight has depth, or is merely a surface, as Berkeley contended. This does not matter for our purposes. Even if we admit that sight alone shows a difference between an object a few inches from the eyes and an object several feet distant, yet you certainly cannot, by sight alone, see that a cloud is less distant than a fixed star, though you may *infer* that it is, because it can hide the star. The world of astronomy, from the point of view of sight, is a surface. If you were put in a dark room with little holes cut in the ceiling in the pattern of the stars letting light come through, there would be nothing in your immediate visual data to show that you were not "seeing the stars." This illustrates what I mean by saying that what you see is *not* "out there". . . .

We learn in infancy that we can sometimes touch objects we see, and sometimes not. When we cannot touch them at once, we can sometimes do so by walking to them. That is to say, we learn to correlate sensations of sight with sensations of touch, and sometimes with sensations of movement followed by sensations of touch. In this way we locate our sensations in a three-dimensional world. Those which involve sight alone we think of as "external," but there is no justification for this view. What you see when you see a star is just as internal as what you feel when you feel a headache. That is to say, it is internal from the standpoint of *physical* space. It is distant in your private space, because it is not associated with sensations of touch, and cannot be associated with them by means of any journey you can perform. . . .

To make the matter definite, let us suppose that a physiologist is observing a living brain—no longer an impossible supposition, as it would have been formerly. It is natural to suppose that what the physiologist sees is in the brain he is observing. But if we are speaking of physical space, what the physiologist sees is in his own brain. It is in no sense in the brain that he is observing, though it is in the percept of that brain, which occupies part of the physiologist's perceptual space. Causal continuity makes the matter perfectly evident: light-waves travel from the brain that is being observed to the eye of the physiologist, at which they only arrive after an interval of time, which is finite though short. The physiologist sees what he is observing only after the light-waves have reached his eye; therefore the event which constitutes his seeing comes at the end of a series of events which travel from the observed brain into the brain of the physiologist. We cannot, without a preposterous kind of discontinuity, suppose that the physiologist's percept, which comes at the end of this series, is anywhere else but in the physiologist's head. . . .

It is extraordinarily difficult to divest ourselves of the belief that the physical world is the world we perceive by sight and touch; even if, in our philosophic moments, we are aware that this is an error, we nevertheless fall into it again as soon as we are off our guard. The notion that what we see is "out there" in physical space is one which cannot survive while we are grasping the difference between what physics supposes to be really happening, and what our senses show us as happening; but it is sure to return and plague us when we begin to forget the argument. Only long reflection can make a radically new point of view familiar and easy.

Our illustrations hitherto have been taken from the sense of sight; let us now take one from the sense of touch. Suppose that, with your eyes shut, you let your finger-tip press against a hard table. What is really happening? The physicist says that your finger-tip and the table consist, roughly speaking, of vast numbers of electrons and protons; more correctly, each electron and proton is to be thought of as a collection of processes of radiation, but we can ignore this for our present purposes. Although you think you are touching the table, no electron or proton in your finger ever really touches an electron or proton in the table, because this would develop an infinite force. When you press, repulsions are set up between parts of your finger and parts of the table. If you try to press upon a liquid or a gas, there is room in it for the parts that are repelled to get away. But if you press a hard solid, the electrons and protons that try to get away, because electrical forces from your finger repel them, are unable to do so, because they are crowded close to others which elbow them back to more or less their original position, like people in a dense crowd. Therefore the more you press the more they repel your finger. The repulsion consists of electrical forces, which set up in the nerves a current whose nature is not very definitely known. This current runs into the brain, and there has effects which, so far as the physiologist is concerned, are almost wholly conjectural. But there is one effect which is not conjectural, and that is the sensation of touch. This effect . . . is associated by us with the finger-tip. But the sensation is the same if, by artificial means, the parts of the nerve nearer the brain are suitably stimulated—e.g., if your hand has been amputated and the right nerves are skillfully manipulated. Thus our confidence that touch affords evidence of the existence of bodies at the place which we think is being touched is quite misplaced. As a rule we are right, but we can be wrong; there is nothing of the nature of an infallible revelation about the matter. And even in the most favorable case, the perception of touch is something very different from the mad dance of electrons and protons trying to jazz out of each other's way, which is what physics maintains is really taking place at your finger-tip. . . .

DISCUSSION QUESTIONS

1. What does Russell mean when he says, "The event which happens when a physiologist observes an eye is an event in him, not on the eye he is observing"?

2. What does Russell mean when he says, "What I see, no one else sees; what I hear, no one else hears"?

3. Why does Russell claim that "sophistication and philosophy come in at the stage at which we realize that the physical world cannot be identified with our percepts"?

4. According to Russell, what is the difference between **perceptual** and **physical** space?

34. THE CLASSICAL DEFENSE OF IDEALISM

George Berkeley

GEORGE BERKELEY (pronounced BARK-lee) (1685–1753) was an Irish philosopher and Anglican bishop noted primarily for his rejection of mind-independent physical objects. A versatile man, Berkeley was active in Irish politics as well as in the Church. He spent two and a half years in the British colony of Rhode Island, vainly attempting to raise money to set up a college in Bermuda. A writer on various subjects, Berkeley is noted for his clear and forceful writing style and his formidable analytic powers. He wrote a poem that contains the famous line "Westward the course of empire takes its way." As a result of this poem, a town in Northern California took Berkeley's name as its own (but pronounced it differently).

As a philosopher, Berkeley's central aim was to reconcile the science of his day with Christianity. Berkeley's immaterialistic philosophy was his attempt to avoid the atheism he saw implicit in the materialism that was taken to underlie science. Berkeley was a strong critic of the philosophic tendency to suppose that abstractions refer to abstract entities. Berkeley utilized his extreme anti-abstractionism to criticize Newton's view of absolute time and space (anticipating Einstein's theory of relativity).[1] He also attacked Newton's concept of infinitesimals (infinitely divisible quantities), which was the central notion in Newton's development of the calculus.

[1]According to Newtonian theory, space and time exist independently of objects—i.e., it is possible to conceive a universe of space and time existing without any objects. Berkeley, as well as Gottfried Leibniz (1646–1716) argued, however, that space and time are merely *relations* between objects, so that if there were no objects, there would be no space and time. Berkeley's and Leibniz' arguments against the Newtonian view of space and time were of a purely conceptual nature. As they saw it, the Newtonian notion of a framework of absolute space and time was a *meaningless* framework. Given the impressive explanatory and predictive power of Newtonian mechanics, the relativistic view of space and time was rejected in favor of the Newtonian view until the twentieth century, when Einstein's theory of relativity marshalled impressive theoretical arguments and empirical evidence in its support.

Although not a mathematician, Berkeley exposed the weak conceptual foundations of this notion. His criticisms influenced mathematicians and contributed to the clarification of the structure of the calculus—the notion of infinitesimals eventually being replaced with the more precise notion of limits.

In addition to his influence on mathematics, Berkeley contributed to the science of optics. As a philosopher of science, he criticized the tendency of scientists and philosophers to see the forces and attractions of Newtonian physics as "real things" that exist and act in nature. They should, he claimed, be seen instead as mathematical formulas that enable us to predict the sequence of our experiences. This view anticipated the influential view of the nature of science known as **instrumentalism,** associated with the American pragmatist John Dewey and his followers.

Berkeley's defense of his idealistic philosophy is contained in his two major philosophical works, **A Treatise Concerning the Principles of Human Knowledge** and his later-published and more lively **Three Dialogues between Hylas and Philonous.** The selection that follows is from the first of these two works. In the Introduction to this work (parts of which are included in our excerpt), Berkeley contends that his, not Locke's, view of perception is the view of common sense. In speaking of physical objects as the external unobservable causes of our sensations, Locke makes it impossible for us to know anything about these physical objects, Berkeley claims. As Berkeley sees it, the way to avoid this scepticism is to equate physical objects with our sense experiences. As Berkeley put it in a memorable phrase, "All the choir of heaven and furniture of the earth, in a word all those bodies which compose the mighty frame of the world have not any subsistence without a mind, that their being is to be perceived." Minds and their ideas are the only things that exist, Berkeley contends. Physical objects exist only as ideas in the mind of some perceiver.

Introduction

Philosophy being nothing else but the study of wisdom and truth, it may with reason be expected, that those who have spent most time and pains in it should enjoy a greater calm and serenity of mind, a greater clearness and evidence of knowledge, and be less disturbed with doubts and difficulties than other men. Yet so it is we see the illiterate bulk of mankind that walk the high-road of plain, common sense, and are governed by the dictates of Nature, for the most part easy and undisturbed. To them nothing that's familiar appears unaccountable or difficult to comprehend. They complain not of any want of evidence in their senses, and are out of all danger of becoming *sceptics.* But no sooner do we depart from sense and instinct to follow the light of a superior principle, to reason, meditate, and reflect on the nature of things, but a thousand scruples spring up in our minds, concerning those things which before we seemed fully to comprehend. Prejudices and errors of sense do from all parts discover themselves to our view; and endeavouring to correct these by reason we are insensibly drawn into uncouth paradoxes, difficulties, and inconsistences, which multiply and grow upon us as we advance in speculation; till at length, having wander'd

Source: George Berkeley's *A Treatise Concerning the Principles of Human Knowledge,* first published in 1710.

through many intricate mazes, we find our selves just where we were, or, which is worse, sit down in a forlorn scepticism. . . .

. . . I am inclined to think that the far greater part, if not all, of those difficulties which have hitherto amused philosophers, and blocked up the way to knowledge, are entirely owing to our selves. That we have first raised a dust, and then complain, we cannot see. . . .

1 It is evident to any one who takes a survey of the objects of human knowledge, that they are either ideas actually imprinted on the senses, or else such as are perceived by attending to the passions and operations of the mind, or lastly ideas formed by help of memory and imagination, either compounding, dividing, or barely representing those originally perceived in the aforesaid ways. By sight I have the ideas of light and colours with their several degrees and variations. By touch I perceive, for example, hard and soft, heat and cold, motion and resistance, and of all these more and less either as to quantity or degree. Smelling furnishes me with odours; the palate with tastes, and hearing conveys sounds to the mind in all their variety of tone and composition. And as several of these are observed to accompany each other, they come to be marked by one name, and so to be reputed as one thing. Thus, for example, a certain colour, taste, smell, figure and consistence having been observed to go together, are accounted one distinct thing, signified by the name *apple.* Other collections of ideas constitute a stone, a tree, a book, and the like sensible things; which, as they are pleasing or disagreeable, excite the passions of love, hatred, joy, grief, and so forth.

2 But besides all that endless variety of ideas or objects of knowledge, there is likewise something which knows or perceives them, and exercises divers operations, as willing, imagining, remembering about them. This perceiving, active being is what I call *mind, spirit, soul* or *my self.* By which words I do not denote any one of my ideas, but a thing entirely distinct from them, wherein they exist, or, which is the same thing, whereby they are perceived; for the existence of an idea consists in being perceived.

3 That neither our thoughts, nor passions, nor ideas formed by the imagination, exist without the mind, is what every body will allow. And it seems no less evident that the various sensations or ideas imprinted on the sense, however blended or combined together (that is, whatever objects they compose) cannot exist otherwise than in a mind perceiving them. I think an intuitive knowledge may be obtained of this, by any one that shall attend to what is meant by the term *exist* when applied to sensible things. The table I write on, I say, exists, that is, I see and feel it; and if I were out of my study I should say it existed, meaning thereby that if I was in my study I might perceive it, or that some other spirit actually does perceive it. There was an odour, that is, it was smelled; there was a sound, that is to say, it was heard; a colour or figure, and it was perceived by sight or touch. This is all that I can understand by these and the like expressions. For as to what is said of the absolute existence of unthinking things without any relation to their being perceived, that seems perfectly unintelligible. Their *esse* is *percipi,*[2] nor is it possible they should have any existence, out of the minds or thinking things which perceive them.

4 It is indeed an opinion strangely prevailing amongst men, that houses, mountains, rivers, and in a word all sensible objects have an existence natural or real, distinct from their being perceived by the understanding. But with how great an assurance and acquiescence soever this principle may be entertained in the world; yet whoever shall find it in his heart to call it in question, may, if I mistake not, perceive it to involve a manifest contradiction. For what are the forementioned objects but the things we

[2]That is, "their existence consists in their being perceived." EDITOR'S NOTE.

perceive by sense, and what do we perceive besides our own ideas or sensations; . . .

5 . . . Light and colors, heat and cold, extension and figures, in a word the things we see and feel, what are they but so many sensations, notions, ideas or impressions on the sense; and is it possible to separate, even in thought, any of these from perception? . . . I may indeed divide in my thoughts or conceive apart from each other those things which, perhaps, I never perceived by sense so divided. Thus I imagine the trunk of a human body without the limbs, or conceive the smell of a rose without thinking on the rose itself. . . . But my conceiving or imagining power does not extend beyond the possibility of . . . perception. Hence as it is impossible for me to see or feel anything without an actual sensation of that thing, so is it impossible for me to conceive in my thoughts any sensible thing or object distinct from the sensation or perception of it.

6 Some truths there are so near and obvious to the mind, that a man need only open his eyes to see them. Such I take this important one to be, to wit, that all the choir of heaven and furniture of the earth, in a word all those bodies which compose the mighty frame of the world, have not any subsistence without a mind, that their being is to be perceived or known; that consequently so long as they are not actually perceived by me, or do not exist in my mind or that of any other created spirit, they must either have no existence at all, or else subsist in the mind of some eternal spirit: it being perfectly unintelligible . . . to attribute to any single part of them an existence independent of a spirit. To be convinced of which, the reader need only reflect and try to separate in his own thoughts the being of a sensible thing from its being perceived.

7 From what has been said, it follows, there is not any other substance than *spirit,* or that which perceives. But for the fuller proof of this point, let it be considered, the sensible qualities are colour, figure, motion, smell, taste, and such like, that is, the ideas perceived by sense. Now for an idea to exist in an unperceiving thing, is a manifest contradiction; for to have an idea is all one as to perceive: that therefore wherein colour, figure, and the like qualities exist, must perceive them; hence it is clear there can be no unthinking substance or *substratum* of those ideas.

8 But say you, though the ideas themselves do not exist without the mind, yet there may be things like them whereof they are copies or resemblances, which things exist without the mind, in an unthinking substance. I answer, an idea can be like nothing but an idea; a colour or figure can be like nothing but another colour or figure. If we look but ever so little into our thoughts, we shall find it impossible for us to conceive a likeness except only between our ideas. Again, I ask whether those supposed originals or external things, of which our ideas are the pictures or representations, be themselves perceivable or no? If they are, then they are ideas, and we have gained our point; but if you say they are not, I appeal to anyone whether it be sense, to assert a colour is like something which is invisible; hard or soft, like something which is intangible; and so of the rest.

9 Some there are who make a distinction betwixt *primary* and *secondary* qualities: by the former, they mean extension, figure, motion, rest, solidity or impenetrability and number: by the latter they denote all other sensible qualities, as colours, sounds, tastes, and so forth. The ideas we have of these they acknowledge not to be the resemblances of any thing existing without the mind or unperceived; but they will have our ideas of the primary qualities to be patterns or images of things which exist without the mind, in an unthinking substance which they call *matter.* By matter therefore we are to understand an inert, senseless substance, in which extension, figure, and motion, do actually subsist. But it is evident from what we have already shewn, that extension, figure and motion are

only ideas existing in the mind, and that an idea can be like nothing but another idea, and that consequently . . . they [cannot] exist in an unperceiving substance. Hence it is plain, that the very notion of what is called *matter* or *corporeal substance,* involves a contradiction in it.

10 They who assert that figure, motion, and the rest of the primary or original qualities do exist without the mind, in unthinking substances, do at the same time acknowledge that colours, sounds, heat, cold, and such like secondary qualities, do not, which they tell us are sensations existing in the mind alone, that depend on and are occasioned by the different size, texture and motion of the minute particles of matter. This they take for an undoubted truth, which they can demonstrate beyond all exception. Now if it be certain, that those original qualities are inseparably united with the other sensible qualities, and not, even in thought, capable of being abstracted from them, it plainly follows that they exist only in the mind. But I desire any one to reflect and try, whether he can by any abstraction of thought, conceive the extension and motion of a body, without all other sensible qualities. For my own part, I see evidently that it is not in my power to frame an idea of a body extended and moved, but I must withal give it some colour or other sensible quality which is acknowledged to exist only in the mind. In short, extension, figure, and motion, abstracted from all other qualities, are inconceivable. Where therefore the other sensible qualities are, there must these be also, to wit, in the mind and no where else. . . .

14 I shall farther add, that after the same manner, as modern philosophers prove certain sensible qualities to have no existence in matter, or without the mind, the same thing may be likewise proved of all other sensible qualities whatsoever. Thus, for instance, it is said that heat and cold are affections only of the mind, and not at all patterns of real beings, existing in the corporeal substances which excite them, for that the same body which appears cold to one hand, seems warm to another. Now why may we not as well argue that figure and extension are not patterns or resemblances of qualities existing in matter, because to the same eye at different stations, or eyes of a different texture at the same station, they appear various, and cannot therefore be the images of any thing settled and determinate without the mind? Again, it is proved that sweetness is not really in the sapid thing, because the thing remaining unaltered the sweetness is changed into bitter, as in case of a fever or otherwise vitiated palate. Is it not as reasonable to say, that motion is not without the mind, since if the succession of ideas in the mind become swifter, the motion, it is acknowledged, shall appear slower without any alteration in any external object.

15 In short, let anyone consider those arguments, which are thought manifestly to prove that colours and tastes exist only in the mind, and he shall find they may with equal force, be brought to prove the same thing of extension, figure, and motion. Though it must be confessed this method of arguing doth not so much prove that there is no extension or colour in an outward object, as that we do not know by sense which is the true extension or colour of the object. But the arguments foregoing plainly shew it to be impossible that any colour or extension at all, or other sensible quality whatsoever, should exist in an unthinking subject without the mind, or in truth, that there should be any such thing as an outward object.

16 But let us examine a little the received opinion. It is said extension is a mode[3] or accident[4] of matter, and that matter is the *substratum* that supports it. Now I desire that you would explain what is meant by matter's *supporting* extension: say you, I have no idea of matter, and therefore cannot explain it. I answer, though you have no positive, yet if you

[3]The manner in which a substance is manifested. EDITOR'S NOTE.

[4]A property of a substance. EDITOR'S NOTE.

have any meaning at all, you must at least have a relative idea of matter; though you know not what it is, yet you must be supposed to know what relation it bears to accidents, and what is meant by its supporting them. It is evident *support* cannot here be taken in its usual or literal sense, as when we say that pillars support a building: in what sense therefore must it be taken?

17 If we inquire into what the most accurate philosophers declare themselves to mean by *material substance;* we shall find them acknowledge, they have no other meaning annexed to those sounds, but the idea of being in general, together with the relative notion of its supporting accidents. The general idea of being appeareth to me the most abstract and incomprehensible of all other; and as for its supporting accidents, this, as we have just now observed, cannot be understood in the common sense of those words; it must therefore be taken in some other sense, but what that is they do not explain. So that when I consider the two parts or branches which make the signification of the words *material substance,* I am convinced there is no distinct meaning annexed to them. But why should we trouble ourselves any farther, in discussing this material *substratum* or support of figure and motion, and other sensible qualities? Does it not suppose they have an existence without the mind? And is not this . . . altogether inconceivable?

18 But though it were possible that solid, figured, moveable substances may exist without the mind, corresponding to the ideas we have of bodies, yet how is it possible for us to know this? Either we must know it by sense, or by reason. As for our senses, by them we have the knowledge only of our sensations, ideas, or those things that are immediately perceived by sense, call them what you will: but they do not inform us that things exist without the mind, or unperceived, like to those which are perceived. This the materialists themselves acknowledge. It remains therefore that if we have any knowledge at all of external things, it must be by reason, inferring their existence from what is immediately perceived by sense. But what reason can induce us to believe the existence of bodies without the mind, from what we perceive, since the very patrons of matter themselves do not pretend, there is any necessary connexion betwixt them and our ideas? I say it is granted on all hands (and what happens in dreams, phrensies, and the like, puts it beyond dispute) that it is possible we might be affected with all the ideas we have now, though no bodies existed without, resembling them. Hence it is evident the supposition of external bodies is not necessary for the producing our ideas: since it is granted they are produced sometimes, and might possibly be produced always in the same order we see them in at present, without their concurrence.

19 But though we might possibly have all our sensations without them, yet perhaps it may be thought easier to conceive and explain the manner of their production, by supposing external bodies in their likeness rather than otherwise; and so it might be at least probable there are such things as bodies that excite their ideas in our minds. But neither can this be said; for though we give the materialists their external bodies, they by their own confession are never the nearer knowing how our ideas are produced: since they own themselves unable to comprehend in what manner body can act upon spirit, or how it is possible it should imprint any idea in the mind. Hence it is evident the production of ideas or sensations in our minds, can be no reason why we should suppose matter or corporeal substances, since that is acknowledged to remain equally inexplicable with, or without this supposition. If therefore it were possible for bodies to exist without the mind, yet to hold they do so, must needs be a very precarious opinion; since it is to suppose, without any reason at all, that God has created innumerable beings that are entirely useless, and serve to no manner of purpose.

20 In short, if there were external bodies, it is impossible we should ever come to know it; and if there were not, we might have the very same reasons to think there were that we have now. Suppose, what no one can deny possible, an intelligence, without the help of external bodies, to be affected with the same train of sensations or ideas that you are, imprinted in the same order and with like vividness in his mind. I ask whether that intelligence hath not all the reason to believe the existence of corporeal substances, represented by his ideas, and exciting them in his mind, that you can possibly have for believing the same thing? Of this there can be no question; which one consideration is enough to make any reasonable person suspect the strength of whatever arguments he may think himself to have, for the existence of bodies without the mind. . . .

22 I am afraid I have given cause to think me needlessly prolix[5] in handling this subject. For to what purpose is it to dilate on that which may be demonstrated with the utmost evidence in a line or two, to anyone that is capable of the least reflexion? It is but looking into your own thoughts, and so trying whether you can conceive it possible for a sound, or figure, or motion, or colour, to exist without the mind, or unperceived. This easy trial may make you see, that what you contend for, is a downright contradiction. Insomuch that I am content to put the whole upon this issue; if you can but conceive it possible for one extended moveable substance, or in general, for any one idea or any thing like an idea, to exist otherwise than in a mind perceiving it, I shall readily give up the cause: And as for [any external body] which you contend for, I shall grant you its existence, though you cannot either give me any reason why you believe it exists, or assign any use to it when it is supposed to exist. I say, the bare possibility of your opinion's being true, shall pass for an argument that it is so.

[5]Wordy. EDITOR'S NOTE.

23 But say you, surely there is nothing easier than to imagine trees, for instance, in a park, or books existing in a closet, and no body by to perceive them. I answer, you may so, there is no difficulty in it: but what is all this, I beseech you, more than framing in your mind certain ideas which you call *books* and *trees,* and at the same time omitting to frame the idea of any one that may perceive them? But do not you your self perceive or think of them all the while? This therefore is nothing to the purpose: it only shows you have the power of imagining or forming ideas in your mind; but it doth not shew that you can conceive it possible, the objects of your thought may exist without the mind: to make out this, it is necessary that you conceive them existing unconceived or unthought of, which is a manifest [contradiction]. When we do our utmost to conceive the existence of external bodies, we are all the while only contemplating our own ideas. But the mind taking no notice of itself, is deluded to think it can and doth conceive bodies existing unthought of or without the mind; though at the same time they are apprehended by or exist in itself. A little attention will discover to any one the truth and evidence of what is here said, and make it unnecessary to insist on any other proofs against the existence of material substances. . . .

25 . . . A little attention will discover to us that the very being of an idea implies passiveness and inertness in it, insomuch that it is impossible for an idea to do any thing, or, strictly speaking, to be the cause of any thing. . . . Whence it plainly follows that extension, figure and motion, cannot be the cause of our sensations. To say therefore, that these are the effects of powers resulting from the configuration, number, motion, and size of corpuscles, must certainly be false.

26 We perceive a continual succession of ideas, some are anew excited, others are changed or totally disappear. There is therefore some cause of these ideas whereon they depend, and

which produces and changes them. That this cause cannot be any quality or idea or combination of ideas, is clear from the preceding section. It must therefore be a substance; but it has been shewn that there is no corporeal or material substance: it remains therefore that the cause of ideas is an incorporeal active substance or spirit.

27 A spirit is one simple, undivided, active being. . . . Hence there can be no idea formed of a soul or spirit: for all ideas whatever, being passive and inert, *vide Sect.* 25, they cannot represent unto us, by way of image or likeness, that which acts. . . . Such is the nature of *spirit* or that which acts, that it cannot be of it self perceived, but only by the effects which it produceth. . . .

28 I find I can excite ideas in my mind at pleasure, and vary and shift the scene as oft as I think fit. It is no more than willing, and straightway this or that idea arises in my fancy: and by the same power it is obliterated, and makes way for another. This making and unmaking of ideas doth very properly denominate the mind active. Thus much is certain, and grounded on experience: but when we talk of unthinking agents, or of exciting ideas exclusive of volition, we only amuse our selves with words.

29 But whatever power I may have over my own thoughts, I find the ideas actually perceived by sense have not a like dependence on my will. When in broad day-light I open my eyes, it is not in my power to choose whether I shall see or no, or to determine what particular objects shall present themselves to my view; and so likewise as to the hearing and other senses, the ideas imprinted on them are not creatures of my will. There is therefore some other will or spirit that produces them.

30 The ideas of sense are more strong, lively, and distinct than those of the imagination; they have likewise a steadiness, order, and coherence, and are not excited at random, as those which are the effects of human wills often are, but in a regular train or series, the admirable connexion whereof sufficiently testifies the wisdom and benevolence of its Author. Now the set rules or established methods, wherein the mind we depend on excites in us the ideas of sense, are called the *Laws of Nature:* and these we learn by experience, which teaches us that such and such ideas are intended with such and such other ideas, in the ordinary course of things.

31 This gives us a sort of foresight, which enables us to regulate our actions for the benefit of life. And without this we should be eternally at a loss: we could not know how to obtain any thing that might procure us the least pleasure, or remove the least pain of sense. That food nourishes, sleep refreshes, and fire warms us; that to sow in the seed-time is the way to reap in the harvest, and, in general, that to obtain such or such ends, such or such means are conducive, all this we know . . . by the observation of the settled laws of Nature, without which we should be all in uncertainty and confusion, and a grown man no more know how to manage himself in the affairs of life, than an infant just born.

32 And yet this consistent uniform working, which so evidently displays the goodness and wisdom of that governing spirit whose will constitutes the Laws of Nature, is so far from leading our thoughts to him, that it rather sends them a wandering after second causes. For when we perceive certain ideas of sense constantly followed by other ideas, and we know this is not of our doing, we forthwith attribute power and agency to the ideas themselves, and make one the cause of another, than which nothing can be more absurd and unintelligible. Thus, for example, having observed that when we perceive by sight a certain round luminous figure, we at the same time perceive by touch the idea or sensation called *heat,* we do from thence conclude the sun to be the cause of heat. And in like manner perceiving the motion and collision of bodies to be attended with sound, we are inclined to think the latter an effect of the former.

33 The ideas imprinted on the senses by the Author of Nature are called *real things:* and those excited in the imagination being less regular, vivid and constant, are more properly termed *ideas,* or *images of things,* which they copy and represent. But then our sensations, be they never so vivid and distinct, are nevertheless *ideas,* that is, they exist in the mind, or are perceived by it, as truly as the ideas of its own framing. The ideas of sense are allowed to have more reality in them, that is, to be more strong, orderly, and coherent than the creatures of the mind; but this is no argument that they exist without the mind. They are also less dependent on the spirit, or thinking substance which perceives them, in that they are excited by the will of another and more powerful spirit: yet still they are *ideas,* and certainly no *idea,* whether faint or strong, can exist otherwise than in a mind perceiving it. . . .

45 . . . it will be objected that from the foregoing principles it follows, things are every moment annihilated and created anew. The objects of sense exist only when they are perceived: the trees therefore are in the garden, or the chairs in the parlour, no longer than while there is some body by to perceive them. Upon shutting my eyes all the furniture in the room is reduced to nothing, and barely upon opening them it is again created. . . .

48 If we consider it, the objection proposed in *Sect.* 45 will not be found reasonably charged on the principles we have premised, so as in truth to make any objection at all against our notions. For though we hold indeed the objects of sense to be nothing else but ideas which cannot exist unperceived; yet we may not hence conclude they have no existence except only while they are perceived by us, since there may be some other spirit that perceives them, though we do not. Wherever bodies are said to have no existence without the mind, I would not be understood to mean this or that particular mind, but all minds whatsoever. It does not therefore follow from the foregoing principles, that bodies are annihilated and created every moment, or exist not at all during the intervals between our perception of them. . . .

60 . . . it will be demanded to what purpose serves that curious organization of plants, and the admirable mechanism in the parts of animals; might not vegetables grow, and shoot forth leaves and blossoms, and animals perform all their motions, as well without as with all that variety of internal parts so elegantly contrived and put together, which being ideas have nothing powerful or operative in them, nor have any necessary connexion with the effects ascribed to them? If it be a spirit that immediately produces every effect by a *fiat,* or act of his will, we must think all that is fine and artificial in the works, whether of man or Nature, to be made in vain. By this doctrine, though an artist hath made the spring and wheels, and every movement of a watch, and adjusted them in such a manner as he knew would produce the motions he designed; yet he must think all this done to no purpose, and that it is an intelligence which directs the index, and points to the hour of the day. If so, why may not the intelligence do it, without his being at the pains of making the movements, and putting them together? Why does not an empty case serve as well as another?. . .

62 . . . [In reply], it must be observed, that though the fabrication of all those parts and organs be not absolutely necessary to the producing any effect, yet it is necessary to the producing of things in a constant, regular way, according to the Laws of Nature. . . . Thus, for instance, it cannot be denied that God, or the intelligence which sustains and rules the ordinary course of things might, if he were minded to produce a miracle, choose all the motions on the dial-plate of a watch, though no body had ever made the movements, and put them in it: but yet if he will act agreeably to the [the Laws of Nature], it is necessary that those actions of the watchmaker, whereby he makes the movements and rightly adjusts them, precede the

production of the aforesaid motions; as also that any disorder in them be attended with the perception of some corresponding disorder in the movements, which being once corrected all is right again. . . .

DISCUSSION QUESTIONS

1. According to Berkeley, what is a physical object (e.g., a table)? How does Berkeley's analysis differ from Russell's? Which seems more reasonable to you? Why?

2. What is Berkeley's reply to those (e.g., Locke) who claim that while our ideas (i.e., sense perceptions) are in the mind, some of these ideas resemble properties of physical objects that exist outside of any mind?

3. What is Berkeley's criticism of Locke's view that physical objects exist unperceived as colorless extended objects that cause our sense perceptions? Do you see any problems with Berkeley's criticisms?

4. Berkeley claims (paragraph 14) "that after the same manner, as modern philosophers [e.g., Locke] prove certain sensible qualities to have no existence in matter, or without the mind, the same thing may be likewise proved of all other sensible qualities." What is Berkeley's argument here? Is it convincing?

5. What reasons does Berkeley give for rejecting the notion of "material substance"?

6. What reply does Berkeley give to those who claim that even though physical objects are unobservable, the belief in their existence serves as an explanation for the order of our sensory experience?

7. In paragraph 22, Berkeley claims that the inconceivability of physical objects existing outside of the mind can be "demonstrated with the utmost evidence in a line or two, to anyone that is capable of the least reflexion." What is Berkeley's argument here? Is it convincing?

8. What reasons does Berkeley give in defense of his claim that only a spirit can cause an idea? Does this seem plausible to you? Why, or why not?

9. According to Berkeley, what accounts for the orderly occurrence of sense experiences? Is this a better explanation than the assumption that these sense experiences are caused by external objects?

10. When asked to refute Berkeley, Samuel Johnson (1709–84) kicked a stone and said, "I refute it thus." Was this a satisfactory refutation? Why, or why not?

35. PHENOMENALISM: ITS ADVANTAGES AND DISADVANTAGES

C.H. Whiteley

C.H. Whiteley (1911-), professor of philosophy at the University of Birmingham, England, is the author of **Introduction to Metaphysics** (1950), **Mind in Action: An Essay in Philosophical Psychology** (1973), and, with W.M. Whiteley, his wife, **The Permissive Morality** (1964) and **Sex and Morals** (1967).

The following selection comes from Whiteley's **Metaphysics,** a general introduction to the problems of metaphysics directed to a lay audience. In this selection, Whiteley presents a very clear exposition and criticism of the phenomenalistic theory of perception. The phenomenalistic view of perception can be traced back to Berkeley who, in the **Principles of Human Knowledge,** claimed that when we say that a table is in a room that we have left, we mean **either** that if we were to return there we would perceive it **or** that "some other spirit actually does perceive it." Consequently, Berkeley proposed two different ways of handling the problem of the continued existence of physical objects that are unperceived by human beings. The second alternative was, however, the view for which he ultimately opted. The first alternative—that is, the phenomenalistic analysis of existence in terms of **hypothetical** perceptions—was to be developed by David Hume and John Stuart Mill. As mentioned in the introduction to this chapter, phenomenalism was a widely held view among the logical positivists of the 1930's to 1950's, but is today considered by most philosophers a fatally flawed theory.

. . . When I am teaching a child the meaning of the word "table," I point to the table, so that he sees it; I put his hand to it, so that he feels it; that is, I cause him to sense certain sense-data. Surely it is with these sense-data that he thereupon associates the sound "table"; when he seems and feels similar sense-data, he repeats "table." It is by the differences in what they look like and feel like that he distinguishes tables from chairs and apples. . . . It is natural to conclude that when he uses the word "table" or "apple," he is using it to describe what he sees, feels, tastes, etc., rather than to propound some theory about an invisible and intangible material substance.

The word "table" *means* a certain visible squareness and brownness, a certain tangible hardness; i.e., it means a certain type of sense-experience. When I say "There is a table in this room" I am describing the sense-data which I am now sensing, and if I do not sense such sense-data, then, being a truthful person, I do not say that there is a table in the room. If someone else says that there is, I test his statement by looking and feeling, i.e., by finding out whether the appropriate sense-data are available; if they are not, I dismiss his statement as false. If I say "Socrates drank his companions under the table," I am not describing any sense-experiences which I have now, but I am describing sense-experiences which I suppose Socrates and his companions to have had at another time and place.

Source: From Chapters VI and VII of C.H. Whiteley's *An Introduction to Metaphysics* (London: Methuen and Co., 1949).

We cannot, of course, identify "the table" with any one single sense-datum; an experience which was entirely unique and did not recur would not be worth naming. The function of words is not to name everything we see or hear, but to pick out the recurrent patterns in our experience. They identify our present sense-data as being of the same group or type as others which we have sensed before. A word, then, describes, not a single experience, but a group or type of experiences; the word "table" describes all the various sense-data which we normally refer to as appearances or sensations "of" the table. So a material thing is not indeed identical with any sense-datum; but neither is it something different in kind from sense-data. It is a group, or class, or system of sense-data; and nothing but sense-data goes to constitute it. So this doctrine may be expressed by saying that every statement we make about a material thing is equivalent to another about sense-data.

Phenomenalism

This analysis of the notion of a material thing is called Phenomenalism, since it makes of a material thing a group of phenomena, appearances, instead of a transcendent reality distinct from appearances. It is a widespread view, and has been accepted by many philosophers who do not call themselves Idealists and are far from accepting Berkeley's view that the fundamental reality is Mind. The term ''idealism'' itself, however, though it has shifted in meaning since, does properly denote just this part of Berkeley's theory, that the material world—''the whole choir of heaven and furniture of the earth'' says Berkeley—consists of what he calls ''ideas'' and I have been calling ''sense-data.'' The word in this sense has nothing to do with ideals, and the theory would have been called ''idealism'' but for considerations of pronunciation.

Phenomenalism, then, is the doctrine that all statements about material objects can be completely analysed into statements about sense-data. The analysis of any such statement must be very complex; and the value of the ''material-object language'' is that it enables us to refer in one word, such as ''table,'' to a vast number of sense-data differing very much among themselves. The group of sense-data constituting the table includes all the different views I can obtain at different distances, from different angles, in different lights, no two of them exactly alike, but all of them variations on one central pattern; it includes sense-data of touch, and those of sound (though these last seem somewhat more loosely connected with the main visuo-tactual group); and with the other kinds of material things, such as apples, sense-data of taste and smell form important constituents of the thing.

Its Advantages

This type of theory has certain clear advantages. On the representative theory, the very existence of a material world or of any given material object must always be in principle doubtful. I am directly aware of my sense-data, and so can be certain of their existence and character: but ''material objects'' are quite different—their existence and character can be known only by an inference, which cannot give the complete certainty which comes from observation. Descartes, for example, accepts this consequence of the theory, and will not allow himself to believe that there is a material world at all, until he has convinced himself that there exists an omnipotent and benevolent God who would never have led him to believe in the material world if it had not been real. But if Descartes really succeeded in keeping up this attitude of doubt for more than a moment, few men have been able to imitate him. We *cannot* believe that the existence of the table is in any way subject to doubt.

The phenomenalist theory, by making the existence of the table *the same thing* as the occurrence of certain sense-data, removes that doubt; for the system of sense-data constituting the table has beyond doubt come under my observation.

The theory not only removes the doubt, but makes it clear why we cannot seriously entertain it. The Plain Man was right after all: material things are seen and touched, are objects of direct awareness, and it is by seeing and touching that we know that they exist, though no material thing is straightforwardly identical with what I am seeing and touching *at this particular moment.*

So, by accepting the phenomenalist analysis, we escape being involved in any reference to an unobservable Matter. We can preserve our empiricism inviolate, and talk about the things we see and hear and smell and touch, and not about other hypothetical things beyond the reach of our observation. Science, the knowledge of nature, on this view becomes the recording, ordering and forecasting of human experiences. Therein lies its interest for us. If the physical world lay outside our experience, why should we be concerned with it?

Criticisms of Phenomenalism

But these advantages of phenomenalism are purchased at a cost. Along several different lines the phenomenalist interpretation of our statements about material things seems to conflict with our usual beliefs, and produces paradoxes not very easy to accept.

"Appearance and Reality"

In ordinary speech we are accustomed to draw a distinction between "appearance and reality," and to allow that a thing may appear to be what it is not, as Descartes' stick half under water may appear bent although it is really straight. Hence we reckon some of our perceptions as "real" or "true" or "genuine," and others as "illusions." The representative theory of perception is in accordance with this way of thinking; for on that theory our sense-data are in some respects copies of material things; some are accurate copies, and so are genuine and true, others are inaccurate copies, and so false and illusory. The representative theory differs from common sense mainly in holding that the discrepancies between the sense-datum and the material object which it represents are greater than we realize.

But what is the phenomenalist to make of this distinction? He can admit no essential difference between appearance and reality; for on his view the appearances *are* the reality. Material things consist of appearances—sense-data—and of nothing else. And these sense-data all actually occur and so are equally real. Moreover, they are what they appear to be; their reality consists in appearing, and the suggestion that they might "really" have qualities which they do not appear to have is without meaning. Thus the phenomenalist has no justification for classifying them into "real" and "unreal", or "genuine" and "counterfeit." The various sense-data which go to constitute a material object, such as my table, are of many different shapes and colours. All of them are equally real, and none of them can be *the* "real shape" or "real colour" of the table. Evidently tables are more versatile objects than we thought, and may have as many different shapes and colours as there are occasions of observing them. Why then should we come by the idea that there is only one "real shape," and the rest are mere appearances?

The phenomenalist solution of this difficulty is to allow that in a strict philosophical sense of the word "real," the distinction between reality and appearance cannot be drawn. But the purpose of the common-sense distinction between appearance and reality is not to pry into the ultimacies of metaphysics, but to enable us to deal with the experiences we encounter. What causes us to condemn an experience as an "illusion" is that it leads us astray. A mirage is an illusion because it causes us to make a mistake. But what kind of mistake? Surely, not the mistake of thinking that we now see trees and water, but the mistake of expecting that we shall soon be able to have a drink and sit in the shade. The mistake consists in the false expectation of certain other sense-data. Thus the illusoriness is not in the sense-datum itself, but in the expectation which we form when we sense it.

Error of this sort is possible because sense-data are not chaotic, but in the main are arranged in orderly series. Normally, when the visual sense-data belonging to water are obtainable, so are the gustatory sense-data of drinking water and relieving one's thirst. The mirage deceives us because, abnormally, we get the visual sense-data without the gustatory ones. Mirror-images may deceive us because the things seen in a mirror cannot be observed from the back and cannot be touched. Thus a "real" table consists of a complete set of sense-data of different senses related to one another in certain systematic ways (e.g., visual sense-data become continuously smaller and auditory ones continuously fainter as we move away from a certain region of space). When, as in the case of a table seen in a mirror, you have some members of the set but not others, you say that what is seen in the mirror is not a "real" table, or is not "really" there.

Again, the stick in water may lead us into error because sticks that "look bent" usually "feel bent" as well; and so we are surprised to find that it "feels straight," and say that though it "looks bent" it is not "really bent."

The precise interpretation of the word "real" is different in different contexts. But in general, say phenomenalists, it will be found that what we call the "real world" is not a world different from that of appearances; it is a selection from the world of appearances, a collection of appearances which are normal, systematic, and so reliable. The "unreal" consists of eccentric appearances which in one way or another fail to fit in with the normal type of sets of sense-data, and therefore cause us to form false expectations.

The Permanence of Material Things

Sensations come and go. Few of them last for very long, and none of them lasts for ever. If we add up all the occasions in my life on which I have been looking at this table, we get a very short period indeed. And, like the rest of my species, I frequently go to sleep, and cease to perceive any material object whatsoever. That is to say, if a material thing consists of sense-data, its existence must be intermittent. . . .

The phenomenalist answer to these difficulties involves a radical reinterpretation of the whole notion of a permanent material thing. . . .

Clearly, when I say that there is a table in the now uninhabited attic, I am not describing the sense-data of anyone. But, though the statement cannot be a description of *actual* sense-data, it can be a description of *possible* sense-data; and this is what it is according to phenomenalists. To say that there is a table there now is to say that *if* there were anyone in the room he *would be* having the kind of experience which we call seeing a table. "There is a table" means "Go and look and you will see a table." And to say that it has been there twenty years means that if at any time during those years anyone had been in the room, he could have seen or touched a table. . . .

Berkeley himself gives another explanation of the permanence of material things. According to his theory, God is eternally perceiving everything, and therefore, at times when neither I nor any other human being or animal is perceiving the table, God is still perceiving it. But whether or not this is really the case, it is obviously not a correct interpretation of what we mean when we attribute continuous existence in time to the table. For if it were, we should not believe in permanent material things at all unless we believed, not only in God, but in an omniscient God such as Berkeley believed in.

Causal Activity

According to our ordinary notions of them, material objects are causally active: they do things. The table supports the tablecloth, the fire warms the room. Material objects exercise force, have influences on one another and incidentally on ourselves, causing, among other things, our sensations of them. This continually active causal interplay makes up the system of nature, which it is the business of science to study and reduce to laws. Does not science explain what happens by referring events to their causes, which in the material realm at least are material things, exercising physical force? Surely, the room cannot be warmed by my visual sense-datum of a fire! Still less can it be warmed by the possibility of a visual sense-datum of a fire during my absence, when I am not looking at the fire but the room gets warmed all the same. When we all sit round the table and sense sense-data very similar in shape, size and colour, what is the explanation of this fact, if not that there is an independent table which is the common cause of all our similar sense-data? Berkeley himself admits, or rather insists, that an "idea" is "inert," and can *do* nothing.

Phenomenalist Analysis of Causation

To deal with this problem, we need a fresh analysis and re-interpretation of the notion of cause, parallel to the phenomenalist re-interpretation of the notion of "substance" or "thing." Such an analysis was given in David Hume's *Treatise of Human Nature* (1739), and modern phenomenalists in the main follow his line of thought. Hume's aim is to interpret statements about cause and effect in such a way that the relation between a cause and its effect shall be an observable fact, and shall contain nothing mysterious or occult. For unless the words "cause and effect" described something we could observe, they would not, according to Hume, be intelligible to us.

What, then, do I observe in cases in which I should naturally use causal language? I am watching a game of billiards. I observe the event which I might naturally describe by saying that one ball A moved across the table and made or caused another ball B to roll into a pocket. What do I actually *see*? I see a certain sequence of events: first the movement of A, then the touching of A and B, then the movement of B. This temporal sequence of movements, the one which I call the effect following on the one I call the cause, seems to be all the visible relation there is between them.

But obviously, mere temporal sequence is not the same thing, as causation . . . plenty of other things preceded the movement of my billiard-ball in time which were not causes of it. Yet nothing seems to be observable but temporal sequence—first one event, then the other. Whence do I get this notion of the ball being made or caused or forced to move?

If I were pushing the ball myself, I should be aware of myself making a certain muscular effort, *trying* to make it move; and, when I observe the collision of the two balls and the ensuing movement of B, I may perhaps have a vague image of a similar kind of pushing going on between the balls. But if I do, it is clear that this feeling of muscular effort is not observed in the situation presented to my senses, but is a "projection" of my own past feelings in similar situations. For billiard balls do not have muscles, or make efforts, and even if they did, I could not observe what efforts they were making, I could only observe their movements.

Certainly when I see the collision, I expect that the second ball will move—there is a "felt tendency of the mind" to pass from the "cause" to the "effect"; but this is a psychological fact about me, not a physical fact about the balls. There seems nothing in the observed situation corresponding to the words "cause," "power," "force," which I am inclined to apply to it; only the observed sequence of one event on the other. But how, then, do I distinguish between those temporal antecedents of an event which are its causes, and those which are not?. . .

The answer is plain enough; I repeat the experiment, and if the same sequence of events recurs, I conclude that it was a causal and not an accidental sequence. The reason I believe that the movement of the ball was caused by the impact of the other ball, and not by somebody lighting a cigarette at the same time, is that I know by long experience that balls always move when they are struck by other balls moving fairly quickly, whereas they do not usually move when men light cigarettes in their neighbourhood. When medical men inquire into the cause of cancer, what they are looking for is something which always happens to a man before he becomes ill with cancer, just as, when they say that malaria is caused by the bite of a mosquito, they mean that a man has always been bitten by a mosquito before developing malaria. The observable fact which leads us to say that C is the cause of E is the fact that events of the kind C are followed by events of the kind E, not once or sometimes, but whenever they occur.

Causality, as a fact about the world, is then, according to Hume, a relation of invariable sequence. . . . To say that every event has a cause is to say that for any event E there is another event (or complex of ''conditions'') C such that whenever an event of the kind C occurs, an event of the kind E follows. It is to say that the sequence of phenomena is patterned, systematic; that there are in nature discoverable regularities.

But these regularities are discoverable among the observed phenomena themselves, and not between phenomena and something transcending phenomena. Causation, thus interpreted, is a relation between sense-data. The causes, that is to say, the invariable antecedents, of sense-experiences, are other sense-experiences.

Of course, not all causes are actually observed phenomena. In the analysis of cause, as in the analysis of substance, we must sometimes refer to possible sense-data which are not actual. But to say, for example, that a burst pipe was caused by the formation of a lump of ice which I have not seen, is not to desert the realm of sense-data; it is only to refer to sense-data which were not actually observed, but which might, in principle, have been observed; if I had been in a position to look at the interior of the pipe, I should have seen a lump of ice there.

Thus Hume and his followers do not deny that the relation of cause and effect is a real feature of the world; but they interpret it as a relation between sense-data, actual or possible. So the principle of causality does not carry us beyond the sphere of the observed and the observable, or compel us to admit the existence of ''material substance'' over and above systems of sense-data.

Thus, on this theory, the material world consists of sets of sense-experiences, together with the fact that an indefinitely large number of other similar sense-experiences might be had under certain specified conditions. Its ''substances'' are orderly groups of sense-data; and its causal relations are relations of regular sequence between sense-data of specified kinds. The main business of science is to discover causal laws, i.e., to reveal the patterns in that complex of experiences we call Nature. Science tells us what experiences to expect as the sequel to the experiences we are now having, and so renders our knowledge of the world systematic. . . .

The Paradoxes of Phenomenalism

If we take the phenomenalist alternative, let us not do so without being clearly and fully aware of what it involves. (1) It involves the denial that physical objects are permanent, or exist unperceived. It must be granted to the phenomenalists that when I say ''There is a table upstairs,'' I am at least implying that if you were to go upstairs and look (given normal eyesight, normal lighting, etc.) you would have certain visual sense-data. But it seems quite clear to me that this is not the whole nor the essential part of what I am asserting. For when I say that the table is there, I am stating something about what exists or happens *in fact, now;* my statement is about the actual present, and not, as the phenomenalists make it, about the possible future. And if the phenomenalist account is to be accepted, we must say that this statement is a mistake. There is nothing at all in the attic now; there is no attic now at all; for there is nobody perceiving it.

(2) We must very seriously revise our opinions about the nature of causality. As a rule, we are in the habit of believing that a cause is something which actually exists or occurs, and that something which does not actually exist or occur can have no effects. This opinion must be given up if we accept the phenomenalist view. For on that view, to say that the bursting of pipes is caused by the formation of ice in them is to say that whenever one observes or could observe sense-data of the set constituting a burst pipe, one either has or could have previously observed sense-data of the set constituting a lump of ice inside that pipe. But quite clearly, in prac-

tically every instance of this rule, nobody does actually observe the ice; the sense-data of the ice are possible, not actual. That is to say, causality in such a case is a relation between something and nothing, between an actually observed burst, and a hypothetical proposition to the effect that if something had happened which did not happen and in practice could not have happened, then something else would have happened which also did not happen. This interpretation flouts our usual assumption that what might have happened but did not happen can have no effects. The actual material agents of physics and common sense must be replaced by a set of hypothetical facts relating to unfulfilled conditions. If this is so, it is difficult to see why we should suppose that these hypothetical propositions are true. If I leave a fire in my room, I expect it to be warm on my return; but is this not because I believe that the fire is still now burning, a real present fire exercising an influence on a real present atmosphere? I cannot see what reason can be given for expecting the room to be warmed, independently of my reasons for supposing that the fire *is* burning *now* (and not that, *if* I went and looked, I should see flame). I can see reason for believing in regularities in nature holding between one event and another; but no reason at all for believing in regularities holding between one event which happened and another which might have happened but did not. . . .

These paradoxical conclusions have been accepted by able philosophers, and one cannot therefore say that they are beyond belief. But they are markedly at variance with the ordinary assumptions, not only of common sense, but also of scientific investigation (for, whatever some scientists may manage to persuade themselves, they are not concerned only with the cataloguing and ordering of phenomena, but believe themselves to be dealing with permanent and independent objects). . . .

DISCUSSION QUESTIONS

1. What is "phenomenalism"?

2. How would a phenomenalist distinguish dreams from waking experiences? How would Berkeley? How would Russell?

3. What is the phenomenalistic analysis of the continued existence of unperceived physical objects?

4. What is the phenomenalistic analysis of causation?

5. According to the phenomenalist, what do we mean when we say that "an orange really has a certain taste," although we have one kind of taste experience when we eat it alone, another if we eat it after eating something very sour, and another if we eat it after eating something very sweet?

6. How would a phenomenalist reply to the following:

> Last night, I left a room where a fire was burning in the fireplace. When I came back an hour later, I saw that only glowing embers were left. This shows that a fire must have existed and went on burning when I was out.

How would Berkeley answer?

36. DESCARTES' EVIL GENIUS HYPOTHESIS REVISITED: THE POSSIBILITY OF SYSTEMATIC HALLUCINATION

Jonathan Harrison

JONATHAN HARRISON (1924–) is the chair of the philosophy department at the University of Nottingham, England. In the selection that follows, Harrison contemplates the possibility of systematic hallucination that so troubled Descartes and has often been a theme of contemporary science fiction writers. Placing Descartes' hypothesis of "the evil genius" in a more plausible science fiction setting, Harrison imagines a healthy, living brain being disconnected from a diseased body and connected to an "electrohallucinator" that creates a systematic stream of hallucinatory perceptions (like Descartes imagined in his dream hypothesis). Deceived by the electrohallucinator into believing that he has a normal body and that the experiences he has are experiences of an external world, the bodyless brain (or, if you prefer, person with a brain, but no other bodily parts), whose name is Ludwig, develops an interest in philosophy, in particular, the philosophy of perception. Harrison's prime aim here is to reveal the inadequacies of contemporary philosophical views of perception which dismiss as logically incoherent Descartes' imagined philosophical nightmare of systematic hallucinatory experiences. In addition, Harrison's article can be seen as an implicit defense of the classical philosophical view, originating with Descartes, which erects a barrier of ideas (or sense data) between the perceiver and the external world. As Ludwig entertains contemporary views of perception which reject the classical view of perception, the reader's awareness of Ludwig's true condition will, Harrison believes, bring out the inadequacies of these twentieth-century attempts to circumvent the classical problem of perception. Harrison's style of writing in this article is refreshingly original and witty.

Once upon a time, in the year 2167 A.D., when the connected disciplines of Physiology, Psychology, Medicine, Cybernetics and Communication Theory were enormously more advanced than they have been before or since, there lived a very famous neurologist. He was so eminent that the conventions which circumscribed the behavior of his less successful colleagues neither worried nor restricted him, and finding even the most difficult tasks which he met in his professional life presented a challenge insufficient adequately to tax his unrivalled knowledge and consummate skill, his ambition led him to embark upon an enterprise which one would have supposed the most dangerous excess of *hubris*[1] could not have aspired to, an enterprise which might almost be deemed to usurp the prerogative of God himself.

One day one of his assistants delivered a baby which, it was immediately obvious, was so deformed that a life even remotely approaching

Source: From Jonathan Harrison, "A Philosopher's Nightmare or The Ghost Not Laid," *Proceedings of The Aristotelian Society*, 67 (1967). Reprinted with the permission of The Aristotelian Society.

[1]Arrogance resulting from excessive pride. EDITOR'S NOTE.

normal was impossible for him. From the neck down, this baby was afflicted with almost every known physiological defect. From the neck up, however, the baby appeared perfectly normal; indeed, in so far as it was possible to tell at this early age, it exhibited features which in Dr. Smythson's experience had been associated with exceptionally high intelligence, and even led him to predict very great philosophical ability. In order that such a genius should not be lost to the world by the premature cessation of his bodily functioning, Dr. Smythson made up his mind to undertake an experiment never before attempted by a human being; he decided to dissolve the unequal marriage between the superb head and mutilated body, and keep the latter alive independently of the former by a process the possibility of which had recently occurred to him. The head was to be kept in a case and to be fed with its necessary blood supply from a reservoir by means of a pump connected to the appropriate arteries.

This having been successfully accomplished, it occurred to him that the life of his protégé–whom he decided to call Alfred Ludwig Gilbert Robinson, in memory of a once well known twentieth century philosopher of that name—must inevitably be circumscribed and dull. Since he was a kindly man as well as an ingenious one, he made up his mind to produce an adaptation—which he christened the endocephalic electrohallucinator—of a twenty-second century means of entertainment and use it for a different and more questionable purpose than mere pleasure-giving. This device was designed to give men and women seeking escape from that small amount of monotony contained even by twenty-second century lives all the experiences which would be involved in participating in the various incidents celebrated in the fiction of the day by stimulating their sense organs in the identical ways in which they would have been stimulated had they actually participated in these scenes. Dr. Smythson modified it so that the necessary stimuli could be fed directly into the nerves communicating with the relevant centres of the brain—a process rather like cutting and tapping a telephone wire except that in the case we are considering the telephone wire had, as it were, already been cut. In order to do this, he found it not only necessary to remove Alfred Ludwig Gilbert Robinson's eyes, ears and tongue, but the whole of his skull, but to a man who had already removed a body from its head, the performance of this operation caused scarcely a vestige of compunction; nor was he disturbed by the fact that the impulses used to stimulate Alfred Ludwig Gilbert Robinson's perceptual apparatus produced scenes which were totally hallucinatory. Dr. Smythson contented himself with the thought that a consistent hallucination was as good as reality—in this case, indeed, even better—and solved his only slightly uneasy conscience by resolving that he would give Alfred Ludwig Gilbert Robinson an experience of life which was not only coherent, but happy as well. In order to find out, among other things, whether Ludwig was happy Dr. Smythson had to introduce another rather elaborate piece of apparatus, a development of the electro-encephalograph, much used by officials in the Department of Justice, which enabled them to detect in detail even the slightest variation in a patient's cerebral activity. Since it had been discovered that there was a correlation between such activity and the symbols used by people in their private thoughts it was possible for his thoughts to be first recorded and then decoded by officials trained for the purpose. Dr. Smythson found that reading the results of this process was a little tedious, and was sometimes distressed at the confusion which he detected, but he contented himself with the knowledge that at least he had an adequate means of telling whether the chemistry of Ludwig's blood was such as to keep him both contented and alert, and to rectify it when it was not.

In this environment Ludwig developed apace. Dr. Smythson saw that he had an excellent education, and stimulated his optic nerve with the contents of only the best books. As Ludwig reached his late 'teens, Dr. Smythson even put in his way—metaphorically speaking, of course—some works on philosophy, and was interested to see the decoded summaries of Ludwig's reflections when these were presented to him by his technical staff. The writings of one philosopher in particular—a now little regarded Frenchman called René Descartes—provoked a crisis in Ludwig's intellectual life. After reading a work of his—called *Meditations*—Ludwig was for many months distressed by the thought that all his most cherished beliefs might be mistaken and that, instead of the benevolent deity whose existence he had previously taken for granted, there was a malicious demon who produced in his mind experience which proceeded just as if he perceived material objects, though in fact no such things existed. Descartes's own reason—that God was incapable of deceit—for rejecting this hypothesis did not greatly impress him. Descartes had to defend it by suggesting that God cannot help but occasionally produce error, since it was impossible to have afferent nerves which would produce sensations by being stimulated at their endings, unless these nerves could produce similar sensations by being stimulated nearer the brain, and this suggestion struck Ludwig, who was almost entirely ignorant of physiology, as fanciful.

However, reading the works of a later Irish philosopher called Berkeley produced some reassurance to his troubled mind, and for a long time he was convinced that since what philosophers called matter was an inert and stupid substance, it could not conceivably have the power to produce in him the ideas of colour and light which he saw when he opened his eyes. Hence he concluded that these perceptions were produced in him directly by God's volitions, and that his perception, since it consisted in participating in God's own perceptual experience, brought him much closer to the deity than appeared possible on the view it was designed to replace. To say that my helicopter—for Dr. Smythson had not deemed it either kind or right not to feed Ludwig with at least the experience of flying, when all round youths of Ludwig's age had their own helicopters—exists unperceived in its heliport, he decided, is simply to say that some other being perceives it. Dr. Smythson, on reading the transcript of these reflections, was both amused and concerned at how profoundly erroneous were Ludwig's conclusions, but did not see fit to disillusion him. Indeed, he was quite sure that, were he to break in upon Ludwig with an account of the true state of affairs, his words would be neither heeded nor believed.

Ludwig did not remain long satisfied with Berkeley's refutation of his first tendency towards scepticism and atheism, and he still often felt inclined to doubt the existence of the world he seemed to experience. Reading the works of a celebrated Scottish sceptic called Hume did a little to reassure him, for the views to which he leaned seemed so preposterous when actually seen in black and white that reading them in Hume's words brought home to him their manifest absurdity. What nonsense to think that the world was composed entirely of impressions, and that, since these impressions were dependent for their existence upon the percipient's brain—at this Dr. Smythson's machine stimulated his nervous system in all the ways in which it would have been stimulated had he in reality been eating an excellent breakfast—the belief in the independent existence of a world of objects is contradictory and impossible! The belief that scepticism was absurd led him for a while to sympathize with the school of Scottish philosophers who, unlike most of their countrymen, believed in common sense, but this sympathy proved only temporary, and a week or so later, after reading a work of John Stuart Mill called *An Examination of Sir William Hamilton's Philosophy*—who Sir William Hamilton was he never discovered—he inclined to the view that material objects were no more than permanent possibilities of sensation. So long, he thought, as it is the case that if I were to go into my study—Dr. Smythson had decided that he would give him the experience of having a study, though such things were usual in the twenty-second century—I would have the sensation of seeing a room with books, etc. my study existed unobserved, for this is all that saying I have an unobserved study can mean. . . .

However, recurring doubts about the reality of those personal belongings and the few friends that Dr. Smythson's apparatus was able to supply him with were eventually banished only by reading the works of a number of twentieth century philosophers, in particular, by one called G. E. Moore. Two papers, one entitled "A Defense of Common Sense," and the other "Proof of the External World" in particular impressed him. Indeed, from the time of reading these his earlier scepticism never again fully returned. It was reading Moore which eventually brought home to him how the existence of things external to our minds could be proved, and in his excitement at the solution of a problem which had long perplexed him, he actually mimicked Moore. "There must be things external to us," he argued under what he supposed was his breath, "for if there are two human hands, then there are at least two things external to us, and that there are two such things," he agreed with Moore, "can be proved as follows: Here," he said (as the machine fed him the experience of holding up one hand), "is a hand, and," as the machine fed him the experience of holding up another, "here is another."

Though this proof of the existence of his hands and so of the external world completely contented him, he nevertheless saw with satisfaction that a number of other philosophers reinforced the conclusion of Moore's argument by considerations of a slightly different nature. Though Moore himself, he realised, held the view that what we saw directly were not external objects themselves, but sense-data, he himself was quickly convinced by the arguments of some of Moore's successors which were designed to show that most of the problems of perception were the products of confusion engendered by the introduction into philosophy of this bastard concept of the sense-datum. Scepticism in particular, he decided, was one of the most undesirable consequences of that piece of philosophical legerdemain[2] which fabricated these entities, and, he thought, that since to talk of sense-data was just an extremely misleading way of talking about how things looked, and since the dots, specks, blotches and coloured shapes he saw about him simply were material things themselves, there was no reason why he should not say he saw material objects *directly,* and the idea that there was an iron curtain of sense-data interposed between him and the external world he concluded to be absurd. Since the only reason he had had for being a sceptic, he believed, was this erroneous delusion—shared it is true, by almost all the philosophers with whom he had so far had any acquaintance—his scepticism was revealed as manifestly unfounded when once this piece of nonsense was exposed for what it was.

Reading the work of other philosophers of roughly the same period also, to his great relief, caused him to reject a number of other opinions, the possible truth of which had been perplexing him more than he cared to admit. Sometimes he had been troubled by the possibility that life was a dream from which he might one day awake, and discover that all the things and persons he thought he saw were mere illusion. This possibility, too, he discounted after a further acquaintance with mid-twentieth century Anglo-Saxon philosophy. It was impossible, he decided, that the whole of his experience could be an illusion, since the terms "real" and "illusory" were so related that it was necessary that some things should be real in order that other things could be illusory; hence that the whole of his experience should be an illusion was as much a logical impossibility as that all

[2]Sleight of hand. EDITOR'S NOTE.

coins should be counterfeit, or all bank notes forged. That unhappy frame of mind into which he had fallen, he now saw, was the product of certain terminological confusions, and he felt grateful to those twentieth century philosophers who had dispelled his anxieties by so successful an application of their benign therapeutic techniques. One argument, sometimes in those days called the argument from standard samples, gave him especial satisfaction, by its apparent simplicity and obviousness. How could he have doubted, he wondered, whether the object he sat on was a chair when it was by being shown such things as these that he had been taught the very meaning of the word "chair"? How could he have wondered whether the chair he saw was perhaps an illusion, when it was by being shown such things as this that he had been taught what was meant by the expression "real" as opposed to "illusory"? How could he have wondered whether it was certain that it was a chair, when it was in these very cases, when the thing he saw continued to appear to be a chair in whatever way he tried to test it, that he had been taught that it was correct to use the expression "It is certain that that is a chair" and that it was incorrect to use such expressions as, "It is highly probable that that is a chair" or "It seems very likely that that is a chair"?

A brief excursion into the works of certain philosophising physiologists of about the same date did for a moment cause him to suspect that all that he saw might be the product of his own cerebral activity, but he soon discounted this possibility as too absurd to contemplate. Dr. Smythson too, took fright at this point, and saw that no more such books were put into the apparatus which was responsible for Ludwig's perceptual experience.

His reading of mid-twentieth century philosophy was not pure gain, however. He had previously been of a religious disposition and, in his unsceptical moments, he had believed in the existence of an omnipotent, omniscient and perfectly benevolent deity who was responsible not only for his own existence, bur for the existence of the whole world and his experience of it. To his great distress, he now saw that this possibility was not after all a real one, and that the words in which it was expressed were in fact meaningless. He now realized that the meaning of a statement was the method of its verification, and that since the statement that there was a being who supported the world, sustained him, and was responsible for the course of his experience being what it was, was unverifiable, it was also meaningless. It was meaningless, he concluded, to talk of a world or a sphere of existence other than his own, as it was meaningless to talk of any causal dependence other than that observed dependence of the things to be found in his perceptual experience upon one another. If indeed you could deduce anything from the hypothesis of a creator, then the large amount of avoidable evil in the world—Dr. Smythson was a little hurt at this—showed that it must be an hypothesis which was false. The existence of God, therefore, was either false or unverifiable. . . .

To his great regret his former much cherished belief that he had an immortal soul which would survive the death of his body quickly went the way of his belief in God. Formerly he had, in moments of depression, consoled himself with the thought that life in this world was a preparation for another, happier life upon which he would enter upon the dissolution of his body. However, after a careful perusal of one of the most influential of twentieth century philosophers, he decided that any such belief rested upon the mistake of thinking that his mind, like his body, was a substance, and so, like his body, capable of an independent existence. Now he realised that this was a mistake, and that his mind was not a hidden ghostly substance, lying behind the solid earthy substance of his body, and to the workings of which he alone—Dr. Smythson smiled at this—had access. Talk about his mind, he realised, was of a different logical type from talk about his body, much as talk about electricity was of a different logical type from talk about wires and electric light bulbs. Just as it was absurd to say "Yes, I know that electric light bulbs light up when wires connect them to the positive and negative cells of a battery, and that electric motors work in the same circumstances, but nevertheless I doubt the existence of electricity" so, he thought, it was equally absurd to suppose that he could know that he was in the presence of something who could talk and act intelligently, solve problems, play games, and make love, but doubt that he was in the presence of a mind. And so, he concluded, he knew the contents of his own mind in a way no more esoteric than that in which he knew the contents of other people's, and, correspondingly, that other people—here Dr. Smythson laughed more heartily than he had done for many a year—knew the contents of his mind in a way no more esoteric than they knew the contents of their own. The corollary to this solution of the mind/body problem, which he found as emotionally distressing as the solution itself was intellectually satisfying, was that his mind could no more exist apart from his body and the variegated activities in which it indulged than electricity could exist apart from such things as wires and television sets and vacuum cleaners and batteries. . . .

He was never disturbed in the state of intellectual equilibrium which he had now reached. Had he been able to continue his researches into the history of philosophy until the end of the twentieth century . . . his naïve faith in the permanence of the intellectual millenium he supposed himself to have discovered would no doubt have been irretrievably shaken. However, he never did see these things. By what was perhaps for him a fortunate coincidence, a young friend of Dr. Smythson's, called Marcus Antonius Richardson, who possessed a body of the most remarkable beauty and power, and whose prowess far outstripped that of any other athlete whose feats had been recorded, contracted a fatal brain disease which even the vast resources of contemporary medicine could not cure. Dr. Smythson was for a while greatly distressed by the thought of the imminent demise of a body physiologically so unique, but it was not long before he formed an idea as brilliant as any which had occurred to him previously. Ludwig, the brain without a body, would be the means of the salvation of Marcus, the body without a brain. A long, difficult and dangerous operation followed. Marcus's head was removed and Ludwig, or Ludwig's head—Dr. Smythson had some hesitation over which was the correct expression—was carefully grafted on to it. Marcus's eyes and ears were fastened to Ludwig's optic nerves in place of the apparatus which was hitherto all they had known, and his face and skull were used to protect and beautify the once disembodied brain. Though the result was indistinguishable from the original Marcus in appearance, it was more like the original Ludwig in behaviour and intellectual capacity, and since these are of so much greater importance than the grosser physical features, we shall continue to call the amalgam Ludwig, despite the fact that actually most of it was Marcus. When Ludwig recovered from the anaesthetic he not unnaturally believed that he had now come to experience a consistent hallucination or dream, and it took Dr. Smythson and his colleagues many months before they could convince him that it was in reality his former experience which had been hallucinatory. At this moment Ludwig's career, though long and, on the whole happy, ceased to be of any philosophical importance. He married and had children—who in character and intellect bore a strong resemblance to Marcus, none at all to him—and was only briefly puzzled by the problems that what had happened to him presented to his former firm belief in the impossibility of the transmigration of souls. But acquiring Marcus' body, though it brought to his life a variety, verve and intensity which, he now discovered, it had formerly lacked, ruined his powers of concentration. Though he occasionally returned to the actual books, the contents of which Dr. Smythson had previously fed into his optic nerve, he found they did not have the same power to excite him, and eventually he gave up altogether such intellectually fatiguing pursuits, and concentrated his powers on a determined attempt to achieve Marcus' former ambition to be the first man to run a three minute mile. He contented himself with the thought that though now his goals were less elevated than they had been previously, his actually having reached them could so much more easily be proved.

DISCUSSION QUESTIONS

1. In the light of Harrison's tale of the plight of Ludwig, critically consider the plausibility of the following conclusion that Ludwig drew while under the influence of the electrohallucinator:

   It was impossible, he decided, that the whole of his experience should be an illusion, since the terms "real" and "illusory" were so related that it was necessary that some things should be real in order that other things could be illusory; hence that the whole of his experience should be an illusion was as much a logical impossibility as that all coins should be counterfeit. . . .

2. In the light of Harrison's tale, consider the plausibility of the realist, idealist, and phenomenalistic views of perception.

3. Consider the plausibility of the following claim: Our experience of the external physical world (including our own physical bodies) is a systematic dream caused by God. While our experiences of physical objects are hallucinatory, we do have contact with other disembodied spirits who share with us the same coherent dream that God projects into our minds. In this common dream, God allows the sequence of experiences to be controlled to some extent by the free choices of the spirits who interrelate in their common hallucinatory world. As religious tradition rightly preaches, our experience in this so-called physical world is a moral test. What people fail to realize, however, is that there was no need for God to actually create a physical world. All he had to do was to create the systematic delusive appearance of living in a common physical world. What we call death is, in reality, waking up from a long dream—a special dream, however, in which, by the omnipotence of God, many have shared and participated.

Is such a story possible? Plausible? In what sense, if any, would our experiences in this world be "hallucinatory," according to this view?

37. THE PROBLEM OF INDUCTION

Bertrand Russell

(For a biographical sketch of Bertrand Russell, see Selection #1.)

The preceding story of Ludwig brings us face to face with the disquieting thought that, however subjectively certain we may be of the nature of the world we inhabit and even of our own natures, **we can never really be sure.** The great lesson of the empiricist tradition seems to be that the search for indubitable knowledge of matters of fact is a search that can never be satisfied, for the evidence is never totally complete. For example, like Descartes, I can even question the apparent "certain fact" that I am typing this now. How do I know this? I see a typewriter and my hands hitting the keys. I feel the resistance of the typewriter against my fingers. I remember getting up from the dinner table and coming to my desk. But, couldn't I be dreaming? Couldn't I be like Ludwig, a disembodied brain connected to an "electrohallucinator"? Couldn't it all be an hallucination? How do I know too that what I **seem to remember** really did happen? Our apparent memories of the past, after all, are sometimes deceptive. For example, I seem to remember burning my hand severely as a small child. But do I really remember this or simply imagine that I do as a result of my mother's later description of this event to me? An awareness of such possibilities can lead to a consideration of much more fanciful possibilities. For example, Bertrand Russell once pointed out that it is possible that the world was created only five minutes ago, complete with false memories of the past. Given this possibility, is there any way one can **know** that one's ostensible memories are generally to be trusted?

Usually our doubts over matters of fact come to an end after a certain amount of observation. The philosophical doubts expressed above, however, seem incapable of ever being put to rest. If one lived one's life compulsively afraid of the possibility that all of life is an hallucination or that ostensible memories can never be trusted or that the past cannot be taken as a justifiable guide to the future, one would be judged "crazy." Yet many philosophers, like Descartes and Hume, have found themselves faced with similar doubts in moments of deep philosophical reflection. Fortunately for them as human beings who want to function in this world, these doubts are purely intellectual and are easily forgotten in the rush of everyday affairs. As Hume once put it,

> The intense view of these manifold contradictions and imperfections in human reason has so wrought upon me, and heated my brain, that I am ready to reject all belief and reasoning, and can look upon no opinion even as more probable or likely than another. Where am I, or what? From what causes do I derive my existence, and to what condition shall I return? . . . I am confounded with all these questions, and begin to fancy myself in the most deplorable condition imaginable, inviron'd with the deepest darkness . . .
>
> Most fortunately it happens, that since reason is incapable of dispelling these clouds, nature herself suffices to that purpose, and cures me of this philosophical melancholy and delirium, either by relaxing this bent of mind, or by some avocation, and lively impression of my senses, which obliterates all these chimeras.[1] I dine, I play a game of backgammon, I converse, and am merry with my friends; and when after three or four hours' amusement, I wou'd return to these speculations, they appear so cold, and strain'd and ridiculous, that I cannot find in my heart to enter into them any further.[2]

Yet Hume, to his credit as a philosopher, could not let these doubts rest indefinitely and he would continually come back to them. Among Hume's most nagging doubts was his doubt about the foundation of our inductive inference that the "future will be like the past."

> Let the course of things be allowed hitherto so regular; that alone, without some new argument or inference, proves not that, for the future, it will continue so. . . . My practice you say, refutes my doubts. But you mistake the purport of my question. As an agent, I am quite satisfied in the point . . .[3]

[1] Foolish fancies. EDITOR'S NOTE.

[2] Hume, *Treatise*, Conclusion of Book I.

[3] Hume, *Enquiry*, Sec. IV.

As an agent, then, Hume had confidence in the laws of nature. Unlike a crazy person, he did not think that it made no difference whether he left a second floor room by the stairs or by the window. Yet, as a philosopher, he vainly sought the rational justification for this practice, leaving himself in the end the sceptic that he was at the beginning of his philosophical reflection.

Hume's scepticism has had a great influence on subsequent philosophers. As mentioned, Kant took it as a prod, "awaking him from his dogmatic slumber." It also had a deep effect upon Bertrand Russell, who in many respects followed in the footsteps of Hume. In the following selection, which comes from his **Problems of Philosophy,** Russell clearly expresses in nontechnical and more modern language the very same sceptical doubts about induction first elucidated by Hume. How, Russell wonders, can we justify our belief that the future will be like the past, a belief that underlies the process of scientific inference no less than our common-sense belief that the sun will rise tomorrow morning or that the next apple we bite will taste as similar apples have tasted in the past and not like a banana or like chocolate ice cream.

In almost all our previous discussions we have been concerned in the attempt to get clear as to our data in the way of knowledge of existence. What things are there in the universe whose existence is known to us owing to our being acquainted with them? So far, our answer has been that we are acquainted with our sense-data, and, probably, with ourselves. These we know to exist. And past sense-data which are remembered are known to have existed in the past. This knowledge supplies our data.

But if we are to be able to draw inferences from these data—if we are to know of the existence of matter, of other people, of the past before our individual memory begins, or of the future, we must know general principles of some kind by means of which such inferences can be drawn. It must be known to us that the existence of some one sort of thing, A, is a sign of the existence of some other sort of thing, B, either at the same time as A or at some earlier or later time, as, for example, thunder is a sign of the earlier existence of lightning. If this were not known to us, we could never extend our knowledge beyond the sphere of our private experience; and this sphere, as we have seen, is exceedingly limited. The question we have now to consider is whether such an extension is possible, and if so, how it is effected.

Let us take as an illustration a matter about which none of us, in fact, feel the slightest doubt. We are all convinced that the sun will rise to-morrow. Why? Is this belief a mere blind outcome of past experience, or can it be justified as a reasonable belief? It is not easy to find a test by which to judge whether a belief of this kind is reasonable or not, but we can at least ascertain what sort of general beliefs would suffice, if true, to justify the judgment that the sun will rise to-morrow, and the many other similar judgments upon which our actions are based.

It is obvious that if we are asked why we believe that the sun will rise to-morrow, we shall naturally answer, 'Because it always has risen every day'. We have a firm belief that it will rise in the future, because it has risen in the past. If we are challenged as to why we believe that it will continue to rise as heretofore, we may appeal to the laws of motion: the earth, we shall say, is a freely rotating body, and such bodies do not cease to rotate unless something interferes from outside, and there is nothing outside to interfere with the earth between now and to-morrow. Of course it might be doubted whether we are quite certain that there is nothing outside to interfere, but this is not the interesting doubt. The interesting doubt is as to whether the laws of motion will remain in operation until to-morrow. If this doubt is raised, we find ourselves in the same position as when the doubt about the sunrise was first raised.

The *only* reason for believing that the laws of motion will remain in operation is that they have operated hitherto, so far as our knowledge of the past enables us to judge. It is true that we have a greater body of evidence from the past in favour of the laws of motion than we have in favour of the sunrise, because the sunrise is merely a particular case of fulfilment of the laws of motion, and there are countless other particular cases. But the real question is: Do *any* number of cases of a law being fulfilled in the past afford evidence that it will be fulfilled in the future? If not, it becomes plain that we have no ground whatever for expecting the sun to rise to-morrow, or for expecting the bread we shall eat at our next meal not to poison us, or for any of the other scarcely conscious expectations that control our daily lives. It is to be observed that all such expectations are only *probable;* thus we have not to seek for a proof that they *must* be fulfilled, but only for some reason in favour of the view that they are *likely* to be fulfilled.

Now in dealing with this question we must, to begin with, make an important distinction, without which we should soon become involved in hopeless confusions. Experience has shown us that, hitherto, the frequent repetition of some uniform succession or coexistence has been a *cause* of our expecting the same succession or coexistence on the next occasion. Food that has a certain appearance generally has a certain taste, and it is a severe shock to our expectations when the familiar appearance is found to be associated with an unusual taste. Things which we see become associated, by habit, with certain tactile sensations which we expect if we touch them; one of the horrors of a ghost (in many ghost-stories) is that it fails to give us any sensations of touch. Uneducated people who go abroad for the first time are so surprised as to be incredulous when they find their native language not understood.

And this kind of association is not confined to men; in animals also it is very strong. A horse which has been often driven along a certain road resists the attempt to drive him in a different direction. Domestic animals expect food when they see the person who usually feeds them. We know that all these rather crude expectations of uniformity are liable to be misleading. The man who has fed the chicken every day throughout its life at last wrings its neck instead, showing that more refined views as to the uniformity of nature would have been useful to the chicken.

But in spite of the misleadingness of such expectations, they nevertheless exist. The mere fact that something has happened a certain number of times causes animals and men to expect that it will happen again. Thus our instincts certainly cause us to believe that the sun will rise to-morrow, but we may be in no better a position than the chicken which unexpectedly has its neck wrung. We have therefore to distinguish the fact that past uniformities *cause* expectations as to the future, from the question whether there is any reasonable ground for giving weight to such expectations after the question of their validity has been raised.

The problem we have to discuss is whether there is any reason for believing in what is called 'the uniformity of nature'. The belief in the uniformity of nature is the belief that everything that has happened or will happen is an instance of some general law to which there are *no* exceptions. The crude expectations which we have been considering are all subject to exceptions, and therefore liable to disappoint those who entertain them. But science habitually assumes, at least as a working hypothesis, that general rules which have exceptions can be replaced by general rules which have no exceptions. 'Unsupported bodies in air fall' is a general rule to which balloons and aeroplanes are exceptions. But the laws of motion and the law of gravitation, which account for the fact that most bodies fall, also account for the fact that balloons and aeroplanes can rise; thus the laws of motion and the law of gravitation are not subject to these exceptions.

The belief that the sun will rise to-morrow might be falsified if the earth came suddenly into contact with a large body which destroyed its rotation; but the laws of motion and the law of gravitation would not be infringed by such an event. The business of science is to find uniformities, such as the laws of motion and the law of gravitation, to which, so far as our experience extends, there are no exceptions. In this search science has been remarkably successful, and it may be conceded that such uniformities have held hitherto. This brings us back to the question: Have we any reason, assuming that they have always held in the past, to suppose that they will hold in the future?

It has been argued that we have reason to know that the future will resemble the past, because what was the future has constantly become the past, and has always been found to resemble the past, so that we really have experience of the future, namely of times which were formerly future, which we may call past futures. But such an argument really begs the very question at issue. We have experience of past futures, but not of future futures, and the question is: Will future futures resemble past futures? This question is not to be answered by an argument which starts from past futures alone. We have therefore still to seek for some principle which shall enable us to know that the future will follow the same laws as the past.

The reference to the future in this question is not essential. The same question arises when we apply the laws that work in our experience to past things of which we have no experience—as, for example, in geology, or in theories as to the origin of the Solar System. The question we really have to ask is: 'When two things have been found to be often associated, and no instance is known of the one occurring without the other, does the occurrence of one of the two, in a fresh instance, give any good ground for expecting the other?' On our answer to this question must depend the validity of the whole of our expectations as to the future, the whole of the results obtained by induction, and in fact practically all the beliefs upon which our daily life is based.

It must be conceded, to begin with, that the fact that two things have been found often together and never apart does not, by itself, suffice to *prove* demonstratively that they will not be found together in the next case we examine. The most we can hope is that the oftener things are found together, the more probable it becomes that they will be found together another time, and that, if they have been found together often enough, the probability will amount *almost* to certainty. It can never quite reach certainty, because we know that in spite of frequent repetitions there sometimes is a failure at the last, as in the case of the chicken whose neck is wrung. Thus probability is all we ought to seek.

It might be urged, as against the view we are advocating, that we know all natural phenomena to be subject to the reign of law, and that sometimes, on the basis of observation, we can see that only one law can possibly fit the facts of the case. Now to this view there are two answers. The first is that, even if *some* law which has no exceptions applies to our case, we can never, in practice, be sure that we have discovered that law and not one to which there are exceptions. The second is that the reign of law would seem to be itself only probable, and that our belief that it will hold in the future, or in unexamined cases in the past, is itself based upon the very principle we are examining.

The principle we are examining may be called the *principle of induction,* and its two parts may be stated as follows:

(a) When a thing of a certain sort A has been found to be associated with a thing of a certain other sort B, and has never been found dissociated from a thing of the sort B, the greater the number of cases in which A and B have been associated, the greater is the probability that

they will be associated in a fresh case in which one of them is known to be present;

(b) Under the same circumstances, a sufficient number of cases of association will make the probability of a fresh association nearly a certainty, and will make it approach certainty without limit.

As just stated, the principle applies only to the verification of our expectation in a single fresh instance. But we want also to know that there is a probability in favour of the general law that things of the sort A are *always* associated with things of the sort B, provided a sufficient number of cases of association are known, and no cases of failure of association are known. The probability of the general law is obviously less than the probability of the particular case, since if the general law is true, the particular case must also be true, whereas the particular case may be true without the general law being true. Nevertheless the probability of the general law is increased by repetitions, just as the probability of the particular case is. We may therefore repeat the two parts of our principle as regards the general law, thus:

(a) The greater the number of cases in which a thing of the sort A has been found associated with a thing of the sort B, the more probable it is (if no cases of failure of association are known) that A is always associated with B;

(b) Under the same circumstances, a sufficient number of cases of the association of A with B will make it nearly certain that A is always associated with B, and will make this general law approach certainty without limit.

It should be noted that probability is always relative to certain data. In our case, the data are merely the known cases of coexistence of A and B. There may be other data, which *might* be taken into account, which would gravely alter the probability. For example, a man who had seen a great many white swans might argue, by our principle, that on the data it was *probable* that all swans were white, and this might be a perfectly sound argument. The argument is not disproved by the fact that some swans are black, because a thing may very well happen in spite of the fact that some data render it improbable. In the case of the swans, a man might know that colour is a very variable characteristic in many species of animals, and that, therefore, an induction as to colour is peculiarly liable to error. But this knowledge would be a fresh datum, by no means proving that the probability relatively to our previous data had been wrongly estimated. The fact, therefore, that things often fail to fulfil our expectations is no evidence that our expectations will not *probably* be fulfilled in a given case or a given class of cases. Thus our inductive principle is at any rate not capable of being *disproved* by an appeal to experience.

The inductive principle, however, is equally incapable of being *proved* by an appeal to experience. Experience might conceivably confirm the inductive principle as regards the cases that have been already examined; but as regards unexamined cases, it is the inductive principle alone that can justify any inference from what has been examined to what has not been examined. All arguments which, on the basis of experience, argue as to the future or the unexperienced parts of the past or present, assume the inductive principle; hence we can never use experience to prove the inductive principle without begging the question. Thus we must either accept the inductive principle on the ground of its intrinsic evidence, or forgo all justification of our expectations about the future. If the principle is unsound, we have no reason to expect the sun to rise to-morrow, to expect bread to be more nourishing than a stone, or to expect that if we throw ourselves off the roof we shall fall. When we see what looks like our best friend approaching us, we shall have no reason to suppose that his body is not inhabited by the mind of our worst enemy or of some total stranger. All our conduct is based upon associations which have worked in the past, and which we therefore regard as likely to work in the future; and this likelihood is dependent for its validity upon the inductive principle.

The general principles of science, such as the belief in the reign of law, and the belief that every event must have a cause, are as completely dependent upon the inductive principle as are the beliefs of daily life. All such general principles are believed because mankind have found innumerable instances of their truth and no instances of their falsehood. But this affords no evidence for their truth in the future, unless the inductive principle is assumed.

Thus all knowledge which, on a basis of experience tells us something about what is not experienced, is based upon belief which experience can neither confirm nor confute, yet which, at least in its more concrete applications, appears to be as firmly rooted in us as many of the facts of experience. The existence and justification of such beliefs—for the inductive principle, as we shall see, is not the only example—raises some of the most difficult and most debated problems of philosophy. . . .

[EDITOR'S NOTE. In the chapter of *Problems of Philosophy* that follows the preceding selection, Russell opts for the rationalistic view, shared by Descartes, Leibniz, and Spinoza, that in addition to knowledge derived from experience "there are certain 'innate ideas' and 'innate principles' which we know independently of experience." In this vein, Russell contends, "Thus, while admitting that all knowledge is elicited . . . by experience, we shall nevertheless hold that some knowledge is *a priori*, in the sense that the experience which makes us think of it does not suffice to prove it, but merely so directs our attention that we see its truth without requiring any proof from experience." Our knowledge of the principle of induction, Russell suggests, is one of these self-evident *a priori* truths. Yet there are passages in Russell's later writings that call into question the *basic a priori* self-evidence of the principle of induction. For example, in his *Human Knowledge: Its Scope and Limits* (London: George Allen and Unwin, 1948), Russell claims that "concentration on induction has very much hindered the progress of the whole inquiry into the postulates of scientific method." In this book, Russell claims that the rationality of the particular type of inductive method employed in science, *follows from* five very abstract presuppositions of scientific inference. He writes "Induction, we have seen, is not quite the universal proposition that we need to justify scientific inference. But we most certainly do need some universal proposition of propositions, whether the five canons suggested . . . or something different. And whatever these principles of inference may be, they certainly cannot be logically deduced from the facts of experience. Either, therefore, we know something independently of experience, or science is moonshine." The conclusion Russell consequently leaves us with is that we must *either* abandon empiricism and embrace a rationalistic view of science or remain a Humean sceptic. While it would appear that Russell takes the former route, there are some critics who see him as rejecting the empiricist view of science, without offering a constructive alternative to it. From the perspective of these critics, the five principles which Russell sees as underlying scientific inference are themselves neither self-evident nor capable of proof. Futhermore, they are suggested, at least in part, by the inductive principle that the future will be like the past, the principle which they are meant to justify and supplant. Consequently, as Hume claimed of all attempts to justify induction, Russell seems to beg the question.]

DISCUSSION QUESTIONS

1. Consider the following argument:
   According to Russell, the principle of induction asserts that:

   > When a thing of a certain sort A has been found to be associated with a thing of a certain sort B, and has never been found dissociated from a thing of the sort B, the greater the number of cases in which A and B have been associated, the greater is the probability that they will be associated in a fresh case in which one of them is known to be present.

   This principle must be rejected since, if it were true, a seventy-year-old man could legitimately argue that it is more probable that he will see the next year go by than a twenty-year-old man, since he has seventy supporting associations of years gone by and years that he has lived, whereas the twenty-year-old man has only twenty of these associations.

What would Russell say in reply?

2. Consider the following criticism:[4]

Inductive sceptics like Hume and Russell neglect the fact that we constantly obtain empirical evidence that the future will be like the past as the future is constantly revealed to us by the passage of time. The inductive sceptic is misled by the picture of the future always hidden behind an impenetrable veil. Fascinated by this picture, the sceptic mistakenly sees the border between past and future as a stationary one. The proper image, however, is that of a constantly moving border which reveals more and more evidence for the belief that the future will be like the past.

What would Russell say? What do you think?

3. Consider the following criticism of inductive scepticism:

Every time I have let go of a heavier-than-air object like a book or a pencil, it has fallen. This, coupled with our knowledge of the law of gravitation, gives me excellent evidence for my belief that if I let my book or pencil go this time, it will drop again. If this is not evidence—if my belief is not reasonable—then what in the world can conceivably count as good evidence or reasonable belief?

What would Russell say? What do you think?

[4]An argument like this is given in F.L. Will's "Will the Future Be Like the Past," *Mind,* Vol. 56 (1947), pp. 332–47.

38. PROPOSED SOLUTIONS TO THE PROBLEM OF INDUCTION

Max Black

MAX BLACK (1909–   ) is a well-known American analytic philosopher who has taught at Cornell University for most of his professional career. Educated in England, Black first specialized in mathematics. This interest led to his first book, **The Nature of Mathematics** (1933). Black came to the United States in 1940 and was naturalized in 1948. He first taught at the University of Illinois and then moved to Cornell in 1946, becoming a Professor Emeritus in 1977. He is, however, still active at Cornell University as Senior Member of its program on **Science, Technology, and Society.** Black has provided philosophical analyses of concepts and issues on a wide range of topics, including formal logic, education, and sociology. His main interest, however, has been in the general area of the philosophy of language and in philosophical issues surrounding the topic of probability and induction.

In the selection that follows, Black sketches the various replies that philosophers have made to the sceptical doubts concerning the justification of induction first elucidated by Hume and echoed in our preceding selection by Russell. Greatly influenced by Wittgenstein's later views concerning language (see the introduction to Selection #3), Black himself sees the problem of induction as a pseudo-problem that is generated by linguistic confusion. In Black's view, Hume's quest for a "general justification" of induction is a quest for the conceptually impossible, which is generated primarily by the futile attempt to convert inductive arguments into deductive ones. Accepting Wittgenstein's view that philosophical problems that are generated by linguistic confusion must be "dissolved" rather than "solved," Black believes that clarity of thought "ought to result in the disappearance of the alleged 'problem of induction.' "

The Importance of Induction

If a dog barks at me each time I pass by, I naturally expect him to bark again the next time he sees me. This is an example of *inductive reasoning* in its most primitive form. From knowledge about a *sample* of cases, those in which the dog has already barked, I draw a conclusion about a case not included in that sample—I anticipate what will happen the next time.

Let us now take a more sophisticated example: On applying a lighted match to a scrap of cellophane, I find that it catches fire; I conclude that any similar piece of cellophane would also burn in a similar situation. Here we have an inference from what happened in *one case* to what would happen in *any* similar case. One last example: An entomologist finds that each examined beetle of a certain species has a green spot on its back and concludes that *all* beetles of that species will have the same marking.

Such familiar examples of inductive reasoning involve a transition from information about a given set of objects or situations to a conclusion about some wider, more inclusive, set. We might say that all of them consist of reasoning from *samples*. Let us therefore agree to understand by an inductive argument one in which the conclusion refers to at least one thing that is not referred to by the premises.

The simplest forms of inductive arguments, on whose correctness the more sophisticated ones ultimately depend, can be represented as follows: "Such and such *A*'s are *B*; therefore another *A* is *B*" or, again, "*Some A*'s (selected in such and such a fashion) are *B*; therefore all *A*'s are *B*." We need not consider ways of improving these formulas, since the problem of justifying induction remains essentially the same in all forms of inductive reasoning, whether primitive or sophisticated.

It has been held, very widely though not universally, that the use of inductive reasoning is a distinctive feature of scientific method, integrally connected with the discovery of scientific laws and generalizations. In strict *deductive* reasoning, we are limited to rearranging information about the data referred to in the premises, and never advance to knowledge about the hitherto unobserved; by means of inductive reasoning, however, we make the leap from "some" to "all"; from the known present to the predicted future; from the finite data of observation to laws covering all that will be and could be. The so-called "inductive leap" (from "some" to "any" and "all") seems indispensable in science no less than in ordinary life.

Indeed, the very language we use to refer to persons and material objects implies a belief in the permanence of objects and the continuity of their properties that can be grounded only in inductive reasoning from experience. There can be no serious question of human beings rejecting inductive reasoning as unsound: to do so would be tantamount to destroying the very language we use to talk about the universe and about ourselves and would lead to the kind of last-ditch skepticism that lacks even the words to express itself.

Source: Max Black, "The Justification of Induction," in *Philosophy of Science Today,* ed. S. Morgenbesser (New York: Basic Books, 1967). Reprinted by permission of Max Black; quotes in Editor's Notes are from Max Black, *Problems of Analysis* (London: Routledge & Kegan Paul Ltd; Ithaca, N.Y.: Cornell University Press, 1954). Reprinted by permission of Max Black and Routledge & Kegan Paul Ltd.

Doubts About Induction

It is altogether reasonable to wonder how the use of this powerful method of reasoning can be justified. Indeed, certain features of inductive argument, as we have defined it, can easily awaken serious disquiet. In logic, we have all been taught that the transition from a "some" in the premises to an "all" in the conclusion is a transparent fallacy: if some men are white-skinned, it by no means follows that *all* men are; how, then, can we be justified in wholesale violation of this plain and simple rule? Again, inductions are notoriously fallible; the gambler who expects a sequence of reds on the roulette wheel to continue indefinitely will soon be undeceived. In our dealings with nature, are we in any stronger position than the gambler who has had a lucky sequence of throws? Are we perhaps about to come to the end of our lucky guesses about nature? How can we possibly *know* that the sun will rise tomorrow?

For the sake of clarity, it is essential to distinguish such sweeping skeptical doubts from practical questions about the reliability of inductive procedures. It is one thing to ask whether a given inductive procedure is sufficiently reliable for a given purpose; different and more basic questions are at issue when we ask how *any* inductive argument can be justified. We have well-tested methods for discriminating random events, such as those that occur on a roulette table, from lawful ones: where practical decision is in question, it would be foolish to consider the contingency that the sun might *not* rise the next day. On the other hand, in cases where inductive conclusions based upon sampling are relatively unreliable, we know in principle how to improve the reliability of the sampling process. There is no difficulty in principle about meeting any practical criticism of a given inductive procedure.

By contrast, the question of justification raised by the philosopher is one of the utmost generality. He is perplexed to understand how *any* inductive reasoning, no matter how satisfactory by the standards of common sense or of good statistical practice, can really count as acceptable. He finds it hard to understand how the "inductive leap," which seems to involve a plain logical fallacy, could *ever* be justified. The problem has no immediate bearing upon scientific practice, but is of the first importance for evaluating the claims of science to be a vehicle of truth about the universe. It seems that unless induction can be justified, our claims to have scientific *knowledge* must be rejected as unfounded and science will have to count as no better than any other unsubstantiated *faith*. However appealing such a skeptical conclusion might be to those who welcome any proof of man's impotence, it is one to be accepted only after the most careful investigation.

Five Attempted Solutions

In the course of the intensive consideration that philosophers of science have given to this problem, almost every conceivable answer has been defended.

1. Perhaps the most drastic solution available consists of a denial that induction plays, or ought to play, any part in scientific method. This view has been most eloquently defended in recent times by Professor Karl Popper, who has argued in numerous writings that the proper business of science is the *deductive testing* of empirical hypotheses. According to him, there is no rational way of arriving at generalizations from the examination of sampled cases—no rational way of making the inductive leap—but once such a generalization has been produced, by whatever means, there *is* a rational way of discovering whether it meets the tests of observation and experiment. Such generalizations or hypotheses can be conclusively *falsified,* but never verified, never shown to be true. The task of empirical science is falsification, putting to the trial of experience bold "conjectures" about the world, and not the impossible task of discovering truth.

For all the ingenuity with which this provocative view has been argued (to which I cannot do justice in this brief essay), the "no induction" view, as it might be called, has not received wide acceptance. It seems too paradoxical a conception of science that it should consist only of the elimination of error, rather than the progressive discovery of approximations to the truth. And induction seems to creep in by the back door in Popper's theory of "corroboration," that is, of the criteria by which we discriminate between the relative strengths of hypotheses, none of which are falsified by the known observational facts.

2. One might think that common sense can provide a simple and satisfactory answer to the problem of induction. If a layman is asked why he trusts an inductive argument from "some" to "all," the chances are he will say that this kind of argument has "always worked in the past." (One might have some doubts about that "always," but no matter.) How foolish it would be, we can imagine the plain man saying, to abandon techniques that have worked so well and have produced such spectacular successes in technology and in pure science. Well, let it be granted that induction *has* "worked" in the past; what grounds does this give us for expecting it to work in the future? If we conclude that induction *will* work because it *has* worked we are arguing—inductively!

As the philosopher David Hume pointed out long ago in a famous discussion of the problem, we seem here to be begging the question. The best method we have for settling specific empirical questions—arguing from the known character of observed instances—leaves us in the lurch when we try to find a *general* justification of induction. To offer an inductive justification to anybody who doubts that induction is *ever* justified is obviously futile. . . .

3. A favorite approach to the problem of justification begins by asserting that inductive arguments, in the form considered in the essay, are basically *incomplete*. Transition from "some" to "all," from a premise about a sample to a conclusion about the population from which that sample was drawn, is held to rely upon unstated *assumptions*. Until such assumptions are made explicit, the inductive inference is unsound—the inductive *leap* is never justified by itself: an inductive argument needs an extra premise in order to become valid. There needs to be supplied some principle that "the future will resemble the past" or some more general principle of "the Uniformity of Nature." Once such a principle has been introduced into the argument, and only then, that argument will become logically respectable. (It will be noticed that this line of attack on the problem tacitly assumes that only *deductive* argument is irreproachable. By implicitly denying the possibility of distinctive arguments, this position resembles the "no induction" view previously mentioned.)

The formulation of general principles that might plausibly play the part of missing premises in inductive arguments is a matter of great difficulty. Since nature obviously exhibits variety as well as uniformity, irregularity as well as order, it is hard to state a principle of uniformity without producing something that is plainly false. For example, the principle that whenever some *A*'s are *B*, all *A*'s are *B* is a grotesque overstatement . . . . It seems fair to say that nobody has yet produced a suitably qualified candidate for the title of the "Basic Principle of Inductive Inference"—although many have tried.

We need not enter into the technicalities of this attempt to bolster induction by supplying an additional grand premise. There is in my opinion a conclusive objection against this whole line of approach. Imagine the desired general principle produced. . . .

How . . . is *its* truth to be known? Only, it seems, by the familiar methods, the best we know, of observation and inductive reasoning. Indeed, we may go further: our confidence in particular laws of nature, the conclusions of inductive inferences, is *better* grounded than our confidence in the truth of any alleged principle about the general uniformity of nature. Such evidence as we have for the orderliness of the universe is derived from our knowledge of particular regularities and not vice versa. The search for grand principles of induction therefore merely shifts the problem without solving it: the problem of establishing such principles is just the old one of justifying induction—in another and even less tractable form.

4. So far, I have made no reference to probability, in order to avoid complicating what is already a sufficiently complicated subject. Yet problems of induction and of probability are intertwined. It is important to notice, for instance, that the conclusion of a sound inductive argument follows from its premises only with a certain probability. Given a good inductive argument for some conclusion, we can always conceive of *stronger* evidence: inductive inferences can sometimes be compared with respect to their relative strengths in a way that would be quite inappropriate for deductive inferences. Some students of the theory of induction have therefore held that a reference to probability should be part of the conclusion of a properly expressed inductive argument. For instance, the correct conclusion from the premise "All examined *A*'s have been *B*," they say, is not "All *A*'s are *B*," but perhaps, "It is more probable than not that all *A*'s are *B*" or something similar. And the suggestion has often been made that neglect of such reference to probability is responsible for the inadequacy of the attempts to justify induction that we have so far considered.

Replacing a conclusion of the form "All *A*'s are *B*" by a conclusion of the form "It is more probable than not that all *A*'s are *B*" amounts to weakening the conclusion. (We may recall here that those who hoped to add an extra premise concerning the uniformity of nature were engaged in strengthening the premises. So both lines of attack aim at bringing inductive arguments closer to satisfying the standards of valid deductive argument.)

Our verdict on this attempt to make induction respectable by introducing probability must depend upon the meaning we attach to the relevant probability statement. According to one conception of the meaning of probability, the conclusion "It is more probable than not that all *A*'s are *B*" follows *strictly* from the premise "All examined *A*'s have been *B*": it is logically impossible that the premise should be true while the probability conclusion is false. On this interpretation, we would have a valid deductive argument, with no "inductive leap," if we introduced reference to probability into the conclusion. But this reading of inductive arguments is useless: our whole attempt has been to understand how it is possible to end in a conclusion that goes beyond the premises, by referring to things or situations that are not covered by those premises. Replacing the original inductive argument by some deductive substitute, however ingeniously constructed, will not be a solution.

There is another way of understanding probability, according to which the probability conclusion makes a genuinely empirical claim about what would be found true in a large number of similar cases. To say that the conclusion is "It is more probable than not that all *A*'s are *B*" would be tantamount to saying something like "In most cases in which the examined *A*'s have been *B*, it will be found subsequently that all *A*'s are *B*." On this view, the argument, as amended by explicit reference to probability, remains genuinely inductive. But by the same token we are confronted once again with the inductive leap. The new conclusion does not follow strictly from the premises, and we are still faced with the troublesome problem of how it can be rational to go beyond the evidence, in the manner that is characteristic of genuinely inductive arguments.

Those who insist that the conclusions of inductive arguments should be probability statements are faced with the same dilemma that bedevils all previous attempts to justify induction: either the argument is left in its original form, and then it seems to be invalid; or else it is replaced by some valid deductive argument (either by strengthening the premises or by weakening the conclusion), and then it is not an inductive argument at all.

5. I turn, finally, to the so-called ''pragmatic'' justifications of induction, which have seemed to many modern students of the problem to provide a satisfactory answer to this ancient puzzle. The basic ideas underlying this approach were independently formulated by Charles Sanders Peirce and by Hans Reichenbach, the latter of whom argued the position with great ingenuity and pertinacity.

Consider the following familiar position in ordinary life. A doctor, who is treating a patient suffering from some serious disease, has reason to believe that the only chance of saving the patient's life is to perform a certain operation; suppose also that there is no guarantee of the operation's proving successful: if the doctor is right in thinking that the patient will die in any case if the operation is not performed, he is justified in operating. To put the matter in another way: If a *necessary condition* for saving the patient's life is performing the operation, then that operation is justified, even though the outcome is unknown and the risks are great. This might be called a case of ''nothing to lose by trying''—resort to the dangerous operation may be a ''forlorn hope,'' but it is a justifiable one.

Those who apply this idea to the justification of induction argue as follows: Hume was right when he said that it was impossible to argue from the present to the future, from the known to the unknown. The ''inductive leap'' cannot be justified in the way that philosophers and scientists have hoped. Nevertheless, we badly need knowledge ranging beyond our observations and nothing can prevent us from trying to obtain it. Suppose it could be shown that the *only way* to reach such knowledge is by following inductive procedures. Then we should be in the position of the doctor or the patient in the original example, with nothing to lose by trying. If following inductive procedures is a *necessary condition* for anticipating the unknown, we shall be practically or—as people say,'' ''pragmatically''—justified in following that procedure.

We may agree that the general line of argument is plausible; its contribution to the problem of justifying induction will depend upon how successful its defenders are in showing that some kind of inductive procedure is a necessary condition for making correct generalizations about the unknown or the unobserved.

The model usually employed has approximately the following character: Suppose we are performing a series of observations and are interested in some property P. If in the first 100 trials we find that P has appeared in 65 cases, we assume provisionally that in the *long run* the proportion of favorable cases will be close to 65/100. As we continue our trials, we may find, say, 87 favorable cases in the first 150 observations: we therefore correct our estimate and now expect the proportion of favorable cases to be near 85/150. We proceed in this same way: whenever we find that k out of l trials exhibit the property P, we provisionally assume that the proportion in the long run will be close to k/l.

Since there is no guarantee that the fractions we progessively find in this way will ultimately converge to a limit, our attempt to anticipate the overall character of the entire series of observations may be defeated after all. But *if* there is a limit (which we cannot know) this procedure of successive correction will eventually bring us close to the true value of that limit. We are justified in following the procedure, because we have nothing to lose. If the series of successive fractions is sufficiently irregular, *no* method of forecasting its ultimate character will be possible; while if it has the regularity of a convergent series, our method will bring us close to the desired answer sooner or later.

This idea is too ingenious and too complicated to be criticized in a few words. I have argued at length elsewhere that it fails. Some of the strongest objections that I and other critics have brought to light are technical ones, having to do with the impossibility, according to the pragmatic view, of preferring one method of estimation to another.[1] But the basic objection is that the whole approach concedes too much to the skeptical critics of induction. Those who agree with Hume that *knowledge* of the unobserved is, strictly speaking, impossible, will always find themselves with empty hands at the conclusion of an inductive procedure no matter how ingeniously they try to wriggle out of their predicament.[2]

The Disappearance of the Problem

We seem now to have arrived at a stalemate. None of the ways of justifying induction that have been explored by a long line of able and acute thinkers seem to offer any prospects of success. Attempts to justify induction by using inductive procedures seem hopelessly circular; attempts to find principles expressing the alleged uniformity of nature simply raise the old questions in a new form; introducing probability statements does not help; and the fashionable "pragmatic" justifications really leave us helpless against skeptical objections to induction. Considering the intensity with which the problem has been studied, there is no hope that we shall do better where so many powerful intellects have labored in vain.

Now when we meet with a situation like this, there is usually reason to suppose that the nature of the problem has been misconceived, and that the apparently insurmountable difficulties arise from misunderstanding. The view is steadily gaining ground that this is the situation with regard to the celebrated problem of justifying induction.

The very notion of justification implies some *standard* of justification: to justify induction must be to show that that kind of reasoning satisfies some relevant criterion of what is regarded as reasonable. Now the long history of the subject shows that nearly everybody who has grappled with the problem has really had before his mind the standards of *deductive* reasoning: however widely the various attempts to justify induction differ, they all assume that the only really reputable mode of reasoning, the only "strict" method, is that in which the conclusion follows by logical necessity from the premises.

But induction, *by definition*, is not deduction: the idea of the so-called "inductive leap" is built into our conception of an inductive argument. To try to convert inductive arguments into deductive ones is as futile an attempt as that of the child who argued that a horse was really a cow—only without horns. The beginning of wisdom in this extremely complicated and controversial domain is therefore the recognition that no *general* justification of induction, of the sort that philosophers of science have hoped to uncover, is either possible or needed. What we *mean* by justifying a specific empirical generalization is an inductive demonstration, using principles that have been found to work in the kind of case in question, that the generalization is true or at least probable. When we try to apply this relatively definite notion of justification to induction itself, the very notion of justification becomes unclear.

It is not so much that we do not know how to justify induction as that we do not know and cannot imagine what we would *accept* as such a justification. Clarity, here—which cannot, of course, be achieved without the hardest intellectual labor—ought to result in the disappearance of the alleged "problem of induc-

[1]For editorial elaboration of this issue see note 1 at the end of the selection.

[2]For editorial elaboration of this issue see note 2 at the end of the selection.

tion.'' If this view is correct, as I hold it to be, the problem of induction will eventually be classified with such famous ''insoluble'' problems as that of squaring the circle or that of inventing perpetual-motion machines. And as in those famous cases, the quest for the impossible does not seem, from the long perspective of history, to have been futile. For the byproducts of serious investigation may be even more important than its ostensible goal. If our knowledge of the character of inductive procedures is as rich and as sophisticated as it is today, no little of the credit must be assigned to those who have labored so long and so unsuccessfully at trying to justify induction.

EDITOR'S NOTES

[1]The difficulty Black refers to is mathematical in nature and relates to the method of selecting the series which hopefully converges to a limit. It has been shown that there are an infinite number of such series. For example, Reichenbach, the most influential defender of the pragmatic solution to the problem of induction, identifies ''the rule of induction'' with what has come to be called ''the straight rule.'' Yet, it is conceded by supporters of the pragmatic approach that Reichenbach does not succeed in justifying his choice of this rule over others. Defenders of the pragmatic approach have attempted to narrow down the class of candidates for basic inductive rules. Foremost among defenders of this approach is Wesley C. Salmon of the University of Arizona. Yet, as Salmon regretfully admits, this approach had not led to success. To illustrate the sort of problem involved, Salmon considers the following initial sequence of heads and tails:

H T T H T H T H H H T H T H H H T H T H

Salmon writes:

> The relative frequency of heads in this observed sequence is 6/10; on the basis of the rule of induction we might infer—or *posit*, to use Reichenbach's term—that the long run frequency of heads, if the sequence is continued, will be somewhere near that value. If, however, we examine the initial section carefully, we note that each toss corresponding to a prime number—the second, third, fifth, seventh, etc.—is a tail, while every other toss yields heads. If we use the rule of induction on the subsequences, we posit that each prime toss will be a tail and all others will be heads. Since it is known that the limiting frequency of primes among the natural numbers is zero, the induction on the subsequences entails that the limiting frequency of heads in the entire sequence is 1. Unless it can be shown how, and why, one of these inductions must supersede the other, adoption of Reichenbach's rule of induction will lead to a genuine paradox. At present, I do not know how to resolve this paradox—or whether it is, in principle, capable of resolution. (''Unfinished Business: The Problem of Induction,'' *Philosophical Studies*, 33 (1978), pp. 14–15)

In his discussion of attempts at pragmatic justification of induction in his *Problems of Analysis* (London: Routledge and Kegan Paul, 1954), Black also argues that the supporters of this point of view (Black calls them *practicalists*) are incapable of showing that the *specific* inductive procedures they provide are necessary for *any* successful prediction. As Black sees it, what they do show is that the specific methods they supply are necessary for successful prediction, which is more narrowly defined by their inductive procedure and, consequently, their claims tend to degenerate into tautologies (i.e., they are true by definition alone). To use Black's own example:

> Suppose a doctor who is treating a certain disease with sulfa drugs were to say that no other measures could achieve the aims of the treatment, i.e., that it was *necessary* to use sulfa drugs to achieve the aims desired. If the doctor informed us that his aim was to *cure* the patient (by any means efficacious), his assertion that sulfa drugs are necessary to achieve that aim would be interesting and significant. But suppose he were to say that his aim was the narrower one of *curing the patient solely by means of sulfa drugs.* In that case, the contention that sulfa drugs are necessary would become trivial. It is an uninteresting tautology that if you intend to use sulfa drugs in effecting a cure, you must use sulfa drugs: the assertion is both uncontroversial and pointless. (*Problems of Analysis*, pp. 174–75.)

Black continues:

> Parallel considerations apply to the case in hand. If practicalists define their aim as that of making predictions about the unobserved *by means of their designated inductive policies,* the contention that adherence to these policies is a necessary condition for success in achieving this aim is trivial, uncontroversial and pointless. If what is said is to deserve attention, the aims to be served by the policies must be more broadly defined. And in fact, being sensible men, practicalists do so define their aims, at least half the time. The chief aim of the inductive procedures (if we neglect our interest in systematic and coherent knowledge) is *successful prediction*. But if this is accepted, it is no longer an empty tautology that the only way to achieve it is by using the inductive policies. (Ibid., p. 175)

Yet Black claims that practicalists are incapable of demonstrating this. Instead, they simply attempt to demonstrate that their specific inductive procedure is capable of achieving their more specific goal. Quoting from Reichenbach, Black writes:

Reichenbach says: "Scientific method pursues the aim of predicting the future: *in order to construct a precise formulation* for this aim we interpret it as meaning that scientific method is intended to find limits to the frequency" (p. 474 of *Theory of Probability,* italics added). He is narrowing the aim, not just formulating it more precisely. This narrowing of the aim makes it possible for Reichenbach to view the search for limits of the frequency as a necessary condition for the success of inductive method. But anybody who says that he wants to predict the future but is not interested in finding the limits of relative frequencies of occurrence of characters in infinite series is not contradicting himself. Reichenbach is not analyzing scientific method but redefining it for his own purposes. (*Problems of Analysis,* p. 175, footnote)

Black continues:

. . . reduced to its simplest terms, the so-called "pragmatic" *proof* that the inductive policies are "reasonable" amounts to no more than this: "These inductive policies are the only ones that could achieve the aims distinguishing these inductive policies from all other policies," and this is not only a tautology but a useless one. Still more simply, what such proofs amount to is the assurance "You can always go on trying, can't you? . . . But why would a person take this advice if he had thought there could be no question of his having any likelihood of success? (Ibid, pp. 186–87)

[2]There are several difficulties here. First, even if the practicalists can justify the selection of a particular rule of induction, there is no guarantee that our short-range estimates of the limit are close to the actual limit of the series. What may be true in the never-to-be-realized "long-run" may be quite unhelpful in the short-run. Second, and most fundamental for Black, the practicalists grant too much to Hume when they concede that it is impossible to *know* the conclusion of inductive arguments to be true or even probable. For example, Reichenbach concedes that:

Hume was right in asserting that the conclusion of the inductive inference cannot be proved to be true, and we may add that it cannot even be proved to be probable . . . The aim of knowing the future is unattainable; there is no demonstrative truth informing us about future happenings. (Reichenbach, *Theory of Probability,* p. 475, 480; quoted in Black, *Problems of Analysis,* pp. 161–62)

Black finds this view unreasonable, for according to it:

. . . we do not and cannot *know* that water is wet, that acorns grow into oaks or that monkeys never argue about induction. And if anybody were to say that pigs can fly, we should not *know* that he was wrong. The same must also be said, according to these writers, about probability statements. If they are right, you do not know that you are unlikely to win the Irish Sweepstake or that it will probably rain before the end of the year. I wonder whether anybody, not excluding Hume and his contemporary followers, has ever really been as sceptical as this? (*Problems of Analysis,* p. 162).

DISCUSSION QUESTION

1. Consider the following three different views on the justification of induction:

A: In discussing the justification of induction it is essential that we distinguish the basic principle of inductive reasoning (**basic induction**) from the particular inductive method utilized by scientific method (**scientific induction**). According to the principle of basic induction, one has good reason to accept a method of predicting the future only insofar as it has proved reliable in the past. This principle is true by definition, while the principle of scientific induction is not. According to the latter principle, one can reliably infer that regularities in nature that have occurred continually in the past will continue to occur continually in the future. In more symbolic language, scientific induction is the mode of inference that enables us to infer that "All **F**s are **G**s" from the fact that "All **F**s have been **G**s in the past," where **F** and **G** stand for either properties of objects or events. The belief in the reliability of scientific induction has often been expressed as the belief in "the uniformity of nature" or in "the law of universal causation." It is the mode of inference that is presupposed by scientists when they assume that the patterns of observed regularities in the past can be counted on to continue in the future. While this mode of inference has proved successful in the past, there is no guarantee that it will continue to be successful in the future. In this Hume was quite right. If scientific induction were to cease being a reliable form of inference and we were lucky enough to survive, we might find ourselves occupying a chaotic and unpredictable universe or a new method of predicting the future might then prove reliable. For example, the course of events might then prove amenable to the method of **inverse induction**, which is utilized by card players whose expectation of future cards of a particular suit that will be drawn varies inversely with the number of cards of that suit already drawn. Or one can imagine a world where a soothsayer is capable of reliably predicting the future through precognitive visions. But the important point to recognize here is that if scientific induction were to be supplanted by some other more successful method of predicting the future, its reliability would have to be supported by the principle of basic induction. For example, we would not and should not trust the soothsayer unless he has a high success rate of accurate predictions. To say that a method of predicting the future is successful **simply means** that it has repeatedly been applied with success. The phrase "successful method of predicting the future which has no inductive support" is self-contradictory. Consequently, the principle of basic induction is true by definition, for to say that one has good reason to accept a method of predicting the future simply means that that method has a record of previous successes; it can mean nothing else. It seems to me that the source of the desire to justify induction stems from the failure to realize this and to confuse basic induction with scientific induction.

B: I don't think A's distinction between what he calls basic and scientific induction comes to grips with Hume's question. A's claim that the principle of basic induction is true by definition seems to me to beg the question at issue. The claim that it is true by definition that "what has occurred in the past gives us reason to assume that it will occur in the future" follows only if one assumes that the only reason one could have for making predictions is the **previous** success of a particular method of inference. But, as Hume pointed out, the whole problem of justifying induction is the problem of uncovering our warrant for assuming that **previous** successes will, at least most likely, lead to **future** successes. It is the failure to recognize this central point in Hume's argument that leads A and other linguistically oriented philosopers to claim that "any successful method of inferring the future would have to be inductively supported." Such a claim begs the question, for the sceptic will say that however successful a method of inferring the future has been in the past, this provides no evidence for its continued success in the future. However irrational we may think a person to be who trusts a method of predicting the future that does not have a record of success, Hume was right that there is no way we can justify basic induction without assuming precisely what is at issue.

C: I agree with B that one cannot adequately dismiss Hume's scepticism concerning the justification of induction by simply turning, as A does, to the ordinary meaning of words. Even though A is quite right that it is self-contradictory **in ordinary language** to say that a reliable, reasonable, or trustworthy mode of prediction has no inductive support, that simply reflects our practice; it does not justify it. Hume would have been quite ready to admit that a person who does not proportion his beliefs to the inductive evidence for them would be considered unreasonable to the ordinary person. Indeed, he would be considered unreasonable to Hume when Hume was not in one of his philosophical moods. But Hume was not misusing language when he sought some vindication for his inductive practice, some way of showing that following the principle of basic induction is likely to lead to success in the future. If basic induction, rather than some other alternative, like reading tea leaves, is constitutive of rationality, we ought to be able to say on what grounds its superiority rests. According to B, it would appear, there are no such grounds. It's all a matter of blind faith, I suppose, whether one trusts a soothsayer who consistently makes unreliable forecasts or chooses to rely on predictive methods that have proven reliable in the past. No doubt, as Hume stressed, we can never be certain that reliable methods will continue to be reliable. But we do have a right to infer that a regularity that has occurred consistently in the past **most probably** will occur in the future. As all students of statistics know, it can be **proven** mathematically that the probability of a generalization increases with the number of instances for which it is found to hold. This is a direct corollary of the mathematical truth that the greater the size of a sample of a given population, the greater the likelihood that the sample will match the entire population. This, in short, is the justification of induction. It's really that simple. All Hume needed for resolving his doubt about induction was a little mathematics.

Critically consider the issues raised by A, B, and C. What's your position on this matter? Why?

FURTHER READINGS

The Encyclopedia of Philosophy (New York: Macmillan, 1967): In addition to entries on Descartes, Locke, Berkeley, Hume, Mill and Kant which cover the epistemological views of these philosophers, *The Encyclopedia of Philosophy* contains the following articles which are related to the topics of this chapter: Critical Realism; Empiricism; Idealism; Illusions; Induction; Perception; Phenomenalism; Primary and Secondary Qualities; Rationalism; Realism; Sensa; Skepticism.

the philosophical problem of distinguishing appearance from reality as expressed in science fiction

Imaginative science fiction tales provide a fertile area for philosophical themes which jar our complacency in drawing the distinctions that we do between appearance and reality. For example, George Henry Smith, in his brief tale "In the Imagicon," imagines a machine ("the Imagicon") that can be programmed to produce desired coherent and vivid dreams that are indistinguishable from "reality." As an added bonus, Smith's story can be read as an allegory that reflects a traditional theological response to the problem of evil. The distinction between real and delusive memories is the central theme of Philip K. Dick's "We Can Remember It for You Wholesale." In this tale, the hero Douglas Quail's decision to have false memories of an adventurous past implanted into his mind has quite unexpected consequences. Smith's and Dick's tales can be found in *Nebula Award Stories, Number Two,* edited by Damon Knight (New York: Doubleday, 1967). The clash of two individuals' conflicting views of reality and the mutual uncertainty it engenders as these two individuals struggle to convince the other, and then themselves, as to who is "really in touch with reality" is the theme of Rog Phillips' "The Yellow Pill" which was originally published in *Astounding Science Fiction* (October, 1958) and reprinted in Tom Beauchamp, William Blackstone, and Joel Feinberg, *Philosophy and the Human Condition* (Englewood Cliffs, N.J.: Prentice-Hall, 1980).

perception-epistemology: classic sources and commentary

Berkeley, George, *Berkeley: Principles, Dialogues and Correspondence.* Indianapolis, Ind.: Bobbs-Merrill, 1965. This book contains Berkeley's *Principles of Human Knowledge* (a formal exposition of Berkeley's idealism), his *Dialogues Between Hylas and Philonous* (a lively, more informal dialogue that expresses the same ideas), and the correspondence between Berkeley and Samuel Johnson. This material is preceded by a good (28-page) introduction by Colin Turbayne. There is also a useful analytic summary of the two works.

Berkeley, George, *The Principles of Human Knowledge and Other Writings.* Cleveland: Meridian Books, 1963. This book also contains Berkeley's *Principles* and *Dialogues.* The (32-page) introduction by G.J. Warnock is very helpful.

Cornford, F.M., *Plato's Theory of Knowledge.* London: Routledge, 1935. This book contains Plato's views on epistemology as expressed in his *Theaetetus* and *Sophist* and Cornford's analyses of these works which, though clear, are geared to a sophisticated reader of philosophy.

Hume, David, *A Treatise of Human Nature.* Oxford: Oxford University Press, 1978. This edition of Hume's *Treatise* consists of the 1888 Selby-Bigge edition with revisions and notes by P.H. Nidditch. Selby-Bigge's analytic index is excellent and quite useful. To find passages relating to Hume's discussion of perception, look up "perception" in the analytic index.

Kenny, Anthony, *Descartes: A Study of His Philosophy.* New York: Random House, 1968. An excellent introduction to Descartes' philosophy with an emphasis on his epistemology.

Locke, John, *An Essay Concerning Human Understanding.* Cleveland: Meridian Books, 1964. See Book II, Chapters 7 to 9 for Locke's theory of perception. The (46-page) introduction by A.D. Woozley is very helpful.

Mackie, J.L., *Problems From Locke.* New York: Oxford University Press, 1976. Mackie discusses topics which figure prominently in John Locke's *Essay Concerning Human Understanding.* The topics discussed are: (1) the distinction between primary and secondary qualities; (2) representative theories of perception; (3) substance, real and nominal essence; (4) abstract ideas, universals, and the meaning of general terms; (5) identity, especially personal identity; (6) the conflict between empiricism and the doctrine of innate ideas. While Mackie examines Locke's arguments carefully, his primary interest is in the problems themselves, and consequently he intertwines his own analyses of the philosophical problems that occupied Locke with Locke's own analyses. The book is clearly written and nontechnical, but the analyses are involved and sophisticated.

Mill, John Stuart, *An Examination of Sir William Hamilton's Philosophy.* London: Longmans, Green, 1872. Mill's classic presentation of phenomenalism is found in Chapters XI and XII.

Stroud, Barry, *Hume.* London: Routledge & Kegan Paul, 1977. This book provides a clear and nontechnical account of Hume's theory of ideas, his views on perception and causality, as well as other aspects of his philosophy.

Warnock, G.J., *Berkeley.* Baltimore: Pelican, 1953. A clearly written and highly recommended commentary on Berkeley's idealism.

perception: twentieth century views

Armstrong, D.M., *Perception and the Physical World.* London: Routledge and Kegan Paul; New York: Humanities Press, 1961. This sophisticated book is for the more advanced reader of philosophy. Armstrong argues for *direct realism* (which he defines as the view that the immediate object of awareness is "a physical existent" which exists independently of our awareness of it) and against views that claim that the direct objects of perception are sense data (or impressions) which do not exist independently of our awareness of them. In the course of defending his view, Armstrong analyzes the nature of perception and the concepts of *sense impressions* and *physical objects.*

Ayer, A.J., *The Foundations of Empirical Knowledge.* London: Macmillan, 1940; *The Problem of Knowledge.* London: Penguin, 1956. *The Central Questions of Philosophy.* New York: Holt, Rinehart and Winston, 1973. Read in sequence, these books are valuable for their demonstration of how Ayer, an early defender of phenomenalism, eventually abandoned this view. With his clear writing style, Ayer directs his book to a wide lay audience, although the arguments he presents are complex enough to generate debate among professional philosophers. While *The Foundations of Empirical Knowledge* deals exclusively with philosophical theories of perception, the other two books range widely over the topic of epistemology. For example, *The Problem of Knowledge* contains an excellent discussion of scepticism and certainty.

Austin, J.L., *Sense and Sensibilia.* New York: Oxford University Press, 1962. A very influential critique of the view that sense data and not physical objects are the direct objects of perception. Austin's criticisms refer, in particular, to Ayer's arguments in *The Foundation of Empirical Knowledge.* (For Ayer's rejoinder, see his "Has Austin Refuted the Sense-Datum Theory," in Ayer, A.J., *Metaphysics and Common Sense.* London: Macmillan, 1969.)

Barnes, W.H.F., "The Myth of Sense-Data," *Proceedings of The Aristotelian Society,* 45 (1944–45), pp. 89–117. As does Austin above, Barnes argues against the view that sense data and not physical objects are the direct objects of perception.

Lewis, C.I., *Mind and the World Order.* New York: Dover, 1956 (originally published in 1929). In this influential book, C.I. Lewis offers a theory of perception that combines the Kantian view that experiences are always interpreted by a system of classification imposed by the mind, with the pragmatic emphasis upon the relativity of these modes of classification to human needs and purposes. This book is geared to the more philosophically sophisticated.

Russell, Bertrand, *The Problems of Philosophy.* London: Oxford University Press, 1917. The first four chapters of this book clearly and engagingly introduce the problem of perception. (Portions of these chapters appear in our first selection.) Russell presents a more technical account of his philosophy of perception in *Our Knowledge of the External World,* London: G. Allen, 1926. Russell's views on perception can also be found in his *The Outline of Philosophy,* London: Allen and Unwin, 1927, and *Human Knowledge,* New York: Simon & Schuster, 1948. Like Ayer's, Russell's theory of perception underwent modification in his many philosophical writings. In Russell's case, one notices a tension between phenomenalism and critical realism. Also like Ayer's, Russell's clear writing style makes him an appealing philosophical writer for beginning philosophy students. References to criticisms of Russell's theory of perception can be found in the annotated bibliography on perception in Paul Edwards, and Arthur Pap, *A Modern Introduction to Philosophy* (3rd ed.), p. 658, New York: Macmillan, 1973.

Ryle, Gilbert, *Dilemmas,* Cambridge: Cambridge University Press, 1954. Chapter V contains Ryle's criticism of the view that critical realism is supported by physics.

general critical surveys of theories of perception

Hospers, John, *An Introduction to Philosophical Analysis* (2nd ed.), Englewood Cliffs, N.J.: Prentice-Hall, 1967. Chapter 6 contains a very good introductory exposition and criticism of philosophical theories of perception.

Mundle, C.W.K., *Perception: Facts and Theories.* London: Oxford University Press, 1971. A critical survey of rival philosophical theories of perception and material drawn from psychology and physiology. Mundle claims that philosophers have neglected relevant data from experimental psychology in formulating their theories of perception. This comprehensive anthology is geared to the more advanced student of the philosophy of perception.

Passmore, John, *A Hundred Years of Philosophy*, 2nd ed. Hammondsworth: Penguin Books, 1968. Chapters 9 through 12 contain an excellent discussion of philosophical theories of perception.

anthologies on the philosophy of perception

Beardsley, D.C., and M. Wertheimer, eds., *Readings in Perception.* Princeton: Van Nostrand, 1958. This anthology is geared to psychology students, but there are many selections of philosophical interest. It would be very useful to students of the philosophy of perception who have an interest and background in psychology.

Hirst, R.J., ed., *Perception and the External World.* New York: Macmillan, 1965. Contained in this anthology are selections from classical and contemporary philosophers as well as from physiologists and psychologists on the subject of perception. The (27-page) editorial introduction provides a good synopsis of the topics covered.

Nagel, E., and R. Brandt, *Meaning and Knowledge.* New York: Harcourt, 1965. This broad general anthology of selections on epistemology has a good section of selections on the philosophy of perception by classical and contemporary philosophers. It also contains sections on meaning, truth, induction, memory, and other minds ("How do we know that other people are conscious?").

Swartz, Robert J., ed., *Perceiving, Sensing and Knowing.* Garden City, N.Y.: Doubleday, 1965. This anthology contains selections on the philosophy of perception by twentieth-century Anglo-American philosophers.

Warnock, G.J., ed., *The Philosophy of Perception.* London: Oxford University Press, 1967. An anthology of articles on the philosophy of perception by contemporary philosophers.

a modern defense of scepticism

Unger, Peter, *Ignorance.* New York: Oxford University Press, 1975. In this provocative but difficult book, Unger argues for the highly sceptical views that nothing can ever be "known" and that no one can ever have any "reason" at all for believing anything.

induction

Black, Max, *Problems of Analysis,* Chapters X and XI. London: Routledge & Kegan Paul, 1954. In Chapter X, Black criticizes pragmatic justifications of induction and, in Chapter XI, he sympathetically discusses attempts to provide inductive support for induction, while escaping the claim that such justifications are circular. The sophistication of the analyses is softened by Black's clear and nontechnical writing style and the wealth of examples he employs.

Hume, David, *An Inquiry Concerning Human Understanding,* Section IV. Indianapolis: Bobbs-Merrill, 1955 (first published 1748). Hume's classic presentation of his sceptical doubts concerning the justification of induction.

Edwards, Paul, "Bertrand Russell's Doubts about Induction," *Mind*, 58 (1949), pp. 141–63. A defense of the view that the problem of induction is a pseudo-problem generated by linguistic confusion.

Popper, Karl, *The Logic of Scientific Discovery*. London: Hutchinson, 1959. In this stimulating and controversial book, Popper denies that the principle of induction plays any role in scientific method and consequently treats sceptical doubts about the justification of induction as idle.

Reichenbach, Hans, *Theory of Probability*. Berkeley: University of California Press, 1949. A technical discussion of the concept of probability and the classic defense of the pragmatic justification of inductive inference.

Russell, Bertrand, *Human Knowledge: Its Scope and Limits.* London: George Allen & Unwin, 1948. This book contains Russell's later thinking on induction.

Salmon, Wesley, "Unfinished Business: The Problem of Induction," *Philosophical Studies,* 33, No. 1 (January 1978), pp. 1-19. A clear and comprehensive survey of current philosophical thinking on the philosophical problem of the justification of induction. Salmon defends the pragmatic approach, following in the footsteps of Reichenbach. He is especially critical of the linguistic approach that dismisses the problem of induction as a pseudo-problem.

Strawson, P.F., *Introduction to Logical Theory,* Chapter 9. New York, Wiley, 1952. A very clear defense of the linguistic approach to the problem of induction which claims that this problem results from linguistic confusion and consequently needs to be "dissolved" through a closer attention to language, rather than "solved."

Will, F.L., "Will the Future Be Like the Past?" *Mind,* 56 (1947), pp. 332–47. Will criticizes Hume's and Russell's doubts concerning the justification of inductive inference. In particular, he argues that they were mistaken in claiming that all attempts to justify induction are circular. Will attributes this (alleged) mistake to the failure to recognize that "the future" is constantly being revealed to us, providing us with more and more evidence for our belief that the future will be like the past.

longer annotated bibliography

Edwards, Paul, and A. Pap, *A Modern Introduction to Philosophy,* (3rd ed.), New York: Macmillan, 1973. See pp. 654–63 for a comprehensive annotated bibliography of reference sources on specific topics in the philosophy of perception and pp. 164–69 for a comprehensive annotated bibliography of philosophical writings on the problem of induction, scepticism, and the lack of conclusive verification of statements about matters of fact.

Chapter V

ETHICS

Reason is, and ought only to be the slave of the passions, and can never pretend to any other office than to serve and obey them. . . . Where a passion is neither founded on false suppositions, nor chooses means insufficient for the end, the understanding can neither justify nor condemn it. 'Tis not contrary to reason to prefer the destruction of the whole world to the scratching of my finger.

David Hume

There cannot be such a thing as ethical science, if by ethical science one means the elaboration of a "true" system of morals. For . . . as ethical judgments are mere expressions of feeling, there can be no way of determining the validity of any ethical system.

A.J. Ayer

. . . . the will is a faculty of choosing only that which reason, independently of inclination, recognizes . . . as good.

Immanuel Kant

All reasoning must be grounded on first principles. . . . There must, therefore, be in morals . . . first or self-evident principles, on which all moral reasoning is grounded. From such self-evident principles, conclusions may be drawn . . . with regard to the moral conduct of life. . . . But without such principles, we can no more establish any conclusion in morals, than we can build a castle in the air, without any foundation.

Thomas Reid

. . . Moral concepts are ultimately generalizations of tendencies to feel either moral approval or disapproval with reference to that of which these concepts are predicated. . . . A moral judgment always has the character of disinterestedness. When pronouncing an act good or bad, I mean that it is so quite independently of any reference to me personally.

Edward Westermarck

God made us and all the world. Because of that he has an absolute claim on our obedience. We do not exist in our own right, but only as His creatures, who ought therefore to do and be what He desires. . . . The pattern of conduct which God has laid down for man is the same for all men. . . . not to follow it [is, by definition] . . . to refuse to do what . . . [is] right . . .

Bishop Robert C. Mortimer

No reason can be given why the general happiness is desirable, except that each person . . . desires his own happiness. This, however,

. . . there is an imperative which, without being based on . . . any . . . purpose to be attained by a certain line of conduct, enjoins this

being a fact, we have . . . all the proof . . . which it is possible to require that happiness is a good; that each person's happiness is a good to that person, and the general happiness, therefore, a good to the aggregate of all persons.

John Stuart Mill

. . . a moral code is "ideal" if its currency in a particular society would produce at least as much good per person (the total divided by the number of persons) as the currency of any other moral code. . . . An act is right if and only if it would not be prohibited by the moral code ideal for the society.

Richard Brandt

conduct immediately. This imperative is ***categorical****. . . . There is only a single categorical imperative and it is this:* ***Act only on that maxim through which you can at the same time will that it should become a universal law****. . . . [This is equivalent to]* ***Act in such a way that you always treat humanity, whether in your person or in the person of any other, never simply as a means, but always at the same time as an end.***

Immanuel Kant

. . . each person possesses an inviolability founded on justice that even the welfare of society as a whole cannot override.

John Rawls

Introduction: The Roles of Reason and Feeling in Moral Reasoning

Caught in the moral crosscurrents of our times, we may think back nostalgically to the comforting days of childhood when moral matters seemed so much clearer. Was it not much easier then to classify actions as right or wrong and people as good or bad? However, as we grow older and become aware of widespread disagreements among individuals and cultures over specific moral issues and the general principles that underlie them, we often become uncertain of our moral compass, fearing that our cherished moral beliefs are incapable of rational justification. After all, we reflect, other people and cultures, equally desirous as we to be good and to do what is right, have rejected these beliefs. Can we be sure then that we are right and they are wrong? In such a disquieting mood, we wonder whether our moral beliefs are no more than reflections of the prevailing, although ever changing mores of our cultures—no more right or wrong than those of innumerable cultures that have existed through the ages.

Such thoughts are reinforced by the claims of many social scientists who deny the possibility of cross-cultural moral evaluation. For example, after describing the vast differences in lifestyles and moral attitudes of various cultures, the cultural anthropologist Ruth Benedict concludes that ". . . most individuals are plastic to the moulding force of the society in which they are born." Morality, she claims, is simply a matter of "conditioned habit." (see Selection #41). Such views filter into the common consciousness and are often offered as support for the common observation today by the cynical and sceptical that "morality is simply a matter of taste" and "taste," they imply, is notoriously fickle and unreasoning.

Those who deny the possibility of rationally distinguishing some moral claims as "true" and others as "false" have their supporters among the ranks of famous philosophers. Foremost among these philosophers is David Hume (1711–1766), who has exerted a great influence on subsequent philosophy. As Hume saw it, there is an unbridgeable gap between the world of "facts" and the world of "values." Values, he believed, are not to be discovered by a faculty of human reason which can discern a "moral order" in the universe that exists apart from human psychological sentiments. Although reason, he claimed, is necessary to guide and direct our sentiments in such a way that we may best achieve our moral ends, it is ultimately sentiment, and not reason, which moves us to judge things as good or bad and right or wrong. As he put it in a well-known passage, "Reason is, and ought only to be the slave of the passions, and can never pretend to any other office than to serve and obey them."[1]

Hume's claim that one's choice of moral ends is determined by sentiment and not by reason, has been criticized by many philosophers who claim that moral ends are capable of rational appraisal, as are the means we employ to achieve them. Indeed, many philosophers sympathetic to Hume's emphasis upon the central role of feelings of approval or disapproval in moral judgments have pointed out that he ignores an essential role that reason must play in the choice of moral ends—the role of criticizing ends when they are mutually inconsistent. Clearly, if one accepts a plurality of moral ends, it is important that these ends not contradict each other. One's view of "the most desirable mode of life" must be *a rational pattern of life* which requires that one's moral ends "hang together" as a coherent whole and this requirement makes it possible to criticize moral ends as unreasonable. In addition, the realization that one's momentary desires can conflict with one's reasoned preferences also requires that one be willing to forego present gratification, however momentarily strong, in order to secure greater future gratification or to avoid greater future suffering, and this, too, requires reasoning. In his preoccupation with drawing a radical dichotomy between "facts" and "values," Hume refused to concede this important point. Nevertheless, he may still be correct that it is logically possible for individuals of different psychological temperaments to reach a point of ultimate moral disagreement—that is, disagreement that would persist even with total agreement on all possibly relevant nonmoral "facts."

While a majority of social scientists would accept this claim, it does not automatically follow, as many of them imply, from the acceptance of the unquestionable diversity of moral beliefs and practices. While it is unquestionable that different societies are and have been guided by very different attitudes concerning *specific* moral issues (e.g., sexual morality and the morality of abortion, suicide, and euthanasia), it is open to question whether these different attitudes on specific moral issues reflect differences in ultimate moral principles or are instead reflections of differing circumstances, or factual or religious beliefs. It has been suggested that if agreement could be obtained on all nonmoral factors, agreement would be obtained on moral issues as well. For example, people today would morally condemn the practice during the Spanish Inquisition of burning people at the stake. However, this does not imply that today's ultimate moral principles are different from those accepted in the past when the Spanish Inquisition was seen as morally justified. Perhaps, in this case, the disagreement stems from a fundamental difference in religious belief. During the period of the Inquisition, when there was widespread fear of eternal damnation, it was fervently believed by many that burning people at the stake was the only way to save them from the far worse fate of eternal damnation. If we shared this religious belief, would we not also approve of this distasteful and desperate action?

While it may be logically possible to attribute

[1]David Hume, *A Treatise of Human Nature* (Oxford: Oxford University Press, 1964), originally published in 1739, p. 415.

all moral disagreements to disagreements over nonmoral factors, such a position is not a widely held one among contemporary social scientists. Ultimate moral disagreements may not be as wide as many anthropologists have suggested; nevertheless such disagreements seem to exist. But even if moral disagreement would *in fact* persist even with total agreement on all nonmoral "facts," this does not imply that such disagreement must be irreconcilable by reason. After all, some people notoriously refuse to be, or are incapable of being, guided by reason. The existence of some moral truth or a coherent system of such truths is quite consistent with human blindness to these truths. Consequently the observation by anthropologists of cultural moral diversity, even if ultimate in nature, does not refute those who believe that they possess that moral truth or system of moral truths. (It does, however, pose a grave difficulty for particular views concerning the nature of objective moral truth. For example, the fact of ultimate moral disagreements would pose a grave difficulty to those philosophers who claim that one can simply "see" or "intuit" what is right. If there are ultimate moral disagreements, how can we distinguish "correct" moral intuitions from "incorrect" ones?)

Regardless of the pronouncements by so many anthropologists of the impossibility of cross-cultural moral evaluation, such a view runs counter to the widespread belief that some moral attitudes are *wrong,* regardless of what people or "societies" of people happen to feel about it. For example, the famous twentieth-century philosopher Bertrand Russell argues that

> . . . if two men differ about values, there is not a disagreement as to any kind of truth, but a difference of taste. If one man says "oysters are good" and another says "I think they are bad," we recognize that there is nothing to argue about. . . . All differences as to values are of this sort, although we do not naturally think them so when we are dealing with matters that seem to us more exalted than oysters.[2]

But he confesses elsewhere that

> Certainly there seems to be something more. Suppose, for example, that someone were to advocate the introduction of bull-fighting in this country. In opposing the proposal, I should *feel,* not only that I was expressing my desires, but that my desires in the matter are *right,* whatever that may mean. As a matter of argument, I can, I think, show that I am not guilty of any logical inconsistency in holding to the above interpretation of ethics and at the same time expressing strong ethical preferences. But in feeling I am not satisfied.[3]

Is Russell's hesitancy to accept his professed view that morality is a matter of "taste" an irrational hesitancy, capable of psychological explanation but not of rational justification, or is there some underlying universal moral truth which makes bull-fighting wrong, regardless of what people happen in a particular place and at a particular time to think and feel about it? Are there any moral assertions like this? Many philosophers have thought so.

Religious Absolutism

For many people, the justification of moral standards is to be found in the will of God. A right action, on this view, consists, *by definition,* in obedience to God's will. This, it has been claimed, is the only genuine basis for morality. An atheist may live according to the moral point of view, but if his life is to have any rational justification, it must come from its correspondence to the will of God. As Dostoyevsky's Ivan Karamazov puts it in the *The Brothers Karam-*

[2]See Selection #43.

[3]Paul Schilpp, ed., *The Philosophy of Bertrand Russell* (New York: Tudor Publishing Company, 1954), p. 724.

azov, "If there is no God, then anything is permissible."

Following Plato's famous argument in the *Euthyphro* (Selection #40), most contemporary philosophers would contend that it is not God commanding an act that makes it right, but the *reasons* God has for commanding it (i.e., an act is not right because God commands it, but rather is commanded by God because it is right). Furthermore, the claim that rightness must be defined in terms of God's will is inconsistent with the traditional Judeo-Christian view that the very concept of God involves reference to his moral attributes (i.e., God is, by definition, a morally perfect being). If such a definition is not to be circular, moral principles must be grounded on standards independent of divine authority. Must we not utilize these standards in determining whether an alleged pronouncement from God truly derives from God? If, on the other hand, God is to be defined without reference to his moral attributes, why should his commands necessarily merit our *respect*? Do we, for example, owe him absolute allegiance simply because he is our creator, regardless of the reasons that he had for creating us? What if he created us simply to see us suffer? Would the commands of such a being be a model of moral perfection? If he commands us to be cruel to others, does that make cruelty right? If we choose to obey the commands of such a being, would it not simply be out of fear and not for a worthy moral reason, for does not morality demand that we choose to act on principles which are worthy of respect in and of themselves and not out of fear of the being who promulgates these principles?

Intuitionism

Accepting the arguments against identifying morality with the will of God, many philosophers have argued that there are certain self-evident moral truths which any rational person, regardless of psychological temperament and social conditioning, can see to be true. Indeed, such a view was a popular one among philosophers in Hume's day and it has continued to exert influence. According to this point of view (called *intuitionism*), one can simply "see" or "intuit" certain unchangeable moral truths which are independent of human desires. Just as Euclid believed that there were self-evident geometrical truths (his axioms or postulates) from which the entire corpus of geometrical knowledge could be deduced (his theorems), so the intuitionist believes that there are self-evident moral truths from which the corpus of moral knowledge can be deduced. Unfortunately, however, philosophers who take this point of view do not agree on what these self-evident moral truths are. Such disagreement gives credence to the cynical observation of other philosophers that the intuitionists are simply expressing their own moral preferences and trying to get others to adopt their attitudes. While an intuitionist may speak of those who do not accept his intuitions as "morally blind," there are no agreed upon tests for determining when this condition exists. Unlike the color-blind person, the morally blind one is not compelled to accept the existence of a capacity in others that he lacks himself.

On the other hand, some principles offered as alleged self-evident moral truths turn out on scrutiny to be true by definition and do not make any substantive moral claim. For example, the principle "murder is always wrong" has been offered as an example of a self-evident moral principle. Yet such a principle can be made self-evident only by defining "murder" as "a wrongful killing," but in that case the principle that "murder is always wrong" reduces to the empty claim that "wrongful killing is always wrong." Similarly, the intuitionist W.D. Ross, in his influential book *The Right and the Good* (1930), claims that "To me it seems as self-evident as anything could be, that to make a promise . . . is to create a moral claim on us in someone else.'' This certainly does seem self-evident, but why? Is it not simply true, by definition, that promising ''creates a moral claim on us in someone else''? Is not the practice of promising, by definition, a vehicle for creating such moral claims? While the existence of such a moral claim follows, by definition, from the acceptance of the practice of promise-keeping and is, for that reason, self-evident, it is not at all self-evident that one is always acting wrongly if one breaks a promise. Most of us believe, as indeed Ross did, that the moral claim we create on us by making a promise to someone can be overridden by an even more stringent moral claim that someone else has upon us. Practically all of us, after all, would admit that promises can be broken in special circumstances. There will, however, be much disagreement as to what these ''special circumstances'' are.

Kantian Ethics: The Categorical Imperative

Like the ethical intuitionists, the immensely influential philosopher Immanuel Kant (1724–1804) believed that the foundations of moral thinking consisted of self-evident moral truths which are independent of human psychology. Consequently, Kant has been called an ethical intuitionist. Unlike those who are commonly known as intuitionists, however, Kant did not simply ''intuit'' moral truths in a philosophical vacuum but attempted to provide some comprehensive theory of the nature of morality which could *explain how* morality, as the common person understood it, was possible and rational.

As Kant saw it, the very concept of morality is inextricably connected to the notions of impartiality, rationality, and respect for the freedom (autonomy) of persons. While human beings are a part of nature and as such are subject to the deterministic laws of nature, human beings differ from other animals, Kant believed, in their capacity for rational moral choice; it is in this capacity that human beings find their special dignity. Although reason is indeed subservient to desire as far as human sensual nature is concerned, this, Kant believed, is not true in the realm of moral actions. Moral principles, as he saw it, are of such a sort that they are binding on all rational persons, regardless of their psychological desires or ends. Like the upright moral person that he was, Kant noticed that a morally good person acts according to moral principles that bind him to act in a certain way, regardless of whether or not he desires to act that way—that is, moral principles act as rational curbs upon our desires. Moral principles, he claimed, are not prudential means to the satisfaction of the sensual desires that we happen to have but are demands that any rational person would see as implicit in the very idea of morality. The demands of morality, Kant claimed, are *categorical* and not *hypothetical,* that is, they are not means for achieving our desires but are independent of any desire that we might happen to have. For example, if one wants to lose weight, then it is rational for one to eat less. The imperative (command) to eat less, Kant would say, is hypothetical in that it will bind us only insofar as we accept the end of losing weight. If we reject this end, the command ''to eat less'' will have no force for us. A demand of morality, on the other hand, Kant asserts, is categorical in the sense that it presents ''an action as of itself objectively necessary, without regard to any other end,'' (that is, it constitutes a rational principle of action even in the absence of any desire in that direction). For example, according to Kant, our moral obligation to keep our promises in no way depends upon whether we desire to keep them.

According to Kant, the various specific categorical demands of morality follow from a supreme categorical moral principle which he called *the categorical imperative*. Kant presents various formulations of this supreme moral principle which he claimed are equivalent in meaning. According to one of these formulations, the categorical imperative enjoins you to "act in such a way that you always treat humanity, whether in your own person, or in the person of any other, never simply as a means, but always at the same time as an end." This formulation of the categorical imperative expresses Kant's view that individuals who are treated "simply as means" are not treated "with respect as persons," as morality demands they should be. An individual is treated simply as a means when our response to him is motivated not by his choices, but by ours in disregard of his. As Kant saw it, since the very dignity of human beings resides in their freedom and rationality, human beings are treated with respect only when they are treated as rational moral agents who are given the freedom to set their own goals. To be "treated as a person" is simply to be afforded this respect.

According to Kant's most influential formulation of the categorical imperative, you should "act as if the maxim of your action [the subjective principle under which you act] were to become through your will a universal law of nature [i.e., that everyone follow that maxim]." In telling you to perform the thought experiment of imagining everyone doing as you contemplate doing, Kant is giving sophisticated expression to the idea, central to the very concept of morality, that morality demands impartiality. As a parent might tell a child, "You were wrong to take Billy's toy away from him. If it's right for you to do it, then it would be right for him to do it to you. How would you like that?" The idea of impartiality and concern for those who might be affected by one's action is at the heart of the Golden Rule of Christian ethics which commands that you "Do unto others as you would have them do unto you." When a person acts on a moral principle, he must, we tend to believe, be willing to accept the right of everyone else to act on the same principle—that is, he must be willing to accept the *universalization* of the rule under which he acts. The categorical imperative was Kant's attempt to formulate in a more precise manner the spirit behind the Golden Rule, without its implicit reference to the variable "subjective tastes" or "likings" of human beings. The categorical imperative, Kant believed, is so basic to moral thinking that all rational persons who understand what it means would accept it as binding, regardless of their specific psychological idiosyncracies.

While Kant's view of morality reflects our intuitive sense that morality is impartial, universal, and rational, there is no consensus among philosophers as to what the categorical imperative, which Kant claims captures this requirement, implies. Many of Kant's examples of moral rules that follow from the categorical imperative are questionable. For example, Kant claims that the categorical imperative leads to a condemnation of suicide. Is it not possible, however, for a rational person who finds life unbearable (and let us assume has no obligations to fulfill to anyone) to be willing to accept the universalization of the maxim "Commit suicide when life becomes unbearable and you have no obligation to others." Is it not the case that the maxims that one is willing to have universalized are a function of individual psychological temperament? Kant denies that this is so. But if the demands of morality are not dependent on the variable psychological desires that human beings *happen to have,* it is unclear how one can derive the specific moral rules that Kant claims follow from the categorical imperative.

Furthermore, Kant believed that the absolutely binding categorical imperative leads to derivative and also absolutely binding moral principles such as "never make a promise which you have no intention of keeping'' and ''never lie, regardless of the beneficial consequences.'' But would it be wrong to make a false promise or to lie to an evil person who threatens your life or the life of someone else? Kant says that it would be wrong, but this is inconsistent with the intuitive moral beliefs of ''the common person,'' whose moral beliefs Kant's theory was meant to explain and justify. In addition, what are we to do if we must choose, as we sometimes do, between making a false promise or lying? If, as Kant claimed, our moral obligations to refrain from making insincere promises and to tell the truth are absolute, regardless of what we do, we will be acting wrongly. The problem of possible conflicts in supposedly absolute moral duties is unfortunately neglected by Kant.

While it has been suggested that the problem here is not with the categorical imperative but with Kant's application of it, the problem seems to go much deeper than this, for there is no agreement among philosophers as to what the categorical imperative should be taken to mean. For example, many scholars have rejected Kant's claim that his various formulations of the categorical imperative are equivalent in meaning. As some see it, the essence of Kantian morality is not its insistence on universalizability but its emphasis upon human *autonomy* and its insistence that individuals have *rights* that protect them from being paternalistically treated and from ''being used as mere instruments in the quest for the maximization of the common good.'' From this perspective, it is Kant's claim that the categorical imperative demands ''respect for persons'' by enjoining us ''never to treat individuals as mere means'' which best expresses the spirit of Kantian morality. Yet there is wide disagreement as to what ''respect for persons'' specifically entails. If, on the other hand, Kant's insistence on universalizability is to be taken as the essence of the categorical imperative, as it often is, we run into the problem of how an act is to be categorized. Although Kant categorizes actions very broadly, he gives no reason why narrower categorizations should be rejected. For example, Kant claims that one cannot universalize an act of lying to achieve one's ends, but does this not depend on what one's ends are—such as, to help others, to save a life, to save a life in the only way possible? The more narrowly one perceives one's act, it would appear, the easier it is to accept ''everyone's doing the same.'' How, then, is one to decide on an act's proper categorization? How, too, is one to morally distinguish the actions of a moral saint from those of a moral fanatic, for both will accept the universalization of their principles of action? As many critics see it, Kant's requirement that moral principles be universalizable is a necessary but not a sufficient condition for determining what is right. The supreme principle(s) of morality, it is often said, must refer directly to subjective psychological desires and to the consequences of human actions. It is this view that is central to the utilitarian moral tradition which has and continues to exert great influence.

Utilitarianism

Taking a position diametrically opposed to that of Kant, the British philosophers Jeremy Bentham (1748–1832) and John Stuart Mill (1806–73), the most influential figures in the development of *utilitarianism,* saw morality as nothing other than an attempt to maximize the satisfaction of human desires. As they saw it, a human desire should only be condemned when it comes into conflict with other human desires which promise to create greater human happiness in the long run. Morality should not be perceived as a conflict between actual human desires and an abstract duty having no reference to such desires, but rather as an attempt to arbitrate between these desires in such a way as to maximize the amount of happiness in this world, counting everyone's happiness equally.

Either in a situation of individual moral choice or in the legislative task of deciding between conflicting laws, the right act or law to choose was that act or law which among all the alternatives produced "the greatest happiness for the greatest number." The principle of "the greatest happiness for the greatest number" played the same role for Bentham and Mill that the categorical imperative played for Kant—that is it was taken as the sole basic principle of moral obligation which provided the justification for all other moral principles.

Since whether an act or law will maximize happiness depends exclusively on its *consequences*, Bentham and Mill believed that the rightness of an act or law, in turn, depends solely on its consequences. Given the possibility of unforeseeable consequences and the difficulty of estimating the probability of foreseeable ones, even the most wisely made moral judgments are subject to error, Bentham believed. This is the inevitable price one must pay for the finiteness of human foresight. Since the rightness of an action depends solely on its consequences, it also follows, Bentham believed, that there are no absolute exceptionless moral rules other than the principle of "the greatest happiness for the greatest number" (*the principle of utility*). It seemed clear to Bentham that in certain circumstances the consequences of breaking conventional moral rules (e.g., always keep your promises) might have the best consequences. Consequently, conventional moral rules are not to be taken as the absolute moral rules that they are often taken to be. Bentham did not, however, totally reject the rules of conventional morality. As he saw it, many of them are useful rules of thumb which serve in most cases to maximize human happiness. Given the difficulty of foreseeing possible consequences, one has need for moral guides other than the principle of utility. The rules of conventional morality often provide these guides. Furthermore, they provide a background of stability and predictability of human behavior which better enables individuals to anticipate the actions of others and to plan their own actions accordingly. Nevertheless, Bentham believed, these rules should not be used blindly. Given important choices or a conflict in the conventional rules themselves, one should always resort to the principle of utility itself in deciding what to do. (See Selection #46 for a modern defense of this point of view.)

In deciding whether a conventional moral rule should be violated, it is essential, Bentham believed, to consider the long-range consequences of such a violation. Quite often, even though the short-range consequences of breaking a rule may be advantageous, its long-range consequences may be quite undesirable. For example, even though in the short-run my refusal to keep my promise to repay a debt of money to a wealthy friend may be justified from a utilitarian perspective if I use this money instead to help a more needy person, such an action may not be justified in the long-run. Among the long-range consequences I should consider the effect of my action on people's confidence in my reliability or in the general practice of promise-keeping which serves the general interest. Whatever short-range beneficial consequences I might have gained in this particular instance of breaking my promise might be more than offset by its undesirable long-range effect on my ability to have my promises accepted in the future. Futhermore, if most people broke promises whenever they thought the beneficial consequences to specific individuals would be maximized—however slightly—public confidence in the practice of promise-keeping, which has great utility, would soon be shattered.

As Bentham saw it, the principle of utility was the only rationally defensible ultimate moral principle. If a particular moral position could not be shown to follow from the principle of utility, there was no other conceivable way it could be justified, Bentham believed. Moral positions not based on the principle of utility, he claimed, were based simply on unjustified (and variable) feelings of approval or disapproval, that is, on caprice or prejudice rather than on principle. Nevertheless, Bentham admitted that he could not offer any direct proof for the principle of utility "for that which is used to prove everything else, cannot itself be proved . . . " However, in some of Bentham's writings, as well as in the writings of his most influential disciple John Stuart Mill, attempts are made to anchor the principle of utility to the doctrine of *psychological hedonism* (which is almost universally rejected by philosophers today but was popular in Bentham's day). According to this doctrine, the pursuit of one's own pleasure is, as a matter of fact, the *sole* human motive for action. As the psychological hedonist sees it, one is concerned about the pleasures of others only insofar as they are thought to be a source of or means to one's own pleasure. Clearly however, individuals do not always, as a matter of fact, care about the pleasure of others either as an end in itself or as a means to their own pleasure. In fact, both Bentham and Mill stress the need to *induce* people (especially children) to develop feelings of sympathy and concern for others, that is, to associate the pleasures and pains of others with their own pleasures and pains. Consequently, they both seem to admit there is no guarantee that people will naturally (i.e., apart from social conditioning) develop a concern for the interests of others, let alone that they will naturally feel inclined to consider *equally* the interests of all human beings, as Bentham says they should. Indeed, even if people could be conditioned to feel this way, some would claim that it is not in one's ultimate interest to feel this way and consequently one ought not to feel this way. (This is, for example, the position of the late philosopher and novelist Ayn Rand.) Consequently, there is a fundamental gap between the doctrine of psychological hedonism and the principle of utility. This gap is not bridged by Bentham and Mill, who never adequately explain the source of our supposed moral obligation to maximize human happiness.[4]

The general consensus among philosophers today is that the principle of utility cannot be "proven" to be correct on the basis either of abstract reason or of brute psychological fact. If we are to accept this principle, it is because we are *willing to choose* it as a guide to moral action. In order to decide if we are so willing, we must inquire into the moral implications of this principle and ask ourselves whether we are willing to accept these implications. (Even if Bentham's utilitarianism has some implications as to what is right in particular situations which go counter to our nonreflective moral feelings, we might still cling to that theory if no better one is available.) The vast majority of ethical philosophers today would contend that the classical utilitarianism of Bentham has morally intolerable implications and should, for that reason, be rejected. (See Selection #46 for a contrary view.) Foremost among the criticisms of classical utilitarianism is the contention that such an

[4]In this regard, it is interesting to note that while Hume, like Bentham and Mill, saw morality as a function of the brute psychological desires of human beings, unlike them, he rejected the view that a concern for the interests of others is based upon primary self-regarding interests. As Hume saw it, (inborn) human nature is such that the vast majority of us are naturally inclined to feel empathy and sympathy for others and consequently are pleased by the happiness of others even when "there is nothing in it for us." It is our natural sympathy for others, Hume believed, that makes morality possible. Nevertheless, Hume did not deny that there are, as a matter of fact, some people in this world who simply do not care about anyone other than themselves. Consistent with his ethical theory, Hume believed that no rational argument would suffice to prove to such people that they are wrong or irrational for not caring for others. Only by appealing to the feelings of such people, Hume believed, can we hope to move them to care about others. Society exists, Hume believed, because, as a matter of fact, the majority of people do so care.

ethical perspective can lead to grave injustice. Indeed, Kant was quite opposed to the utilitarian way of thinking for precisely this reason.

The utilitarian precept that one should always act in a manner most likely to produce "the greatest happiness for the greatest number" suffers from an inherent ambiguity, for there are two notions conflated into this formula—the maximization of the *total happiness* of all individuals and the *total number of individuals* who share in that happiness. Bentham and Mill never distinguished these two factors nor realized the possibility of conflict when one must choose between a greater total amount of happiness for those involved or a wider distribution of it. Since Bentham often spoke of "the greatest happiness" principle, deleting reference to "the greatest number," it appears that the meaning he intended for his formula was that one should always attempt to maximize the total amount of happiness, regardless of its method of distribution. Bentham's discussion of the manner in which pleasures are to be measured and acts evaluated points to this interpretation. Yet, it is clearly inadequate to neglect consideration of the distribution of happiness in determining what is right. The same quantity of happiness can be distributed in many different ways. One arrangement might give all, or most, of that happiness to a relatively small number of people who do not especially deserve it, while another arrangement might spread it more evenly or more in accord with merit. Certainly, it is possible that an act which maximizes the total amount of human happiness is, nevertheless, wrong, if that happiness is *unjustly distributed.*

Consider, for example, the practice in communist Russia under Stalin of repressing civil liberties and unjustly imprisoning and executing individuals who were seen as a threat to the social order, a practice which was justified as a necessary means to the maximization of the general happiness in the long run. Yet even if this were true, it would not guarantee that such a practice was right. Even if we grant, as most of us will, that justice should at times be sacrificed for the common good (for example, killing innocent people in war), the point is that there are different and possibly conflicting principles involved here—general utility versus individual justice. Bentham and Mill, in their attempt to reduce all moral value to the principle of utility, never did recognize this. Although Mill attempted to reconcile the principle of utility with a principle guaranteeing extensive individual freedom in his famous essay *On Liberty,* there is no guarantee that these two principles will always coincide. Given today's more pessimistic view of human rationality, one may reject Mill's fundamental premise in *On Liberty* that each individual is the best judge of his own happiness. Without this premise, a possible implication of the principle of utility is that we ought to force people to be happy "in spite of themselves." The conflict between governmental paternalism and individual freedom is for most of us a conflict over differing moral principles and not a question of the proper application of the single utilitarian principle, as Mill suggested. Similarly, although Bentham and Mill were strong proponents of greater equality, particularly of a more even distribution of wealth, their theoretical justification for this aim was that a more equal distribution of goods was the most likely *means* toward a greater total happiness for society as a whole. There is again no good reason to believe that these two values will necessarily coincide. When they do not, some of us will choose to sacrifice some degree of equality to achieve a greater total of happiness, whereas others will choose to accept a smaller sum of happiness for a more equal distribution of it. Such situations of moral choice seem to involve a conflict of independent moral principles that cannot be resolved by an appeal to a higher moral principle.

Rule-Utilitarianism

Dissatisfied both with the potential injustice of classical utilitarianism (or *act-utilitarianism,* as it is generally called) and the Kantian attempt to reduce all of morality to an abstract principle of reason (the categorical imperative), which makes no reference to the actual desires of human beings, many contemporary philosophers have turned to one of several versions of *rule-utilitarianism* which have been developed by philosophers within this century. Although utilitarian in their ultimate concern with beneficial consequences, the various versions of rule-utilitarianism incorporate this concern with a Kantian requirement either that moral actions must be capable of universalization or that they must be guided by specific moral rules and not by a direct appeal to the principle of utility. These latter versions of rule-utilitarianism draw a fundamental distinction between the proper procedures to be employed in justifying specific actions on the one hand and moral rules on the other. As these theories see it, when determining how one ought to act, one should not appeal directly to the principle of utility, focusing on whether a specific action is likely to have the best consequences. Instead, one should determine what one ought to do on the basis of specific moral rules which are themselves justified in terms of their utility. Some of these theories claim that actions should be justified in terms of the actual and recognized rules of a given society, while others claim that actions should be justified in terms of moral rules, which would be ideal for a given society from a utilitarian point of view.

While some of the most influential of contemporary philosophers have, at one time or another, defended some rule-utilitarian theory, such theories have also been subjected to sharp criticism. Indeed, it has been argued that some versions of rule-utilitarianism reduce to act-utilitarianism (i.e., their moral implications are the same) and that those theories that are different from act-utilitarianism involve a valueless type of "rule-worship." Furthermore, it has been claimed, if the principle of utility is the sole standard to be used in justifying moral rules, then these rules can allow unjust social practices that most of us would consider clearly wrong. As these critics see it, utilitarianism, in any of its forms, must be supplemented by independent and possibly conflicting principles of justice.

Two Contemporary Theories of Justice in the Kantian Tradition: Rawls and Nozick

Recognizing the dangers of an absolute commitment to "the common good," unlimited by a concern for the *rights* of individuals, many contemporary philosophers have turned to ethical theories which emphasize the notions of justice, individual moral rights, and the freedom and dignity of human beings. Like the framers of the United States Constitution, who amended it with "The Bill of Rights," such philosophers are united in their belief that principles of justice (or "inalienable rights") ought to act as constraints upon the pursuit of the common welfare. (Recall the fear of "the tyranny of the majority" on the part of the framers of the United States Constitution.[5]) Echoing Kant, these philosophers believe that underlying any legitimate legal system are principles of justice which are *independent* of any particular theory of the common good. (Indeed, many contemporary philosophers are quite sceptical of the possibility of framing some notion of "the common good," which is itself value-free, and consequently are sceptical of those who claim that the realization of "the common good" is a purely "scientific" question.)

In the past decade, two competing theories of justice, the liberal-welfare-state theory of John

[5]For example, see James Madison's *Federalist #10.*

Rawls[6] and the libertarian theory of Robert Nozick[7] have generated much interest among contemporary moral philosophers. Fundamental to both theories is an acceptance of the Kantian view of human beings as autonomous rational moral agents and a rejection of the utilitarian view of them as mere pleasure-seekers. Following Kant, both Rawls and Nozick see justice and not utility as the primary moral value. Like Kant, they see justice as the cornerstone of human dignity and self-respect. Yet their theories of justice are very different.

The central notion in Nozick's theory of justice is that of "entitlement." Like Kant before him, Nozick equates justice with the respecting of people's rights. As he sees it, people's rights are respected only when they are allowed to keep and control that to which they are *entitled.* An individual is entitled to those things which he has acquired without resort to force, theft, and fraud, Nozick believes. This is all one can demand *by right.* Although individuals can demand by right that they be left alone to make their own decisions as to how they are to live their lives, they cannot demand by right that the state provide them with assistance in the pursuit of their ends, Nozick declares, echoing Kant. Such positive interferences by the state are illegitimate impositions upon personal autonomy, since the state can help some only by violating the entitlements of others. Given this extreme anti-utilitarian view and concern for human freedom, Nozick argues for a "minimum state" which is limited to the narrow passive functions of the enforcement of contracts and protection against force, theft, and fraud. Nozick argues first that a minimum state would naturally arise out of an association of human beings "even though no one intended this or tried to bring it about, by a process which need not violate anyone's rights." He then goes on to argue that a more extensive state cannot be justified. In particular, he argues that a state is not justified in redistributing the wealth of its citizens or in restricting human freedom through paternalistic legislation which aims at protecting people from themselves. Consequently, for Nozick, the progressive income tax, publicly supported education and welfare, and mandatory seatbelts in automobiles are all unjustified infringements of human liberty. If people want education and health or employment insurance, they will be free in Nozick's minimal state voluntarily to contract for it themselves. Nozick's extreme libertarianism is shared today by members of the Libertarian Party, a United States political party, who are united in their commitment to individual freedom and opposition to the welfare state.

Unlike Nozick, Rawls is quite concerned with human welfare in his theory of justice. Nevertheless, like Nozick, he accepts the basic Kantian view that individual liberty takes precedence over the utilitarian concern with "the common good." As Rawls puts it,

> Each person possesses an inviolability founded on justice that even the welfare of society as a whole cannot override. For this reason justice denies that the loss of freedom for some is made right by a greater good shared by others . . . the rights secured by justice are not subject to political bargaining or to the calculus of social interests.[8]

Like Kant, Rawls attempts to show that the value of justice can be derived from the idea of rationality. As the *social contract* theorists before him, Rawls tries to derive principles of morality from a hypothetical consideration of the moral principles that purely self-interested, rational people would unanimously choose to regulate the practices of their society. Realizing that fully knowledgeable self-interested people,

[6]John Rawls, *A Theory of Justice* (Cambridge, Mass.: Harvard University Press, 1971).

[7]Robert Nozick, *Anarchy, State and Utopia* (New York: Basic Books, 1974).

[8]Rawls, op. cit., pp. 3-4.

seeking to maximize their own vested interests would never unanimously agree on any specific principles, Rawls hypothesizes that they are ignorant of their individual mental and physical attributes, their conceptions of the good life and of the particular places they will occupy in their society. Furthermore, he assumes that, while the framers of his hypothetical social contract do not know the particular economic or political circumstances of their own society, they do "know the general facts of human society," and, in particular, "understand political affairs and the principles of economic theory; they know the basis of social organization and the laws of human psychology."[9] Subject to certain other constraints, Rawls argues that, given this *veil of ignorance,* rational and purely self-interested persons would choose certain principles of justice to rule their lives over utilitarian principles and would commit themselves to abide by these principles when the veil of ignorance is lifted. According to Rawls, the participants would accept the following two principles:

> 1. *First Principle:* Each person is to have an equal right to the most extensive total system of equal basic liberties compatible with a similar system of liberty for all.
>
> 2. *Second Principle:* Social and economic inequalities are to be arranged so that they are both:
> (a) to the greatest benefit of the least advantaged, consistent with the just savings principle,[10] and
> (b) attached to offices and positions open to all under conditions of fair equality and opportunity.[11]

The most widely discussed part of these two principles is part (a) of the second principle, according to which inequalities in power, wealth, and other resources must not exist unless they work out to the advantage of the worst-off members of society. For example, imagine a rather inefficient society in which everyone shares equally. This society can be made more efficient only by rewarding people unequally. According to part (a) of the second principle, such unequal rewards would be justified only if the worst-off members of society fare better in this unequal society than they did in the previous society where everyone shared equally. Similarly, this unequal society can be made more unequal only if the worst-off members still fare better than they did before. No greater disadvantage, however small, for the worst-off members of society can justify a greater advantage, however large, for those better-off. From this perspective, Rawls views rational people acting under the constraint of the veil of ignorance as very cautious people who plan their lives on the basis of the least favorable possibility about how things will turn out.[12]

Rawls' and Nozick's theories of justice are works of intellectual brilliance. But perhaps, like Kant, they overplay the role of reason in moral judgment and underplay the role of feeling. Neither Rawls nor Nozick seems willing to accept the existence of conflicts of basic moral principles, irreconcilable by reason alone. As such they construct elaborate moral systems that do justice to some of our moral intuitions only at the expense of conflicting ones that most of us are unwilling to abandon. For example, Nozick in his preoccupation with individual freedom and entitlement to the goods that one produces in the "free market," finds no place for benevolence in his moral system, while

[9]Ibid., p. 137.

[10]The *just savings principle* obligates present generations to deal justly with future generations (e.g., by conserving natural resources).

[11]Ibid., p. 302.

[12]After agreeing to the two basic principles of justice mentioned, Rawls imagines the participants of his social contract moving on to a constitutional convention to decide upon the most effective, just constitution. At this point, the veil of ignorance is partially lifted to allow the participants, still ignorant of their own natural abilities, social positions, and conceptions of the good life, to "know the relevant general facts about society, that is, its natural circumstances and resources, its level of economic advance and political culture, and so on" (Ibid., p. 197).

Rawl's in his preoccupation with freedom and equality finds no place for an individual's right to control that which he has produced. Both systems seem inadequate to the complexity of the moral life and for that reason do not seem to provide a pattern for living to which most of us would be willing to fully commit ourselves. Indeed, perhaps the truth for most of us is that the principles we choose to live by cannot be reconciled into a single coherent moral system.

39. A CLASH OF CONFLICTING MORAL IMPERATIVES: A LITERARY PORTRAYAL

Herman Melville

HERMAN MELVILLE (1819–91) is considered one of America's greatest authors. His masterpiece **Moby Dick** is a literary classic. The struggle between good and evil is a theme that is found in many of Melville's writings, including his last (short) novel **Billy Budd,** which is ranked as his finest book after **Moby Dick.** In this memorable tale, Melville dramatizes the poignant moral dilemma individuals sometimes face when they must choose between conflicting moral demands or natural sympathies. Is there some uniquely rational and correct way to resolve all questions of moral choice or are some of these questions incapable of uniquely rational and correct answers? This is the central question of ethics that has preoccupied moral philosophers since philosophy began.

Billy Budd is set aboard the English warship **Indomitable** in 1797 when England was at war with France. Billy Budd is a sailor on board the **Indomitable** who, because of his good personality and willingness to work, is well regarded by both his shipmates and the officers under whom he serves. For some unknown reason, however, Claggart, the master-at-arms (the equivalent of the chief-of-police aboard a warship) takes a strong dislike to Billy. After apparently attempting to entrap Billy into joining a fictitious mutiny, Claggart falsely reports to the ship's captain, Vere, that Billy is fomenting a mutiny. Calling Billy into his cabin along with Claggart, Vere asks Claggart to repeat his accusation to Billy's face. When he does so, Billy, greatly emotionally upset, finds himself tongue-tied. In frustration at being unable to answer, Billy forcefully strikes Claggart, who is killed when he falls heavily to the floor.

Captain Vere is now faced with an unpleasant duty, for according to military law, Billy is guilty of assaulting and murdering a superior officer, a capital crime. In addition, to allow Billy to escape the punishment military law demands might have bad consequences by encouraging mutinous sentiments. This is especially troubling to Vere since England is at war and two mutinies had already occurred in the British navy that year. On the other hand, Vere is convinced that Billy does not deserve to be punished, that, to use his own words, "Billy is innocent in the eyes of God." Furthermore, Vere has a special fondness for Billy. Several times in his previous dealings with Billy, Vere is described as fatherly and this aspect of Vere is recognized by the orphan Billy, "doubtless touching Billy's heart to the quick."

With his own great misgivings, Vere convenes a court-martial consisting of three officers of the ship. Our excerpt consists of the trial and Vere's own passionate testimony before the court-martial's officers. In Vere's testimony, we see the conflict in Vere between what he sees as the clear call of military duty on one hand and his natural sympathies and private conscience on the other. Opting for military duty, Vere argues for Billy's conviction. Billy is then convicted and hanged. Billy bears no animosity toward the Captain, with whose anguish he sympathizes. Indeed, just prior to being hanged, Billy calls out a blessing on Captain Vere. Some months later, Vere is wounded in action. As he dies from this wound, he is heard to murmur Billy Budd's name over and over again. Melville, however, does not give any indication that Vere has changed his mind as to the rightness of Billy's execution. The nagging question that remains with the reader is whether this is indeed the case, and the philosophical question that remains in the background, is "Why?"

All being quickly in readiness, Billy Budd was arraigned, Captain Vere necessarily appearing as the sole witness in the case. . . . Concisely he narrated all that had led up to the catastrophe, omitting nothing in Claggart's accusation and deposing as to the manner in which the prisoner had received it. At this testimony the three officers glanced with no little surprise at Billy Budd, the last man they would have suspected either of the mutinous design alleged by Claggart or the undeniable deed he himself had done. The first lieutenant, taking judicial primacy and turning toward the prisoner, said, "Captain Vere has spoken. Is it or is it not as Captain Vere says?"

In response came syllables not so much impeded in the utterance as might have been anticipated. They were these: "Captain Vere tells the truth. It is just as Captain Vere says, but it is not as the master-at-arms said. I have eaten the King's bread and I am true to the King."

"I believe you, my man," said the witness, his voice indicating a suppressed emotion not otherwise betrayed.

"God will bless you for that, your honor!" not without stammering said Billy, and all but broke down. But immediately he was recalled to self-control by another question, to which with the same emotional difficulty of utterance he said, "No, there was no malice between us. I never bore malice against the master-at-arms. I am sorry that he is dead. I did not mean to kill him. Could I have used my tongue I would not have struck him. But he foully lied to my face and in presence of my captain, and I had to say something, and I could only say it with a blow, God help me!"

In the impulsive aboveboard manner of the frank one the court saw confirmed all that was implied in words that just previously had perplexed them, coming as they did from the testifier to the tragedy and promptly following Billy's impassioned disclaimer of mutinous intent—Captain Vere's words, "I believe you, my man.". . .

"One question more," said the officer of marines, now first speaking and with a troubled earnestness. "You tell us that what the master-at-arms said against you was a lie. Now why should he have so lied, so maliciously lied, since you declare there was no malice between you?"

At that question, unintentionally touching on a spiritual sphere wholly obscure to Billy's thoughts, he was nonplussed, evincing a confusion indeed that some observers, such as can

Source: Herman Melville's *Billy Budd,* published in 1924, after Melville's death.

readily be imagined, would have construed into involuntary evidence of hidden guilt. Nevertheless, he strove some way to answer, but all at once relinquished the vain endeavor, at the same time turning an appealing glance towards Captain Vere as deeming him his best helper and friend. Captain Vere, who had been seated for a time, rose to his feet, addressing the interrogator. "The question you put to him comes naturally enough. But how can he rightly answer it?—or anybody else, unless indeed it be he who lies within there," designating the compartment where lay the corpse. "But the prone one there will not rise to our summons. In effect, though, as it seems to me, the point you make is hardly material. Quite aside from any conceivable motive actuating the master-at-arms, and irrespective of the provocation to the blow, a martial court must needs in the present case confine its attention to the blow's consequence, which consequence justly is to be deemed not otherwise than as the striker's deed."

This utterance, the full significance of which it was not at all likely that Billy took in, nevertheless caused him to turn a wistful interrogative look toward the speaker, a look in its dumb expressiveness not unlike that which a dog of generous breed might turn upon his master, seeking in his face some elucidation of a previous gesture ambiguous to the canine intelligence. Nor was the same utterance without marked effect upon the three officers, more especially the soldier. Couched in it seemed to them a meaning unanticipated, involving a prejudgment on the speaker's part. It served to augment a mental disturbance previously evident enough.

The soldier once more spoke, in a tone of suggestive dubiety addressing at once his associates and Captain Vere: "Nobody is present—none of the ship's company, I mean—who might shed lateral light, if any is to be had, upon what remains mysterious in this matter."

"That is thoughtfully put," said Captain Vere; "I see your drift. Ay, there is a mystery; but, to use a scriptural phrase, it is a 'mystery of iniquity,' a matter for psychologic theologians to discuss. But what has a military court to do with it? Not to add that for us any possible investigation of it is cut off by the lasting tongue-tie of—him—in yonder," again designating the mortuary stateroom. "The prisoner's deed—with that alone we have to do."

To this, and particularly the closing reiteration, the marine soldier, knowing not how aptly to reply, sadly abstained from saying aught. The first lieutenant, who at the outset had not unnaturally assumed primacy in the court, now overrulingly instructed by a glance from Captain Vere, a glance more effective than words, resumed that primacy. Turning to the prisoner, "Budd," he said, and scarce in equable tones, "Budd, if you have aught further to say for yourself, say it now."

Upon this the young sailor turned another quick glance toward Captain Vere; then, as taking a hint from that aspect, a hint confirming his own instinct that silence was now best, replied to the lieutenant, "I have said all, sir."

The marine . . . was now directed to take [Billy] back to the after compartment originally assigned to the prisoner and his custodian. As the twain disappeared from view, the three officers, as partially liberated from some inward constraint associated with Billy's mere presence, simultaneously stirred in their seats. They exchanged looks of troubled indecision, yet feeling that decide they must and without long delay. For Captain Vere, he for the time stood—unconsciously with his back toward them, apparently in one of his absent fits—gazing out from a sashed porthole to windward upon the monotonous blank of the twilight sea. But the court's silence continuing, broken only at moments by brief consultations, in low earnest tones, this served to arouse him and energize him. Turning, he to-and-fro paced the cabin athwart; in the returning ascent to windward climbing the slant deck in the ship's lee roll, without knowing it symbolizing thus in his action a mind resolute to surmount difficulties even if against primitive instincts strong as the wind and the sea. Presently he came to a stand before the three. After scanning their faces he stood less as mustering his thoughts for expression than as one deliberating how best to put them to well-meaning men not intellectually mature, men with whom it was necessary to demonstrate certain principles that were axioms to himself. Similar impatience as to talking is perhaps one reason that deters some minds from addressing any popular assemblies.

When speak he did, something, both in the substance of what he said and his manner of saying it, showed the influence of unshared studies modifying and tempering the practical training of an active career. This, along with his phraseology, now and then was suggestive of the grounds whereon rested that imputation of a certain pedantry socially alleged against him by certain naval men of wholly practical cast, captains who nevertheless would frankly concede that His Majesty's navy mustered no more efficient officer of their grade than Starry Vere.

What he said was to this effect: "Hitherto I have been but the witness, little more; and I should hardly think now to take another tone, that of your coadjutor for the time, did I not perceive in you—at the crisis too—a troubled hesitancy, proceeding, I doubt not, from the clash of military duty with moral scruple—scruple vitalized by compassion. For the compassion, how can I otherwise than share it? But, mindful of paramount obligations, I strive against scruples that may tend to enervate[1] decision. Not, gentlemen, that I hide from myself that the case is an exceptional one. Speculatively regarded, it well might be referred to a jury of casuists.[2] But for us here, acting not as casuists or moralists, it is a case practical, and under martial law practically to be dealt with.

"But your scruples: do they move as in a dusk? Challenge them. Make them advance and declare themselves. Come now; do they import something like this: If, mindless of palliating[3] circumstances, we are bound to regard the death of the master-at-arms as the prisoner's deed, then does that deed constitute a capital crime whereof the penalty is a mortal one. But in natural justice is nothing but the prisoner's overt act to be considered? How can we adjudge to summary and shameful death a fellow creature innocent before God, and whom we feel to be so?—Does that state it aright? You sign sad assent. Well, I too feel that, the full force of that. It is Nature. But do these buttons that we wear attest that our allegiance is to Nature? No, to the King. Though the ocean, which is inviolate Nature primeval, though this be the element where we move and have our being as sailors, yet as the King's officers lies our duty in a sphere correspondingly natural? So little is that true, that in receiving our commissions we in the most important regards ceased to be natural free agents. When war is declared are we the commissioned fighters previously consulted? We fight at command. If our judgments approve the war, that is but coincidence. So in other particulars. So now. For suppose condemnation to follow these present proceedings. Would it be so much we ourselves that would condemn as it would be martial law operating through us? For that law and the rigor of it, we are not responsible. Our vowed responsibility is in this: That however pitilessly that law may operate in any instances, we nevertheless adhere to it and administer it.

"But the exceptional in the matter moves the hearts within you. Even so too is mine moved. But let not warm hearts betray heads that should be cool. Ashore in a criminal case, will an upright judge allow himself off the bench to be waylaid by some tender kinswoman of the accused seeking to touch him with her tearful plea? Well, the heart here, sometimes the femi-

[1]Weaken. EDITOR'S NOTE.

[2]An expert in utilizing general moral principles in determining what is morally required in particular circumstances. EDITOR'S NOTE.

[3]Extenuating. EDITOR'S NOTE.

nine in man, is as that piteous woman, and hard though it be, she must here be ruled out.''

He paused, earnestly studying them for a moment; then resumed.

''But something in your aspect seems to urge that it is not solely the heart that moves in you, but also the conscience, the private conscience. But tell me whether or not, occupying the position we do, private conscience should not yield to that imperial one formulated in the code under which alone we officially proceed?''

Here the three men moved in their seats, less convinced than agitated by the course of an argument troubling but the more the spontaneous conflict within.

Perceiving which, the speaker paused for a moment; then abruptly changing his tone, went on.

''To steady us a bit, let us recur to the facts.—In wartime at sea a man-of-war's man strikes his superior in grade, and the blow kills. Apart from its effect the blow itself is, according to the Articles of War, a capital crime. Furthermore ——''

''Ay, sir,'' emotionally broke in the officer of marines, ''in one sense it was. But surely Budd purposed neither mutiny nor homicide.''

''Surely not, my good man. And before a court less arbitrary and more merciful than a martial one, that plea would largely extenuate. At the Last Assizes[4] it shall acquit. But how here? We proceed under the law of the Mutiny Act. In feature no child can resemble his father more than that Act resembles in spirit the thing from which it derives—War. In His Majesty's service—in this ship, indeed—there are Englishmen forced to fight for the King against their will. Against their conscience, for aught we know. Though as their fellow creatures some of us may appreciate their position, yet as navy officers what reck[5] we of it? Still less recks the enemy. Our impressed men he would fain cut down in the same swath with our volunteers. As regards the enemy's naval conscripts, some of whom may even share our own abhorrence of the regicidal[6] French Directory,[7] it is the same on our side. War looks out to the frontage, the appearance. And the Mutiny Act, War's child, takes after the father. Budd's intent or non-intent is nothing to the purpose.

''But while, put to it by those anxieties in you which I cannot but respect, I only repeat myself—while thus strangely we prolong proceedings that should be summary—the enemy may be sighted and an engagement result. We must do; and one of two things must we do—condemn or let go.''

''Can we not convict and yet mitigate the penalty?'' asked the sailing master, here speaking, and falteringly, for the first.

''Gentlemen, were that clearly lawful for us under the circumstances, consider the consequences of such clemency. The people'' (meaning the ship's company) ''have native sense; most of them are familiar with our naval usage and tradition; and how would they take it? Even could you explain to them—which our official position forbids—they, long molded by arbitrary discipline, have not that kind of intelligent responsiveness that might qualify them to comprehend and discriminate. No, to the people the foretopman's deed, however it be worded in the announcement, will be plain homicide committed in a flagrant act of mutiny. What penalty for that should follow, they know. But it does not follow. *Why?* they will ruminate. You know what sailers are. Will they not revert to the recent outbreak at the Nore? Ay. They

[4]In previous English law, an *assizes* was a court session held periodically in each county of England to try civil and criminal cases. Melville's expression ''the last assizes'' was meant to refer to the Christian notion of the ''last (or final) judgment'' of human beings by God. EDITOR'S NOTE.

[5]To be concerned about. EDITOR'S NOTE.

[6]Pertaining to the killing of a king. (The reference is to the execution of Lous XVI during the French Revolution.) EDITOR'S NOTE.

[7]The Directory was the form of government established in France after the French Revolution. EDITOR'S NOTE.

know the well-founded alarm—the panic it struck throughout England. Your clement sentence they would account pusillanimous.[8] They would think that we flinch, that we are afraid of them—afraid of practicing a lawful rigor singularly demanded at this juncture, lest it should provoke new troubles. What shame to us such a conjecture on their part, and how deadly to discipline. You see then, whither, prompted by duty and the law, I steadfastly drive. But I beseech you, my friends, do not take me amiss. I feel as you do for this unfortunate boy. But did he know our hearts, I take him to be of that generous nature that he would feel even for us on whom in this military necessity so heavy a compulsion is laid.''

With that, crossing the deck he resumed his place by the sashed porthole, tacitly leaving the three to come to a decision. On the cabin's opposite side the troubled court sat silent. Loyal lieges, plain and practical, though at bottom they dissented from some points Captain Vere had put to them, they were without the faculty, hardly had the inclination, to gainsay one whom they felt to be an earnest man, one too not less their superior in mind than in naval rank. But it is not improbable that even such of his words as were not without influence over them, less came home to them than his closing appeal to their instinct as sea officers: in the forethought he threw out as to the practical consequences to discipline, considering the unconfirmed tone of the fleet at the time, should a man-of-war's man's violent killing at sea of a superior in grade be allowed to pass for aught else than a capital crime demanding prompt infliction of the penalty. . . .

Says a writer whom few know, ''Forty years after a battle it is easy for a noncombatant to reason about how it ought to have been fought. It is another thing personally and under fire to have to direct the fighting while involved in the obscuring smoke of it. Much so with respect to other emergencies involving considerations both practical and moral, and when it is imperative promptly to act. The greater the fog the more it imperils the steamer, and speed is put on though at the hazard of running somebody down. Little ween the snug card players in the cabin of the responsibilities of the sleepless man on the bridge.''

In brief, Billy Budd was formally convicted and sentenced to be hung at the yardarm in the early morning watch. . . . In wartime on the field or in the fleet, a mortal punishment decreed by a drumhead court . . . follows without delay on the heel of conviction, without appeal.

[8]Cowardly. EDITOR'S NOTE.

DISCUSSION QUESTIONS

1. What reasons does Captain Vere give in support of his decision that Billy should be hanged? Do you agree? Why?

2. Was Vere's decision a morally correct one? In general, what makes a decision morally correct? Are some decisions which involve choosing between conflicting obligations neither morally correct nor morally incorrect or is there some objective way to resolve all moral conflicts?

3. Does a military officer have a moral obligation to abide by military regulations when he believes that these regulations will lead to unjust suffering? If so, is this obligation absolute? If not, when can it be overridden?

4. How would you resolve the following moral dilemmas? What underlying moral principle would you appeal to as a justification for the moral position you take?

   a. **The Fat Man and the Impending Doom.** A fat man leading a group of people out of a cave on a coast is stuck in the mouth of that cave. In a very short time high tide will be upon them, and unless he is promptly unstuck, they will all be drowned, except the fat man, whose head is out of the cave. But, fortunately, or unfortunately, someone has with him a stick of dynamite. There seems to be no way to get the fat man loose from the opening without using that dynamite which will inevitably kill him; but if they do not use it, everyone will drown. What should they do?

b. **Jean Val jean's Conscience.** In Victor Hugo's **Les Miserables,** the hero, Jean Val jean, is an ex-convict living illegally under an assumed name and wanted for a robbery he committed many years ago. Although he will be returned to prison, probably for life, if he is caught, he is a good man who does not deserve to be punished. He has established himself in a town, becoming mayor and a public benefactor. One day, Jean learns that another man, a vagabond, has been arrested for a minor crime and identified as Jean Val jean. Jean is first tempted to remain silent, reasoning to himself that since he had nothing to do with the false identification of the hapless vagabond, he has no obligation to save him. Perhaps this man's false identification, Jean reflects, is "an act of Providence meant to save me." Upon reflection, however, Jean judges such reasoning "monstrous and hypocritical." He now feels certain that it is his duty to reveal his identity, regardless of the disastrous personal consequences. His resolve is disturbed, however, as he reflects on the shattering and irreparable harm his return to prison will mean to so many people who depend upon him for their livelihood. He now reproaches himself for being too selfish, for thinking only of his own conscience and not of others. The right thing to do, he now claims to himself, is to remain quiet, to continue making money, while using it to help others. The vagabond, he now comforts himself, is not a worthy person, anyway. Still unconvinced, and tormented by the decision he must make, Jean goes to the trial and confesses. Did he do the right thing?

c. **The Torture of the Mad Bomber.** A madman, who has killed many people by planting bombs in crowded areas, has finally been apprehended. It is known that this fiend has planted several more bombs which are scheduled to go off in a very short time. It is possible that hundreds of people may die. The authorities seem unable to make him divulge the location of the bomb by conventional and legal methods. He refuses to say anything and his lawyer is there to protect his fifth amendment right against self-incrimination. Finally, in exasperation, some official suggests that truth serum or, if necessary, torture, be used to prevent the looming tragedy. This would, of course, be illegal, but the official thinks that it is nevertheless the right thing to do in this desperate situation. Do you agree? If you do, would it also be morally justifiable to torture the mad bomber's innocent wife or child if that is the only way to make him talk? If you believe that this would be wrong, how do you square this with your view concerning the morality of war?

40. A CRITICISM OF RELIGIOUS ABSOLUTISM

Plato

PLATO (427–347 B.C.), along with his foremost student Aristotle, was one of the two most influential philosophers of the ancient Western world. The breadth of Plato's many philosophical works led the twentieth-century philosopher Alfred North Whitehead to remark that "The safest general characterization of the European philosophical tradition is that it consists of a series of footnotes to Plato." Born into an aristocratic family in the period of political turmoil and moral degeneration that coincided with the Greek Peloponnesian Wars, Plato originally planned to enter a life of politics. These plans, however, were given up when, as a young man of twenty, Plato met the philosopher Socrates, who was then sixty-two.

Like many other young men, Plato followed Socrates through the streets of Athens as Socrates practiced his method of critical philosophy upon passers-by. While never professing knowledge himself, Socrates **questioned** the pretensions to knowledge of others, forcing people in the process to recognize the imprecision and inconsistencies of their beliefs. As one would expect, this was often an embarrassment to those whose pretensions to knowledge were deflated by Socrates' skillful questioning. Yet Socrates believed that by acting as a "gadfly," stinging his contemporaries into thinking more clearly and logically about their beliefs, he was actually providing them with a great service. As Socrates saw it, being a gadfly was instrumental to his true aim, that of being "a midwife to knowledge" who, by his skillful probing of unexamined beliefs, delivers knowledge from the minds of others. Socrates' use of his dialectic method of questioning, which has come to be called the **Socratic method,** left a strong imprint on Plato, most of whose philosophical writings are in the form of conversational dialogues. Like Socrates, Plato believed that truth best emerges when divergent points of view are made to clash. By attempting to defend one's point of view against the points of view of others, one is forced to examine its presuppositions and implications. In this way, positions are often abandoned or modified until the truth emerges.

Plato's main philosophical interests like Socrates' were in ethics and political philosophy. Plato defends his view of morality in his most well known philosophical writing, the **Republic.** In this work, Plato criticizes democracy (government by the many) and advocates government by "philosopher kings" (i.e., the wise). Plato's strong distrust of democracy was, no doubt, motivated by his own personal experience of the corruption of Athenian democracy. Unlike our democracy which is **representative,** Athenian democracy in Plato's day was a **direct participatory one** in which all **free** adult **male** Athenian citizens voted in a legislative assembly. In this assembly, skillful but ignorant orators had the power to sway the beliefs of the masses. It was the Athenian democracy, in which power was in the hands of the easily swayed ignorant masses, that executed Socrates on the trumped up charges of "impiety" and "corrupting the youth" when Socrates' activity in questioning moral and political beliefs became too unsettling for those in power. In Plato's early dialogues, a picture of the historical Socrates emerges. This is especially the case in several dialogues that center around the trial and death of Socrates—**Euthyphro, Apology, Crito,** and **Phaedo.** (Since Socrates did not put any of his philosophical ideas in writing, our knowledge of the character of the historical Socrates and his philosophical beliefs is restricted to what others have written about him. Unfortunately, such evidence is contradictory. While some scholars fully accept the picture Plato paints of Socrates in his early dialogues, others do not.)

The selection that follows is an edited version of the **Euthyphro.** The setting of this dialogue is the chance meeting of Socrates and Euthyphro at the Athenian courthouse. As is Socrates' way, he soon engages Euthyphro in a philosophical conversation. In this case, it is over the meaning of "piety." (The Greek word which is translated as "piety" had a much broader meaning for the ancient Greeks than it has for us today. Believing that all moral obligations stem from the authority of the gods, the ancient Greeks naturally saw all moral obligation as a species of devotion to the gods. In reading the **Euthyphro,** it might be best to substitute the more general word "rightness" for "piety.") With his sharp analytic skill, Socrates criticizes the traditional religious authoritarianism of his day, accepted by Euthyphro, which equated morality with what is pleasing to the gods. It is a mistake, Socrates argues, for Euthyphro to **define** "piety" as "what is pleasing to the gods," for Euthyphro, like everyone else who bases morality on religious authority, also claims that "the gods are pleased with acts **because** they are pious." But, if this is so, "piety" cannot be defined as "that which is pleasing to the gods." What makes an act pious is not the fact that the gods are pleased with it, but the **reasons** they have for being pleased with it, Socrates claims. These reasons can be studied apart from religion. In defending this position, Plato (through the voice of Socrates) claims that one need not embrace the religious authoritarianism of the traditionalists of his day to avoid the devastating ethical relativism of the **Sophists** of his day, who saw morality as nothing but a "racket" that the powerful employ to get their way.

Euthyphro. What in the world are you doing here in the king's hall,[1] Socrates? Why have you left your haunts in the Lyceum? You surely cannot have a suit before him, as I have.

Socrates. The Athenians, Euthyphro, call it an indictment, not a suit.

Euth. What? Do you mean that someone is prosecuting you? I cannot believe that you are prosecuting anyone yourself.

Socr. Certainly I am not.

Euth. Then is someone prosecuting you?

Socr. Yes.

Euth. Who is he?

Socr. I scarcely know him myself, Euthyphro; I think he must be some unknown young man. His name, however, is Meletus, and his district Pitthis, if you can call to mind any Meletus of that district—a hook-nosed man with lanky hair and rather a scanty beard.

Euth. I don't know him, Socrates. But tell me, what is he prosecuting you for?

Socr. What for? Not on trivial grounds, I think. It is no small thing for so young a man to have formed an opinion on such an important matter. For he, he says, knows how the young are corrupted, and who are their corrupters. He must be a wise man who, observing my ignorance, is going to accuse me to the state . . . of corrupting his friends. . . .

Euth. . . . [H]ow, tell me, does he say that you corrupt the youth?

Socr. In a way which sounds absurd at first, my friend. He says that I am a maker of gods; and so he is prosecuting me, he says, for inventing new gods and for not believing in the old ones.

Euth. I understand, Socrates. It is because you say that you always have a divine guide. So he is prosecuting you for introducing religious reforms; and he is going into court to arouse prejudice against you, knowing that the multitude are easily prejudiced about such matters. Why, they laugh even at me, as if I were out of my mind, when I talk about divine things in the assembly and tell them what is going to happen; and yet I have never foretold anything which has not come true. But they are resentful of all people like us. We must not worry about them; we must meet them boldly.

Socr. My dear Euthyphro, their ridicule is not a very serious matter. The Athenians, it seems to me, may think a man to be clever without paying him much attention, so long as they do not think that he teaches his wisdom to others. But as soon as they think that he makes other people clever, they get angry, whether it be from

Source: Plato's *Euthyphro,* trans. F.J. Church, in Plato's *Euthyphro, Apology and Crito* (Indianapolis, Ind.: Bobbs-Merrill, 1948). Reprinted with permission.

[1]The anachronistic title "king" was retained by the magistrate who had jurisdiction over crimes affecting the state religion—Ed.

resentment, as you say, or for some other reason.

Euth. I am not very anxious to test their attitude toward me in this matter.

Socr. No, perhaps they think that you are reserved, and that you are not anxious to teach your wisdom to others. But I fear that they may think that I am; for my love of men makes me talk to everyone whom I meet quite freely and unreservedly, and without payment. Indeed, if I could I would gladly pay people myself to listen to me. If then, as I said just now, they were only going to laugh at me, as you say they do at you, it would not be at all an unpleasant way of spending the day—to spend it in court, joking and laughing. But if they are going to be in earnest, then only prophets like you can tell where the matter will end.

Euth. Well, Socrates, I dare say that nothing will come of it. Very likely you will be successful in your trial, and I think that I shall be in mine.

Socr. And what is this suit of yours, Euthyphro? Are you suing, or being sued?

Euth. I am suing.

Socr. Whom?

Euth. A man whom people think I must be mad to prosecute.

Socr. What? Has he wings to fly away with?

Euth. He is far enough from flying; he is a very old man.

Socr. Who is he?

Euth. He is my father.

Socr. Your father, my good man?

Euth. He is indeed.

Socr. What are you prosecuting him for? What is the accusation?

Euth. Murder, Socrates.

Socr. Good heavens, Euthyphro! Surely the multitude are ignorant of what is right. I take it that it is not everyone who could rightly do what you are doing; only a man who was already well advanced in wisdom.

Euth. That is quite true, Socrates.

Socr. Was the man whom your father killed a relative of yours? But, of course, he was. You would never have prosecuted your father for the murder of a stranger?

Euth. You amuse me, Socrates. What difference does it make whether the murdered man were a relative or a stranger? The only question that you have to ask is, did the murderer kill justly or not? If justly, you must let him alone; if unjustly, you must indict him for murder, even though he share your hearth and sit at your table. The pollution is the same if you associate with such a man, knowing what he has done, without purifying yourself, and him too, by bringing him to justice. In the present case the murdered man was a poor laborer of mine, who worked for us on our farm in Naxos. While drunk he got angry with one of our slaves and killed him. My father therefore bound the man hand and foot and threw him into a ditch, while he went to Athens to ask the priest what he should do. While the messenger was gone, he entirely neglected the man, thinking that he was a murderer, and that it would be no great matter, even if he were to die. And that was exactly what happened; hunger and cold and his bonds killed him before the messenger returned. And now my father and the rest of my family are indignant with me because I am prosecuting my father for the murder of this murderer. They assert that he did not kill the man at all; and they say that, even if he had killed him over and over again, the man himself was a murderer, and that I ought not to concern myself about such a person because it is impious for a son to prosecute his father for murder. So little, Socrates, do they know the divine law of piety and impiety.

Socr. And do you mean to say, Euthyphro, that you think that you understand divine things and piety and impiety so accurately that, in such a case as you have stated, you can bring your father to justice without fear that you yourself may be doing something impious?

Euth. If I did not understand all these matters accurately, Socrates, I should not be worth much—Euthyphro would not be any better than other men.

Socr. Then, my dear Euthyphro, I cannot do better than become your pupil and challenge Meletus on this very point before the trial begins. I should say that I had always thought it very important to have knowledge about divine things; and that now, when he says that I offend by speaking carelessly about them, and by introducing reforms, I have become your pupil. And I should say, "Meletus, if you acknowledge Euthyphro to be wise in these matters and to hold the correct belief, then think the same of me and do not put me on trial; but if you do not, then bring a suit, not against me, but against my master, for corrupting his elders—namely, myself whom he corrupts by his teaching, and his own father whom he corrupts by admonishing and punishing him." And if I did not succeed in persuading him to release me from the suit or to indict you in my place, then I could repeat my challenge in court.

Euth. Yes, by Zeus! Socrates, I think I should find out his weak points if he were to try to indict me. I should have a good deal to say about him in court long before I spoke about myself.

Socr. Yes, my dear friend, and knowing this I am anxious to become your pupil. I see that Meletus here, and others too, seem not to notice you at all, but he sees through me without difficulty and at once prosecutes me for impiety. Now, therefore, please explain to me what you were so confident just now that you knew. Tell me what are righteousness and sacrilege with respect to murder and everything else. I suppose that piety is the same in all actions, and that impiety is always the opposite of piety, and retains its identity, and that, as impiety, it always has the same character, which will be found in whatever is impious.

Euth. Certainly, Socrates, I suppose so.

Socr. Tell me, then, what is piety and what is impiety?

Euth. Well, then, I say that piety means prosecuting the unjust individual who has committed murder or sacrilege, or any other such crime, as I am doing now, whether he is your father or your mother or whoever he is; and I say that impiety means not prosecuting him. And observe, Socrates, I will give you a clear proof, which I have already given to others, that it is so, and that doing right means not letting off unpunished the sacrilegious man, whosoever he may be. Men hold Zeus to be the best and the most just of the gods; and they admit that Zeus bound his own father, Cronos, for wrongfully devouring his children; and that Cronos, in his turn, castrated his father for similar reasons. And yet these same men are incensed with me because I proceed against my father for doing wrong. So, you see, they say one thing in the case of the gods and quite another in mine.

Socr. Is not that why I am being prosecuted, Euthyphro? I mean, because I find it hard to accept such stories people tell about the gods? I expect that I shall be found at fault because I doubt those stories. Now if you who understand all these matters so well agree in holding all those tales true, then I suppose that I must yield to your authority. What could I say when I admit myself that I know nothing about them? But tell me, in the name of friendship, do you really believe that these things have actually happened?

Euth. Yes, and more amazing things, too, Socrates, which the multitude do not know of.

Socr. Then you really believe that there is war among the gods, and bitter hatreds, and battles, such as the poets tell of, and which the great painters have depicted in our temples, notably in the pictures which cover the robe that is carried up to the Acropolis at the great Panathenaic festival? Are we to say that these things are true, Euthyphro?

Euth. Yes, Socrates, and more besides. As I was saying, I will report to you many other stories about divine matters, if you like, which I am sure will astonish you when you hear them.

Socr. I dare say. You shall report them to me at your leisure another time. At present please try to give a more definite answer to my question which I asked you just now. What I asked you, my friend, was, What is piety? and you have not explained it to me to my satisfaction. You only tell me that what you are doing now, namely, prosecuting your father for murder, is a pious act.

Euth. Well, that is true, Socrates.

Socr. Very likely. But many other actions are pious, are they not, Euthyphro?

Euth. Certainly.

Socr. Remember, then, I did not ask you to tell me one or two of all the many pious actions that there are; I want to know what is characteristic of piety which makes all pious actions pious. You said, I think, that there is one characteristic which makes all pious actions pious, and another characteristic which makes all impious actions impious. Do you not remember?

Euth. I do.

Socr. Well, then, explain to me what is this characteristic, that I may have it to turn to, and to use as a standard whereby to judge your actions and those of other men, and be able to say that whatever action resembles it is pious, and whatever does not, is not pious.

Euth. Yes, I will tell you that if you wish, Socrates.

Socr. Certainly I do.

Euth. Well, then, what is pleasing to the gods is pious, and what is not pleasing to them is impious.

Socr. Fine, Euthyphro. Now you have given me the answer that I wanted. Whether what you say is true, I do not know yet. But, of course, you will go on to prove that it is true.

Euth. Certainly.

Socr. Come, then, let us examine our statement. The things and the men that are pleasing to the gods are pious, and the things and the men that are displeasing to the gods are impious. But piety and impiety are not the same; they are as opposite as possible—was not that what we said?

Euth. Certainly.

Socr. And it seems the appropriate statement?

Euth. Yes, Socrates, certainly.

Socr. Have we not also said, Euthyphro, that there are quarrels and disagreements and hatreds among the gods?

Euth. We have.

Socr. But what kind of disagreement, my friend, causes hatred and anger? Let us look at the matter thus. If you and I were to disagree as to whether one number were more than another, would that make us angry and enemies? Should we not settle such a dispute at once by counting?

Euth. Of course.

Socr. And if we were to disagree as to the relative size of two things, we should measure them and put an end to the disagreement at once, should we not?

Euth. Yes.

Socr. And should we not settle a question about the relative weight of two things by weighing them?

Euth. Of course.

Socr. Then what is the question which would make us angry and enemies if we disagreed about it, and could not come to a settlement? Perhaps you have not an answer ready; but listen to mine. Is it not the question of the just and unjust, of the honorable and the dishonorable, of the good and the bad? Is it not questions about these matters which make you and me and everyone else quarrel, when we do quarrel, if we differ about them and can reach no satisfactory agreement?

Euth. Yes, Socrates, it is disagreements about these matters.

Socr. Well, Euthyphro, the gods will quarrel over these things if they quarrel at all, will they not?

Euth. Necessarily.

Socr. Then, my good Euthyphro, you say that some of the gods think one thing just, the others another; and that what some of them hold to be honorable or good, others hold to be dishonorable or evil. For there would not have been quarrels among them if they had not disagreed on these points, would there?

Euth. You are right.

Socr. And each of them loves what he thinks honorable, and good, and just; and hates the opposite, does he not?

Euth. Certainly.

Socr. But you say that the same action is held by some of them to be just, and by others to be unjust; and that then they dispute about it, and so quarrel and fight among themselves. Is it not so?

Euth. Yes.

Socr. Then the same thing is hated by the gods and loved by them; and the same thing will be displeasing and pleasing to them.

Euth. Apparently.

Socr. Then, according to your account, the same thing will be pious and impious.

Euth. So it seems.

Socr. Then, my good friend, you have not answered my question. I did not ask you to tell me what action is both pious and impious; but it seems that whatever is pleasing to the gods is also displeasing to them. And so, Euthyphro, I should not be surprised if what you are doing now in punishing your father is an action well pleasing to Zeus, but hateful to Cronos and Uranus, and acceptable to Hephaestus, but hateful to Hera; and if any of the other gods disagree about it, pleasing to some of them and displeasing to others.

Euth. But on this point, Socrates, I think that there is no difference of opinion among the gods: they all hold that if one man kills another unjustly, he must be punished.

Socr. What, Euthyphro? Among mankind, have you never heard disputes whether a man ought to be punished for killing another man unjustly, or for doing some other unjust deed?

Euth. Indeed, they never cease from these disputes, especially in courts of justice. They do all manner of unjust things; and then there is nothing which they will not do and say to avoid punishment.

Socr. Do they admit that they have done something unjust, and at the same time deny that they ought to be punished, Euthyphro?

Euth. No, indeed, that they do not.

Socr. Then it is not the case that there is nothing which they will not do and say. I take it, they do not dare to say or argue that they must not be punished if they have done something unjust. What they say is that they have not done anything unjust, is it not so?

Euth. That is true.

Socr. Then they do not disagree over the question that the unjust individual must be punished. They disagree over the question, who is unjust, and what was done and when, do they not?

Euth. That is true.

Socr. Well, is not exactly the same thing true of the gods if they quarrel about justice and injustice, as you say they do? Do not some of them say that the others are doing something unjust, while the others deny it? No one, I suppose, my dear friend, whether god or man, dares to say that a person who has done something unjust must not be punished.

Euth. No, Socrates, that is true, by and large.

Socr. I take it, Euthyphro, that the disputants, whether men or gods, if the gods do disagree, disagree over each separate act. When they quarrel about any act, some of them say that it was just, and others that it was unjust. Is it not so?

Euth. Yes.

Socr. Come, then, my dear Euthyphro, please enlighten me on this point. What proof have you that all the gods think that a laborer who has been imprisoned for murder by the master of the man whom he has murdered, and who dies from his imprisonment before the master has had time to learn from the religious authorities what he should do, dies unjustly? How do you know that it is just for a son to indict his father and to prosecute him for the murder of such a man? Come, see if you can make it clear to me that the gods necessarily agree in thinking that this action of yours is just; and if you satisfy me, I will never cease singing your praises for wisdom.

Euth. I could make that clear enough to you, Socrates; but I am afraid that it would be a long business.

Socr. I see you think that I am duller than the judges. To them, of course, you will make it clear that your father has committed an unjust action, and that all the gods agree in hating such actions.

Euth. I will indeed, Socrates, if they will only listen to me.

Socr. They will listen if they think that you are a good speaker. But while you were talking, it occurred to me to ask myself this question: suppose that Euthyphro were to prove to me as clearly as possible that all the gods think such a death unjust, how has he brought me any nearer to understanding what piety and impiety are? This particular act, perhaps, may be displeasing to the gods, but then we have just seen that piety and impiety cannot be defined in that way; for we have seen that what is displeasing to the gods is also pleasing to them. So I will let you off on this point, Euthyphro; and all the gods shall agree in thinking your father's action wrong and in hating it, if you like. But shall we correct our definition and say that whatever all the gods hate is impious, and whatever they all love is pious; while whatever some of them love, and others hate, is either both or neither? Do you wish us now to define piety and impiety in this manner?

Euth. Why not, Socrates?

Socr. There is no reason why I should not, Euthyphro. It is for you to consider whether that definition will help you to teach me what you promised.

Euth. Well, I should say that piety is what all the gods love, and that impiety is what they all hate.

Socr. Are we to examine this definition, Euthyphro, and see if it is a good one? Or are we to be content to accept the bare statements of other men or of ourselves without asking any questions? Or must we examine the statements?

Euth. We must examine them. But for my part I think that the definition is right this time.

Socr. We shall know that better in a little while, my good friend. Now consider this question. Do the gods love piety because it is pious, or is it pious because they love it?

Euth. I do not understand you, Socrates.

Socr. I will try to explain myself: we speak of a thing being carried and carrying, and being led and leading, and being seen and seeing; and you understand that all such expressions mean different things, and what the difference is.

Euth. Yes, I think I understand.

Socr. And we talk of a thing being loved, of a thing loving, and the two are different?

Euth. Of course.

Socr. Now tell me, is a thing which is being carried in a state of being carried because it is carried, or for some other reason?

Euth. No, because it is carried.

Socr. And a thing is in a state of being led because it is led, and of being seen because it is seen?

Euth. Certainly.

Socr. Then a thing is not seen because it is in a state of being seen: it is in a state of being seen because it is seen; and a thing is not led because it is in a state of being led: it is in a state of being led because it is led; and a thing is not carried because it is in a state of being carried: it is in a state of being carried because it is carried. Is my meaning clear now, Euthyphro? I mean this: if anything becomes or is affected, it does not become because it is in a state of becoming: it is in a state of becoming because it becomes; and it is not affected because it is in a state of being affected: it is in a state of being affected because it is affected. Do you not agree?

Euth. I do.

Socr. Is not that which is being loved in a state either of becoming or of being affected in some way by something?

Euth. Certainly.

Socr. Then the same is true here as in the former cases. A thing is not loved by those who love it because it is in a state of being loved; it is in a state of being loved because they love it.

Euth. Necessarily.

Socr. Well, then, Euthyphro, what do we say about piety? Is it not loved by all the gods, according to your definition?

Euth. Yes.

Socr. Because it is pious, or for some other reason?

Euth. No, because it is pious.

Socr. Then it is loved by the gods because it is pious; it is not pious because it is loved by them?

Euth. It seems so.

Socr. But, then, what is pleasing to the gods is pleasing to them, and is in a state of being loved by them, because they love it?

Euth. Of course.

Socr. Then piety is not what is pleasing to the gods, and what is pleasing to the gods is not pious, as you say, Euthyphro. They are different things.

Euth. And why, Socrates?

Socr. Because we are agreed that the gods love piety because it is pious, and that it is not pious because they love it. Is not this so?

Euth. Yes.

Socr. And that what is pleasing to the gods because they love it, is pleasing to them by reason of this same love, and that they do not love it because it is pleasing to them.

Euth. True.

Socr. Then, my dear Euthyphro, piety and what is pleasing to the gods are different things. If the gods had loved piety because it is pious, they would also have loved what is pleasing to them because it is pleasing to them; but if what is pleasing to them had been pleasing to them because they loved it, then piety, too, would have been piety because they loved it. But now you see that they are opposite things, and wholly different from each other. For the one is of a sort to be loved because it is loved, while the other is loved because it is of a sort to be loved. My question, Euthyphro, was, What is piety? But it turns out that you have not explained to me the essential character of piety; you have been content to mention an effect which belongs to it—namely, that all the gods love it. You have not yet told me what its essential character is. Do not, if you please, keep from me what piety is; begin again and tell me that. Never mind whether the gods love it, or whether it has other effects: we shall not differ on that point. Do your best to make clear to me what is piety and what is impiety.

Euth. But, Socrates, I really don't know how to explain to you what is in my mind. Whatever statement we put forward always somehow moves round in a circle, and will not stay where we put it. . . .

Socr. Then we must begin again and inquire what piety is. I do not mean to give in until I have found out. Do not regard me as unworthy; give your whole mind to the question, and this time tell me the truth. For if anyone knows it, it is you. . . . It cannot be that you would ever have undertaken to prosecute your aged father for the murder of a laboring man unless you had known exactly what piety and impiety are. You would have feared to risk the anger of the gods, in case you should be doing wrong, and you would have been afraid of what men would say. But now I am sure that you think that you know exactly what is pious and what is not; so tell me, my good Euthyphro, and do not conceal from me what you think.

Euth. Another time, then, Socrates. I am in a hurry now, and it is time for me to be off. . . .

DISCUSSION QUESTIONS

1. Consider the following passage from the book of Genesis in the Bible relating to God's test of Abraham's faith:

> And it came to pass . . . that God did tempt Abraham, and said unto him . . . Take now thy son, thine only son Isaac, whom you lovest, and get thee into the land of Moriah; and offer him there for a burnt offering upon one of the mountains which I will tell thee of. And Abraham . . . took . . . Isaac his son . . . and went unto the place of which God had told him . . . and Abraham built an altar there, and laid the wood in order, and bound Isaac his son, and laid him on the altar upon the wood. And Abraham stretched forth his hand, and took the knife to slay his son. And the Angel of the Lord called into him out of heaven, and said, Abraham, Abraham: and he said, Here am I. And he said, Lay not thine hand upon the lad, neither do thou any thing unto him: for now I know that thou fearest God . . .[2]

a. Could Abraham know for certain that the command to sacrifice Isaac came from God? Could Abraham ever have good evidence for this belief? Why, or why not?

b. What does Abraham's willingness to sacrifice Isaac indicate as to the nature of Abraham's belief in God? Is he simply afraid of God or does he have faith that God has good reasons for what he has commanded or is there some other alternative?

c. Assuming that Abraham carried through the sacrifice and then in great anguish asked God, "Why?" and was told something like "I hate kids" or "I was bored" or "I enjoy tormenting people," or "No reason," what ought Abraham to think? What does this indicate about the relationship of God to morality?

2. Consider the following dialogue:

A: God commanded me to kill Jones.

B: God couldn't have commanded you to do such a thing because it is wrong.

A: Since God commanded me to do it, it can't be wrong.

Critically discuss the philosophical implications of this dialogue.

3. Why does Socrates reject Euthyphro's definition of "piety" as "doing what I am doing; that is to say, prosecuting any one who is guilty of murder, sacrilege, or any similar crime"?

4. According to Socrates should one say that the gods love things because they are pious or that they are pious because the gods love them? What is the difference in the meanings of these two claims and why does Socrates dismiss one of them as inadequate?

5. Consider the following dialogue:

God: Do X.

Jones: But you told me not to do Y and X does not appear to differ in any morally relevant respect from Y. Since you make a moral distinction between the two cases, I assume there must be something different about them.

God: The only difference between X and Y is that I approve of X and disapprove of Y and that's what makes X right and Y wrong.

Jones: In that case your approval of X and disapproval of Y is not moral in nature. You are misusing moral language.

Critically discuss the implications of Jones' criticism. (This criticism is developed in Selection #44.)

6. Assuming that what is right can indeed be identified (factually, if not definitionally) with the will of God, can one utilize one's knowledge of God's will in a given situation to project God's will in a different situation? If so, how?

[2]Genesis 22.

41. A DEFENSE OF ETHICAL RELATIVISM

Ruth Benedict

RUTH BENEDICT (1887–1948) was an American cultural anthropologist whose works stress the role of culture in personality development. Her book **Patterns of Culture** (1934) is a classic of anthropology. In the following selection, which is from an article published in the same year in which **Patterns of Culture** appeared, Benedict expresses and defends her belief that individuals are very adaptable to divergent cultural patterns of behavior and moral standards. As Benedict sees it, a culture's morality does not derive from some "inevitable constitution of human nature" or from the apprehension of certain moral truths, but from the human tendency to accept prevailing modes of behavior which vary from culture to culture.

Benedict's view of the nature of morality is often referred to by social scientists and philosophers as **ethical relativism.** This concept is, however, often used with different meanings which should be clarified. First, it is sometimes used to refer to the thesis that **as a matter of fact** the moral views of individuals and societies differ in fundamental ways—that is, that such disagreements would persist even with full agreement on all non-moral facts. (In the introduction to this chapter, such disagreements were called **ultimate ethical disagreements**—see p. 325.) This thesis is referred to by philosophers as **descriptive relativism.** A specific form of this thesis is **cultural relativism** which has been embraced by many anthropologists. According to this thesis, ultimate ethical disagreements are **primarily dependent** upon **variable** cultural factors.[1]

Those who accept the existence of ultimate ethical disagreements often go on to draw the **philosophical** conclusion that there is no **uniquely correct** moral view, or to put it another way, that **equally rational** individuals can arrive at ultimate ethical disagreements. Philosophers call such a view **metaethical relativism** and distinguish it from the view called **normative relativism** which contends that the ultimate standard for determining what **actually is right** (and not simply **believed to be right**) for an individual is what his or her society says is right. The distinction between metaethical and normative relativism comes from the distinction that contemporary philosophers make between the two branches of ethics—**metaethics** and **normative ethics.** Normative ethics is that branch of ethics which attempts to supply correct (or justifiable) answers to moral questions, while metaethics is the study of the **meaning** of ethical terms and the **logic** of moral reasoning.

In reading Benedict's article, the reader should keep these distinctions in mind and attempt to locate which types of ethical relativism Benedict accepts.

[1]The reader should notice the weasel word "primarily" in our definition. At one logical extreme, a cultural relativist would claim that a person's moral beliefs are *totally (fully)* dependent (determined) by cultural factors. As we have defined it, however, a cultural relativist need not deny that some ultimate ethical disagreements among individuals arise from biological or individual psychological differences, as long as the influence of these factors is seen to be less than the influence of the cultural factors. One could define "cultural relativism" even more broadly as the view that moral beliefs are *influenced by* cultural factors—leaving open the relative importance of other factors. As always in philosophy, conceptual clarification is the first prerequisite of careful philosophical reflection.

Modern social anthropology has become more and more a study of the varieties and common elements of cultural environment and the consequences of these in human behavior. For such a study of diverse social orders primitive peoples fortunately provide a laboratory not yet entirely vitiated by the spread of a standardized worldwide civilization. Dyaks and Hopis, Fijians and Yakuts are significant for psychological and sociological study because only among these simpler peoples has there been sufficient isolation to give opportunity for the development of localized social forms. In the higher cultures the standardization of custom and belief over a couple of continents has given a false sense of the inevitability of the particular forms that have gained currency, and we need to turn to a wider survey in order to check the conclusions we hastily base upon this near-universality of familiar customs. Most of the simpler cultures did not gain the wide currency of the one which, out of our experience, we identify with human nature, but this was for various historical reasons, and certainly not for any that gives us as its carriers a monopoly of social good or of social sanity. Modern civilization, from this point of view, becomes not a necessary pinnacle of human achievement but one entry in a long series of possible adjustments. . . .

The most spectacular illustrations of the extent to which normality may be culturally defined are those cultures where an abnormality of our culture is the cornerstone of their social structure. It is not possible to do justice to these possibilities in a short discussion. A recent study of an island of northwest Melanesia . . . describes a society built upon traits which we regard as beyond the boder of paranoia. In this tribe the [family] groups look upon each other as prime manipulators of black magic, so that one marries always into an enemy group which remains for life one's deadly and unappeasable foes. They look upon a good garden crop as a confession of theft, for everyone is engaged in making magic to induce into his garden the productiveness of his neighbors'; therefore no secrecy in the island is so rigidly insisted upon as the secrecy of a man's harvesting of his yams. Their polite phrase at the acceptance of a gift is, "And if you now poison me, how shall I repay you this present?" Their preoccupation with poisoning is constant; no woman ever leaves her cooking pot for a moment untended. . . . They have even rigorous religiously enforced customs that forbid the sharing of seed even in one family group. Anyone else's food is deadly poison to you, so that communality of stores is out of the question. For some months before harvest the whole society is on the verge of starvation, but if one falls to the temptation and eats up one's seed yams, one is an outcast and a beachcomber for life. There is no coming back. It involves, as a matter of course, divorce and the breaking of all social ties.

Now in this society where no one may work with another and no one may share with another, [there was an] individual who was regarded by all his fellows as crazy. He was not one of those who periodically ran amok and, beside himself and frothing at the mouth, fell with a knife upon anyone he could reach. Such behavior they did not regard as putting anyone outside the pale. They did not even put the individuals who were known to be liable to these attacks under any kind of control. They merely fled when they saw the attack coming on and kept out of the way. "He would be all right tomorrow." But there was one man of sunny, kindly disposition who liked work and liked to be helpful. The compulsion was too strong for him to repress it in favor of the opposite tendencies of his culture. Men and women never spoke of him without laughing; he was silly and simple and definitely crazy. Nevertheless, to the ethnologist used to a culture that has, in Christianity, made his type the model of all virtue, he seemed a pleasant fellow.

An even more extreme example, because it is of a culture that has built itself upon a more

Source: From Ruth Benedict, "Anthropology and the Abnormal," *Journal of General Psychology,* 1934, 10, 59–82.

complex abnormality, is that of the North Pacific Coast of North America. The civilization of the Kwakiutl . . ., at the time when it was first recorded in the last decades of the nineteenth century, was one of the most vigorous in North America. It was built up on an ample economic supply of goods, the fish which furnished their food staple being practically inexhaustible and obtainable with comparatively small labor, and the wood which furnished the material for their houses, their furnishings, and their arts being, with however much labor, always procurable. . . .

It was one of the most vigorous and zestful of the aboriginal cultures of North America, with complex crafts and ceremonials, and elaborate and striking arts. It certainly had none of the earmarks of a sick civilization. The tribes of the Northwest Coast had wealth, and exactly in our terms. That is, they had not only a surplus of economic goods, but they made a game of the manipulation of wealth. It was by no means a mere direct transcription of economic needs and the filling of those needs. It involved the idea of capital, of interest, and of conspicuous waste. It was a game with all the binding rules of a game, and a person entered it as a child. His father distributed wealth for him, according to his ability, at a small feast or potlatch, and each gift the receiver was obliged to accept and to return after a short interval with interest that ran to about 100 per cent a year. By the time the child was grown, therefore, he was well launched, a larger potlatch had been given for him on various occasions of exploit or initiation, and he had wealth either out at usury or in his own possession. Nothing in the civilization could be enjoyed without validating it by the distribution of this wealth. . . . It was the game of validating and exercising all the privileges one could accumulate from one's various forbears, or by gift, or by marriage, that made the chief interest of the culture. Everyone in his degree took part in it, but many, of course, mainly as spectators. In its highest form it was played out between rival chiefs representing not only themselves and their family lines but their communities, and the object of the contest was to glorify oneself and to humiliate one's opponent. . . .

Every contingency of life was dealt with in . . . two traditional ways. To them the two were equivalent. Whether one fought with weapons or "fought with property," as they say, the same idea was at the bottom of both. In the olden times, they say, they fought with spears, but now they fight with property. One overcomes one's opponents in equivalent fashion in both, matching forces and seeing that one comes out ahead, and one can thumb one's nose at the vanquished rather more satisfactorily at a potlatch than on a battle field. Every occasion in life was noticed, not in its own terms, as a stage in the sex life of the individual or as a climax of joy or of grief, but as furthering this drama of consolidating one's own prestige and bringing shame to one's guests. Whether it was the occasion of the birth of a child, or a daughter's adolescence, or of the marriage of one's son, they were all equivalent raw material for the culture to use for this one traditionally selected end. They were all to raise one's own personal status and to entrench oneself by the humiliation of one's fellows. . . .

In their behavior at great bereavements this set of the culture comes out most strongly. Among the Kwakiutl it did not matter whether a relative had died in bed of disease, or by the hand of an enemy, in either case death was an affront to be wiped out by the death of another person. The fact that one had been caused to mourn was proof that one had been put upon. A chief's sister and her daughter had gone up to Victoria, and either because they drank bad whiskey or because their boat capsized they never came back. The chief called together his warriors. "Now I ask you, tribes, who shall wail? Shall I do it or shall another?" The spokesman answered, of course, "Not you, Chief. Let some other of the tribes." Immediately they set up the war pole to announce their intention of wiping out the injury, and gathered a war party.

They set out, and found seven men and two children asleep and killed them. "Then they felt good when they arrived at Sebaa in the evening."

The point which is of interest to us is that in our society those who on that occasion would feel good when they arrived at Sebaa that evening would be the definitely abnormal. There would be some, even in our society, but it is not a recognized and approved mood under the circumstances. On the Northwest Coast those are favored and fortunate to whom that mood under those circumstances is congenial, and those to whom it is repugnant are unlucky. This latter minority can register in their own culture only by doing violence to their congenial responses and acquiring others that are difficult for them. The person, for instance, who, like a Plains Indian whose wife has been taken from him, is too proud to fight, can deal with the Northwest Coast civilization only by ignoring its strongest bents. If he cannot achieve it, he is the deviant in that culture, their instance of abnormality.

This head-hunting that takes place on the Northwest Coast after a death is no matter of blood revenge or of organized vengeance. There is no effort to tie up the subsequent killing with any responsibility on the part of the victim for the death of the person who is being mourned. A chief whose son has died goes visiting wherever his fancy dictates, and he says to his host, "My prince has died today, and you go with him." Then he kills him. In this, according to their interpretation, he acts nobly because he has not been downed. He has thrust back in return. The whole procedure is meaningless without the fundamental paranoid reading of bereavement. Death, like all the other untoward accidents of existence, confounds man's pride and can only be handled in the category of insults. . . .

These illustrations, which it has been possible to indicate only in the briefest manner, force upon us the fact that normality is culturally defined. An adult shaped to the drives and standards of either of these cultures, if he were transported into our civilization, would fall into our categories of abnormality. . . .

No one civilization can possibly utilize in its mores the whole potential range of human behavior. Just as there are great numbers of possible phonetic articulations, and the possibility of language depends on a selection and standardization of a few of these in order that speech communication may be possible at all, so the possibility of organized behavior of every sort, from the fashions of local dress and houses to the dicta of a people's ethics and religion, depends upon a similar selection among the possible behavior traits. In the field of recognized economic obligations or sex tabus this selection is as nonrational and subconscious a process as it is in the field of phonetics. It is a process which goes on in the group for long periods of time and is historically conditioned by innumerable accidents of isolation or of contact of peoples. In any comprehensive study of psychology, the selection that different cultures have made in the course of history within the great circumference of potential behavior is of great significance.

Every society, beginning with some slight inclination in one direction or another, carries its preference farther and farther, integrating itself more and more completely upon its chosen basis, and discarding those types of behavior that are uncongenial. Most of those organizations of personality that seem to us most incontrovertibly abnormal have been used by different civilizations in the very foundations of their institutional life. Conversely the most valued traits of our normal individuals have been looked on in differently organized cultures as aberrant. Normality, in short, within a very wide range, is culturally defined. It is primarily a term for the socially elaborated segment of human behavior in any culture; and abnormality, a term for the segment that that particular civilization does not use. The very eyes with which we see the problem are conditioned by the long traditional habits of our own society.

It is a point that has been made more often in relation to ethics than in relation to psychiatry. We do not any longer make the mistake of deriving the morality of our own locality and decade directly from the inevitable constitution of human nature. We do not elevate it to the dignity of a first principle. We recognize that morality differs in every society, and is a convenient term for socially approved habits. Mankind has always preferred to say, "It is a morally good," rather than "It is habitual," and the fact of this preference is matter enough for a critical science of ethics. But historically the two phrases are synonymous. . . .

I have spoken of individuals as having sets toward certain types of behavior, and of these sets as running sometimes counter to the types of behavior which are institutionalized in the culture to which they belong. From all that we know of contrasting cultures it seems clear that differences of temperament occur in every society. The matter has never been made the subject of investigation, but from the available material it would appear that these temperament types are very likely of universal recurrence. That is, there is an ascertainable range of human behavior that is found wherever a sufficiently large series of individuals is observed. But the proportion in which behavior types stand to one another in different societies is not universal. The vast majority of the individuals in any group are shaped to the fashion of that culture. In other words, most individuals are plastic to the moulding force of the society into which they are born. In a society that values trance, as in India, they will have supernormal experience. In a society that institutionalizes homosexuality, they will be homosexual. In a society that sets the gathering of possessions as the chief human objective, they will amass property. The deviants, whatever the type of behavior the culture has institutionalized, will remain few in number, and there seems no more difficulty in moulding the vast malleable majority to the "normality" of what we consider an aberrant trait, such as delusions of reference, than to the normality of such accepted behavior patterns as acquisitiveness. The small proportion of the number of the deviants in any culture is not a function of the sure instinct with which that society has built itself upon the fundamental sanities, but of the universal fact that, happily, the majority of mankind quite readily take any shape that is presented to them . . . .

The problem of understanding abnormal human behavior in any absolute sense independent of cultural factors is still far in the future. The categories of borderline behavior which we derive from the study of the neuroses and psychoses of our civilization are categories of prevailing local types of instability. They give much information about the stresses and strains of Western civilization, but no final picture of inevitable human behavior. Any conclusions about such behavior must await the collection by trained observers of psychiatric data from other cultures. Since no adequate work of the kind has been done at the present time, it is impossible to say what core of definition of abnormality may be found valid from the comparative material. It is as it is in ethics: all our local conventions of moral behavior and of immoral are without absolute validity, and yet it is quite possible that a modicum of what is considered right and what wrong could be disentangled that is shared by the whole human race. When data are available in psychiatry, this minimum definition of abnormal human tendencies will be probably quite unlike our culturally conditioned, highly elaborated psychoses such as those that are described, for instance, under the terms of schizophrenia and manic-depressive.

DISCUSSION QUESTIONS

1. Critically discuss the meaning and implications of Ruth Benedict's claim that

> We recognize that morality differs in every society, and is a convenient term for socially approved habits. Mankind has always preferred to say, "It is morally good," rather than "it is habitual". . . . But historically the two phrases are synonymous.

Do you agree with this claim? Why, or why not?

2. What bearing do the examples of cultural diversity presented by Benedict have on the view that

a. as a matter of fact, different societies have fundamentally different moralities.

b. the morality of an individual's behavior can only be judged by the moral standards of that individual's society, for an individual's moral standards are correct when they conform to the moral standards of that individual's society and wrong when they do not. The correctness of an individual's moral standards are subject to objective testing, but the moral standards of societies are not.

c. a person never has any rational justification for criticizing the value judgments of others.

d. there is no single uniquely correct morality that can be used as a standard for rationally appraising the moralities of societies or individuals.

3. In speaking of a particular pattern of behavior of the Kwakiutl, Ruth Benedict claims that, "The whole procedure is meaningless without the fundamental paranoid reading of bereavement." Is she not, by utilizing the word "paranoid," making an implicit judgment that the Kwakiutl are **mistaken** in their view of the world? Is this consistent with the position she maintains in her article? Critically discuss.

4. According to Ruth Benedict, can there be any justification for war crimes trials such as those conducted at Nuremburg by the victorious Allies against vanquished Nazi officials who admittedly obeyed the laws of their government? What do you think Benedict would say about the Nuremburg trials?

5. Assuming that, as a matter of fact, all societies and individuals shared the same moral standards, what bearing would such a fact have on the question of whether such standards were **correct**?

6. Are there some moral principles or values which every reasonable person would accept? If so, what are they and how would you account for their universal acceptability? Are all ethical disagreements rationally resolvable on the basis of these moral principles? Why?

7. In **Patterns of Culture**, Benedict writes that

> The recognition of cultural relativity carries with it its own values. . . . [In recognizing it,] we shall arrive then at a more realistic social faith, accepting as grounds of hope and as new bases for tolerance the coexisting and equally valid patterns of life which mankind has created for itself from the raw materials of existence.[2]

Is it true that the recognition of cultural relativity leads (as a matter of fact) to greater tolerance of divergent moral opinions? Does Benedict think that it **should** lead in that direction? If so, does this imply that she is not an ethical relativist since she believes that (all) people, regardless of their own cultural heritage, should be tolerant of divergent moralities?

7. Some philosophers have suggested the following definition of "X is right":

> "X is right" means that an ideal observer would approve of it. An "ideal observer" is defined to be impartial, fully informed, and vividly aware of the relevant facts, and in a calm frame of mind.

Does such a standard enable anthropologists to make judgments about the correctness or incorrectness of the moralities of different societies? Why?

8. Do you see the disagreement between principled vegetarians, who believe that animals have a right not be killed by humans for food, and those who do not agree with this belief as one that would be resolved if the disputants agreed on all their nonmoral facts? Explain.

9. Solomon Asch, a social psychologist, argues that the apparent divergence of moral beliefs of different societies over the rightness of particular ac-

[2]Ruth Benedict, *Patterns of Culture* (New York: Pelican Books, 1946), p. 257.

tions can be explained away as a function of the different psychological meanings that these societies place on the same action. For example, he writes:

> If . . . we are to speak of relativism with reference to infanticide we must assume that the **same** action which is tolerated under one set of conditions is outlawed under other conditions. This assumption is . . . dubious. . . . In the first few days of life, an infant may be regarded as not yet human. . . . Therefore, the act of killing will not have the same meaning . . . [3]

[3]Solomon E. Asch, *Social Psychology* (Englewood Cliffs, N.J.: Prentice-Hall, Inc., 1952), pp. 376–77.

Is Asch right that even though individuals may disagree as to the morality of infanticide, this may not indicate a difference in basic moral value, if there is disagreement as to the "humanity" of an infant (i.e., in one society a newborn infant may be seen as a "human being," while in a different society, an infant may be seen as something less than a "human being")? Is Asch right in his apparent assumption that one's perception of the nature of an infant as "human" or "nonhuman" is a nonmoral perception that determines one's moral attitude toward infanticide or is this perception itself a moral one? If so, is it at all informative to claim that "Whenever individuals disagree as to the morality of an action, there is a difference in **the meaning** they attribute to this action," as Asch does? Carefully explain.

42. A CRITICISM OF ETHICAL RELATIVISM

W.T. Stace

W(ALTER) T(ERENCE) STACE (1886–1967) was born in Great Britain and served in the British Civil Service in Ceylon before accepting a position to teach philosophy at Princeton University. The author of many books, Stace had very wide philosophical interests. During the latter part of his life, he became a defender of mysticism as a scientifically acceptable view of the world.

In the following selection from his book **The Concept of Morals** (1937), Stace criticizes ethical relativism. He argues that an acceptance of this doctrine entails a rejection of our ordinary concept of morality and, if pressed to its logical conclusion, can only end "in taking the life-blood out of every ideal and every aspiration which has ever ennobled the life of man." While Stace does not defend his own ethical theory in our excerpt, in other parts of **The Concept of Morals** he argues for the belief in a single correct morality for human beings based on a **universal human nature** which is not a function of cultural factors.

Any ethical position which denies that there is a single moral standard which is equally applicable to all men at all times may fairly be called a species of ethical relativity. There is not, the relativist asserts, merely one moral law, one code, one standard. There are many moral laws, codes, standards. What morality ordains in one place or age may be quite different from what morality ordains in another place or age. . . . Any morality, therefore, is relative to the age, the place, and the circumstances in which it is found. It is in no sense absolute.

This does not mean merely—as one might at first sight be inclined to suppose—that the very same kind of action which is *thought* right in one country and period may be *thought* wrong in another. This would be a mere platitude, the truth of which everyone would have to admit. Even the absolutist would admit this—would even wish to emphasize it—since he is well aware that different people have different sets of moral ideas, and his whole point is that some of these sets of ideas are false. What the relativist means to assert is, not this platitude, but that the very same kind of action which *is* right in one country and period may *be* wrong in another. And this, far from being a platitude, is a very startling assertion.

It is very important to grasp thoroughly the difference between the two ideas. For there is reason to think that many minds tend to find ethical relativity attractive because they fail to keep them clearly apart. It is so very obvious that moral ideas differ from country to country and from age to age. And it is so very easy, if you are mentally lazy, to suppose that to say this means the same as to say that no universal moral standard exists,—or in other words that it implies ethical relativity. We fail to see that the word ''standard'' is used in two different senses. It is perfectly true that, in one sense, there are many variable moral standards. We speak of judging a man by the standard of his time. And this implies that different times have different standards. And this, of course, is quite true. But when the word ''standard'' is used in this sense it means simply the set of moral ideas current during the period in question. It means what people *think* right, whether as a matter of fact it *is* right or not. On the other hand when the absolutist asserts that there exists a single universal moral ''standard,'' he is not using the word in this sense at all. He means by ''standard'' what *is* right as distinct from what people merely think right. His point is that although what people think right varies in different countries and periods, yet what actually is right is everywhere and always the same. And it follows that when the ethical relativist disputes the position of the absolutist and denies that any universal moral standard exists he too means by ''standard'' what actually is right. But it is exceedingly easy, if we are not careful, to slip loosely from using the word in the first sense to using it in the second sense; and to suppose that the variability of moral beliefs is the same thing as the variability of what really is moral. And unless we keep the two senses of the word ''standard'' distinct, we are likely to think the creed of ethical relativity much more plausible than it actually is.

The genuine relativist, then, does not merely mean that Chinamen may think right what Frenchmen think wrong. He means that what *is* wrong for the Frenchman may *be* right for the Chinaman. And if one enquires how, in those circumstances, one is to know what actually is right in China or in France, the answer comes quite glibly. What is right in China is the same as what people think right in China; and what is right in France is the same as what people think right in France. So that, if you want to know what is moral in any particular country or age all you have to do is to ascertain what are the moral ideas current in that age or country.

Source: Excerpted with permission of Macmillan Publishing Co., Inc. from *The Concept of Morals* by W.T. Stace.

Those ideas are, *for that age or country,* right. Thus what is morally right is identified with what is thought to be morally right, and the distinction which we made above between these two is simply denied. To put the same thing in another way, it is denied that there can be or ought to be any distinction between the two senses of the word "standard." There is only one kind of standard of right and wrong, namely, the moral ideas current in any particular age or country. . . .

When it is said that, according to the ethical relativist, what is thought right in any social group is right for that group, one must be careful not to misinterpret this. The relativist does not, of course, mean that there actually is an objective moral standard in France and a different objective standard in England, and that French and British opinions respectively give us correct information about these different standards. His point is rather that there are no objectively true moral standards at all. There is no single universal objective standard. Nor are there a variety of local objective standards. All standards are subjective. People's subjective feelings about morality are the only standards which exist.

To sum up. The ethical relativist consistently denies, it would seem, whatever the ethical absolutist asserts. For the absolutist there is a single universal moral standard. For the relativist there is no such standard. There are only local, ephemeral, and variable standards. For the absolutist there are two senses of the word "standard." Standards in the sense of sets of current moral ideas are relative and changeable. But the standard in the sense of what is actually morally right is absolute and unchanging. For the relativist no such distinction can be made. There is only one meaning of the word standard, namely, that which refers to local and variable sets of moral ideas. Or if it is insisted that the word must be allowed two meanings, then the relativist will say that there is at any rate no actual example of a standard in the absolute sense, and that the word as thus used is an empty name to which nothing in reality corresponds; so that the distinction between the two meanings becomes empty and useless. Finally—though this is merely saying the same thing in another way—the absolutist makes a distinction between what actually is right and what is thought right. The relativist rejects this distinction and identifies what is moral with what is thought by certain human beings or groups of human beings. . . .

I shall now proceed to consider, first, the main arguments which can be urged in favour of ethical relativity; and secondly, the arguments which can be urged against it. . . . The first is that which relies upon the actual varieties of moral "standards" found in the world. It was easy enough to believe in a single absolute morality in older times when there was no anthropology, when all humanity was divided clearly into two groups, Christian peoples and the "heathen." Christian peoples knew and possessed the one true morality. The rest were savages whose moral ideas could be ignored. But all this is changed. Greater knowledge has brought greater tolerance. We can no longer exalt our own morality as alone true, while dismissing all other moralities as false or inferior. The investigations of anthropologists have shown that there exist side by side in the world a bewildering variety of moral codes. On this topic endless volumes have been written, masses of evidence piled up. Anthropologists have ransacked the Melanesian Islands, the jungles of New Guinea, the steppes of Siberia, the deserts of Australia, the forests of central Africa, and have brought back with them countless examples of weird, extravagant, and fantastic "moral" customs with which to confound us. We learn that all kinds of horrible practices are, in this, that, or the other place, regarded as essential to virtue. We find that there is nothing, or next to nothing, which has always and everywhere been regarded as morally good by all men. Where then is our universal morality? Can we, in face of all this evidence, deny that it is nothing but an empty dream?

This argument, taken by itself, is a very weak one. It relies upon a single set of facts—the variable moral customs of the world. But this variability of moral ideas is admitted by both parties to the dispute, and is capable of ready explanation upon the hypothesis of either party. The relativist says that the facts are to be explained by the non-existence of any absolute moral standard. The absolutist says that they are to be explained by human ignorance of what the absolute moral standard is. And he can truly point out that men have differed widely in their opinions about all manner of topics including the subject-matters of the physical sciences—just as much as they differ about morals. And if the various different opinions which men have held about the shape of the earth do not prove that it has no one real shape, neither do the various opinions which they have held about morality prove that there is no one true morality.

Thus the facts can be explained equally plausibly on either hypothesis. There is nothing in the facts themselves which compels us to prefer the relativistic hypothesis to that of the absolutist. And therefore the argument fails to prove the relativist conclusion. If that conclusion is to be established, it must be by means of other considerations. . . .

[Another] argument in favour of ethical relativity is also a very strong one. . . . It consists in alleging that no one has ever been able to discover upon what foundation an absolute morality could rest, or from what source a universally binding moral code could derive its authority.

If, for example, it is an absolute and unalterable moral rule that all men ought to be unselfish, from whence does this *command* issue? For a command it certainly is, phrase it how you please. There is no difference in meaning between the sentence "You ought to be unselfish" and the sentence "Be unselfish." Now a command implies a commander. An obligation implies some authority which obliges. Who is this commander, what this authority? Thus the vastly difficult question is raised of *the basis of moral obligation*. Now the argument of the relativist would be that it is impossible to find any basis for a universally binding moral law; but that it is quite easy to discover a basis for morality if moral codes are admitted to be variable, ephemeral, and relative to time, place, and circumstance.

. . . I am assuming that it is no longer possible to solve this difficulty by saying naïvely that the universal moral law is based upon the uniform commands of God to all men. There will be many, no doubt, who will dispute this. But I am not writing for them. I am writing for those who feel the necessity of finding for morality a basis independent of particular religious dogmas. And I shall therefore make no attempt to argue the matter.

The problem which the absolutist has to face, then, is this. The religious basis of the one absolute morality having disappeared, can there be found for it any other, any secular, basis? If not, then it would seem that we cannot any longer believe in absolutism. We shall have to fall back upon belief in a variety of perhaps mutually inconsistent moral codes operating over restricted areas and limited periods. No one of these will be better, or more true, than any other. Each will be good and true for those living in those areas and periods. We shall have to fall back, in a word, on ethical relativity.

For there is no great difficulty in discovering the foundations of morality, or rather of moralities, if we adopt the relativistic hypothesis. Even if we cannot be quite certain *precisely* what these foundations are—and relativists themselves are not entirely agreed about them—we can at least see in a general way the *sort* of foundations they must have. We can see that the question on this basis is not in principle impossible of answer—although the details may be obscure;

while, if we adopt the absolutist hypothesis—so the argument runs—no kind of answer is conceivable at all. . . .

This argument is undoubtedly very strong. It is absolutely essential to solve the problem of the basis of moral obligation if we are to believe in any kind of moral standards other than those provided by mere custom or by irrational emotions. It is idle to talk about a universal morality unless we can point to the source of its authority—or at least to do so is to indulge in a faith which is without rational ground. To cherish a blind faith in morality may be, for the average man whose business is primarily to live aright and not to theorize, sufficient. Perhaps it is his wisest course. But it will not do for the philosopher. His function, or at least one of his functions, is precisely to discover the rational grounds of our everyday beliefs—if they have any. Philosophically and intellectually, then, we cannot accept belief in a universally binding morality unless we can discover upon what foundation its obligatory character rests.

But in spite of the strength of the arguments thus posed in favour of ethical relativity, it is not impregnable. For it leaves open one loophole. It is always possible that some theory, not yet examined, may provide a basis for a universal moral obligation. The argument rests upon the negative proposition that *there is no theory which can provide a basis for a universal morality.* But it is notoriously difficult to prove a negative. How can you prove that there are no green swans? All you can show is that none have been found so far. And then it is always possible that one will be found tomorrow. . . .

It is time that we turned our attention from the case in favour of ethical relativity to the case against it. Now the case against it consists, to a very large extent, in urging that, if taken seriously and pressed to its logical conclusion, ethical relativity can only end in destroying the conception of morality altogether, in undermining its practical efficacy, in rendering meaningless many almost universally accepted truths about human affairs, in robbing human beings of any incentive to strive for a better world, in taking the life-blood out of every ideal and every aspiration which has ever ennobled the life of man. . . .

First of all . . . , ethical relativity, in asserting that the moral standards of particular social groups are the only standards which exist, renders meaningless all propositions which attempt to compare these standards with one another in respect to their moral worth. And this is a very serious matter indeed. We are accustomed to think that the moral ideas of one nation or social group may be "higher" or "lower" than those of another. We believe, for example, that Christian ethical ideals are nobler than those of the savage races of central Africa. . . . In short we habitually compare one civilization with another and judge the sets of ethical ideas to be found in them to be some better, some worse. The fact that such judgments are very difficult to make with any justice, and that they are frequently made on very superficial and prejudiced grounds, has no bearing on the question now at issue. The question is whether such judgments have any *meaning*. We habitually assume that they have.

But on the basis of ethical relativity they can have none whatever. For the relativist must hold that there is no *common* standard which can be applied to the various civilizations judged. Any such comparison of moral standards implies the existence of some superior standard which is applicable to both. And the existence of any such standard is precisely what the relativist denies. According to him the Christian standard is applicable only to Christians, the Chinese standard only to Chinese, the New Guinea standard only to the inhabitants of New Guinea.

What is true of comparisons between the moral standards of different races will also be true of comparisons between those of different ages. It is not unusual to ask such questions as whether the standard of our own day is superior to that which existed among our ancestors five hundred years ago. And when we remember that our ancestors employed slaves, practiced barbaric physical tortures, and burnt people alive, we may be inclined to think that it is. At any rate we assume that the question is one which has meaning and is capable of rational discussion. But if the ethical relativist is right, whatever we assert on this subject must be totally meaningless. For here again there is no common standard which could form the basis of any such judgments.

This in its turn implies that the whole notion of moral *progress* is a sheer delusion. Progress means an advance from lower to higher, from worse to better. But on the basis of ethical relativity it has no meaning to say that the standards of this age are better (or worse) than those of a previous age. For there is no common standard by which both can be measured. Thus it is nonsense to say that the morality of the New Testament is higher than that of the Old. And Jesus Christ, if he imagined that he was introducing into the world a higher ethical standard than existed before his time, was merely deluded. . . .

I come now to a second point. Up to the present I have allowed it to be taken tacitly for granted that, though judgments comparing different races and ages in respect of the worth of their moral codes are impossible for the ethical relativist, yet judgments of comparison between individuals living within the same social group would be quite possible. For individuals living within the same social group would presumably be subject to the same moral code, that of their group, and this would therefore constitute, as between these individuals, a common standard by which they could both be measured. We have not here, as we had in the other case, the difficulty of the absence of any common standard of comparison. It should therefore be possible for the ethical relativist to say quite meaningfully that President Lincoln was a better man than some criminal or moral imbecile of his own time and country, or that Jesus was a better man than Judas Iscariot.

But is even this minimum of moral judgment really possible on relativist grounds? It seems to me that it is not. For when once the whole of humanity is abandoned as the area covered by a single moral standard, what smaller areas are to be adopted as the [area covered by] different standards? Where are we to draw the lines of demarcation? We can split up humanity, perhaps,—though the procedure will be very arbitrary—into races, races into nations, nations into tribes, tribes into families, families into individuals. Where are we going to draw the *moral* boundaries? Does the [area covered by] a particular moral standard reside in a race, a nation, a tribe, a family, or an individual? Perhaps the blessed phrase ''social group'' will be dragged in to save the situation. Each such group, we shall be told, has its own moral code which is, for it, right. But what *is* a ''group''? Can any one define it or give its boundaries? This is the seat of that ambiguity in the theory of ethical relativity to which reference was made on an earlier page.

The difficulty is not, as might be thought, merely an academic difficulty of logical definition. If that were all, I should not press the point. But the ambiguity has practical consequences which are disastrous for morality. No one is likely to say that moral codes are confined within the arbitrary limits of the geographical divisions of countries. Nor are the notions of race, nation, or political state likely to help us. To bring out the essentially practical character of the difficulty let us put it in the form of concrete questions. Does the American nation constitute a ''group'' having a single moral standard? Or does the standard of what I ought to do change continuously as I cross the continent in a railway train? Do different States of the Union have different moral codes? Perhaps every town and village has its own peculiar standard. This may at first sight seem reasonable enough. "In Rome do as Rome does" may seem as good a rule in morals as it is in etiquette. But can we stop there? Within the village are numerous cliques each having its own set of ideas. Why should not each of these claim to be bound only by its own special and peculiar moral standards? And if it comes to that, why should not the gangsters of Chicago[1] claim to constitute a group having its own morality, so that its murders and debaucheries must be viewed as "right" by the only standard which can legitimately be applied to it? And if it be answered that the nation will not tolerate this, that may be so. But this is to put the foundation of right simply in the superior force of the majority. In that case whoever is stronger will be right, however monstrous his ideas and actions. And if we cannot deny to any set of people the right to have its own morality, is it not clear that, in the end, we cannot even deny this right to the individual? Every individual man and woman can put up, on this view, an irrefutable claim to be judged by no standard except his or her own.

If these arguments are valid, the ethical relativist cannot really maintain that there is anywhere to be found a moral standard binding upon anybody against his will. And he cannot maintain that, even within the social group, there is a common standard as between individuals. And if that is so, then even judgments to the effect that one man is morally better than another become meaningless. All moral valuation thus vanishes. There is nothing to prevent each man from being a rule unto himself. The result will be moral chaos and the collapse of all effective standards. . . .

But even if we assume that the difficulty about defining moral groups has been surmounted, a further difficulty presents itself. Suppose that we have now definitely decided what are the exact boundaries of the social group within which a moral standard is to be operative. And we will assume—as is invariably done by relativists themselves—that this group is to be some actually existing social community such as a tribe or nation. How are we to know, even then, what actually *is* the moral standard within that group? How is anyone to know? How is even a member of the group to know? For there are certain to be within the group—at least this will be true among advanced peoples—wide differences of opinion as to what is right, what wrong. Whose opinion, then, is to be taken as representing *the* moral standard of the group? Either we must take the opinion of the majority within the group, or the opinion of some minority. If we rely upon the ideas of the majority, the results will be disastrous. Wherever there is found among a people a small band of select spirits, or perhaps one man, working for the establishment of higher and nobler ideals than those commonly accepted by the group, we shall be compelled to hold that, for that people at that time, the majority are right, and that the reformers are wrong and are preaching what is immoral. We shall have to maintain, for example, that Jesus was preaching immoral doctrines to the Jews. Moral goodness will have to be equated always with the mediocre and sometimes with the definitely base and ignoble. If on the other hand we said that the moral standard of the group is to be identified with the moral opinions of some minority, then what minority is this to be? We cannot answer that it is to be the minority composed of the best and most enlightened individuals of the group. This would involve us in a palpably vicious circle. For by what standard are these individuals to be judged the best and the most enlightened? There is no principle by which we could select the right minority. And therefore we should have to consider every minority as good as every other. And this means that we should have no logical right whatever to resist the claim of the gangsters of Chicago—if such a claim were made—that their practices represent the high-

[1]This book was written in the 1930's, when organized crime flourished in Chicago. EDITOR'S NOTE.

est standards of American morality. It means in the end that every individual is to be bound by no standard save his own. . . .

Finally, not only is ethical relativity disastrous in its consequences for moral theory. It cannot be doubted that it must tend to be equally disastrous in its impact upon practical conduct. If men come really to believe that one moral standard is as good as another, they will conclude that their own moral standard has nothing special to recommend it. They might as well then slip down to some lower and easier standard. It is true that, for a time, it may be possible to hold one view in theory and to act practically upon another. But ideas, even philosophical ideas, are not so ineffectual that they can remain for ever idle in the upper chambers of the intellect. In the end they seep down to the level of practice. They get themselves acted on.

DISCUSSION QUESTIONS

1. Stace draws a distinction between two different notions of "moral standards." What are these two notions and why does Stace think that it is important to distinguish between them?

2. In the very first sentence of the preceding selection, Stace defines "ethical relativism" as "any ethical position which denies that there is a single moral standard which is equally applicable to all men at all times." What is the meaning Stace attributes to "moral standard" in this definition? Does ethical relativism, so defined, lead inevitably, as Stace claims, to the view that one can never have a rational justification for criticizing a given morality as "incorrect" and that "moral right means what people think morally right"? Why?

3. What reasons does Stace have for claiming that ". . . if taken seriously and pressed to its logical conclusion, ethical relativity can only end in destroying the conception of morality altogether, in undermining its practical efficacy, in rendering meaningless many almost universally accepted truths about human affairs, in robbing human beings of any incentive to strive for a better world, in taking the life-blood out of every ideal and every aspiration which has ever ennobled the life of man. . . ." To what extent do you agree with this assessment? Critically defend your position.

4. Do you think that the doctrine of ethical relativism is dangerous, as Stace suggests? If so, is this at all relevant to the question of whether or not ethical relativism is true? Is there a justification, at times, for suppressing the truth when it is harmful?

5. Why does Stace believe that the view that an individual's actions are subject to moral appraisal only according to the moral standard of his society is a logically unstable one, which leads inevitably to the view that any individual can be judged by no standard except his own?

43. A DEFENSE OF MORAL SUBJECTIVISM

Bertrand Russell

(For a biographical sketch of Bertrand Russell, see Selection #1.)

In the selection that follows, Russell defends the view that there are no moral facts which exist independently of human desires. It is this doctrine that Russell refers to as the doctrine of **the subjectivity of values** (or, as other philosophers often call it, **moral subjectivism**). As is the case with so much of Russell's philosophy, David Hume had a great influence on Russell's ethical philosophy.

On the basis of the belief that moral judgments depend on subjective human desires or tastes, Russell claims that moral disagreements are incapable of rational resolution. As he sees it, assertions about moral values can be seen either as **statements** about personal preferences (e.g., "I like X") or as nonfactual expressions of one's desires or emotions (e.g., "Would that everyone approve of X!"). The second view **(the emotive theory of ethics)** was a popular view among the logical positivists of the early twentieth century. Sharing the view that moral assertions are nonfactual (i.e., they cannot meaningfully be said to be either true or false), the emotivists differed in the analyses they offered for moral assertions. For example, moral assertions have been analyzed by emotivists as: (1) expressions of desires, emotions, or attitudes; (2) linguistic devices for arousing feelings of approval or disapproval; (3) commands; and (4) universal prescriptions (i.e., recommendations that **everyone** ought to behave in a particular way in a given situation). It is the first of these emotive analyses that Russell suggests as a possible analysis of moral assertions. After presenting his subjectivistic view of ethics, Russell goes on to disagree with those (e.g., Stace in the preceding selection) who claim that the acceptance of a subjective (and, implicitly, relativistic) view of ethics is bound (or, at least, is likely) to lead to a decay of all sense of moral obligation.

The study of ethics, traditionally, consists of two parts, one concerned with moral rules, the other with what is good on its own account. Rules of conduct, many of which have a ritual origin, play a great part in the lives of savages and primitive peoples. It is forbidden to eat out of the chief's dish . . .; it is commanded to offer sacrifices to the gods, which, at a certain stage of development, are thought most acceptable if they are human beings. Other moral rules, such as the prohibition of murder and theft, have a more obvious social utility, and survive the decay of the primitive theological systems with which they were originally associated. But as men grow more reflective there is a tendency to lay less stress on rules and more on states of mind. This comes from two sources—philosophy and mystical religion. We are all familiar with passages in the prophets and the gospels, in which purity of heart is set above meticulous observance of the Law; and St. Paul's famous praise of charity, or love, teaches the same principle. The same thing will be found in all great mystics, Christian and non-Christian; what they value is a state of mind, out of which, as they hold, right conduct must ensue; rules seem to them external, and insufficiently adaptable to circumstances.

One of the ways in which the need of appealing to external rules of conduct has been avoided has been the belief in "conscience," which has been especially important in Protestant ethics. It has been supposed that God reveals to each human heart what is right and what is wrong, so that, in order to avoid sin, we have only to listen to the inner voice. There are, however, two difficulties in this theory: first, that conscience says different things to different people; secondly, that the study of the unconscious has given us an understanding of the mundane causes of conscientious feelings.

As to the different deliverances of conscience: George III's conscience told him that he must

Source: From *Religion and Science* by Bertrand Russell (1935). Reprinted by permission of Oxford University Press.

not grant Catholic Emancipation, as, if he did, he would have committed perjury in taking the Coronation Oath, but later monarchs have had no such scruples. Conscience leads some to condemn the spoliation of the rich by the poor, as advocated by communists; and others to condemn exploitation of the poor by the rich, as practised by capitalists. It tells one man that he ought to defend his country in case of invasion, while it tells another that all participation in warfare is wicked. . . .

The diversity in the deliverances of conscience is what is to be expected when its origin is understood. In early youth, certain classes of acts meet with approval, and others with disapproval; and by the normal process of association, pleasure and discomfort gradually attach themselves to the acts, and not merely to the approval and disapproval respectively produced by them. As time goes on, we may forget all about our early moral training, but we shall still feel uncomfortable about certain kinds of actions, while others will give us a glow of virtue. To introspection, these feelings are mysterious, since we no longer remember the circumstances which originally caused them; and therefore it is natural to attribute them to the voice of God in the heart. But in fact conscience is a product of education, and can be trained to approve or disapprove, in the great majority of mankind, as educators may see fit. While, therefore, it is right to wish to liberate ethics from external moral rules, this can hardly be satisfactorily achieved by means of the notion of "conscience."

Philosophers, by a different road, have arrived at a different position in which, also, moral rules of conduct have a subordinate place. They have framed the concept of the Good, by which they mean (roughly speaking) that which, in itself and apart from its consequences, we should wish to see existing—or, if they are theists, that which is pleasing to God. Most people would agree that happiness is preferable to unhappiness, friendliness to unfriendliness, and so on. Moral rules, according to this view, are justified if they promote the existence of what is good on its own account, but not otherwise. The prohibition of murder, in the vast majority of cases, can be justified by its effects, but the practice of burning widows on their husband's funeral pyre cannot. The former rule, therefore, should be retained, but not the latter. Even the best moral rules, however, will have *some* exceptions, since no class of action *always* has bad results. . . .

Different philosophers have formed different conceptions of the Good. Some hold that it consists in the knowledge and love of God; others in universal love; others in the enjoyment of beauty; and yet others in pleasure. The Good once defined, the rest of ethics follows: we ought to act in the way we believe most likely to create as much good as possible, and as little as possible of its correlative evil. The framing of moral rules, so long as the ultimate Good is supposed known, is a matter for science. For example: should capital punishment be inflicted for theft, or only for murder, or not at all? Jeremy Bentham, who considered pleasure to be the Good, devoted himself to working out what criminal code would most promote pleasure, and concluded that it ought to be much less severe than that prevailing in his day. All this, except the proposition that pleasure is the Good, comes within the sphere of science.

But when we try to be definite as to what we mean when we say that this or that is "the Good," we find ourselves involved in very great difficulties. Bentham's creed that pleasure is the Good roused furious opposition, and was said to be a pig's philosophy. Neither he nor his opponents could advance any argument. In a scientific question, evidence can be adduced on both sides, and in the end one side is seen to have the better case—or, if this does not happen, the question is left undecided. But in a question as to whether this or that is the ultimate Good, there is no evidence either way;

each disputant can only appeal to his own emotions, and employ such rhetorical devices as shall rouse similar emotions in others.

Take, for example, a question which has come to be important in practical politics. Bentham held that one man's pleasure has the same ethical importance as another man's, provided the quantities are equal; and on this ground he was led to advocate democracy. Nietzsche, on the contrary, held that only the great man can be regarded as important on his own account, and that the bulk of mankind are only means to his well-being. He viewed ordinary men as many people view animals: he thought it justifiable to make use of them, not for their own good, but for that of the superman, and this view has since been adopted to justify the abandonment of democracy. We have here a sharp disagreement of great practical importance, but we have absolutely no means, of a scientific or intellectual kind, by which to persuade either party that the other is in the right. There are, it is true, ways of altering men's opinions on such subjects, but they are all emotional, not intellectual.

Questions as to "values"—that is to say, as to what is good or bad on its own account, independently of its effects—lie outside the domain of science, as the defenders of religion emphatically assert. I think that in this they are right, but I draw the further conclusion, which they do not draw, that questions as to "values" lie wholly outside the domain of knowledge. That is to say, when we assert that this or that has "value," we are giving expression to our own emotions, not to a fact which would still be true if our personal feelings were different. To make this clear, we must try to analyze the conception of the Good.

It is obvious, to begin with, that the whole idea of good and bad has some connection with *desire*. *Prima facie,*[1] anything that we all desire is "good," and anything that we all dread is "bad." If we all agreed in our desires, the matter could be left there, but unfortunately our desires conflict. If I say "what I want is good," my neighbor will say "No, what I want." Ethics is an attempt—though not, I think, a successful one—to escape from this subjectivity. I shall naturally try to show, in my dispute with my neighbor, that my desires have some quality which makes them more worthy of respect than his. If I want to preserve a right of way, I shall appeal to the landless inhabitants of the district; but he, on his side, will appeal to the landowners. I shall say: "What use is the beauty of the countryside if no one sees it?" He will retort: "What beauty will be left if trippers are allowed to spread devastation?" Each tries to enlist allies by showing that his own desires harmonize with those of other people. When this is obviously impossible, as in the case of a burglar, the man is condemned by public opinion, and his ethical status is that of a sinner.

Ethics is thus closely related to politics; it is an attempt to bring the collective desires of a group to bear upon individuals; or, conversely, it is an attempt by an individual to cause his desires to become those of his group. This latter is, of course, only possible if his desires are not too obviously opposed to the general interest . . . . When our desires are for things which all can enjoy in common, it seems not unreasonable to hope that others may concur; thus the philosopher who values Truth, Goodness and Beauty seems, to himself, to be not merely expressing his own desires, but pointing the way to the welfare of all mankind. Unlike the burglar, he is able to believe that his desires are for something that has value in an impersonal sense.

Ethics is an attempt to give universal, and not merely personal, importance to certain of our desires. I say "certain" of our desires, because in regard to some of them this is obviously impossible, as we saw in the case of the burglar.

[1]Adequate to establish a fact unless refuted. EDITOR'S NOTE.

The man who makes money on the Stock Exchange by means of some secret knowledge does not wish others to be equally well informed . . . .

. . . Every attempt to persuade people that something is good (or bad) in itself, and not merely in it effects, depends upon the art of rousing feelings, not upon an appeal to evidence. In every case the preacher's skill consists in creating in others emotions similar to his own—or dissimilar, if he is a hypocrite. I am not saying this as a criticism of the preacher, but as an analysis of the essential character of his activity.

When a man says "this is good in itself," he *seems* to be making a statement, just as much as if he said "this is square" or "this is sweet." I believe this to be a mistake. I think that what the man really means is: "I wish everybody to desire this," or rather "Would that everybody desired this." If what he says is interpreted as a statement, it is merely an affirmation of his own personal wish; if, on the other hand, it is interpreted in a general way, it states nothing, but merely desires something. The wish as an occurrence, is personal, but what it desires is universal. It is, I think, this curious interlocking of the particular and the universal which has caused so much confusion in ethics.

The matter may perhaps become clearer by contrasting an ethical sentence with one which makes a statement. If I say "all Chinese are Buddhists," I can be refuted by the production of a Chinese Christian or Mohammedan. If I say "I believe that all Chinese are Buddhists," I cannot be refuted by any evidence from China, but only by evidence that I do not believe what I say; for what I am asserting is only something about my own state of mind. If, now, a philosopher says "Beauty is good," I may interpret him as meaning either "Would that everybody loved the beautiful" . . . or "I wish that everybody loved the beautiful." . . . The first of these makes no assertion, but expresses a wish; since it affirms nothing, it is logically impossible that there should be evidence for or against it, or for it to possess either truth or falsehood. The second sentence, instead of being merely optative,[2] does make a statement, but it is one about the philosopher's state of mind, and it could only be refuted by evidence that he does not have the wish that he says he has. This second sentence does not belong to ethics, but to psychology or biography. The first sentence, which does belong to ethics, expresses a desire for something, but asserts nothing.

Ethics, if the above analysis is correct, contains no statements, whether true of false, but consists of desires of a certain general kind, namely such as are concerned with the desires of mankind in general—and of gods, angels, and devils, if they exist. Science can discuss the causes of desires, and the means for realizing them, but it cannot contain any genuinely ethical sentences, because it is concerned with what is true or false.

The theory which I have been advocating is a form of the doctrine which is called the "subjectivity" of values. This doctrine consists in maintaining that, if two men differ about values, there is not a disagreement as to any kind of truth, but a difference of taste. If one man says "oysters are good" and another says "I think they are bad," we recognize that there is nothing to argue about. The theory in question holds that all differences as to values are of this sort, although we do not naturally think them so when we are dealing with matters that seem to us more exalted than oysters. The chief ground for adopting this view is the complete impossibility of finding any arguments to prove that this or that has intrinsic value. If we all agreed, we might hold that we know values by intuition. We cannot *prove*, to a colour-blind man, that grass is green and not red. But there are various ways of proving to him that he lacks a power of discrimination which most men

[2]A grammatical mood for expressing a wish or desire. EDITOR'S NOTE.

possess, whereas in the case of values there are no such ways, and disagreements are much more frequent than in the case of colours. Since no way can be even imagined for deciding a difference as to values, the conclusion is forced upon us that the difference is one of tastes, not one as to any objective truth.

The consequences of this doctrine are considerable. In the first place, there can be no such thing as "sin" in any absolute sense; what one man calls "sin" another may call "virtue" and though they may dislike each other on account of this difference, neither can convict the other of intellectual error. Punishment cannot be justified on the ground that the criminal is "wicked," but only on the ground that he has behaved in a way which others wish to discourage, Hell, as a place of punishment for sinners, becomes quite irrational. . . .

Those who believe in "objective" values often contend that the view which I have been advocating has immoral consequences. This seems to me to be due to faulty reasoning. There are, as has already been said, certain ethical consequences of the doctrine of subjective values, of which the most important is the rejection of vindictive punishment and the notion of "sin." But the more general consequences which are feared, such as the decay of all sense of moral obligation, are not to be logically deduced. Moral obligation, if it is to influence conduct, must consist not merely of a belief, but of a desire. The desire, I may be told, is the desire to be "good" in a sense which I no longer allow. But when we analyse the desire to be "good" it generally resolves itself into a desire to be approved, or, alternatively, to act so as to bring about certain general consequences which we desire. We have wishes which are not purely personal, and, if we had not, no amount of ethical teaching would influence our conduct except through fear of disapproval. The sort of life that most of us admire is one which is guided by large impersonal desires; now such desires can, no doubt, be encouraged by example, education, and knowledge, but they can hardly be created by the mere abstract belief that they are good, nor discouraged by an analysis of what is meant by the word "good."

When we contemplate the human race, we may desire that it should be happy, or healthy, or intelligent, or warlike, and so on. Any one of these desires, if it is strong, will produce its own morality; but if we have no such general desires, our conduct, whatever our ethic may be, will only serve social purposes in so far as self-interest and the interests of society are in harmony. It is the business of wise institutions to create such harmony as far as possible, and for the rest, whatever may be our theoretical definition of value, we must depend upon the existence of impersonal desires. When you meet a man with whom you have a fundamental ethical disagreement—for example, if you think that all men count equally, while he selects a class as alone important—you will find yourself no better able to cope with him if you believe in objective values than if you do not. In either case, you can only influence his conduct through influencing his desires; if you succeed in that, his ethic will change, and if not, not.

Some people feel that if a general desire, say for the happiness of mankind, has not the sanction of absolute good, it is in some way irrational. This is due to a lingering belief in objective values. A desire cannot, in itself, be either rational or irrational. It may conflict with other desires, and therefore lead to unhappiness; it may rouse opposition in others, and therefore be incapable of gratification. But it cannot be considered "irrational" merely because no reason can be given for feeling it. We may desire A because it is a means to B, but in the end, when we have done with mere means, we must come to something which we desire for no reason, but not on that account "irrationally." All systems of ethics embody the desires of those who advocate them, but this fact is concealed in a mist of words. Our desires are, in fact, more general and less purely selfish than many moralists imagine; if it were not so, no theory of ethics would make moral improvement possible. It is, in fact, not by ethical theory, but by the cultivation of large and generous desires through intelligence, happiness, and freedom from fear, that men can be brought to act more than they do at present in a manner that is consistent with the general happiness of mankind. Whatever our definition of the ''Good,'' and whether we believe it to be subjective or objective, those who do not desire the happiness of mankind will not endeavour to further it, while those who do desire it will do what they can to bring it about.

I conclude that, while it is true that science cannot decide questions of value, that is because they cannot be intellectually decided at all, and lie outside the realm of truth and falsehood. Whatever knowledge is attainable, must be attained by scientific methods; and what science cannot discover, mankind cannot know.

DISCUSSION QUESTIONS

1. What difficulties does Russell see with the view that "conscience" is the standard for determining what is right? Can these difficulties be overcome?

2. Is it impossible, as Russell claims, to rationally resolve the question of whether all human beings should count equally, as Bentham claimed, or whether some human beings should count more than others, as Neitzsche claimed?

3. Russell claims that "ethics is an attempt to give universal, and not merely personal, importance to certain of our desires." What does he mean? Does he think that this is possible? Do you think that ethics is an attempt to do more than Russel suggests? If so, what?

4. Russell claims that when a person says "This is good in itself," he really means "I wish everybody to desire this" or "Would that everybody desired this." According to Russell, what is the difference in these two ways of expressing his thesis? Do you agree with Russell's thesis? Why, or why not?

5. Russell claims that:

> . . .[I]f two men differ about values, there is not a disagreement as to any kind of truth, but a difference of taste. If one man says "oysters are good" and another says "I think they are bad," we recognize that there is nothing to argue about. . . . [A]ll differences as to values are of this sort, although we do not naturally think so when we are dealing with matters that seem to us more exalted than oysters.

To what extent, if at all, do you agree with this statement? In what respects, if at all, are moral values different from one's preferences for foods such as oysters?

6. According to Russell, what distinction, if any, can be made between a "rational moral judgement" and a mere "prejudice"? How, if at all, would you draw this distinction?

7. If there are no objective moral truths, what explanation can be given for the fact that so many people think that there are such truths?

8. If one accepts Russell's analysis of moral language, does it indeed follow, as he claims, that

> Punishment cannot be justified on the ground that the criminal is "wicked" but only on the ground that he has behaved in a way which others wish to discourage. Hell, as a place of punishment for sinners, becomes quite irrational.

44. MORAL REASONING AND THE OBJECTIVITY OR SUBJECTIVITY OF MORAL JUDGMENTS

Editorial Comment

A perennial question of ethical philosophy concerns the proper classification of moral judgments as either "objective" or "subjective." As is often the case in philosophy, however, there is no universal agreement among philosophers as to the meanings of these two concepts. When people (be they philosophers or not) argue over whether moral judgments are objective or subjective, one should always be alert to the possibility that they may be attributing different meanings to these concepts. For example, even though philosophers X and Y may call themselves moral objectivists, while philosopher Z calls herself a moral subjectivist, it may be that X's view is more like Z's than Y's, and that they define these concepts differently. As such, philosophical labels can at times cause more confusion than understanding. This is the case with the familiar distinction often presented between moral objectivism and moral subjectivism.

Consider, for example, the following characterization of this distinction by the philosopher Arthur J. Minton:

> Moral subjectivism interprets our [moral] reactions as nonrational emotional responses which have been conditioned by training and which can be altered by training. . . .Thus for the moral subjectivist, our moral judgments are but expressions of taste, and taste is capricious and arbitrary. On the other hand, objectivists view our moral judgments in the same way as other judgments. Moral judgments are true or false, depending upon the objective nature of things. Although disagreeing in detail, objectivists all agree that moral evaluation can be a rational affair.[1]

[1]Arthur J. Minton, *Philosophy: Paradox and Discovery* (New York: McGraw-Hill, 1976), p. 184.

While Minton does not explicitly state this, the implication created is that these two views are mutually exhaustive (i.e., if one rejects one view, one must accept the other). This is not so, for there clearly are other possible views which cannot be placed in either of these two conceptual categories. Indeed, many philosophers would claim, as I will claim in this essay, that moral judgments are neither objective nor subjective in Minton's senses. In choosing among competing philosophical views, an essential part of one's task is often to *clarify and refine the philosophical choices that are possible.* Let us attempt to do this with Minton's distinction between moral subjectivism and moral objectivism.

First, one should realize that there are two different and logically separable notions conflated into Minton's characterization of "moral subjectivism," the notion that moral judgments are *nonrational emotional responses* and the notion that these responses are *dependent upon environmental conditioning.* While Minton does not say this, his remarks might very well be taken to mean that moral judgments are *completely dependent* upon environmental conditioning. This, however, prejudges the controversial psychological question of the relative influence of "nature" versus "nurture" (i.e., inborn biological nature vs. environmental conditioning) in the formation of psychological characteristics. Even if it were true that all moral judgments are (at least "in the last analysis") nonrational emotional responses, it is possible that such emotional responses are at least in part a function of inborn human nature. If one takes this position, as some have, it becomes possible to accept *both* the existence of universal (and not environmentally "capricious") moral judgments (biologically determined) and the view that such judgments are emotional responses.

As to the more central element in Minton's characterization of moral subjectivism, there are some philosophers who contend that moral judgments are "nonrational emotional responses" or "expressions of taste." Russell says this quite clearly in the preceding selection, assimilating moral judgments to the same category as one's tastes for foods. He writes:

> The theory which I have been advocating is a form of the doctrine which is called the "subjectivity" of values. This doctrine consists in maintaining that, if two men differ about values, there is not a disagreement as to any kind of truth, but a difference of taste. If one man says "oysters are good" and another says "I think they are bad," we recognize that there is nothing to argue about. The theory in question holds that all differences as to values are of this sort, although we do not naturally think them so when we are dealing with matters that seem to us more exalted than oysters.[2]

This characterization of moral judgment is inadequate. Morality, after all, is not simply something most of us deeply care about; it is also something we *argue* about and indeed believe requires argument. In this respect, moral judgments are quite unlike purely "subjective" preferences, such as one's choice of ice cream flavors. Preferences for ice cream flavors, we would all agree, are appropriately described as subjective for they cannot be said to be either "true" or "false," but are merely reflections of individual taste. However, this is not the case with moral judgments. Consider, for example, the difference between the following two dialogues:

A: Oysters are good.

B: I don't like them at all.

A: Really? How can that be? I know you like clams and scallops, and oysters have a similar taste.

B: Yes, but not quite the same. Nothing but an oyster tastes exactly like an oyster and I don't care for that unique taste. I may have very idiosyncratic tastes as far as foods go, but there's nothing wrong with that.

A: Of course not; there's no arguing over taste.

A: It's wrong to place any restrictions on a woman's right to have an abortion.

B: What reasons do you have for your position?

A: I have no reasons; that's just how I feel. I'm entitled to my feelings on this matter just as you're entitled to yours.

B: If you can't give reasons for your position, then it's simply a prejudice and not a rational moral judgment. Let me ask you, do you think a woman should have the unrestricted right to kill her unwanted newborn baby?

A: Heavens, no.

B: But what is the relevant moral difference between a late-term fetus and a newborn baby? I don't think there's any and if there isn't, your moral position is inconsistent.

In the first dialogue, which is concerned about an individual's taste for foods, argument clearly seems out of place. (Consider, for example two people arguing in an ice cream parlor over whether or not pistachio ice cream is "better" than butter pecan ice cream. The inappropriateness of such an argument makes the imagined scene laughable.) Nevertheless, as this dialogue indicates, there is at least the possibility of questioning the *consistency* of an individual's tastes for foods; but this line of questioning need not lead us anywhere, for a person who says that I do not like a particular food is not logically obligated to believe that there is some specific, identifiable property of that food that makes him dislike it. The matter is quite different, however, with moral judgments. For example, imagine a parent giving a toy to one of her children but not to another.

[2]See p. 370.

If the parent believes the discrimination to be a *just* one, the parent is obligated *by the very meaning of the concept of justice* to acknowledge that there is some morally relevant characteristic of these two children which justifies the discrimination. This essential characteristic of moral judgments is brought out in the second dialogue. As we see in this dialogue, those who make specific moral claims are logically obligated to acknowledge the appropriateness of the demand to give *reasons* in support of these claims. If, for example, a person claims that abortion is wrong, that person must by the very nature of moral discourse believe that there is a general universal moral principle which together with a true statement about some particular characteristic of abortions entails this moral judgment. Consider, for example, the following dialogue:

A: Abortion is wrong.

B: Why?

A: Because it is the killing of an innocent person and it's always wrong to kill an innocent person.

B: But do you really believe that it's always wrong to kill an innocent person? Are you against wars, for example, which involve the killing of innocent persons?

Notice the procedure here. First A presents an argument consisting of two premises. The first premise is a general moral principle that asserts that all things that have a particular property are wrong. The second premise asserts that abortions have this property. The conclusion is then validly drawn that abortions are wrong. B then proceeds to challenge the soundness of the argument by challenging the truth of the general principle. He does this by offering an alleged *counterexample* to the principle which he hopes A will accept as a counterexample (i.e., as something that has the property in question, but is not wrong). The alleged counterexample B chooses in the preceding dialogue is the death of innocent people in wars. At this point, A could accept the conclusion that if abortion is wrong because it involves the death of innocent people then, for the same reason, so are wars (at least modern ones), which also involve the death of innocent people. B could then proceed to question A as to whether there are any conceivable circumstances in which it would be right to kill an innocent person, in wars or elsewhere. If A is willing to make exceptions to his principle, B can then attempt to draw an analogy between these exceptions and the case of abortion, and the argument will continue.

Let us assume, however, that A does not take this line but continues as follows:

A: No, I think wars are sometimes morally justifiable, even though they involve the death of innocent persons. This case is, however, different from that of abortions.

B: How is it different?

A: Well, one may rightfully fight a war knowing that innocent people are going to die, as long as one does not intend these deaths, but simply accepts them as a by-product of one's action which is motivated by some good intention. In abortions, however, one intends the death of a fetus.

B: So the principle you hold is not "It is always wrong to perform an action which in point of fact will result in the death of an innocent person," but rather the principle that "It is always wrong to act with the intention (purpose) of causing the death of an innocent person."

A: Yes, I guess that's really what I believe.

B: But is it not possible to perform an abortion, knowing that a fetus will die, without intending that death, no less than it is possible to engage in a war, knowing that innocent people will die, but not intending their deaths. For example, imagine a three-months pregnant woman with cancer of the uterus. She has her uterus removed with the intention of protecting herself from cancer, knowing that the fetus she is carrying will die as a result, but not intending (wanting) this death.

A: Yes, I see what you mean. I didn't think of that before. I suppose there are some abortions—if by "abortion" one means "any medical intervention with a pregnancy that will in point of fact result in the death of a fetus''—that can be morally justified. On the other hand, I don't think I would want to call such procedures as the removal of a pregnant woman's cancerous uterus an ''abortion.'' I would prefer to define an ''abortion'' as ''an action whose purpose is the death of a fetus,'' in which case I would maintain my absolute moral prohibition against abortion.

Notice that in this dialogue A initially appears willing to accept the counterexample to his moral principle and attempts to circumvent it by *refining his moral principle* so that a relevant moral distinction can be drawn between the cases of abortion he judges to be wrong and the wars he judges to be right. Notice, too, in A's last remark how an alleged counterexample can be absorbed by a modification in the meaning of a key concept as well as by a modification of a moral principle. For example, the debate over the morality of abortion often hinges on the meaning to be attributed to the concept of a ''person.'' Consequently, instead of pressing A on his acceptance of the principle that ''It is always wrong to kill an innocent person,'' B could have pressed A to defend his characterization of a fetus as a person. Indeed, the question of whether or not a fetus should be called a person is often the central one in debates over the morality of abortion.

As we have seen, it is essential that those who make specific moral judgments believe that there are reasons supporting these judgments and acknowledge as appropriate the demand for them. Consequently, contrary to Russell, it is a mistake to claim that moral judgments are in the same logical category as one's tastes for foods. Similarly, if, following Russell and Minton, ''subjectivism'' is defined as the view that moral judgments are ''nonrational emotional responses,'' subjectivism is false. Nevertheless, many philosophers, while agreeing that moral judgments are different from purely subjective tastes for foods, would also agree that moral judgments are still very much like such subjective tastes in another respect. While the very distinction between a legitimate moral judgment and a mere moral prejudice hinges on the giving of cogent reasons for one's judgment, in the last analysis, it will be said, the ultimate reasons one chooses to accept for one's moral judgments are a function not of reason but of psychological disposition or emotion. Consider, for example, the following excerpt from Russell:

> Bentham held that one man's pleasure has the same ethical importance as another man's, provided the quantities are equal; and on this ground he was led to advocate democracy. Nietzsche, on the contrary, held that only the great man can be regarded as important on his own account, and that the bulk of mankind are only means to his well-being. He viewed ordinary men as many people view animals: he thought it justifiable to make use of them, not for their own good, but for that of the superman, and this view has since been adopted to justify the abandonment of democracy. We have here a sharp disagreement of great practical importance, but we have absolutely no means, of a scientific or intellectual kind, by which to persuade either party that the other is in the right. There are, it is true, ways of altering men's opinions on such subjects, but they are all emotional, not intellectual.[3]

As Russell sees it, there is no way to ''prove'' that all human beings should have equal ethical importance (as Bentham, the founder of modern utilitarianism, claimed) or whether some human beings should have more ethical importance than others (as Nietzsche, whose philosophy was perverted by the Nazis for their own purposes, claimed). While Bentham and Nietzsche would give reasons for their views, there is no way, Russell claims, for either of them to persuade the other by rational means that he is right. As Bentham would see it, human beings should count equally because of their similar capacities to feel pleasure and pain, while as Nietzsche would see it, it is not the mere capacity to feel pleasure and pain (which animals also possess) which confers ethical im-

[3]See p. 369.

portance upon human beings, but the capacity for certain qualities of character that human beings do not at all possess to the same degree. There is, Russell claims, an ultimate moral disagreement between Bentham and Nietzsche which is irreconcilable by reason alone. Focusing upon the similarities in the abilities of all human beings to experience pleasure and pain and *feeling* a certain universal benevolence toward all mankind, Bentham afforded all human beings an equal moral importance. Nietzsche, on the other hand, did not share Bentham's basic benevolent feelings toward all humanity and a different ethical perspective was the result. Struck by the vast differences in the psychological and intellectual capabilities of human beings, Nietzsche's *emotional reaction* to some human beings was very much like the reaction of most human beings to animals. Persons sharing the benevolent sentiments of Bentham may shake their heads in moral disagreement and in moral disgust, but, nevertheless, rational means alone cannot suffice to generate the feeling for the happiness of the average human being that is required to cause a Nietzschean to change his views.

Along with many philosophers, I would agree that the possibility of rationally irreconciliable ultimate moral disagreement is indeed real. For example, as a student at the height of the Vietnamese War, I remember listening to a defense of the war by the then Secretary of State, Dean Rusk, and being struck by the realization that the disagreement between Rusk and the antiwar movement reached a fundamental impasse which went deeper than their obvious disagreements over the likely effects of our actions in Vietnam upon our own national interests. At that moment, it appeared to me that the Secretary of State simply did not *feel* sufficient sympathy for the vast suffering of human beings who were being sacrificed for unclear ideals of American security. As I listened to Rusk, my predominant reaction was not to argue with him rationally but in some sense to shake him into an emotional realization of the enormity of human suffering we as a nation were creating in Vietnam. An emotional conversion was required here, not simply cold rational arguments, for there are no rational arguments or calculations that can tell us how much human suffering should be sacrificed for the achievement of certain desired ends.

The insight that rationally irreconcilable ultimate moral disagreements are possible is an important one. One should admit that human desires are various and often conflicting and that this plurality of desires can generate a plurality of ideals. Where there is no background of mutually accepted ideals, rational argument reaches an impasse and the various techniques of emotional arousal are our only recourse. It is a mistake, however, to overplay the importance of emotion in moral judgments, as Russell does, following in the tradition of Hume. Even though our initial unrefined desires or emotions are the raw materials from which our values are constructed, a moral *judgment* is more than the mere reflection of some strong, and possibly transitory, desire or emotion. One must use reason to organize one's desires and emotions into some coherent whole (one's *reasoned preferences*) which can withstand rational scrutiny. This means, at the very least, that our moral preferences should be informed, mutually consistent, and capable of providing long-range satisfaction. As the philosopher Morris R. Cohen (1880–1947) rightly observed:

> One of the obvious facts of human nature is that our unhappiness comes not only from the fact that we cannot have what we want, but very often we are most miserable because we succeed in getting what we thought we wanted. Wisdom, therefore, consists in surveying our various conflicting desires with a view to the attainment of a harmony, or a maximum of happiness. A man may prefer a short but a merry life. Another may prefer suicide. But, if we regard our life as a continuing one, that is, if we have some regard for our own personality, we must integrate all of our desires into one coherent system, so that we can attain self-respect. Just as all of our judgments of percepton of nature can be integrated by physical

science into a view of the world, so may our judgments of preference be integrated with them into a view of the most desirable mode of life.[4]

Although Russell, following Hume, is right that the ultimate source of our moral principles resides in our feelings, it is a mistake to assume that we must be slaves to our feelings. One not only can change one's moral principles when they conflict intolerably with one's natural feelings,[5] one can also discount strong initial moral sentiments when they prove incompatible with one's reasoned preferences and can acquire strong desires for those things which are necessary for the fulfillment of our reasoned preferences. The moral life is a constant interplay between reason and feeling.

Furthermore, it is quite unlikely that two ethical disputants will not share certain moral sentiments which can provide some basis for rational argument. For example, while many of Nietzsche's claims (e.g., "You want to decrease suffering; I want precisely to increase it.") will, *if taken in isolation*, be repulsive to our moral sensibilities, such remarks were not made in isolation but within the context of a *comprehensive* world view and way of thinking about the value of human life. The value Nietzsche placed on suffering was not an end in itself but a means to such noble virtues as strength rather than weakness and to individuality or originality as opposed to "sheeplike conformity." These values are, of course, values we all profess to share. Consequently, to reject Nietzsche's ethical philosophy, one must either find some flaw in the arguments he presents for connecting moral values as he does or, if one accepts these connections, one must take the moral stand that the Nietzschean view of morality exacts too high a price from other moral values. Whether or not one is willing to pay the moral price of a particular view of morality or pattern of living is a question of moral choice and not of intellectual perception. Such is the core of truth in the "subjectivistic" view of morality, in my opinion.

Consistent with these sentiments, shared by Russell and other philosophers who have called themselves "moral subjectivists," this view can be defined as the view that

1. There are ultimate ethical disagreements which are incapable of rational resolution.

Those who accept such a view would, like Russell, attribute the existence of rationally irresolvable ethical disagreement to the

[4]Morris R. Cohen, *A Preface to Logic* (New York: Holt, Rinehart & Winston, 1944), p. 170.

[5] The view that morality should not be seen as something external to our feelings, but rather as an attempt to organize feelings into some coherent whole, is lost on Mark Twain's fictionalized character Huck Finn when he helps his slave friend Jim escape. Although Huck's natural sympathies are clearly with Jim, his socially conditioned conscience tells him that he is acting wrongly. Incapable of realizing that he can and should reconsider the promptings of his socially conditioned conscience in the light of his natural sympathies and criticize the morality of his day as wrong, Huck sees himself as a person of weak moral will who is sacrificing an "objective" morality for the promptings of his own personal feelings. Consider, for example, the following passage:

> Jim was saying how the first thing he would do when he got to a free state he would go to saving up money . . . and when he got enough he would buy his wife . . . and then they would both work to buy the two children and if their master wouldn't sell them, they'd get an Ab'litionist to go and steal them.
>
> It most froze me to hear such talk . . . . Thinks I, this is what comes of my not thinking. Here was this nigger, which I had as good as helped to run away, coming right out flat-footed and saying he would steal his children—children that belonged to a man I didn't even know; a man that hadn't ever done me no harm. I was sorry to hear Jim say that, it was such a lower of him. My conscience got to stirring me up hotter than ever . . . .
>
> . . . I go aboard the raft, feeling bad and low, because I knowed very well I had done wrong . . . . Then I thought a moment, and says to myself, hold on; s'pose you'd 'a' done right and give Jim up, would you have felt better than what you do now? No, says I, I'd feel bad . . . .

(Samuel L. Clemens. *The Adventures of Huckleberry Finn*, New York: Dodd, Mead, 1953 edition, pp. 97, 100)

dependence of moral judgments upon psychologically determined feelings or emotions. Consequently, moral subjectivists would also embrace the following view:

2. Morality depends, at least in part, upon feelings or emotions.

Denying both principles 1 and 2, most philosophers who have called themselves "moral objectivists" have believed that

3. There are moral facts which are true or false apart from human feelings or emotions (and, some would add, capable of cognition by some special moral sense).

4. All moral disagreements are capable (in theory, if not in practice) of rational resolution.

One should note, however, that if the acceptance of both views 1 and 2 is taken as the definition of "moral subjectivism" and the acceptance of views 3 and 4 is taken as the definition of "moral objectivism," then it is possible to be neither a moral subjectivist nor a moral objectivist since it is possible to simultaneously hold views 1 and 3 or views 2 and 4. As mentioned before, a person who holds views 2 and 4 would claim that while morality is dependent upon the feelings or emotions of human beings, given (so they would claim) certain invariable features of human nature and/or of environmental circumstance, all moral disagreements are capable of rational resolution. On the other hand, a person who holds views 1 and 3 could claim that there are certain duties—for example, to be just, to be benevolent, to keep one's promises—which report moral facts that all rational people, regardless of psychological temperament, would recognize as true, but that the possibility of conflicting duties can give rise to rationally irresolvable ultimate ethical disagreements. For example, such a disagreement may arise over when, if ever, a desire to be benevolent can justify breaking a promise.

In light of these possibilities, if we are to define "moral subjectivism" and "moral objectivism" in such a manner as to make them mutually exhaustive, it is wise to take view 1 alone as the defining characteristic of moral subjectivism and its denial, view 4, as the defining characteristic of moral objectivism.[6] As mentioned, however, there is no consensus among philosophers as to the best way to draw this distinction. As always in philosophy, the way we choose to draw our conceptual distinctions must ultimately be a function of the usefulness of these distinctions in getting us to see what we believe to be most important. The lack of consensus among philosophers as to the meaning of basic philosophical distinctions is often a reflection of the fact that rational people may disagree on the standards to be employed in determining what is "most important." If the moral subjectivist is right, in this respect, philosophical disagreements can be very much like the ultimate moral disagreements that divide people.

DISCUSSION QUESTIONS

1. Consider the following quotations from David Hume and Immanuel Kant:

> Reason is . . . the slave of the passions . . . . Where a passion is neither founded on false suppositions, nor chooses means insufficient for the end, the understanding can neither justify nor condemn it. 'Tis not contrary to reason to prefer the destruction of the whole world to the scratching of my finger.[7]

> . . . the will is a faculty of choosing only that

[6]Notice the circularity of Minton's definition of moral objectivism" as the view that "moral judgments are true or false, depending upon the objective nature of things" (i.e., Minton uses the very term "objective" as a defining characteristic of "moral objectivism.")

[7]David Hume, *A Treatise of Human Nature* (Oxford: Oxford University Press, 1964, originally published in 1739), pp. 415–16.

which reason, independently of inclination [i.e., of psychologically determined temperament or desire], recognizes as . . . good.[8]

Do you accept either of these two claims? If not, can either (or both) of them be qualified or made more precise so as to make it (or them) acceptable? If not, do you think one of the two claims is closer to the truth? Why?

2. Compare the similarities and differences between one's "moral tastes" and one's tastes for specific foods or drink. In this connection, consider the existence of such seeming arbiters of taste as wine, tea, whiskey, or tobacco tasters, who give reasons for the judgments they make.

3. How exactly do rational "moral judgments" differ from mere "prejudices"? Give some examples.

4. Consider the following dialogue:

Meat Eater: There you go again with your obsessive concern about the killing of animals for food. It might be wrong for you to eat meat, but it's not wrong for me. Let's leave it at that.

Principled Vegetarian: You can call my concern "obsessive," but I think your lack of concern is improper and your belief that it's all right to eat meat a prejudice that allows you to do as you like with a clear conscience.

Meat Eater: Look, you and I have an ultimate moral disagreement in this matter that reflects differences in our attitudes toward animals. Since such differences are not over facts, you have no right to call my attitude toward animals a "prejudice." I know you don't like my attitude, but there's no way you can prove it to be mistaken, just as I can't prove your opposed attitude mistaken. That's the way it is when you come to basic moral principles.[9]

Principled Vegetarian: That's not so. If I told you that people with brown eyes should be afforded less respect than people with blue eyes and that this was a basic moral principle with me, you'd think me crazy. Basic moral principles must themselves be rational. I do not think it is any more rational for you to draw a moral distinction between animals and human beings than it would be to draw a moral distinction between brown- and blue-eyed people.

How would you resolve this issue?

[8]See p. 385.

[9]A basic moral principle is a moral principle that is used to justify other moral principles but is incapable itself of justification by a more general moral principle.

45. CONSCIENTIOUSNESS AND THE CATEGORICAL IMPERATIVE

Immanuel Kant

IMMANUEL KANT (1724–1804) was a profoundly influential German philosopher whose ideas marked a major turning point in Western philosophy. Born in Königsberg, East Prussia, into a devoutly religious family of modest means, Kant originally studied for the ministry at the University of Königsberg, but his interests shifted to the natural sciences and philosophy. Between 1746 and 1755, when he was appointed to a teaching position in the University of Königsberg, Kant supported himself as a private tutor for various aristocratic families in Königsberg. At the University, Kant lectured on an incredibly broad range of subjects—mathematics, physics, astronomy, anthropology, geography, theology, logic, metaphysics, and ethics. A man of severe self-discipline and routine, Kant rarely left Königsberg, the city of his birth and death. As the German writer Heine said of Kant, "Rising from bed, coffee-drinking, writing, lecturing, dining, walking, everything has its set time; and the neighbors knew that it must be exactly half past four when they saw Professor Kant, in his gray coat, with his cane in his hand, step out of his housedoor, and move toward the little lime tree avenue, which is named after him, the Philosopher's Walk."

Kant's philosophical masterpiece, **The Critique of Pure Reason,** was published when he was fifty-seven and was followed rapidly by many other books on philosophical topics. Believing that the structure of the human mind imposes a particular order on human experience, Kant's main thesis in **The Critique of Pure Reason** is that the empiricist David Hume was wrong when he claimed that all knowledge of matters of fact (Kant calls this **synthetic knowlege**) is **a posteriori** (i.e., dependent upon experience) and for that reason can never be certain. As Kant sees it, however, it is possible to have **certain a priori** knowledge (i.e., knowledge that is not dependent upon experience) of matters of fact. It was Kant's belief that his argument for the existence of synthetic, **a priori** knowledge offered a solution to the rationalist-empiricist controversy that began with Descartes.

Kant's masterpiece of ethics, **The Fundamental Principles** (or **Foundations** or **Groundwork,** depending on the translation) **of the Metaphysics of Morals,** was first published in 1785. In our selection from this work, Kant considers two questions which he sees as very much interrelated: What makes a person morally worthy and what makes an act right? Kant's answer to the first question is that a person is morally worthy only when he acts **from a sense of duty** (i.e., **conscientiously**). In making this assertion, Kant distinguishes conscientious persons from those who do as duty demands (i.e., act **in accord with duty**) out of either immediate natural inclination or calculated self-interest. Such individuals, however exemplary their external conduct may be, are not morally worthy individuals, Kant claims. Kant's answer to the second question is that an action is right if and only if it satisfies his **categorical imperative** , which closely resembles the golden rule (i.e., do unto others as you would have others do unto you). As Kant sees it, the categorical imperative is the foundation of any adequate morality since it is presupposed by the very notion of what it is to be a rational and free agent. Seeing the categorical imperative as deducible from this notion alone, which makes no reference to subjective human desires, Kant goes on to claim that the categorical imperative is the fundamental moral principle from which all other correct moral principles can be deduced. In our selection, Kant attempts to derive four more specific moral principles from the categorical imperative.

While the following selection is edited to make it more readable for introductory philosophy students (Kant's philosophical writings are not addressed to the philosophical novice!), there are some technical terms that he employs in his discussion which are important for the reader to understand before tackling our selection. For example, the reader should be aware of Kant's distinction between **categorical** and **hypothetical imperatives** (which is explained on p. 328 of the introduction to this chapter). In addition to this distinction, Kant also employs in our selection the distinction between **necessary** or **rigorous** duties on one hand and **contingent** or **meritorious** duties, on the other. As Kant uses these terms, a necessary or rigorous duty is a duty that is binding **in all circumstances**. For example, Kant believed that we have a necessary (rigorous) duty to keep our promises—that is one must keep one's promises, regardless of the circumstances. A contingent or meritorious duty, however, is a duty that one need not fulfill in all circumstances, although one is obligated to fulfill it sometimes. For example, as Kant saw it, the duty to be benevolent to others is a contingent (meritorious) duty—that is, although it is our duty to be benevolent to other human beings, one does not have a duty to be benevolent to **any** human being who would benefit from an act of benevolence. While it is one's duty to be benevolent sometimes, it is not one's duty to be benevolent in all circumstances, Kant believed.

[The Good Will]

It is impossible to conceive anything at all in the world, or even out of it, which can be taken as good without qualification, except a *good will*. Intelligence, wit, judgement, and any other *talents* of the mind we may care to name, or courage, resolution, and constancy of purpose, as qualities of *temperament,* are without doubt good and desirable in many respects; but they can also be extremely bad and hurtful when the will is not good which has to make use of these gifts of nature, and which for this reason has the term *'character'* applied to its peculiar quality. It is exactly the same with *gifts of fortune*. Power, wealth, honour, even health and that complete well-being and contentment with one's state which goes by the name of *'happiness'*, produce boldness, and as a consequence often over-boldness as well, unless a good will is present by which their influence on the mind—and so too the whole principle of action—may be corrected and adjusted to universal ends; not to mention that a rational and impartial spectator can never feel approval in contemplating the uninterrupted prosperity of a being graced by no touch of a pure and good will, and that consequently a good will seems to constitute the indispensable condition of our very worthiness to be happy.

Source: Immanuel Kant, *The Moral Law,* being a translation of *The Groundwork of the Metaphysics of Morals,* trans. H.J. Paton. London: Hutchinson Publishing Group Limited.

Some qualities are even helpful to this good will itself and can make its task very much easier. They have none the less no inner unconditioned worth, but rather presuppose a good will which sets a limit to the esteem in which they are rightly held and does not permit us to regard them as absolutely good. Moderation in affections and passions, self-control, and sober reflexion are not only good in many respects; they may even seem to constitute part of the *inner* worth of a person. Yet they are far from being properly described as good without qualification (however unconditionally they have been commended by the ancients). For without the principles of a good will they may become exceedingly bad; and the very coolness of a scoundrel makes him, not merely more dangerous, but also immediately more abominable in our eyes than we should have taken him to be without it.

[The Good Will and Its Results]

A good will is not good because of what it effects or accomplishes—because of its fitness for attaining some proposed end: it is good through its willing alone—that is, good in itself. Considered in itself it is to be esteemed beyond comparison as far higher than anything it could ever bring about merely in order to favour some inclination or, if you like, the sum total of inclinations. Even if, by some special disfavour of destiny or by the niggardly endowment of step-motherly nature, this will is entirely lacking in power to carry out its intentions; if by its utmost effort it still accomplishes nothing, and only good will is left (not, admittedly, as a mere wish, but as the straining of every means so far as they are in our control); even then it would still shine like a jewel for its own sake as something which has its full value in itself. Its usefulness or fruitlessness can neither add to, nor subtract from, this value. Its usefulness would be merely, as it were, the setting which enables us to handle it better in our ordinary dealings or to attract the attention of those not yet sufficiently expert, but not to commend it to experts or to determine its value. . . .

[The Good Will and the Motive of Duty]

We have now to elucidate the concept of a will estimable in itself and good apart from any further end . . . [In order to do this, we will] take up the concept of *duty,* which includes that of a good will. . . .

I will pass over all actions already recognized as contrary to duty . . . . I will also set aside actions which in fact accord with duty, yet for which men have *no immediate inclination*, but perform them because impelled to do so by some other inclination. For there it is easy to decide whether the action which accords with duty has been done *from duty* or from some purpose of self-interest. This distinction is far more difficult to perceive when the action accords with duty and the subject has in addition an *immediate* inclination to the action. For example, it certainly accords with duty that a grocer should not overcharge his inexperienced customer; and where there is much competition a sensible shopkeeper refrains from so doing and keeps to a fixed and general price for everybody so that a child can buy from him just as well as anyone else. Thus people are served *honestly*; but this is not nearly enough to justify us in believing that the shopkeeper has acted in this way from duty or from principles of fair dealing; his interests required him to do so. We cannot assume him to have in addition an immediate inclination towards his customers, leading him, as it were out of love, to give no man preference over another in the matter of price. Thus the action was done neither from duty nor from immediate inclination, but solely from purposes of self-interest.

On the other hand, to preserve one's life is a duty, and besides this every one has also an immediate inclination to do so. But on account of this the often anxious precautions taken by the greater part of mankind for this purpose have no inner worth, and the maxim of their action is without moral content. They do protect their lives *in conformity with duty,* but not *from the motive of duty.* When on the contrary, disappointments and hopeless misery have quite taken away the taste for life; when a wretched man, strong in soul and more angered at his fate than faint-hearted or cast down, longs for death and still preserves his life without loving it—not from inclination or fear but from duty; then indeed his maxim has a moral content.

To help others where one can is a duty, and besides this there are many spirits of so sympathetic a temper that, without any further motive of vanity or self-interest, they find an inner pleasure in spreading happiness around them and can take delight in the contentment of others as their own work. Yet I maintain that in such a case an action of this kind, however right and however amiable it may be, has still no genuinely moral worth. It stands on the same footing as other inclinations—for example, the inclination for honour, which if fortunate enough to hit on something beneficial and right and consequently honourable, deserves praise and encouragement, but not esteem; for its maxim lacks moral content, namely, the performance of such actions, not from inclination, but *from duty.* Suppose then that the mind of this friend of man were overclouded by sorrows of his own which extinguished all sympathy with the fate of others, but that he still had power to help those in distress, though no longer stirred by the need of others because sufficiently occupied with his own; and suppose that, when no longer moved by an inclination, he tears himself out of this deadly insensibility and does the action without any inclination for the sake of duty alone; then for the first time his action has its genuine moral worth. Still further; if nature had implanted little sympathy in this or that man's heart; if (being in other respects an honest fellow) he were cold in temperament and indifferent to the sufferings of others—perhaps because, being endowed with the special gift of patience and robust endurance in his own sufferings, he assumed the like in others or even demanded it; if such a man (who would in truth not be the worst product of nature) were not exactly fashioned by her to be a philanthropist, would he not still find in himself a source from which he might draw a worth far higher than any that a good-natured temperament can have? Assuredly he would. It is precisely in this that the worth of character begins to show—a moral worth and beyond all comparison the highest—namely, that he does good, not from inclination, but from duty.

[Reverence for the Law]

. . . An action done from duty has its moral worth, *not in the purpose* to be attained by it, but in the maxim in accordance with which it is decided upon; it depends therefore, not on the realization of the object of the action, but solely on the *principle of volition* in accordance with which, irrespective of all objects to the faculty of desire, the action has been performed. . . .

. . . [A]n action done from duty has to set aside altogether the influence of inclination, and along with inclination every object of the will; so there is nothing left able to determine the will except objectively the *law* and subjectively *pure reverence* for this pratical law, and therefore the maxim[1] of obeying this law even to the detriment of all my inclinations.

Thus the moral worth of an action does not depend on the result expected from it, and so too does not depend on any principle of action that needs to borrow its motive from this expected result. For all these results (agreeable states and even the promotion of happiness in others) could have been brought about by other causes as well, and consequently their production did not require the will of a rational being, in which, however, the highest and unconditioned good can alone be found. Therefore nothing but the *idea of law* in itself, *which admittedly is present only in a rational being*—so far as it, and not an expected result, is the ground determining the will—can constitute that pre-eminent good which we call moral, a good which is already present in the person acting on this idea and has not to be awaited merely from the result.

[The Categorical Imperative]

But what kind of a law can this be the thought of which, even without regard to the results expected from it, has to determine the will if this is to be called good absolutely and without qualification? Since I have robbed the will of every inducement that might arise for it as a consequence of obeying any particular law, nothing is left but the conformity of actions to universal law as such, and this alone must serve the will as its principle. That is to say, I ought never to act except in such a way *that I can also will that my maxim should become a universal law.* Here bare conformity to universal law as such

[1]A maxim is a subjective principle of volition; an objective principle (i.e., one which would also serve subjectively as a practical principle for all rational beings if reason had full control over the faculty of desire) is a practical *law.* EDITOR'S NOTE.

(without having as its base any law prescribing particular actions) is what serves the will as its principle, and must so serve it if duty is not to be everywhere an empty delusion. . . .

. . . Unless we wish to deny the concept of morality all truth and all relation to a possible object, we cannot dispute that its law is of such widespread significance as to hold, not merely for men, but for all *rational beings as such*—not merely subject to contingent conditions and exceptions, but *with absolute necessity*. . . .

. . . All moral concepts have their seat and origin in reason completely *a priori* [i.e., independent of experience], and indeed in the most ordinary human reason just as much as in the most speculative . . . In this purity of their origin is to be found their very worthiness to serve as supreme practical principles, and everything empirical [i.e., relating to experience] added to them is just so much taken away from their genuine influence and from the absolute value of the corresponding actions. . . . We ought never . . . to make principles depend on the special nature of human reason. Since moral laws have to hold for every rational being as such, we ought rather to derive our principles from the general concept of a rational being as such, and on this basis to expound the whole of ethics—which requires anthropology for its *application to man* . . .

Everything in nature works in accordance with laws. Only a rational being has the power to act *in accordance with his idea* of laws—that is, in accordance with principles—and only so has he a will. . . . [T]he will is . . . a power to choose *only that* which reason independently of inclination recognizes to be . . . good. . . .

All imperatives are expressed by an "ought". . . . By this they mark the relation of an objective law of reason to a will which is not necessarily determined by this law in virtue of its subjective constitution. . . . They say that something would be good to do or to leave undone; only they say it to a will which does not always do a thing because it has been informed that this is a good thing to do. . . .

All imperatives command either *hypothetically* or *categorically*. Hypothetical imperatives declare a possible action to be practically necessary as a means to the attainment of something else that one wills (or that one may will). A categorical imperative would be one which represented an action as objectively necessary in itself apart from its relation to a further end. . . . [Consequently,] if the action would be good solely as a means to *something else*, the imperative is *hypothetical*; if the action is represented as good *in itself* and therefore as necessary, in virtue of its principle, for a will which of itself accords with reason, then the imperative is *categorical*. . . .

There is . . . *one* end that can be presupposed as actual in all rational beings. . . . and thus there is one purpose which they not only *can* have, but which we can assume with certainty that they all *do* have by a natural necessity—the purpose, namely, of *happiness*. . . . Now skill in the choice of means to one's own greatest well-being can be called *prudence* in the narrowest sense. Thus an imperative concerned with the choice of means to one's own happiness—that is, a precept of prudence—still remains *hypothetical*; an action is commanded, not absolutely but only as a means to a further purpose.

Finally, there is an imperative which, without being based on, and conditioned by, any further purpose to be attained by a certain line of conduct, enjoins this conduct immediately. This imperative is *categorical*. It is concerned, not with the matter of the action and its presumed results, but with its form and with the principle from which it follows; and what is essentially good in the action consists in the mental disposition, let the consequences be what they may. This imperative may be called the imperative of *morality*. . . .

There is . . . only a single categorical imperative and it is this: "*Act only on that maxim through which you can at the same time will that it should become a universal law.*" . . . [T]he universal imperative of duty may also run as follows: "*Act as if the maxim of your action were to become through your will a universal law of nature* [i.e., everyone were to follow that maxim]."

[Illustrations]

We will now enumerate a few duties. . . .

1. A man feels sick of life as the result of a series of misfortunes that has mounted to the point of despair, but he is still so far in possession of his reason as to ask himself whether taking his own life may not be contrary to his duty to himself. He now applies the test 'Can the maxim of my action really become a universal law of nature?' His maxim is 'From self-love I make it my principle to shorten my life if its continuance threatens more evil than it promises pleasure.' The only further question to ask is whether this principle of self-love can become a universal law of nature. It is then seen at once that a system of nature by whose law the very same feeling whose function . . . is to stimulate the furtherance of life should actually destroy life would contradict itself and consequently could not subsist as a system of nature. Hence this maxim cannot possibly hold as a universal law of nature and is therefore entirely opposed to the supreme principle of all duty.

2. Another finds himself driven to borrowing money because of need. He well knows that he will not be able to pay it back; but he sees too that he will get no loans unless he gives a firm promise to pay it back within a fixed time. He is inclined to make such a promise; but he has still enough conscience to ask 'Is it not unlawful and contrary to duty to get out of difficulties in this way?' Supposing, however, he did resolve to do so, the maxim of his action would run thus; 'Whenever I believe myself short of money, I will borrow money and promise to pay it back, though I know that this will never be done.' Now this principle of self-love or personal advantage is perhaps quite compatible with my own entire future welfare; only there remains the question 'Is it right?' I therefore transform the demand of self-love into a universal law and frame my questions thus: 'How would things stand if my maxim became a universal law?' I then see straight away that this maxim can never rank as a universal law of nature and be self-consistent, but must necessarily contradict itself. For the universality of a law that every one believing himself to be in need can make any promise he pleases with the intention not to keep it would make promising, and the very purpose of promising, itself impossible, since no one would believe he was being promised anything, but would laugh at utterances of this kind as empty shams.

3. A third finds in himself a talent whose cultivation would make him a useful man for all sorts of purposes. But he sees himself in comfortable circumstances, and he prefers to give himself up to pleasure rather than to bother about increasing and improving his fortunate natural aptitudes. Yet he asks himself further 'Does my maxim of neglecting my natural gifts, besides agreeing in itself with my tendency to indulgence, agree also with what is called duty?' He then sees that a system of nature could indeed always subsist under such a universal law, although (like the South Sea Islanders) every man should let his talents rust and should be bent on devoting his life solely to idleness, indulgence, procreation, and, in a word, to enjoyment. Only he cannot possibly *will* that this should become a universal law of nature or should be implanted in us as such a law by a natural instinct. For as a rational being he necessarily wills that all his powers should be developed, since they serve him, and are given him, for all sorts of possible ends.

4. Yet a *fourth* is himself flourishing, but he sees others who have to struggle with great hardships (and whom he could easily help); and he thinks 'What does it matter to me? Let every

one be as happy as Heaven wills or as he can make himself; I won't deprive him of anything; I won't even envy him; only I have no wish to contribute anything to his well-being or to his support in distress!' Now admittedly if such an attitude were a universal law of nature, mankind could get on perfectly well—better no doubt than if everybody prates about sympathy and goodwill, and even takes pains, on occasion, to practise them, but on the other hand cheats where he can, traffics in human rights, or violates them in other ways. But although it is possible that a universal law of nature could subsist in harmony with this maxim, yet it is impossible to *will* that such a principle should hold everywhere as a law of nature. For a will which decides in this way would be in conflict with itself, since many a situation might arise in which the man needed love and sympathy from others, and in which, by such a law of nature sprung from his own will, he would rob himself of all hope of the help he wants for himself.

[The Canon of Moral Judgement]

These are some of the many actual duties—or at least of what we take to be such—whose derivation from the single principle cited above leaps to the eye. We must *be able to will* that a maxim of our action should become a universal law—this is the general canon for all moral judgement of action. Some actions are so constituted that their maxim cannot even be *conceived* as a universal law of nature without contradiction, let alone be *willed* as what *ought* to become one. In the case of others we do not find this inner impossibility, but it is still impossible to *will* that their maxim should be raised to the universality of a law of nature; because such a will would contradict itself. It is easily seen that the first kind of action is opposed to strict or narrow (rigorous) duty, the second only to wider (meritorious) duty; and thus that by these examples all duties—so far as the type of obligation is concerned . . . are fully set out in their dependence on our single principle.

If we now attend to ourselves whenever we transgress a duty, we find that we in fact do not will that our maxim should become a universal law—since this is impossible for us—but rather that its opposite should remain a law universally: we only take the liberty of making an *exception* to it for ourselves (or even just for this once) to the advantage of our inclination. . . .

[The Formula of the End in Itself]

. . . Practical principles are *formal* if they abstract from all subjective ends; they are *material*, on the other hand, if they are based on such ends. . . . Ends that a rational being adopts arbitrarily as *effects* of his action (material ends) are in every case only relative; for it is solely their relation to . . . [subjective inclination] which gives them their value. Hence this value can provide no universal principles, no principles valid and necessary for all rational beings and also for every volition—that is, no practical laws. Consequently all these relative ends can be the ground only of hypothetical imperatives.

Suppose, however, there were something *whose existence* has *in itself* an absolute value, something which as *an end in itself* could be a ground of determinate laws; then in it, and in it alone, would there be the ground of a possible categorical imperative—that is, of a practical law.

Now I say that man, and in general every rational being, *exists* as an end in himself, *not merely as a means* for arbitrary use by this or that will: he must in all his actions, whether they are directed to himself or to other rational beings, always be viewed *at the same time as an end.* All the objects of inclination have only a conditioned value; for if there were not these inclinations and the needs grounded on them, their object would be valueless. Inclinations themselves, as sources of needs, are so far from having an absolute value to make them desirable for their own sake that it must rather be the universal wish of every rational being to be wholly free from them. Thus the value of all objects that can *be produced* by our action is always conditioned. Beings whose existence depends, not on our will, but on nature, have none the less, if they are non-rational beings, only a relative value as means and are consequently called *things*. Rational beings, on the other hand, are called *persons* because their nature already marks them out as ends in themselves—that is, as something which ought not to be used merely as a means—and consequently imposes to that extent a limit on all arbitrary treatment of them (and is an object of reverence.) Persons therefore are not merely subjective ends whose existence as an object of our actions has a value *for us*: they are *objective ends*—that is, things whose existence is in itself an end, and indeed an end such that in its place we can put no other end to which they should serve *simply* as means; for unless this is so, nothing at all of *absolute* value would be found anywhere. But if all value were conditioned—that is, contingent—then no supreme principle could be found for reason at all.

If then there is to be a supreme practical principle and—so far as the human will is concerned—a categorical imperative, it must be such that from the idea of something which is necessarily an end for every one because it is an *end in itself* it forms an *objective* principle of the will and consequently can serve as a practical law. The ground of this principle is: *Rational nature exists as an end in itself.* This is the way in which a man necessarily conceives his own existence: it is therefore so far a *subjective* principle of human actions. But it is also the way in which every other rational being conceives his existence on the same rational ground which is valid also for me; hence it is at the same time an *objective* principle, from which, as a supreme practical ground, it must be possible to derive all laws for the will. The practical imperative will therefore be as follows: *Act in such a way that you always treat humanity, whether in your own person or in the person of any other, never simply as a means, but always at the same time as an end.* We will now consider whether this can be carried out in practice.

[Illustrations]

Let us keep to our previous examples.

First, as regards the concept of necessary duty to oneself, the man who contemplates suicide will ask 'Can my action be compatible with the Idea of humanity *as an end in itself?*' If he does away with himself in order to escape from a painful situation, he is making use of a person merely as *a means* to maintain a tolerable state of affairs till the end of his life. But man is not a thing—not something to be used *merely* as a means: he must always in all his actions be regarded as an end in himself. Hence I cannot dispose of man in my person by maiming, spoiling, or killing. (A more precise determination of this principle in order to avoid all misunderstanding—for example, about having limbs amputated to save myself or about exposing my life to danger in order to preserve it, and so on—I must here forego: this question belongs to morals proper.)

Secondly, so far as necessary or strict duty to others is concerned, the man who has a mind to make a false promise to others will see at once that he is intending to make use of another man *merely as a means* to an end he does not share. For the man whom I seek to use for my own purposes by such a promise cannot possibly agree with my way of behaving to him, and so cannot himself share the end of the action. This incompatibility with the principle of duty to others leaps to the eye more obviously when we bring in examples of attempts on the freedom and property of others. For then it is manifest that a violator of the rights of man intends to use the person of others merely as a means without taking into consideration that, as rational beings, they ought always at the same time to be rated as ends—that is, only as beings who must themselves be able to share in the end of the very same action.

Thirdly, in regard to contingent (meritorious) duty to oneself, it is not enough that an action should refrain from conflicting with humanity in our own person as an end in itself: it must also *harmonize with this end*. Now there are in humanity capacities for greater perfection which form part of nature's purpose for humanity in our person. To neglect these can admittedly be compatible with the *maintenance* of humanity as an end in itself, but not with the *promotion* of this end.

Fourthly, as regards meritorious duties to others, the natural end which all men seek is their own happiness. Now humanity could no doubt subsist if everybody contributed nothing to the happiness of others but at the same time refrained from deliberately impairing their happiness. This is, however, merely to agree negatively and not positively with *humanity as an end in itself* unless every one endeavours also, so far as in him lies, to further the ends of others. For the ends of a subject who is an end in himself must, if this conception is to have its *full* effect in me, be also, as far as possible, *my* ends.

DISCUSSION QUESTIONS

1. Consider the following disagreement:

   Kantian: Man's greatest moral virtue is his capacity to be rational and self-governing. It is this capacity which enables him to adopt moral principles and to live by them, regardless of the contingencies of his feelings.

   Critic: The most important moral virtue is the capacity to feel sympathy for one's fellow creatures. Conscientiousness itself is unimportant. What is important is that one be conscientious about the right things and this requires that one be motivated by feelings of benevolence.

   What do you think?

2. Are there any moral principles that have no exceptions? If so, what are they? If not, why not?

3. Kant utilizes the categorical imperative to tell us what we cannot do. Does Kant tell us that we are **required** to perform all actions that are in accord with the categorical imperative? Does he claim that we are **permitted** to perform them? What do you think the most reasonable position is in this regard?

4. Carefully consider the various examples Kant supplies of applications of the categorical imperative. Do you find any difficulties with Kant's application of the categorical imperative to these examples? Do you see any difference between the categorical imperative and the golden rule?

5. In a well-known passage, Jean-Paul Sartre, the famous French existentialist, writes:

   To give you an example which will enable you to understand forlornness better, I shall cite the case of one of my students who came to see me under the following circumstances: his father was on bad terms with his mother, and, moreover, was inclined to be a collaborationist; his older brother had been killed in the German offensive of 1940, and the young man, with somewhat immature but generous feelings, wanted to avenge him. His mother lived alone with him, very much upset by the half-treason of her husband and the death of her older son; the boy was her only consolation.

   The boy was faced with the choice of leaving for England and joining the Free French Forces—that is, leaving his mother behind—or remaining with his mother and helping her to carry on. He was fully aware that the woman lived only for him and that his going-off—and perhaps his death—would plunge her into despair. He was also aware that every act that he did for his mother's sake was a sure thing, in the sense that it was helping her to carry on, whereas every effort he made toward going off and fighting was an uncertain move which might run aground and prove completely useless; for example, on his way to England he might, while passing through Spain, be detained indefinitely in a Spanish camp; he might reach England or Algiers and be stuck in an office at a desk job. As a result, he was faced with two very different kinds of action: one, concrete, immediate, but concerning only one individual; the other concerned an incomparably vaster group, a national collectivity, but for that very reason was dubious, and might be interrupted en route. And, at the same time, he was wavering between two kinds of ethics. On the one hand, an ethics of sympathy, of personal devotion; on the other, a broader ethics, but one whose efficacy was more dubious. He had to choose between the two.

Who could help him choose? Christian doctrine? No. Christian doctrine says, "Be charitable, love your neighbor, take the more rugged path, etc., etc." But which is the more rugged path? Whom should he love as a brother? The fighting man or his mother? Which does the greater good, the vague act of fighting in a group, or the concrete one of helping a **particular** human being to go on living? Who can decide **a priori?** Nobody. No book of ethics can tell him. The Kantian ethics says, "Never treat any person as a means, but as an end." Very well, if I stay with my mother, I'll treat her as an end and not as a means; but by virtue of this very fact, I'm running the risk of treating the people around me who are fighting as means; and, conversely, if I go to join those who are fighting, I'll be treating them as an end, and, by doing that, I run the risk of treating my mother as a means.

If values are vague, and if they are always too broad for the concrete and specific case that we are considering, the only thing left for us is to trust our instincts. That's what this young man tried to do; and when I saw him, "In the end, feeling is what counts. I ought to choose whichever pushes me in one direction. If I feel that I love my mother enough to sacrifice everything else for her—my desire for vengeance, for action, for adventure—then I'll stay with her. If, on the contrary, I feel that my love for my mother isn't enough, I'll leave."

But how is the value of a feeling determined? What gives his feeling for his mother value? Precisely the fact that he remained with her. I may say that I like so-and-so well enough to sacrifice a certain amount of money for him, but I may say so only if I've done it. I may say "I love my mother well enough to remain with her" if I have remained with her. The only way to determine the value of this affection is, precisely, to perform an act which confirms and defines it. But, since I require this affection to justify my fact, I find myself caught in a vicious circle.[2]

Do you share Sartre's scepticism as to the practical guidance provided by general moral principles—in particular, Kant's categorical imperative? Why? Are there any claims Sartre makes in the preceding passage with which you disagree? If so, why?

6. Consider the following dialogue:

> A: I know it would be right for me to lie in these circumstances, but I don't know if it would be right for anyone else in the same circumstances.
>
> B: What you say makes no sense. If you really thought that all the relevant circumstances were the same, you would have to make the same moral judgment, otherwise, you're simply misusing moral language. What is right for one person cannot be wrong for someone else unless there is some relevant difference in their circumstances. The very meaning of moral language requires this.

Critically discuss.

7. Kant tells us that we should never treat individuals as "mere means." Are soldiers who are drafted into the army treated as "mere means"? Are criminals who are punished? Explain.

8. Critically consider the following claim:

> Kant's picture of human beings as autonomous rational moral agents unfortunately does not fit most human beings who tend to be quite irrational. Although Kant says that human beings should be "respected as persons," most human beings should be treated as children.

9. Argue as forcefully as you can either for or against the claim: "Let justice be done though the heavens may fall" (in less poetic language, "When justice and utility conflict, as they may, always choose justice over utility, even if the consequences would be disastrous.")

[2]Jean-Paul Sartre, *The Philosophy of Existentialism* (New York: Philosophical Library, 1965).

10. Consider the following criticism of Kantian morality:

> As Kant saw it, moral rights can only be rightfully conferred upon those who are worthy of respect—that is, only upon rational creatures. I disagree. Influenced by Christian philosophy, Kant places too much emphasis on the **rationality** that supposedly separates human beings from other animals, while he wrongfully neglects their similar capacity **to feel** pleasure and pain. Compare, for example, the following quotations from Bentham and Kant:
>
>> The day may come when the rest of the animal creation may acquire those rights which never could have been withholden from them but by the hand of tyranny. The French have already discovered that the blackness of the skin is no reason why a human being should be abandoned without redress to the caprice of a tormentor. It may come one day to be recognized that the number of legs, the villosity of the skin, or the termination of the **os sacrum,** are reasons equally insufficient for abandoning a sensitive being to the same fate. What else is it that should trace the insuperable line? Is it the faculty of reason, or perhaps the faculty of discourse? But a full-grown horse or dog is beyond comparison a more rational, as well as a more conversable animal, than an infant of a day, or a week, or even a month old. But suppose the case were otherwise, what would it avail? The question is not, Can they **reason**? nor, Can they talk? but, Can they **suffer**?[3]
>>
>> But so far as animals are concerned, we have no direct duties. Animals. . . . are merely as a means to an end. That end is man. . . . Our duties towards animals are merely indirect duties towards humanity. Animal nature has analogies to human nature, and by doing our duties to animals . . . , we indirectly do our duty towards humanity. Thus, if a dog has served his master long and faithfully, his service, on the analogy of human service, deserves reward, and when the dog has grown too old to serve, his master ought to keep him until he dies. Such action helps to support us in our duties towards human beings. . . . If a man shoots his dog because the animal is no longer capable of service, he does not fail in his duty to the dog, for the dog cannot judge, but his act is inhuman and damages in himself that humanity which it is his duty to show towards mankind. If he is not to stifle his human feelings, he must practice kindness towards animals, for he who is cruel to animals becomes hard also in his dealings with men.[4]
>
> I must say that my sympathies lie with Bentham and not with Kant. Can we really say, as Kant does, that we do not have a duty to a dog and that decent behavior to a dog is merely practice for decent behavior towards human beings? Dogs may not be able to "judge," as Kant puts it, but neither can many human beings (consider children and the mentally retarded), but certainly we have duties to them. No, Bentham was right. The important moral question is not "Is that creature rational?" but, rather, "Can it feel?"

What do you think?

[3]Jeremy Bentham, *The Principles of Morals and Legislation* (New York: Hafner Publishing Co., 1948), p. 311, footnote 1.

[4]Immanuel Kant, "Duties Towards Animals and Spirits" in *Lectures on Ethics* (New York: Harper & Row, Publishers, 1963), pp. 239-40.

46. A DEFENSE OF UTILITARIANISM

J.J.C. Smart

(For a biographical sketch of J.J.C. Smart, see Selection #33)

In the selection that follows, J.J.C. Smart, the foremost contemporary advocate of act-utilitarianism, presents and defends this ethical perspective which had its classical formulation in the writings of Jerry Bentham and John Stuart Mill (see p. 334 of this chapter's introduction for the distinction between act- and rule-utilitarianism). In the process of defending his version of act-utilitarianism, Smart tries to meet the challenges of critics that act-utilitarianism is inconsistent with natural moral sentiments.

Act-Utilitarianism and Rule-Utilitarianism

The system of normative ethics which I am here concerned to defend is . . . *act*-utilitarianism. Act-utilitarianism is to be contrasted with rule-utilitarianism. Act-utilitarianism is the view that the rightness or wrongness of an action is to be judged by the consequences, good or bad, of the action itself. Rule-utilitarianism is the view that the rightness or wrongness of an action is to be judged by the goodness and badness of the consequences of a rule that everyone should perform the action in like circumstances. . . .

I have argued elsewhere the objections to rule-utilitarianism as compared with act-utilitarianism. Briefly they boil down to the accusation of rule worship: the rule-utilitarian presumably advocates his principle because his is ultimately concerned with human happiness: why then should he advocate abiding by a rule when he knows that it will not in the present case be most beneficial to abide by it? The reply that in most cases it is most beneficial to abide by the rule seems irrelevant. And so is the reply that it would be better that everybody should abide by the rule than that nobody should. This is to suppose that the only alternative to 'everybody does *A*' is 'no one does *A*'. But clearly we have the possibility 'some people do *A* and some don't'. Hence to refuse to break a generally beneficial rule in those cases in which it is not most beneficial to obey it seems irrational and to be a case of rule worship. . . .

Hedonistic and Non-Hedonistic Utilitarianism

An act-utilitarian judges the rightness or wrongness of actions by the goodness and badness of their consequences. But is he to judge the goodness and badness of the consequences of an action solely by their pleasantness and unpleasantness? Bentham, who thought that quantity of pleasure being equal, the experience of playing pushpin was as good as that of reading poetry, could be classified as a hedonistic act-utilitarian.[1] Moore, who believed that some states of

Source: J.J.C. Smart, "An Outline of a System of Utilitarian Ethics," in *Utilitarianism: For and Against* by J.J.C. Smart and Bernard Williams (New York: Cambridge University Press, 1973). Reprinted by permission.

[1]Bentham's remark about pushpin and poetry can be found in *The Works of Jeremy Bentham* (Edinburgh: Tait, 1838-43), vol. 2, pp. 253-54. EDITOR'S NOTE.

mind, such as those of acquiring knowledge, had intrinsic value quite independent of their pleasantness, can be called an ideal utilitarian.[2] Mill seemed to occupy an intermediate position. He held that there are higher and lower pleasures. . . .

. . . Let us consider Mill's contention that it is 'better to be Socrates dissatisfied than a fool satisfied.'[3] Mill holds that pleasure is not to be our sole criterion for evaluating consequences: the state of mind of Socrates might be less pleasurable than that of the fool, but, according to Mill, Socrates would be happier than the fool.

It is necessary to observe, first of all, that a purely hedonistic utilitarian, like Bentham, might agree with Mill in preferring the experiences of discontented philosophers to those of contented fools. His preference for the philosopher's state of mind, however, would not be an *intrinsic* one. He would say that the discontented philosopher is a useful agent in society and that the existence of Socrates is responsible for an improvement in the lot of humanity generally. Consider two brothers. One may be of a docile and easy temperament: he may lead a supremely contented and unambitious life, enjoying himself hugely. The other brother may be ambitious, may stretch his talents to the full, may strive for scientific success and academic honours, and may discover some invention or some remedy for disease or improvement in agriculture which will enable innumerable men of easy temperament to lead a contented life, whereas otherwise they would have been thwarted by poverty, disease or hunger. Or he may make some advance in pure science which will later have beneficial practical applications. Or, again, he may write poetry which will solace the leisure hours and stimulate the brains of practical men or scientists, thus indirectly leading to an improvement in society. That is, the pleasures of poetry or mathematics may be *extrinsically* valuable in a way in which those of pushpin or sun-bathing may not be. Though the poet or mathematician may be discontented, society as a whole may be the more contented for his presence.

Again, a man who enjoys pushpin is likely eventually to become bored with it, whereas the man who enjoys poetry is likely to retain this interest throughout his life. Moreover the reading of poetry may develop imagination and sensitivity, and so as a result of his interest in poetry a man may be able to do more for the happiness of others than if he had played pushpin and let his brain deteriorate. In short, both for the man immediately concerned and for others, the pleasures of poetry are, to use Bentham's word, more *fecund*[4] than those of pushpin. . . .

. . . [T]o call a person 'happy' is to say more than that he is contented for most of the time, or even that he frequently enjoys himself and is rarely discontented or in pain. It is, I think, in part to express a favourable attitude to the idea of such a form of contentment and enjoyment. That is, for *A* to call *B* 'happy', *A* must be contented at the prospect of *B* being in his present state of mind and at the prospect of *A* himself, should the opportunity arise, enjoying that sort of state of mind. That is, 'happy' is a word which is mainly descriptive (tied to the concepts of contentment and enjoyment) but which is also partly evaluative. It is because Mill approves of the 'higher' pleasures, e.g., intellectual pleasures, so much more than he approves of the more simple and brutish pleasures, that, quite apart from consequences and side effects, he can pronounce the man who enjoys the

[2]G.E. Moore was an influential twentieth century philosopher whose ethical theory is presented in his *Principia Ethica* (Cambridge: Cambridge University Press, 1903). Moore's *ideal utilitarianism* is developed in Chapter VII of this book. EDITOR'S NOTE.

[3]Mill's remark about Socrates dissatisfied and a fool satisfied can be found in his *Utilitarianism* (Indianapolis: Bobbs-Merrill, 1957), p. 12. This book was first published in 1863. EDITOR'S NOTE.

[4]Fruitful. EDITOR'S NOTE.

pleasures of philosophical discourse as 'more happy' than the man who gets enjoyment from pushpin or beer drinking. . . .

. . . [Since] happiness is partly an evaluative concept, . . . the utilitarian maxim 'You ought to maximize happiness' is doubly evaluative [i.e., disagreement is possible both over whether the utilitarian maxim ought to be followed as well as over what is to count as 'happiness' in applying the utilitarian maxim]. There is the possibility of an ultimate disagreement between two utilitarians who differ over the question of pushpin versus poetry, or Socrates dissatisfied versus the fool satisfied. . . .

Average Happiness Versus Total Happiness

Another type of ultimate disagreement between utilitarians, whether hedonistic or ideal, can arise over whether we should try to maximize the *average* happiness of human beings . . . or whether we should try to maximize the *total* happiness . . . . Would you be quite indifferent between (a) a universe containing only one million happy sentient beings, all equally happy, and (b) a universe containing two million happy beings, each neither more nor less happy than any in the first universe? Or would you, as a humane and sympathetic person, give a preference to the second universe? I myself cannot help feeling a preference for the second universe. But if someone feels the other way I do not know how to argue with him. It looks as though we have yet another possibility of disagreement within a general utilitarian framework.

This type of disagreement might have practical relevance. It might be important in discussions of the ethics of birth control. This is not to say that the utilitarian who values total, rather than average, happiness may not have potent arguments in favour of birth control. But he will need more arguments to convince himself than will the other type of utilitarian.

In most cases the difference between the two types of utilitarianism will not lead to disagreement in practice. For in most cases the most effective way to increase the total happiness is to increase the average happiness, and vice versa. . . .

Rightness and Wrongness of Actions

I shall now state the act-utilitarian doctrine. Purely for simplicity of exposition I shall put it forward in a broadly hedonistic form. If anyone values states of mind such as knowledge independently of their pleasurableness he can make appropriate verbal alterations to convert it from hedonistic to ideal utilitarianism. . . .

Let us say, then, that the only reason for performing an action *A* rather than an alternative action *B* is that doing *A* will make mankind (or, pehaps, all sentient beings) happier than will doing *B*. (Here I put aside the consideration that in fact we can have only probable belief about the effects of our actions, and so our reason should be more precisely stated as that doing *A* will produce more probable benefit than will doing *B*. . . .) This is so simple and natural a doctrine that we can surely expect that many of my readers will have at least some propensity to agree. For I am talking, as I said earlier, to sympathetic and benevolent men, that is, to men who desire the happiness of mankind. Since they have a favourable attitude to the general happiness, surely they will have a tendency to submit to an ultimate moral principle which does no more than express this attitude. . . .

Suppose we could predict the future consequences of actions with certainty. Then it would be possible to say that the total future consequences of action *A* are such-and-such and that the total future consequences of action *B* are so-and-so. In order to help someone to decide whether to do *A* or to do *B* we could say to him: 'Envisage the total consequences of *A*, and think them over carefully and imaginatively. Now envisage the total consequences of *B*, and think them over carefully. As a benevolent and humane man, and thinking of yourself just as one man among others, would you prefer the consequences of *A* or those of *B?*' That is, we are asking for a comparison of one (present and future) *total* situation with another (present and future) *total* situation. So far we are not asking for a *summation* or *calculation* of pleasures or happiness. We are asking only for a comparison of total situations. And it seems clear that we can frequently make such a comparison and say that one total situation is better than another. For example few people would not prefer a total situation in which a million people are well-fed, well-clothed, free of pain, doing interesting and enjoyable work, and enjoying the pleasures of conversation, study, business, art, humour, and so on, to a total situation where there are ten thousand such people only, or perhaps 999,999 such people plus one man with toothache, or neurotic, or shivering with cold. In general, we can sum things up by saying that if we are humane, kindly, benevolent people, we want as many people as possible now and in the future to be as happy as possible. . . .

Sometimes, of course, more needs to be said. For example one course of action may make some people very happy and leave the rest as they are or perhaps slightly less happy. Another course of action may make all men rather more happy than before but no one very happy. Which course of action makes mankind happier on the whole? Again, one course of action may make it highly probable that everyone will be made a little happier whereas another course of action may give us a much smaller probability that everyone will be made very much happier. In the third place, one course of action may make everyone happy in a pig-like way, whereas another course of action may make a few people happy in a highly complex and intellectual way.

It seems therefore that we have to weigh the maximizing of happiness against equitable distribution, to weigh probabilities with happiness, and to weigh the intellectual and other qualities of states of mind with their pleasurableness. Are we not therefore driven back to the necessity of some calculus of happiness? Can we just say: "envisage two total situations and tell me which you prefer"? If this were possible, of course there would be no need to talk of summing happiness or of a calculus. All we should have to do would be to put total situations in an order of preference. . . .

. . . The non-hedonistic utilitarian may evaluate the total situations differently from the hedonistic utilitarian, in which case there will be an ultimate ethical disagreement. This possibility of ultimate disagreement is always there, though we have given reasons for suspecting that it will not frequently lead to important disagreement in practice.

Let us now consider the question of equity. Suppose that we have the choice of sending four equally worthy and intelligent boys to a medium-grade public school or of leaving three in an adequate but uninspiring grammar school and sending one to Eton.[5] (For sake of the example I am making the almost certainly incorrect assumption that Etonians are happier than other public-school boys and that these other public-school boys are happier than grammar-school boys.). . . . Should we prefer the greater happiness of one boy to the moderate happiness of all four? Clearly one parent may prefer one total situation (one boy at Eton and three at the grammar school) while another may prefer the other total situation (all four at the medium-grade public school). Surely both parents have an equal claim to being sympathetic and benevolent, and yet their difference of opinion here is not founded on an empirical disagreement about facts. I suggest, however, that there are not in fact many cases in which such a disagreement could arise. Probably the parent who wished to send one son to Eton would draw the line at sending one son to Eton plus giving him

[5]An exclusive, private British prep school. EDITOR'S NOTE.

expensive private tuition during the holidays plus giving his other sons no secondary education at all. It is only within rather small limits that this sort of disagreement about equity can arise. Furthermore, the cases in which we can make one person *very* much happier without increasing *general* happiness are rare ones. The law of diminishing returns comes in here. So, in most practical cases, a disagreement about what should be done will be an empirical disagreement about what total situation is likely to be brought about by an action, and will not be a disagreement about which total situation is preferable. For example the inequalitarian parent might get the other to agree with him if he could convince him that there was a much higher probability of an Etonian benefiting the human race, such as by inventing a valuable drug or opening up the mineral riches of Antarctica, then there is of a non-Etonian doing so. . . . I must again stress that since disagreement about what causes produce what effects is in practice so much the most important sort of disagreement, to have intelligent moral discussion with a person we do not in fact need complete agreement with him about ultimate ends: an approximate agreement is sufficient.

Rawls[6] has suggested that we must maximize the general happiness only if we do so in a *fair* way. An *unfair* way of maximizing the general happiness would be to do so by a method which involved making some people less happy than they might be otherwise. As against this suggestion a utilitarian might make the following rhetorical objection: if it is rational for me to choose the pain of a visit to the dentist in order to prevent the pain of toothache, why is it not rational of me to choose a pain for Jones, similar to that of my visit to the dentist, if that is the only way in which I can prevent a pain, equal to that of my toothache, for Robinson? Such situations continually occur in war, in mining, and in the fight against disease, when we may often find ourselves in the position of having in the general interest to inflict suffering on good and happy men. However it must be conceded that these objections against fairness as an *ultimate* principle must be rhetorical only, and that Rawls's principle could perhaps be incorporated in a restrained system of deontological ethics,[7] which would avoid the artificiality of the usual forms of deontology. There are in any case plenty of good utilitarian reasons for adopting the principle of fairness as an important, but not inviolable, rule of thumb. . . .

The Place of Rules in Act-Utilitarianism

According to the act-utilitarian, then, the rational way to decide what to do is to decide to perform that one of those alternative actions open to us (including . . . the doing of nothing) which is likely to maximize the probable

[6] "Justice as Fairness," *Philosophical Review,* 67 (1958), pp. 164–94, especially p. 168. EDITOR'S NOTE.

[7] Philosophers distinguish *deontological* moral systems from *teleological* ones. A teleological moral system is a moral system which claims that one ought *always* to act in a manner which appears most likely to have the best consequences—or, to put it slightly differently, one ought always to attempt to maximize the good. The most well-known teleological system of ethics is *utilitarianism,* which asserts that everyone's good is to count equally. Since the classical utilitarians, Bentham and Mill, were also *hedonists* who believed that pleasure *alone* is good in and of itself, apart from its consequences (i.e., intrinsically good), they took the obligation to maximize pleasure (or happiness, which they took to be equivalent in meaning) to be the only ultimate (basic) moral obligation. While philosophers have used the notion of a deontological moral system in different senses, it is perhaps best defined simply as a non-teleological moral system—that is, a moral system that does not accept the moral obligation to maximize the good as the only ultimate moral obligation. Such systems can either deny that there is any ultimate moral obligation to maximize the good or can assert that there is a plurality of ultimate moral principles, not all of which are teleological (i.e., forward-looking ones which attempt to maximize the good). EDITOR'S NOTE.

happiness or well-being of humanity as a whole, or more accurately, of all sentient beings. The utilitarian position is here put forward as a criterion of rational choice. It is true that we may choose to habituate ourselves to behave in accordance with certain rules, such as to keep promises, in the belief that behaving in accordance with these rules is generally optimific,[8] and in the knowledge that we most often just do not have time to work out individual pros and cons. When we act in such an habitual fashion we do not of course deliberate or make a choice. The act-utilitarian will, however, regard these rules as mere rules of thumb, and will use them only as rough guides. Normally he will act in accordance with them when he has no time for considering probable consequences or when the advantages of such a consideration of consequences are likely to be outweighed by the disadvantage of the waste of time involved. He acts in accordance with rules, in short, when there is no time to think, and since he does not think, the actions which he does habitually are not the outcome of moral thinking. When he has to think what to do, then there is a question of deliberation or choice, and it is precisely for such situations that the utilitarian criterion is intended.

It is, moreover, important to realize that there is no inconsistency whatever in an act-utilitarian's schooling himself to act, in normal circumstances, habitually and in accordance with stereotyped rules. He knows that a man about to save a drowning person has no time to consider various possibilities, such as that the drowning person is a dangerous criminal who will cause death and destruction, or that he is suffering from a painful and incapacitating disease from which death would be a merciful release, or that various timid people, watching from the bank, will suffer a heart attack if they see anyone else in the water. No, he knows that it is almost always right to save a drowning man, and in he goes. Again, he knows that we would go mad if we went in detail into the probable consequences of keeping or not keeping every trivial promise: we will do most good and reserve our mental energies for more important matters if we simply habituate ourselves to keep promises in all normal situations. Moreover he may suspect that on some occasions personal bias may prevent him from reasoning in a correct utilitarian fashion. Suppose he is trying to decide between two jobs, one of which is more highly paid than the other, though he has given an informal promise that he will take the lesser paid one. He may well deceive himself by underestimating the effects of breaking the promise (in causing loss of confidence) and by overestimating the good he can do in the highly paid job. He may well feel that if he trusts to the accepted rules he is more likely to act in the way that an unbiased act-utilitarian would recommend than he would be if he tried to evaluate the consequences of his possible actions himself. . . .

Utilitarianism and the Future

The chief persuasive argument in favour of utilitarianism has been that the dictates of any deontological ethics will always, on some occasions, lead to the existence of misery that could, on utilitarian principles, have been prevented. Thus if the deontologist says that promises always should be kept (or even if, like Ross, he says that there is a *prima facie* duty[9] to keep them) we may confront him with a situation like the following, the well-known 'desert island promise': I have promised a dying man on a desert island, from which subsequently I alone

[8]That is, have the best consequences. EDITOR'S NOTE.

[9]For David Ross in his *The Right and the Good* (Oxford Oxford University Press, 1930), a *prima facie* duty is a duty that can be overridden by a more stringent competing duty. EDITOR'S NOTE.

am rescued, to give his hoard of gold to the South Australian Jockey Club. On my return I give it to the Royal Adelaide Hospital, which, we may suppose, badly needs it for a new X-ray machine. Could anybody deny that I had done rightly without being open to the charge of heartlessness? (Remember that the promise was known only to me, and so my action will not in this case weaken the general confidence in the social institution of promising.) Think of the persons dying of painful tumours who could have been saved by the desert island gold! . . .

Utilitarianism and Justice

It is not difficult to show that utilitarianism could, in certain exceptional circumstances, have some very horrible consequences. In a very lucid and concise discussion note, H.J. McCloskey has considered such a case. Suppose that the sheriff of a small town can prevent serious riots (in which hundreds of people will be killed) only by 'framing' and executing (as a scapegoat) an innocent man. In actual cases of this sort the utilitarian will usually be able to agree with our normal moral feelings about such matters. He will be able to point out that there would be some possibility of the sheriff's dishonesty being found out, with consequent weakening of confidence and respect for law and order in the community, the consequences of which would be far worse even than the painful deaths of hundreds of citizens. But as McCloskey is ready to point out, the case can be presented in such a way that these objections do not apply. For example, it can be imagined that the sheriff could have first-rate empirical evidence that he will not be found out. So the objection that the sheriff *knows* that the man he 'frames' will be killed, whereas he has only probable belief that the riot will occur unless he frames the man, is not a sound one. Someone like McCloskey can always strengthen his story to the point that we would just have to admit that if utilitarianism is correct, then the sheriff must frame the innocent man. (McCloskey also has cogently argued that similar objectionable consequences are also implied by rule-utilitarianism. That is, an unjust *system* of punishment might be more *useful* than a just one. Hence even if rule-utilitarianism can be clearly distinguished from act-utilitarianism, a utilitarian will not be able to avoid offensive consequences of his theory by retreating from the 'act' form to the 'rule' form.) Now though a utilitarian might argue that it is empirically unlikely that some such situation as McCloskey envisages would ever occur, McCloskey will point out that it is *logically* possible that such a situation will arise. If the utilitarian rejects the unjust act (or system) he is clearly giving up his utilitarianism. McCloskey then remarks: "But as far as I know, only J.J.C. Smart among the contemporary utilitarians, is happy to adopt this 'solution'." Here I must lodge a mild protest. McCloskey's use of the word 'happy' surely makes me look a most reprehensible person. Even in my most utilitarian moods I am not *happy* about this consequence of utilitarianism. Nevertheless, however unhappy about it he may be, the utilitarian must admit that he draws the consequence that he might find himself in circumstances where he ought to be unjust. Let us hope that this is a logical possibility and not a factual one. In hoping thus I am not being inconsistent with utilitarianism, since any injustice causes misery and so can be justified only as the lesser of two evils. The fewer the situations in which the utilitarian is forced to choose the lesser of two evils, the better he will be pleased. . . .

It is also true that we should probably dislike and fear a man who could bring himself to do the right utilitarian act in a case of the sort envisaged by McCloskey. Though the man in this case might have done the right utilitarian act, his act would betoken a toughness and lack of squeamishness which would make him a dangerous person. We must remember that people have egoistic tendencies as well as beneficent ones, and should such a person be tempted to act wrongly he could act very wrongly indeed. A utilitarian who remembers the possible moral weakness of men might quite consistently prefer to be the sort of person who would not always be able to bring himself to do the right utilitarian act and to surround himself by people who would be too squeamish to act in a utilitarian manner in such extreme cases.

No, I am not happy to draw the conclusion that McCloskey quite rightly says that the utilitarian must draw. But neither am I happy with the anti-utilitarian conclusion. For if a case really *did* arise in which injustice was the lesser of two evils (in terms of human happiness and misery), then the anti-utilitarian conclusion is a very unpalatable one too, namely that in some circumstances one must choose the greater misery, perhaps the *very much* greater misery, such as that of hundreds of people suffering painful deaths.

Still, to be consistent, the utilitarian must accept McCloskey's challenge. Let us hope that the sort of possibility which he envisages will always be no more than a logical possibility and will never become an actuality. At any rate, even though I have suggested that in ethics we should test particular feelings by general attitudes, McCloskey's example makes me somewhat sympathetic to the opposite point of view. Perhaps indeed it is too much to hope that there is *any* possible ethical system which will appeal to all sides of our nature and to all our moods. It is perfectly possible to have conflicting attitudes within oneself. It is quite conceivable that there is *no* possible ethical theory which will be conformable with all our attitudes. If the theory is utilitarian, then the possibility that sometimes it would be right to commit injustice will be felt to be acutely unsatisfactory by someone with a normal civilized upbringing. If on the other hand it is not utilitarian but has deontological elements, then it will have the unsatisfactory implication that sometimes avoidable misery (perhaps very great avoidable misery) ought not to be avoided. . . .

DISCUSSION QUESTIONS

1. Do you agree with Smart that it is irrational "rule-worship" to feel morally obligated to abide by a moral rule when it appears that such an action would not have the best consequences? Why?

2. Unlike Bentham, Smart does not claim that there is any mechanical way of objectively weighing the consequences of alternative courses of action. He admits that utilitarians can disagree as to (1) whether quantity of pleasure is the only intrinsic good, (2) whether average happiness or total happiness should be considered, and (3) the weight, if any, that equitable distribution of happiness should have when weighed against the maximization of happiness.

   a. What does Smart have to say about these possible points of disagreement among utilitarians? Do you agree? Why?

   b. Smart downplays the frequency of such disagreements, claiming that "[The] possibility of ultimate disagreement is always there, though we have given reasons for suspecting that it will not frequently lead to important disagreement in practice." Do you agree? Why?

   c. Even if such disagreement will turn out, in practice, to be infrequent, as Smart claims, would this fact serve to adequately undercut the objections to utilitarianism as an adequate and complete moral theory? Why?

3. In reply to John Rawls' claim that the general happiness should be maximized only in a **fair** way, Smart replies:

> As against this suggestion a utilitarian might make the following rhetorical objection: if it is rational for me to choose the pain of a visit to the dentist in order to prevent the pain of a toothache, why is it not rational of me to choose a pain for Jones, similar to that of my visit to the dentist, if that is the only way in which I can prevent a pain, equal to that of my toothache, for Robinson? Such situations continually occur in war, in mining, and in the fight against disease, when we may often find ourselves in the position of having in the general interest to inflict suffering on good and happy men.

What do you think of this reply? Do you agree with

Smart that "there are . . . good utilitarian reasons for adopting the principle of fairness as an important, but not inviolable, rule of thumb." Would it always be right, as Smart suggests, to violate the principle of fairness when it seems clear that the violation of this principle would have the best consequences?

4. In the example, well-known to philosophers, of "the desert island promise," Smart suggests that only a "heartless" person would think that it was wrong to break the promise (see pp. 397–98). Do you agree? When, if ever, do you think that it is right to break promises?

5. What is Smart's reaction to McCloskey's well-known example of the sheriff who contemplates framing an innocent man to save the lives of many innocent people? Do you agree? Why?

6. Do you agree with Smart that the punishment of criminals is justified **only** by the beneficial results of this punishment? If so, how, if at all, does "punishment" differ from the imposition of inconveniences on those committed to mental hospitals and those whose liberty is restricted by quarantine regulations?

7. Consider the following criticism of utilitarianism by the American philosopher William James:

> If the hypothesis were offered us of a world in which Messrs. Fourier's and Bellamy's and Morris's utopias should be all outdone, and millions kept permanently happy on the one simple condition that a certain lost soul on the far-off edge of things should lead a life of lonely torture, . . . [would we not] immediately feel, even though an impulse arose within us to clutch at the happiness so offered, how hideous a thing would be its enjoyment when deliberately accepted as the fruit of such a bargain.[10]

Do you agree with James? If so, what is your reaction to the following claim by the American philosopher Morris R. Cohen?

> Moral feelings are very strong, but this does not prevent them from appearing as irrational taboos to those who do not share our conventions. This should warn us against the tendency to make ethical philosophy an apology or justification of the conventional customs that happen to be established. Suppose that someone were to offer our country a wonderfully convenient mechanism, but demand in return the privilege of killing thousands of our people every year. How many of those who would indignantly refuse such a request will condemn the use of the automobile now that it is already with us?[11]

Can you see any relevant moral differences between the cases James and Cohen mention?

8. No doubt, most of us feel strongly that our obligation not **to harm** people is much more stringent than our obligation **to help** people. Can a utilitarian give any justification for this moral distinction? Similarly, do you think a utilitarian can give a plausible defense of our tendency to distinguish the claim that "It would be **morally ideal** for Jones to do X" from the claim that "Jones is **morally obligated** to do X"? If so, how do you think a utilitarian would analyze the different meanings of these two claims?

9. There is an unresolved question that utilitarianism must face concerning whether the principle of utility should apply only to human beings and not to animals. How do you think we should weigh the rights of animals against those of human beings? If, let us fancifully imagine, beating animals before killing them resulted in making the animals' meat far more tender and succulent, would we be morally justified in this sort of action? If not, what justifies us in eating them at all? If you think we are justified in using animals for our benefit as we do, would it be morally correct for beings from some other part of our universe whose abilities are vastly superior to ours to use us in a similar manner? If not, why not?

10. If one were committed to the view that the right thing to do is always to act so as to maximize the general happiness, would not one be acting immorally whenever one spends money on some personal luxury when this same money could create greater general happiness if given to the poor of

[10] William James, *The Will to Believe and Other Essays in Popular Philosophy* (New York: Longmans, 1896), p. 188.

[11] Morris R. Cohen, *Studies in Philosophy and Science* (New York: Frederick Ungar Publishing Co., Inc., 1949), pp. 24–25.

this world? If so, is the principle of utility a principle that the average person can reasonably be expected to follow or is it one for saints?

11. Consider the following quotation from Ayn Rand's **Atlas Shrugged**:

> . . . "the good of others" is a magic formula that transforms anything into gold. . . . Your code hands out, as its version of the absolute, the following rule of moral conduct; if **you** wish it, it's evil; if others wish it, it's good; if the motive of your action is **your** welfare, don't do it; if the motive is the welfare of others, then anything goes. . . . For those of you who might ask questions, your code provides a consolation prize and booby-trap; it is your own happiness, it says, that you serve the happiness of others; the only way to achieve your joy is to give it up to others . . . and if you find no joy in this procedure, it is your fault and the proof of your evil. . . . [A] morality that teaches you to scorn a whore who gives her body indiscriminately to all men—this same morality demands that you surrender your soul to promiscuous love for all comers.[12]

a. To what extent does the code of morality Rand criticizes differ from utilitarianism?

b. If you were a utilitarian, how would you respond to Rand's criticisms?

c. To what extent, if at all, do you agree with Rand?

12. In upholding the involuntary sterilization of a retarded sixteen-year-old girl, a 1925 Michigan court (**Smith v. Command**) claimed in justification that "No citizen has any right superior to the common welfare." First argue for or against this general claim and then consider its application to the particular question of the involuntary sterilization of the mentally retarded.

13. In his discussion of the possibility of disagreement between those who prefer to maximize the **average** happiness of human beings and those who prefer to maximize the **total** happiness, Smart considers a situation in which one is forced to choose between a larger or smaller number of people each equally happy, but neglects the more problematic case where one must choose between a world of more people, experiencing less average happiness but more total happiness and a world of a lesser number of individually happier people who share in a lesser total happiness. Which of these two possible worlds would you choose? If it is better to maximize the average happiness and not the total happiness, should a government have the right to compel birth control measures? Why, or why not?

14. From the perspective of a hedonistic utilitarian, is a couple acting immorally if they refuse to bring children into the world, even if it is quite likely that by having children they would increase the amount of happiness in the world—since it is probable that their children will lead pleasant lives which would not be outweighed by whatever unhappiness their existence would cause others? Would a couple be acting immorally if they refuse to abort a seriously physically or mentally deformed fetus and devote themselves to its care when born, at the price of not having the other children they originally planned to have who would most likely have a much more pleasant life than the defective child? Do such cases bring out some inadequacy of the hedonistic utilitarian point of view or of utilitarianism itself?

15. In Dostoyevsky's **Crime and Punishment,** a young and poor student, Raskolnikov, kills an old woman for her money. Raskolnikov's resolve in committing this crime is reinforced when he overhears another student arguing with an officer for the morality of killing this old woman. The student argues:

> "Listen, I want to ask you a serious question," the student said hotly. "I was joking of course, but look here; on one side we have a stupid, senseless, worthless, spiteful, ailing, horrid old woman, not simply useless but doing actual mischief, who has not an idea what she is living for herself. . . . On the other side, fresh young lives thrown away for want of help and by thousands, on every side! A hundred thousand good deeds could be done and helped, on that old woman's money which will be buried in a monastery! Hundreds, thousands, perhaps, might be set on the right path; dozens of families saved from

[12] Ayn Rand, *Atlas Shrugged* (New York: Random House, 1957), pp. 1030, 1031, 1033.

destitution, from ruin, from vice. . . . Kill her, take her money and with the help of it devote oneself to the service of humanity and the good of all. What do you think, would not one tiny crime be wiped out by thousands of good deeds? . . . Besides, what value has the life of that sickly, stupid, ill-natured old woman in the balance of existence? No more than the life of a louse, of a black beetle, less in fact because the old woman is doing harm. She is wearing out the lives of others; the other day she bit Lizaveta's finger out of spite, it almost had to be amputated."

"Of course she does not deserve to live," remarked the officer, "but there it is, it's nature."

"Oh well, brother, but we have to correct and direct nature . . ."

Do you think Smart would accept the student's argument? How would he justify his answer? How would you reply to the student's argument?

47. MORALITY AND RATIONAL SELF-INTEREST

Baruch Brody

(For a biographical sketch of Baruch Brody, see Selection #2.)

Is everyone selfish? Can the demands of morality really, in the long run, conflict with self-interest? If such conflicts are possible, can any good reason be given for choosing the demands of morality over self-interest or is self-interest the only good reason for being moral? It is these questions and the answers that influential philosophers have given to them that Brody discusses and clarifies in the following selection. In this selection, we turn our attention for the first time to the connection between morality and human motivation. Our previous selections centered on the objectivity or subjectivity of moral assertions and on the attempt to provide some supreme moral principle. But even if we could all agree on some uniquely correct way to resolve all moral problems (at least in principle), the preceding questions concerning the scope of psychologically possible and rational motives for choosing to act on the demands of morality remain to be considered.

Suppose for a moment that you are competing for a very important job. This job would advance your career considerably. The final choice is between you and one other candidate. Suppose, moreover, that you have an opportunity to spread a vicious lie about your opponent. If the lie is believed, you'll get the job. Why shouldn't you spread the lie? No doubt doing so would be morally wrong. But isn't it foolish to be concerned with morality when your career and so much of your own happiness is at stake? If it is not foolish to be concerned about morality in this situation, why isn't it?

In situations like this, one course of action seems to be morally correct while a different course of action seems to be in one's own self-interest. The question that naturally arises, then, is which course of action to follow. Should one

Source: Baruch A. Brody, *Beginning Philosophy*, © 1977, pp. 33-55. Reprinted by permission of Prentice-Hall, Inc., Englewood Cliffs, N.J.

do the right action even at a great cost to oneself? If so why? What rational purpose can there be for sacrificing one's self-interest?

Philosophers have been troubled by this question for a long time. It is not surprising, because this is a dilemma faced by all of us on many occasions throughout our lives. Indeed, this problem is at the root of the first great philosophical classic, Plato's *Republic.* At the beginning of that book, one of the main characters makes the following claim:

> All men believe in their hearts that injustice is far more profitable to the individual than justice. . . . If you could imagine anyone obtaining the power of becoming invisible, and never doing any wrong or taking what was another's, he would be thought by the onlookers to be a most wretched idiot, although they would praise him to one another's face.

. . . .

Obviously, no one . . . [has the power of becoming invisible at will]. But we all have opportunities to profit by acting immorally. In all of these cases, we have to ask ourselves "why should I be moral?"

The Conventional Answers

There are a variety of conventional attempts to meet this problem. The simplest is the plain denial that it exists. Consider, for example, the familiar maxim "Honesty is the best policy." This and other such sayings essentially claim that, if we look at the matter fully, considering long-range as well as short-range considerations, we will see that our self-interest is best served by doing the right thing. There is clearly some truth to these maxims. There are cases in which doing the wrong action will clearly hurt us in the long run.

For example, many students know that it is often possible to get a good grade, with much less work, by cheating on an exam. And this dishonest course of action might at first seem to be in their self-interest. But look carefully at the long-range consequences of cheating. Suppose, for example, you really need to know the material you were being tested on at some later time, perhaps in another course, or outside of school. You may lose out then because you cheat now. Marital infidelity is another example. Many people have found they can be unfaithful to their spouses and "get away with it." The immediate pleasures obtained from doing so have made it seem as though this dishonest act is really in their self-interest. But again, one should carefully examine the long-range consequences, for example, the psychological effects on one's relationship with one's spouse. This might well reveal that faithfulness is really in one's true interest.

There may well be many such cases in which "honesty pays." But it would be rash to conclude that this is true in all cases. At first glance, in fact, it would seem that there are many cases in which the opposite is true. Consider some of your actions that you know to have been wrong. Did you really always lose because you did them? If you didn't lose, then wasn't it the smart thing to do? Why shouldn't we perform the wrong action in such cases?

Let's consider these questions more closely. First of all, does the fear of being caught and punished enter into the issue? Perhaps we shouldn't do the wrong action because the punishment we will receive for doing it outweighs any gain we receive? I suspect that this answer is widely believed. It seems, for example, to lie behind the belief that a strong system of criminal justice will deter crime. The trouble with this answer is that it assumes that we will always be caught and punished. It doesn't address itself to the cases in which we have a good chance of getting away with our wrongdoings. When the probability of being caught is low enough, and the gain from wrongdoing large enough, it would seem rational to gamble on getting away with the wrong action. . . .

Things would be very different, of course, if we knew that we would *always* be caught and punished. However, the opposite is true; all too often, we have a good chance of avoiding punishment, at least the ordinary forms of punishment. This last remark will suggest to many that there may be other forms of punishment, ones that always work, and that our problem can be solved if we will turn our attention to them.

What could these super-effective forms of punishment be? One is the internal pangs of conscience. After all, say some moralists, we always know when we do wrong, and our conscience bothers us about it. The reason then for doing the right action, even if we could get away with wrongdoing, is that we will be punished by our consciences for doing the wrong action. Another kind of punishment is divine retribution. According to some religious moralists, we shouldn't do wrong, even if we can get away with it, because God will always know about it. He will punish us, if not in this life, then in the afterlife.

There is no doubt that some wrongdoers suffer greatly from pangs of conscience. But as a general solution to the question of why one should be moral, this appeal to the pangs of conscience is insufficient because: (1) it does not apply to all people, since the voice of conscience seems to be weak in many people; (2) it does not apply to all cases, since in many cases one's conscience is not particularly bothered and the gain from wrongdoing may outweigh the slight stirrings of conscience; (3) it does not take into account the way our consciences come to terms with our shortcomings. As I think we all know from our own experience, we tend to find justifications for our shortcomings, especially when they are repeated. After a while, our consciences no longer bother us. It is this malleability of conscience that makes it an uncertain basis for doing the right action.

The appeal to divine punishment is a different matter. For if God does exist and does punish all evildoers, then we always have a powerful reason—and one based on self-interest—for doing the right action. However, most philosophers have not wanted to rest the case for being moral on our desire to avoid divine retribution. To begin with, no matter how sound that case may be logically, it does not seem to be psychologically effective. Perhaps this is because divine punishment seems so far away, belonging to some unknown existence after death. At any rate, the fear of divine punishment does not deter even religious people from doing at times what they know to be wrong. Secondly, if we were to take this approach, then we would be justified in making moral sacrifices only if we could prove (or make it likely) that God exists [and] doing that is not so easy. It seems preferable, then, to find another basis for acting morally. Finally, and perhaps most important, this type of argument would force us to reevaluate our feelings about the nobility of moral behavior. If the reason for behaving morally is just to avoid punishment (even divine punishment), then we have no reason to treat moral self-sacrifice as a noble form of behavior. . . .

Two Philosophical Theories

There have been, in the history of philosophy, two especially notable attempts to deal with our problem. One is to be found in Plato's *Republic,* and the other is found in Thomas Hobbes's *Leviathan.* While these two attempts are very different, they share the theme that a proper solution to the problem must begin with an understanding of human nature.

Plato's analysis of human nature begins with a phenomenon that we are all familiar with, self-conflict. Consider, the person who desires something but who recognizes that satisfying this desire would be a great mistake. Such a person both wants and doesn't want to satisfy his desire. How is this phenomenon to be explained? Plato felt that we can explain it only by supposing that the human psyche, or soul, is not a simple, unified thing. It must be composed, Plato felt, out of several potentially conflicting elements. Self-conflict comes about when these potentially conflicting elements actually do come into conflict with each other.

What different elements does Plato find in our psyche? There are three of them: desire, reason, and spirited feelings. The first two are easy to understand. Take as an example a person who wants to be unfaithful to his spouse but who knows that unbearable marital conflicts will result. This person is moved to commit adultery by desire but is moved to refrain from it by reason. This, of course, is a familiar pattern. The third element is harder to understand, but Plato seemed to have felt that it must be present in those cases where we have a spirited nonrational (not necessarily irrational) opposition to our own desires. His example of this is a person who feels a morbid desire (e.g., to see dead bodies) and a feeling of disgust at his own desire.

Plato is not alone in thinking that self-conflict can only be understood by reference to different parts of the human psyche. Indeed, a very similar approach is to be found in Freud's theory of the structure of the human personality. Freud's *id* is like Plato's desire; it is a faculty of passions and desires. Freud's *superego* is like Plato's spirited element, a faculty of strong feelings of opposition to various desires. And Freud's ego is like Plato's reason, the factor forced to consider things rationally, including the reality surrounding the person. Without overdoing the analogy, then, I think it does point out that Plato's theory of human nature is still today an appealing one.

Such a conception of human nature obviously gives rise to the question of how these different elements should relate to each other. Plato felt that this relation must be hierarchical, that reason must with the aid of our spirited element rule over desire. And he felt that this should be so because it was in the interest of the individual. Why does Plato believe this? . . . First of all, in this way, the individual "sets in order his own inner life, and is his master and his own law, and at peace with himself." The point seems to be this: when desires rule, a person never knows any peace. On one day, one desire rules and the person follows one course of action. The next day, a different desire rules and the person pursues still a different course of action. On still other days, no desire rules over the others, they all conflict, and the person cannot follow any consistent course of action.

The second argument for reason's ruling over desire is that the person in whom reason rules would pursue intellectual pleasures. And the pursuit of such pleasures would be in his self-interest. It would be in his self-interest because those who have experienced all the different pleasures perceive from their experiences that these intellectual pleasures are not only the most rewarding but the most pleasurable. . . .

Suppose, then, that on the basis of . . . these arguments we agree with Plato's conception of how the ideal soul works. Suppose that we agree that we are best off when reason rules. What follows from this? Plato felt that this provided a reason, based on self-interest, for acting morally. After all, he argued, a man in whom reason rules would never act immorally. A person who acts immorally must not have his psyche in proper working order. But we have just seen how disadvantageous such a psychic disorder is. So a life of moral behavior must be truly in our own self-interest.

The Platonic argument is a fascinating one. Plato, in effect, claimed that we must turn our attention from the particular action to the type of personality that lies behind its performance. It is only when we do that, said Plato, that we can see the reason for behaving morally. For the real shortcoming of immoral behavior lies in the type of person we have to be in order to behave immorally.

Although this idea is attractive, there is a serious difficulty with the argument as Plato actually presented it. Plato's argument clearly rests on the assumption that a person in whom reason rules, a person whose psyche is well-ordered, will not behave immorally. Is there any reason to believe that this is so? As we look back at the text of Plato, we find that he treated that assumption as self-evident.

> Will the just man [the man in whom reason rules] or citizens ever be guilty of sacrilege or theft, or treachery either to his friends or to his country?
>
> Never.
>
> Never will he ever break faith where there have been oaths.
>
> Impossible.
>
> No one will be less likely to commit adultery or to dishonor his father and mother, or to fail in his religious duties?
>
> No one.
>
> And the reason is that each part of him is doing his own business, whether in ruling or being ruled? (*Republic,* Book IV)

One can even see why Plato thought that this was so. His idea of the thief or the adulterer was of a person who was swept away by desire and did what reason forbade. But why couldn't there be a calm and rational thief or adulterer, one in whom reason rules but whose reason tells him to perform the immoral action? Unless Plato can rule out this possibility—and it is hard to see how he can—then the rational life and the moral life are not necessarily identical. In terms of self-interest, the benefits of the former are not the same as the benefits of the latter. . . .

We turn now to the argument offered by Thomas Hobbes. Hobbes begins with a fundamental assumption about human nature: that human beings are essentially self-interested agents, each acting to obtain what he thinks is in his self-interest and prepared to harm other human beings in order to obtain it. Now this would be okay if there were enough goods to completely satisfy everyone. But since there are not, human beings compete for what is available and come into armed conflict with each other. Hobbes calls this state of human conflict the state of nature. . . .

Now, said Hobbes, it is clear that no rational person would want to live in the state of nature. It would not be so bad if we could be sure of winning. But no person is so strong that he doesn't have to fear conflicts with other people (or groups of people). So the state of nature is something we should want to avoid.

The basic idea behind Hobbes's argument for acting morally is then very simple: the rational self-interested person should agree to abide by certain moral principles, which would regulate his relations with other human beings, in order to be able to live without this fear of conflict. Or, to put this point another way, if we are to live with other people, we must follow certain moral rules respecting the rights and interests of other people. Only in that way can people live in peace with one another.

Hobbes clearly has an important point. Even if we do give up something by behaving morally, and even if we would in a particular case gain by behaving immorally, we know that we would lose even more if everyone behaved immorally. And it is this knowledge that leads us to behave morally.

But isn't there a confusion here? Hobbes is right in saying that we would be better off if everyone behaved morally than if everyone pursued his own self-interest without regard to morality. But wouldn't *I* be better off if I could follow my own self-interest while others worried about morality? And if so, isn't it rational for me to do just that? Shouldn't I try to get away with advantageous acts of immorality while urging others to be moral? . . .

More Radical Approaches

We have so far examined several attempts to show that being moral is always in our self-interest. These we have found lacking. This leads us to wonder if it's even possible to connect morality and self-interest. Suppose that it's not. What does that mean?

There are philosophers who feel that this failure is not really very important. Some believe, in fact, that the whole attempt was a mistake. One such philosopher was H. A. Prichard. He wrote:

> A general but not very critical familiarity with the literature of Moral Philosophy might well lead to the remark that much of it is occupied with attempts either to prove that there is a necessary connexion between duty and interest or in certain cases even to exhibit the connexion as something self-evident. . . . When we read the attempts referred to we naturally cannot help in a way wishing them to succeed; and we might express our wish in the form that we should all like to be able to believe that honesty is the best policy. At the same time we also cannot help feeling that somehow they are out of place, so that the real question is not so much whether they are successful, but whether they ought ever to have been made. *(Duty and Interest)*

Philosophers like Prichard feel there is no need to prove that morality is identical with self-interest because we have reason to be moral even if it is not in our self-interest. They say that Plato, Hobbes, and others were mistaken in claiming that self-interest is ultimately the only reason for acting. Prichard and his followers believe that there are other reasons for acting morally. And, they say, since there are these other reasons, it is not very important if we cannot prove that morality is in our self-interest.

What are these other reasons? Prichard says, for one thing, that we want to do the right thing:

> We obviously are referring to a fact when we speak of someone as possessing a sense of duty and, again, a strong sense of duty. And if we consider what we are thinking of in these individuals whom we think of as possessing it, we find that we cannot exclude from it a desire to do what is a duty, as such, for its own sake, or, more simply, a desire to do what is a duty . . . if we admit the existence of a desire to do what is right, then there is no longer any reason for maintaining as a general thesis that in any case in which a man knows some action to be right, he must, if he is to be led to do it, be convinced that he will gain by doing it. For we shall be able to maintain that his desire to do what is right, if strong enough, will lead him to do the action in question in spite of any aversion from doing it which he may feel on account of its disadvantages. *(ibid.)*

Other philosophers have said the reason is that we have a concern for the welfare of others. Francis Hutcheson, for example, said that the true reason for virtuous action is "some determination of our nature to study the good of others, or some instinct, antecedent to all reason from interest, which influences us to the love of others."

Let us return now to our case of the two competitors for the one job. According to Prichard, the one competitor should not spread the damaging lie about the other because doing so will fly in the face of his desire to do the right thing. According to Hutcheson, the one competitor should not spread the damaging lie about the other because doing so will fly in the face of his concern for the well-being of others.

This whole approach, if accepted, would certainly affect our ideas about moral training. We have already remarked that in the moral training of a child, it is a mistake to emphasize the personal benefits that come from being moral. If we do emphasize this, of course, we do not provide the child with a reason for being moral in cases where morality and self-interest conflict. Prichard's theory suggests, as an alternative, that moral training should develop in the child a desire to do the right thing. Hutcheson's views suggest that moral training should develop the child's concern for the well-being of others. . . .

The Prichard-Hutcheson view also helps explain an important fact about morality. Because of their motives, we often distinguish between two people who have performed the same action, praising one while not praising the other. A philanthropist who gives to gain public acclaim is not as praiseworthy as one who gives for truly charitable motives. Now if self-interest were really the only motive for human action, there could be no such distinction. All actions would be selfishly motivated and no one would deserve praise for moral behavior. But if Prichard or Hutcheson is right, we can distinguish those who deserve praise from those who do not. Those who act with motives other than self-interest will clearly be the ones deserving praise. . . .

We have seen attractive features in the views of Prichard and Hutcheson. They seem to provide us with a reason for being moral even against our own self-interest. They offer us an interesting approach to moral training and education. And they provide us with a satisfactory account of when actions and people are truly praiseworthy. There are, nevertheless, two large problems which they must face:

1. Assume that one of their theories is true. That means that we have at least two radically different types of motives: self-interest, on the one hand, and, on the other, duty or benevolence. How then are we to choose between them when they conflict? No doubt these theories provide us with a reason for being moral. But we are also left with a reason for being immoral. What rational basis is there for choosing between these reasons? Consider again the competitors for the job. If either Hutcheson or Prichard is right, then the competitors have a reason for not spreading the lie (concern for the "good of others," or the "desire to do what is right"). But they also have a reason for spreading it (self-interest). So how shall they decide between these two reasons?

2. Are their theories correct? Do we ever really act from any motive other than self-interest? From our own experiences we all are painfully aware of people who seem to be acting from the loftiest of motives but who are really acting out of self-interest. Maybe that is true in all cases.

In the final sections of this chapter, we will deal with these two objections.

What Really Are Our Motives?

Let us begin with the second objection, which raises the question of human motives. Hutcheson and Prichard are attacking the thesis of *psychological egoism,* the view that the only reason or motive for any action is self-interest. They insist that there must be other reasons for human actions.

What arguments do they offer for their views? To begin with, they think that the truth of their views is something that we can experience in our own feelings. Thus, Hutcheson writes:

> But what will most effectually convince us of the truth on this point is reflection upon our own hearts, whether we have not a desire of the good of others, generally without any consideration or intention of obtaining these pleasant reflections on our own virtue.

Secondly, they feel that we can see in the actions of others clear examples of actions not based on self-interest. Finally, they appeal to the fact that only their views explain (as we saw above) the fact that some people are praiseworthy.

Prichard and Hutcheson certainly recognize that those who act out of nonselfish motives are often motivated by self-interest, too. All that they want to claim is that this does leave a place open for the nonselfish motives. . . .

Many people are skeptical about these claims. They suggest that the only thing that we really desire is what is in our own self-interest. Such people offer three arguments for this view:

1. When we look at examples of supposedly nonselfish actions, we often find that they are motivated by hidden considerations of self-interest.

2. People who supposedly act from benevolent motives or from a sense of duty are really acting to obtain the pleasure of seeing others happy or the pleasure of feeling that they are virtuous. So they are really acting to obtain their own pleasure, and that is an act motivated by self-interest.

3. In any case, we act to satisfy our desires, whatever they are, and that makes our action motivated by self-interest.

The first of these arguments has a great deal of intuitive appeal. After all, we have all been fooled that way. We have all admired people for their supposedly noble and generous actions only to discover the truly selfish motives that have moved them. Nevertheless, these experiences, while enough to make us somewhat skeptical about people's motives, are not enough to establish the general truth of egoism. They do not establish that people only act from selfish motives. And there is, after all, the evidence that Hutcheson and Prichard appeal to that suggests that egoism is not valid.

The second argument is more substantial. It concedes that there is some psychological truth in the Hutcheson-Prichard thesis, but it claims that the thesis distorts the nature of that truth. We are not moved, says this argument, by a desire to do what is right or to see others happy; what really moves us is the pleasure we get from thinking of ourselves as doing the right thing or from seeing others happy. Since it is this desire for our own pleasure that moves us, egoism is still correct. . . .

Nevertheless, this second argument does not really succeed. To begin with, even if its claims were true, we would still have a reason for acting morally. After all, the pleasure we get from thinking of ourselves as righteous or from seeing others happy is just as much a reason for doing the right action as Prichard's sense of duty or Hutcheson's sense of benevolence. But more important, there is evidence from both introspection and our observations of others to suggest that these claims are false. Hutcheson, for example, seems correct when he writes:

Reflections in our minds again will best discover the truth. Many have never thought upon this connection; nor do we ordinarily intend the obtaining of any such pleasure when we do generous offices. We all often feel delight upon seeing others happy, but during our pursuit of their happiness we have no intention of obtaining this delight. We often feel the pain of compassion, but were our sole ultimate intention or desire the freeing ourselves from this pain, would the deity offer us either wholly to blot out all memory of the person in distress, or to take away this connection, so that we should be easy during the misery of our friend, on the one hand, or on the other would relieve him from his misery, we should be as ready to choose the former way as the latter, since either of them would free us from our pain, which upon this scheme is the sole end proposed by the compassionate person. Don't we find in ourselves that our desire does not terminate upon the removal of our own pain? Were this our sole intention, we would run away, shut our eyes, or divert our thoughts from the miserable object, as the readiest way of removing our pain.

The third of the arguments noted above rests on a common confusion. It supposes that if I do an action to satisfy some desire of mine, then, no matter what the nature of the desire, the action is based on self-interest. But this supposition is a mistake. A "self-interested action" is one done to satisfy certain interests of mine, or certain desires for my own happiness, and not merely one done to satisfy any desire.

This point can also be put as follows: Those who make this third objection have the following picture in mind:

self-interested	other
action done to satisfy a desire	action not done to satisfy a desire

Given this picture, and the plausible assumption that all actions satisfy a desire, they conclude that the "other" category is empty and that all actions are self-interested actions. The trouble with this argument is that they are working with the wrong picture. The correct picture of the distinction is rather this one:

self-interested	other
action done to satisfy a desire for my own well-being	action done to satisfy a desire for something other than my own well-being

Given this picture, we can agree that all actions are done to satisfy some desire of the agent and still claim that not all actions are self-interested. All we need to suppose is that the agent can have desires for something other than his own well-being. And this certainly seems reasonable.

Reasons and Motives

We can conclude, then, that the egoist's arguments have failed. There is no reason to doubt that we have reasons for action other than self-interest. Now, we have still to deal with the first objection which we were left with at the end of [the section "More Radical Approaches"]: How can we decide between the reasons for action given by Hutcheson and Prichard, on the one hand, and self-interest, on the other?

This is a question that the Hutcheson-Prichard approach does not answer. It says instead that there is no basis for preferring one type of reason to the other. We may decide to follow the one type of reason or we may decide to follow the other. We may decide to follow self-interest or we may decide to be moral. Which we will decide to do depends primarily on the strength of our various desires. But whatever we do, we will have a reason for doing it, although we will not have a reason for letting *that* reason prevail.

Let us return one more time to the competitor for the job. He has a reason (his self-interested desires) for spreading the lie about his rival. He probably also has a reason (his benevolent desires or his desire to do what is right) for not doing so. Given these conflicting reasons, he will have to choose which course of action he will follow; presumably, that choice will be determined by the strength of his various desires. But if he does choose to be moral, his action will have been based upon a good reason; there will be a good answer to the question "why should he have behaved morally?"

Not everyone is satisfied with such a conclusion. There are many who feel that philosophy must provide us with an account of the reasons we have for all our choices. On this conception of the goals of philosophy, the Hutcheson-Prichard approach is unsatisfactory. It admits the existence of a choice for which we have no reasons: the choice between following our reasons for doing what is in our own interest and following our reasons for doing what is moral. The Hutcheson-Prichard approach seems to leave us with some choices that are decided solely upon the basis of the strength of our conflicting desires.

Those who follow the Hutcheson-Prichard approach are not persuaded by this objection, however. It is fundamental to that approach to accept the idea that our reasons for actions will be based on desires, and that conflicts between fundamental desires cannot be resolved by further reasons. We have, that approach says, reasons for our actions, whether they be moral or immoral. We do not have reasons for *preferring* some reasons over other reasons.

DISCUSSION QUESTIONS

1. How does Brody define the distinction between an action motivated by "self-interest" and one that is not so motivated? Do you accept this definition? Does it account for unconscious motivation or ulterior motives?

2. Consider the following often-quoted incident attributed to Abraham Lincoln:

> Mr. Lincoln once remarked to a fellow-passenger in an old-time mud coach that all men were prompted by selfishness in doing good. His fellow-passenger was antagonizing this position when they were passing over a corduroy bridge that spanned a slough. As they crossed this bridge they espied an old razor-backed sow on

the bank making a terrible noise because her pigs had got into the slough and were in danger of drowning. As the old coach began to climb the hill, Mr. Lincoln jumped out, ran back and lifted the little pigs out of the mud and water, and placed them on the bank. When he returned, his companion remarked: "Now, Abe, where does selfishness come in on this little episode?" "Why, bless your soul, Ed, that was the very essence of selfishness. I should have had no peace of mind all day had I gone on and left that suffering old sow worrying over those pigs. I did it to get peace of mind, don't you see?"[1]

Do you agree with Lincoln that his action was a selfish one or would you say, as some philosophers have, that his action was definitely an unselfish one or do you think that it depends? If so, on what does it depend? Can you think of some test that would decide the issue?

3. Consider the following argument:

[1]Quoted from the *Springfield* (Ill.) *Monitor* in the *Outlook*, 56, p. 1059.

> The doctrine of psychological egoism is incompatible with true friendship. True friendship, by definition, involves a concern for the welfare of someone else that is an end in itself. A concern for the welfare of someone else that is purely self-regarding is not true friendship. Yet the psychological egoist claims that all motives for action are self-regarding. Consequently, the psychological egoist rules out the possibility of true friendship.

How do you think a psychological egoist would reply? What do you think?

4. In depicting a person who successfully feigns an unselfish concern for the feelings and interests of others, Glaucon, a character in Plato's **Republic,** imagines a thoroughly unjust person who cunningly deceives others into believing him just. Is it at all likely in the real world for a person to successfully practice such duplicity over a long period of time? Are such dishonest people likely to be as happy as those who are motivated by a genuine unselfish concern for others? Explain.

FURTHER READINGS

classic sources and commentaries

Ayer, A.J., *Language, Truth and Logic*. New York: Dover Publications, 1952, originally published 1935. Ayer defends the (emotivist) view that ethical assertions are nothing more than "expressions of feeling" on pp. 102-13 of this highly influential and lucidly written book, which contributed greatly to the popularization of the school of philosophical thought known as *logical positivism* that flourished in the years following its publication. Ayer's defense of his view of the nature of ethical assertions provides an excellent and nontechnical introduction to the main features of the *emotivist* conception of ethics which was associated with logical positivism. Those interested in a more refined emotivist theory of ethics (which makes distinctions lacking in Ayer's book) should turn to C.L. Stevenson's *Ethics and Language*.

Bentham, Jeremy, *An Introduction to the Principles of Morals and Legislation.* New York: Hafner Press, 1948, first published in 1789. This long and rather tedious classical exposition of utilitarianism is not as well suited for the beginning philosophy student as is Mill's *Utilitarianism*. However, the detailed table of contents in the work makes it a good reference source for the serious student of utilitarianism. Of special interest in Bentham's discussion of the hedonistic underpinnings of his utilitarianism. Of special interests is Bentham's disbe compared to Mill's quite different view in *Utilitarianism*.

Butler, Joseph, Fifteen Sermons Upon Human Nature. London: Macmillan, 1900. Sermon XI contains the classical criticism of psychological egoism (the psychological view that self-interest is the only motive for action).

Hume, David, *A Treatise of Human Nature*. Oxford: Oxford University Press, 1964, first published in 1739. Hume's most provocative presentation of his thesis that moral questions are decided by *sentiment* and not *reason* is found in Book II, Part III, Section III. (The quotation from Hume at the beginning of this chapter comes from this section of the *Treatise*—pp. 415-16 of this edition.) Disappointed by the poor literary reception of the *Treatise*, Hume reformulated his ideas on ethics into the more popular form of his *Inquiries* (or *Enquiries,* depending on the edition) *Concerning Human Understanding*. Hume's treatment of the relationship between reason and feeling is found in Appendix I of this work. Since Hume believed that the moral *sentiments* which determine our allegience to moral principles are *in point of fact* aroused only by what is considered "pleasant or useful to ourselves or to others," Hume's moral philosophy foreshadowed the utilitarianism of Bentham and Mill.

Kant, Immanuel, *Groundwork of the Metaphysics of Morals,* trans. H.J. Paton. New York: Harper & Row, 1964, first published in 1785. Kant's classical theoretical discussion of the underpinnings of morality. While there are several translations of this work (in one translation the word "foundations" is used instead of "groundwork," in another the word "fundamental principles" is used), this is the best for students since it also contains a section-by-section short summary and analysis of the work by the Kantian scholar H.J. Paton, who also provided the translation.

Kant, Immanuel, *The Metaphysical Elements of Justice*, trans. John Ladd. Indianapolis: Bobbs-Merrill, 1965, first published in 1797. In this work, Kant applies the categorical imperative introduced in the *Groundwork of the Metaphysics of Morals* to derive specific moral principles relating to the states's moral right to use coercion to limit the freedom of individuals.

Kant, Immanuel, *The Metaphysical Principles of Virtue*, trans, James Ellington. Indianapolis: Bobbs-Merrill, 1964, first published in 1797. Kant's discussion of the moral virtues that he claims should be enforced not by the state but from the moral agent's own sense of duty. Kant considers "duties to oneself" as well as "duties to others."

Kant, Immanuel, *Lectures on Ethics*, trans. Louis Infield. New York: Harper and Row, 1963. Kant's application of his ethical theory to specific moral questions (e.g., the morality of suicide and duties to animals). This work, which consists of lecture notes of three of Kant's students, helps put flesh on the bare bones of Kant's theoretical discussions of ethics.

Mill, John Stuart, *Utilitarianism*. Indianapolis: Hackett, 1979, first published in 1863. A short and readable classical exposition of utilitarianism. The seven-page introduction by George Sher, the editor, is clear and helpful. (The quotation from Mill at the beginning of this chapter comes from the first paragraph of Chapter IV of this work.)

Moore, G.E., *Principia Ethica*. Cambridge, Mass. Cambridge University Press, 1959, first published in 1903. A classical defense of the view that there are unique *nonnatural* (nonscientific) properties that are discerned through a faculty of moral intuition.

Murphy, Jeffrie, *Kant: The Philosophy of Right*. London: Macmillan, 1970. A good, short, and lucid account of Kant's ethical theory in *The Groundwork of the Metaphysics of Morals* and its application to *The Metaphysical Elements of Justice* which should prove quite helpful to beginning students.

Plato, *The Republic*, trans. Francis MacDonald Cornford. New York: Oxford University Press, 1945. Books 2 and 9 contain Plato's classical defense of the ultimate convergence of morality and self-interest.

Randall, J.H., *Aristotle*. New York: Columbia University Press, 1960. A good exposition of Aristotle's moral theory and its place in his general philosophy.

Reid, Thomas, *Essays on the Active Powers of the Human Mind.* Cambridge, Mass. M.I.T. Press, 1969, originally published in 1788 and republished in other editions. Reid was a Scottish philosopher who is noted for his defense of common sense beliefs and their metaphysical underpinnings. In this capacity, he was sharp in his criticisms of the central ideas in the British empiricist tradition that flourished around him and was especially critical of the philosophical views of his Scottish contemporary, David Hume. Reid's defense of his objectivistic view of ethics and criticism of Hume's subjectivistic view is found in Essays III and IV of his *Essays on the Active Powers of the Human Mind.* (The quotation from Reid at the beginning of this chapter comes from Essay III, Chapter VI, Section II.)

Ross, David, *The Right and the Good.* Oxford: Oxford University Press, 1930. In this influential book, Ross defends an intuitionistic view of ethics, coupled with the belief that there is a plurality of *basic* moral principles. In so doing, Ross attempts to mediate between traditional utilitarian and Kantian ethics.

Stevenson, C.L., *Ethics and Language*. New Haven, Conn.: Yale University Press, 1943. The classic and most refined defense of an emotivist theory of ethics.

Westermarck, Edward, *Ethical Relativity*. New York: Harcourt, Brace and Company, 1932. Westermarck (1862–1939) was an influential anthropologist, sociologist, and philosopher. As a philosopher, he is noted for his sophisticated defense of a subjectivistic theory of ethics. This theory was first presented, illustrated, and supported by a wealth of anthropological examples in Westermark's *The Origin and Development of the Moral Ideas* (1906–8) and then in his most exclusively philosophical work *Ethical Relativity* (1932). Unlike many other defenses of subjectivism by anthropologists who are struck by the variability of moral beliefs among different cultures, Westermarck formulates his position with considerable philosophical sophistication. According to his position, since "all moral concepts are ultimately based on emotions" and since "no objectivity can come from an emotion" (p. 60 of *Ethical Relativism*), it follows that moral principles cannot be said to be objectively valid or invalid (i.e., there are no "moral truths"). Nevertheless, as the quotation at the beginning of this book indicates (Ibid, p. 90), Westermarck also believed that moral emotions must necessarily be disinterested ones.

contemporary viewpoints

Baier, Kurt, *The Moral Point of View*, Chapter 8. Ithaca, N.Y.: Cornell University Press, 1958. Following Kant, Baier sees the moral point of view as one of acting from rational principles that are *universalizable*. Baier specifies certain conditions which he sees as implicit requirements of universalization. For example, he says that moral rules must be "universally teachable" and cannot be "self-frustrating" or "self-defeating." This book is geared to the more advanced philosophy student.

Brandt, Richard, *A Theory of the Right and the Good.* New York: Oxford University Press, 1979. In this sophisticated book, Brandt elaborately defends the version of rule-utilitarianism that is expressed in the quotation from him at the beginning of this chapter. Brandt presents a less elaborate defense of the same view in his article "Some Merits of One Form of Rule-Utilitarianism," which originally appeared in *University of Colorado Series in Philosophy,* 3 (1967), pp. 39–65. This article has been reprinted in several anthologies, including Joel Feinberg and Henry West, eds., *Moral Philosophy: Classic Texts and Contemporary Problems* (Encino, Ca.: Dickenson, 1977).

Hare, R.M., *The Language of Morals*. London: Oxford Univeristy Press, 1952. In this influential book, Hare incorporates his view that moral principles are *by definition universalizable* with the subjectivistic view that one must choose one's moral principles and not discover them. In this respect, Hare's point of view is quite different from that of Baier.

Mortimer, Robert C., *Christian Ethics*. London: Hutchison's University Library, 1950. In this exposition of Christian ethics, Mortimer defends the view that there is an objective morality which derives its legitimacy from the will of God. (This is the position Plato argues against in his *Euthyphro*.) The section in *Christian Ethics* in which Mortimer defends this position appears in Raziel Abelson and Marie-Louise Friquegnon, eds., *Ethics for Modern Life* (New York: St. Martin's Press, 1975). (The quotation from Mortimer at the beginning of this chapter can be found on pp. 127–28 of this anthology.)

Nozick, Robert, *Anarchy, State and Utopia.* New York: Basic Books, 1974. A modern and often discussed theoretical defense of a "minimum state," which is limited to the passive functions of protection against force, theft, and fraud, and the enforcement of contracts. Nozick's theoretical disdain for the welfare state is shared today by members of the Libertarian Party.

Rand, Ayn, *The Virtue of Selfishness.* New York: New American Library, 1964. A defense of the view that people *ought* to be selfish, by an influential contemporary novelist.

Rawls, John, "Two Concepts of Rules," *Philosophical Review*, 64 (1955). In this influential article, Rawls argues for the merits of a type of rule-utilitarianism over act-utilitarianism. As he sees it, some of our actions (but not all of them) can only be morally evaluated in terms of certain rules or practices (which are justified in terms of their utility) that *define* these actions as the sorts of actions they are taken to be. This article is reprinted in the Bayles and Feinberg-West anthologies listed in this bibliography.

Rawls, John, *A Theory of Justice*. Cambridge, Mass: Harvard University Press, 1970. The most talked about book in ethical theory in the last several decades. Rawls argues for the priority of individual freedom and justice over utility and for a liberal-welfare-state. In his acceptance of the view that justice and not utility is the primary moral value, Rawls' ethical theory is like Nozick's. In his emphasis upon the value of social welfare, however, Rawls' theory is radically different from Nozick's.

Smart, J.J.C., and Bernard Williams, *Utilitarianism: For and Against*. Cambridge: Cambridge University Press, 1973. This book consists of an essay by Smart defining and defending a utilitarian point of view and one by Williams in criticism. An excerpt from Smart's essay is one of this chapter's selections.

general texts

Bayles, Michael D., ed., *Contemporary Utilitarianism.* Garden City, N.Y.: Doubleday, 1968. A good collection of pro and con essays on utilitarianism by contemporary philosophers.

Brandt, Richard, *Ethical Theory*. Englewood Cliffs, N.J.: Prentice-Hall, 1959. A very clear and comprehensive discussion of the main issues of ethical theory for the serious philosophy student.

Broad, C.D., *Five Types of Ethical Theory*. New York: Littlefield, 1965. An excellent discussion of the moral theories of Spinoza, Butler, Hume, Kant, and Sidgwick.

Frankena, W., *Ethics*. Englewood Cliffs, N.J.: Prentice-Hall, 1963. A popular short introduction to the central problems and theories of ethics.

Grassian, Victor, *Moral Reasoning*, Part I. Englewood Cliffs, N.J.: 1981. A concise discussion of the central problems and theories of ethics and of the nature and pitfalls of moral reasoning.

Hospers, John, *Human Conduct*. New York: Harcourt, 1972. An engaging, though long, discussion of the central problems and theories of ethics.

Ladd, John, ed., *Ethical Relativism*. Belmont, Ca.: Wadsworth, 1973. An anthology of selections by philosophers, anthropologists, and other social scientists on the issue of ethical relativism. Ladd's introduction to the anthology and his own article, which is included in it, provide especially good philosophical clarifications of the issues involved in debates over the validity of ethical relativism.

MacIntyre, A., *A Short History of Ethics.* New York: Macmillan, 1966. A brief, but comprehensive, history of ethics.

Warnock G., *Contemporary Moral Philosophy*. New York: St. Martins, 1967. This analytically oriented, but very clearly written, book is a good complement to the historically oriented *Ethics Since 1900* by Mary Warnock. The topics covered are: intuitionism, emotivism, prescriptivism, the content of morals, and naturalism.

Warnock, Mary, *Ethics Since 1900*. Oxford: Oxford University Press, 1960. In this clear and useful book, Mary Warnock briefly traces the history of twentieth-century Anglo-American viewpoints on ethics. The topics covered (by chapter headings) are: The Metaphysical Ethics of F. H. Bradley; G. E. Moore, Intuitionism; The Emotive Theory; After the Emotivists; The Free Will Issue; Sartre.

anthologies

Alston, W., and R. Brandt, eds.*The Problems of Philosophy*, 3rd ed. Boston: Allyn and Bacon, 1978. This general anthology for introductory philosophy has an extensive and well-rounded collection of selections on ethics, covering ethical relativism, the meaning and justification of ethical statements, types of normative ethics, and the rationality of being moral. It provides a good supplement to our anthology's selection on ethics for the serious student.

Brandt, R. ed., *Value and Obligation*. New York: Harcourt, 1961. This excellent anthology of classical and contemporary readings in ethics provides a good companion to Brandt's excellent ethics text *Ethical Theory*. Each selection is prefaced by a brief editorial introduction which explains the main ideas of the selection and gives some background on its author. The topics covered (in order) are: What is Worthwhile; Which Acts are Right; Justification of Ethical Beliefs; Ethical Relativism; Human Rights; Morality of Institutions; and Moral Responsibility and Free Choice.

Edwards, P., and A. Pap, eds., *A Modern Introduction to Philosophy.* New York: Macmillan, 1973. The selections on ethics in this general anthology for introductory philosophy are restricted to the topic of the meaning and justification of ethical statements. The selections are well chosen for this topic.

Feinberg, J., and Henry West, eds., *Moral Philosophy: Classical Texts and Contemporary Problems*. Encino, Ca.: Dickenson, 1977. A good collection of classical and contemporary selections on the central problems and theories of ethics.

encyclopedia of philosophy

The *Encyclopedia of Philosophy* (New York: Macmillan, 1967) has a multitude of articles on various topics in the broad field of ethics. Check pp. 427–28 in the Index at the end of Volume 8.

longer bibliographies

Alston, W., and R. Brandt, eds., *The Problems of Philosophy*, 3rd ed. Boston: Allyn and Bacon, 1978. See pp. 273–80 for an unannotated bibliography, which is divided into topics.

Cornman, J., and K. Lehrer, *Philosophical Problems and Arguments: An Introduction*, 2nd ed. New York: Macmillan, 1974. See pp. 514–27 for an extensive annotated bibliography.

Edwards, P., and A. Pap, eds., *A Modern Introduction to Philosophy*, 3rd ed. New York: Macmillan, 1973. See pp. 364–72 for an extensive annotated bibliography.

Chapter VI

DETERMINISM, FREE WILL, AND MORAL RESPONSIBILITY

The actions of men . . . are determined in conformity with the order of nature, by their empirical character and by the other causes which co-operate with that character; and if we could exhaustively investigate all the appearances of men's will, there would not be found a single human action which we could not predict with certainty.

Immanuel Kant

It is . . . for want of recurring to the causes that move him; for want of being able to analyze, from not being competent to decode the complicated motion of his machine, that man believes himself a free agent; it is only upon his own ignorance that he founds the . . . deceitful notion that he has . . . free agency.

Paul-Henri Holbach

It is impossible for me to think when I am making a free choice that my volition is completely determined by my formed character and the motives acting upon it.

Henry Sidgwick

. . . there has never been any ground for the controversy between the doctrine of free will and determinism . . . . It is based upon a misapprehension . . . . Acts are free only in so far as they are determined.

R.E. Hobart

Freedom means the opposite of compulsion; a man is free if he does not act under compulsion, and he is compelled or unfree when he is hindered from without in the realization of his natural desires.

Moritz Schlick

When we reason about the liberty of the will, or about the free will, we do not ask if the man can do what he wills, but if there is enough independence in his will itself.

Gottfried Leibniz

In the case of an action that is free, it must be such that it is caused by the agent who performs it, but such that no antecedent conditions

If . . . man's nature . . . makes him do what he does, how does his action differ from that of a stone or tree? Have we not parted with any

were sufficient for his performing just that action . . . . When I believe that I have done something, I believe that it was I who caused it to be done, I who made something happen, and not merely something within me, such as one of my subjective states . . .

Richard Taylor

ground for responsibility? . . . Holding men to responsibility may make a decided difference in their **future** *behavior; holding a stone or tree to responsibility is a meaningless performance . . . it makes no difference . . . . Infants, idiots, the insane . . . are not held to liability; the reason is that . . . to do so . . . has no effect on their further actions.*

John Dewey

In his play *Long Day's Journey into Night*, one of Eugene O'Neill's characters, Mary Tyrone, expresses O'Neill's own sentiments when she laments:

> I suppose life has made him like that, and he can't help it. None of us can help the things life has done to us. They're done before you realize it, and once they're done they make you do other things until at last everything comes between you and what you'd like to be.

Many other literary figures, for example, Mark Twain and Thomas Hardy, have shared O'Neill's pessimistic and fatalistic view of the human condition. For example, in his essay "Reflections on Religion," Twain wrote:

> Man is not to blame for what he is. He didn't make himself. He has no control over himself. All the control is vested in his temperament—which he did not create—and in the circumstances which hedge him round from the cradle to the grave and which he did not devise . . . . He is as purely a piece of automatic mechanism as is a watch. . . . He is a subject for pity, not blame.

Twain's deeply held view that our cherished belief in human free will and moral responsibility is an illusion discredited by modern science finds its supporters among contemporary behavioral psychologists. For example, in his best seller *Beyond Freedom and Dignity*, American's foremost contemporary behavioral psychologist B.F. Skinner writes:

> We admire beauty, grace and sensitivity, but we do not blame a person because he is ugly, spastic, or color blind. Less conspicuous forms of genetic endowment nevertheless cause trouble. Individuals presumably differ . . . in the extent to which they respond aggressively . . . or in the extent to which they . . . are affected by sexual reinforcement. Are they, therefore, equally responsible for controlling their aggressive or sexual behavior, and is it fair to punish them to the same extent? If we do not punish a person for a clubfoot, should we punish him for being quick to anger or highly susceptible to sexual reinforcement? . . . The concept of responsibility offers little help. The issue is controllability . . . . What must be changed is not the responsibility of autonomous man but the conditions, environmental or genetic, of which a person's behavior is a function.

Skinner's rejection of the concepts of human freedom and responsibility is reinforced by contemporary sociobiologists, who believe that many human personality traits and actions are genetically determined. From their point of view, just as a helpless moth is propelled by its genetic programming toward a flame that will ultimately envelop and destroy it, so too are human beings often helplessly propelled by their genetic programming to embark on behavior that ultimately will prove self-destructive. If the responsibility for undesirable human actions cannot be placed on our genetic programming, many psychologists and psychiatrists have placed this responsibility on environmental forces that mold our personalities before we develop the capacity for reasoned self-determination. For example, Sigmund Freud, the founder of psychoanalysis, emphasized the effect of early childhood environment upon the development of the adult human personality. As he once wrote:

> Analytic experience has convinced us of the complete truth of the common assertion that the child is psychologically the father of the man and that the events of his first years are of paramount importance for his whole subsequent life.

While the view of human beings as pawns of environmental and hereditary factors ultimately beyond their control is a quite common one in literature, psychology, and philosophy, existing side-by-side with it is the view of human beings as free and morally responsible agents. For example, according to Christian religious tradition, human beings are distinguished from other animals precisely by virtue of their status as free and morally responsible creatures. It is in this that our dignity as persons resides, we are told. Indeed, according to this religious tradition, our ultimate destiny rests on the manner in which we utilize the gift of freedom that God has bestowed upon us. The world, we are told, is a moral testing ground for free human beings, with the reward of heaven for those who "pass" and hell for those who "fail." The assumption of human freedom is, thus, at the very core of the fabric of Christian theology. It is also at the core of Freudian psychology.

While psychoanalysts emphasize the strong influence upon human beings of unconscious factors beyond their control, they emphasize as well the belief that these unconscious factors can be brought to consciousness and then be subject to rational control. From the psychoanalytic perspective, it is precisely our capability to understand and rationally control the impulses we find within ourselves that makes us free and morally responsible; as this understanding and rational control increases, so does our degree of freedom and moral responsibility. Indeed, Freud, who was an atheist, followed Jesus in preaching that human beings should accept responsibility for what they *find themselves thinking* as well as for what they *deliberately do*. For example, in a well known passage Freud tells us that we must accept responsibility for the content of our dreams, writing:

> Must one assume responsibility for the content of one's dreams? . . . Obviously one must hold oneself responsible for the evil impulses of one's dreams. What else is one to do with them? Unless the content of the dream (rightly understood) is inspired by alien spirits, it is part of my own being . . . . [An unconscious impulse revealed in a dream] not only "is" in me but sometimes "acts" out of me as well . . . . The physician will leave it to the jurist to construct for social purposes a responsibility that is artificially limited to the . . . [conscious] ego. It is notorious that the greatest difficulties are encountered by the attempts to derive from such a construction practical consequences which are not in contradiction to human feeling.

The conflicting themes of human freedom on one hand and of human helplessness before the forces of heredity and environment on the other find expression in many spectacular murder trials that generate popular interest and often result in a battle of psychological experts who debate the question of whether or not a perpetrator of an evil deed acted of his own "free will' or was "insane" or had "diminished capacity" to refrain from his action. For example, a front page headline in the *Los Angeles Times* reads, "Bianchi Ties to Mother Termed Pathological." The person referred to is

Kenneth Bianchi (the "Hillside Strangler"), who confessed to murdering a number of women during a murder spree that terrorized southern California in 1977 and 1978. In the story is the following comment:

> What Bianchi's mother saw as love, say psychiatrists who have examined him, was smothering control and largely responsible for his hostility toward women and its murderous results. "That boy was my life," Bianchi's mother told *The Times* in a recent interview. "I put him *first* before my husband . . . I raised him on a pedestal."

What are we to make of this? Are all people who were similarly "put on a pedestal" by their adoring mothers incipient murderers? If Bianchi's relationship with his mother was "the cause" of his subsequent spree of homicide, what then distinguishes this relationship from countless other mother-son relationships? Unlike the more developed sciences of chemistry and physics, there are, alas, few agreed upon scientific laws to which psychiatrists can turn to resolve such questions of causation. Instead, like the rest of us, psychiatrists often engage in a highly subjective process of organizing the diverse and conflicting strands of a human personality into a more intuitively understandable and coherent picture. Psychiatrists for the defense will paint a picture of the defendent as a victim of circumstances who is *driven* toward the commission of his heinous crime, while psychiatrists for the prosecution will paint a picture of a person who, regardless of the obstacles in his way, "freely chose" to do as he did. The jury is then told to choose which of these conflicting pictures best describes "the facts." How this is to be done, juries are rarely told. While there are legal standards for determining such things as "insanity" and "diminished capacity," the justification and very meaning of these standards have generated much legal debate. This debate touches upon the philosophical underpinnings of our current philosophy of punishment and the conception of human nature that it presupposes.

The disagreement today among jurists, psychologists, psychiatrists, and others as to whether human beings really are free and morally responsible is one that has always generated heated debate among philosophers. At the heart of this debate are conflicting views of human nature and conflicting ethical views concerning the proper conditions for holding individuals morally responsible. As the perceptive reader may have already noticed, the disagreement as to whether human beings are free and morally responsible cannot be resolved without first coming to grips with the question of what these concepts *mean or should be taken to mean*. Often when people argue as to whether or not people are free and morally responsible, they fail to consider the possibility that they may be attributing different meanings to these concepts. If people are free and morally responsible in some senses of these terms but not in others, how do we decide which sense is "correct"? Is it, perhaps, a mistake to assume that there is a single correct answer to this question which can be determined apart from a consideration of the shifting purposes and attitudes of human beings? Such questions are at the very heart of the classical philosophical problem of human free will, a problem that, unfortunately, is rarely thought out clearly and deeply enough by the many jurists, psychologists, and psychiatrists who make influential assertions as to the freedom and moral responsbility of human beings.

Traditionally, philosophical debates as to the existence and nature of human "free will" and "moral responsibility" have centered on the compatibility of these notions with the doctrine of determinism. Determinism is the philosophical theory that everything in the universe, including human choices and actions, is entirely governed by causal laws of the sort that science attempts to discover. To put this thesis in another way, determinism is the belief that for any event, E, in this universe, there is some *cause* C. C, in turn, is called a cause of E, because there is a *law of nature* which asserts that "whenever C occurs, E will occur." According to determinism then, nothing ever happens purely by chance, if "by chance" one means "without any cause." Although we do, of course, often say that events happen "without any cause," if we accept determinism such assertions cannot be taken literally. When we say, for example, that "Jones quit his job without any cause," the determinist will take such a statement to mean not that Jones' action was an uncaused one, but rather that the cause is either unknown to the speaker or that Jones' reasons for leaving his job appear unjustified to the speaker. If determinism is true, every event that happens in this universe is in principle predictable if one knows the relevant laws of nature and the events leading up to that event. If, for example, there were some type of superscientist who knew everything that was happening in the universe at a given moment and every causal law, then he could predict the entire future of the universe from that moment on. This would be so, for any event, E, that will occur from that moment on will be related to some cause, C, through a law of nature that asserts that "whenever C occurs, E will occur"; and our superscientist will, according to our assumption, know of this law and of the existence of the event C which this law says will cause E.

Now, although it is impossible to prove that determinism is true, for there are clearly many things that happen whose causes are at present unknown to us, this doctrine is, nevertheless, a fundamental presupposition of scientific method as well as the reasoning of the ordinary person. For example, whenever we plug in a machine or plant seeds or mix certain chemicals, we act in accordance with the belief that events will occur in accordance with laws of nature. Indeed, without the knowledge of such laws, we would be powerless to control the future. Although there are many events whose causes we do not know, we rarely consider the possibility that these events are uncaused, and seek to discover a cause which we believe exists but is simply unknown to us. For example, although we do not know what the cause or causes of cancer are, we naturally assume that cancer is always caused by some condition or set of conditions. Similarly, we tend to accept readily the claim that human physical characteristics such as the color of one's eyes, one's height, and general health and susceptibility to diseases are fully determined by heredity and environment.

Is it not equally true that human temperament, intelligence, and behavior are fully determined by causal laws? Is it not possible that the developing science of psychology will one day enable us to predict the behavior of human beings just as we can now predict the motion of physical objects according to the laws of mechanics? Many philosophers and scientists have thought so, believing that a human being is a complex conscious machine whose feelings, thoughts, choices, and behavior are subject to scientific explanation no less than other parts of nature. Given the complexity of the human organism and the innumerable forces that act upon it in complex and ever-changing combinations, there will, most likely, always be some element of uncertainty in the predictions scientists make about human behavior. Nevertheless, many philosophers have claimed that human behavior is in principle subject to scientific laws no less than is a pebble which once thrown up in the air with a particular force and particular air resistence, eventually begins to fall at a velocity and rate of acceleration predictable by the science of mechanics. As the sciences of psychology, sociology, and anthropology advance, we learn more and more about how human behavior is part of an order of causes and effects that is subject to scientific study.

While we appear to assume the doctrine of determinism in our everyday judgments about so many different things, we also assume that individuals perform actions ''of their own free will'' in situations in which they were quite capable of doing something other than what they in fact did, and, therefore, are proper subjects of judgments of moral responsibility and blame. Yet many philosophers have found it impossible to reconcile the assumption that people act freely with the doctrine of determinism, which seems to imply that every event that occurs is *the only one that could have occurred* in the circumstances. For example, assuming that determinism is true, if Jones kills Smith at time *t*, given the forces both internal and external acting on Jones just prior to *t*, his killing of Smith had to happen. Given the causal factors at work in this situation, as in all situations of human choice, nothing can happen except what does happen. Thus, it seems to follow that if determinism is true, human beings can never act differently from the way they do act—that what occurs must occur, given the causal factors involved—and that consequently people are not really morally responsible or morally praiseworthy or blameworthy for their actions. Given the causal antecedents of their actions, they really have no choice but to act as they do. If determinism is true, the argument continues, then the feeling a person has that there are a number of alternative courses of action open to him is an illusion. Actually, only one of the imagined alternatives is possible—and indeed inevitable—given the causal law or laws involved.

Many philosophers have accepted the soundness of the preceding argument and have, as a consequence, argued that one must choose between the belief in universal determinism and that of human freedom of choice (''free will''). Others have disagreed and have held that any apparent conflict between determinism and human freedom is itself an illusion. There are, thus, three possible positions one can take on the determinism-free will issue and one can find influential supporters of all three.

First, there are those who, agreeing that determinism is incompatible with human freedom and moral responsibility, accept freedom and moral responsibility and reject determinism. Utilizing the generally accepted philosophical terminology, we shall call this the *libertarian* position. Many who take this position assert that the existence of free choice is a given fact of immediate experience. As the philosopher Henry Sidgwick put it, ''It is impossible for me to think when I am making a free choice that my volition is completely determined by my formed character and the motives acting upon it. The opposite conviction is so strong as to be absolutely unshaken by the evidence brought against it; I cannot believe it to be illusory.'' Since free choice seems to be so intuitively certain and is incompatible with determinism, a doctrine that is unproved and believed on scientific faith, one should reject determinism. Many who take this point of view emphasize the feeling of freedom that we have when engaged in a moral choice. Our belief that we are moral agents, they say, presupposes that we have free choice. As the philosopher Immanuel Kant (1724–1804) put it, ''ought implies can'' (i.e., to tell a person that he ought to do something makes sense only when that person has the freedom to do that act or to refrain from doing it). If an abstract and unproven theory such as determinism conflicts with our consciousness of being moral beings, the scientific theory must be discarded and not the immediate and strong testimony of our consciousness. Such a view has been defended, for example, by the philosopher William James (1842–1910) and the English physicist Sir Arthur Eddington (1882–1944), who believed that the ideas of contemporary quantum physics are incompatible with determinism. While James and Eddington were willing to identify freedom with chance, this is not true of all libertarians. For example, Kant and his twentieth-century disciple C.A. Campbell, insist that ''acts of will' are neither capable of a full causal scientific explanation nor are they mere chance occurrences. According to this point of view, free acts are caused by "acts of will" of an autonomous "self" ("soul"?) that can transcend the biological, psychological, and social conditions of one's being.

Second, there are those who, agreeing that determinism is incompatible with freedom and moral responsibility, accept determinism and reject freedom and moral responsibility. Following William James' terminology, such individuals are often called *hard determinists*.[1] According to this point of view, the constant advance in scientific explanation of phenomena, including human behavior, strongly favors belief in determinism. Any feeling that we may have of freedom of choice and action that transcends causal determination by physical, psychological, and social conditions is a reflection of our ignorance of the causes that act through us. Human choices and actions are simply the determined responses of complex machines subject to scientific understanding and control. Since we do not choose the hereditary and environmental factors that fully determine our psychological makeup, which in turn determines our choices and actions, we are not ultimately morally responsible for what we do. We do what we do because we are what we are; but what we are is what our genes and environment have made us. In holding people morally responsible for their actions and in praising them for their good actions and blaming them for their bad ones, we like to think that people are morally praiseworthy or morally blameworthy for their actions; in doing this, we forget that those who do well are simply those who have been *lucky* enough to inherit desirable characteristics or to be exposed to environmental circumstances which cause them to develop the wherewithal to do well. This hard deterministic perspective was held by the philosophers Hobbes (1588–1679) and Spinoza (1632–77). The famous twentieth-century lawyer, Clarence Darrow, often expressed such a view, both in his writings and in his successful court pleas, in particular, in his defense of the kidnap-murderers Leopold and Loeb.

Third, there are those who maintain that determism is compatible with freedom and moral responsibility and that any appearance of conflict is a result of various philosophical confusions. Following the widely used terminology, we will call those who hold such a view *soft determinists.* According to this point of view, once we clearly consider what we mean—or at least ought to mean, if we are thinking clearly—when we call an act or choice free, we shall see that we in no way imply that free choices or actions are uncaused. It is specific types of causes that make acts or choices unfree, not the mere fact that they are caused. Yet soft determinists disagree as to what these causes are and therefore disagree as to proper analysis of the notion of free choice (or action). According to the classic soft deterministic viewpoint held by the philosophers David Hume (1711–76) and John Stuart Mill (1806–73), a free action is one that is not due to external compulsion. Even though all human actions are caused, those many human actions which are not a result of compulsion are free. Other soft determinists choose different analyses of the notion of a free action. For example, a "free action" has been defined as:

1. one in which the agent could (or would) have done otherwise if he had chosen otherwise or tried

[1]James called those determinists who believe that determinism and free will are compatible *soft determinists.* Although the terms James coined are currently used with no evaluative connotations, they were not intended as such. As a libertarian, James rejected the attempt to reconcile determinism with free will and in calling those who attempted this soft determinists, James meant to imply that they were "soft-headed" thinkers who refused to accept the unpleasant, but inevitable, consequences of the belief in determinism. On the other hand, James believed, hard determinists were "hard-headed" enough to accept these unpleasant consequences.

to do otherwise. For instance, X's knee reflex was not a free action. If he had tried (chosen) not to move his leg when the doctor hit his knee, he would have failed. (Freedom as hypothetical behavior.)

2. one in which the agent had the power to decide and act otherwise. For instance, X's raising his hand when told to was not a free action. He was under hypnotic suggestion and even though he would not have raised his hand if he had chosen not to, he did not have the power to make this choice. (Freedom as power to do otherwise.)

3. one in which the agent could have been persuaded to act otherwise in the light of rational considerations which would make it reasonable to act otherwise. For instance, the neurotic's continual washing of his hands is not a free action. (Freedom as capacity for rational action.)

Libertarians and hard determinists protest that the freedom soft determinists offer us is a specious type of freedom that cannot support the judgments of moral responsibility that we make about human beings or assume that God will ultimately make. As libertarians see it, such judgments are justifiable precisely because human beings can transcend the hereditary and environmental factors that predispose but do not necessitate their actions. While a knowledge of the laws of human psychology and physiology can enable us to make predictions as to what an individual is likely to do, it is in principle impossible for science to tell us what an individual definitely will do, if he is acting freely, libertarians assert. As hard determinists see it, on the other hand, the judgments of moral responsibility we make about people and the attitudes of resentment and righteous indignation that we naturally feel toward wrongdoers are a function of our ignorance as to the causes of human behavior. Once we realize that people's behavior can be traced back to hereditary and environmental causes belonging to a world they had no part in making, it becomes apparent that there is no distinction that can be made between free and unfree actions that can sustain the moral weight it is made to bear when we hold individuals morally responsible or unresponsible for their actions, hard determinists contend. While there can be a practical justification for holding some individuals morally accountable for their actions as a way of affecting their future behavior, if we put aside any practical concerns about the future and simply try to rank individuals in terms of their moral responsibility for their actions, as many people believe God ultimately will do, we will find that the distinction between free and unfree acts must be meaningless to an all-knowing God who can grasp the full network of causes that serve to explain why individuals behave as they do. For such a being, the feelings of righteous indignation and resentment that we so naturally feel toward those whom we perceive to have freely acted wrongly must be replaced by an understanding that transcends such feelings and makes it impossible to rank people in terms of their relative moral worth. At the highest level of moral development, the notion of a type of divine justice which dispenses rewards and punishments to individuals in accordance with their moral deserts must be seen as unintelligible, hard determinists argue. This claim is in turn hotly challenged by soft determinists and libertarians, who see the notion of moral desert in a different light.

As you ponder the various defenses of the hard deterministic, soft deterministic, and libertarian viewpoints that follow this introduction, you may conclude that every position has its strengths and weaknesses, finding yourself pulled first one way and then another by what you read, unable to come to any firm resolution of the issues involved. Such is often the case with perennial philosophical questions that have been debated through the ages by the best of philosophers, without any ultimate resolution. Perhaps, in the last analysis, wisdom in this issue comes with the realization that judgments about whether or not people acted freely or were morally responsible or morally blameworthy for their actions are made from varying moral perspectives, reflecting different human concerns and attitudes. Furthermore, it may be that no single perspective can be picked out as the uniquely correct approach to this vexing problem, a problem whose solution has profound practical bearings on the very attitude we assume toward human beings and especially toward criminals. Is the traditional legal and religious picture of human beings as free and morally responsible persons who deserve moral praise or blame for their actions compatible with the scientific picture of human actions as completely subject to deterministic laws of nature? What meaning are you attributing to the notions of freedom and moral responsibility in your answer to the preceding question? Stop and reflect upon your answers to both of these questions now and reconsider the adequacy of your answers after you have read the various selections.

48. AN ATTORNEY'S HARD DETERMINISTIC PLEA FOR THE LIVES OF TWO MURDERERS

Clarence Darrow

(For a biographical sketch of Clarence Darrow, see Selection #22.)

The following selection is an excerpt from Darrow's summation to the jury in his famous defense of Nathan Leopold, Jr., eighteen, and Richard Loeb, seventeen, the two confessed kidnappers and murderers of fourteen-year-old Bobby Franks in Chicago in 1924. The Leopold-Loeb trial was a sensational one that captured the interest of the entire nation and was attended by many representatives of the press. The Chicago newspapers and many others throughout the United States printed in full or in part Darrow's more then twelve-hour plea that Leopold and Loeb be spared the death penalty.

Leopold and Loeb, both from wealthy Chicago families, were brilliant students who had the distinction of being the youngest graduates of the Universities of Chicago and Michigan. In order to demonstrate their contempt for conventional morality, the two planned to commit "the perfect crime." Their attempt proved flawed, however, and captured, they confessed. The state demanded the death penalty, while the attorney for the defense, Clarence Darrow, already famous for his defense of unpopular causes, pleaded that the killers' lives be spared. Darrow's plea proved successful and the defendants were sentenced to life imprisonment. (Indeed, is is said that Darrow's passionate plea for mercy was so effective that tears were streaming down the judge's face as Darrow finished his plea.) Over and over again in his summation, Darrow, arguing from a hard deterministic perspective, implored that Leopold and Loeb were helpless victims of hereditary and environmental forces they did not choose, but which, nevertheless, molded them into the murderers that they became. (Loeb was killed in prison 12 years after his sentence to life imprisonment; Leopold was released on parole in 1958, married in 1961, and died in 1971.)

I have tried to study the lives of these two most unfortunate boys. Three months ago, if their friends and the friends of the family had been asked to pick out the most promising lads of their acquaintance, they probably would have picked these two boys. With every opportunity, with plenty of wealth, they would have said that those two would succeed.

In a day, by an act of madness, all this is destroyed. . . .

How did it happen?

Let us take Dickie Loeb first.

I do not claim to know how it happened; I have sought to find out. I know that something, or some combination of things, is responsible for this mad act. I know that there are no accidents in nature. I know that effect follows cause. I know that, if I were wise enough, and knew enough about this case, I could lay my finger on the cause. I will do the best I can, but it is largely speculation.

The child, of course, is born without knowledge.

Impressions are made upon its mind as it goes along. Dickie Loeb was a child of wealth and opportunity. Over and over in this court Your Honor has been asked, and other courts have been asked, to consider boys who have no chance; they have been asked to consider the poor, whose home had been the street, with no education and no opportunity in life, and they have done it, and done it rightfully.

But, Your Honor, it is just as often a great misfortune to be the child of the rich as it is to be the child of the poor. Wealth has its misfortunes. Too much, too great opportunity and advantage, given to a child has its misfortunes. . . .

Can I find what was wrong [in this case]? I think I can. Here was a boy at a tender age, placed in the hands of a governess, intellectual, vigorous, devoted, with a strong ambition for the welfare of this boy. He was pushed in his studies, as plants are forced in hothouses. He had no pleasures, such as a boy should have, except as they were gained by lying and cheating.

Now, I am not criticizing the nurse. I suggest that some day Your Honor look at her picture. It explains her fully. Forceful, brooking no interference, she loved the boy, and her ambition was that he should reach the highest perfection. No time to pause, no time to stop from one book to another, no time to have those pleasures which a boy ought to have to create a normal life. And what happened? Your Honor, what would happen? Nothing strange or unusual. This nurse was with him all the time, except when he stole out at night, from two to fourteen years of age. He, scheming and planning as healthy boys would do, to get out from under her restraint; she, putting before him the best books, which children generally do not want; and he, when she was not looking, reading detective stories, which he devoured, story after story, in his young life. Of all this there can be no question.

What is the result? Every story he read was a story of crime. We have a statute in this state, passed only last year, if I recall it, which forbids minors reading stories of crime. Why? There is only one reason. Because the legislature in its wisdom felt that it would produce criminal tendencies in the boys who read them. The legislature of this state has given its opinion, and forbidden boys to read these books. He read them day after day. He never stopped. While he was passing through college at Ann Arbor he was still reading them. . . .

Now, these facts are beyond dispute. He early developed the tendency to mix with crime, to be a detective; as a little boy shadowing people on the street; as a little child going out with his fantasy of being the head of a band of criminals and directing them on the street. How did

Source: From Clarence Darrow, "The Crime of Compulsion," in *Attorney for the Damned,* edited by Arthur Weinberg,

this grow and develop in him? Let us see. It seems to be as natural as the day following the night. Every detective story is a story of a sleuth getting the best of it: trailing some unfortunate individual through devious ways until his victim is finally landed in jail or stands on the gallows. They all show how smart the detective is, and where the criminal himself falls down.

This boy early in his life conceived the idea that there could be a perfect crime, one that nobody could ever detect; that there could be one where the detective did not land his game—a perfect crime. He had been interested in the story of Charley Ross, who was kidnapped. He was interested in these things all his life. He believed in his childish way that a crime could be so carefully planned that there would be no detection, and his idea was to plan and accomplish a perfect crime. It would involve kidnapping and involve murder. . . .

There had been growing in Dickie's brain, dwarfed and twisted—as every act in this case shows it to have been dwarfed and twisted—there had been growing this scheme, not due to any wickedness of Dickie Loeb, for he is a child. It grew as he grew; it grew from those around him; it grew from the lack of the proper training until it possessed him. He believed he could beat the police. He believed he could plan the perfect crime. He had thought of it and talked of it for years—had talked of it as a child, had worked at it as a child—this sorry act of his, utterly irrational and motiveless, a plan to commit a perfect crime which must contain kidnaping, and there must be ransom, or else it could not be perfect, and they must get the money. . . .

The law knows and has recognized childhood for many and many a long year [as an excuse for criminal responsibility]. What do we know of childhood? The brain of the child is the home of dreams, of castles, of illusions and of delusions. . . .

The whole life of childhood is a dream and an illusion, and whether they take one shape or another shape depends not upon the dreamy boy but on what surrounds him. As well might I have dreamed of burglars and wished to be one as to dream of policemen and wished to be one. Perhaps I was lucky, too, that I had no money. We have grown to think that the misfortune is in not having it. The great misfortune in this terrible case is the money. That has destroyed their lives. That has fostered these illusions. That has promoted this mad act. And, if Your Honor shall doom them to die, it will be because they are the sons of the rich. . . .

I know where my life has been molded by books, amongst other things. We all know where our lives have been influenced by books. The nurse, strict and jealous and watchful, gave him one kind of book; by night he would steal off and read the other.

Which, think you, shaped the life of Dickie Loeb? Is there any kind of question about it? A child. Was it pure maliciousness? Was a boy of five or six or seven to blame for it? Where did he get it? He got it where we all get our ideas, and these books became a part of his dreams and a part of his life, and as he grew up his visions grew to hallucinations. . . .

Suppose, Your Honor, that instead of this boy being here in this court, under the plea of the State that Your Honor shall pronounce a sentence to hang him by the neck until dead, he had been taken to a pathological hospital to be analyzed, and the physicians had inquired into his case. What would they have said? There is only one thing that they could possibly have said. They would have traced everything back to the gradual growth of the child. . . .

Where is the man who has not been guilty of delinquencies in youth? Let us be honest with ourselves. Let us look into our own hearts. How many men are there today—lawyers and congressmen and judges, and even state's attorneys—who have not been guilty of some mad act in youth? And if they did not get caught, or the consequences were trivial, it was their good fortune.

We might as well be honest with ourselves, Your Honor. Before I would tie a noose around the neck of a boy I would try to call back into my mind the emotions of youth. I would try to remember what the world looked like to me when I was a child. I would try to remember how strong were these instinctive, persistent emotions that moved my life. I would try to remember how weak and inefficient was youth in the presence of the surging, controlling feelings of the child. One that honestly remembers and asks himself the question and tries to unlock the door that he thinks is closed, and calls back the boy, can understand the boy.

But, Your Honor, that is not all there is to boyhood. Nature is strong and she is pitiless. She works in her own mysterious way, and we are her victims. We have not much to do with it ourselves. Nature takes this job in hand, and we play our parts. In the words of old Omar Khayyam, we are only:

But helpless pieces in the game He plays
Upon this checkerboard of nights and days;
Hither and thither moves, and checks, and slays,
And one by one back in the closet lays.

What had this boy to do with it? He was not his own father; he was not his own mother; he was not his own grandparents. All of this was handed to him. He did not surround himself with governesses and wealth. He did not make himself. And yet he is to be compelled to pay. . . .

Your Honor, I am almost ashamed to talk about it. I can hardly imagine that we are in the twentieth century. And yet there are men who seriously say that for what nature has done, for what life has done, for what training has done, you should hang these boys.

Now, there is no mystery about this case. Your Honor. I seem to be criticizing their parents. They had parents who were kind and good and wise in their way. But I say to you seriously that the parents are more responsible than these boys. And yet few boys had better parents.

Your Honor, it is the easiest thing in the world to be a parent. We talk of motherhood, and yet every woman can be a mother. We talk of fatherhood, and yet every man can be a father. Nature takes care of that. It is easy to be a parent. But to be wise and farseeing enough to understand the boy is another thing; only a very few are so wise and so farseeing as that. When I think of the light way nature has of picking our parents and populating the earth, having them born and die, I cannot hold human beings to the same degree of responsibility that young lawyers hold them when they are enthusiastic in a prosecution. I know what it means.

I know there are no better citizens in Chicago than the fathers of these poor boys. I know there were no better women than their mothers. But I am going to be honest with this court, if it is at the expense of both. I know that one of two things happened to Richard Loeb: that this terrible crime was inherent in his organism, and came from some ancestor; or that it came through his education and his training after he was born. . . .

To believe that any boy is responsible for himself or his early training is an absurdity that no lawyer or judge should be guilty of today. Somewhere this came to the boy. If his failing came from his heredity. I do not know where or how. None of us are bred perfect and pure; and the color of our hair, the color of our eyes, our stature, the weight and fineness of our brain, and everything about us could, with full knowledge, be traced with absolute certainty to somewhere. If we had the pedigree it could be traced just the same in a boy as it could in a dog, a horse or a cow.

I do not know what remote ancestors may have sent down the seed that corrupted him, and I do not know through how many ancestors it may have passed until it reached Dickie Loeb.

All I know is that it is true, and there is not a biologist in the world who will not say that I am right.

If it did not come that way, then I know that if he was normal, if he had been understood, if he had been trained as he should have been it would not have happened. Not that anybody may not slip, but I know it and Your Honor knows it, and every schoolhouse and every church in the land is an evidence of it. Else why build them?

Every effort to protect society is an effort toward training the youth to keep the path. Every bit of training in the world proves it, and it likewise proves that it sometimes fails. I know that if this boy had been understood and properly trained—properly for him—and the training that he got might have been the very best for someone; but if it had been the proper training for him he would not be in this courtroom today with the noose above his head. If there is responsibility anywhere, it is back of him; somewhere in the infinite number of his ancestors, or in his surroundings, or in both. And I submit, Your Honor, that under every principle of natural justice, under every principle of conscience, of right, and of law, he should not be made responsible for the acts of someone else. . . .

DISCUSSION QUESTIONS

1. Darrow claims that the idea of committing a perfect crime grew in Loeb's mind "until it possessed him." What does it mean to speak of a person being "possessed" by an idea or some psychological state? What sort of evidence would be required to establish that a person is so possessed? On the basis of Darrow's remarks in the preceding selection, do you believe that Darrow had such evidence in this case? Does the fact that a person is so possessed always relieve him of responsibility for actions that stem from his being so possessed?

2. Darrow writes:

> What has this boy to do with it. . . . He did not make himself and yet he is to be compelled to pay.

What does Darrow mean by "He did not make himself?" What, if anything, would Darrow count as an instance of a person making himself?

3. Speaking of Loeb, Darrow pleads:

> If there is responsibility anywhere, it is back of him; somewhere in the infinite number of his ancestors, or in his surroundings, or in both. And I submit, Your Honor, that under every principle of natural justice . . . he should not be made responsible for the acts of someone else.

Can Darrow consistently place responsibility for Loeb's crime on his ancestors? Do you think that Darrow believes that responsibility ultimately can be placed anywhere? If so, where? If not, why? Do you agree? Why? What do you take the notion of "responsibility" to mean?

4. According to Darrow's reasoning, is there anything special about Loeb's background that makes him more deserving of being exempted from responsibility than other criminals?

5. If one accepts Darrow's view of responsibility, can a plausible case be made for maintaining the death penalty? What justification, if any, do you see for the death penalty?

6. In criticism of Darrow's position, the philosopher Sidney Hook writes:

> The belief that because men are determined they cannot be morally responsible is a mistaken one. Not only is it a mistaken belief, it is a mischievous one. For far from diminishing the amount of needless suffering and cruelty in the world, it is quite certain to increase it. It justifies the infamous dictum of Smerdyakov in **The Brothers Karamazov**: "All things are permissible," if only one can get away with them. One of the commonest experiences of teachers, if not parents, is to observe young men and women whose belief that they can't help doing what they are doing, or failing to do, is often an excuse for not doing as well as they can do, or at the very least better than they are at present doing. When we have, as we often do, independent evidence that

they are capable of doing better, is it so absurd to hold them at least partly responsible for not doing better? Do we not know from our own experience that our belief that we are responsible, or that we will be held responsible, enables us to do things which had previously seemed beyond our power?[1]

What do you think Darrow would say in reply? What do you think?

[1]Sidney Hook, "Moral Freedom in a Determined World" in his *The Quest for Being* (New York: St. Martins Press, 1961), pp. 45-46. Hook expresses the same point of view in his essay "Necessity, Indeterminism and Sentimentalism," in *Determinism and Freedom in the Age of Modern Science*, ed. Sidney Hook (New York: Collier Books, 1958), p. 191.

49. A CONTEMPORARY PHILOSOPHER'S DEFENSE OF HARD DETERMINISM

John Hospers

JOHN HOSPERS (1918–) is presently the chair of the philosophy department at the University of Southern California. He is the author of numerous articles on philosophy, primarily on topics in the fields of ethics and aesthetics. His two popular introductory philosophy texts, **An Introduction to Philsophical Analysis** and **Human Conduct,** are noted for their clarity and engaging style.

The following selection is from Hospers' widely reprinted article, "What Means This Freedom," which presents a more sophisticated defense of hard determinism than that found in the preceding selection from Darrow. Willing to admit that for practical purposes we must hold individuals responsible for their actions, Hospers claims that when we reflect more deeply about the determinants of behavior, we realize that in a deeper sense people are never morally responsible for their actions. Although those of us who are good like to look down upon wrongdoers from a position of moral superiority, believing them to be proper recipients of our moral feelings of righteous indignation and resentment, such feelings, Hospers claims, are out of place on deeper-level reflection. Since determinism is true, there is a causal chain stretching from conditions that existed before our birth to our present characters and present choices. This means that if we go back far enough we will find our characters to be causally determined by conditions over which we had no control. Thoughtful persons, Hospers contends, once recognizing this fact, will find feelings of moral superiority out of place. In making this claim, Hospers echoes the famous French saying "tout comprendre, tout pardonner" (i.e, to understand all is to forgive all).

We Are Not Responsible for Actions that Are Unconsciously Motivated

. . . There are many actions—not those of an insane person (however the term ''insane'' be defined), nor of a person ignorant of the effects of his action, nor ignorant of some relevant fact about the situation, nor in any obvious way mentally deranged—for which human beings in general and the courts in particular are inclined to hold the doer responsible, and for which, I would say, he should not be held responsible. The deed may be planned, it may be carried out in cold calculation, it may spring from the agent's character and be continuous with the rest of his behavior, and it may be perfectly true that he could have done differently *if* he had wanted to; nonetheless his behavior was brought about by unconscious conflicts developed in infancy, over which he had no control and of which (without training in psychiatry) he does not even have knowledge. He may even *think* he knows why he acted as he did, he may *think* he has conscious control over his actions, he may even *think* he is fully responsible for them; but he is not. Psychiatric casebooks provide hundreds of examples. The law and common sense, though puzzled sometimes by such cases, are gradually becoming aware that they exist; but at this early stage countless tragic blunders still occur because neither the law nor the public in general is aware of the genesis of criminal actions. The mother blames her daughter for choosing the wrong men as candidates for husbands; but though the daughter thinks she is choosing freely and spends a considerable amount of time ''deciding'' among them, the identification with her sick father, resulting from Oedipal fantasies in early childhood, prevents her from caring for any but sick men, twenty or thirty years older than herself. Blaming her is beside the point; she cannot help it, and she cannot change it. Countless criminal acts are thought out in great detail; yet the participants are (without their own knowledge) acting out fantasies, fears, and defenses from early childhood, over whose coming and going they have no conscious control . . . .

Source: John Hospers, ''What Means This Freedom,'' in *Determinism and Freedom in the Age of Modern Science*, ed. Sidney Hook (New York: Collier Books, 1958). Reprinted by permission of New York University Press, the publisher of the hardcover edition of the book and holder of the copyright.

In a Deep Sense, No One Is Ever Morally Responsible, Since No One Chooses His Character

. . . [Even if an action is not unconsciously motivated], there remains a question in our minds whether we are, in the final analysis, *responsible for any of our actions at all*. The issue may be put this way: How can anyone be responsible for his actions, since they grow out of his character, which is shaped and molded and made what it is by influences—some hereditary, but most of them stemming from early parental environment—that were not of his own making or choosing? This question, I believe, still troubles many people . . . .

They have the uneasy suspicion that there is a more ultimate sense, a ''deeper'' sense, in which we are *not* responsible for our actions, since we are not responsible for the character out of which those actions spring . . . .

Let us take as an example a criminal who, let us say, strangled several persons and is himself now condemned to die in the electric chair. Jury and public alike hold him fully responsible . . . for the murders were planned down to the minutest detail, and the defendant tells the jury exactly how he planned them. But now we find out how it all came about; we learn of parents who rejected him from babyhood, of the childhood spent in one foster home after another, where it was always plain to him that he was not wanted; of the constantly frustrated early desire for affection, the hard shell of nonchalance and bitterness that he assumed to cover the painful and humiliating fact of being unwanted, and his subsequent attempts to heal these wounds to his shattered ego through defensive aggression . . . . The poor victim is not conscious of the inner forces that exact from him this ghastly toll; he battles, he schemes, he revels in pseudo-aggression, he is miserable, but he does not know what works within him to produce these catastrophic acts of crime. His aggressive actions are the wriggling of a worm on a fisherman's hook. And if this is so, it seems difficult to say any longer, "He is responsible." Rather, we shall put him behind bars for the protection of society, but we shall no longer flatter our feeling of moral superiority by calling him personally responsible for what he did.

Let us suppose it were established that a man commits murder only if, sometime during the previous week, he has eaten a certain combination of foods—say, tuna fish salad at a meal also including peas, mushroom soup, and blueberry pie. What if we were to track down the factors common to all murders committed in this country during the last twenty years and found this factor present in all of them, and only in them? The example is of course empirically absurd; but may it not be that there is *some* combination of factors that regularly leads to homicide. . . . When such specific factors are discovered, won't they make it clear that it is foolish and pointless, as well as immoral, to hold human beings responsible for crimes? Or, if one prefers biological to psychological factors, suppose a neurologist is called in to testify at a murder trial and produces X-ray pictures of the brain of the criminal; anyone can see, he argues, that the *cella turcica* was already calcified at the age of nineteen; it should be a a flexible bone, growing, enabling the gland to grow. All the defendant's disorders might have resulted from this early calcification. Now, this particular explanation may be empirically false; but who can say that no such factors, far more complex, to be sure, exist?

When we know such things as these, we no longer feel so much tempted to say that the criminal is responsible for his crime; and we tend also (do we not?) to excuse him—not legally (we still confine him to prison) but morally; we no longer call him a monster or hold him personally responsible for what he did. Moreover, we do this in general, not merely in the case of crime: "You must excuse Grandmother for being irritable; she's really quite ill and is suffering some pain all the time." Or: "The dog always bites children after she's had a litter of pups; you can't blame her for it: she's not feeling well, and besides she naturally wants to defend them." Or: "She's nervous and jumpy, but do excuse her: she has a severe glandular disturbance."

Let us note that the more *thoroughly* and *in detail* we know the causal factors leading a person to behave as he does, the more we tend to exempt him from responsibility. When we know nothing of the man except what we see him do, we say he is an ungrateful cad who expects much of other people and does nothing in return, and we are usually indignant. When we learn that his parents were the same way and, having no guilt feelings about this mode of behavior themselves, brought him up to be greedy and avaricious, we see that we could hardly expect him to have developed moral feelings in this direction. When we learn, in addition, that he is not aware of being ungrateful or selfish, but unconsciously represses the memory of events unfavorable to himself, we feel that the situation is unfortunate but "not really his fault." When we know that this behavior of his, which makes others angry, occurs more constantly when he feels tense or insecure, and that he now feels tense and insecure, and that relief from pressure will diminish it, then we tend to "feel sorry for the poor guy'' and say he's more to be pitied than censured. We no longer want to say that he is personally responsible; we might rather blame nature or his parents for having given him an unfortunate constitution or temperament . . . .

And so, it would now appear, neither of the parties is responsible: ''they acted as their neurotic difficulties forced them to act.'' The patients are not responsible for their neurotic manifestations, but then neither are the parents responsible for theirs; and so, of course, for their parents in turn, and theirs before them . . . .

''But,'' a critic complains, ''it's immoral to exonerate people indiscriminately in this way. I might have thought it fit to excuse somebody because he was born on the other side of the tracks, if I didn't know so many bank presidents who were also born on the other side of the tracks.'' Now, I submit that the most immoral thing in this situation is the critic's caricature of the conditions of the excuse. Nobody is excused merely because he was born on the other side of the tracks. But if he was born on the other side of the tracks *and* was a highly narcissistic infant to begin with *and* was repudiated or neglected by his parents *and* . . . (here we list a finite number of conditions), and if this complex of factors is *regularly* followed by certain behavior traits in adulthood, and moreover *unavoidably* so—that is, they occur no matter what he or anyone else tries to do—then we excuse him morally and say he is not responsible for his deed. If he is not responsible for *A*, a series of events occurring in his babyhood, then neither is he responsible for *B*, a series of things he does in adulthood, provided that *B*, inevitably—that is, unavoidably—follows upon the occurrence of *A*. And according to psychiatrists and psychoanalysts, this often happens.

But one may still object that so far we have talked only about neurotic behavior. Isn't nonneurotic or normal or not unconsciously motivated (or whatever you want to call it) behavior still within the area of responsibility? There are reasons for answering ''No'' even here, for the normal person no more than the neurotic one has caused his own character, which makes him what he is. Granted that neurotics are not responsible for their behavior (that part of it which we call neurotic) because it stems from undigested infantile conflicts that they had no part in bringing about, and that are external to them just as surely as if their behavior had been forced on them by a malevolent deity (which is indeed one theory on the subject); but the so-called normal person is equally the product of causes in which his volition took no part. And if, unlike the neurotic's, his behavior is changeable by rational considerations, and if he has the will power to overcome the effects of an unfortunate early environment, this again is no credit to him; he is just lucky. If energy is available to him in a form in which it can be mobilized for constructive purposes, this is no credit to him, for this too is part of his psychic legacy. Those of us who can discipline ourselves and develop habits of concentration of purpose tend to blame those who cannot, and call them lazy and weak-willed; but what we fail to see is that they literally *cannot* do what we expect . . . . We cannot with justification blame them for their inability, any more than we can congratulate ourselves for our ability. This lesson is hard to learn, for we constantly and naïvely assume that other people are constructed as we ourselves are . . . .

But, one persists, it isn't a matter simply of luck; it *is* a matter of effort. Very well then, it's a matter of effort; without exerting the effort you may not overcome the deficiency. But whether or not you are the kind of person who has it in him to exert the effort is a matter of luck.

All this is well known to psychoanalysts. They can predict, from minimal cues that most of us don't notice, whether a person is going to turn out to be lucky or not. ''The analyst,'' they say, ''must be able to use the residue of the patient's unconscious guilt so as to remove the symptom or character trait that creates the guilt. The guilt must not only be present, but *available* for use, *mobilizable*. If it is used up (absorbed) in criminal activity, or in an excessive amount of self-damaging tendencies, then it cannot be used for therapeutic purposes, and the prognosis is negative.'' Not all philosophers will relish the analyst's way of putting the matter, but at least as a physician he can soon detect whether the patient is lucky or unlucky—and he knows that whichever it is, it *isn't the patient's fault*. The patient's conscious volition cannot remedy the deficiency. Even whether he will co-operate with the analyst is really out of the patient's hands: if he continually projects the denying-mother fantasy on the analyst and unconsciously identifies him always with the cruel, harsh forbidder of the nursery, thus frustrating any attempt at impersonal observation, the sessions are useless; yet if it happens that way, he can't help that either. That fatal projection is not under his control; whether it occurs or not depends on how his unconscious identifications have developed since his infancy. He can try, yes—but the ability to try enough for the therapy to have effect is also beyond his control; the capacity to try more than just so much is either there or it isn't—and either way ''it's in the lap of the gods.''

The position, then, is this: if we *can* overcome the effects of early environment, the ability to do so is itself a product of the early environment. We did not give ourselves this ability; and if we lack it we cannot be blamed for not having it. Sometimes, to be sure, moral exhortation brings out an ability that is there but not being used, and in this lies its *occasional* utility; but very often its use is pointless, because the ability is not there. The only thing that can overcome a desire, as Spinoza said, is a stronger contrary desire; and many times there simply is no wherewithal for producing a stronger contrary desire. Those of us who do have the wherewithal are lucky.

There is one possible practical advantage in remembering this. It may prevent us (unless we are compulsive blamers) from indulging in righteous indignation and committing the sin of spiritual pride, thanking God that we are not as this publican here. And it will protect from our useless moralizings those who are least equipped by nature for enduring them. As with responsibility, so with deserts. Someone commits a crime and is punished by the state; ''he deserved it,'' we say self-righteously—as if we were moral and he immoral, when in fact we are lucky and he is unlucky—forgetting that there, but for the grace of God and a fortunate early environment, go we. . . .

The Two Levels of Moral Discourse

I want to make it quite clear that I have not been arguing for determinism. Though I find it difficult to give any sense to the term ''indeterminism,'' because I do not know what it would be like to come across an uncaused event, let us grant indeterminists everything they want, at least in words—influences that suggest but do not constrain, a measure of acausality in an otherwise rigidly causal order, and so on—whatever these phrases may mean. With all this granted, exactly the same situation faces the indeterminist and the determinist; all we have been saying would still hold true. ''Are our powers innate or acquired?''

> Suppose the powers are declared innate; then the villain may sensibly ask whether he is responsible for what he was born with. A negative reply is inevitable. Are they then acquired? Then the ability to acquire them—was *that* innate? or acquired? It is innate? Very well then. . . .

The same fact remains—that we did not cause our characters, that the influences that made us what we are are influences over which we had no control and of whose very existence we had no knowledge at the time. This fact remains for "determinism" and "indeterminism" alike. . . .

"But," it may be asked, "isn't it your view that nothing ultimately *could* be other than it is? And isn't this deterministic? And isn't it deterministic if you say that human beings could never act otherwise than they do, and that their desires and temperaments could not, when you consider their antecedent conditions, be other than they are?"

I reply that all these charges rest on confusions.

1. To say that nothing *could* be other than it is, is, taken literally, nonsense; and if taken as a way of saying something else, misleading and confusing. If you say, "I can't do it," this invites the question, "No? Not even if you want to?" "Can" and "could" are power words, used in the context of human action; when applied to nature they are merely anthropomorphic. "Could" has no application to nature—unless, of course, it is uttered in a theological context: one might say that God *could* have made things different. But with regard to inanimate nature "could" has no meaning. . . .

2. What of the charge that we could never have acted otherwise than we did? This, I submit, is simply not true. Here the exponents of . . . "soft determinism" are quite right. I could have gone to the opera today instead of coming here; that is, if certain conditions had been different, I should have gone. I could have done many other things instead of what I did, if some condition or other had been different, specifically if my desire had been different. I repeat that "could" is a power word, and "I could have done this" means approximately "I *should* have done this *if* I had wanted to." In this sense, all of us could often have done otherwise than we did. I would not want to say that I should have done differently even if *all* the conditions leading up to my action had been the same (this is generally not what we mean by "could" anyway); but to assert that I could have is empty, for if I *did* act different from the time before, we would automatically say that one or more of the conditions were different, whether we had independent evidence for this or not, thus rendering the assertion immune to empirical refutation. . . .

3. Well, then, could we ever have, not acted, but *desired* otherwise than we did desire? This gets us once again to the heart of the matter we were discussing in the previous section. Russell said, "We can do as we please but we can't please as we please." But I am persuaded that even this statement conceals a fatal mistake. Let us follow the same analysis through. "I could have done *X*" means "I should have done *X* if I had wanted to." "I could have wanted *X*" by the same analysis would mean "I should have wanted *X* if I had wanted to"—which seems to make no sense at all. (What does Russell want? To please as he doesn't please?)

What does this show? It shows, I think, that the only meaningful context of "can" and "could have" is that of *action*. "Could have acted differently" makes sense; "could have desired differently," as we have just seen, does not. Because a word or phrase makes good sense in one context, let us not assume that it does so in another.

I conclude . . . with the following suggestion: that we operate on two levels of moral discourse, which we shouldn't confuse; one (let's call it the upper level) is that of actions; the other (the lower, or deeper, level) is that of the springs of action. Most moral talk occurs on the upper level. . . . As we have just seen, "can" and "could" acquire their meaning on this level; so, I suspect, does "freedom.". . . [and the various senses of "responsibility" we use in practical circumstances to distinguish those who should and should not be held responsible for their actions]. All these distinctions are perfectly valid on this level . . . of moral discourse; and it is, after all, the usual one—we are practical beings interested in changing the course of human behavior, so it is natural enough that 99 per cent of our moral talk occurs here.

But when we descend to what I have called the lower level of moral discourse, as we occasionally do in thoughtful moments when there is no immediate need for action, then we must admit that we are ultimately the kind of persons we are because of conditions occurring outside us, over which we had no control. But while this is true, we should beware of extending the moral terminology we used on the other level to this one also. ''Could'' and ''can,'' as we have seen, no longer have meaning here. . . .I suspect that the same is true of ''responsibility,'' for now that we have recalled often forgotten facts about our being the product of outside forces, we must ask in all seriousness what would be added by saying that we are not *responsible* for our own characters and temperaments. What would it mean even? Has it a significant opposite? What would it be like to be responsible for one's own character? What possible situation is describable by this phrase? Instead of saying that it is *false* that we are responsible for our own characters, I should prefer to say that the utterance is meaningless—meaningless in the sense that it describes no possible situation, though it *seems* to because the word ''responsible'' is the same one we used on the upper level, where it marks a real distinction. If this is so, the result is that *moral* terms—at least the terms ''could have'' and ''responsible''—simply drop out on the lower level. What remains, shorn now of moral terminology, is the point we tried to bring out in Part II: whether or not we have personality disturbances, whether or not we have the ability to overcome deficiencies of early environment, is like the answer to the question whether or not we shall be struck down by a dread disease: ''it's all a matter of luck.'' It is important to keep this in mind, for people almost always forget it, with consequences in human intolerance and unnecessary suffering that are incalculable.

DISCUSSION QUESTIONS

1. Do you agree with Hospers that "the more thoroughly and in detail we know the causal factors leading a person to behave as he does, the more we tend to exempt him from responsibility"? Is this a reasonable **private attitude** to take? Should our **response** to people reflect this attitude?

2. Is Hospers right that if "some combination of factors regularly leads to homicide," it is "pointless, as well as immoral, to hold human beings responsible for crimes?" In what relevant respects, if any, are the causes of most criminal actions unlike the fanciful examples Hospers gives of the possible causal connection between eating a certain combination of foods and committing murder?

3. What reason does Hospers offer in justification of his claim that even when an individual can, through some personal effort, alter a personality deficiency or refrain from an action that stems from that personality deficiency, he is still not morally responsible for not making that effort? Do you agree? Why, or why not? If you do agree, would you, nevertheless, want to draw a moral distinction between such individuals and those who are incapable through any "act of will" from acting otherwise or altering a personality deficiency? If so, how would you draw this distinction?

4. What do you think Hospers would say in reply to Hook's criticism of the hard deterministic point of view? (See question 6 of the preceding selection.)

5. Critically consider the plausibility of Hosper's remark that " . . . I find it difficult to give any sense to the term 'indeterminism,' because I do not know what it would be like to come across an uncaused event." Do you believe that "free acts" or "free choices" must be undetermined or do you think they must be determined (i.e., caused) in a particular way. (Reconsider this question after reading the remainder of the selections in this chapter.)

6. According to Hospers, what does it mean to claim that "X could have acted otherwise"? Do you see any difficulties with this analysis?

7. What reason does Hospers give for dismissing as meaningless Russell's claim that "We can do as

we please but we can't please as we please"? Do you agree? Why? If you disagree, what meaning do you attribute to this claim? Is it true?

8. Why does Hospers claim at the end of the preceding selection that the notion of "responsibility" has no meaning in the lower level of moral discourse? Is the notion of "it's all a matter of luck" any more meaningful, as Hospers employs it at this level of discourse, than the notion of "responsibility" he believes has no place here? If not, what are we to make of what he is claiming?

50. THE FREE WILL-DETERMINISM ISSUE IS A PSEUDOPROBLEM

Moritz Schlick

MORITZ SCHLICK (1882–1936) was born in Germany and shot to death in Vienna by a deranged graduate student to whom he had denied a doctoral degree. At the age of twenty-two, Schlick received his doctorate in physics from the University of Berlin, under the supervision of the famous physicist Max Planck. Schlick's interests turned, however, to philosophical questions concerning the nature of knowledge in general, and scientific knowledge in particular. After his appointment in 1922 to a chair in philosophy at the University of Vienna, Schlick soon became a central figure in **The Vienna Circle,** a group of philosophers and scientists that gathered in Vienna in the 1920's to discuss philosophy. It was this group of thinkers who began the philosophical movement that came to be called **logical positivism.** The unifying belief of the logical positivists was that the meanings of statements should be identified when their method of empirical verification, a view whose roots can be found in David Hume. Believing that many philosophical claims (e.g., the claim that God exists) were incapable of empirical verification, the positivists claimed that these statements were actually meaningless. As one would expect, such contentions created quite a stir.

In our selection, Schlick defends the classical Hume-Mill soft deterministic analysis of freedom as lack of compulsion. Schlick is more concerned, however, to reveal what he sees as the confusions which generate the mistaken belief that determinism is incompatible with human freedom. (The belief that many traditional philosophical problems were **pseudoproblems** brought about by a confused use of language or by muddled thinking was central to the logical positivist philosophy.) As Schlick sees it, the main source of this confusion is the mistaken assimilation of laws of psychological science to legal laws. Whereas the latter can serve to compel our actions, the former do not compel our actions but simply describe the psychological factors on the basis of which we regularly choose to act, Schlick asserts.

The Pseudoproblem of Freedom of the Will

With hesitation and reluctance I prepare to add this chapter to the discussion of ethical problems. For in it I must speak of a matter which, even at present, is thought to be a fundamental ethical problem, but which got into ethics and has become a much discussed problem only because of a misunderstanding. This is the so-called problem of the freedom of the will. Moreover, this pseudo-problem has long since been settled by the efforts of certain sensible persons; and, above all, the state of affairs just described has been often disclosed—with exceptional clarity by Hume. Hence it is really one of the greatest scandals of philosophy that again and again so much paper and printer's ink is devoted to this matter. . . . Thus I should truly be ashamed to write a chapter on "freedom." In the chapter heading, the word "responsible" indicates what concerns ethics, and designates the point at which misunderstanding arises. Therefore the concept of responsibility constitutes our theme, and if in the process of its clarification I must also speak of the concept of freedom I shall, of course, say only what others have already said better; consoling myself with the thought that in this way alone can anything be done to put an end at last to that scandal.

The main task of ethics is to explain moral behavior.[1] To explain means to refer back to laws: every science, including psychology, is possible only in so far as there are such laws to which the events can be referred. Since the assumption that all events are subject to universal laws is called the principle of causality, one can also say, "Every science presupposes the principle of causality." Therefore every explanation of human behavior must also assume the validity of causal laws; in this case the existence of psychological laws. All of our experience strengthens us in the belief that this presupposition is realized, at least to the extent required for all purposes of practical life in intercourse with nature and human beings, and also for the most precise demands of technique. Whether, indeed, the principle of causality holds universally, whether, that is, determinism is true, we do not know; no one knows. But we do know that it is impossible to settle the dispute between determinism and indeterminism by mere reflection and speculation. . . .

Fortunately, it is not necessary to lay claim to a final solution of the causal problem in order to say what is necessary in ethics concerning responsibility; there is required only an analysis of the concept, the careful determination of the meaning which is in fact joined to the words "responsibility" and "freedom," as these are actually used. If men had made clear to themselves the sense of these propositions, which we use in everyday life, that pseudo-argument which lies at the root of the pseudo-problem, and which recurs thousands of times within and outside philosophical books, would never have arisen.

The argument runs as follows: "If determinism is true, if, that is, all events obey immutable laws, then my will too is always determined, by my innate character and my motives. Hence my decisions are necessary, not free. But if so, then I am not responsible for my acts, for I would be accountable for them only if I could do something about the way my decisions went; but I can do nothing about it, since they proceed with necessity from my character and the motives. And I have made neither, and have no power over them: the motives come from with-

Source: From Moritz Schlick, *Problems of Ethics,* trans. David Rynin (New York: Dover Publications, 1962; English translation originally published in 1939 by Prentice-Hall, Inc.). Reprinted with the permission of David Rynin.

[1]Schlick was an emotivist who claimed that ethical assertions were noncognitive ones, making it impossible to view ethics as the *rational criticism* of ethical assertions. The proper task of ethics, as he saw it, was that of describing and explaining the value-ascribing forms of behavior that happen to exist among human beings. EDITOR'S NOTE.

out, and my character is the necessary product of the innate tendencies and the external influences which have been effective during my lifetime. Thus determinism and moral responsibility are incompatible. Moral responsibility presupposes freedom, that is, exemption from causality."

This process of reasoning rests upon a whole series of confusions, just as the links of a chain hang together. We must show these confusions to be such, and thus destroy them.

Two Meanings of the Word "Law"

It all begins with an erroneous interpretation of the meaning of "law." In practice this is understood as a rule by which the state prescribes certain behavior to its citizens. These rules often contradict the natural desires of the citizens (for if they did not do so, there would be no reason for making them), and are in fact not followed by many of them; while others obey, but under compulsion. The state does in fact compel its citizens by imposing certain sanctions (punishment) which serve to bring their desires into harmony with the prescribed laws.

In natural science, on the other hand, the word "law" means something quite different. The natural law is not a prescription as to how something should behave, but a formula, a description of how something does in fact behave. The two forms of "laws" have only this in common: both tend to be expressed in formulae. Otherwise they have absolutely nothing to do with one another, and it is very blameworthy that the same word has been used for two such different things; but even more so that philosophers have allowed themselves to be led into serious errors by this usage. Since natural laws are only descriptions of what happens, there can be in regard to them no talk of "compulsion." The laws of celestial mechanics do not prescribe to the planets how they have to move, as though the planets would actually like to move quite otherwise, and are only forced by these burdensome laws of Kepler to move in orderly paths; no, these laws do not in any way "compel" the planets, but express only what in fact planets actually do.

If we apply this to volition, we are enlightened at once, even before the other confusions are discovered. When we say that a man's will "obeys psychological laws," these are not civic laws, which compel him to make certain decisions, or dictate desires to him, which he would in fact prefer not to have. They are laws of nature, merely expressing which desires he actually has under given conditions; they describe the nature of the will in the same manner as the astronomical laws describe the nature of planets. "Compulsion" occurs where man is prevented from realizing his natural desires. How could the rule according to which these natural desires arise itself be considered as "compulsion"?

Compulsion and Necessity

But this is the second confusion to which the first leads almost inevitably: after conceiving the laws of nature, anthropomorphically, as order imposed *nolens volens*[2] upon the events, one adds to them the concept of "necessity." This word, derived from "need," also comes to us from practice, and is used there in the sense of inescapable compulsion. To apply the word with this meaning to natural laws is of course senseless, for the presupposition of an opposing desire is lacking, and it is then confused with something altogether different, which is actually an attribute of natural laws. That is, universality. It is of the essence of natural laws to be universally valid, for only when we have found a rule which holds of events without exception do we call the rule a law of nature. Thus when we say "a natural law holds necessarily" this has but

[2]Unwillingly. EDITOR'S NOTE.

one legitimate meaning: "It holds in all cases where it is applicable." It is again very deplorable that the word "necessary" has been applied to natural laws (or, what amounts to the same thing, with reference to causality), for it is quite superfluous, since the expression "universally valid" is available. Universal validity is something altogether different from "compulsion"; these concepts belong to spheres so remote from each other that once insight into the error has been gained one can no longer conceive the possibility of a confusion.

The confusion of two concepts always carries with it the confusion of their contradictory opposites. The opposite of the universal validity of a formula, of the existence of a law, is the nonexistence of a law, indeterminism, acausality; while the opposite of compulsion is what in practice everyone calls "freedom." Here emerges the nonsense, trailing through centuries, that freedom means "exemption from the causal principle," or "not subject to the laws of nature." Hence it is believed necessary to vindicate indeterminism in order to save human freedom.

Freedom and Indeterminism

This is quite mistaken. Ethics has, so to speak, no moral interest in the purely theoretical question of "determinism or indeterminism," but only a theoretical interest, namely: in so far as it seeks the laws of conduct, and can find them only to the extent that causality holds. But the question of whether man is morally free (that is, has that freedom which, as we shall show, is the presupposition of moral responsibility) is altogether different from the problem of determinism. . . . Freedom means the opposite of compulsion; a man is free if he does not act under compulsion, and he is compelled or unfree when he is hindered from without in the realization of his natural desires. Hence he is unfree when he is locked up, or chained, or when someone forces him at the point of a gun to do what otherwise he would not do. This is quite clear, and everyone will admit that the everyday or legal notion of the lack of freedom is thus correctly interpreted, and that a man will be considered quite free and responsible if no such external compulsion is exerted upon him. There are certain cases which lie between these clearly described ones, as, say, when someone acts under the influence of alcohol or a narcotic. In such cases we consider the man to be more or less unfree, and hold him less accountable, because we rightly view the influence of the drug as "external," even though it is found within the body; it prevents him from making decisions in the manner peculiar to his nature. If he takes the narcotic of his own will, we make him completely responsible for this act and transfer a part of the responsibility to the consequences, making, as it were, an average or mean condemnation of the whole. In the case of a person who is mentally ill we do not consider him free with respect to those acts in which the disease expresses itself, because we view the illness as a disturbing factor which hinders the normal functioning of his natural tendencies. We make not him but his disease responsible.

The Nature of Responsibility

But what does this really signify? What do we mean by this concept of responsibility which goes along with that of "freedom," and which plays such an important role in morality? It is easy to attain complete clarity in this matter; we need only carefully determine the manner in which the concept is used. What is the case in practice when we impute "responsibility" to a person? What is our aim in doing this? The judge has to discover who is responsible for a given act in order that he may punish him. We are inclined to be less concerned with the inquiry as to who deserves reward for an act, and we have no special officials for this; but of course the principle would be the same. But let us stick to punishment in order to make the idea clear. What is punishment, actually? The view still often expressed, that it is a natural retaliation for past wrong, ought no longer to be defended in cultivated society; for the opinion that an increase in sorrow can be ''made good again'' by further sorrow is altogether barbarous. Certainly the origin of punishment may lie in an impulse of retaliation or vengeance; but what is such an impulse except the instinctive desire to destroy the cause of the deed to be avenged, by the destruction of or injury to the malefactor? Punishment is concerned only with the institution of causes, of motives of conduct, and this alone is its meaning. Punishment is an educative measure, and as such is a means to the formation of motives, which are in part to prevent the wrongdoer from repeating the act (reformation) and in part to prevent others from committing a similar act (intimidation). Analogously, in the case of reward we are concerned with an incentive.

Hence the question regarding responsibility is the question: Who in a given case, is to be punished? Who is to be considered the true wrongdoer? This problem is not identical with that regarding the original instigator of the act; for the great-grandparents of the man, from whom he inherited his character, might in the end be the cause, or the statesmen who are responsible for his social milieu, and so forth. But the ''doer'' is the one upon whom the motive must have acted in order, with certainty, to have prevented the act (or called it forth, as the case may be). Consideration of remote causes is of no help here, for in the first place their actual contribution cannot be determined, and in the second place they are generally out of reach. Rather, we must find the person in whom the decisive junction of causes lies. The question of who is responsible is the question concerning the correct point of application of the motive. . . . It is a matter only of knowing who is to be punished or rewarded, in order that punishment and reward function as such—be able to achieve their goal.

Thus, all the facts connected with the concepts of responsibility and imputation are at once made intelligible. We do not charge an insane person with responsibility, for the very reason that he offers no unified point for the application of motive. It would be pointless to try to affect him by means of promises or threats, when his confused soul fails to respond to such influence because its normal mechanism is out of order. We do not try to give him motives, but try to heal him (metaphorically, we make his sickness responsible, and try to remove its causes). When a man is forced by threats to commit certain acts we do not blame him, but the one who held the pistol at his breast. The reason is clear: the act would have been prevented had we been able to restrain the person who threatened him; and this person is the one whom we must influence in order to prevent similar acts in the future.

The Consciousness of Responsibility

But much more important than the question of when a man is said to be responsible is that of when he himself feels responsible. Our whole treatment would be untenable if it gave no explanation of this. It is, then, a welcome confirmation of the view here developed that the subjective feeling of responsibility coincides with objective judgment. It is a fact of experience that, in general, the person blamed or condemned is conscious of the fact that he was ''rightly'' taken to account—of course, under the supposition that no error has been made, that the assumed state of affairs actually occurred. What is this consciousness of having been the true doer of the act, the actual instigator? Evidently not merely that it was he who took the steps required for its performance; but there must be added the awareness that he did it "independently," "of his own initiative," or however it be expressed. This feeling is simply the consciousness of freedom, which is merely the knowledge of having acted on one's own desires. And "one's own desires" are those which have their origin in the regularity of one's character in the given situation, and are not imposed by an external power, as explained above. The absence of the external power expresses itself in the well-known feeling (usually considered characteristic of the consciousness of freedom) that one could also have acted otherwise. How this indubitable experience ever came to be an argument in favor of indeterminism is incomprehensible to me. It is of course obvious that I should have acted differently had I willed something else; but the feeling never says that I could also have willed something else, even though this is true, if, that is, other motives had been present. And it says even less that under exactly the same inner and outer conditions I could also have willed something else. How could such a feeling inform me of anything regarding the purely theoretical question of whether the principle of causality holds or not? Of course, after what has been said on the subject, I do not undertake to demonstrate the principle, but I do deny that from any such fact of consciousness the least follows regarding the principle's validity. This feeling is not the consciousness of the absence of a cause, but of something altogether different, namely, of freedom, which consists in the fact that I can act as I desire.

Thus the feeling of responsibility assumes that I acted freely, that my own desires impelled me; and if because of this feeling I willingly suffer blame for my behavior or reproach myself, and thereby admit that I might have acted otherwise, this means that other behavior was compatible with the laws of volition—of course granted other motives. And I myself desire the existence of such motives and bear the pain (regret and sorrow) caused me by my behavior so that its repetition will be prevented. To blame oneself means just to apply a motive of improvement to oneself, which is usually the task of the educator. But if, for example, one does something under the influence of torture, feelings of guilt and regret are absent, for one knows that according to the laws of volition no other behavior was possible—no matter what ideas, because of their feeling tones, might have functioned as motives. The important thing, always, is that the feeling of responsibility means the realization that one's self, one's own psychic processes constitute the point at which motives must be applied in order to govern the acts of one's body.

Causality as the Presupposition of Responsibility

We can speak of motives only in a causal context; thus it becomes clear how very much of the concept of responsibility rests upon that of causation, that is, upon the regularity of volitional decisions. In fact if we should conceive of a decision as utterly without any cause (this would in all strictness be the indeterministic presupposition) then the act would be entirely a matter of chance, for chance is identical with the absence of a cause; there is no other opposite of causality. Could we under such conditions make the agent responsible? Certainly not. Imagine a man, always calm, peaceful and blameless, who suddenly falls upon and begins to beat a stranger. He is held and questioned regarding the motive of his actions, to which he answers, in his opinion truthfully, as we assume: "There was no motive for my behavior. Try as I may I can discover no reason. My volition was without any cause—I desired to do so, and there is simply nothing else to be said about it." We should shake our heads and call him insane, because we have to believe that there was a cause, and lacking any other we must assume some mental disturbance as the only cause remaining; but certainly no one would hold him to be responsible. If decisions were causeless there would be no sense in trying to influence men; and we see at once that this is the reason why we could not bring such a man to account, but would always have only a shrug of the shoulders in answer to his behavior. One can easily determine that in practice we make an agent the more responsible the more motives we can find for his conduct. If a man guilty of an atrocity was an enemy of his victim, if previously he had shown violent tendencies, if some special circumstance angered him, then we impose severe punishment upon him; while the fewer the reasons to be found for an offense the less do we condemn the agent, but make "unlucky chance," a momentary aberration, or something of the sort, responsible. We do not find the causes of misconduct in his character, and therefore we do not try to influence it for the better: this and only this is the significance of the fact that we do not put the responsibility upon him. And he too feels this to be so, and says, "I cannot understand how such a thing could have happened to me."

In general we know very well how to discover the causes of conduct in the characters of our fellow men; and how to use this knowledge in the prediction of their future behavior, often with as much certainty as that with which we know that a lion and a rabbit will behave quite differently in the same situation. From all this it is evident that in practice no one thinks of questioning the principle of causality, that, thus, the attitude of the practical man offers no excuse to the metaphysician for confusing freedom from compulsion with the absence of a cause. If one makes clear to himself that a causeless happening is identical with a chance happening, and that, consequently, an indetermined will would destroy all responsibility, then every desire will cease that might be father to an indeterministic thought. No one can prove determinism, but it is certain that we assume its validity in all our practical life, and that in particular we can apply the concept of responsibility to human conduct only in as far as the causal principle holds of volitional processes. . . .

DISCUSSION QUESTIONS

1. Do you agree with Schlick that ". . . every explanation of human behavior must . . . assume the validity of causal laws" (i.e., human behavior can be explained only by being shown to fall under some universal law of nature)? If not, what other type or types of explanation of human behavior are possible?

2. According to Schlick, how does the confusion between legal laws and natural laws (i.e., laws of nature) contribute to the mistaken belief that determinism is incompatible with freedom?

3. According to Schlick, "Freedom means the opposite of compulsion; a man is free if he does not act under compulsion, and he is compelled or unfree when he is hindered from without in the realization of his natural desires. Hence he is unfree when he is locked up, or chained, or when someone forces him at the point of a gun to do what otherwise he would not do."

   a. Schlick admits that the notion of "compulsion" is vague; as a result it is not always clear whether or not a human action should be said to be "free." Give some examples of human actions that are clearly a result of compulsion, others that are clearly not a result of compulsion, and yet others for which it is unclear whether or not they are a result of compulsion. Then attempt to define as precisely as possible what "acting under compulsion" means. Must a person be aware of the fact that he is acting under compulsion? What bearing, if any, does the existence of unconscious motives for actions that psychiatrists emphasize have on the scope of human compulsive behavior? What would Hospers say here? Do you agree? Why?

   b. Do you agree with Schlick that freedom "means nothing more than the absence of compulsion"? Is a person acting "freely" if he acts without compulsion but is incapable of realizing why he should behave differently? If not, how should Schlick's definition of "freedom" be modified?

4. According to Schlick, when is a person "responsible"? Why does Schlick believe that responsibility is not only compatible with determinism, but presupposes it? Do you agree?

5. Consider the following criticisms of Schlick's view of responsibility by the libertarian philosopher C.A. Campbell:

> We do not ordinarily consider the lower animals to be morally responsible. But **ought** we not to do so if Schlick is right about what we mean by moral responsibility? It is quite possible, by punishing the dog who absconds with the succulent chops designed for its master's luncheon, favourably to influence its motives in respect of its future behavior in like circumstances. If moral responsibility is to be linked with punishment as Schlick links it, and punishment conceived as a form of education, we should surely hold the dog morally responsible? The plain fact, of course, is that we don't. We don't, because we suppose that the dog "couldn't help it": that its action (unlike what we usually believe to be true of human beings) was simply a link in a continuous chain of causes and effects. In other words, we do commonly demand the contra-causal sort of freedom as a condition of moral responsibility.[3]

Do you agree with Campbell that Schlick's view of punishment and moral responsibility is defective? How would you define these concepts? Do you accept the reason Campbell gives for the appropriateness of holding human beings responsible, but not dogs? If not, what reason would you give?

6. If, as Schlick claims, the question of who is responsible "is a matter only of knowing who is to be punished or rewarded," what sense, if any, can be made of the common practice of holding responsible individuals who are dead or inaccessible to our influence? What do you think Schlick would say? What do you think?

7. Is it reasonable to excuse individuals or to mitigate their degree of responsibility on the basis of the biological and environmental obstacles with which they had to cope? Does Schlick's analysis of responsibility allow for this?

8. According to Schlick, a person's consciousness of his or her own freedom of action is simply the knowledge of having acted on "one's own desires"—that is, free actions are "those which have their origin in the regularity of one's character in the given situation." Does this mean that one is not responsible for acting out of character? What do you think Schlick would say? What do you think? What do you think the subjective feeling of freedom and responsibility signifies?

9. Schlick claims that, ". . . in practice we make an agent the more responsible the more motives we can find for his conduct. . . . While the fewer the reasons to be found for an offense the less do we condemn the agent. . . ." Do you agree?

10. Schlick claims that, when a person does something under the influence of torture, "feelings of guilt and regret are absent, for one knows that according to the laws of volition no other behavior was possible. . ." Is it not possible for a person to refuse to succumb to torture? Do we not at times consider it a person's responsibility not to so succumb? (Imagine a trained captured spy.) What do you think Schlick would say? What do you think?

11. Consider the following two analyses of "freedom and moral responsibility":

a. People are free and morally responsible if they are capable of **doing as they choose.**

b. People are free and morally responsible if they are **free to choose** what they shall do.

What differences, if any, do you see between these two views? Which, if any, would Schlick accept? Which do you think is more adequate? Why?

[3]C.A. Campbell, "Is 'Free Will' a Pseudo-Problem?" (*Mind*, 1951).

51. FREEDOM AS CHANCE

William James

(For a biographical sketch of William James, see Selections #12 and 20.)

The following selection is from James' classic libertarian defense, "The Dilemma of Determinism." In arguing for his position, James is motivated, as he was in so much of his writing, by the desire to preserve traditional religious and moral beliefs against the onslaught of the naturalism of his day.

Dismissing with scorn the attempt to reconcile determinism with freedom, James, as the pragmatist that he was, stresses the practical consequences of the acceptance of determinism. As he sees it, since determinism entails that whatever **is,** however bad it might be, **must be,** it follows that if determinism is true, it is irrational to have feelings of regret over what happens—that is, feelings that some things that happen ought not have happened. But if feelings of regret are irrational, there is no moral sense to the universe. Conversely, if there is moral sense to the universe, regret must be appropriate. And, if regret is appropriate, then the universe must be an open unfolding system which cannot be completely predicted from past events. While James argues that the acceptance of an indeterministic universe seems to be suggested by our immediate experience of freedom, he is willing to admit that he cannot demonstrate that the belief in indeterminism is more rational than the belief in determinism, just as his opponents cannot demonstrate that determinism is more rational than indeterminism. Since reason cannot decide the choice between determinism and indeterminism, we have a right to believe in the doctrine that is more in accord with our natural feelings or desires, James believes. (Notice that this is the same argument James utilizes for belief in God in "The Will to Believe"—Selection #20.) Since the desire to make moral sense out of the universe is a deeply natural human desire, we have the right to believe in human freedom and the indeterminism that it requires, James concludes.

A common opinion prevails that the juice has ages ago been pressed out of the free-will controversy, and that no new champion can do more than warm up stale arguments which every one has heard. This is a radical mistake. I know of no subject less worn out, or in which inventive genius has a better chance of breaking open new ground—not, perhaps, of forcing a conclusion or of coercing assent, but of deepening our sense of what the issue between the two parties really is, of what the ideas of fate and of free will imply . . . .

. . . The arguments I am about to urge all proceed on two suppositions: first, when we make theories about the world and discuss them with one another, we do so in order to attain a conception of things which shall give us subjective satisfaction; and, second, if there be two conceptions, and the one seems to us, on the whole, more rational than the other, we are en-

Source: William James, "The Dilemma of Determinism," an address to the Harvard Divinity Students, published in the *Unitarian Review,* September 1884.

titled to suppose that the more rational one is the truer of the two . . . . I cannot stop to argue the point; but I myself believe that all the magnificent achievements of mathematical and physical science—our doctrines of evolution, of uniformity of law, and the rest—proceed from our indomitable desire to cast the world into a more rational shape in our minds than the shape into which it is thrown there by the crude order of our experience. The world has shown itself, to a great extent, plastic to this demand of ours for rationality. How much farther it will show itself plastic no one can say. Our only means of finding out is to try; and I, for one, feel as free to try conceptions of moral as of mechanical or of logical rationality. If a certain formula for expressing the nature of the world violates my moral demand, I shall feel as free to throw it overboard, or at least to doubt it, as if it disappointed my demand for uniformity of sequence, for example; the one demand being, so far as I can see, quite as subjective and emotional as the other is. The principle of causality, for example—what is it but a postulate. . . . All our scientific and philosophic ideals are altars to unknown gods. Uniformity is as much so as is free will. If this be admitted, we can debate on even terms. But if any one pretends that while freedom and variety are, in the first instance, subjective demands, necessity and uniformity are something altogether different, I do not see how we can debate at all.

To begin, then, I must suppose you acquainted with all the usual arguments on the subject. I cannot stop to take up the old proofs from causation, from statistics, from the certainty with which we can foretell one another's conduct, from the fixity of character, and all the rest. But there are two *words* which usually encumber these classical arguments, and which we must immediately dispose of if we are to make any progress. One is the eulogistic word *freedom,* and the other is the opprobrious [1] word *chance*. The word "chance" I wish to keep, but I wish to get rid of the word "Freedom." Its eulogistic associations have so far overshadowed all the rest of its meaning that both parties claim the sole right to use it, and determinists today insist that they alone are freedom's champions . . . .

Now, all this is a quagmire of evasion under which the real issue of fact has been entirely smothered . . . . But there *is* a problem, an issue of fact and not of words, an issue of the most momentous importance, which is often decided without discussion in one sentence—nay, in one clause of a sentence—by those very writers who spin out whole chapters in their efforts to show what "true" freedom is; and that is the question of determinism, about which we are to talk tonight.

Fortunately, no ambiguities hang about this word or about its opposite, indeterminism. Both designate an outward way in which things may happen, and their cold and mathematical sound has no sentimental associations that can bribe our partiality either way in advance. Now, evidence of an external kind to decide between determinism and intermission is, as I intimated a while back, strictly impossible to find. Let us look at the difference between them and see for ourselves. What does determinism profess?

It professes that those parts of the universe already laid down absolutely appoint and decree what the other parts shall be. The future has no ambiguous possibilities hidden in its womb: the part we call the present is compatible with only one totality . . . .

With earth's first clay they did the last man knead,
And there of the last harvest sowed the seed.
And the first morning of creation wrote
What the last dawn of reckoning shall read.

Indeterminism, on the contrary, says that the parts have a certain amount of loose play on one another, so that the laying down of one of them does not necessarily determine what the others

[1] Abusive. EDITOR'S NOTE.

shall be. It admits that possibilities may be in excess of actualities, and that things not yet revealed to our knowledge may really in themselves be ambiguous. Of two alternative futures which we conceive, both may now be really possible; and the one become impossible only at the very moment when the other excludes it by becoming real itself. Indeterminism thus denies the world to be one unbending unit of fact. It says there is a certain ultimate pluralism in it; and, so saying, it corroborates our ordinary unsophisticated view of things. To that view, actualities seem to float in a wider sea of possibilities from out of which they are chosen; and, *somewhere*, indeterminism says, such possibilities exist, and form a part of truth.

Determinism, on the contrary, says they exist *nowhere*, and that necessity on the one hand and impossibility on the other are the sole categories of the real. Possibilities that fail to get realized are, for determinism, pure illusions: they never were possibilities at all . . . .

The issue, it will be seen, is a perfectly sharp one, which no eulogistic terminology can smear over or wipe out. The truth *must* lie with one side or the other, and its lying with one side makes the other false.

The question relates solely to the existence of possibilities, in the strict sense of the term, as things that may, but need not, be. Both sides admit that a volition, for instance, has occurred. The indeterminists say another volition might have occurred in its place; the determinists swear that nothing could possibly have occurred in its place . . . .

The sting of the word "chance" seems to lie in the assumption that it means something positive, and that if anything happens by chance, it must needs be something of an intrinsically irrational and preposterous sort. Now, chance means nothing of the kind. It is a purely negative and relative term, giving us no information about that of which it is predicated, except that it happens to be disconnected with something else—not controlled, secured, or necessitated by other things in advance of its own actual presence . . . .

Nevertheless, many persons talk as if the minutest dose of disconnectedness of one part with another, the smallest modicum of independence, the faintest tremor of ambiguity about the future, for example, would ruin everything, and turn this goodly universe into a sort of insane sand-heap . . . . Since future human volitions are as a matter of fact the only ambiguous things we are tempted to believe in, let us stop for a moment to make ourselves sure whether their independent and accidental character need be fraught with such direful consequences to the universe as these.

What is meant by saying that my choice of which way to walk home after the lecture is ambiguous and matter of chance as far as the present moment is concerned? It means that both Divinity Avenue and Oxford Street are called; but that only one, and that one *either* one, shall be chosen. Now, I ask you seriously to suppose that this ambiguity of my choice is real; and then to make the impossible hypothesis that the choice is made twice over, and each time falls on a different street. In other words, imagine that I first walk through Divinity Avenue, and then imagine that the powers governing the universe annihilate ten minutes of time with all that it contained, and set me back at the door of this hall just as I was before the choice was made. Imagine then that, everything else being the same, I now make a different choice and traverse Oxford Street. You, as passive spectators, look on and see the two alternative universes—one of them with me walking through Divinity Avenue in it, the other with the same me walking through Oxford Street. Now, if you are determinists you believe one of these universes to have been from eternity impossible: you believe it to have been impossible because of the intrinsic irrationality or accidentality somewhere involved in it. But looking outwardly at these universes, can you say which is the impossible and accidental one, and which the rational and necessary one? I doubt if the most iron-clad determinist among you could have the slightest glimmer of light on this point. In other words, either universe *after the fact* and once there would, to our means of observation and understanding, appear just as rational as the other. There would be absolutely no criterion by which we might judge one necessary and the other matter of chance. Suppose now we relieve the gods of their hypothetical task and assume my choice, once made, to be made forever. I go through Divinity Avenue for good and all. If, as good determinists, you now begin to affirm what all good determinists punctually do affirm, that in the nature of things I *couldn't* have gone through Oxford Street—had I done so it would have been chance, irrationality, insanity, a horrid gap in nature—I simply call your attention to this, that your affirmation is what the Germans call a *Machtspruch*, a mere conception fulminated as a dogma and based on no insight into details. Before my choice, either street seemed as natural to you as to me. Had I happened to take Oxford Street, Divinity Avenue would have figured in your philosophy as the gap in nature; and you would have so proclaimed it with the best deterministic conscience in the world . . . .

And this at last brings us within sight of our subject. We have seen that indeterminism is rightly described as meaning chance; and we have seen that chance, the very name of which we are urged to shrink from as from a metaphysical pestilence, means only the negative fact that no part of the world, however big, can claim to control absolutely the destinies of the whole. But although, in discussing the word "chance," I may at moments have seemed to be arguing for its real existence, I have not meant to do so yet. We have not yet ascertained whether this be a world of chance or no; at most, we have agreed that it seems so. And I now repeat what I said at the outset, that, from any strict theoretical point of of view, the question is insoluble. To deepen our theoretic sense of the *difference* between a world with chances in it and a deterministic world is the most I can hope to do; and this I may now at last begin upon, after all our tedious clearing of the way.

I wish first of all to show you just what the notion that this is a deterministic world implies. The implications I call your attention to are all bound up with the fact that it is a world in which we constantly have to make what I shall, with your permission, call judgments of regret. Hardly an hour passes in which we do not wish that something might be otherwise; and happy indeed are those of us whose hearts have never echoed the wish of Omar Khayam—

> That we might clasp, ere closed, the book of fate,
>   And make the writer on a fairer leaf
> Inscribe our names, or quite obliterate.
>
> Ah! Love, could you and I with fate conspire
> To mend this sorry scheme of things entire,
>   Would we not shatter it to bits, and then
> Remould it nearer to the heart's desire?

Now, it is undeniable that most of these regrets are foolish . . . . Even from the point of view of our own ends, we should probably make a botch of remodeling the universe. How much more then from the point of view of ends we cannot see! Wise men therefore regret as little as they can. But still some regrets are pretty obstinate and hard to stifle—regrets for acts of wanton cruelty or treachery, for example, whether performed by others or by ourselves. Hardly any one can remain *entirely* optimistic after reading the confession of the murderer at Brockton the other day: how, to get rid of the wife whose continued existence bored him, he inveigled her into a desert spot, shot her four times, and then, as she lay on the ground and said to him, "You didn't do it on purpose, did you, dear?" replied, "No, I didn't do it on purpose," as he raised a rock and smashed her skull. Such an occurrence, with the mild sentence and self-satisfaction of the prisoner, is a field for a crop of regrets, which one need not take up in detail. We feel that, although a perfect mechanical fit to the rest of the universe, it is a bad moral fit, and that something else would really have been better in its place.

But for the deterministic philosophy the murder, the sentence, and the prisoner's optimism were all necessary from eternity; and nothing else for a moment had a ghost of a chance of being put into their place. To admit such a chance, the determinists tell us, would be to make a suicide of reason; so we must steel our hearts against the thought. And here our plot thickens, for we see the first of those difficult implications of determinism . . . which it is my purpose to make you feel. If this Brockton murder was called for by the rest of the universe, if it had to come at its preappointed hour, and if nothing else would have been consistent with the sense of the whole, what are we to think of the universe? Are we stubbornly to stick to our judgment of regret, and say, though it *couldn't* be, yet it *would* have been a better universe with something different from this Brockton murder in it? That, of course, seems the natural and spontaneous thing for us to do; and yet it is nothing short of deliberately espousing a kind of pessimism. The judgment of regret calls the murder bad. Calling a thing bad means, if it means anything at all, that the thing ought not to be, that something else ought to be in its stead. Determinism, in denying that anything else can be in its stead, virtually defines the universe as a place in which what ought to be is impossible . . . . Regret for the murder must transform itself, if we are determinists and wise, into a larger regret. It is absurd to regret the murder alone. Other things being what they are, *it* could not be different. What we should regret is that whole frame of things of which the murder is one member. I see no escape whatever from this pessimistic conclusion if, being determinists, our judgement of regret is to be allowed to stand at all . . . .

Let me, then, without circumlocution say just this. The world is enigmatical enough in all conscience, whatever theory we may take up toward it. The indeterminism I defend, the free-will theory of popular sense based on the judgment of regret, represents that world as vulnerable, and liable to be injured by certain of its parts if they act wrong. And it represents their acting wrong as a matter of possibility or accident, neither inevitable nor yet to be infallibly warded off. In all this, it is a theory devoid either of transparency or of stability. It gives us a pluralistic, restless universe, in which no single point of view can ever take in the whole scene; and to a mind possessed of the love of unity at any cost, it will, no doubt, remain forever inacceptable . . . .

But while I freely admit that the pluralism and the restlessness are repugnant and irrational in a certain way, I find that every alternative to them is irrational in a deeper way . . . . [I]ndeterminism offends only the native absolutism of my intellect—an absolutism which, after all, perhaps, deserves to be snubbed and kept in check. But . . . determinism . . . violates my sense of moral reality through and through. When, for example, I imagine . . . the Brockton murder, I cannot conceive it as an act by which the universe, as a whole, logically and necessarily expresses its nature without shrinking from complicity with such a whole. And I deliberately refuse to keep on terms of loyalty with the universe by saying blankly that the murder, since it does flow from the nature of the whole, is not [bad]. There are *some* instinctive reactions which I, for one, will not tamper with . . . .

. . . Make as great an uproar about chance as you please, I know that chance means pluralism and nothing more. If some of the members of the pluralism are bad, the philosophy of pluralism, whatever broad views it may deny me permits me, at least, to turn to the other members with a clean breast of affection and an unsophisticated moral sense. And if I still wish to think of the world as a totality, it lets me feel that a world with a *chance* in it of being altogether good, even if the chance never come to pass, is better than a world with no such chance at all. That "chance" whose very notion I am exhorted and conjured to banish from my view of the future as the suicide of reason concerning it, that "chance" is—what? Just this—the chance that in moral respects the future may be other and better than the past has been. This is the only chance we have any motive for supposing to exist. Shame, rather, on its repudiation and its denial! For its presence is the vital air which lets the world live, the salt which keeps it sweet. . . .

DISCUSSION QUESTIONS

1. James writes:

> Determinism . . . says . . . that necessity on the one hand and impossibility on the other are the sole categories of the real. Possibilities that fail to get realized are, for determinism, pure illusions . . . .

What would Schlick say in reply? What do you think?

2. Why does James believe that feelings of regret are inappropriate in a determined world? Would they be more appropriate in an undetermined world, as James believes? Why, or why not?

3. Do you agree with James that freedom and moral responsibility have no place in a determined world? Do you agree with his identification of freedom with chance? Why, or why not?

4, Does James' example of the choice he will make between going home by way of Divinity Avenue and by way of Oxford Street support indeterminism? Why?

52. FREEDOM AS CAUSATION BY A SELF WHOSE CHOICES ARE UNCAUSED

Richard Taylor

(For a biographical sketch of Richard Taylor, see Selection #10.)

In the following selection which comes from his introductory book **Metaphysics,** Taylor defends libertarianism and criticizes soft determinism. As Taylor sees it, in claiming that actions are free if and only if they are chosen without impediment or constraint, soft determinists neglect to consider the fact that if determinism is true, then every choice we make, however free of impediment or constraint, is itself the inevitable outcome of inner physiological or psychological states that **make** us behave as we do. Taylor then goes on to reinforce this traditional abstract argument for the incompatibility of freedom and determinism with a specific counterexample—that is, he imagines a concrete case of a person acting without impediment or constraint which he believes all rational people would agree is an unfree act (the case of "the ingenious physiologist"). Having presented his reasons for rejecting soft determinism, Taylor goes on to discuss and dismiss James' **simple indeterminism,** which equates freedom with chance, a view which he sees as replacing the determinist's distressing view of human beings as "puppets" with the equally distressing view of human beings as "erratic and jerking phantoms."

Claiming that any adequate view of freedom must be compatible with the efficacy of human deliberation and the belief that some things that happen are **up to us** and not caused by things that **happen to us,** Taylor claims that the only conception of free action which is compatible with these apparently self-evident facts of human experience is the view he calls **the theory of agency,** according to which human beings can be "self-determining beings." This in turn, he claims, entails that "In the case of an action that is free, it must be such that no antecedent conditions were sufficient for performing just that action. In the case of an action that is both free and rational, it must be such that the agent who performed it did so for some reason, but this reason cannot have been the cause of it." In taking this view, Taylor presupposes a conception of the nature of causation and of the distinction between reasons and causes which would generate heated debate among contemporary philosophers who accept different metaphysical frameworks.

Freedom

To say that it is, in a given instance, up to me what I do, is to say that I am in that instance *free* with respect to what I then do. Thus, I am sometimes free to move my finger this way and that, but not, certainly, to bend it backward or into a knot. But what does this mean?

It means, first, that there is no *obstacle* or *impediment* to my activity. Thus, there is sometimes no obstacle to my moving my finger this way and that, though there are obvious obstacles to my moving it far backward or into a knot. Those things, accordingly, that pose obstacles to my motions limit my freedom. If my hand were strapped in such a way as to permit only a leftward motion of my finger, I would not then be free to move it to the right. If it were encased in a tight cast that permitted no motion, I would not be free to move it at all. Freedom of motion, then, is limited by obstacles.

Further, to say that it is, in a given instance, up to me what I do, means that nothing *constrains* or *forces* me to do one thing rather than another. Constraints are like obstacles, except that while the latter prevent, the former enforce. Thus, if my finger is being forcibly bent to the left—by a machine, for instance, or by another person, or by any force that I cannot overcome—then I am not free to move it this way and that. I cannot, in fact move it at all; I can only watch to see how it is moved, and perhaps vainly resist. Its motions are not up to me, or within my control, but in the control of some other thing or person.

Obstacles and constraints, then, both obviously limit my freedom. To say I am free to perform some action thus means at least that there is no obstacle to my doing it, and that nothing constrains me to do otherwise.

Now if we rest content with this observation, as many have, and construe free activity simply as activity that is unimpeded and unconstrained, there is evidently no inconsistency between affirming both the thesis of determinism and the claim that I am sometimes free. For to say that some action of mine is neither impeded nor constrained does not by itself imply that it is not causally determined. The absence of obstacles and constraints are mere negative conditions, and do not by themselves rule out the presence of positive causes. It might seem, then, that we can say of some of my actions that there are conditions antecedent to their performance so that no other actions were possible, and also that these actions were unobstructed and unconstrained. And to say that would logically entail that such actions were both causally determined, and free.

Source: Richard Taylor, *Metaphysics,* 3rd ed., © 1983, pp. 41–50. Reprinted by permission of Prentice-Hall, Inc., Englewood Cliffs, N.J.

Soft Determinism

It is this kind of consideration that has led many philosophers to embrace what is sometimes called "soft determinism." All versions of this theory have in common three claims, by means of which, it is naively supposed, a reconciliation is achieved between determinism and freedom. Freedom being, furthermore, a condition of moral responsibility and the only condition that metaphysics seriously questions, it is supposed by the partisans of this view that determinism is perfectly compatible with such responsibility. This, no doubt, accounts for its great appeal and wide acceptance, even by some men of considerable learning.

The three claims of soft determinism are (1) that the thesis of determinism is true, and that accordingly all human behavior, voluntary or other, like the behavior of all other things, arises from antecedent conditions, given which no other behavior is possible—in short, that all human behavior is caused and determined; (2) that voluntary behavior is nonetheless free to the extent that it is not externally constrained or impeded; and (3) that, in the absence of such obstacles and constraints, the causes of voluntary behavior are certain states, events, or conditions within the agent himself; namely, his own acts of will or volitions, choices, decisions, desires, and so on.

Thus, on this view, I am free, and therefore sometimes responsible for what I do, provided nothing prevents me from acting according to my own choice, desire or volition, or constrains me to act otherwise. There may, to be sure, be other conditions for my responsibility—such as, for example, an understanding of the probable consequences of my behavior, and that sort of thing—but absence of constraint or impediment is, at least, one such condition. And, it is claimed, it is a condition that is compatible with the supposition that my behavior is caused—for it is, by hypothesis, caused by my own inner choices, desires, and volitions.

The Refutation of This

The theory of soft determinism looks good at first—so good that it has for generations been solemnly taught from numberless philosophical chairs and implanted in the minds of students as sound philosophy—but no great acumen is needed to discover that far from solving any problem, it only camouflages it.

My free actions are those unimpeded and unconstrained motions that arise from my own inner desires, choices, and volitions; let us grant this provisionally. But now, whence arise those inner states that determine what my body shall do? Are they within my control or not? Having made my choice or decision and acted upon it, could I have chosen otherwise or not?

Here the determinist, hoping to surrender nothing and yet to avoid the problem implied in that question, bids us not to ask it; the question itself, he announces, is without meaning. For to say that I could have done otherwise, he says, means only that I *would* have done otherwise *if* those inner states that determined my action had been different; if, that is, I had decided or chosen differently. To ask, accordingly, whether I could have chosen or decided differently is only to ask whether, had I decided to decide differently or chosen to choose differently, or willed to will differently, I would have decided or chosen or willed differently. And this, of course, is unintelligible nonsense.

But it is not nonsense to ask whether the causes of my actions—my own inner choices, decisions and desires—are themselves caused. And of course they are, if determinism is true, for on that thesis everything is caused and determined. And if they are, then we cannot avoid concluding that, given the causal conditions of those inner states, I could not have decided, willed, chosen, or desired otherwise than I in fact did, for this is a logical consequence of the very definition of determinism. Of course we can still say that, *if* the causes of those inner states, whatever they were, had been different, then their effects, those inner states themselves, would have been different, and that in this hypothetical sense I could have decided, chosen, willed, or desired differently—but that only pushes our problem back still another step. For we will then want to know whether the causes of those inner states were within my control; and so on, *ad infinitum*. We are, at each step, permitted to say ''could have been otherwise'' only in a provisional sense—provided, that is, something else had been different—but must then retract it and replace it with ''could not have been otherwise'' as soon as we discover, as we must at each step, that whatever would have to have been different could not have been different.

Examples

Such is the dialectic of the problem. The easiest way to see the shadowy quality of soft determinism, however, is by means of examples.

Let us suppose that my body is moving in various ways, that these motions are not externally constrained or impeded, and that they are all exactly in accordance with my own desires, choices, or acts of will and what not. When I will that my arm should move in a certain way, I find it moving in that way, unobstructed and unconstrained. When I will to speak, my lips and tongue move, unobstructed and unconstrained, in a manner suitable to the formation of the words I choose to utter. Now given that this is a correct description of my behavior, namely, that it consists of the unconstrained and unimpeded motions of my body in response to my own volitions, then it follows that my behavior is free, on the soft determinist's definition of ''free.'' It follows further that I am responsible for that behavior; or at least, that if I am not, it is not from any lack of freedom on my part.

But if the fulfillment of these conditions renders my behavior free—that is to say, if my behavior satisfies the conditions of free action set forth in the theory of soft determinism—then my behavior will be no less free if we assume further conditions that are perfectly consistent with those already satisfied.

We suppose further, accordingly, that while my behavior is entirely in accordance with my own volitions, and thus ''free'' in terms of the conception of freedom we are examining, my volitions themselves are caused. To make this graphic, we can suppose that an ingenious physiologist can induce in me any volition he pleases, simply by pushing various buttons on an instrument to which, let us suppose, I am attached by numerous wires. All the volitions I have in that situation are, accordingly, precisely the ones he gives me. By pushing one button, he evokes in me the volition to raise my hand; and my hand, being unimpeded, rises in response to that volition. By pushing another, he induces the volition in me to kick, and my foot, being unimpeded, kicks in response to that volition. We can even suppose that the physiologist puts a rifle in my hands, aims it at some passer-by, and then, by pushing the proper button, evokes in me the volition to squeeze my finger against the trigger, whereupon the passer-by falls dead of a bullet wound.

This is the description of a man who is acting in accordance with his inner volitions, a man whose body is unimpeded and unconstrained in its motions, these motions being the effects of those inner states. It is hardly the description of a free and responsible agent. It is the perfect description of a puppet. To render a man your puppet, it is not necessary forcibly to constrain the motions of his limbs, after the fashion that real puppets are moved. A subtler but no less effective means of making a man your puppet would be to gain complete control of his inner states, and ensuring, as the theory of soft determinism does ensure, that his body will move in accordance with them.

The example is somewhat unusual, but it is no worse for that. It is perfectly intelligible, and it does appear to refute the soft determinist's conception of freedom. One might think that, in such a case, the agent should not have allowed himself to be so rigged in the first place, but this is irrelevant; we can suppose that he was not aware that he was, and was hence unaware of the source of those inner states that prompted his bodily motions. The example can, moreover, be modified in perfectly realistic ways, so as to coincide with actual and familiar cases. One can, for instance, be given a compulsive desire for certain drugs, simply by having them administered to him over a course of time. Suppose, then, that I do, with neither my knowledge nor consent, thus become a victim of such a desire and act upon it. Do I act freely, merely by virtue of the fact that I am unimpeded in my quest for drugs? In a sense I do, surely, but I am hardly free with respect to whether or not I shall use drugs. I never chose to have the desire for them inflicted upon me.

Nor does it, of course, matter whether the inner states which allegedly prompt all my "free" activity are evoked in me by another agent or by perfectly impersonal forces. Whether a desire which causes my body to behave in a certain way is inflicted upon me by another person, for instance, or derived from hereditary factors, or indeed from anything at all, matters not the least. In any case, if it is in fact the cause of my bodily behavior, I cannot but act in accordance with it. Wherever it came from, whether from personal or impersonal origins, it was entirely caused or determined, and not within my control. Indeed, if determinism is true, as the theory of soft determinism holds it to be, all those inner states which cause my body to behave in whatever ways it behaves must arise from circumstances that existed before I was born; for the chain of causes and effects is infinite, and none could have been the least different, given those that preceded.

Simple Indeterminism

We might at first now seem warranted in simply denying determinism, and saying that, insofar as they are free, my actions are not caused; or that, if they are caused by my own inner states—my own desires, impulses, choices, volitions, and whatnot—then these, in any case, are not caused. This is a perfectly clear sense in which a man's action, assuming that it was free, could have been otherwise. If it was uncaused, then, even given the conditions under which it occurred and all that preceded, some other act was nonetheless possible, and he did not have to do what he did. Or if his action was the inevitable consequence of his own inner states, and could not have been otherwise given these, we can nevertheless say that these inner states, being uncaused, could have been otherwise, and could thereby have produced different actions.

Only the slightest consideration will show, however, that this simple denial of determinism has not the slightest plausibility. For let us suppose it is true, and that some of my bodily motions—namely, those that I regard as my free acts—are not caused at all or, if caused by my own inner states, that these are not caused. We shall thereby avoid picturing a puppet, to be sure—but only by substituting something even less like a man; for the conception that now emerges is not that of a free man, but of an erratic and jerking phantom, without any rhyme or reason at all.

Suppose that my right arm is free, according to this conception; that is, that its motions are uncaused. It moves this way and that from time to time, but nothing causes these motions. Sometimes it moves forth vigorously, sometimes up, sometimes down, sometimes it just drifts vaguely about—these motions all being wholly free and uncaused. Manifestly I have nothing to do with them at all; they just happen, and neither I nor anyone can ever tell what this arm will be doing next. It might seize a club and lay it on the head of the nearest bystander, no less to my astonishment than his. There will never be any point in asking why these motions occur, or in seeking any explanation of them, for under the condition assumed there is no explanation. They just happen, from no causes at all.

This is no description of free, voluntary, or responsible behavior. Indeed, so far as the motions of my body or its parts are entirely uncaused, such motions cannot even be ascribed to me as my behavior in the first place, since I have nothing to do with them. The behavior of my arm is just the random motion of a foreign object. Behavior that is mine must be behavior that is within my control, but motions that occur from no causes are without the control of anyone. I can have no more to do with, and no more control over, the uncaused motions of my limbs than a gambler has over the motions of an honest roulette wheel. I can only, like him, idly wait to see what happens.

Nor does it improve things to suppose that my bodily motions are caused by my own inner states, so long as we suppose these to be wholly uncaused. The result will be the same as before. My arm, for example, will move this way and that, sometimes up and sometimes down, sometimes vigorously and sometimes just drifting about, always in response to certain inner states, to be sure. But since these are supposed to be wholly uncaused, it follows that I have no control over them and hence none over their effects. If my hand lays a club forcefully on the nearest bystander, we can indeed say that this motion resulted from an inner club-wielding desire of mine; but we must add that I had nothing to do with that desire, and that it arose, to be followed by its inevitable effect, no less to my astonishment than to his. Things like this do, alas, sometimes happen. We are all sometimes seized by compulsive impulses that arise we know not whither, and we do sometimes act upon these. But since they are far from being examples of free, voluntary, and responsible behavior, we need only to learn that behavior was of this sort to conclude that it was not free, voluntary, nor responsible. It was erratic, impulsive, and irresponsible.

Determinism and Simple Indeterminism as Theories

Both determinism and simple indeterminism are loaded with difficulties, and no one who has thought much on them can affirm either of them without some embarrassment. Simple indeterminism has nothing whatever to be said for it, except that it appears to remove the grossest difficulties of determinism, only, however, to imply perfect absurdities of its own. Determinism, on the other hand, is at least initially plausible. Men seem to have a natural inclination to believe in it; it is, indeed, almost required for the very exercise of practical intelligence. And beyond this, our experience appears always to confirm it, so long as we are dealing with everyday facts of common experience, as distinguished from the esoteric researches of theoretical physics. But determinism, as applied to human behavior, has implications which few men can casually accept, and they appear to be implications which no modification of the theory can efface.

Both theories, moreover, appear logically irreconcilable to [two apparently self-evident facts of experience]; namely, (1) that my behavior is sometimes the outcome of my deliberation, and (2) that in these and other cases it is sometimes up to me what I do. . . .

I can deliberate only about my own futue actions, and then only if I do not already know what I am going to do. If a certain nasal tickle warns me that I am about to sneeze, for instance, then I cannot deliberate whether to sneeze or not; I can only prepare for the impending convulsion. But if determinism is true, then there are always conditions existing antecedently to everything I do, sufficient for my doing just that, and such as to render it inevitable. If I can know what those conditions are and what behavior they are sufficient to produce, then I can in every such case know what I am going to do and cannot then deliberate about it.

By itself this only shows, of course, that I can deliberate only in ignorance of the causal conditions of my behavior; it does not show that such conditions cannot exist. It is odd, however, to suppose that deliberation should be a mere substitute for clear knowledge. . . .

Worse yet, however, it now becomes clear that I cannot deliberate about what I am going to do, if it is even possible for me to find out in advance, whether I do in fact find out in advance or not. I can deliberate only with the view to deciding what to do, to making up my mind; and this is impossible if I believe that it could be inferred what I am going to do, from conditions already existing, even though I have not made that inference myself. If I believe that what I am going to do has been rendered inevitable by conditions already existing, and could be inferred by anyone having the requisite sagacity, then I cannot try to decide whether to do it or not, for there is simply nothing left to decide. I can at best only guess or try to figure it out myself or, all prognostics failing, I can wait and see; but I cannot deliberate. I deliberate in order to *decide* what to do, not to *discover* what it is that I am *going* to do. But if determinism is true, then there are always antecedent conditions sufficient for everything that I do, and this can always be inferred by anyone having the requisite sagacity; that is, by anyone having knowledge of what those conditions are and what behavior they are sufficient to produce.

This suggests what in fact seems quite clear, that determinism cannot be reconciled with our [belief] that it is sometimes up to me what I am going to do. For if it is ever really up to me whether to do this thing or that, then, as we have seen, each alternative course of action must be such that I can do it; not that I can do it in some abstruse or hypothetical sense of "can"; not that I could do it if only something were true that is not true; but in the sense that it is then and there within my power to do it. But this is never so, if determinism is true, for on the very formulation of that theory whatever happens at any time is the only thing that can then happen, given all that precedes it. It is simply a logical consequence of this that whatever I do at any time is the only thing I can then do, given the conditions that precede my doing it. Nor does it help in the least to interpose, among the causal antecedents of my behavior, my own inner states, such as my desires, choices, acts of will, and so on. For even supposing these to be always involved in voluntary behavior—which is highly doubtful in itself—it is a consequence of determinism that these, whatever they are at any time, can never be other than what they then are. Every chain of causes and effects, if determinism is true, is infinite. This is why it is not now up to me whether I shall a moment hence be male or female. The conditions determining my sex have existed through my whole life, and even prior to my life. But if determinism is true, the same holds of anything that I ever am, ever become, or ever do. It matters not whether we are speaking of the most patent facts of my being, such as my sex; or the most subtle, such as my feelings, thoughts, desires, or choices. Nothing could be other than it is, given what was; and while we may indeed say, quite idly, that something—some inner state of mine, for instance—*could* have been different, had only something *else* been different, any consolation of this thought evaporates as soon as we add that whatever would have to have been different could not have been different.

It is even more obvious that our data cannot be reconciled to the theory of simple indeterminism. I can deliberate only about my own actions; this is obvious. But the random, uncaused motion of any body whatever, whether it be a part of my body or not, is no action of mine and nothing that is within my power. I might try to guess what these motions will be, just as I might try to guess how a roulette wheel will behave, but I cannot deliberate about them or try to decide what they shall be, simply because these things are not up to me. Whatever is not caused by anything is not caused by me, and nothing could be more plainly inconsistent with saying that it is nevertheless up to me what it shall be.

The Theory of Agency

The only conception of action that accords with our data is one according to which men—and perhaps some other things too—are sometimes, but of course not always, self-determining beings; that is, beings which are sometimes the causes of their own behavior. In the case of an action that is free, it must be such that it is caused by the agent who performs it, but such that no antecedent conditions were sufficient for his performing just that action. In the case of an action that is both free and rational, it must be such that the agent who performed it did so for some reason, but this reason cannot have been the cause of it.

Now this conception fits what men take themselves to be; namely, beings who act, or who are agents, rather than things that are merely acted upon, and whose behavior is simply the causal consequence of conditions which they have not wrought. When I believe that I have done something, I do believe that it was I who caused it to be done, I who made something happen, and not merely something within me, such as one of my own subjective states, which is not identical with myself. If I believe that something not identical with myself was the cause of my behavior—some event wholly external to myself, for instance, or even one internal to myself, such as a nerve impulse, volition, or what not—then I cannot regard that behavior as being an act of mine, unless I further believe that I was the cause of that external or internal event. My pulse, for example, is caused and regulated by certain conditions existing within me, and not by myself. I do not, accordingly, regard this activity of my body as my action, and would be no more tempted to do so if I became suddenly conscious within myself of those conditions or impulses that produce it. This is behavior with which I have nothing to do, behavior that is not within my immediate control, behavior that is not only not free activity, but not even the activity of an agent to begin with; it is nothing but a mechanical reflex. Had I never learned that my very life depends on this pulse beat, I would regard it with complete indifference, as something foreign to me, like the oscillations of a clock pendulum that I idly contemplate.

Now this conception of activity, and of an agent who is the cause of it, involves two rather strange metaphysical notions that are never applied elsewhere in nature. The first is that of a *self* or *person*—for example, a man—who is not merely a collection of things or events, but a substance and a self-moving being. For on this view it is a man himself, and not merely some part of him or something within him, that is the cause of his own activity. Now we certainly do not know that a man is anything more than an assemblage of physical things and processes, which act in accordance with those laws that describe the behavior of all other physical things and processes. Even though a man is a living being, of enormous complexity, there is nothing, apart from the requirements of this theory, to suggest that his behavior is so radically different in its origin from that of other physical objects, or that an understanding of it must be sought in some metaphysical realm wholly different from that appropriate to the understanding of nonliving things.

Second, this conception of activity involves an extraordinary conception of causation, according to which an agent, which is a substance and not an event, can nevertheless be the cause of an event. Indeed, if he is a free agent then he can, on this conception, cause an event to occur—namely, some act of his own—without anything else causing him to do so. . . .

. . . The theory of agency avoids the absurdities of simple indeterminism by conceding that human behavior is caused, while at the same time avoiding the difficulties of determinism by denying that every chain of causes and effects is infinite. Some such causal chains, on this view, have beginnings, and they begin with agents themselves. Moreover, if we are to suppose that it is sometimes up to me what I do, and understand this in a sense which is not consistent with determinism, we must suppose that I am an agent or a being who initiates his own actions, sometimes under conditions which do not determine what action I shall perform. Deliberation becomes, on this view, something that is not only possible but quite rational, for it does make sense to deliberate about activity that is truly my own and that depends in its outcome upon me as its author, and not merely upon something . . . that is supposed to be intimately associated with me, such as my thoughts, volitions, choices, or whatnot. . . .

DISCUSSION QUESTIONS

1. What reasons does Taylor give for rejecting soft determinism? Do you agree? Why?

2. What reasons does Taylor give for claiming that determinism is incompatible with the belief that a person's behavior is sometimes the outcome of his deliberation and that in such cases what a person will do is "up to that person"? Do you find any faults with his reasoning here?

3. According to Taylor, when is an action "free"?

4. What does Taylor mean by "a self?" Do you think this concept makes sense and can be utilized in the manner in which Taylor uses it? Why?

5. If one accepts Taylor's view of freedom, how can one know in a given instance whether or not a person acted freely?

6. Do you think Taylor would accept the possibility that an act of the self can itself be unfree? If not, is this plausible? If so, would there be any possible way that he could distinguish a free from an unfree act of the self?

7. According to Taylor, a rational and free act is an act caused by the self "for some reason, but this reason cannot have been the cause of it." Is it possible on such a view to distinguish "true reasons" for acting from "rationalizations"—that is, reasons which are given to justify one's action, but, in point of fact, have no effect upon one's motive for acting?

8. Does Taylor's view of freedom allow us to draw a distinction between degrees of freedom and degrees of moral responsibility? Does it allow us to make allowances for bad environmental or hereditary factors which have made it more than ordinarily difficult for a person to act otherwise than he did?

9. A common criticism of libertarianism is that such a view is inconsistent with the fact that human behavior, including human deliberation, is to a large extent predictable on the basis of a knowledge of an agent's psychological traits. If libertarianism were true, it is claimed, human behavior would appear chaotic. How do you think Taylor would reply? What do you think?

10. Consider the following criticism of Taylor:

> The example Taylor presents of the "ingenious physiologist who can induce in me any volition he pleases, simply by pushing various buttons on an instrument to which, let us suppose, I am attached by numerous wires" does not refute **soft determinism** (i.e., the view that even though determinism is true, human beings can still be free), but a particular unrefined soft deterministic analysis of freedom as lack of compulsion or constraint, which would compel us to describe Taylor's example as a "free act." On a more sophisticated analysis, however, such an example would be described as an "unfree act," as it should, and consequently would not serve as a counterexample to soft determinism.[1]

Critically discuss. If you agree with the above criti-

[1]Criticism was composed by the editor.

cism, present a soft deterministic analysis of freedom, under which Taylor's example would count as an unfree act.

11. If, as Taylor claims, a self's choices are themselves uncaused, how, if at all, can we distinguish a self's **own** choices from those choices which the self finds itself making or is imposed upon it? Is Taylor's view immune from the criticism that Taylor himself makes to the "simple indeterminism" of someone like James?

12. If free acts are not to be attributed to a person's psychological states, how then do we justify the infliction of punishment? Do we not inflict punishment on the assumption that it will act upon a person's psychological states?

13. Attempting to leave scope for the predictability of human behavior, the libertarian C.A. Campbell claims that free actions are restricted to choices between one's sense of duty and one's natural inclination, writing:

> Here, and here alone, as far as I can see, in the act of deciding whether to put forth or withhold the moral effort required to resist temptation and rise to duty, is to be found an act which is free in the sense required for moral responsibility. . . . There is X, the course which we believe we ought to follow, and Y, the course towards which we feel our desire is strongest. The freedom which we ascribe to the agent is the freedom to put forth or refrain from putting forth the moral effort required to resist the pressure of desire and do what he thinks he ought to do.
>
> But then there is surely an immense range of practical situations—covering by far the greater part of life—in which there is no question of a conflict within the self between what he most desires to do and what he thinks he ought to do. . . . Yet over that whole range there is nothing whatever in our version of Libertarianism to prevent our agreeing that character determines conduct. In the absence, real or supposed, of any "moral" issue, what a man chooses will be simply that course which, after reflection as seems called for, he deems most likely to bring him what he most strongly desires; and that is the same as to say the course to which his present character inclines him.[2]

Do you find this view plausible? Why, or why not?

[2]C.A. Campbell, *On Selfhood and Godhood* (London: George Allen and Unwin, Ltd., 1957)

53. SOME REFLECTIONS ON THE FREE WILL ISSUE

Editorial Comment

Clearly, we cannot hope to resolve the question of whether or not human actions are free until we agree on what it means to say that an action is free. While many philosophers write as if there is a single "correct" meaning of this concept, this is a mistake. Certainly, it makes sense to say that a person's action is free from one perspective but unfree (or free to a much lesser extent) from another perspective. For example, a person's action may be free in the sense that he could easily have avoided this action if he tried, but unfree in the sense that he is incapable of attending to considerations which would lead him to realize why he ought to try. What then is the sense of "freedom" that is relevant to the free will problem? As our exposure to the conflicting viewpoints of philosophers on this problem has demonstrated, the sense of "freedom" that philosophers and others are concerned about when they argue over whether or not human beings have a free will is that sense of "freedom" that they see as relevant to judgments of moral responsibility.

Although philosophers have often made it appear that the question of whether or not an individual's action is free is a ''factual'' one that can justify ascriptions of moral responsibility, the fact of the matter is that a judgment of whether or not an individual is free *presupposes* some view of the conditions under which it is ''proper'' to hold individuals morally responsible. The resolution of the question of when an individual should ''properly'' be held morally responsible, however, involves taking a moral position and not simply uncovering the relevant facts, for it is our moral decision that will specify which of the facts are to be considered relevant.

Consider, for example, a typical case of an individual acting under external ''compulsion.'' Smith is informed that if he does not assist in a particular crime he will be beaten. Smith, acting ''under compulsion,'' commits the crime. Did he act ''freely''? Did he have a choice? The answer we give to this question will depend *on what we are willing to excuse.* Those who want to excuse Smith may say, ''he really didn't have a choice'' or claim that his choice was ''forced'' and hence ''unfree.'' Those who do not want to excuse him will not call his choice a ''forced'' one, attributing it to an unpleasant but nevertheless ''free'' choice. If the crime Smith was pressured to commit involved some horrid act like killing several people, most of us would say that he acted ''freely,'' but if the crime were a minor one, that he acted ''unfreely.''

Similarly, consider a prisoner of war who is tortured into giving the enemy some intelligence. Did he have a choice? Did he act ''freely''? ''He was free to remain silent and suffer; he had a choice,'' some of us will say, while others will say, ''He was not free; he had no choice.'' It is very important to realize that what we say will depend on what we think a reasonable person ought to do in such circumstances. (If the prisoner were a spy, we would expect much more of him and consequently be much less inclined to excuse him by saying he acted ''unfreely.'') Consider, too, the possible excuses of accident and mistake. It might seem that in such cases a person clearly has no choice—for one does not choose to be careless or to make mistakes. Assuming this to be the case (psychiatrists would say that it is not always the case), this is still not the whole story. Even though accidents and mistakes are not (consciously) chosen, we can still make a distinction between ''avoidable'' and ''unavoidable'' accidents and mistakes as the law does. For example, if an intoxicated person gets himself involved in an automobile accident which would not have occurred but for his intoxication, the law will claim that his accident was ''avoidable,'' for he did not have to drink (i.e., the law takes the view that even though an accident is not in itself chosen, one can choose the events leading to it). Such an action is considered ''avoidable'' because we demand that reasonable people should refrain from driving when they are intoxicated or, at the very least, be prepared to accept responsibility for any accident they might cause as a result of that intoxication. In general, whether a given accident or mistake is said to be ''avoidable'' in the law is decided on the basis of our judgment of whether or not it was a ''reasonable'' one, and what one considers ''reasonable'' depends upon what one is willing to excuse.

Consider, too, the excuse of insanity. A person might say, ''Jones was not morally responsible; he did not act freely as a result of his insanity.'' For such a person, the judgment that an individual is insane will often be seen as a factual psychiatric one that justifies the claim that an individual is not morally responsible. But the fact of the matter is that ''insanity'' is not a psychiatric term at all, but is a legal one which is defined on the basis of an insanity rule. There is, however, much legal disagreement as to which insanity rule best picks out those who *morally ought* to be considered insane.

Since the decision as to whether or not an individual "acted freely" presupposes a moral standard under which the proper conditions for moral responsibility are defined, the question of whether or not a person "really" acted freely reduces to the question of whether or not there is some single uniquely justifiable moral perspective from which judgments of moral responsibility should be made. It is my opinion that there is not—that any single perspective will prove inadequate to achieve all reasonable human purposes and to express all reasonable human attitudes; as a consequence, we move from perspective to perspective as our shifting purposes and attitudes lead us. With this claim as a backdrop, let us critically consider the traditional soft deterministic, hard deterministic, and libertarian positions on the free will issue.

Soft Determinism

Soft determinists are, I think, quite right that *if* the distinction between free and unfree actions is to have any meaning at all, it must be understood in terms of the differences in the nature of the causes behind one's acts—causes which are, in principle, capable of scientific understanding and prediction. While many things can interfere with a person's freedom, the mere fact that these decisions and actions are capable of scientific explanation and prediction does not in itself interfere with that freedom. For example, every morning when I awake I "freely" choose to have a cup of coffee. Anyone who has lived with me knows that this is what I will do (assuming that I am not ill and that the coffee is available). I assume that my morning ritual of having a cup of coffee as I browse through the paper is caused by certain psychological and physiological factors that are capable of detailed scientific explanation. If this is so, I see no good reason to say that I am "unfree" when I groggily make my way to the kitchen to get that cup of coffee. (I am not "addicted" to the coffee. I could get the same result by taking a cold shower; I just prefer the coffee.) Since I am not acting under any type of *compulsion* or *ignorance* as to the nature of what I am doing, I look at myself as acting freely. In short, a free act is not a (scientifically) uncaused act, it is rather an act that is not *caused in some special way* that renders judgments of moral responsibility inappropriate. In this, soft determinists are quite right. The problem with soft-determinists, however, is that they tend to provide oversimplified analyses of the notion of *free agency* which disguise the diversity of the various causal factors that reasonable people take as relevant to ascriptions of moral responsibility.

Consider, for example, the influential soft deterministic analysis of freedom as the absence of compulsion. As Moritz Schlick, following both David Hume and John Stuart Mill put it, "Freedom means the opposite of compulsion; a man is free if he does not act under compulsion, and he is compelled or unfree when he is hindered from without in the realization of his natural desires." From this perspective, as long as an individual can do as he pleases, without external compulsion, he is (by definition) acting freely or has "free will." Supporters of this point of view, however, usually leave the notion of compulsion unanalysed, assuming, quite mistakenly, that this notion has a transparently clear definition.

There are, no doubt, clear cases of human behavior that we would all agree are due to compulsion and, for that reason, clearly unfree. For example, we would all agree that an epileptic is behaving under the influence of a compulsion and, consequently, acting unfreely when he finds himself helplessly in the midst of a seizure. In this clear-cut example of unfree behavior due to some external compulsive force, there is no element of choice at all. Once we turn away from such clear-cut examples of involuntary behavior, however, and turn to those actions which do involve some element of choice, it becomes very difficult to understand exactly what we mean or ought to mean when we say that an action is due to external compulsion. An example often given of such an action by soft determinists is that of a person doing something under the threat of death—such as, when someone is pointing a gun at you and asks you to divulge some information. When a person acts as a result of such compulsion, the act is an unfree one for which the actor is not morally responsible, it is said. This is, however, problematic. A person who chooses to divulge information rather than to face the clear and immediate prospect of his death could have chosen death rather than divulge the information if he had wanted to. Indeed, if the actor were a captured spy, it would be his obligation to make such a choice. As mentioned before, whether or not we call such an action free depends upon what we are willing to excuse. Since we are often faced with unpleasant choices that we perceive as being at least to some extent imposed on us from without, we must make a decision as to what type or degree of external constraint upon our behavior renders that behavior unfree. This decision is a moral one that cannot be resolved simply by looking at the facts.

For example, attorney F. Lee Bailey argued in defense of Patty Hearst that she was brainwashed into robbing a bank with members of the radical group that kidnapped her. According to Bailey, the pressures under which Ms. Hearst was forced to choose whether or not to accept the wishes of her captors were so compulsive as to render her action an unfree one. Given the coercive nature of her captivity, Ms. Hearst's only avenue of self-preservation was to *identify* with her captors, Bailey asserted, with the backing of psychiatric testimony. No doubt, Ms. Hearst was in a very unpleasant coercive situation when she allowed herself to be influenced by her captors to become the seemingly self-assured and proud radical that she became, but was she not also in a very unpleasant coercive situation when she was influenced by her attorney and parents to appear in court as a humble, timid girl who repentantly became again the dutiful daughter that she once was? If Ms. Hearst joined her captors out of fear for her own safety, is it not possible that she went along with her attorney and parents out of fear of imprisonment? If this is so, and if the first choice can properly be called compulsive, why shouldn't the second one qualify as compulsive as well?

It is precisely because the answer to such a question requires a moral decision as to the causal factors that affect a person's moral responsibility that psychiatric "experts" find themselves in the unflattering position of never agreeing on their judgments of a defendant's criminal responsibility. "Yes, she was brainwashed," "Yes, she did act under compulsion," some say. "No, she was not brainwashed," "No, she did not act under compulsion," others say. And though such a debate is often presented in courts of law as being over a purely factual issue for which psychiatrists are especially qualified to offer testimony, this is simply not the case. The fact of the matter is that psychiatrists, like the rest of us, simply do not agree on what *ought* to count as rendering an action "unfree as a result of compulsion." Two psychiatrists might very well agree on the nature of the pressures that a person faced and disagree over whether or not these pressures had compulsive force, for they, like the rest of us, *do not clearly know what is meant by a compulsive force.*

As we grapple with what it means to say that an act is due to compulsion, our heads may swim in a swirl of conceptual confusion. If acting under compulsion is to be identified with acting under an "irresistible impulse," am I acting under compulsion when I run to help my small child who has severely hurt himself? Clearly, we do not want to say this, for we tend to call actions compulsive only when an individual's choices are determined by needs, desires, or motives with which he does not identify himself or of which he does not approve. Consequently, the notion of a compulsive action carries along the suggestion of fighting against alien and strong desires which incline one to do something that does not fit in with one's normal personality or which go against one's value system. Yet, one may wonder, why should a person's failure to identify with his desires be considered an excusing factor, for is not the decisive factor in the determination of moral responsibility whether an individual has the power to control his desires and not that he consider them as parts of his normal self? After all, we all, at one time or another, find within ourselves very strong desires which seem alien to our nature, which seem as if they were imposed upon us from without. Yet as long as we have some degree of control over them, should we not be responsible for them?

But as our minds continue swimming in philosophical confusion, we wonder how we can determine the degree of control individuals have over their desires. This becomes especially puzzling when we realize that a person can appear to us and herself as acting free of any external compulsion but nevertheless be a victim of some type of internal compulsion over which she is unaware—for instance, she might be acting under the influence of a hypnotic suggestion. But if acting under a hypnotic suggestion renders an action as due to internal compulsion and for that reason unfree, what if someone acts in a particular way because of some childhood experience or purely biochemical condition which exerts its influence on a purely unconscious level? Are these not unfree actions as well? Is it not also the case that many actions which appear to be under deliberate conscious control are in fact more like compulsive actions in that rational control is absent because the true significance of the action is not realized? If Freud and other psychiatrists are right, is it not the case that the sphere of compulsive actions is much wider than most of us think? How wide is it? Are any of our actions ever totally free of internal unconscious influences that can be said to function as compulsive forces? Even if they sometimes are free of such forces, how can we ever know when this is so?

In addition, even if we could clearly agree upon a definition of that sort of internal or external compulsion that negates human freedom and could specify a range of human actions which is exempt from it, it still would seem to be wrong to claim that all acts which are performed free of compulsion are free actions which justify the ascription of moral responsibility. If we accept this point of view, it follows that nonrational creatures such as animals and very young children act freely and are morally responsible, for they often act without internal or external compulsion. Clearly, however, such a conclusion would be rejected. Why is this so? Is it not because animals and very young children are not *rational* creatures that have a capacity for reasoned choice and moral reflection? If animals and very young children are not ordinarily considered free and morally responsible agents because they are incapable (or not sufficiently capable) of altering their behavior in accordance with rational considerations, cannot the same sometimes be said of human beings? Would we call a person free who acts as he chooses, without any compulsion, but is incapable of perceiving and rationally weighing alternative courses of action? I would think not. Consequently, it would appear that individuals should not be said to act freely unless they are capable of rationally considering the nature and consequences of possible courses of action. Many philosophers have thought so, identifying the notion of free action with the capacity for rational choice.

For many philosophers who accept this identification, a free and morally responsible person is (by definition) a person whose actions are guided by rational considerations and, as such, is capable of modifying his behavior through rational persuasion. Such a view of freedom and moral responsibility has often been embraced by legal theorists seeking some rationale for legal excuses. As they have seen it, such legal excuses as duress and insanity which free an offender of criminal responsibility for his actions are justified by virtue of the fact that individuals who act under such conditions are incapable of modifying their behavior through the fear of punishment—that is, are nondeterrable.

The notions of capacity for rational choice and deterrability are, however, no less exasperating to analyze than the notion of compulsion. In particular, it is not at all clear how we should distinguish those who are *incapable* of being affected by rational reasons (or the threat of punishment) from those who are merely *indisposed* to be so affected. For example, would we not want to say that some free individuals are so courageous that no threat or infliction of punishment could ever intimidate them or cause them to modify their behavior in the future? For example, an ''incorrigible'' civil disobedient such as Gandhi would seem to be a model of nondeterrability, but we would not consider him a model of the unfree and nonresponsible individual who does not deserve praise or blame for his actions.

Hard Determinism

Even if we could clearly distinguish free from unfree actions in the manner in which soft determinists propose, a hard determinist would argue that any distinction that a soft determinist makes is too narrow in focusing attention only on the present capacities or incapacities of an individual without focusing on the causal antecedents of these capacities or incapacities. Clearly, the hard determinist will contend, we are often willing to lessen our harsh moral judgment of an individual when we find that he suffered from certain environmental or hereditary disadvantages from which most of us have been spared. But, the hard determinist will contend, if we attempt to trace back the causes of why an individual chooses to act in one way rather than another we will find that his character is ultimately the product of factors over which he had no control, namely heredity and early childhood experiences. Since a person is not responsible for these factors, how can he justifiably be held responsible for his later actions which stem from a character that was molded by these forces, the hard determinist will protest. As the philosopher Schopenhauer (1780–1860) put it, ''A man can surely do what he wills to do, but he cannot determine what he wills.'' Since a human being does not choose his character or make himself, the hard determinist will claim, it is improper to hold him morally responsible for his actions.

The notion that individuals are not ultimately morally responsible for their actions in a determined world, since in such a world individuals do not ''choose their own characters,'' is a central idea that one finds in expressions of the hard deterministic point of view. Yet the notion of ''choosing one's [entire] character'' seems to be self-contradictory, for in order to choose something, one would seem to need to already possess some type of character. Consequently, when we speak of ''choosing one's character,'' are we not already assuming that one already has some type of character? Although we can attach meaning to the notion of an individual who already has a particular type of character choosing to change or develop certain personality traits, the idea of a characterless blob (which cannot be identified as a *person*) choosing its entire character from scratch seems to be nonsensical. It would seem to be as self-contradictory to talk about ''choosing one's [entire] character'' as it is to talk of a four-sided triangle. Yet it seems to be this notion that hard determinists have in mind. Hard determinists bemoan the fact that if determinism is true, people cannot ''choose their character'' but even if determinism were false, it would appear that people would be equally incapable of choosing their characters, for this notion appears self-contradictory. Consequently, it is misleading for a hard determinist to make it appear that the validity of determinism has any bearing on a person's free will and moral responsibility. The real problem here is to understand what possible sense can be attributed to this puzzling notion of ''choosing one's [entire] character.''

Hard determinists can also be criticized for their tendency to move illegitimately and without warning from the idea that individuals are not morally responsible because they do not "make themselves" to the idea that individuals are not morally responsible because they have "no control" over themselves (see Twain, p. 417, Darrow, p. 427, and Hospers p. 435). One can, however, have the power to control or alter aspects of one's personality, however free of responsibility one may be for having these personality traits. For example, even though Jones may not have chosen to have the violent temper that he does, if he has the power to control that temper, we expect him to utilize that power. It is a common experience that the more people see themselves as helpless pawns of external forces, the less apt they are to make an effort to change themselves.[1]

A sophisticated hard determinist can grant that there is a certain dignity in being considered a morally responsible being who has control over his destiny and that human beings are indeed morally responsible in this sense. Furthermore, he might well agree that since a human being's conception of himself as a morally responsible being can motivate him to redirect his future behavior, the practice of holding individuals morally responsible is practically useful. Nevertheless, he would say that no one is morally responsible in the sense that justifies judgments of comparative moral worth and the common attitudes of righteous indignation and resentment that the "good" feel toward the "bad" (see Hospers, p. 433). From this perspective, as we learn more and more about the environmental and hereditary factors that produce a person's defective character, we often, quite rightly find ourselves inclined to "feel sorry for the poor guy," while feeling fortunate in having avoided the same causal influences ourselves. If we are good at empathy, we might be able to imagine ourselves turning out no different from the person we originally judged with feelings of moral superiority, saying, "there but for the grace of God, go I," or perhaps, more appropriately, "there, but for the grace of my causal antecedents, go I." When we see things this way, as so many of us can at times, the righteous indignation and resentment that we initially feel toward a wrongdoer undergoes a metamorphosis into a sort of cosmic sadness that the forces of the world created such a person. It is not the individual as a locus of responsibility to whom we direct our scorn but to those causes that molded him. "If only his physiology were different, or his early environment, or his parents . . . , he would not have turned out as he did," we muse. And if there is anything at all that we find redeeming about this person, as we often will, we can imagine *him* existing without his "bad" qualities and direct our sorrow for the loss of what could have been at that "good" part of him we see before us. From this point of view, the notion of a type of divine justice which distributes reward and punishment in accordance with a person's ultimate moral worth or desert is, in the last analysis, unintelligible. While one may make distinctions as to the relative desert or moral worth of human beings on the basis of *partial* and varying moral standards, reflecting different human purposes and attitudes, there is no single coherent way of ranking people in terms of their moral worth and desert, *all things considered.* This claim is, in my opinion, correct.

Libertarianism

The hard determinist's reasons for rejecting the soft determinist's attempt to reconcile freedom with determinism are shared by libertarians. Like hard determinists, libertarians see moral responsibility in terms of whether a person *deserves* praise or blame for his actions, apart from the consequences of praising or blaming him. (Consider that we often "punish" animals or

[1]See the quotation from Sidney Hook on pp. 428–29.

little children in order to modify their future behavior without judging them morally responsible for their actions.) Like the hard determinist, the libertarian would point out that we often renounce or soften our harsh moral judgment of people when we consider the causal antecedents of their actions—causal antecedents which may lead us to the conclusion that an evildoer ''did not have a reasonable chance'' to choose differently than he did. If we were concerned only with the practical utility of holding people morally responsible and punishing them, it would follow that such people should often be judged even more harshly than those who performed the same act but could have more easily avoided it, since more counteracting influences are often needed to influence those who find it more difficult to behave otherwise. Yet such a practice would be seen as *unjust.*

While the law may be justified in ignoring the causal antecedents of a person's power to do otherwise (or to be affected by rational reasons) in the formulations of standards of *legal* responsibility, the libertarian would echo the hard determinist in claiming that judgments of moral responsibility cannot ignore such considerations. In judging the moral responsibility of individuals we must focus not only on what they are capable of doing but also on why they have the capabilities that they do. If determinism were true, all human actions could ultimately be traced to factors over which human beings have no control and consequently self-determination would, in the last analysis, be impossible. Jones may, for example, kill because he is the sort of person who desires to kill. Even if Jones accepts his desire to kill as part of his own natural personality and does not see it as an alien force imposing itself upon him unwillingly, *he* cannot ultimately be held responsible for this desire if determinism is true, the libertarian claims. This is so, it is argued, because according to determinism there must be a cause for Jones' desire to kill and, even if that cause is itself an element of Jones' personality and not external to it, that cause too must have a cause, and so on, until we find ourselves focusing on the factors that *made* Jones the sort of person that he is. If determinism were true and we could grasp the entire scheme of causes that resulted in Jones' desire to kill, the notion of Jones as a responsible agent would disappear and be replaced by a network of ''inputs'' and ''outputs'' governed by inflexible and impersonal laws of nature. In this the libertarian and hard determinist are in total agreement. They disagree only in whether or not one should accept the doctrine of determinism, which both see as leading inevitably to the logical incoherence of the notion of self-determination and as a consequence to the notion of moral responsibility. Like the hard determinist, however, the libertarian does not clearly define the notion of self-determination that he sees threatened by the assumption of universal determinism. As soft determinists have claimed, various conceptual confusions underlie many of the libertarian's arguments for the view that human self-determination and moral responsibility are incompatible with determinism.

Consider, for example, William James' classic defense of indeterminism. The introspective feeling of freedom that James relies upon does not support his belief that human choices are undetermined. According to the soft determinist, this feeling is nothing more than the feeling that one can do as one pleases. Although it is conceptually impossible for a person who is in the course of deliberating to know what the outcome of that deliberation will be, this does not mean that the result of an act of deliberation is not determined and could consequently not be known beforehand by some superscientist who was aware of all the factors influencing this deliberation. The fact that one is not aware of the causes of one's action in no way shows that there is no cause for that action. For example, it was Freud's contention that many apparently random slips of the tongue were quite significant revelations of unconscious mental processes that were capable of causal explanation.

Most fundamentally, it is unreasonable to identify free actions with those that are due to chance, as James does. If, for example, Jones' decision to murder Smith was due to chance—to, let us say, some random firing of certain neurons in his brain—how can we call such an action a free one for which Jones is morally responsible? As one soft determinist put it, "in proportion as an act of volition starts of itself without cause it is exactly, so far as freedom of the individual is concerned, as if it had been thrown into his mind from without—'suggested to him by a freakish demon!' " If, as James contends, our feelings of regret that a murder occurred would be inappropriate in a determined world, would they be appropriate in a world governed by chance? Certainly not. If undesirable events are due to chance, we would have no control over the future. On the other hand, if they are determined, we can learn how to prevent similar events from occurring *again.* Is it not the case that the intelligibility of feelings of regret resides precisely in the fact that the future is open to our control through a knowledge of causes?

As soft determinists have pointed out, it is essential that one distinguish, as James does not, the doctrine of determinism from that of fatalism—that is, the doctrine that human choices are powerless to affect the future. Determinism need not, however, entail such a bleak view. The determinist is committed to the view that all events are caused, not that they will occur *in spite of* human actions to avoid them. Quite often, the nonfatalistic determinist would assert, human choices and actions can act as causes. While we cannot erase what has already happened, we can study the cause that made it happen and utilize this knowledge to create the causal conditions that will eliminate, or at least make less probable, that type of occurrence in the future. From such a perspective, human freedom resides in human control, which presupposes a deterministic universe and not one ruled by chance.

Given the implausibility of equating freedom of action with chance, most libertarians would grant that free acts are caused but would insist that they are caused not by one's psychological states but by a self (or soul) whose choices are themselves uncaused and, as a result, are incapable of scientific prediction. The main elements of such a point of view are succinctly expressed by the contemporary philosopher Richard Taylor when he writes, "When I believe that I have done something, I do believe that it was I who caused it to be done, I who made something happen, and not merely something within me, such as one of my own subjective states." Implicit in such a view are quite controversial metaphysical assumptions as to the nature of personal identity and causation. First, many philosophers, following David Hume, would deny that we have any subjective evidence for the existence of a self (or soul) which is distinct from our states of consciousness. Second, many philosophers would challenge the intelligibility of the notion of a *self*, rather than some physical or mental *event, causing* a particular human action. While it is my own belief that Taylor's point of view is a confused one, there are many reputable philosophers who would disagree.

So let us assume, for the sake of argument, that one can speak meaningfully of a self, distinct from one's psychological or physical states, causing an action, as Taylor claims. Does such an assumption help us in distinguishing free from unfree actions? What reason do we have to assume that the self, whose choices are uncaused, is always free to act one way or the other? Even if Taylor is right that the self cannot be identified with one's subjective states and character traits, he cannot reasonably deny that the self's choices are influenced by the promptings of one's subjective states and character traits. Indeed, Campbell quite readily admits that the self is influenced by the promptings of character which make it more or less difficult for the self "to rise to duty."[2] But is it not possible that these promptings are so strong that the self is powerless to overcome them? Certainly, some people clearly see what they think they ought to do, try very hard to overcome desires that lead them to do otherwise, but fail. Are they free? Certainly, Campbell would have to concede that a person who is in some manner involuntarily "programmed" to consider his duty, but to decide not to do it, is not acting of his own "free will." Are we to say then that such an action was caused by an unfree act of the self, or are we perhaps to say that the self had no causal role in this action? It would seem that Campbell and Taylor will have the same sorts of problems in deciding when a self is free or when a choice is a choice of a self and not a result of some physiological or psychological state that we had in deciding when a human being is free. Campbell and Taylor have not solved our problem; they have simply sidestepped it.

If we can turn neither to the notion of a self whose choices are incapable of scientific explanation nor to the notion of chance to provide an adequate analysis of the freedom required for self-determination and moral responsibility, then why are so many people attracted to the libertarian point of view? No doubt, as I have suggested, part of the attraction can be attributed to various conceptual confusions, in particular to the failure to distinguish determinism from fatalism and to distinguish descriptive (noncoercive) laws from prescriptive (coercive) laws (see Schlick, Selection #50). I suspect, however, that the widespread attraction to the libertarian point of view cannot be attributed solely to conceptual confusion. It is no accident, for example, that believers in the traditional Judeo-Christian God are practically always libertarians, for this seems to be the only way to logically reconcile the belief in an all-powerful, all-knowing, and perfectly good God with the traditional conception of a God who stands in ultimate judgment of the moral worth of human beings. The difficulty does not reside, as many have thought, with the belief in God's foreknowledge of our actions but with the assumption that he is our creator and is ultimately responsible for giving us the biological natures with which we were born and the environment in which we must struggle. As so many theologians have seen it, if human behavior were completely determined by hereditary and environmental forces, God would have to accept ultimate responsibility for human actions. Since they assume on faith that this is not the case, they draw the logical conclusion that human actions are not fully determined, that human beings can in some mysterious way transcend the laws of psychology and physiology that scientists seek as explanations for human behavior. As the libertarian sees it, it is in this transcendence from the laws of nature that human freedom, responsibility, and dignity reside. What distinguishes this transcendence from the fickle dictates of chance, we are not told. Yet it is this question that the libertarian must answer if his view is to be rendered intelligible.

[2]Campbell's version of libertarianism is presented in a quotation from him on p. 458.

DISCUSSION QUESTIONS

1. Argue for or against the claim made in this selection that:

> . . . the notion of a type of divine justice which distributes reward and punishment in accordance with a person's ultimate moral worth or desert is, in the last analysis, unintelligible. While one may make distinctions as to the relative desert or moral worth of human beings on the basis of **partial** and varying moral standards, reflecting different human purposes and attitudes, there is no single coherent way of ranking people in terms of their moral worth and desert, **all things considered.**

2. Consider the following excerpt from this selection:

> . . . every morning when I awake I "freely" choose to have a cup of coffee . . . . I am not "addicted" to the coffee. I could get the same result by taking a cold shower; I just prefer the coffee.

How does the speaker know that he is not a coffee addict who acts under the illusion of his freedom when he describes his choice of coffee as simply a preferred choice?

3. How can a free action be distinguished from an action performed as a result of brainwashing, subliminal suggestion, or other forms of coercive pressure?

4. Apart from coercive pressures, what factors affect one's freedom? Give some examples.

5. How do you think a libertarian would reply to the claim that our reliance upon conditioning techniques, education, and law makes sense only if we assume that human actions and choices are determined? What do you think?

6. Consider the following two claims:

> A: I had no choice in what I did, but I am morally responsible for it.
>
> B: I had a choice in what I did, but I'm not morally responsible for it.

Can you think of occasions in which either or both of these claims would be appropriate?

7. Consider the following imaginary dialogue:

> A: I wish I could take a pill which would make me always want to do what I morally should.
>
> B: The cost of such a pill would be the loss of your freedom as a human being.
>
> A: On the contrary, it would provide me with the freedom I've always sought.

What do A and B mean by "freedom"? Can a person ever be "forced to be free"? Explain.

8. If it were possible to alter the behavior of criminals by biochemical means (e.g., by giving criminals specific pills or by electronically interfering with their brain processes), would such methods make punishment superfluous? Should criminals have a right to refuse such treatments? If so, when? If such treatments were to become commonplace, would we still be inclined to speak of criminals as "deserving to be punished"? Would anything of value be lost if we ceased to look at criminals as deserving of punishment?

9. What does the following story indicate about the notions of freedom and responsibility:

> During World War I, a Jewish army doctor was sitting in a foxhole with his gentile friend, an aristocratic colonel, and heavy shooting began. Teasingly the colonel said, "You are afraid, aren't you? That's just another proof that the Aryan race is superior to the Semitic one." "Sure I'm afraid," was the doctor's answer. "But who is superior? If you, my dear colonel, were as afraid as I am, you would have run away long ago."[3]

10.a. Which of the following attempts to reconcile the belief in God's omniscience and omnipotence with the conception of God as moral judge and of human beings as free and morally responsible before God do you find the most plausible? Why?

> (1.) God does not have foreknowledge of our actions. This is not, however, a limitation on his omniscience, for it is logically impossible to have foreknowledge of the actions of free beings. Since human actions are free, they cannot be totally determined.
>
> (2.) God has foreknowledge of our actions, and since we are free beings, our actions cannot be fully determined.
>
> (3.) God has foreknowledge of our actions and, since we are free beings, our actions must be determined.
>
> (4.) God has foreknowledge of our actions and we are free. It is irrelevant whether our actions are fully determined or not.
>
> b. Are any of these positions acceptable to you? Assuming that God does have foreknowledge of our actions, can this fact be reconciled with the belief that God sees us as morally responsible individuals who **deserve** punishment or reward for our actions? If this reconciliation can be made

[3]Victor Frankl, quoted in Irving D. Yalom, *Existential Psychotherapy* (New York: Basic Books, 1980).

as far as God's foreknowledge of our actions goes, can it still be made once one adds the fact that God is conceived as an all-powerful creator of all else that exists?

11. Do you see any connection between the view a person has of the mind-body relationship and his view of the free will-determinism issue? Is a libertarian, for example, apt to be an interactionist?

FURTHER READINGS

articles and books

Campbell, C.A., *On Selfhood and Godhood*, Lecture IX. New York: Macmillan, 1957. (Reprinted in the Dworkin anthology.) Campbell defends his version of libertarianism and criticizes soft-deterministic analyses of *free action* as hypothetical behavior (i.e., "could have . . . if"). Campbell also defends his libertarian position and attacks soft determinism in general, and Schlick's position in particular, in his earlier (1951) article "Is 'Free Will' a Pseudo-Problem," which originally appeared in *Mind*, 60 (1951), pp. 441–65. It is also reprinted in the Berofsky anthology.

Dostoevsky, Fyodor, *Notes from Underground*. New York: Dell Publishing Co., 1960, originally published 1864. (The reference here is to the Dell paperback, which is one of many editions.) In this short novel, which demonstrates Dostoevsky's incisive powers of psychological analysis, the nameless hero confronts the (existential) anguish of his freedom. Convinced of the irrationality of human beings and the psychological supremacy of will over reason, Dostoevsky's hero rejects the reasoned panaceas for the ills of society provided by the socialists of Dostoevsky's day. For example, at one point the hero proclaims, " . . . man everywhere and at all times, whoever he may be, has preferred to act as he chose and not in the least as his reason and advantage dictated. . . . One's own free unfettered choice, one's own caprice—however wild it may be, one's own fancy worked up at times to frenzy—is that very 'most advantageous advantage' . . . which comes under no classification and against which all systems and theories are continually being shattered to atoms." Human beings want, Dostoevsky claims, not "rationally advantageous choice," but "independent choice." Even if our self-interest were made clear to us through scientific demonstration, we would tend to ignore it in order to demonstrate that we are *free beings* and not *mechanical objects* whose interests are scientifically determined. These sentiments, so elegantly described by Dostoevsky, provide insight into one of the factors that makes libertarianism such a psychologically appealing doctrine.

Frankfurt, Harry, "Freedom of the Will and the Concept of a Person," *Philosophical Review*, LXVIII, No. 1 (Jan. 14, 1971), pp. 5–20. In this influential article, Frankfurt equates freedom with rationality in action and downplays the challenge of determinism. Central to Frankfurt's analysis is the distinction between the desires one happens to find within oneself (first-order desires) and those self-reflective judgments one makes as to the sort of desires one would like to have (second-order desires). Frankfurt claims that the human capacity for reflective second-order desires is central to the concept of *a free person*.

Hobart, R.B., "Free Will as Involving Determination and Inconceivable without It," *Mind,* 43 (1934), pp. 1–27. (Reprinted in the Berofsky anthology.) A defense of the view that actions can be free *only when* they are determined, directed to the philosophically sophisticated.

Hospers, John, "What Means This Freedom," was first published in 1961 in the Hook anthology and is reprinted in the Dworkin anthology. Our selection is excerpted from this article. In his earlier (1950) article "Free Will and Psychoanalysis" (reprinted in the Berofsky anthology), Hospers attacks soft-determinists for neglecting unconscious influences. It would be worthwhile to compare the tougher, hard-deterministic stance Hospers takes in "What Means This Freedom" to the weaker stance he takes in "Free Will and Psychoanalysis."

Melden, A.I., *Free Action*. London: Routledge and Kegan Paul, 1961. Melden argues that while *bodily movements* are *caused*, it is logically impossible for *actions* to be *caused*. In drawing a radical logical distinction between the domain of bodily movements which can be explained in terms of (scientific) causes and the domain of actions which can be explained only in terms of *reasons*, Melden's view of the determinism-free will issue is similar to Kant's. Melden's point of view is subjected to forceful criticism by D. Davidson in his 1963 article in the *Journal of Philosophy*, "Actions, Reasons and Causes." Excerpts from both Melden and Davidson are included in the Berofsky anthology. This controversy will appeal only to the more advanced philosophy student.

Ofstad, Harold, *An Inquiry into the Freedom of Decision*. London: George Allen and Unwin, 1961. An excellent detailed analysis and survey of various positions on the determinism-free will issue for the philosophically sophisticated.

Ofstad, Harold, "Recent Work on the Free Will Problem," *American Philosophical Quarterly*, 4 (1967), pp. 179–207. An excellent and comprehensive critical analysis of different contemporary perspectives on the determinism-free will issue.

Twain, Mark, "What Is Man?" in *What Is Man? and Other Philosophical Writings*. Berkeley: University of California Press, 1973. In his typically amusing fashion, Twain presents in dialogue form a hard-deterministic picture of human nature.

anthologies

Berofsky, Bernard, ed., *Free Will and Determinism*. New York: Harper and Row, 1966. The most comprehensive anthology of material on the free will-determinism issue.

Dworkin, Gerald, ed., *Determinism, Free Will and Moral Responsibility*. Englewood Cliffs, N.J.: Prentice-Hall, 1970. A good anthology of classical and contemporary sources.

Enterman, Willard F., ed., *The Problem of Free Will*. New York: Scribners, 1967. A good collection of readable selections on the free will issue makes this anthology the best suited of those in this bibliography for the beginning philosophy student.

Hook, Sidney, ed., *Determinism and Freedom in the Age of Modern Science*. New York: Collier Books, 1961. This anthology contains the proceedings of a symposium devoted to the determinism-free will issue that took place at New York University in 1957. Many well-known philosophers and scientists were participants. Included are the ten papers presented at the symposium on the general concept of determinism; the notion of determinism in physics; and the notions of determinism, freedom, and responsibility in ethics and law. Also included are seventeen papers by participants of the symposium in reply to these papers.

Morris, Herbert, ed., *Freedom and Responsibility: Readings in Philosophy and Law*. Stanford, Ca.: Stanford University Press, 1961. A good collection of selections by philosophers, legal theorists, and psychologists on the notions of causation, freedom, and responsibility, geared to those with some prior exposure to philosophy or law.

encyclopedia of philosophy

Articles in *The Encyclopedia of Philosophy* (New York: Macmillan, 1967):, Can; Causation; Chance; Choosing; Deciding and Doing; Determinism; Freedom; Intentionality: Reasons and Causes; Responsibility, Moral and Legal; Self-Prediction; Volition; Voluntarism (i.e., the conception of the *will as a faculty of the mind*).

longer bibliographies

Alston, W., and R. Brandt, eds., *The Problems of Philosophy,* 3rd ed. Boston: Allyn and Bacon, 1978. See pp. 478–80 for an unannotated bibliography, topically arranged.

Edwards, P., and A. Pap, eds., *A Modern Introduction to Philosophy,* 3rd ed. New York: Macmillan, 1973. See pp. 99–114 for an extensive annotated bibliography.

Chapter VII

POLITICAL PHILOSOPHY: GOVERNMENTAL AUTHORITY AND INDIVIDUAL AUTONOMY

Suppose the laws . . . were to come . . . to me as I was preparing to run away . . . and were to ask ". . . Do you think that a state can exist and not be overthrown, in which the decisions of law are . . . disregarded and undermined by private individuals." . . . Shall I reply, "But the state has injured me by judging my case unjustly?" . . . . And suppose the laws were to reply, "Was that our agreement? Or was it that you would abide by whatever judgments the state should pronounce?" . . . . "[Y]ou must do whatever your state and country tell you to do, or you must persuade them that their commands are unjust . . . " . . . . [The laws] would say, "Are you breaking your contracts and agreements with us? . . . . You had seventy years in which you might have gone away if you had been dissatisfied with us, or if the agreement had seemed to you unjust . . . "

Plato

Should it be said, that, by living under the dominion of a prince which one might leave, every individual has given a tacit *consent to his authority, and promised him obedience; it may be answered, that such an implied consent can only have place where a man imagines that the matter depends on his choice . . . . Can we seriously say, that a poor peasant or artisan has a free choice to leave his country, when he knows no foreign language or manners, and lives, from day to day, by the small wages which he acquires? We might as well assert that a man, by remaining in a vessel, freely consents to the dominion of the master; though he was carried on board while asleep, and must leap into the ocean and perish, the moment he leaves her.*

David Hume

If one claims the right to disobey laws for the sake of one's conscience, one must grant to others as well the right to disobey laws opposed by their consciences . . . . Relations among citizens would rest on their divergent consciences —and on whatever power each group might

I think that we should be men first, and subjects afterward. . . . A common and natural result of an undue respect for law is, that you may see a file of soldiers . . . marching in admirable order over hill and dale to the wars, against their wills, ay, against their common

muster to make its conscience prevail . . . . Once they are not regarded as morally binding, laws are hard to enforce without a police state . . . . The outcome would be a social organization depending on naked power alone, therefore exceedingly precarious as well as brutal, perhaps unviable, and certainly immoral.

Ernest Van Der Haag

If a man is to treat other men as ends in themselves, and not merely as means to his own moral self-fulfillment, a man must recognize them as independent agents by being prepared on occasion to do what they want and what they deem best, and not be entirely a moral law unto himself . . . . Loyalty and friendship, at least among finite, fallible, imperfect beings, are necessarily heteronomous [i.e., subject to external law, nonautonomous] virtues. If I am to be human, I cannot be completely captain of my soul, but must submit myself in part to the judgment of others.

J.R. Lucas

sense and consciences, which makes it very steep marching indeed, and produces a palpitation of the heart . . . . The mass of men serve the state thus, not as men mainly, but as machines, with their bodies. . . . In most cases there is not free exercise whatever of the judgment or of the moral sense. . . . Such command no more respect than men of straw. . . . Yet such as these even are commonly esteemed good citizens. Others—as most legislators, politicians, lawyers, ministers, and officeholders—serve the state chiefly with their heads; and as they rarely make any moral distinctions, they are as likely to serve the Devil, without ***intending*** *it, as God.*

Henry D. Thoreau

A promise to abide by the will of the majority creates an obligation, ***but it does so precisely by giving up one's autonomy*** *. . . . [Citizens by making such a promise] have bound themselves to obey laws which they do not will, and indeed even laws which they vigorously reject. Insofar as democracy originates in such a promise, it is no more than voluntary slavery.*

Robert Paul Wolff

The sole end for which mankind are warranted, individually or collectively, in interfering in the liberty of action of any of their number, is self protection . . . the only purpose for which power can be rightfully exercised on any member of a civilized community, against his will, is to prevent harm to others. . .

John Stuart Mill

. . . society is . . . kept together . . . by the invisible bonds of common thought. If the bonds were too far relaxed, the members would drift apart. A common morality is part of the bondage. The bondage is part of the price of society, and mankind, which needs society, must pay its price.

Patrick Devlin

The methods of education, moral discourse, and persuasion are acceptable not because they recognize the freedom of the individual . . . but because they make only partial contributions to the control of his behavior . . . . When they show too much strength to permit disguise,

Experience should teach us to be most on our guard to protect liberty when the government's purposes are beneficent. Men born to freedom are naturally alert to repel invasion of their liberty by evil-minded rulers. The greatest dangers to liberty lurk in insidious encroach-

we give them other names and suppress them as energetically as we suppress the use of force. Education grown too powerful is rejected as propaganda . . . . We are all controlled by the world in which we live, and part of that world has been and will be constructed by men. The question is this: Are we to be controlled by accident, by tyrants, or by ourselves in effective cultural design?

B. F. Skinner

ment by men of zeal, well-meaning but without understanding.

Louis D. Brandeis

Introduction: Individual Conscience and the Obligation to Obey the Law

In periods of political tranquility, most of us in the United States unquestioningly accept our obligation to obey the laws promulgated by our government, even when we disagree with those laws. While some of us obey laws that we find to be disagreeable only out of fear of the vast power our government has to compel us to obey, the vast majority of us recognize our government's *authority* or *right* to compel us to obey. The power of our government, we tend to believe, is not like the naked coercive power of a bandit with a gun, but is *legitimate* power. In tranquil times, few stop to ponder the source of the governmental authority so readily taken for granted. Discussions over the source and limits of governmental authority become widespread, however, in periods of political turmoil, when large numbers of people find themselves dissatisfied with governmental institutions, laws, or actions.

For example, during the turbulent decade of the 1960's, people hotly debated the issue of whether and to what extent citizens in our American democracy had a moral right to disobey the law. In the civil rights movement of that decade, Martin Luther King, protesting against racial discrimination, advocated a citizen's moral right to nonviolent public disobedience of valid laws as a vehicle of protest. In his emphasis upon nonviolence and public disobedience, as well as in his passive acceptance of punishment for his disobedience of law, King was following in the respected tradition of Gandhi in India in the earlier part of the twentieth century and of Henry David Thoreau in Massachusetts in the 1840's. It was Thoreau who first coined the term *civil disobedience* to describe such action. Believing that King's peaceful civil disobedience would prove incapable of eradicating the legacy of racial injustice, other more radical blacks preached the moral right of violent disobedience of the law.

The spirit of political protest of the civil rights movement struck a sympathetic chord of idealism in young college students throughout our country. Infused with the belief in the moral superiority of conscience over legality, many students turned the weapon of civil disobedience against the ever-escalating war in Vietnam and the military draft that supported it and threatened their own future. One should not sit back, they said, and complacently accept the colossal injustice of the Vietnam war, even if a majority of our citizens do accept it. A young man, they continued, has the right, and indeed the moral obligation, to refuse to fight in a war to which he is morally opposed.

The arguments of the idealistic young for the supremacy of conscience over law were countered by those who preached the need for "law and order." For example, in the earlier days of the civil rights movement, President Kennedy proclaimed:

> . . . Our nation is founded on the principle that observance of the law is the eternal safeguard of liberty and defiance of the law is the surest road to tyranny.
>
> The law which we obey includes the final rulings of the courts as well as the enactments of our legislative bodies. Even among law-abiding men few laws are universally loved. But they are universally respected and not resisted.
>
> Americans are free, in short, to disagree with the law, but not to disobey it. For in a government of laws and not of men, no man, however prominent or powerful . . . is entitled to defy a court of law.
>
> If this country should ever reach the point where any man or group of men, by force or threat of force, could long deny the commands of our court and our Constitution, then no law would stand free from doubt . . . and no citizen would be safe from his neighbors.[1]

Behind such sentiments was an often heard philosophic argument. A commitment to democracy, the argument went, entails a commitment to abide by the wishes of the majority. If everyone reserved for himself the right to disobey laws he believed to be unjust, anarchy would be the result. Since everyone's reserving for himself the right to disobey laws he considers to be unjust would have disastrous consequences, it is wrong for anyone to do so, for morality demands that one grant to others the same rights that one assumes for oneself.

The supporters of disobedience to the law countered the preceding argument with arguments of their own. At the heart of the debate that ensued was an apparent dilemma. On the one hand a commitment to any mode of government involves a willingness to give up a degree of one's autonomy to the state. On the other hand, any political decision procedure, even the democracy we learn as children to cherish, can lead to grave injustice that seems to demand noncompliance. How then is one to weigh one's obligation as a citizen to obey the law against one's obligation as a human being to do what justice demands? How can one claim a commitment to democracy and at the same time reserve for oneself the right to go against the results of the democratic process? Can such a commitment really be justified? Does the state really have the right (authority) to compel us to forfeit our moral autonomy? If so, what is the source of that right and what are its limits?

Some Historical Background: The Emergence of Political Liberalism

The question of the legitimacy of governmental authority is the central question in *political philosophy,* that branch of philosophy concerned with questions of moral justification and conceptual analysis in the context of the relationships between individuals, society, and government. As is the case with Western philosophy in general, the history of Western political philosophy begins with the ancient Greeks. As they and the Romans that followed them saw it, human beings are by their very natures "social animals" bound to each other through relations of mutual dependence, respect, and sympathy. Since from this perspective, a society is as much an organic whole as human beings are themselves, the need for some central authority coordinating the parts of an organic group of human beings called a society is as obvious as is the need for the human body to be subjected to the central control of human reason. This *or-*

[1] *New York Times,* October 1, 1962, p. 22.

ganic view of social relations finds its classic expression in Plato's (427?–347 B.C.) most famous dialogue, *The Republic*, and is echoed in (his student) Aristotle's (384–322 B.C.) writings on political philosophy. Taking for granted the legitimacy of governmental authority, Plato and Aristotle turned their attention to the questions of who should exercise that authority, under what conditions, and within what limits.

In the theological world view of the Middle Ages, which saw all authority deriving ultimately from God, secular governmental authority was naturally seen as a trust from God, whether that authority be the power of a feudal lord over his serf or an absolute monarch over his subjects. As absolute monarchy became the mode of government in Western Europe, the brute physical power that brought such monarchies into power was legitimized through the general belief in "the divine right of kings" to rule. As a result of both the decline of the Church's influence at the end of the Middle Ages in the fifteenth century and the Protestant Reformation (i.e., the religious movement that resulted in the establishment of the various sects of Protestantism) in the sixteenth century, a new *liberal* tradition of political philosophy emerged, a tradition greatly influenced by the new Protestant doctrine of the equal priesthood of all believers before God and of equal access to divine revelation and moral truth. At the core of this new liberal political philosophy was a commitment to individualism. Unlike the organic political theorist, who saw human beings as inherent parts of a greater social whole, the individualistic political theorist saw government and law as instruments for the satisfaction of private human needs that are independent of a specific social setting. Influenced by the new ideology of individual freedom that justified the growing power of the new middle class, the liberal political theorist, unlike his organic predecessor, saw the coercive power of government that curbs individual freedom as an intrinsic evil that cried out for justification. The central question from the liberal perspective was how human beings could justify the loss of freedom entailed by submission to governmental authority. As Jean-Jacques Rousseau (1712–78) put it at the very beginning of his classic treatise on political philosophy, *The Social Contract*, "Man is born free, and everywhere he is in chains." Can such "chains" really be justified? political theorists now asked. Indeed, are they really chains, or is submission to authority self-imposed, that is, a result of some type of mutual agreement or consent?

The idea that the legitimacy of a state derives from the mutual agreement or consent of the governed is the key idea of various *social contract* theories of political obligation, which attempt to answer the central question posed by political liberalism. As the words of the American Declaration of Independence state, "Governments are instituted among men, deriving their just powers from the consent of the governed. . . ." The Declaration's assumptions of a social contract view of political obligation and of the doctrine of *natural rights* ("We hold these truths to be self-evident, that all men . . . are endowed by their Creator with certain unalienable rights. . .") reflect the intellectual debt its author Thomas Jefferson (1743–1826) owed to the political philosophy of the classical social contract theorist John Locke (1632–1704), as expressed in his famous *Two Treatises of Government* (1690). This classic of Western political liberalism was in turn greatly influenced by Thomas Hobbes' (1588–1679) classic of political theory *Leviathan* (1651), of which Locke was highly critical. Beginning with the same view that the legitimacy of government derives from the consent of the governed, Hobbes saw the necessity for unlimited and undivided sovereignty while Locke saw the necessity for limited powers of government and for the "checks and balances" that so strongly motivated the framers of our American Constitution.

Hobbes: The Classical Social Contract Justification for Unlimited Sovereignty

Written in a period of great political unrest and discussion in England, when social contract theorists attempted to undercut the power of the English monarchy, Hobbes' *Leviathan* employed the same social contract perspective to argue for the absolutism that defenders of the monarchy argued for on the grounds of tradition and divine rights. As is the case in all great classics of political philosophy, underlying the arguments of *Leviathan* is a particular theory of human nature. Committed to a deterministic, materialistic world view, Hobbes painted a very bleak and pessimistic picture of human nature. Human beings are, he believed, complex causal mechanisms, motivated only by self-interest. Unconcerned about anyone but themselves, human beings are incapable of renouncing their selfish appetites for the common good or for moral principles that transcend their own egotistical concerns. Consequently, *the state of nature* (i.e., conditions in the world prior to the institution of government) is for Hobbes an amoral condition in which everyone attempts to satisfy his purely selfish appetites. Alas, however, the realities of limited resources make this impossible and human beings come into conflict. The result is a jungle-like existence that is, in Hobbes' memorable words, ''solitary, poor, nasty, brutish and short.'' Given the fact that human beings are equal enough in physical strength, mental shrewdness, and vulnerability to render negligible the strengths of others, everyone is dissatisfied with this state of affairs. Wanting above all else the security and freedom from fear that is impossible in a state of nature, human beings desperately seek an alternative to their miserable state of existence. Since they are fortunately rational as well as selfish, human beings realize that peace with their fellows is necessary for a tolerable existence. As Hobbes saw it, it is precisely our overriding fear of the insecurity of the state of nature that prompts us to accept the civilizing coercion of an external government. Revealingly, Hobbes is said to have often jested that ''fear and I were born twins,'' referring to the fact that he was born prematurely when, in great fear, his mother heard about the approach of the menacing Spanish Armada.

As Hobbes saw it, the insecurity of the state of nature can be eliminated only when human beings submit to absolute and undivided governmental power. If human beings were morally perfect, a mutual promise to refrain from violence would suffice to provide the security which human beings are so desirous of obtaining, but given their amoral nature, ''covenants, without the sword, are but words, and of no strength to secure man at all,'' Hobbes wrote. Given the total selfishness of human beings, matters must be so arranged that it will never be to anyone's advantage to break his promise. This is possible, Hobbes believed, only if there is an absolute and unlimited government to enforce the promise. Anything less, he believed, would invite anarchy. While Hobbes himself was a strong defender of a monarchy (a view, it has been suggested, he may have adopted to curry favor with the king), what was essential, as Hobbes saw it, was that sovereignty be unlimited and undivided and not that it be given to a single individual rather than to a group of individuals. Nevertheless, it seemed to Hobbes that if the power of government were in the hands of more than one person, it would be much more difficult to assure the secrecy and constancy of policy that effective government requires, and the ever-present possibility of disagreement among the rulers would provide the potential for civil war and the dreaded anarchy that government was meant to eliminate.

Having consented to (or having agreed that it would be rational to so consent[2]) absolute sovereignty, citizens can justifiably revolt, Hobbes believed, only when the sovereign can no longer protect their lives and physical security. As Hobbes was well aware, a government's ability to provide its citizens with security is consistent with great tyranny; nevertheless, the tyranny of a government that assures its citizens physical protection is less obnoxious than the tyranny of the amoral law of the jungle and its resultant anarchy, Hobbes believed.

Locke: The Classical Social Contract Justification of Limited Sovereignty and the Separation of Powers

Like Hobbes' *Leviathan,* Locke's *Two Treatises of Government* (1690) was written in a time of political turmoil. This work served as a philosophical justification for the middle-class-inspired Glorious Revolution (Bloodless Revolution) of 1688, which increased the power of the English parliament relative to that of the monarchy. Locke's arguments for limited government had great influence in the United States and France as well as in Great Britain. Locke's influence upon such American political theorists as Jefferson and Paine was reflected in the Declaration of Independence and the United States Constitution, which accepted all of Locke's major proposals for an ideal government. In France, Locke's influence was reflected in the political writings of Montesquieu and Rousseau, which in turn provided the philosophical justification for the French Revolution (1789–99).

Rejecting Hobbes' bleak picture of human nature, Locke saw human beings as motivated by feelings of benovolence and empathy as well as by self-interest. Most importantly, he believed that people have the capacity to renounce their selfish interests for the demands of an objective morality that could be used as a standard for judging the legitimacy of the actual laws of a society. At the core of Locke's political philosophy was his commitment to the notion of *natural law,* whose roots go back to antiquity. According to the natural law tradition, all existing laws are subject to appraisal by an objective and self-evident code of morality that is inherent in the rational fabric of the universe. Accepting the theological underpinning for this viewpoint that was widely held in the Middle Ages, Locke saw the Judeo-Christian god as the ultimate source of natural law and the natural rights which flowed from it. As he saw it, human beings are God's property. Because of this, no human being can rightfully have complete control over another human being, who has such natural rights as the right to life, liberty, and property. It is these natural rights which provide God's ordained limits to the power of any government over its subjects, Locke believed.

Like Hobbes before him, Locke built his political philosophy upon the foundations of his conception of human beings in a state of nature. Locke's natural man, unlike Hobbes' natural man, recognizes the moral legitimacy of the natural rights of other people. In particular, he recognizes their right to life and to the

[2]It is unclear whether Hobbes believed that the agreement of human beings to abide by the directives of an absolute sovereign actually occurred or was rather a *hypothetical* account of the rationality of such an agreement. The first view, as Hume sharply pointed out in his criticism of social contract theories, is in practically all cases refuted by the historical facts. According to the second view, however, the actual genesis of government is not at issue. What is at issue is whether it would be rational for a person to consent to his government. If we answer this question in the affirmative, then, it is claimed, we have the same moral obligation to abide by the directives of our government that we would have had if we had actually promised to so abide. Such a view was explicitly held by Spinoza, who was greatly influenced by Hobbes.

ownership of those goods with which he "has mixed his labor."[3] In addition, he recognizes that he has a natural, God-given right to punish transgressors of the natural law. Indeed, as Locke saw it, there are actually two distinct rights here, "the one of punishing the crime, for restraint and preventing the like offense, which right of punishing is in everybody; the other of taking reparation, which belongs only to the injured party." While painting a much more optimistic picture of the state of nature than Hobbes, Locke too saw such a state as one that rational people would find less desirable than the institution of governmental authority for protecting life and property and punishing transgressions of the natural law. This is so, Locke claimed, because in a state of nature, there is no uniform and impartial administration of the natural law and often inadequate force for punishing its transgressors. In order to remedy the inadequacies of the state of nature, a government is required to lay down uniform and specific laws which follow from the laws of nature, to interpret and administer these laws, and to enforce them. In short, a legislature, judiciary and executive are required. Realizing the need for these governmental functions, human beings in a state of nature would find it reasonable to delegate their own natural right of enforcing the natural law to some centralized government, as long as no single branch of government is given absolute power, for absolute power, Locke believed, is an invitation to tyranny. Ridiculing Hobbes' contention that individual security requires absolute government, Locke wrote:

> . . . The hypothesis is that the timid individual would exchange the possible threat to life presented by 100,000 men, all of whom individually might attack him, for the threat to his life made possible by the authority of one man, who has 100,000 men under his command and can do anything he pleases, without fear. . .

[3]It is interesting to note that Locke's strong emphasis upon the natural right to property provided a philosophical justification for the legitimacy of the growing English middle class and the Whig party, which reflected its interests. As Karl Marx would later provocatively charge, Locke's political theory may be seen as an *after the fact* attempt at philosophical justification for a change in social relations actually caused by underlying economic currents.

A firm believer in majority rule, Locke saw the contractual surrender of individual authority to centralized government as a two-step procedure. First, there is the commitment to abide by the will of the majority. Second, the specific features and relative powers of the various branches of government are decided upon by the will of the majority. Insisting only on governmental "checks and balances" and on the separation of powers, Locke did not think it essential that the majority choose a specific form of government. For example, Locke was not in principle opposed to putting the power to make law into the hands of one or a very small number of people. Clearly influenced by the British form of government, however, Locke expressed his preference for dual legislatures, consisting of "an assembly of hereditary nobility" and "an assembly of representatives chosen pro tempore by the people" and for a "single hereditary person having the constant, supreme, executive power." (As Locke saw it, the supreme branch of government should be the legislature. The executive branch, he believed should be extremely limited, its principal function being to act in national emergencies.)

The Dilemma of Civil Disobedience for Citizens Who Accept the Legitimacy of Their Government

While having quite different views of the conditions that nullify a citizen's obligation to obey the law, both Hobbes and Locke appear to have seen these conditions only in the light of a citizen's decision to reject totally the authority of his government—that is, in the context of the right to revolution. Yet, as the issue of civil disobedience makes clear, many people who do not challenge the general authority of their government would also claim that we have a moral right to disobey specific laws that we consider unjust, even if these laws are valid according to the procedures of law. Indeed, many would go further, claiming that we have a moral right to violate just laws as a vehicle for protesting unjust laws or unjust conditions (e.g., blocking traffic in order to protest a war).

At the center of the debate concerning the legitimacy of civil disobedience is that apparant dilemma with which this introduction began. If one rejects the right to disobey laws one believes to be unjust or laws whose violation can be a vehicle of protest, one foregoes a potent weapon for awakening people to injustice. Thus, at least in some cases, one would seem to share in the responsibility for the continuation of that injustice. On the other hand, there seems to be a threat of anarchy when individual conscience reigns supreme over the authority of a legitimate governmental decisions procedure. Can such a dilemma be resolved? Is there some middle way? The reader should ponder this question while reading this chapter's selections on civil disobedience, consisting of (1) Plato's classic defense of the supremacy of law over human conscience in his *Crito*, (2) the similar, though seemingly more moderate, position of Abe Fortas in his book *Concerning Dissent and Civil Disobedience*, written in 1968 when Fortas was a Justice of the United States Supreme Court, and (3) the heated rebuttal to Fortas by Howard Zinn, a professor of political science, in his book *Disobedience and Democracy* (1968).

The Legitimate Scope of Governmental Authority: A Government's Right to Enforce a Moral Code

Given the fallibility of human judgment and the apparent existence of rationally irreconcilable divergence in basic moral principles, the dilemma of having to choose between the conflicting moral demands of individual conscience and of governmental authority is an ineradicable one. Yet, the mark of a viable and generally accepted government is that such conflicts are infrequent. In order to minimize these moral conflicts, governments often encourage acceptance of a common moral code that serves as a type of social cement, binding its citizens together in common moral commitment. This is especially so in totalitarian governments. Unwilling to accept the existence of moral diversity and the free discussion upon which it thrives, totalitarian governments tend to be ruthless in their suppression of the moral outcast who marches to a different drummer. One of the greatest strengths of democracy, it is often said, is its tolerance of divergence. Given its fundamental commitment to "government by the people," a democracy must publicly justify its political decisions. This fact in turn encourages citizens to conduct political debates in moral terms. Accepting a citizen's right to participate in these moral debates, democratic governments tend to be much more tolerant of moral diversity than totalitarian ones, since they recognize that if a citizen is to freely choose among governmental policies, he must be free to hear unorthodox as well as orthodox opinions.

Nevertheless, a strongly morally committed democratic majority, no less than an unlimited dictator who has no legal obligation to answer to anyone, can be exceedingly repressive, denying individuals any rights other than those which the majority deems fit. Indeed, it was the fear of the possible "tyranny of the majority" that led the framers of the United States Constitution to amend that Constitution with a Bill of Rights, which provides citizens with *rights* protecting them against the majority will.

The classic philosophical defense of the right of the nonconformist in a democracy is found in John Stuart Mill's *On Liberty* (1859). It was Mill's belief that democratically inclined political philosophers, such as John Locke, in their attempt to defend majority rule over the power of absolute monarchy, failed to place sufficient safeguards upon the possible tyranny of the majority. It is essential, Mill believed, that the rights of minorities to unconventional styles of living and to free expression should be protected, however offensive such styles of living and believing might be to the majority. Although afraid of the possibility of repressive laws, Mill was more afraid of the indirect power of societal pressure directed against nonconforming individuals—pressure which can be strong enough to deprive people of such rights as that of living where they choose, obtaining employment, and teaching what they believe. Without such rights, Mill believed, a democracy could easily exchange the tyranny of an absolute monarchy for the potentially even greater tyranny of a majority that, convinced of its claim to moral superiority by the force of its numbers, is capable of employing the most efficient means of social control—the pressure of public opinion. Underlying Mill's fervent plea for individual freedom was his belief that the on-going search for truth and happiness requires an unrestricted competition among differing ideas and lifestyles. As long as people do not interfere with the liberty of others, Mill believed, they should be allowed the right to be idiosyncratic and to live their lives as they see fit. Since we have not obtained full perfection and indeed can never hope to in this world, the maximization of human happiness (Mill was a committed utilitarian) requires that individuals be allowed the freedom to form their own "experiments in living" and not be forced into a stifling "tendency to conformity which breeds only withered capacities."

Mill's faith in the utilitarian value of individual freedom has been rejected by many political philosophers. For example, Plato believed that societies which encourage individual freedom and diversity of thought tend to degenerate into societies of selfish egotists who seek private and hollow self-gratification. Finding no lasting fulfillment in the satisfaction of purely private impulses, the socially unstructured libertine seeks more and more intense private pleasures which ultimately prove self-destructive. From Plato's point of view, the very liberty and individuality which Mill celebrates tends to lead first to lack of moral discipline, then to individual unhappiness and self-destructiveness, and finally to social anarchy. Plato's view in this regard is reflected in the conservative philosophy of the influential English political philosopher Edmund Burke (1729–97) and the French sociologist Emile Durkheim (1858–1917), both of whom emphasized the human need to enfold oneself within the structure of moral values provided by an established community. Seeing the acceptance of a diversity of morals and lifestyles as a threat to social stability, Burke and Durkheim believed that most individuals, freed of the meaning and warmth that shared values provide, will find themselves alone, anchorless, and adrift in a sea of unstructured desires. Individual reason will prove sadly incapable of unifying these desires into a coherent whole and the quest for individuality will tend to lead, not as Mill thought it would, to an invigorating feeling of freedom, but rather to the cold, barren feeling of isolation. When this feeling of isolation from shared values becomes widespread in a society, the society loses its reason for existence as a collective unit and disintegrates from within.

This conservative perspective was given fresh expression in 1958, when Patrick Devlin, an English judge, gave a lecture in criticism of a governmental report (The Wolfenden Report) made public the year before. Accepting Mill's general libertarian perspective, the Wolfenden Report recommended that homosexuality and prostitution should not, in and of themselves, be illegal. Although not questioning the immorality of homosexuality and prostitution, the committee, echoing Mill, asserted that "there must remain a realm of private morality and immorality which is, in brief and crude terms, not the law's business." Devlin's lecture aroused great interest and controversy and led him to write a series of supporting and amplifying essays which were published in 1965 in a book entitled *The Enforcement of Morals*. This book in turn generated much comment and criticism in Great Britain and the United States and in particular generated a rebuttal from the English legal philosopher H.L.A. Hart in his book *Law, Liberty and Morality*. Underlying this debate is the fundamental and perennial issue of where the line is to be drawn between individual freedom and governmental authority—the same issue that underlies the Fortas–Zinn debate. In reading our selections from Mill and Devlin, the reader should ponder the principles that should be utilized in drawing the line between a society's right to control its citizens' behavior to some extent and a human being's right to live, think, and advocate what he or she chooses.

Individual Freedom and Social Control through Behavioral Conditioning

The classical liberal view of individual freedom presented in Mill's *On Liberty* is the freedom to be left alone to do as one deems best. Implicit in Mill's arguments for this type of freedom is his optimistic faith in the rationality of human beings and their capacity to choose what is best for themselves, if given full exposure to diverse points of view. Yet Mill realized that people are not always rational and do not always know and choose what is in their best interest. Consequently, he claimed that his plea that individuals should be left alone as long as they do not harm others applies only to human beings "in the maturity of their faculties." This is, however, a very open-ended qualification. Given the pessimistic twentieth-century emphasis upon the irrationality of human beings, we are much less apt than Mill to accept his assumption that each individual is the best judge of his own interests. As the success of modern day advertising seems to confirm, it is not necessarily the best products that sell or the truth that always wins out in the end, but rather the best packaged product or that version of the truth which best appeals to the subliminal and often irrational desires of the masses. Given such a pessimistic view of the rationality of the masses, a person who accepts Mill's proviso that his principle should apply only to rational and mature individuals may go on to assert that this, unfortunately, excludes most of us.

Defining freedom as the lack of external compulsion, Mill neglected the fact that some people lack freedom not because they are coerced from without, but because they are, so to speak, empty within—that is, incapable of recognizing what alternatives of action are open to them or of feeling any desire to do what is in their own ultimate self-interest. It has been claimed that freedom requires not only the *negative freedom* to be left alone that Mill advocated, but the *positive freedom* to be able, and indeed to have the capacity to want, to do certain things. Yet this positive freedom in turn depends upon environmental conditions that greatly contribute to one's personality structure. One can, for example, imagine a society of ant-like creatures who, having been conditioned from infancy onwards to behave in a particular way and to have no desire to behave differently, complacently accept a way of life, incapable of appreciating more desirable alternative ways of life. Many philosophers, including Plato, Rousseau, and Marx, have seen the preceding not as merely a hypothetical scenerio of a dark future but as the historical reality of human beings and society.

Marx, for example, believed that certain social arrangements (which he saw as determined primarily by underlying economic forces) lead human beings to develop "false needs" that interfere with the realization of their "true needs." For example, he thought that capitalistic societies foster greediness and competitiveness that dehumanize people and alienate them from the products of their labor and from themselves and others. In a capitalistic society, Marx believed, the negative freedom to be left alone, as advocated by Mill, could only contribute to human unhappiness in the long run. If human beings are to find lasting happiness, society itself, he believed, must be restructured so that human desires which are greatly influenced by social forces can themselves be restructured into a form that leads human beings to recognize their true needs.

It was Marx's fundamental belief that human beings are *social* animals who define themselves and find fulfillment only through their social relations. As Marx saw it, human desires should never be taken as the starting point of moral inquiry, as the utilitarian tradition took them to be, but rather should be seen as the *byproduct* of particular social relations. As Marx put it, "It is not the consciousness of men that determines their social being but rather their social being that determines their consciousness." From Marx' point of view, the "freedom" advocated by Mill was, in practice, *bourgeois* (middle class) *freedom*—that is, the liberation of the middle class merchant from the constraints of an outdated feudal social structure and the provision for him of the maximum room for maneuver, consistent with a similar maneuverability for others, in seeking to fulfill his selfish capitalistic aims.

Marx' belief that human desires are determined by one's social relations, which are themselves capable of moral evaluation and change, is the central belief in the organic tradition of political philosophy. Plato, for example, was firmly committed to such a point of view. In his classic of political philosophy, *The Republic,* Plato presents his utopian vision of a controlled society in which principles of eugenics are utilized to determine who should be brought into the world and where principles of behavioral conditioning and education are utilized to train people to voluntarily act in the common good. Rousseau, too, was a strong advocate of educating citizens to desire what is in the common interest. Like Marx and Plato, Rousseau believed that freedom implies more than merely the ability to act as one chooses, whatever these choices happen to be, but also the ability to choose and act as one would *rationally* want to choose. This in turn requires that individuals be shaped and disciplined by a social system which promotes certain ends and discourages others.

The foremost contemporary advocate of utopia through social conditioning is the famed behavioral psychologist B.F. Skinner, whose books *Walden Two* (1961) and *Beyond Freedom and Dignity* (1971) have generated much heated discussion. As some see it, the evil of totalitarianism lurks behind the benevolent sounding rhetoric of contemporary advocates of behavioral conditioning, like Skinner. As Skinner and his supporters see it, however, it is only through the conscious and intelligent manipulation of the means of social control that human beings can ever hope to find lasting happiness. Skinner contends that the proper utilization of the techniques of behavioral conditioning does not take away whatever real "freedom" human beings possess, but enhances it. Accepting a deterministic viewpoint, Skinner claims that the question is not whether human beings should be "controlled" by social forces—for they will be regardless of what we as a society choose to do—but whether they should be controlled intelligently and in the best interests of all or haphazardly, or by demagogues. In their pronouncements on the bearing of environmental forces upon human freedom, Skinner and his supporters and critics in the field of psychology often do not attempt to clarify or defend the meanings they attribute to the concept of freedom—a concept which, as we have seen in the previous chapter, has perennially occupied the attention of philosophers. Here, as elsewhere, philosophers can provide the needed conceptual clarification and analysis upon which scientific theorizing and political policy-making can build.

54. THE DECLARATION OF INDEPENDENCE

When in the Course of human events it becomes necessary for one people to dissolve the political bands which have connected them with another, and to assume among the powers of the earth, the separate and equal station to which the Laws of Nature and of Nature's God entitle them, a decent respect to the opinions of mankind requires that they should declare the causes which impel them to the separation.

We hold these truths to be self-evident, that all men are created equal, that they are endowed by their Creator with certain unalienable Rights, that among these are Life, Liberty and the pursuit of Happiness. That to secure these rights, Governments are instituted among Men, deriving their just powers from the consent of the governed. That whenever any Form of Government becomes destructive of these ends, it is the Right of the People to alter or to abolish it, and to institute new Government, laying its foundation on such principles, and organizing its powers in such form, as to them shall seem most likely to effect their Safety and Happiness. Prudence, indeed, will dictate that Governments long established should not be changed for light and transient causes; and accordingly all experience hath shewn, that mankind are more disposed to suffer, while evils are sufferable, than to right themselves by abolishing the forms to which they are accustomed. But when a long train of abuses and usurpations, pursuing invariably the same Object, evinces a design to reduce them under absolute Despotism, it is their right, it is their duty, to throw off such Government, and to provide new Guards for their future security. Such has been the patient sufferance of these Colonies; and such is now the necessity which constrains them to alter their former Systems of Government. The history of the present King of Great Britain is a history of repeated injuries and usurpations, all having in direct object the establishment of an absolute Tyranny over these States. To prove this, let Facts be submitted to a candid world.

[Omitted is the list of the colonies' grievances against the King of England.]

We, therefore, the Representatives of the United States of America, in General Congress, Assembled, appealing to the Supreme Judge of the world for the rectitude of our intentions, do, in the Name and by authority of the good People of these Colonies solemnly publish and declare That these United Colonies are and of Right ought to be free and independent states; that they are Absolved from all Allegiance to the British Crown, and that all political connection between them and the State of Great Britain, is and ought to be totally dissolved; and that as Free and Independent States, they have full Power to levy War, conclude Peace, contract Alliances, establish Commerce, and to do all other Acts and Things which Independent States may of right do. And for the support of this Declaration, with a firm reliance on the protection of divine Providence, we mutually pledge to each other our Lives, our Fortunes, and our sacred Honor.

55. THE BILL OF RIGHTS

Amendment I.

Congress shall make no law respecting an establishment of religion, or prohibiting the free exercise thereof; or abridging the freedom of speech, or of the press; or the right of the people peaceably to assemble, and to petition the Government for a redress of grievances.

Amendment II.

A well regulated Militia, being necessary to the security of a free State, the right of the people to keep and bear Arms, shall not be infringed.

Amendment III.

No Soldier shall, in time of peace be quartered in any house, without the consent of the Owner, nor in time of war, but in a manner to be prescribed by law.

Amendment IV.

The right of the people to be secure in their persons, houses, papers, and effects, against unreasonable searches and seizures, shall not be violated, and no Warrants shall issue, but upon probable cause, supported by Oath or affirmation, and particularly describing the place to be searched, and the persons or things to be seized.

Amendment V.

No person shall be held to answer for a capital, or otherwise infamous crime, unless on a presentment or indictment of a Grand Jury, except in cases arising in the land or naval forces, or in the Militia, when in actual service in time of War or public danger; nor shall any person be subject for the same offence to be twice put in jeopardy of life or limb; nor shall be compelled in any criminal case to be a witness against himself, nor be deprived life, liberty, or property, without due process of law; nor shall private property be taken for public use, without just compensation.

Amendment VI.

In all criminal prosecutions, the accused shall enjoy the right to a speedy and public trial, by an impartial jury of the State and district wherein the crime shall have been committed, which district shall have been previously ascertained by law, and to be informed of the nature and cause of the accusation; to be confronted with the witnesses against him; to have compulsory process for obtaining witnesses in his favor, and to have the Assistance of Counsel for his defence.

Amendment VII.

In Suits at common law, where the value in controversy shall exceed twenty dollars, the right of trial by jury shall be preserved, and no fact tried by a jury, shall be otherwise re-examined in any Court of the United States, than according to the rules of the common law.

Amendment VIII.

Excessive bail shall not be required, nor excessive fines imposed, nor cruel and unusual punishments inflicted.

Amendment IX.

The enumeration in the Constitution, of certain rights, shall not be construed to deny or disparage others retained by the people.

Amendment X.

The powers not delegated to the United States by the Constitution, nor prohibited by it to the States, are reserved to the States respectively, or to the people.

56. A SOCIAL CONTRACT JUSTIFICATION OF UNLIMITED SOVEREIGNTY

Thomas Hobbes

THOMAS HOBBES (1588–1679) was a very influential English philosopher. Upon his graduation from Oxford University, Hobbes served as secretary to Sir Francis Bacon and as tutor to William Cavendish, who was later to become Earl of Devonshire. Traveling widely with Cavendish, Hobbes met many European philosophers and scientists, including Galileo. His leisurely life also gave him time to read widely and to write. Living during a period of great political tension between Parliament and King Charles I, Hobbes was forced to flee to France because he feared the displeasure of the parliamentary forces over his written support of absolute monarchy. In France, Hobbes became acquainted with the philosophy of his contemporary Descartes, whose philosophical writings he criticized. This led to an acrimonious exchange between the two philosophers. While in France, Hobbes also acted for a brief time as a tutor in mathematics to the future Charles II, who, like many royalists, had fled to Paris until it was safe to return to England.

Exposed to the same seventeenth-century science to which Descartes was exposed, Hobbes' reaction to it was quite different. Instead of Descartes' dualism of mind and body, Hobbes took the mechanistic and deterministic materialism which underlay the new science as the **single** fundamental principle of nature, seeing everything as ultimately reducible to material bodies in motion. In particular, Hobbes was the first philosopher to apply the mechanistic and deterministic materialism of the new science to human behavior, seeing human beings as completely determined mechanical systems of material particles. Greatly enamored of the deductive method of Euclidean geometry, Hobbes envisioned a unified science from whose mechanistic roots the laws of human psychology could be deduced and from which, in turn, the principles of morality and political theory could be deduced. Hobbes' attempt to carry out this vision in his writings led him to the view that human nature is totally selfish and to a subjective and relativistic view of morality.

The following selection comes from Hobbes' masterpiece of political philosophy, **Leviathan,** which was published in 1651 in a period of political flux and discussion in England, between the time of the execution of Charles I in 1649 and the appointment of Oliver Cromwell as Protector in 1653. (See pp. 476–77 of this chapter's introduction for an outline of Hobbes' political philosophy as expressed in **Leviathan.**)

Chapter XIII: Of the Natural Condition of Mankind as Concerning Their Felicity, and Misery

Nature hath made men so equal, in the faculties of the body, and mind; as that though there be found one man sometimes manifestly stronger in body, or of quicker mind than another; yet when all is reckoned together, the difference between man, and man, is not so considerable, as that one man can thereupon claim to himself any benefit, to which another may not pretend, as well as he. . . .

From this equality of ability, ariseth equality of hope in attaining our ends. And therefore if any two men desire the same thing, which nevertheless they cannot both enjoy, they become enemies; and in the way to their end, which is principally their own conservation. . . , endeavour to destroy, or subdue one another. And from hence it comes to pass, that where an invader hath no more to fear, than another man's single power; if one plant, sow, build, or possess a convenient seat, others may probably be expected to come prepared with forces united, to dispossess and deprive him, not only of the fruit of his labour, but also of his life, or liberty. And the invader again is in the like danger of another.

And from this diffidence of one another, there is no way for any man to secure himself, so reasonable, as anticipation; that is, by force, or wiles, to master the persons of all men he can, so long, till he sees no other power great enough to endanger him. . . .

Hereby it is manifest, that during the time men live without a common power to keep them all in awe, they are in that condition which is called war; and such a war, as is of every man, against every man. . . .

. . . [In a state of war] men live without other security, than what their own strength, and their own invention shall furnish them withal. In such a condition, there is no place for industry, because the fruit thereof is uncertain; and consequently no culture of the earth . . . no arts; no letters; no society; and which is worst of all, continual fear, and danger of violent death; and the life of man, solitary, poor, nasty, brutish, and short. . . .

To this war of every man, against every man, this also is consequent; that nothing can be unjust. The notions of right and wrong, justice and injustice have there no place. Where there is no common power, there is no law: where no law, no injustice. Force, and fraud, are in war the two cardinal virtues. Justice, and injustice are none of the faculties neither of the body, nor mind. If they were, they might be in a man that were alone in the world, as well as his senses, and passions. They are qualities, that relate to men in society, not in solitude. It is consequent also to the same condition, that there be no propriety, no dominion, no *mine* and *thine* distinct; but only that to be every man's, that he can get: and for so long, as he can keep it. And thus much for the ill condition, which man by mere nature is actually placed in; though with a possibility to come out of it, consisting partly in the passions, partly in his reason.

The passions that incline men to peace, are fear of death; desire of such things as are necessary to commodious[1] living; and a hope by their industry to obtain them. And reason suggesteth convenient articles of peace, upon which men may be drawn to agreement. These articles are . . . called the Laws of Nature. . . .

Source: The Molesworth edition (1841) of Thomas Hobbes' *Leviathan,* first published in 1651.

[1]Suitable. EDITOR'S NOTE.

Chapter XIV: Of the First and Second Natural Laws, and of Contracts

The Right of Nature . . . is the liberty each man hath, to use his own power, as he will himself, for the preservation of his own nature; that is to say, of his own life; and consequently of doing any thing, which in his own judgment, and reason, he shall conceive to be the aptest means thereunto. . . .

And because the condition of man, as hath been declared in the precedent chapter, is a condition of war of every one against every one; in which case every one is governed by his own reason; and there is nothing he can make use of, that may not be a help unto him, in preserving his life against his enemies; it followeth, that in such a condition, every man has a right to every thing; even to one another's body. And therefore, as long as this natural right of every man to every thing endureth, there can be no security to any man, how strong or wise soever he be, of living out the time, which nature ordinarily alloweth men to live. And consequently it is a precept, or general rule of reason, *that every man, ought to endeavor peace, as far as he has hope of obtaining it; and when he cannot obtain it, that he may seek, and use, all helps, and advantages of war.* The first branch of which rule, containeth the first, and fundamental law of nature; which is, *to seek peace, and follow it.* The second, the sum of the right of nature; which is, *by all means we can, to defend ourselves.*

From this fundamental law of nature, by which men are commanded to endeavour peace, is derived this second law; *that a man be willing, when others are so too, as far-forth, as for peace, and defence of himself he shall think it necessary, to lay down this right to all things; and be contented with so much liberty against other men, as he would allow other men against himself.* For as long as every man holdeth this right, of doing any thing he liketh; so long are all men in the condition of war. But if other men will not lay down their right, as well as he; then there is no reason for any one, to divest himself of his: for that were to expose himself to prey, which no man is bound to, rather than to dispose himself to peace. This is that law of the Gospel; *whatsoever you require that others should do to you, that do ye to them.* From that law of nature, by which we are obliged to transfer to another such rights as being retained, hinder the peace of mankind, there followeth a third; which is this, *that men perform their covenants made,* without which, covenants are in vain, and but empty words; and the right of all men to all things remaining, we are still in the condition of war.

And in this law of nature, consisteth the fountain and original of JUSTICE. For where no covenant hath preceded, there hath no right been transferred, and every man has right to every thing; and consequently no action can be unjust. But when a covenant is made, then to break it is *unjust:* and the definition of INJUSTICE, is no other than *the not performance of covenant.* And whatsoever is not unjust, is *just.*

But because covenants of mutual trust, where there is a fear of not performance on either part, as hath been said in the former chapter, are invalid; though the original of justice be the making of covenants; yet injustice actually there can be none, till the cause of such fear be taken away; which while men are in the natural condition of war, cannot be done. Therefore before the names of just, and unjust can have place there must be some coercive power, to compel men equally to the performance of their covenants, by the terror of some punishment, greater than the benefit they expect by the breach of their covenant; and to make good that propriety, which by mutual contract men acquire, in recompense of the universal right they abandon: and such power there is none before the erection of a commonwealth. . . .

Chapter XVII: Of the Causes, Generation, and Definition of a Commonwealth

The final . . . end . . . of men, who naturally love liberty, and dominion over others, in the introduction of that restraint upon themselves, in which we see them live in commonwealths, is the foresight of their own preservation, and of a more contented life thereby; that is to say, of getting themselves out from that miserable condition of war, which is necessarily consequent . . . to the natural passions of men, when there is no visible power to keep them in awe, and tie them by fear of punishment to the performance of their covenants, and observation of those laws of nature set down in the fourteenth and fifteenth chapters.

For the laws of nature, as *justice, equity, modesty, mercy,* and, in sum, *doing to others, as we would be done to,* of themselves, without the terror of some power to cause them to be observed, are contrary to our natural passions. . . . And covenants, without the sword, are but words, and of no strength to secure a man at all. Therefore notwithstanding the laws of nature (which every one hath then kept, when he has the will to keep them, when he can do it safely) if there be no power erected, or not great enough for our security; every man will, and may lawfully rely on his own strength and art, for caution against all other men. . . . there be somewhat else required, besides covenant, to make their agreement constant and lasting; which is a common power, to keep them in awe, and to direct their actions to the common benefit.

The only way to erect such a common power, as may be able to defend them from the invasion of foreigners, and the injuries of one another, and thereby to secure them in such sort, as that by their own industry, and by the fruits of the earth, they may nourish themselves and live contentedly; is, to confer all their power and strength upon one man, or upon one assembly of men, that may reduce all their wills, by plurality of voices, unto one will: which is as much as to say, to appoint one man, or assembly of men, to bear their person; and every one to own, and acknowledge himself to be author of whatsoever he that so beareth their person, shall act, or cause to be acted, in those things which concern the common peace and safety; and therein to submit their wills, every one to his will, and their judgments, to his judgment. This is more than consent, or concord; it is a real unity of them all, in one and the same person, made by covenant of every man with every man, in such manner, as if every man should say to every man, *I authorize and give up my right of governing myself, to this man, or to this assembly of men, on this condition, that thou give up thy right to him, and authorize all his actions in like manner.* This done, the multitude so united in one person, is called a COMMONWEALTH. . . . This is the generation of that great LEVIATHAN, or rather, to speak more reverently, of that *mortal god,* to which we owe under the *immortal God,* our peace and defence. For by this authority, given him by every particular man in the commonwealth, he hath the use of so much power and strength conferred on him, that by terror thereof, he is enabled to form the wills of them all, to peace at home, and mutual aid against their enemies abroad. And in him consisteth the essence of the commonwealth; which, to define it, is *one person, of whose acts a great multitude, by mutual covenants one with another, have made themselves every one the author, to the end he may use the strength and means of them all, as he shall think expedient, for their peace and common defence.*

And he that carrieth this person, is called SOVEREIGN, and said to have *sovereign power;* and every one besides, his SUBJECT. . . .

Chapter XVIII: Of the Rights of Sovereigns . . .

From this institution of a commonwealth are derived all the *rights*, and *faculties* of him, or them, on whom the sovereign power is conferred by the consent of the people assembled.

First, because they covenant, it is to be understood, they are not obliged by former covenant to any thing repugnant hereunto. And consequently they that have already instituted a commonwealth, being thereby bound by covenant, to own the actions, and judgments of one, cannot lawfully make a new covenant, amongst themselves, to be obedient to any other, in any thing whatsoever, without his permission. Whereas some men have pretended for their disobedience to their sovereign, a new covenant, made, not with men, but with God; this also is unjust: for there is no covenant with God, but by mediation of somebody that representeth God's person; which none doth but God's lieutenant, who hath the sovereignty under God. . . . Because every subject is by this institution author of all the actions, and judgments of the sovereign instituted; it follows, that whatsoever he doth, it can be no injury to any of his subjects; nor ought he to be by any of them accused of injustice. For he that doth anything by authority from another; doth therein no injury to him by whose authority he acteth. . . . It is true that they that have sovereign power may commit iniquity; but not injustice, or injury in the proper signification.

Chapter XXI: Of the Liberty of Subjects

. . . The obligation of subjects to the sovereign is understood to last as long, and no longer, than the power lasteth by which he is able to protect them. For the right men have by nature to protect themselves, when none else can protect them, can by no convenant be relinquished. . . .

DISCUSSION QUESTIONS

1. What is Hobbes' view of the nature of morality? Does he believe that acts can be morally appraised apart from the laws of a particular government? Is Hobbes' view of the nature of morality plausible? If not, why do you think he accepted it?

2. What does Hobbes mean by "The Right of Nature"? Is this alleged "right" a moral one for Hobbes or is it simply a description of the brute facts of nature?

3. What does Hobbes think about the possibility and/or rationality of a person voluntarily giving up his or her life for others or for some cause? Is such a view defensible?

4. Hobbes is noted for his advocacy of **psychological egoism**—that is, the doctrine that human beings are motivated only by self-interest. It is alleged that Hobbes was once asked by a person who saw him give alms to a beggar why he did so. Hobbes, it is said, claimed that he did so in order to relieve his own distress at seeing the beggar's distress. Does such a claim eliminate the apparent inconsistency of Hobbes' action and his professed belief in psychological egoism? (Look over pp. 408–10 of Brody's "Morality and Rational Self-Interest" in our anthology and question 2 which follows the Brody selection.)

5. Does Hobbes believe that we have a moral obligation to keep our promises (or abide by our covenants)? Is this view consistent with his acceptance of psychological egoism?

6. What is Hobbes' view of the obligations that exist between sovereign and subjects?

7. In criticism of Hobbes' contention that the human desire for security would lead rational people to put all their collective power in the hands of an absolute sovereign, John Locke argued:

> Whereas by supposing they have given up themselves to the absolute arbitrary power and will of a legislator, they have disarmed themselves, and armed him to make a prey of them when he pleases; he being in a much worse condition that is exposed to the arbitrary power of one man who has the command of a hundred thousand than he that is exposed to the arbitrary power of a hundred thousand single men, nobody being secure, that his will who has such a command

> is better than that of other men, though his force be a hundred thousand times stronger." (paragraph #137 of Locke's **Second Treatise of Civil Government**)

Do you agree? Do you think Hobbes could have a plausible reply?

8. Do you agree with Hobbes that the desire for security is the only rational motive human beings could have for consenting to subject themselves to governmental authority? If not, what other motives are involved?

9. Consider the following criticism of the social contract view of political obligation:

> Such a view assumes the consent of every individual who is subject to governmental authority. This is, however, absurd. If some individual were to say "I choose not to enter into the contract; I prefer to defend myself as I am able," such an individual would still be subjected to the law of the land. The social contract view of political obligation is only valid in those very rare situations (never realized in any actually existing government) in which there is universal consent to the laws of one's government.[1]

What do you think?

10. Is there any plausibility in claiming that people who are born into an existing governmental structure have, by remaining in their society, implicitly consented to its laws? Even if it can reasonably be said that an individual has either explicitly or implicitly consented to abide by the laws of his government, is this consent irrevocable? If not, when is it revocable? What would Hobbes say here? What do you think?

[1]Criticism composed by editor.

57. A SOCIAL CONTRACT JUSTIFICATION OF LIMITED SOVEREIGNTY AND THE SEPARATION OF GOVERNMENTAL POWERS

John Locke

(See Selection #28 for biographical information on John Locke and pp. 477–78 of this chapter's introduction for an outline of Locke's political philosophy.)

The following selection is from Locke's **The Second Treatise of Government.** Since Locke's **Two Treatises of Government** was published a year after the Glorious Revolution of 1688, it was originally thought to have been written as an after-the-fact justification for that revolution. An earlier draft of this work has, however, been found, dated 1681, indicating that Locke's political theory predated its practical application in the Glorious Revolution. In our selection, Locke discusses the purposes for which human beings set up a state and the conditions under which they are justified in overthrowing it. Arguing for a limited constitutional and democratic government, Locke advocates the separation of powers (checks and balances) that so influenced the framers of the United States Constitution who, like Locke, were motivated by the ideal of democratic law and order, free of the tyranny implicit in absolute government.

Chapter 2: Of the State of Nature

4. To understand political power aright, and derive it from its original, we must consider what estate all men are naturally in, and that is, a state of perfect freedom to order their actions, and dispose of their possessions and persons as they think fit, within the bounds of the law of Nature, without asking leave or depending upon the will of any other man.

A state also of equality, wherein all the power and jurisdiction is reciprocal, no one having more than another, there being nothing more evident than that creatures of the same species and rank, promiscuously born to all the same advantages of Nature, and the use of the same faculties, should also be equal one amongst another, without subordination or subjection, unless the lord and master of them all should, by any manifest declaration of his will, set one above another, and confer on him, by an evident and clear appointment, an undoubted right to dominion and sovereignty . . . .

6. But though this be a state of liberty, yet it is not a state of licence; though man in that state have an uncontrollable liberty to dispose of his person or possessions, yet he has not liberty to destroy himself, or so much as any creature in his possession, but where some nobler use than its bare preservation calls for it. The state of Nature has a law of Nature to govern it, which obliges every one, and reason, which is that law, teaches all mankind who will but consult it, that being all equal and independent, no one ought to harm another in his life, health, liberty or possessions; for men being all the workmanship of one omnipotent and infinitely wise Maker; all the servants of one sovereign Master, sent into the world by His order and about His business; they are His property, whose workmanship they are made to last during His, not one another's pleasure. And, being furnished with like faculties, sharing all in one community of Nature, there cannot be supposed any such subordination among us that may authorise us to destroy one another, as if we were made for one another's uses, as the inferior ranks of creatures are for ours. Every one as he is bound to preserve himself, and not to quit his station willfully so by the like reason, when his own preservation comes not in competition, ought he as much as he can to preserve the rest of mankind, and not unless it be to do justice on an offender, take away or impair the life, or what tends to the preservation of the life, the liberty, health, limb, or goods of another.

7. And that all men may be restrained from invading others' rights, and from doing hurt to one another, and the law of Nature be observed, which willeth the peace and preservation of all mankind, the execution of the law of Nature is in that state put into every man's hands, whereby every one has a right to punish the transgressors of that law to such a degree as may hinder its violation. For the law of Nature would, as all others laws that concern men in this world, be in vain if there were nobody that in the state of Nature had a power to execute that law, and thereby preserve the innocent and restrain offenders; and if any one in the state of Nature may punish another for any evil he has done, every one may do so. For in that state of perfect equality, where naturally there is no superiority or jurisdiction of one over another, what any may do in prosecution of that law, every one must needs have a right to do . . . .

Chapter 7: Of Political or Civil Society

. . . 87. Man being born, as has been proved, with a title to perfect freedom and an uncontrolled enjoyment of all the rights and privileges

Source: John Locke's *Two Treatises of Government,* first published in 1689.

of the law of Nature, equally with any other man, or number of men in the world, hath by nature a power not only to preserve his property—that is, his life, liberty, and estate, against the injuries and attempts of other men but to judge of and punish the breaches of that law in others, as he is persuaded the offence deserves . . . . But because no political society can be, nor subsist, without having in itself [this power] . . . there, and there only, is political society where every one of the members hath quitted this natural power, resigned it up into the hands of the community . . . . And thus . . . the community comes to be umpire, and by understanding indifferent rules and men authorised by the community for their execution, decides all the differences that may happen between any members of that society concerning any matter of right, and punishes those offences which any member hath committed against the society with such penalties as the law has established . . . .

89. Wherever . . . any number of men so unite into one society as to quit every one his executive power of the law of Nature, and to resign it to the public, there and there only is a political or civil society . . . . And this puts men out of a state of Nature into that of a commonwealth, by setting up a judge on earth with authority to determine all the controversies and redress the injuries that may happen to any member of the commonwealth, which judge is the legislative or magistrates appointed by it. And wherever there are any number of men, however associated, that have no such decisive power to appeal to, there they are still in the state of Nature.

90. And hence it is evident that absolute monarchy, which by some men is counted for the only government in the world, is indeed inconsistent with civil society, and so can be no form of civil government at all. For the end of civil society being to avoid and remedy those inconveniences of the state of Nature which necessarily follow from every man's being judge in his own case, by setting up a known authority to which every one of that society may appeal upon any injury received, or controversy that may arise, and which every one of the society ought to obey. Wherever any persons are who have not such an authority to appeal to, and decide any difference between them there, those persons are still in the state of Nature. And so is every absolute prince in respect of those who are under his dominion.

Chapter 8: Of the Beginning of Political Societies

95. Men being, as has been said, by nature all free, equal, and independent, no one can be put out of this estate and subjected to the political power of another without his own consent, which is done by agreeing with other men, to join and unite into a community for their comfortable, safe, and peaceable living, one amongst another, in a secure enjoyment of their properties, and a greater security against any that are not of it. This any number of men may do, because it injures not the freedom of the rest; they are left, as they were, in the liberty of the state of Nature. When any number of men have so consented to make one community or government, they are thereby presently incorporated, and make one body politic, wherein the majority have a right to act and conclude the rest.

96. For, when any number of men have, by the consent of every individual, made a community, they have thereby made that community one body, with a power to act as one body, which is only by the will and determination of the majority. For that which acts any community, being only the consent of the individuals of it, and it being one body, must move one way, it is necessary the body should move that way whither the greater force carries it, which is the consent of the majority, or else it

is impossible it should act or continue one body, one community, which the consent of every individual that united into it agreed that it should; and so every one is bound by that consent to be concluded by the majority.

98. [If] the consent of the majority shall not in reason be received as the act of the whole, and conclude every individual, nothing but the consent of every individual can make anything to be the act of the whole, which, considering the infirmities of health and avocations of business, which in a number though much less than that of a commonwealth, will necessarily keep many away from the public assembly; and the variety of opinions and contrariety of interests which unavoidably happen in all collections of men, it is next to impossible ever to be had . . . .

99. Whosoever, therefore, out of a state of Nature unite into a community, must be understood to give up all the power necessary to the ends for which they unite into society to the majority of the community, unless they expressly agreed in any number greater than the majority . . . .

119. Every man being, as has been showed, naturally free, and nothing being able to put him into subjection to any earthly power, but only his own consent; it is to be considered, what shall be understood to be a sufficient declaration of a man's consent, to make him subject to the laws of any government. There is a common distinction of an express and a tacit consent, which will concern our present case. Nobody doubts but an express consent of any man entering into any society, makes him a perfect member of that society, a subject of that government. The difficulty is, what ought to be looked upon as a tacit consent, and how far it binds, *i.e.* how far anyone shall be looked on to have consented, and thereby submitted to any government, where he has made no expressions of it at all. And to this I say, that every man, that hath any possessions, or enjoyment of any part of the dominions of any government, doth thereby give his tacit consent, and is as far forth obliged to obedience to the laws of that government, during such enjoyment, as anyone under it; whether this his possession be of land, to him and his heirs forever, or a lodging only for a week; or whether it be barely travelling freely on the highway; and, in effect, it reaches as far as the very being of anyone within the territories of that government . . . .

Chapter 9: Of the Ends of Political Society and Government

123. If man in the state of Nature be so free as has been said, if he be absolute lord of his own person and possessions, equal to the greatest and subject to nobody, why will he part with his freedom, this empire, and subject himself to the dominion and control of any other power? To which it is obvious to answer, that though in the state of Nature he hath such a right, yet the enjoyment of it is very uncertain and constantly exposed to the invasion of others . . . .

124. The great and chief end . . . of men uniting into commonwealths, and putting themselves under government, is the preservation of their property; to which in the state of Nature there are many things wanting.

Firstly, there wants an established, settled, known law, received and allowed by common consent to be the standard of right and wrong, and the common measure to decide all controversies between them. For though the law of Nature be plain and intelligible to all rational creatures, yet men, being biased by their interest, as well as ignorant for want of study of it, are not apt to allow of it as a law binding to them in the application of it to their particular cases.

125. Secondly, in the state of Nature there wants a known and indifferent judge, with authority to determine all differences according

to the established law. For every one in that state being both judge and executioner of the law of Nature, men being partial to themselves, passion and revenge is very apt to carry them too far, and with too much heat in their cases, as well as negligence and unconcernedness, make them too remiss in other men's.

126. Thirdly, in the state of Nature there often wants power to back and support the sentence when right, and to give it due execution. They who by any injustice offended will seldom fail where they are able by force to make good their injustice. Such resistance many times makes the punishment dangerous, and frequently destructive to those who attempt it.

127. Thus mankind, notwithstanding all the privileges of the state of Nature, being but in an ill condition while they remain in it are quickly driven into society. Hence it comes to pass, that we seldom find any number of men live any time together in this state. The inconveniencies that they are therein exposed to by the irregular and uncertain exercise of the power every man has of punishing the transgressions of others, make them take sanctuary under the established laws of government, and therein seek the preservation of their property. It is this makes them so willingly give up every one his single power of punishing to be exercised by such alone as shall be appointed to it amongst them, and by such rules as the community, or those authorised by them to that purpose, shall agree on. And in this we have the original right and rise of both the legislative and executive power as well as of the governments and societies themselves . . . .

131. But though men when they enter into society give up the equality, liberty, and executive power they had in the state of Nature into the hands of the society, to be so far disposed of by the legislative as the good of the society shall require, yet it being only with an intention in every one the better to preserve himself, his liberty and property (for no rational creature can be supposed to change his condition with an intention to be worse), the power of the society or legislative constituted by them can never be supposed to extend farther than the common good, but is obliged to secure every one's property by providing against those three defects above mentioned that made the state of Nature so unsafe and uneasy. And so, whoever has the legislative or supreme power of any commonwealth, is bound to govern by established standing laws, promulgated and known to the people, and not by extemporary decrees, by indifferent and upright judges, who are to decide controversies by those laws; and to employ the force of the community at home only in the execution of such laws, or abroad to prevent or redress foreign injuries and secure the community from inroads and invasion. And all this to be directed to no other end but the peace, safety, and public good of the people . . . .

135. Though the legislative . . . be the supreme power in every commonwealth, yet, first, it is not, nor can possibly be, absolutely arbitrary over the lives and fortunes of the people. For it being but the joint power of every member of the society given up to that person or assembly which is legislator, it can be no more than those persons had in a state of Nature before they entered into society, and gave it up to the community. For nobody can transfer to another more power than he has in himself, and nobody has an absolute arbitrary power over himself, or over any other, to destroy his own life, or take away the life or property of another. A man, as has been proved, cannot subject himself to the arbitrary power of another; and having, in the state of Nature, no arbitrary power over the life, liberty, or possession of another, but only so much as the law of Nature gave him for the preservation of himself and the rest of mankind, this is all he doth, or can give up to the commonwealth, and by it to legislative power, so that the legislative can have no

more than this. Their power in the utmost bounds of it is limited to the public good of the society. It is a power that hath no other end but preservation, and therefore can never have a right to destroy, enslave, or designedly to impoverish the subjects; the obligations of the law of Nature cease not in society . . . . Thus the law of Nature stands as an eternal rule to all men, legislators as well as others. The rules that they make for other men's actions must, as well as their own and other men's actions, be conformable to the law of Nature—*i.e.,* to the will of God, of which that is a declaration, and the fundamental law of Nature being the preservation of mankind, no human sanction can be good or valid against it . . . .

137. Absolute arbitrary power, or governing without settled standing laws, can neither of them consist with the ends of society and government, which men would not quit the freedom of the state of Nature for, and tie themselves up under, were it not to preserve their lives, liberties, and fortunes, and by stated rules of right and property to secure their peace and quiet. It cannot be supposed that they should intend, had they a power so to do, to give any one or more an absolute arbitrary power over their persons and estates, and put a force into the magistrate's hand to execute his unlimited will arbitrarily upon them; this were to put themselves into a worse condition than the state of Nature, wherein they had a liberty to defend their right against the injuries of others, and were upon equal terms of force to maintain it, whether invaded by a single man or many in combination. Whereas by supposing they have given up themselves to the absolute arbitrary power and will of a legislator, they have disarmed themselves, and armed him to make a prey of them when he pleases; he being in a much worse condition that is exposed to the arbitrary power of one man who has the command of a hundred thousand than he that is exposed to the arbitrary power of a hundred thousand single men, nobody being secure, that his will who has such a command is better than that of other men, though his force be a hundred thousand times stronger. And, therefore, whatever form the commonwealth is under, the ruling power ought to govern by declared and received laws, and not by extemporary dictates and undetermined resolutions, for then mankind will be in a far worse condition than in the state of Nature if they shall have armed one or a few men with the joint power of a multitude, to force them to obey at pleasure the exorbitant and unlimited decrees of their sudden thoughts, or unrestrained, and till that moment, unknown wills, without having any measures set down which may guide and justify their actions. For all the power the government has, being only for the good of the society, as it ought not to be arbitrary and at pleasure, so it ought to be exercised by established and promulgated laws, that both the people may know their duty, and be safe and secure within the limits of the law, and the rulers, too, kept within their due bounds . . . .

140. It is true governments cannot be supported without great charge, and it is fit every one who enjoys his share of the protection should pay out of his estate his proportion for the maintenance of it. But still it must be with his own consent—*i.e.,* the consent of the majority, giving it either by themselves or their representatives chosen by them; for if any one shall claim a power to lay and levy taxes on the people by his own authority, and without such consent of the people, he thereby invades the fundamental law of property, and subverts the end of government. For what property have I in that which another may by right take when he pleases to himself? . . .

221. There is . . . another way whereby governments are dissolved, and that is, when the legislative, or the prince, either of them, act contrary to their trust.

For, the legislative acts against the trust reposed in them, when they endeavour to invade the property of the subject, and to make themselves, or any part of the community, masters, or arbitrary disposers of the lives, liberties, or fortunes of the people.

222. The reason why men enter into society is the preservation of their property; and the end why they choose and authorize a legislative is that there may be laws made, and rules set, as guards and fences to the properties of all the members of the society: to limit the power, and moderate the dominion, of every part and member of the society: for since it can never be supposed to be the will of the society that the legislative should have a power to destroy that which everyone designs to secure by entering into society, and for which the people submitted themselves to legislators of their own making; whenever the legislators endeavour to take away and destroy the property of the people, or to reduce them to slavery under arbitrary power, they put themselves into a state of war with the people, who are thereupon absolved from any farther obedience, and are left to the common refuge, which God hath provided for all men, against force and violence. Whensoever therefore the legislative shall trangress this fundamental rule of society; and either by ambition, fear, folly, or corruption, endeavour to grasp themselves, or put into the hands of any other, an absolute power over the lives, liberties, and estates of the people; by this breach of trust they forfeit the power the people had put into their hands for quite contrary ends, and it devolves to the people, who have a right to resume their orginal liberty, and, by the establishment of a new legislative, (such as they shall think fit) provide for their own safety and security, which is the end for which they are in society . . . .

DISCUSSION QUESTIONS

1. Critically compare Locke's and Hobbes' views of the state of nature. What is your position on this matter?

2. Both Locke and Hobbes speak of the "equality" of human beings in the state of nature. Do they mean the same thing by this?

3. What is Locke's view of the morality of homicide and suicide? Do you agree? Why, or why not?

4. What argument(s) does Locke provide as a justification for majority rule (see paragraphs, 96, 98, and 99). Do you see any difficulty with this (these) argument(s)?

5. According to Locke (see paragraph 119), while governmental authority is justified only by the consent of its subjects, this consent can be tacit as well as expressed. Consent is tacit, he claims, whenever a person accepts the benefits of living in a given society. Implicit in this view is the assumption that people are free to reject the benefits of that society (by leaving it) and, consequently, if they choose to accept them (by remaining), justice demands that they accept the burden of abiding by the laws which make these benefits possible. The classic objection to this point of view was made by David Hume in his essay "Of the Original Contract" (1748). Hume wrote:

> Should it be said, that, by living under the dominion of a prince which one might leave, every individual has given a **tacit** consent to his authority, and promised him obedience; it may be answered, that such an implied consent can only have place where a man imagines that the matter depends on his choice. But where he thinks (as all mankind do who are born under established governments) that, by his birth, he owes allegiance to a certain prince or certain form of government; it would be absurd to infer a consent or choice, which he expressly, in this case, renounces or disclaims.
>
> Can we seriously say, that a poor peasant or artisan has a free choice to leave his country, when he knows no foreign language or manners, and lives, from day to day, by the small wages which he acquires? We may as well assert that a man, by remaining in a vessel, freely consents to the dominion of a master; though he was carried on board while asleep, and must leap into the ocean and perish, the moment he leaves her.[1]

[1]David Hume, "Of the Original Contract," in *Social Contract: Essays by Locke, Hume and Rousseau*, Introduction by Sir Ernest Barker (New York: Oxford University Press, 1962), pp. 155–56.

Critically consider the implications of Hume's claim upon Locke's conception of tacit consent.

6. Compare Locke's and Hobbes' view of the purpose(s) of government. Are either of these two views fully adequate? Why?

7. According to Locke, what features must any adequate government possess? Do you agree? Are there any other features you would add?

8. Compare Locke's and Hobbes' views of the extent of a citizen's obligation to obey the laws of his government. Do you find either view fully adequate? Why, or why not?

58. A CONSERVATIVE DEFENSE OF THE MORAL OBLIGATION TO OBEY THE LAW

Plato

(For a biographical sketch of Plato, see Selection #40.)

The following selection is from Plato's **Crito,** one of several early Socratic dialogues to which the trial and death of Socrates form the backdrop. The dialogue that precedes the **Crito,** the **Apology,** consists of Socrates' trial and conviction for impiety and corrupting the youth. In the **Apology,** Socrates defends his innocence of the charges brought against him, and, in the process, defends his method of doing philosophy.

At the time of Socrates' trial (399 B.C.), Athens had just recently returned to the democratic form of government that it had prior to the Peloponnesian War between Athens and Sparta, which ended in Athens' defeat in 404 B.C. Unlike our own representative democracy, the Athenian government was a participatory democracy in which all free male Athenian citizens had a vote in the legislative body, the Assembly. Juries consisted of a rotating group of hundreds of Athenian citizens. As in our law courts, the prosecution would present its case for conviction before the jury and the defense its case for acquittal. The jury would then vote to convict or acquit, a majority vote being sufficient to convict. (In Socrates' trial, the vote was 281 for conviction and 200 for acquittal.) If the decision were for conviction, the prosecution would first be asked to suggest an appropriate penalty and then the defense would be allowed to suggest an alternative penalty. The jury would then be compelled to choose one of the two penalties.

In the **Apology,** Socrates' prosecutors suggest death as the appropriate penalty. The obvious alternative penalty that Socrates could have suggested (which most likely would have been accepted) was exile. But Socrates refuses to suggest this penalty, claiming that since he will never give up his method of philosophical questioning, it would be foolish for him to believe that any other state would tolerate his presence when the most enlightened state of them all, Athens, will not. So, in taunting mockery of the injustice of his conviction, Socrates proudly declares that he actually deserves to be rewarded and not punished by the state. It would be appropriate, he suggests, for the state to give him a pension. Recognizing that this will not be accepted, he nonchalantly suggests a fine which his friends have pledged to pay, since he is poor. Insulted by Socrates' arrogant refusal to plead for mercy, the jury overwhelmingly votes for Socrates' execution, and the **Apology** ends. (The mode of capital punishment in ancient Athens was by compelling the accused to drink a cup of hemlock, a poison.)

Though death sentences were usually carried out within a short period of time, the Athenians had a superstition about executing prisoners while a sacred ship was out of port, as was true at the time of Socrates's conviction. Consequently, several weeks lapsed between the conviction and execution of Socrates. During this period of time, Socrates' friends plotted his escape. The **Crito** consists of a dialogue between Socrates and Crito, a wealthy businessman who has come to inform Socrates (who was seventy-one years old at the time of his conviction) of the plot and to gain his cooperation. Socrates, however, refuses to cooperate, arguing that it would be wrong for him to disobey the law, even though his conviction was an unjust one. Socrates offers various arguments in defense of this belief, including the social contract view, later to be echoed in Hobbes and Locke, that, by remaining in Athens and accepting its benefits when he could have left, he has implicitly made a contract (or promised) to abide by its laws. Although the **Crito** was written long ago, its conservative arguments for respect for law are timeless.

Incapable of meeting Socrates' arguments, Crito eventually comes to accept them and the plot is forgotten as the **Crito** closes. (The death of Socrates is dramatized in Plato's dialogue the **Phaedo,** in which Socrates, in the presence of his friends, argues for the immortality of the soul.)

Crito. But, O my good Socrates, I beg you for the last time to listen to me and save yourself. For to me your death will be more than a single disaster; not only shall I lose a friend the like of whom I shall never find again, but many persons who do not know you and me well will think that I might have saved you if I had been willing to spend money, but that I neglected to do so. And what reputation could be more disgraceful than the reputation of caring more for money than for one's friends? The public will never believe that we were anxious to save you, but that you yourself refused to escape.

Socr. But, my dear Crito, why should we care so much about public opinion? Reasonable men, of whose opinion it is worth our while to think, will believe that we acted as we really did. . . .

Crito. Well, as you wish. But tell me this, Socrates. You surely are not anxious about me and your other friends, and afraid lest, if you escape, the informers would say that we stole you away, and get us into trouble and involve us in a great deal of expense. . . .

Socr. I am anxious about that, Crito, and about much besides.

Crito. Then have no fear on that score. There are men who, for no very large sum, are ready to bring you out of prison into safety. And then, you know, these informers are cheaply bought, and there would be no need to spend much upon them. My fortune is at your service, and I think that it is adequate; and if you have any feeling about making use of my money, there are strangers in Athens whom you know, ready

Source: Plato's *Crito*, trans. F. J. Church, in Plato's *Euthyphro, Apology and Crito* (Indianapolis, Ind.: Bobbs-Merrill, 1948). Reprinted with permission.

to use theirs . . . And therefore, I repeat, do not shrink from saving yourself on that ground. And do not let what you said in the court—that if you went into exile you would not know what to do with yourself—stand in your way; for there are many places for you to go to, where you will be welcomed. If you choose to go to Thessaly, I have friends there who will make much of you and protect you from any annoyance from the people of Thessaly.

And besides, Socrates, I think that you will be doing what is unjust if you abandon your life when you might preserve it. You are simply playing into your enemies' hands; it is exactly what they wanted—to destroy you. And what is more, to me you seem to be abandoning your children, too. You will leave them to take their chance in life, as far as you are concerned, when you might bring them up and educate them. Most likely their fate will be the usual fate of children who are left orphans. But you ought not to bring children into the world unless you mean to take the trouble of bringing them up and educating them. It seems to me that you are choosing the easy way, and not the way of a good and brave man, as you ought, when you have been talking all your life long of the value that you set upon human excellence. For my part, I feel ashamed both for you and for us who are your friends. Men will think that the whole thing which has happened to you—your appearance in court to face trial, when you need not have appeared at all; the very way in which the trial was conducted; and then last of all this, the crowning absurdity of the whole affair—is due to our cowardice. It will look as if we had shirked the danger out of miserable cowardice; for we did not save you, and you did not save yourself, when it was quite possible to do so if we had been good for anything at all. Take care, Socrates, lest these things be not evil only, but also dishonorable to you and to us. Reflect, then, or rather the time for reflection is past; we must make up our minds. And there is only one plan possible. Everything must be done tonight. If we delay any longer, we are lost. Socrates, I implore you not to refuse to listen to me.

Socr. My dear Crito, if your anxiety to save me be right, it is most valuable; but if not, the greater it is the harder it will be to cope with. We must reflect, then, whether we are to do as you say or not; for I am still what I always have been—a man who will accept no argument but that which on reflection I find to be truest. I cannot cast aside my former arguments because this misfortune has come to me. They seem to me to be as true as ever they were, and I respect and honor the same ones as I used to. And if we have no better argument to substitute for them, I certainly shall not agree to your proposal. . . . I am anxious, Crito, to examine our former argument with your help, and to see whether my present circumstance will appear to me to have affected its truth in any way or not; and whether we are to set it aside, or to yield assent to it. Those of us who thought at all seriously always used to say . . . that we ought to respect some of the opinions which men form, and not others. Tell me, Crito . . . do you not think it reasonable to say that we should not respect all the opinions of men but only some, nor the opinions of all men but only of some men? What do you think? Is not this true?

Crito. It is.

Socr. And we should respect the good opinions, and not the worthless ones?

Crito. Yes. . . .

Socr. And what did we say about this? Does a man who is in training, and who is serious about it, pay attention to the praise and blame and opinion of all men, or only of the one man who is a doctor or a trainer?

Crito. He pays attention only to the opinion of the one man.

Socr. Then he ought to fear the blame and welcome the praise of this one man, not of the multitude?

Crito. Clearly. . . .

Socr. Good. But if he disobeys this one man,

and disregards his opinion and his praise, and respects instead what the many say, who understand nothing of the matter, will he not suffer for it?

Crito. Of course he will.

Socr. And how will he suffer? In what way and in what part of himself?

Crito. Of course in his body. That is disabled.

Socr. You are right. And, Crito, to be brief, is it not the same in everything? And, therefore, in questions of justice and injustice, and of the base and the honorable, and of good and evil, which we are now examining, ought we to follow the opinion of the many and fear that, or the opinion of the one man who understands these matters (if we can find him), and feel more shame and fear before him than before all other men? For if we do not follow him, we shall corrupt and maim that part of us which, we used to say, is improved by justice and disabled by injustice.[1] Or is this not so?

Crito. No, Socrates, I agree with you.

Socr. Now, if by listening to the opinions of those who do not understand, we disable that part of us which is improved by health and corrupted by disease, is our life worth living when it is corrupt? It is the body, is it not?

Crito. Yes.

Socr. Is life worth living with the body corrupted and crippled?

Crito. No, certainly not.

Socr. Then is life worth living when that part of us which is maimed by injustice and benefited by justice is corrupt? Or do we consider that part of us, whatever it is, which has to do with justice and injustice to be of less consequence than our body?

Crito. No, certainly not.

Socr. But more valuable?

Crito. Yes, much more so.

Socr. Then, my good friend, we must not think so much of what the many will say of us; we must think of what the one man who understands justice and injustice, and of what truth herself will say of us. And so you are mistaken, to begin with, when you invite us to regard the opinion of the multitude concerning the just and the honorable and the good, and their opposites. But, it may be said, the multitude can put us to death?

Crito. Yes, that is evident. That may be said, Socrates.

Socr. True. But, my good friend, to me it appears that the conclusion which we have just reached is the same as our conclusion of former times. Now consider whether we still hold to the belief that we should set the highest value, not on living, but on living well?

Crito. Yes, we do.

Socr. And living well and honorably and justly mean the same thing: do we hold to that or not?

Crito. We do.

Socr. Then, starting from these premises, we have to consider whether it is just or not for me to try to escape from prison, without the consent of the Athenians. If we find that it is just, we will try; if not, we will give up the idea. I am afraid that considerations of expense, and of reputation, and of bringing up my children, of which you talk, Crito, are only the opinions of the many—who casually put men to death, and who would, if they could, as casually bring them to life again, without a thought. But reason, which is our guide, shows us that we can have nothing to consider but the question which I asked just now—namely, shall we be acting justly if we give money and thanks to the men who are to aid me in escaping, and if we ourselves take our respective parts in my escape? Or shall we in truth be acting unjustly if we do all this? And if we find that we should be acting unjustly, then we must not take any account either of death, or of any other evil that may be the consequence of remaining here, where we are, but only of acting unjustly.

Crito. I think that you are right, Socrates. But what are we to do?

Socr. Let us examine this question together,

[1]That is, the "soul." EDITOR'S NOTE.

my friend, and if you can contradict anything that I say, do so, and I shall be persuaded. But if you cannot, do not go on repeating to me any longer, my dear friend, that I should escape without the consent of the Athenians. I am very anxious to act with your approval and consent. I do not want you to think me mistaken. But now tell me if you agree with the premise from which I start, and try to answer my questions as you think best.

Crito. I will try.

Socr. Ought we never to act unjustly voluntarily? Or may we act unjustly in some ways, and not in others? Is it the case, as we have often agreed in former times, that it is never either good or honorable to act unjustly?. . . . Is not what we used to say most certainly the truth, whether the multitude agrees with us or not? Is not acting unjustly evil and shameful in every case, whether we incur a heavier or a lighter punishment as the consequence? Do we believe that?

Crito. We do.

Socr. Then we ought never to act unjustly?

Crito. Certainly not.

Socr. If we ought never to act unjustly at all, ought we to repay injustice with injustice, as the multitude thinks we may?

Crito. Clearly not.

Socr. Well, then, Crito, ought we to do evil to anyone?

Crito. Certainly I think not, Socrates.

Socr. And is it just to repay evil with evil, as the multitude thinks, or unjust?

Crito. Certainly it is unjust. . . .

Socr. Then we ought not to repay injustice with injustice or to do harm to any man, no matter what we may have suffered from him. And in conceding this, Crito, be careful that you do not concede more than you mean. For I know that only a few men hold, or ever will hold, this opinion. And so those who hold it and those who do not have no common ground of argument; they can of necessity only look with contempt on each other's belief. Do you therefore consider very carefully whether or not you agree with me and share my opinion. Are we to start in our inquiry from the premise that it is never right either to act unjustly, or to repay injustice with injustice. . . . Or do you disagree with me and dissent from my premise? I myself have believed in it for a long time, and I believe in it still. But if you differ in any way, explain to me how. If you still hold to our former opinion, listen to my next point.

Crito. Yes, I hold to it, and I agree with you. Go on.

Socr. Then, my next point, or rather my next question, is this: Ought a man to carry out his just agreements, or may he shuffle out of them?

Crito. He ought to carry them out.

Socr. Then consider. If I escape without the state's consent, shall I be injuring those whom I ought least to injure, or not? Shall I be abiding by my just agreements or not?

Crito. I cannot answer your question, Socrates. I do not understand it.

Socr. Consider it in this way. Suppose the laws and the commonwealth were to come and appear to me as I was preparing to run away (if that is the right phrase to describe my escape) and were to ask, "Tell us, Socrates, what have you in your mind to do? What do you mean by trying to escape but to destroy us, the laws and the whole state, so far as you are able? Do you think that a state can exist and not be overthrown, in which the decisions of law are of no force, and are disregarded and undermined by private individuals?" How shall we answer questions like that, Crito? Much might be said, especially by an orator, in defense of the law which makes judicial decisions supreme. Shall I reply, "But the state has injured me by judging my case unjustly?" Shall we say that?

Crito. Certainly we will, Socrates.

Socr. And suppose the laws were to reply, "Was that our agreement? Or was it that you would abide by whatever judgments the state should pronounce?" And if we were surprised by their words, perhaps they would say, "Socrates, don't be surprised by our words, but answer us; you yourself are accustomed to ask questions and to answer them. What complaint have you against us and the state, that you are trying to destroy us? Are we not, first of all, your parents? Through us your father took your mother and brought you into the world. Tell us, have you any fault to find with those of us that are the laws of marriage?'' ''I have none,'' I should reply. ''Or have you any fault to find with those of us that regulate the raising of the child and the education which you, like others, received? Did we not do well in telling your father to educate you in music and athletics?'' ''You did,'' I should say. ''Well, then, since you were brought into the world and raised and educated by us, how, in the first place, can you deny that you are our child and our slave, as your fathers were before you? And if this be so, do you think that your rights are on a level with ours? Do you think that you have a right to retaliate if we should try to do anything to you? . . . If we try to destroy you, because we think it just, will you in return do all that you can to destroy us, the laws, and your country, and say that in so doing you are acting justly—you, the man who really thinks so much of excellence? Or are you too wise to see that your country is worthier, more to be revered, more sacred, and held in higher honor both by the gods and by all men of understanding, than your father and your mother and all your other ancestors; and that you ought to reverence it, and to submit to it, and to approach it more humbly when it is angry with you than you would approach your father; and either to do whatever it tells you to do or to persuade it to excuse you; and to obey in silence if it orders you to endure flogging or imprisonment, or if it sends you to battle to be wounded or to die? That is just. You must not give way, nor retreat, nor desert your station. In war, and in the court of justice, and everywhere, you must do whatever your state and your country tell you to do, or you must persuade them that their commands are unjust. But it is impious to use violence against your father or your mother; and much more impious to use violence against your country.'' What answer shall we make, Crito? Shall we say that the laws speak the truth, or not?

Crito. I think that they do.

Socr. ''Then consider, Socrates,'' perhaps they would say, ''if we are right in saying that by attempting to escape you are attempting an injustice. We brought you into the world, we raised you, we educated you, we gave you and every other citizen a share of all the good things we could. Yet we proclaim that if any man of the Athenians is dissatisfied with us, he may take his goods and go away wherever he pleases; we give that privilege to every man who chooses to avail himself of it, so soon as he has reached manhood, and sees us, the laws, and the administration of our state. No one of us stands in his way or forbids him to take his goods and go wherever he likes, whether it be to an Athenian colony or to any foreign country, if he is dissatisfied with us and with the state. But we say that every man of you who remains here, seeing how we administer justice, and how we govern the state in other matters, has agreed, by the very fact of remaining here, to do whatsoever we tell him. And, we say, he who disobeys us acts unjustly on three counts: he disobeys us who are his parents, and he disobeys us who reared him, and he disobeys us after he has agreed to obey us, without persuading us that we are wrong. Yet we did not tell him sternly to do whatever we told him. We offered him an alternative; we gave him his choice either to obey us or to convince us that we were wrong; but he does neither.

''These are the charges, Socrates, to which we say that you will expose yourself if you do what you intend; and you are more exposed to these charges than other Athenians.'' And if I were to ask, ''Why?'' they might retort with justice that I have bound myself by the agreement with them more than other Athenians. They would say, ''Socrates, we have very strong evidence that you were satisfied with us and with the state. You would not have been content to stay at home in it more than other Athenians unless you had been satisfied with it more than they. You never went away from Athens to the festivals, nor elsewhere except on military service; you never made other journeys like other men; you had no desire to see other states or other laws; you were contented with us and our state. . . . Besides, if you had wished, you might at your trial have offered to go into exile. At that time you could have done with the state's consent what you are trying now to do without it. But then you gloried in being willing to die. You said that you preferred death to exile. And now you do not honor those words: you do not respect us, the laws, for you are trying to destroy us. . . . First, therefore, answer this question. Are we right, or are we wrong, in saying that you have agreed not in mere words, but in your actions, to live under our government?'' What are we to say, Crito? Must we not admit that it is true?

Crito. We must, Socrates.

Socr. Then they would say, ''Are you not breaking your contracts and agreements with us? And you were not led to make them by force or by fraud. You did not have to make up your mind in a hurry. You had seventy years in which you might have gone away if you had been dissatisfied with us, or if the agreement had seemed to you unjust. But you preferred neither Sparta nor Crete. . . .

''Reflect now. What good will you do yourself or your friends by thus transgressing and breaking your agreement? It is tolerably certain that they, on their part, will at least run the risk of exile, and of losing their civil rights, or of forfeiting their property. You yourself might go to one of the neighboring states, to Thebes or to Megara, for instance—for both of them are well governed—but, Socrates, you will come as an enemy to these governments, and all who care for their city will look askance at you, and think that you are a subverter of law. You will confirm the judges in their opinion, and make it seem that their verdict was a just one. For a man who is a subverter of law may well be supposed to be a corrupter of the young and thoughtless. Then will you avoid well-governed states and civilized men? Will life be worth having, if you do? Will you associate with such men, and converse without shame—about what, Socrates? About the things which you talk of here? Will you tell them that excellence and justice and institutions and law are the most valuable things that men can have? And do you not think that that will be a disgraceful thing for Socrates? You ought to think so. But you will leave these places; you will go to the friends of Crito in Thessaly. For there is found the greatest disorder and license, and very likely they will be delighted to hear of the ludicrous way in which you escaped from prison, dressed up in peasant's clothes, or in some other disguise which people put on when they are running away, and with your appearance altered. But will no one say how you, an old man, with probably only a few more years to live, clung so greedily to life that you dared to break the highest laws? Perhaps not, if you do not annoy them. But if you do, Socrates, you will hear much that will make you blush. You will pass your life as the flatterer and the slave of all men. . . . And where will be all our old arguments about justice and excellence then? But you wish to live for the sake of your children? You want to bring them up and educate them? What? Will you take them with you to Thessaly, and bring them up and educate them there? Will you make them strangers to their own country, that you may bestow this benefit of exile on them too? Or supposing that you leave them in Athens, will they be brought up and educated better if you are alive, though you are not with them? Yes, your friends will take care of them. Will your friends take care of them if you make a journey to Thessaly, and not if you make a journey to Hades?[2] You ought not to

[2]In Greek mythology, the home of the dead, beneath the earth. EDITOR'S NOTE.

think that, at least if those who call themselves your friends are worth anything at all.

"No, Socrates, be persuaded by us who have reared you. Think neither of children nor of life, nor of any other thing before justice, so that when you come to the other world you may be able to make your defense before the rulers who sit in judgment there. . . . Now you will go away a victim of the injustice, not of the laws, but of men. But if you repay evil with evil, and injustice with injustice in this shameful way, and break your agreements and covenants with us, and injure those whom you should least injure, yourself and your friends and your country and us, and so escape, then we shall be angry with you while you live, and when you die our brothers, the laws in Hades, will not receive you kindly; for they will know that on earth you did all that you could to destroy us. Listen then to us, and let not Crito persuade you to do as he says."

Be sure, my dear friend Crito, that this is what I seem to hear . . . and the sound of these arguments rings so loudly in my ears, that I cannot hear any other arguments. And I feel sure that if you try to change my mind you will speak in vain. Nevertheless, if you think that you will succeed, speak.

Crito. I have nothing more to say, Socrates.

Socr. Then let it be, Crito, and let us do as I say, since the god is our guide.

DISCUSSION QUESTIONS

1. According to Socrates, in deciding whether he ought to follow Crito's advice to escape, which considerations are relevant and which irrelevant? Do you agree? Why?

2. Critically consider Socrates' arguments against disobeying the judgment of the Athenian court. Do any of these arguments establish Socrates' conclusion? Why?

3. Does Socrates believe that as long as he accepts the benefits of Athenian citizenship, he has a moral obligation to obey all of its laws, even if he believes them unjust, or does he believe that a person should disobey laws that he believes to be unjust but submit to the punishment prescribed by law for disobedience? What is your position on this matter? Why?

4. Consider the following two positions on the issue of individual conscience versus governmental authority:

> Must the citizen never . . . resign his conscience to the legislator? Why has every man a conscience, then? I think we should be men first and subjects afterwards. It is not desirable to cultivate a respect for the law, so much as for the right. The only obligation which I have a right to assume, is to do at any time what I think right.[3]

> The defining mark of the state is authority. The primary obligation of man is autonomy, the refusal to be ruled. . . . Insofar as a man fulfills his obligation to make himself the author of his decisions, he will resist the state's claim to have authority over him.[4]

What **exactly** do the preceding two claims assert? Is it possible to attribute more than one meaning to one or both of these claims? Is there some interpretation of either or both of these claims with which you agree? What do you think Plato would have said about them?

[3]Henry D. Thoreau, "Civil Disobedience" in *Civil Disobedience,* ed. Hugo Bedau (N.Y.: Pegasus, 1969.)

[4]Robert Paul Wolff, *In Defense of Anarchism* (New York: Harper and Row, 1979), p. 18.

59. THE PROPER LIMITS OF CIVIL DISOBEDIENCE IN THE AMERICAN DEMOCRACY

Abe Fortas

ABE FORTAS (1910–82) was born in Memphis, Tennessee, and received a law degree from Yale University, where he was an assistant professor of law from 1933 to 1937. He then held many government posts, including that of Undersecretary of the Interior in 1942. In 1947, he entered private practice, establishing a reputation for himself as an outstanding appeals lawyer and defender of civil liberties. He was the defense attorney who argued before the Supreme Court in the landmark case of **Gideon vs. Wainwright** (1962) in which the Supreme Court ruled unanimously that states must assure free legal counsel to the poor in every criminal trial.

In 1965, Fortas was appointed an Associate Justice of the Supreme Court after being nominated by President Lyndon B. Johnson, to whom he was a close friend and advisor. Upon the retirement of Chief Justice Earl Warren, Johnson nominated Fortas for the position of Chief Justice in 1968, but withdrew the nomination when Republicans and Southern Democrats held a filibuster against the nomination. Fortas resigned in controversy the following year, after it was revealed that while on the Supreme Court he had accepted $20,000, part of a life-stipend, from a private foundation.

The following selection comes from Fortas' short book **Concerning Dissent and Civil Disobedience,** published in 1968 while Fortas was on the Supreme Court. At that time there was widespread civil disobedience in the United States over matters of racial equality, the war in Vietnam, and the draft. As Fortas points out in the introduction to his book, the issue of civil disobedience raises moral problems for most of us because we are neither absolute legalists who believe that the law can never rightfully be disobeyed nor absolute individualistic moralists who believe that one should always do what one thinks right, regardless of the dictates of law. Seeing the potential tyranny of absolute legalism and the potential chaos of a society whose citizens always place their own individual consciences above law, we try to draw some middle line. As a spokesman for the establishment, Fortas attempts to draw that line, a line which he hopes can provide a moral rudder to restrain the widespread and, as he saw it, often unjustified civil disobedience that was so much a part of the American scene when his book was written.

The Paradox: The Duty to Obey and to Disobey

I am a man of the law. I have dedicated myself to uphold the law and to enforce its commands. I fully accept the principle that each of us is subject to law; that each of us is bound to obey the law enacted by his government.

But if I had lived in Germany in Hitler's days, I hope I would have refused to wear an armband, to *Heil Hitler,* to submit to genocide. This I hope, although Hitler's edicts were law until allied weapons buried the Third Reich.

If I had been a Negro living in Birmingham or Little Rock or Plaquemines Parish, Louisiana, I hope I would have disobeyed the state laws that said that I might not enter the public waiting room in the bus station reserved for "Whites."

I hope I would have insisted upon going into the parks and swimming pools and schools which state or city law reserved for "Whites."

I hope I would have had the courage to disobey, although the segregation ordinances were presumably law until they were declared unconstitutional.

How, then, can I reconcile my profound belief in obedience to law and my equally basic need to disobey *these* laws? Is there a principle, a code, a theory to which a man, with honor and integrity, may subscribe? Or is it all a matter of individual judgment? Do we live in a trackless jungle? Is there, or is there not, a path that law and integrity mark out through the maze of tangled obligations and conflicting loyalties?. . .

The Simplicities: The Right to Dissent and Its Limitations

the right

In the United States, under our Constitution, the question is not "may I dissent?" or "may I oppose a law or a government?" I *may* dissent. I *may* criticize. I *may* oppose. Our Constitution and our courts guarantee this.

The question is: "*How* may I do so?"

Each of us owes a duty of obedience to law. This is a moral as well as a legal imperative. So, first, we must seek to know which methods of protest are lawful: What are the means of opposition and dissent that are permissible under our system of law and which, therefore, will not subject us to punishment by the state and will not violate our duty of obedience to law?

There is another question. Are there occasions when we, with moral justification, may resort to methods of dissent, such as direct disobedience of an ordinance, even though the methods are unlawful?. . .

From our earliest history, we have insisted that each of us is and must be free to criticize the government, however sharply; to express dissent and opposition, however brashly; even to advocate overthrow of the government itself. We have insisted upon freedom of speech and of the press. . . .

. . . Ultimately, the basic means of protest under our system is the ballot box: the right to organize and to join with others to elect new officials to enact and administer the law. . . .

the limitations

There are limitations, however, even on the freedom of speech. The state may prescribe reasonable regulations as to when and where the right to harangue the public or to assemble a crowd may be exercised. It may require a permit for a mass meeting. But it can't use this housekeeping power for any purpose except to reduce the public inconvenience which any large assemblage involves.

And it is not true that anyone may say what's on his mind anytime and anywhere. According to the famous dictum of Justice Holmes, no one may falsely cry "Fire" in a crowded theater and thereby cause a panic. This is so even though

Source: From *Concerning Dissent and Civil Disobedience* by Abe Fortas.

the person's action may have been prompted by the highest motives. . . .

But good motives do not excuse action which will injure others. The individual's conscience does not give him a license to indulge individual conviction without regard to the rights of others. . . .

. . . [T]he Constitution seeks to accommodate two conflicting values, each of which is fundamental: the need for freedom to speak freely, to protest effectively, to organize, and to demonstrate; and the necessity of maintaining order so that other people's rights, and the peace and security of the state, will not be impaired. . . .

civil disobedience

At the beginning of this book, I said that if I had been a Negro in the South, I hope I would have disobeyed the state and local laws denying to Negroes equal access to schools, to voting rights, and to public facilities. If I had disobeyed those laws, I would have been arrested and tried and convicted. Until the Supreme Court ruled that these laws were unconstitutional, I would have been a law violator.

As it turned out, my refusal to obey those laws would have been justified by the courts. But suppose I had been wrong. Suppose the Supreme Court had decided that the laws were constitutional. Despite the deep moral conviction that motivated me—despite the fact that my violation of the discriminatory racial laws would have been in a great cause—I would have been consigned to jail, with no possible remedy except the remote prospect of a pardon.

This may seem harsh. It may seem especially harsh if we assume that I profoundly believe that the law I am violating is immoral and unconstitutional, and if we assume that the question of its constitutionality is close. *But this is what we mean by the rule of law:* both the government and the individual must accept the result of procedures by which the courts, and ultimately the Supreme Court, decide that the law is such and such, and not so and so; that the law has or has not been violated in a particular situation, and that it is or is not constitutional; and that the individual defendant has or has not been properly convicted and sentenced.

This is the rule of law. The state, the courts, and the individual citizen are bound by a set of laws which have been adopted in a prescribed manner, and the state and the individual must accept the courts' determinations of what those rules are and mean in specific instances. *This is the rule of law,* even if the ultimate judicial decision is by the narrow margin of five to four!

The term "civil disobedience" has been used to apply to a person's refusal to obey a law which the person believes to be immoral or unconstitutional. . . .

The phrase "civil disobedience" has been grossly misapplied in recent years. Civil disobedience, even in its broadest sense, does not apply to efforts to overthrow the government or to seize control of areas or parts of it by force, or by the use of violence to compel the government to grant a measure of autonomy to part of its population. These are programs of revolution. They are not in the same category as the programs of reformers who—like Martin Luther King—seek changes within the established order.

The term "civil disobedience" has not been limited to protests in the form of refusal to obey a law because of disapproval of that particular law. It has been applied to another kind of civil disobedience. This is the violation of laws which the protester does not challenge because of their own terms or effect. The laws themselves are not the subject of attack or protest. They are violated only as a means of protest, like carrying a picket sign. They are violated in order to publicize a protest and to bring pressure on the public or the government to accomplish purposes which have nothing to do with the law that is breached. The great exponent of this type of civil disobedience was Gandhi. He protested the British rule in India by a general program of disobedience to the laws governing ordinary civil life. . . .

Let me first be clear about a fundamental proposition. The motive of civil disobedience, whatever its type, does not confer immunity for law violation. Especially if the civil disobedience involves violence or a breach of public order prohibited by statute or ordinance, it is the state's duty to arrest the dissident. If he is properly arrested, charged, and convicted, he should be punished by fine or imprisonment, or both, in accordance with the provisions of law, unless the law is invalid in general or as applied.

He may be motivated by the highest moral principles. He may be passionately inspired. He may, indeed, be right in the eyes of history or morality or philosophy. These are not controlling. It is the state's duty to arrest and punish those who violate the laws designed to protect private safety and public order. . . .

Just as we expect the government to be bound by all laws, so each individual is bound by all of the laws under the Constitution. He cannot pick and choose. He cannot substitute his own judgment or passion, however noble, for the rules of law. . . . A citizen cannot demand of his government or of other people obedience to the law, and at the same time claim a right in himself to break it by lawless conduct, free of punishment or penalty.

Let me elaborate this by reference to an article written by Dr. Martin Luther King, Jr., and published in September of 1961. In this article, Dr. King set forth the guiding principles of his approach to effective protest by civil disobedience. He said that many Negroes would disobey "unjust laws." These he defined as laws which a minority is compelled to observe but which are not binding on the majority. He said that this must be done openly and peacefully, and that those who do it must accept the penalty imposed by law for their conduct.

This is civil disobedience in a great tradition. It is peaceful, nonviolent disobedience of laws which are themselves unjust and which the protester challenges as invalid and unconstitutional.

Dr. King was involved in a case which illustrated this conception. He led a mass demonstration to protest segregation and discrimination in Birmingham. An injunction had been issued by a state court against the demonstration. But Dr. King disregarded the injunction and proceeded with the march as planned. He was arrested. He was prosecuted in the state court, convicted of contempt, and sentenced to serve five days in jail. He appealed, claiming that the First Amendment protected his violation of the injunction.

I have no doubt that Dr. King violated the injunction in the belief that it was invalid and his conduct was legally as well as morally justified. But the Supreme Court held that he was bound to obey the injunction unless and until it was set aside on appeal; and that he could not disregard the injunction even if he was right that the injunction was invalid. Dr. King went to jail and served his time.

I have no moral criticism to make of Dr. King's action in this incident, even though it turned out to be legally unjustified. He led a peaceable demonstration. He acted in good faith. There was good, solid basis for his belief that he did not have to obey the injunction—until the Supreme Court ruled the other way. The Court disagreed with him by a vote of five to four. I was one of the dissenters. Then Dr. King, without complaint or histrionics, accepted the penalty of misjudgment. This, I submit, is action in the great tradition of social protest in a democratic society where all citizens, including protesters, are subject to the rule of law. . . .

Conclusion

The story of man is the history, first, of the acceptance and imposition of restraints necessary to permit communal life; and second, of the emancipation of the individual within that system of necessary restraints. . . .

. . . The achievement of liberty is man's indispensable condition of living; and yet, liberty cannot exist unless it is restrained and restricted. The instrument for balancing these two conflicting factors is the law.

So we must end as we began, with an acknowledgment that the rule of law is the essential condition of individual liberty as it is of the existence of the state. . . .

Procedure is the bone structure of a democratic society; and the quality of procedural standards which meet general acceptance—the quality of what is tolerable and permissible and acceptable conduct—determines the durability of the society and the survival possibilities of freedom within the society. . . .

We must accept the discomforts necessarily implicit in a large, *lawful* demonstration because, in a sense, it is part of the dynamics of democracy which depends for its vitality upon the vigorous confrontation of opposing forces. But we cannot and should not endure physical assault upon person or property. This sort of assault is ultimately counter-productive. It polarizes society, and in any polarization, the minority group, although it may achieve initial, limited success, is likely to meet bitter reprisal and rejection of its demands.

In my judgment civil disobedience—the deliberate violation of law—is never justified in our nation, where the law being violated is not itself the focus or target of the protest. So long as our governments obey the mandate of the Constitution and assure facilities and protection for the powerful expression of individual and mass dissent, the disobedience of laws which are not themselves the target of the protest—the violation of law merely as a technique of demonstration—constitutes an act of rebellion, not merely of dissent.

Civil disobedience is violation of law. Any violation of law must be punished, whatever its purpose, as the theory of civil disobedience recognizes. But law violation directed not to the laws or practices that are the subject of dissent, but to unrelated laws which are disobeyed merely to dramatize dissent, may be morally as well as politically unacceptable.

At the beginning of this discussion, I presented the dilemma of obedience to law and the need that sometimes may arise to disobey profoundly immoral or unconstitutional laws. This is another kind of civil disobedience, and the only kind that, in my view, is ever truly defensible as a matter of social morality.

It is only in respect to such laws—laws that are basically offensive to fundamental values of life or the Constitution—that a moral (although not a legal) defense of law violation can possibly be urged. Anyone assuming to make the judgment that a law is in this category assumes a terrible burden. He has undertaken a fearful moral as well as legal responsibility. He should be prepared to submit to prosecution by the state for the violation of law and the imposition of punishment if he is wrong or unsuccessful. He should even admit the correctness of the state's action in seeking to enforce its laws, and he should acquiesce in the ultimate judgment of the courts.

For after all, each of us is a member of an organized society. Each of us benefits from its existence and its order. And each of us must be ready, like Socrates, to accept the verdict of its institutions if we violate their mandate and our challenge is not vindicated.

Animating all of this in our society is the principle of tolerance. The state must tolerate the individual's dissent, appropriately expressed. The individual must tolerate the majority's verdict when and as it is settled in accordance with the laws and the procedures that have been established. . . .

DISCUSSION QUESTIONS

1. Fortas begins his essay by presenting the paradox that can be generated by the conflict between a citizen's obligation to obey the law, even if he thinks it wrong, and one's recognition as a moral being that laws can be quite unjust and not worthy of being obeyed. How, if at all, does Fortas resolve this paradox?

2. In his famous essay on civil disobedience, Thoreau writes:

> A wise man will not leave the right to the mercy of chance, nor wish it to prevail through the power of the majority.[1]

How do you think Fortas would reply to such a statement? What is your opinion of it?

3. Fortas writes:

> . . . If I had been a Negro in the South, I hope I would have disobeyed the state and local laws denying to Negroes equal access to schools, to voting rights, and to public facilities. . . . Until the Supreme Court ruled that these laws were unconstitutional, I would have been a law violator. As it turned out, my refusal to obey these laws would have been justified by the courts. But suppose I had been wrong. Suppose the Supreme Court had decided that the laws were constitutional. Despite the deep moral conviction that motivated me. . .I would have been consigned to jail. . . . This may seem harsh. . . . **But this is what we mean by the rule of law:** both the government and the individual must accept the result of procedures by which the courts, and ultimately the Supreme Court, decide that the law is such and such. . . .[2]

What does Fortas mean when he says "Suppose I had been wrong"? Does he mean that a person can disobey the law only when he believes that the Supreme Court will most likely declare that law unconstitutional or in some other way invalid? According to Fortas, can a person justifiably disobey a law he believes to be constitutional, but unjust? What do you think of Fortas' position here?

5. **Civil disobedience** has been defined as follows: Anyone commits an act of civil disobedience if and only if he acts illegally, publicly, nonviolently, and conscientiously with the intent to frustrate (one of) the laws, policies, or decisions of his government.[3]

a. Would you modify this definition in any way? In particular would you describe an act as one of civil disobedience if the reason for disobedience was not to frustrate a given law but to refrain from being an instrument of injustice? In this regard, consider the following quotation from Thoreau's famous essay "On Civil Disobedience":

> If the injustice is . . . of such a nature that it requires you to be the agent of injustice to another, then, I say, break the law. Let your life be a counter friction to stop the machine. What I have to do is to see, at any rate, that I do not lend myself to the wrong which I condemn.[4]

b. According to Fortas, when would an act of civil disobedience be justified? Do you agree?

c. Would Fortas accept any other type of disobedience of the law as morally justified? Would you?

6. Fortas praises Martin Luther King's passive willingness to accept punishment for his act of civil disobedience in Birmingham, Alabama. According to Fortas, would it ever be right for a citizen of our American democracy to attempt to avoid punishment for an act of civil disobedience that the Supreme Court judges properly punishable? Do you agree? If not, do you think that King would have been right to attempt to avoid punishment, if he could? Why do you think that King did passively accept punishment?

7. According to Fortas, must a person exhaust legal channels for protest before engaging in an act of civil disobedience or is it sometimes morally permissible to engage in an act of civil disobedience simultaneously with acts of legal protest? Do you agree?

8. Thoreau is often criticized for his disdain of the democratic process and his complacency in accepting the right of an individual to do as he thinks right, regardless of what the law says. Consider, for example, the following:

> As for adopting the ways which the State has provided for remedying the evil, I know not of such ways. They take too much time. . . . I have other affairs to attend to. I came into this world, not chiefly to make this a good place to live in,

[1]Henry D. Thoreau, "Civil Disobedience" in *Civil Disobedience,* ed. Hugo Bedau (New York: Pegasus, 1969), p. 32.

[2]See p. 507.

[3]This definition is provided by Hugo Bedau on p. 218 of *Civil Disobedience,* which he edited.

[4]Henry D. Thoreau, Ibid., p. 35.

but to live in it, be it good or bad. A man has not everything to do, but something; and because he cannot do **everything**, it is not necessary that he should do **something** wrong. It is not my business to be petitioning the Governor or the Legislature any more than it is theirs to petition me.[5]

What would Fortas say? What do you think?

[5]Henry D. Thoreau, Ibid., p. 35.

60. A REJOINDER TO FORTAS: THE FALLACIES OF HIS "LAW AND ORDER" APPROACH

Howard Zinn

HOWARD ZINN (1922–) is a professor of government at Boston College who is noted for his liberal political views. He is a recipient of an Air Force medal for his conduct as an officer in World War II and a recipient of an award by The American Historical Association in 1958 in recognition of his original historical research.

The following selection is excerpted from Zinn's **Disobedience and Democracy: Nine Fallacies on Law and Order** (1968), which was written in rebuttal to Fortas' **Concerning Dissent and Civil Disobedience.** As Zinn sees it, in spite of Fortas' disclaimers, the positions Fortas defends put him squarely on the side of those "law and order" conservatives who proclaim the supremacy of the rule of law over individual conscience. Claiming that Fortas misleads his readers into believing that he is more tolerant of civil disobedience than he really is, Zinn accuses Fortas of committing nine specific fallacies in his book and passionately defends this accusation.

It is strange. On Mondays, Wednesday and Fridays, thoughtful Americans speak earnestly about how much *change* is needed, not just elsewhere, but here in the United States. On Tuesdays, Thursdays, and Saturdays, disturbed by the tumult of the previous evenings, when various people (blacks, students, draft resisters, mothers on welfare) have, in a disorderly way, *demanded* change, the same people call for "law and order.". . .

This current rush back to "law and order" finds its theoretical exposition in a recent booklet by Justice Abe Fortas of the Supreme Court, *Concerning Dissent and Civil Disobedience.* Having been made uncomfortable on certain days by war, racism, poverty, and politics, and on other days by disorderly demonstrations, we seek comfort in the balanced judgment of Mr. Fortas. His essay has been widely distributed across the nation; his views on civil disobedience are probably those of the majority of the Supreme Court; the tone of his essay is very close to the statements on law and order we find everywhere today—in newspaper editorials, on radio and television, in the pronouncements of political leaders. Therefore, what Mr. Fortas says is important. If he misled us, that would be very serious.

Mr. Fortas does mislead us, on nine counts that I can see, in the fifty-five pages of his booklet. These nine fallacies, I believe, are not only harmful to the liberty of dissident minorities, but stifling to the growth of democracy for the majority of Americans. . . .

First fallacy: *that the rule of law has an intrinsic value apart from moral ends. (By "moral ends" I mean the needs of human beings, not the mores of our culture.)*

Fortas conceals this premise at first, noting in his opening paragraphs that on the one hand he is "a man of the law," but that he would have disobeyed Hitler's laws, and the Southern segregation laws. He asks: "How, then, can I reconcile my profound belief in obedience to law and my equally basic need to disobey *these* laws? Is there a principle, a code, a theory to which a man, with honor and integrity, may subscribe?"

Thus, Fortas leads us to expect from him a set of moral criteria by which both adherence to law and violation of law would be tested, the assumption being that neither is self-justifying but requires some larger anchor of support. His essay never supplies this, however. What he gives us instead is an exposition of what the *legal* limits of dissent are; then he lays down the conditions for civil disobedience, in which the limits are very close to what is *legally* permissible.

Fortas' reluctance to go beyond legal limits is shown when he formulates, with some inconsistency, the grounds for civil disobedience. On page [508] he says the "great tradition" of civil disobedience is invoked when laws are challenged as "invalid and unconstitutional." So here, the laws we disobey must be unconstitutional as well as invalid; Fortas, as a lawyer, must understand how crucial is the conjunction *and.* But on page [509] he talks of "the need . . . to disobey profoundly immoral or unconstitutional laws." Here, apparently, if a law is "profoundly immoral" it may be disobeyed even if it is constitutional. Yet, even in this instance, Fortas says, the disobedient one, when found guilty, "should acquiesce in the ultimate judgment of the courts." Should we acquiesce even where the law is "profoundly immoral"? We might return at this point, although Fortas does not, to his initial example: Should we "acquiesce in the ultimate judgment of the courts" even where the law gives Jews a yellow armband? Or where, as in the Dred Scott decision, the Supreme Court declares Negroes have no rights? Or where a law compels men to fight in an immoral war? To insist we must, at some point, "acquiesce," that even a "profoundly immoral" law is ultimately to be obeyed, must mean that "the rule of law" in general supersedes the immorality of the particular law which represents it, and *in itself* constitutes a higher morality, a supreme value. . . .

If Fortas were really concerned with values, with a moral system, with "a principle, a code, a theory," then there would be circumstances where the rule of law could not be obeyed, where *disobedience* might be the "essential condition" for individual liberty. But Fortas finds no such circumstance. As we have seen, even in those rare instances where we have a "profoundly immoral" law, if the courts uphold it, the verdict and punishment must be accepted. . . .

A common argument [for the view that we ought to obey immoral laws] is that disobedience even of bad laws is wrong because that fosters a general disrespect for all laws, including good ones, which we need. But this is like arguing that children should be made to eat rotten fruit along with the good, lest they get the idea *all* fruit should be thrown away. Isn't it likely that someone forced to eat the rotten fruit may because of that develop a distaste for all fruit?

In fact, there is no evidence that violations

of law in the spirit of civil disobedience lead to a general contempt for all laws. If this were so, we might expect either that persons engaging in civil disobedience become general law violators, or that other persons are encouraged by these acts to become indiscriminate violators of law. There is no indication that this has happened. . . .

In fact, however, an act of civil disobedience, like any move towards reform, is more like the first push up a hill. Society's tendency is to maintain what has been. Rebellion is only an occasional reaction to suffering in human history; we have infinitely more instances of forbearance to exploitation, and submission to authority, than we have examples of revolt. Measure the number of peasant insurrections against the centuries of serfdom in Europe—the millennia of landlordism in the East; match the number of slave revolts in America with the record of those millions who went through their lifetime of toil without outward protest. What we should be most concerned about is not some natural tendency towards violent uprising, but rather the inclination of people, faced with an overwhelming environment, to submit to it. . . .

Our perception is a problem of balance. The magnitude of the grievance must be weighed against the degree of disruption which civil disobedience represents. When people idolize the "rule of law" it is usually because they not only minimize the existing grievances, but magnify the scariness of the act of civil disobedience.

I am arguing for a civil disobedience measured to the size of the evil it is intended to eliminate. When someone criticized William Lloyd Garrison for his militancy, he replied: "Sir, slavery will not be overthrown without excitement, a most tremendous excitement.". . .

We in America are so far removed from our own revolutionary tradition, and the abolitionist tradition, and also from the reality of suffering among other people, that we consider as unpardonable transgressions of law and order what are really mild acts, measured against the exciting evils. For students to occupy a university building in protest against that University's long-time policy of pushing black people from their homes while it accumulated enormous wealth—that is a mild action. For black Mississippians to occupy government property in protest against their poverty is a pitifully moderate act. For a young person to burn a draft card is a rather weak form of protest against a government which drops bombs on villages, destroys crops, kills thousands in war.

Yet all of these actions I have named fall outside Justice Fortas' boundaries for permissible civil disobedience. The reason he would exclude them, I suggest, is that some mystical value has been attached to "the rule of law", beyond those human rights which law, way back in our democratic tradition, was set up to support. Fortas speaks weakly, guardedly of civil disobedience and morality, but in the end what counts with him is power and the law. Until American citizens can overcome this idolization of law, until they begin to see that law is, like other institutions and actions, to be measured against moral principles, against human needs, we will remain a static society in a world of change, a society deaf to the rising cries for justice—and therefore, a society in serious trouble. . . .

Second fallacy: *the person who commits civil disobedience must accept his punishment as right.*

Fortas tells us at the outset that he would have disobeyed the Southern segregation laws. And he tells us later in the essay that even if the Supreme Court had upheld the segregation laws as constitutional, his violation of the racial laws "would have been in a great cause." However, since the Supreme Court decided on behalf of those laws, he would have to go to jail. And this result "the individual must accept." (As Fortas puts it: "But suppose I had been wrong." Why is he so willing to call himself "wrong" just because the Supreme Court decided the other way? Was Dred Scott wrong because the Taney court decided he was property and not a human being?)

To be punished in such an instance "may seem harsh," Fortas says, "*But this is what we mean by the rule of law:* [his emphasis] both the government and the individual must accept the result of procedures by which the courts, and ultimately the Supreme Court, decide that the law is such and such, and not so and so. . . ." . . .

Fortas cites the example of Dr. Martin Luther King's violation of a state court injunction in Alabama. It was an injunction forbidding him from exercising his right of free assembling (as a higher court later agreed). But he was sentenced to jail for violating the injunction before that higher court made its decision, and the Supreme Court upheld his by a 5-4 verdict, after which "Dr. King, without complaint or histrionics, accepted the penalty of misjudgment. This, I submit, is action in the great tradition of social protest in a democratic society where all citizens, including protestors, are subject to the rule of law."

But why was it right for Dr. King to accept an unjust verdict corroborating an unjust injunction, resulting in an unjust jail sentence, "without complaint or histrionics"? Why should there not have been bitter, forceful complaint across the country against this set of oppressive acts? Is the general notion of obedience to law more important than the right of free assembly? Does quiet acceptance in such a case not merely perpetuate the notion that transgressions of justice by the government must be tolerated by citizens?. . .

Third fallacy: *that civil disobedience must be limited to laws which are themselves wrong.*

One of the conditions Fortas sets for civil disobedience is that it should be confined to "disobedience of laws which are themselves unjust." At the end of his essay he is even more explicit: "In my judgment civil disobedience—the deliberate violation of law—is never justified in our nation where the law being violated is not itself the focus or target of the protest."

To violate a law which is itself not being protested "as a technique of warfare in a social and political conflict over other issues" is not only constitutionally unprotected, but morally wrong according to Fortas. He does not say why. Because he gives us no moral principle which makes that wrong, we are left to assume that he is invoking his standard principle, the "rule of law." More and more, Fortas' definition of what is moral coincides almost exactly with what is constitutional, and what is constitutional is what the Supreme Court decides. Thus is morality reduced to law, and law to the current opinions of the Court.

If (to return to an earlier example) after a child had been killed by a speeding automobile, housewives blocked traffic on a street to pressure the city fathers into installing a traffic light, this would not be justified, according to Fortas' criteria, because they would be violating a reasonable law (against obstructing traffic) in order to protest something else (the absence of a traffic signal).

Here is a stark surrender of human values to "the rule of law." Is human life (the lives of those children in danger on this street) not more important than the observance of the traffic-obstruction law by these women? Perhaps Fortas would argue that the housewives' action is so dangerous to the general respect for law and order that even a supreme value—the preservation of life—must be subordinated to "the rule of law." But is this reasonable? Are we really to believe that the housewives' action will lead to a general breakdown in traffic control—or a general wave of disobedience to all laws, in the neighborhood, or in the city? Surely the Constitution does not require us to forego common sense. Perhaps such an action might stimulate another obstruction of traffic on another street, where a traffic light is also needed. But wouldn't this be a good thing? . . .

Fortas is left in the position of failing to distinguish between important and unimportant laws, between trivial and vital issues, because the distinction between legal and illegal seems far more important to him. By his rule he would find himself *supporting* an act of civil disobedience aimed directly at a relatively unimportant law, and *opposing* an act aimed indirectly at a profoundly immoral law. He would find himself opposing violations of the smallest of laws (a trespass law, let us say) for the biggest of reasons (mass murder). . . .

Related to this is another important distinction which Fortas ignores: between bad *laws* and bad *conditions.* He is willing to countenance defiance of a profoundly immoral law, like a segregation law. But what if there is a profoundly immoral situation, as evil in its way as segregation—like hunger, or poor housing, or lack of medical care? Here there is no law that one can challenge to call attention directly to the situation; it can only be done by violating some law which ordinarily is reasonable. . . .

Fourth fallacy: *that civil disobedience must be absolutely nonviolent.*

Mr. Fortas reminds us that Gandhi, Martin Luther King, and Thoreau, did not believe in violence. He then says: "This is civil disobedience in a great tradition. It is peaceful, nonviolent disobedience of laws which are themselves unjust and which the protester challenges as invalid and unconstitutional.". . . If Fortas wants to define civil disobedience as having this limitation, this is his right. But others need not accept his definition, and indeed have not.

I would define civil disobedience more broadly, as "the deliberate violation of law for a vital social purpose." Unlike Fortas' definition, this would include violating laws which are immoral whether constitutional or not, and laws which themselves are not at issue as well as those that are. It would leave open the question of the *means* of disobedience, but with two thoughts in mind: 1. that one of the moral principles guiding the advocate of civil disobedience is his belief, that a nonviolent world is one of his ends, and that nonviolence is more desirable than violence as a means; 2. that in the inevitable tension accompanying the transition from a violent world to a nonviolent one, the choice of means will almost never be pure, and will involve such complexities that the simple distinction between violence and nonviolence does not suffice as a guide. . . .

My point in all this is not at all to establish a case for violence. To me one of the cardinal principles in any moral code is the reduction and elimination of violence. The burden of proof in any argument about social tactics should rest on that person who wants to stray from nonviolence. What I have tried to show is that the problem of tactics in civil disobedience is far more complicated than Mr. Fortas leads us to believe with his easy and righteous dismissal of violence.

What is required is that a set of distinctions be made which will enable us to be more precise in evaluating the problem of violence and nonviolence in civil disobedience. If Mr. Fortas wants to say that civil disobedience must limit itself to nonviolent activity, then he is required to explain the moral principles which say why this should be so. This he does not do; he merely asserts his position.

One soon begins to see why he stays away from a careful discussion. When we attempt to put together a set of principles on violence from the scattered remarks in his essay, contradictions and simplifications appear.

For instance, we might conclude from Mr. Fortas' absolute insistence on nonviolence and civil disobedience that it requires no explanation because in his view nonviolence is an ultimate value, *the* supreme value, and therefore self-justifying. But if this were Mr. Fortas' belief, we would expect him to oppose violence in all forms, all the time. We know this is not his credo, because, as we shall see later in more detail, he defends the massive violence of a number of wars. . . .

There is another point which he slides over—one which is very important, I believe, in drawing up a set of principles on violence and nonviolence in civil disobedience. That is the distinction between violence to people and violence to things; destruction of life, or destruction of property. . . .

At one point, Mr. Fortas mentions as intolerable "breaking windows in the Pentagon." Surely that is a mild form of violence compared to the violence a window-breaker might be protesting against—the decisions made in the Pentagon which result in thousands of American men returning to their families in coffins. . . .

There is an argument for excluding violence from civil disobedience which Justice Fortas does make: that it is impractical; it is not effective in achieving its ends. "But widespread violence—whether it is civil disobedience, or street riots, or guerrilla warfare—will, I am persuaded, lead to repression.". . .

The historical evidence is far from supporting the idea that violence is not effective in producing change. True, there are many instances when violence is completely ineffective, and does result only in repression. But there are other instances when it does seem to bring results. . . .

Barrington Moore's elaborate study of modern social change (*Social Origins of Dictatorship and Democracy*) concludes that violence is an important factor in change. He points out that presumably "peaceful" transitions to modernism, as in England and the United States, really involved large amounts of violence. Certainly this country has not progressed purely on the basis of nonviolent constitutional development. We do not know what effect John Brown's violence had in that complex of events leading to the end of slavery, but it is certainly an open question. Independence, emancipation, labor unions—these basic elements in the development of American democracy all involved violent actions by aggrieved persons. . . .

Fifth fallacy: *that the political structure and procedures in the United States are adequate as they stand to remedy the ills of our society.*

Mr. Fortas says: "Despite the limits which the requirements of an ordered society impose, the protected weapons of protest, dissent, criticism and peaceable assembly are enormously powerful.". . .

We now can understand the restrictions Mr. Fortas has placed on civil disobedience. They are based on a supposition about the facts of life in the United States: that the American political system has been successful, that no more is required for the remedy of existing grievances than existing channels of dissent: "the rights to speak, to publish, to protest, to assemble peaceably, and to participate in the electoral process."

The truth or falsity of this supposition is crucial to Mr. Fortas' limits on civil disobedience, and also to my argument for a broader view of civil disobedience. If the United States has no need for more avenues of protest than the present system allows, then it doesn't really matter if theoretically one can make a case that the restricted view is illogical. On the other hand, if the moral ends we claim to cherish—an equitable distribution of wealth, an end to racism, the abolition of war, the ability as well as the right of an individual to pursue his own happiness in the mass society—seem not achievable at all, or at an intolerably slow pace, with our present channels of protest, then we must widen those channels beyond Mr. Fortas' limits. . . .

Sixth fallacy: *that we can depend on the courts, especially the Supreme Court, to protect our rights to free expression under the First Amendment.*

If we are naive enough to think that the First

Amendment means what it says—that Congress "shall make no law abridging the freedom of speech"—Mr. Fortas himself prepares us for the realities. "It is not true that anyone may say what's on his mind anytime and anywhere. According to the famous dictum of Justice Holmes, no one may falsely cry 'Fire' in a crowded theater and thereby cause a panic." Fortas goes on to elaborate this somewhat, by saying "good motives do not excuse action which will injure others" and a citizen may not say anything that constitutes "a clear and present danger of physical injury to others."

All this sounds reasonable. If there is to be *any* restriction on free speech, certainly it should be directed to speech which in some way injures others—like shouting "Fire" in a crowded theater. The trouble is: the Supreme Court has repeatedly interpreted this in such a way as to curtail free speech even where there was no "clear and present danger" to others. Holmes himself (and Fortas neglects to tell us this) applies his "Fire" analogy so loosely as to approve the jailing of radicals because they criticized the first World War. . . .

Let us take for example the Supreme Court ruling of Monday, May 27, 1968, on the case of David P. O'Brien, who burned his draft card on the steps of the South Boston Courthouse in violation of a recently-enacted federal statute forbidding the burning of draft cards. His motive was quite clear; he was not trying to hide information about himself, or prevent the application of the Selective Service Act to himself, because he did this publicly, hiding nothing from the Government, which was hardly interfered with for more than a few minutes of paper work. O'Brien did this as an expression of protest against the war in Vietnam and the drafting of men to serve in that war. One could hardly find a more apt illustration of an act fitting Fortas' own words: "symbolic speech for the communication of ideas to persuade others.". . .

. . . Does anyone in his right mind believe that O'Brien's action constituted a *clear and present danger* (even if one could have nightmares of *ultimate* chains of draft-card burners reaching into the hundreds of thousands) to the government or to any other person but himself?

Mr. Fortas' tests for free speech exist in theory, in our romantic dreams about how our courts operate, and in his book. But not in the hurly-burly of the real world. In that world. the Supreme Court decided 7–1, with Mr. Fortas on the side of the majority, that O'Brien's act of protest . . . must be punished. . . .

The Court was reluctant to expand the right of symbolic speech to draft-card burning, but it was willing to make "the assumption that the alleged communicative element [to use the word "alleged" in this case is absurd; there was no doubt about O'Brien's intent to communicate something to the public] in O'Brien's conduct is sufficient to bring into play the First Amendment" but it went on to say that this must be balanced against "a sufficiently important governmental interest." In other words, even if someone's free expression is at stake, if the law restricting that expression "furthers an important or substantial governmental interest" then the restriction is okay.

Note how far we have come from the "clear and present danger" test which Fortas assured us we could count on to protect our right of free speech. Now, in this decision (which came out after Fortas' book was published) he goes along with an idea the Court has expressed a number of times, and which he doesn't tell us about in his book, that even if an act of expression does *not* constitute a clear and present danger, if it merely violates some regulation which "furthers an important or substantial governmental interest," the speech may be forbidden.

True, the job of the Court is to "balance" the right of free expression against the rights of others; hence the "clear and present danger" test, hence the idea that free expression may not do injury to others. "We have entrusted the courts," Mr. Fortas tells us, "with the task of striking the balance in individual cases." Well, if the courts are going to strike the balance as it did, with Mr. Fortas' agreement, in the *O'Brien* case, then we had better not depend on them to defend free expression. Not if the principle of free expression weighs so lightly in the Court's mind that it is overpowered by the necessity to protect draft cards against those admittedly few individuals who burned them to protest the war. . . .

DISCUSSION QUESTIONS

1. Zinn accuses Fortas of over-idolizing "the rule of law" as an end in itself, having value apart from any moral end. Is this true? How do you think Fortas would defend himself? What do you think?

2. What is Zinn's reply to the common argument that disobedience even of bad laws is wrong because such disobedience fosters a general disrespect for all laws, even good ones? What do you think of Zinn's reply?

3. Consider the following two general moral principles relating to civil disobedience:

> In deciding whether to break a law one considers to be wrong, one should consider the likely consequences of that act of disobedience. It is wrong to break a law if and only if such an action is likely, in point of fact, to cause more harm than good.
>
> In deciding whether to break a law one considers to be wrong, one should consider the likely consequences, not of one's act of disobedience in isolation, but of the **universalization** of one's act of disobedience—that is, one must consider what the consequences would be **if everyone were to act** under the same principle that one would be acting under were one to break the law in question. If the universalization of this principle of action would cause more harm than good, then it would be wrong to break that law.

Which of these two principles does Zinn seem inclined to accept? Do you agree? Why, or why not?

4. In his discussion of the morality of civil disobedience, Zinn contrasts on the one side those "intent on violence and exploitation" and on the other side those "with the highest motivations." In making this contrast, Zinn neglects those who see their own interest as a demand for justice (e.g., higher wages for certain jobs as opposed to others). Does Zinn's position on civil disobedience adequately take into account the differing conceptions that citizens have of "the demands of justice" and the human tendency to rationalize and to clothe one's naked self-interest in the garbs of a demand for justice?

5. What criticism does Zinn make against Fortas' view that civil disobedience must be limited to laws which are themselves wrong? Can any legitimate criticisms be raised against Zinn's view?

6. What broad definition of "civil disobedience" does Zinn offer? Why does Zinn define this concept so broadly? Does he give us any principle to guide us in deciding when civil disobedience, as he defines it, is justifiable? What limits, if any, does he place on the right of an individual to do as he thinks right, regardless of what the law says? Does he believe that we ever have an obligation to obey a law which we think unjust? Do you agree? Why, or why not?

7. Consider the following position on civil disobedience by the contemporary philosopher John Rawls:

> Assuming that the constitution is just and that we have accepted and plan to continue to accept its benefits, we then have both an obligation and a natural duty to comply with what the majority enacts even though it may be unjust. In this way we become bound to follow unjust laws, not always, of course, but provided the injustice does not exceed certain limits.[1]

In what respects, if any, does this position differ from Zinn's? Do you see any difficulties with this position?

8. Consider the following claim:

> Both a concern for the stability of society and for the equal worth of human beings requires that a person must be prepared to do on occasion what others want and not what he wants. Indeed, paradoxically, the demands of justice and human autonomy actually require the forfeiture of autonomy that commitment to governmental

[1]John Rawls, "The Justification of Civil Disobedience" in *Civil Disobedience*, ed. Bedau (New York: Pegasus, 1969), p. 245.

authority requires, for without the general commitment of human beings to forfeit some degree of their autonomy, the natural result would be the much greater injustice and loss of freedom that results from the lack of governmental authority.[2]

Would Zinn agree? Would Fortas? Would Plato? What do you think?

9. According to Zinn, if a civil disobedient is justified in breaking a law, does he, nevertheless, have a moral obligation to willingly accept punishment for his disobedience? Do you agree? Even if the acceptance of punishment is not **always** a necessary requirement of justifiable civil disobedience, is it, nevertheless, **often** a required or desirable feature of justifiable civil disobedience? Does the acceptance of punishment serve some concrete purpose or symbolically serve to demonstrate something? When, if at all, should a civil disobedient attempt to avoid punishment?

10. Do you agree with Zinn that civil disobedience can legitimately take the form of breaking laws to which one has no moral objection (i.e., indirect civil disobedience as a vehicle of protest) as well as breaking the very laws one is protesting (direct civil disobedience)?

11. What is the difference between a "violent" and "nonviolent" act? What is Zinn's view of the moral justification of the use of violence as a mode of protest? What do you think?

12. How adequate do you think the political structure and procedures of American democracy are to remedy the ills of our society? How morally bound do you think a citizen should be to this structure and these procedures?

13. What principle should the courts utilize in determining when, if ever, speech should be restricted? Elaborate on the meaning of your principle by applying it to specific hypothetical cases.

14. Zinn accuses Fortas of utilizing "a double standard" in his choice of principles that should be utilized in morally appraising the behavior of citizens within our nation and the behavior of our nation in its dealings with other countries. What do you think about this matter?

[2]Composed by the editor.

61. THE CLASSICAL LIBERAL POSITION ON THE LEGITIMATE LIMITS OF GOVERNMENTAL AUTHORITY OVER THE INDIVIDUAL

John Stuart Mill

JOHN STUART MILL (1806–73) was the most influential British philosopher in the nineteenth century. Rigorously educated at home under the tutelage of his father James Mill, a contemporary and disciple of Jeremy Bentham, the bright young Mill studied Greek and arithmetic at the age of three. At eight, he began his study of Latin, and at twelve, he had mastered the classics and was reading extensively in such subjects as philosophy, logic, and economic theory. Exposed to the philosophical writings of Bentham, at the age of fifteen, Mill became a committed utilitarian, out to reform the world. At the age of twenty, however, he went through a severe emotional crisis that lasted for several months. In his autobiography, Mill attributes this crisis to the fact that his father, in his determination to train his son's mind in the rigors of analytic thought, failed to take into account the need for emotional development as well. During this sad period in his life, Mill, while intellectually still committed to the utilitarian point of view, found himself incapable of **caring,** as he once did, about the application of utilitarianism to the problems of the world; indeed, Mill found himself incapable of caring about anything. Greatly depressed by the realization of his emotional emptiness, Mill turned to literature, finding solace in German and English romantic literature, in particular, in the literary works of Wordsworth and Coleridge. Eventually his exposure to romantic literature rekindled his passion for life. At twenty-five, Mill was introduced to Harriet Taylor, the wife of a successful merchant. A strong Platonic relationship developed between the two, in spite of the element of scandal and gossip that a close relationship between a married woman and a single man naturally elicited in the England of Mill's day. Convinced of her brilliance, Mill discussed all his works with Mrs. Taylor, whom he claimed had a great influence in the development of his own thought. Eventually the two married in 1852, three years after the death of Mrs. Taylor's husband. She died, however, only six years later.

For over half of his life (1823–58), Mill held responsible administrative posts with The East India Company, eventually becoming the head of one of its departments . (The East India Company was a royally chartered company responsible for increasing British trade and influence in India.) While so employed, Mill devoted his spare time to writing. Upon retirement from The East India Company, Mill was proposed as a Liberal Party candidate for Parliament. Even though he refused to campaign, he was elected to office. In office, he consistently sided with the liberal forces for social equality and individual freedom. William Gladstone, the British Prime Minister, once said of him, "He had the good sense and practical tact of politics, together with the high independent thought of a recluse. He did us all good."

Mill wrote on many philosophical topics. In his major contribution to ethics, **Utilitarianism** (1861), he presents the classic defense of utilitarianism, attempting to refine Bentham's utilitarian theory and to answer criticisms. His earlier **System of Logic** (1843) provides the model empiricist analysis of the nature of logic and mathematics. His works, **On Liberty** (1859) and **Considerations on Representative Government** (1861) are masterpieces of liberal political philosophy. In addition, Mill wrote influential works on economics **(Principles of Political Economy,** 1848, 7th ed., 1871) and on religion **(Three Essays on Religion,** published posthumously, as was his **Autobiography).**

Believing that it was her sex alone that prevented his beloved wife, Harriet Taylor Mill, from receiving the recognition she deserved, Mill was an early defender of women's rights. While a member of Parliament, he submitted the first bill on the enfranchisement of women to the House of Commons. His essay "The Subjection of Women" is an early influential feminist defense. Mill's interest in causes that are associated with the feminist movement preceded his acquaintance with Harriet, however. As a seventeen-year-old, Mill was arrested for distributing birth control information—a case of civil disobedience. Mill was led to his bold act, despite the embarrassment it caused him, by his strong commitment to the issue of controlling overpopulation, an issue that occupied him throughout his life. This interest was precipitated by a walk with his father through the streets of London. Along the way, the young Mill saw the dead body of a newly born infant, wrapped in rags. Further along, he passed the hanging bodies of several criminals. As he walked, the young Mill was struck with the realization that both of these sad sights were connected with overpopulation. Overpopulation, he came to believe, is one of the greatest causes of misery and vice in this world. This misery and vice, he thought, could be prevented if people were educated to realize the need for voluntary family planning—a topic too indelicate for the sensibilities of the English citizens of his day. From that moment on, Mill became firmly committed to the importance of a public education that could undercut the unthinking attitudes and ways of life of the masses.

While originally committed to laissez-faire capitalism, as Mill grew older he became more and more sensitive to the futility of political freedom without economic opportunity and security. At the end of his life, Mill became a socialist. Yet unlike other idealistic socialists of his day, Mill's advocacy of socialism was tempered by his fear of the tendency of socialism to go hand-in-hand with the suppression of individuality—a fear which the triumph of communism in Russia and China in the twentieth century would later prove to be quite justified. However, as Mill's commitment to socialism grew, he became more and more hopeful that this tendency could be avoided. Yet in his later writings, most notably his later editions of his **Principles of Political Economy,** one notes a tension between his commitment to the value of liberty and to that of economic equality. While he remained steadfast in his advocacy of the right of individuals to lead their **private** lives as they see fit, he came to view the scope of a "person's private life" more narrowly than he did as a younger man. For example, believing in the great power of education to reduce the poverty and misery of the masses, he came to advocate **compulsory** education and the legitimacy of **compelling** parents to provide for the education of their children.

The following selection is from Mill's defense of individual freedom, **On Liberty** (which he dedicated to his recently deceased wife). In his preface to this essay, Mill disclaims any appeal to the moral intuitionism of his predecessor John Locke, who saw individual freedom as a self-evident "natural right." Instead, as the committed utilitarian that he was, Mill attempts to demonstrate that his view of the value of individual freedom **follows from** his basic commitment to the principle of utility (i.e., "the greatest happiness for the greatest number"). While philosophers have come to question the concepts and arguments he employs in defending his plea for individual freedom, Mill's own passionate conviction of the value of individual freedom tends to engender a similar passion in his readers. As indicated by the many people who quote from it, nowhere in the English language can a stronger and more elegant defense of the value of individual freedom be found than in **On Liberty**—Mill's most enduring philosophical legacy to this generation and to generations to come. (See pp. 479–80 of this chapter's introduction for additional editorial comments on **On Liberty**).

The object of this essay is to assert one very simple principle, as entitled to govern absolutely the dealings of society with the individual in the way of compulsion and control, whether the means used be physical force in the form of legal penalties or the moral coercion of public opinion. That principle is that the sole end for which mankind are warranted, individually or collectively, in interfering with the liberty of action of any of their number is self-protection. That the only purpose for which power can be rightfully exercised over any member of a civi-

Source: John Stuart Mill's *On Liberty,* originally published in London in 1859. Many editions.

lized community, against his will, is to prevent harm to others. His own good, either physical or moral, is not a sufficient warrant. He cannot rightfully be compelled to do or forbear because it will be better for him to do so, because it will make him happier, because, in the opinions of others, to do so would be wise or even right. These are good reasons for remonstrating[1] with him, or reasoning with him, or persuading him, or entreating him, but not for compelling him or visiting him with any evil in case he do otherwise. To justify that, the conduct from which it is desired to deter him must be calculated to produce evil to someone else. The only part of the conduct of anyone for which he is amenable to society is that which concerns others. In the part which merely concerns himself, his independence is, of right, absolute. Over himself, over his own body and mind, the individual is sovereign.

It is, perhaps, hardly necessary to say that this doctrine is meant to apply only to human beings in the maturity of their faculties. We are not speaking of children or of young persons below the age which the law may fix as that of manhood or womanhood. Those who are still in a state to require being taken care of by others must be protected against their own actions as well as against external injury. For the same reason we may leave out of consideration those backward states of society in which the race itself may be considered as in its nonage. The early difficulties in the way of spontaneous progress are so great that there is seldom any choice of means for overcoming them; and a ruler full of the spirit of improvement is warranted in the use of any expedients that will attain an end perhaps otherwise unattainable. Despotism is a legitimate mode of government in dealing with barbarians, provided the end be their improvement and the means justified by actually effecting that end. Liberty, as a principle, has no application to any state of things anterior to the time when mankind have become capable of being improved by free and equal discussion. . . .

It is proper to state that I forego any advantage which could be derived to my argument from the idea of abstract right as a thing independent of utility. I regard utility as the ultimate appeal on all ethical questions; but it must be utility in the largest sense, grounded on the permanent interests of man as a progressive being. Those interests, I contend, authorize the subjection of individual spontaneity to external control only in respect to those actions of each which concern the interest of other people. . . . There are also many positive acts for the benefit of others which he may rightfully be compelled to perform, such as to give evidence in a court of justice, to bear his fair share in the common defense or in any other joint work necessary to the interest of the society of which he enjoys the protection, and to perform certain acts of individual beneficence, such as saving a fellow creature's life or interposing to protect the defenseless against ill usage—things whenever it is obviously a man's duty to do he may rightfully be made responsible to society for not doing. A person may cause evil to others not only by his actions but by his inaction, and in either case he is justly accountable to them for the injury. The latter case, it is true, requires a much more cautious exercise of compulsion than the former. To make anyone answerable for doing evil to others is the rule; to make him answerable for not preventing evil is, comparatively speaking, the exception. Yet there are many cases clear enough and grave enough to justify that exception. . . .

But there is a sphere of action in which society, as distinguished from the individual, has, if any, only an indirect interest: comprehending all that portion of a person's life and conduct which affects only himself or, if it also affects others, only with their free, voluntary, and undeceived consent and participation. When I say only himself, I mean directly and in the first instance; for whatever affects himself may af-

[1]Protesting. EDITOR'S NOTE.

fect others through himself; and the objection which may be grounded on this contingency will receive consideration in the sequel. This, then, is the appropriate region of human liberty. It comprises, first, the inward domain of consciousness, demanding liberty of conscience in the most comprehensive sense, liberty of thought and feeling, absolute freedom of opinion and sentiment on all subjects, practical or speculative, scientific, moral, or theological. The liberty of expressing and publishing opinions may seem to fall under a different principle, since it belongs to that part of the conduct of an individual which concerns other people, but, being almost of as much importance as the liberty of thought itself and resting in great part on the same reasons, is practically inseparable from it. Secondly, the principle requires liberty of tastes and pursuits, of framing the plan of our life to suit our own character, of doing as we like, subject to such consequences as may follow, without impediment from our fellow creatures, so long as what we do does not harm them, even though they should think our conduct foolish, perverse, or wrong. Thirdly, from this liberty of each individual follows the liberty, within the same limits, of combination among individuals; freedom to unite for any purpose not involving harm to others; the persons combining being supposed to be of full age and not forced or deceived.

No society in which these liberties are not, on the whole, respected is free, whatever may be its form of government; and none is completely free in which they do not exist absolute and unqualified. The only freedom which deserves the name is that of pursuing our own good in our own way, so long as we do not attempt to deprive others of theirs or impede their efforts to obtain it. Each is the proper guardian of his own health, whether bodily *or* mental and spiritual. Mankind are greater gainers by suffering each other to live as seems good to themselves than by compelling each to live as seems good to the rest. . . .

. . . [T]here is . . . in the world at large an increasing inclination to stretch unduly the powers of society over the individual both by the force of opinion and even by that of legislation; and as the tendency of all the changes taking place in the world is to strengthen society and diminish the power of the individual, this encroachment is not one of the evils which tend spontaneously to disappear, but, on the contrary, to grow more and more formidable. . . .

It will be convenient for the argument if, instead of at once entering upon the general thesis, we confine ourselves in the first instance to a single branch of it on which the principle here stated is, if not fully, yet to a certain point, recognized by the current opinions. This one branch is the Liberty of Thought, from which it is impossible to separate the cognate liberty of speaking and of writing. . . .

Of the Liberty of Thought and Discussion

The time, it is to be hoped, is gone by when any defense would be necessary of the "liberty of the press" as one of the securities against corrupt or tyrannical government. No argument, we may suppose, can now be needed against permitting a legislature or an executive, not identified in interest with the people, to prescribe opinions to them and determine what doctrines or what arguments they shall be allowed to hear. . . . [S]peaking generally, it is not, in constitutional countries, to be apprehended that the government, whether completely responsible to the people or not, will often attempt to control the expression of opinion, except when in doing so it makes itself the organ of the general intolerance of the public. Let us suppose, therefore, that the government is entirely at one with the people, and never thinks of exerting any power of coercion unless in agreement with what it conceives to be their voice. But I deny the right of the people to exercise such coercion, either by themselves or by their government. The power itself is illegitimate. The best government has no more title to it than the worst. It is as noxious, or more noxious, when exerted in accordance with public opinion than when in oppostion to it. If all mankind minus one were of one opinion, mankind would be no more justified in silencing that one person than he, if he had the power, would be justified in silencing mankind. Were an opinion a personal possession of no value except to the owner, if to be obstructed in the enjoyment of it were simply a private injury, it would make some difference whether the injury was inflicted only on a few persons or on many. But the peculiar evil of silencing the expression of an opinion is that it is robbing the human race, posterity as well as the existing generation—those who dissent from the opinion, still more than those who hold it. If the opinion is right, they are deprived of the opportunity of exchanging error for truth; if wrong, they lose, what is almost as great a benefit, the clearer perception and livelier impression of truth produced by its collision with error.

It is necessary to consider separately these two hypotheses, each of which has a distinct branch of the argument corresponding to it. We can never be sure that the opinion we are endeavoring to stifle is a false opinion; and if we were sure, stifling it would be an evil still.

First, the opinion which it is attempted to suppress by authority may possibly be true. Those who desire to suppress it, of course, deny its truth; but they are not infallible. . . .

. . . There is the greatest difference between presuming an opinion to be true because, with every opportunity for contesting it, it has not been refuted, and assuming its truth for the purpose of not permitting its refutation. Complete liberty of contradicting and disproving our opinion is the very condition which justifies us in assuming its truth for purposes of action; and on no other terms can a being with human faculties have any rational assurance of being right.

. . . Why is it . . . that there is on the whole a preponderance among mankind of rational opinions and rational conduct? If there really is this preponderance . . . it is owing to a quality of the human mind, the source of everything respectable in man either as an intellectual or as a moral being, namely, that his errors are corrigible. He is capable of rectifying his mistakes by discussion and experience . . . .

Let us now pass to the second division of the argument, and dismissing the supposition that any of the received opinions may be false, let us assume them to be true and examine into the worth of the manner in which they are likely to be held when their truth is not freely and openly canvassed. However unwillingly a person who has a strong opinion may admit the possibility that his opinion may be false, he ought to be moved by the consideration that, however true it may be, if it is not fully, frequently, and fearlessly discussed, it will be held as a dead dogma, not a living truth. . . .

. . . He who knows only his own side of the case knows little of that. His reasons may be good, and no one may have been able to refute them. But if he is equally unable to refute the reasons on the opposite side, if he does not so much as know what they are, he has no ground for preferring either opinion. The rational position for him would be suspension of judgment, and unless he contents himself with that, he is either led by authority or adopts, like the generality of the world, the side to which he feels most inclination. Nor is it enough that he should hear the arguments of adversaries from his own teachers, presented as they state them, and accompanied by what they offer as refutations. That is not the way to do justice to the arguments or bring them into real contact with his own mind. He must be able to hear them from persons who actually believe them, who defend them in earnest and do their very utmost for them. He must know them in their most plausible and persuasive form. . . . So essential is this discipline to a real understanding of moral and human subjects that, if opponents of all-important truths do not exist, it is indispensable to imagine them and supply them with the strongest arguments which the most skillful devil's advocate can conjure up. . . .

. . . The fact, however, is that not only the grounds of the opinion are forgotten in the absence of discussion, but too often the meaning of the opinion itself. The words which convey it cease to suggest ideas, or suggest only a small portion of those they were originally employed to communicate. Instead of a vivid conception and a living belief, there remain only a few phrases retained by rote; or, if any part, the shell and husk only of the meaning is retained, the finer essence being lost.

. . . We have hitherto considered only two possibilities; that the received opinion may be false and some other opinion, consequently, true; or that, the received opinion being true, a conflict with the opposite error is essential to a clear apprehension and deep feeling of its truth. But there is a commoner case than either of these; when the conflicting doctrines, instead of being one true and the other false, share the truth between them, and the nonconforming opinion is needed to supply the remainder of the truth of which the received doctrine embodies only a part. . . .

We have now recognized the necessity to the mental well-being of mankind (on which all their other well-being depends) of freedom of opinion, and freedom of the expression of opinion, on four distinct grounds, which we will now briefly recapitulate:

First, if any opinion is compelled to silence, that opinion may, for aught we can certainly know, be true. To deny this is to assume our own infallibility.

Secondly, though the silenced opinion be an error, it may, and very commonly does, contain a portion of truth; and since the general or prevailing opinion on any subject is rarely or never the whole truth, it is only by the collision of adverse opinions that the remainder of the truth has any chance of being supplied.

Thirdly, even if the received opinion be not only true, but the whole truth; unless it is suffered to be, and actually is, vigorously and earnestly contested, it will, by most of those who receive it, be held in the manner of a prejudice, with little comprehension or feeling of its rational grounds. And not only this, but, fourthly, the meaning of the doctrine itself will be in danger of being lost or enfeebled, and deprived of its vital effect on the character and conduct the dogma becoming a mere formal profession, inefficacious for good. . . .

Of Individuality, as One of the Elements of Well-Being

. . . No one pretends that actions should be as free as opinions. On the contrary, even opinions lose their immunity when the circumstances in which they are expressed are such as to constitute their expression a positive instigation to some mischievous act. An opinion that corn dealers are starvers of the poor, or that private property is robbery, ought to be unmolested when simply circulated through the press, but may justly incur punishment when delivered orally to an excited mob assembled before the house of a corn dealer, or when handed about among the same mob in the form of a placard. Acts, of whatever kind, which without justifiable cause do harm to others may be, and in the more important cases absolutely require to be, controlled by the unfavorable sentiments, and, when needful, by the active interference of mankind. The liberty of the individual must be thus far limited; he must not make himself a nuisance to other people. But if he refrains from molesting others in what concerns them, and merely acts according to his own inclination and judgment in things which concern himself, the same reasons which show that opinion should be free prove also that he should be allowed, without molestation, to carry his opinions into practice at his own cost. . . . As it is useful that while mankind are imperfect there should be different opinions, so it is that there should be different experiments of living; that free scope should be given to varieties of character, short of injury to others; and that the worth of different modes of life should be proved practically, when anyone thinks fit to try them. It is desirable, in short, that in things which do not primarily concern others individuality should assert itself. Where not the person's own character but the traditions or customs of other people are the rule of conduct, there is wanting one of the principle ingredients of human happiness, and quite the chief ingredient of individual and social progress. . . .

Of the Limits to the Authority of Society Over the Individual

What, then, is the rightful limit to the sovereignty of the individual over himself? Where does the authority of society begin? How much of human life should be assigned to individuality, and how much to society? . . .

Though society is not founded on a contract, and though no good purpose is answered by inventing a contract in order to deduce social obligations from it, everyone who receives the protection of society owes a return for the benefit, and the fact of living in society renders it indispensable that each should be bound to observe a certain line of conduct toward the rest. This conduct consists, first, in not injuring the interests of one another, or rather certain interests which, either by express legal provision or by tacit understanding, ought to be considered as rights; and secondly, in each person's bearing his share (to be fixed on some equitable principle) of the labors and sacrifices incurred for defending the society or its members from injury and molestation. These conditions society is justified in enforcing at all costs to those who endeavor to withhold fulfillment. Nor is this all that society may do. The acts of an individual may be hurtful to others or wanting in due consideration for their welfare, without going to the length of violating any of their constituted rights. The offender may then be justly punished by opinion, though not by law. As soon as any part of a person's conduct affects prejudicially the interests of others, society has jurisdiction over it, and the question whether the general welfare will or will not be promoted by interfering with it becomes open to discussion. But there is no room for entertaining any such question when a person's conduct affects the interests of no persons besides himself. . . .

. . . [N]either one person, nor any number of persons, is warranted in saying to another human creature of ripe years that he shall not do with his life for his own benefit what he chooses to do with it. He is the person most interested in his own well-being: the interest which any other person, except in cases of strong personal attachment, can have in it is trifling compared with that which he himself has; the interest which society has in him individually (except as to his conduct to others) is fractional and altogether indirect, while with respect to his own feelings and circumstances the most ordinary man or woman has means of knowledge immeasurably surpassing those that can be possessed by anyone else. . . .

The distinction here pointed out between the part of a person's life which concerns only himself and that which concerns others, many persons will refuse to admit. How (it may be asked) can any part of the conduct of a member of society be a matter of indifference to the other members? No person is an entirely isolated being; it is impossible for a person to do anything seriously or permanently hurtful to himself without mischief reaching at least to his near connections, and often far beyond them. If he injures his property, he does harm to those who directly or indirectly derived support from it, and usually diminishes, by a greater or less amount, the general resources of the community. If he deteriorates his bodily or mental faculties, he not only brings evil upon all who depended on him for any portion of their happiness, but disqualifies himself for rendering the services which he owes to his fellow creatures generally, perhaps becomes a burden on their affection or benevolence; and if such conduct were very frequent hardly any offense that is committed would detract more from the general sum of good. Finally, if by his vices or follies a person does no direct harm to others, he is nevertheless (it may be said) injurious by his example, and ought to be compelled to control himself for the sake of those whom the sight or knowledge of his conduct might corrupt or mislead.

And even (it will be added) if the consequences of misconduct could be confined to the vicious or thoughtless individual, ought society to abandon to their own guidance those who are manifestly unfit for it? If protection against themselves is confessedly due to children and persons under age, is not society equally bound to afford it to persons of mature years who are equally incapable of self-government? If gambling, or drunkenness, or incontinence, or idleness, or uncleanliness are as injurious to happiness, and as great a hindrance to improvement, as many or most of the acts prohibited by law, why (it may be asked) should not law, so far as is consistent with practicability and social convenience, endeavor to repress these also? . . . There is no question here (it may be said) about restricting individuality, or impeding the trial of new and original experiments in living. The only things it is sought to prevent are things which have been tried and condemned from the beginning of the world until now—things which experience has shown not to be useful or suitable to any person's individuality. . . .

I fully admit that the mischief which a person does to himself may seriously affect, both through their sympathies and their interests, those nearly connected with him and, in a minor degree, society at large. When, by conduct of this sort, a person is led to violate a distinct and assignable obligation to any other peson or persons, the case is taken out of the self-regarding class and becomes amenable to moral disapprobation in the proper sense of the term. If, for example, a man, through intemperance or extravagance, becomes unable to pay his debts, or, having undertaken the moral responsibilty of a family, becomes from the same cause incapable of supporting or educating them, he is deservedly reprobated and might be justly punished; but it is for the breach of duty to his family or creditors, not for the extravagance . . . . No person ought to be punished simply for being drunk; but a soldier or a policeman should be punished for being drunk on duty. Whenever, in short, there is a definite damage, or a definite risk of damage, either to an individual or to the public, the case is taken out of the province of liberty and placed in that of morality or law.

But with regard to the . . . injury which a person causes to society by conduct which neither violates any specific duty to the public, nor occasions perceptible hurt to any assignable individual except himself, the inconvenience is one which society can afford to bear, for the sake of the greater good of human freedom. . . .

But the strongest of all the arguments against the interference of the public with purely personal conduct is that, when it does interfere, the odds are that it interferes wrongly and in the wrong place. On questions of social morality, of duty to others, the opinion of the public, that is, of an overruling majority, though often wrong, is likely to be still oftener right, because on such questions they are only required to judge of their own interests, of the manner in which some mode of conduct, if allowed to be practiced, would affect themselves. But the opinion of a similar majority, imposed as a law on the minority, on questions of self-regarding conduct is quite as likely to be wrong as right, for in these cases public opinion means, at the best, some people's opinion of what is good or bad for other people. . . .

Applications

. . . [The question of the legitimacy] of the sale of poisons, opens a new question: the proper limits of what may be called the functions of police; how far liberty may legitimately be invaded for the prevention of crime, or of accident. It is one of the undisputed functions of government to take precautions against crime before it has been committed, as well as to detect and punish it afterwards. The preventive function of government, however, is far more liable to be abused, to the prejudice of liberty, than the punitory function; for there is hardly any part of the legitimate freedom of action of a human being which would not admit of being represented, and fairly, too, as increasing the facilities for some form or other of delinquency. Nevertheless, if a public authority, or even a private person, sees anyone evidently preparing to commit a crime, they are not bound to look on inactive until the crime is committed, but may interfere to prevent it. If poisons were never bought or used for any purpose except the commission of murder, it would be right to prohibit their manufacture and sale. They may, however, be wanted not only for innocent but for useful purposes, and restrictions cannot be imposed in the one case without operating in the other. Again, it is a proper office of public authority to guard against accidents. If either a public officer or anyone else saw a person attempting to cross a bridge which had been ascertained to be unsafe, and there were no time to warn him of his danger, they might seize him and turn him back, without any real infringement of his liberty; for liberty consists in doing what one desires, and he does not desire to fall into the river. Nevertheless, when there is not a certainty, but only a danger of mischief, no one but the person himself can judge of the sufficiency of the motive which may prompt him to incur the risk; in this case, therefore (unless he is a child, or delirious, or in some state of excitement or absorption incompatible with the full use of the reflecting faculty), he ought, I conceive, to be only warned of the danger; not forcibly prevented from exposing himself to it. Similar considerations, applied to such a question as the sale of poisons, may enable us to decide which among the possible modes of regulation are or are not contrary to principle. Such a precaution, for example, as that of labeling the drug with some word expressive of its dangerous character may be enforced without violation of liberty: the buyer cannot wish not to know that the thing he possesses has poisonous qualities. . . .

. . . [T]here are many acts which, being directly injurious only to the agents themselves, ought not to be legally interdicted, but which, if done publicly, are a violation of good manners and, coming thus within the category of offenses against others, may rightly be prohibited. Of this kind are offenses against decency; on which it is unnecessary to dwell. . . .

There is another question to which an answer must be found, consistent with the principles which have been laid down. In cases of personal conduct supposed to be blamable, but which respect for liberty precludes society from preventing or punishing because the evil directly resulting falls wholly on the agent; what the agent is free to do, ought other persons to be equally free to counsel or instigate? This question is not free from difficulty. The case of a person who solicits another to do an act is not strictly a case of self-regarding conduct. To give advice or offer inducements to anyone is a social act and may, therefore, like actions in general which affect others, be supposed amenable to social control. But a little reflection corrects the first impression, by showing that if the case is not strictly within the definition of individual liberty, yet the reasons on which the principle of individual liberty is grounded are applicable to it. If people must be allowed, in whatever concerns only themselves, to act as seems best to themselves, at their own peril, they must equally be free to consult with one another about what is fit to be so done; to exchange opinions, and give and receive suggestions. Whatever it is permitted to do, it must be permitted to advise to do. The question is doubtful only when the instigator derives a personal benefit from his advice, when he makes it his occupation, for subsistence or pecuniary gain, to promote what society and the State consider to be an evil. . . . Ought this to be interfered with, or not? Fornication, for example, must be tolerated, and so must gambling; but should a person be free to be a pimp, or to keep a gambling house? The case is one of those which lie on the exact boundary line between two principles, and it is not at once apparent to which of the two it properly belongs. There are arguments on both sides. On the side of toleration it may be said that the fact of following anything as an occupation, and living or profiting by the practice of it, cannot make that criminal which would otherwise be admissible; that the act should either be consistently permitted or consistently prohibited; that if the principles which we have hitherto defended are true, society has no business, *as* society, to decide anything to be wrong which concerns only the individual; that it cannot go beyond dissuasion, and that one person should be as free to persuade as another to dissuade. In opposition to this it may be contended that, although the public, or the State, are not warranted in authoritatively deciding, for purposes of repression or punishment, that such or such conduct affecting only the interests of the individual is good or bad, they are fully justified in assuming, if they regard it as bad, that its being so or not is at least a disputable question: that, this being supposed, they cannot be acting wrongly in endeavoring to exclude the influence of solicitations which are not disinterested, of instigators who cannot possibly be impartial—who have a direct personal interest on one side, and that side the one which the State believes to be wrong, and who confessedly promote it for personal objects only. . . .

A further question is whether the State, while it permits, should nevertheless indirectly discourage conduct which it deems contrary to the best interests of the agent; whether, for example, it should take measures to render the means of drunkenness more costly, or add to the difficulty of procuring them by limiting the number of the places of sale. On this, as on most other practical questions, many distinctions require to be made. To tax stimulants for the sole purpose of making them more difficult to be obtained is a measure differing only in degree from their entire prohibition, and would be justifiable only if that were justifiable. Every increase of cost is a prohibition to those whose means do not come up to the augmented price; and to those who do, it is a penalty laid on them for gratifying a particular taste. Their choice of pleasures and their mode of expending their income, after satisfying their legal and moral obligations to the State and to individuals, are their own concern and must rest with their own judgment. These considerations may seem at first sight to condemn the selection of stimulants as special subjects of taxation for purposes of revenue. But it must be remembered that taxation for fiscal purposes is absolutely inevitable; that in most countries it is necessary that a considerable part of that taxation should be indirect; that the State, therefore, cannot help imposing penalties, which to some persons may be prohibitory, on the use of some articles of consumption. It is hence the duty of the State to consider, in the imposition of taxes, what commodities the consumers can best spare; and *a fortiori*,[2] to select in preference those of which it deems the use, beyond a very moderate quantity, to be positively injurious. . . .

[2]All the more. EDITOR'S NOTE.

It was pointed out in an early part of this essay that the liberty of the individual, in things wherein the individual is alone concerned, implies a corresponding liberty in any number of individuals to regulate by mutual agreement [or contract] such things as regard them jointly, and regard no persons but themselves. . . . It is fit, as a general rule, that those engagements [i.e., contracts] should be kept. Yet, in the laws, probably, of every country, this general rule has some exceptions. Not only persons are not held to engagements which violate the rights of third parties, but it is sometimes considered a sufficient reason for releasing them from an engagement that it is injurious to themselves. In this and most other civilized countries, for example, an engagement by which a person should sell himself, or allow himself to be sold, as a slave would be null and void, neither enforced by law nor by opinion. The ground for thus limiting his power of voluntarily disposing of his own lot in life is apparent, and is very clearly seen in this extreme case. The reason for not interfering, unless for the sake of others, with a person's voluntary acts is consideration for his liberty. His voluntary choice is evidence that what he so chooses is desirable, or at least endurable, to him and his good is on the whole best provided for by allowing him to take his own means of pursuing it. But by selling himself for a slave, he abdicates his liberty; he foregoes any future use of it beyond that single act. He therefore defeats, in his own case, the very purpose which is the justification of allowing him to dispose of himself. . . .The principle of freedom cannot require that he should be free not to be free. It is not freedom to be allowed to alienate his freedom. These reasons, the force of which is so conspicuous in this peculiar case, are evidently of far wider application, yet a limit is everywhere set to them by the necessities of life, which continually require, not indeed that we should resign our freedom, but that we should consent to this and the other limitation of it. . . .

DISCUSSION QUESTIONS

1. According to Mill, what principle should be utilized in determining when society is morally justified in interfering with the liberty of an individual? Is the meaning of Mill's principle clear? In particular, what does Mill mean by the concepts of "harm," "affects others," "affects the interests of others," and "an offense against the rights of others"—concepts which he utilizes in his discussion of the meaning of his principle? Does Mill use these concepts interchangeably? Should he? Do any (or all) of these expressions presuppose some moral position or are they morally neutral factual notions?

2. Mill claims that his argument for guaranteeing citizens wide individual freedom rests not on "natural rights" (as in Locke) but on utility. "I regard utility as the ultimate appeal on all ethical questions," Mill wrote. Yet, he went on to modify this claim, writing, "but it must be utility in the largest sense, grounded on the permanent interests of man as a progressive being." What does this mean?

3. Consider the following activities:

   a. the smoking of marijuana

   b. the use of heroin and other hard drugs

   c. gambling

   d. polygamy

   e. the desecration of the national flag

   f. the handling of poisonous snakes by adults as an exercise of faith

   g. the rejection by an adult Jehovah's Witness of a life-saving blood transfusion

   h. the rejection by a child of a Jehovah's Witness of a life-saving blood transfusion, accompanied with the parents' refusal that the child be so treated

Which of the preceding activities would Mill be willing to make illegal? Why? Do you disagree with any of these positions? If so, why?

4. Would Mill be against restricting the freedom of a rich homosexual to rent a billboard on a major city street or road upon which he graphically depicts the techniques and pleasures of homosexual behavior? Why? Would you favor a law re-

stricting behavior that is highly offensive to many people? If so, what principle would you employ in deciding when to interfere with the freedom of individuals in order to prevent offending others?

5. Would Mill, in principle, be opposed to the banning of handguns? If not, how would he look at the issue? How do you look at it?

6. Would Mill, in principle, be opposed to making cigarette smoking illegal? Taxing cigarette smoking very stiffly to discourage smoking? What do you think is proper here?

7. Would Mill be against mandatory social security and mandatory income tax withholding? What is your position here? What principle(s) would you utilize to justify your position?

8. Would Mill have any objection to legalized prostitution? To "houses of prostitution" run for private gain? To pimps? What is your position on this matter?

9. Consider the following three reasons for compelling motorcyclists to wear helmets:

> A: It is in the best interests of the motorcyclists. Motorcyclists should not have the right to make the clearly stupid decision not to use a helmet. I see no problem in sacrificing a person's freedom of choice whenever this is clearly in his self-interest.
>
> B: Laws requiring motorcyclists to wear helmets should not be seen as infringements of freedom, but as attempts to prevent people from making capricious choices which do not reflect their own rational desires. When we tell a motorcyclist that he is required by law to wear a helmet, we are only telling him to do what he himself would choose to do if he rationally reflected on the matter.
>
> C: It is in the best interests of society to compel motorcyclists to wear helmets. If we did not have such a requirement, inevitably some motorcyclists would become seriously hurt and either they or their dependents would become public charges. Motorcycle helmet laws should not be seen as paternalistic laws concerned with purely self-regarding actions but should be seen instead as an attempt to prevent action that is likely to cause harm to others.

Which, if any, of the preceding reasons would Mill find satisfactory? Which do you?

10. The Model Penal Code of the American Law Institute penalizes mistreatment of a corpse "in a way that [the actor]. . . knows would outrage ordinary. . . sensibilities," **even if** the offender takes every precaution for secrecy. The Model Penal Code also penalizes the cruel treatment of an animal in private, as well as in public. Does Mill provide any grounds for justifying such prohibitions? Do you agree with the American Law Institute's decision to penalize such activities? What principle(s) would you utilize to justify your position?

11. The late Supreme Court Justice William Douglas claims (in his autobiography) that "The right of free speech, all are agreed, does have limitations. Statutes which proscribe the use of epithets such as profanity, libel and 'fighting words' have generally been excluded from constitutional protection." Would Mill agree with such sentiments? Do you?

12. In **Roth** v. **United States** (1957), the Supreme Court of the United States ruled that the First Amendment to the Constitution does not protect "obscenity" which they defined as follows:

> a) The dominant theme of the material taken as a whole appeals to a prurient[3] interest in sex; b) the material is patently offensive because it affronts contemporary community standards relating to the description or representation of sexual matters; and c) The material is utterly without redeeming social value.

Would Mill accept such a view? Would you? Why, or why not? If not, do you object simply to the Roth definition of obscenity or to the very idea that "obscenity" is not protected by the First Amendment? If your objection is to the Roth definition of "obscenity," how would you define it?

13. What principle does Mill give for refusing to allow a person to sell himself or herself into slavery? Could the same reason be utilized to make the use of automobile seatbelts mandatory? Could it be utilized to prevent people from attempting suicide?

14. In Greek mythology, Odysseus, afraid of his inability to resist the seductive lure of the sirens,

[3]Lewd or lustful. EDITOR'S NOTE.

ordered his men to bind him and ignore any of his subsequent pleas to be untied. Bound and lured by the sirens, he later begged his men to untie him, but they refused. What do you think Mill would say here? What bearing does this example have on Mill's position?

15. Why does Mill think that it is very important that we allow individuals who have eccentric opinions to freely express these opinions, even when we believe these opinions to be wrong? Under what conditions, if at all, would Mill restrict freedom of speech? Do you agree?

16. Consider the following imaginary dialogue:

A: Judged on the basis of the purely utilitarian goal of maximizing the general welfare, the communists have succeeded spectacularly in transforming Chinese society. Nevertheless, a stiff price in terms of individual liberty has been paid to make these achievements possible. Molded into preset collectivistic roles, the Chinese people lack the individuality and commitment to liberty that is an essential aspect of human dignity. Communism, no doubt, promises the Chinese people greater security, but only at the morally unjustified price of the forfeiture of their freedom and individuality.

B: Your sentiments are an expression of a bourgeois, capitalistic ideology. The "freedom" you so extol turns out, in practice, to be the freedom to be selfish and exploitative. True human fulfillment, and yes, "human dignity," comes not from the lonely pursuit of individual pleasures but rather from the willingness to share and sacrifice for the common good. Western philosophers may speak of "liberty as the first virtue of social institutions," but for the ordinary person that virtue is protection or security—a virtue that can best be achieved through a commitment to collectivistic goals that transcend our purely selfish desires.

What do you think?

62. A CONSERVATIVE'S REJOINDER TO MILL: A SOCIETY'S RIGHT TO ENFORCE A MORAL CODE

Lord Patrick Devlin

LORD PATRICK DEVLIN (1905–) is a British jurist who has held various high positions in the British courts. Since 1966, he has held a high administrative post at Cambridge University.

The following selection is an edited version of Devlin's "The Enforcement of Morals" (see pp. 480–81 of this chapter's introduction for background information on this article). In our selection, Devlin begins his inquiry by isolating the question that will be the focus of his concern: What is the connection between crime and sin and to what extent, if at all, should the criminal law of England concern itself with the enforcement of morals and punish sin or immorality as such? In answer to his own question, Devlin first points out various features of existing law which he believes clearly demonstrate that existing law does **in fact** "punish sin or immorality as such." He then goes on to argue, contrary to Mill and the Wolfenden Report from which he quotes, that such a practice is **morally justified**. In presenting his argument for this moral claim, Devlin defines a society as a collection of people who share a common morality. After presenting this definition, Devlin argues for the moral right of a society to preserve its underlying morality because it is essential for its very existence. Claiming that "there are no theoretical limits to the power of the state to legislate against immorality," Devlin is willing to admit that the rights of the individual must be balanced against society's right to "punish immorality as such" and presents three "elastic principles" supporting the rights of the individual against the state.

What is the connexion between crime and sin and to what extent, if at all, should the criminal law of England concern itself with the enforcement of morals and punish sin or immorality as such?

The statements of principle in the Wolfenden Report provide an admirable and modern starting-point for such an inquiry. . . .

Early in the Report the Committee put forward:

> Our own formulation of the function of the criminal law so far as it concerns the subjects of this enquiry. In this field, its function, as we see it, is to preserve public order and decency, to protect the citizen from what is offensive or injurious, and to provide sufficient safeguards against exploitation and corruption of others, particularly those who are specially vulnerable because they are young, weak in body or mind, inexperienced, or in a state of special physical, official or economic dependence.
>
> It is not, in our view, the function of the law to intervene in the private lives of citizens, or to seek to enforce any particular pattern of behaviour, further than is necessary to carry out the purposes we have outlined.

The Committee preface their most important recommendation

> that homosexual behaviour between consenting adults in private should no longer be a criminal offence, [by stating the argument] which we believe to be decisive, namely, the importance which society and the law ought to give to individual freedom of choice and action in matters of private morality. Unless a deliberate attempt is to be made by society, acting through the agency of law, to equate the sphere of crime with that of sin, there must remain a realm of private morality and immorality which is, in brief and crude terms, not the law's business. To say this is not to condone or encourage private immorality.

Similar statements of principle are set out in the chapters of the Report which deal with prostitution. No case can be sustained, the Report says, for attempting to make prostitution itself illegal . . . They quote with approval the report of the Street Offences Committee, which says: 'As a general proposition it will be universally accepted that the law is not concerned with private morals. . . . ' It will be observed that the emphasis is on *private* immorality. By this is meant immorality which is not offensive or injurious to the public in the ways defined or described in the first passage which I quoted. In other words, no act of immorality should be made a criminal offence unless it is accompanied by some other feature such as indecency, corruption, or exploitation. This is clearly brought out in relation to prostitution: 'It is not the duty of the law to concern itself with immorality as such . . . it should confine itself to those activities which offend against public order and decency or expose the ordinary citizen to what is offensive or injurious.'. . .

If this view is sound, it means that the criminal law cannot justify any of its provisions by reference to the moral law . . . . Why not define the function of the criminal law in simple terms as the preservation of order and decency and the protection of the lives and property of citizens . . . . The criminal law in carrying out these objects will undoubtedly overlap the moral law. Crimes of violence are morally wrong and they are also offences against good order; therefore they offend against both laws. But this is simply because the two laws in pursuit of different objectives happen to cover the same area. Such is the argument.

Is the argument consistent or inconsistent with the fundamental principles of English criminal law as it exists today? That is the first way of testing it, though by no means a conclusive one. In the field of jurisprudence one is at liberty to overturn even fundamental conceptions if they are theoretically unsound. But to see how the argument fares under the existing law is a good starting-point.

It is true that for many centuries the criminal law was much concerned with keeping the peace and little, if at all, with sexual morals. But it would be wrong to infer from that that it had no moral content or that it would ever have tolerated the idea of a man being left to judge for himself in matters of morals. The criminal law of England has from the very first concerned itself with moral principles. A simple way of testing this point is to consider the attitude which the criminal law adopts towards consent.

Subject to certain exceptions inherent in the nature of particular crimes, the criminal law has never permitted consent of the victim to be used as a defence. In rape, for example, consent negatives an essential element [of the definition of "rape"]. But consent of the victim is no defence to a charge of murder. It is not a defence to any form of assault that the victim thought his punishment well deserved and submitted to it; to make a good defence the accused must prove that the law gave him the right to chastise and that he exercised it reasonably. . . .

. . . The reason why a man may not consent to the commission of an offence against himself beforehand or forgive it afterwards is because it is an offence against society. It is not that society is physically injured; that would be impossible. Nor need any individual be hocked, corrupted, or exploited; everything may be done in private. Nor can it be explained on the practical ground that a violent man is a potential danger to others in the community who have therefore a direct interest in his apprehension and punishment as being necessary to their own protection. That would be true of a man whom the victim is prepared to forgive but not of one who gets his consent first; a murderer who acts only upon the consent, and maybe the request, of his victim is no menace to others, but he does threaten one of the great moral principles upon which society is based, that is, the sanctity of human life. There is only one explanation of what has hitherto been accepted as the basis of the criminal law and that is that there are certain standards of behaviour or moral principles which society requires to be observed; and the breach of them is an offence not merely against the person who is injured but against society as a whole.

Thus, if the criminal law were to be reformed so as to eliminate from it everything that was not designed to preserve order and decency or to protect citizens (including the protection of youth from corruption), it would overturn a fundamental principle. It would also end a number of specific crimes. Euthanasia or the killing of another at his own request, suicide, attempted suicide and suicide pacts, duelling, abortion, incest between brother and sister, are all acts which can be done in private and without offence to others and need not involve the corruption of others. Many people think that the law on some of these subjects is in need of reform, but no one hitherto has gone so far as to suggest that they should all be left outside the criminal law as matters of private morality. They can be brought within it only as a matter of moral principle. . . .

I think it is clear that the criminal law as we know it is based upon moral principle. In a number of crimes its function is simply to enforce a moral principle and nothing else. The law, both criminal and civil, claims to be able to speak about morality and immorality generally. Where does it get its authority to do this and how does it settle the moral principles which it enforces? Undoubtedly, as a matter of history, it derived both from Christian teaching. But I think . . . that the law can no longer rely on doctrines in which citizens are entitled to disbelieve. It is necessary therefore to look for some other source.

In jurisprudence, as I have said, everything is thrown open to discussion and, in the belief that they cover the whole field, I have framed three interrogatories addressed to myself to answer:

1. Has society the right to pass judgement at all on matters of morals? Ought there, in other words, to be a public morality, or are morals always a matter of private judgement?

2. If society has the right to pass judgement, has it also the right to use the weapon of the law to enforce it?

3. If so, ought it to use that weapon in all cases or only in some; and if only in some, on what principles should it distinguish?

I shall begin with the first interrogatory and consider what is meant by the right of society to pass a moral judgement, that is, a judgement about what is good and what is evil. The fact that a majority of people may disapprove of a practice does not of itself make it a matter for society as a whole. . . . There is a case for collective judgement (as distinct from a large number of individual opinions which sensible people may even refrain from pronouncing at all if it is upon somebody else's private affairs) only if society is affected. . . .

The language used in the passages I have quoted from the Wolfenden Report suggests the view that there ought not to be a collective judgement about immorality *per se*. Is this what is meant by 'private morality' and 'individual freedom of choice and action'? Some people sincerely believe that homosexuality is neither immoral nor unnatural. Is the 'freedom of choice and action' that is offered to the individual, freedom to decide for himself what is moral or immoral, society remaining neutral; or is it freedom to be immoral if he wants to be? The language of the Report may be open to question, but the conclusions at which the Committee arrive answer this question unambiguously. If society is not prepared to say that homosexuality is morally wrong, there would be no basis for a law protecting youth from 'corruption' or punishng a man for living on the 'immoral' earnings of a homosexual prostitute, as the Report recommends. This attitude the Committee make even clearer when they come to deal with prostitution. In truth, the Report takes it for granted that there is in existence a public morality which condemns homosexuality and prostitution. What the Report seems to mean by private morality might perhaps be better described as private behaviour in matters of morals.

This view—that there is such a thing as public morality—can also be justified by *a priori* argument.[1] What makes a society of any sort is community of ideas, not only political ideas but also ideas about the way its members should behave and govern their lives; these latter ideas are its morals. Every society has a moral structure as well as a political one: or rather, since that might suggest two independent systems, I should say that the structure of every society is made up both of politics and morals. Take, for example, the institution of marriage. Whether a man should be allowed to take more than one wife is something about which every society has to make up its mind one way or the other. In England we believe in the Christian idea of marriage and therefore adopt monogamy as a moral principle. Consequently the Christian institution of marriage has become the basis of family life and so part of the structure of our society. It is there not because it is Christian. It has

[1]That is, an argument that makes no appeal to experience, but relies only on the meaning of concepts. EDITOR'S NOTE.

got there because it is Christian, but it remains there because it is built into the house in which we live and could not be removed without bringing it down. The great majority of those who live in this country accept it because it is the Christian idea of marriage and for them the only true one. But a non-Christian is bound by it, not because it is part of Christianity but because, rightly or wrongly, it has been adopted by the society in which he lives. It would be useless for him to stage a debate designed to prove that polygamy was theologically more correct and socially preferable; if he wants to live in the house he must accept it as built in the ways in which it is. . . .

The institution of marriage is a good example for my purpose because it bridges the division, if there is one, between politics and morals. Marriage is part of the structure of our society and it is also the basis of a moral code which condemns fornication and adultery. The institution of marriage would be gravely threatened if individual judgements were permitted about the morality of adultery; on these points there must be a public morality. But public morality it not to be confined to those moral principles which support institutions such as marriage. People do not think of monogamy as something which has to be supported because our society has chosen to organize itself upon it; they think of it as something that is good in itself and offering a good way of life and that it is for that reason that our society has adopted it. I return to the statement that I have already made, that society means a community of ideas; without shared ideas on politics, morals, and ethics no society can exist. Each one of us has ideas about what is good and what is evil; they cannot be kept private from the society in which we live. If men and women try to create a society in which there is no fundamental agreement about good and evil they will fail; if, having based it on common agreement, the agreement goes, the society will disintegrate. For society is not something that is kept together physically; it is held by the invisible bonds of common thought. If the bonds were too far relaxed the members would drift apart. A common morality is part of the bondage. The bondage is part of the price of society; and mankind, which needs society, must pay its price. . . .

You may think that I have taken far too long in contending that there is such a thing as public morality, a proposition which most people would readily accept, and may have left myself too little time to discuss the next question which to many minds may cause greater difficulty: to what extent should society use the law to enforce its moral judgements? But I believe that the answer to the first question determines the way in which the second should be approached and may indeed very nearly dictate the answer to the second question. If society has no right to make judgements on morals, the law must find some special justification for entering the field of morality; if homosexuality and prostitution are not in themselves wrong, then the onus is very clearly on the lawgiver who wants to frame a law against certain aspects of them to justify the exceptional treatment. But if society has the right to make a judgement and has it on the basis that recognized morality is as necessary to society as, say, a recognized government, then society may use the law to preserve morality in the same way as it uses it to safeguard anything else that is essential to its existence. If therefore the first proposition is securely established with all its implications, society has a prima facie right[2] to legislate against immorality as such.

The Wolfenden Report, notwithstanding that it seems to admit the right of society to condemn homosexuality and prostitution as immoral, requires special circumstances to be shown to justify the intervention of law. I think that this

[2]That is, an apparent right which should be taken as an actual right, unless some good reason can be given as to why it should not be so taken. EDITOR'S NOTE.

is wrong in principle and that any attempt to approach my second interrogatory on these lines is bound to break down. I think that the attempt by the Committee does break down and that this is shown by the fact that it has to define or describe its special circumstances so widely that they can be supported only if it is accepted that the law *is* concerned with immorality as such.

The widest of the special circumstances are described as the provision of 'sufficient safeguards against exploitation and corruption of others, particularly those who are specially vulnerable because they are young, weak in body or mind, inexperienced, or in a state of special physical, official or economic dependence'. The corruption of youth is a well-recognized ground for intervention by the State and for the purpose of any legislation the young can easily be defined. But if similar protection were to be extended to every other citizen, there would be no limit to the reach of the law. The 'corruption and exploitation of others' is so wide that it could be used to cover any sort of immorality which involves, as most do, the co-operation of another person. Even if the phrase is taken as limited to the categories that are particularized as 'specially vulnerable', it is so elastic as to be practically no restriction. This is not merely a matter of words. For if the words used are stretched almost beyond breaking-point, they still are not wide enough to cover the recommendations which the Committee make about prostitution.

Prostitution is not in itself illegal and the Committee do not think that it ought to be made so. If prostitution is private immorality and not the law's business, what concern has the law with the ponce[3] or the brothel-keeper or the householder who permits habitual prostitution? The Report recommends that the laws which make these activities criminal offences should be maintained or strengthened and brings them . . . under the head of exploitation. There may be cases of exploitation in this trade, as there are or used to be in many others, but in general a ponce exploits a prostitute no more than an impresario exploits an actress. The Report finds that 'the great majority of prostitutes are women whose psychological makeup is such that they choose this life because they find in it a style of living which is to them easier, freer and more profitable than would be provided by any other occupation. . . . In the main the association between prostitute and ponce is voluntary and operates to mutual advantage.' The Committee would agree that this could not be called exploitation in the ordinary sense. They say; 'It is in our view an over-simplification to think that those who live on the earnings of prostitution are exploiting the prostitute as such. What they are really exploiting is the whole complex of the relationship between prostitute and customer; they are, in effect, exploiting the human weaknesses which cause the customer to seek the prostitute and the prostitute to meet the demand.'

All sexual immorality involves the exploitation of human weaknesses. The prostitute exploits the lust of her customers and the customer the moral weakness of the prostitute. If the exploitation of human weaknesses is considered to create a special circumstances, there is virtually no field of morality which can be defined in such a way as to exclude the law.

I think, therefore, that it is not possible to set theoretical limits to the power of the State to legislate against immorality. It is not possible to settle in advance exceptions to the general rule or to define inflexibly areas of morality into which the law is in no circumstances to be allowed to enter. Society is entitled by means of its laws to protect itself from dangers, whether from within or without. Here again I think that the political parallel is legitimate. The law of treason is directed against aiding the king's

[3]Pimp. EDITOR'S NOTE.

enemies and against sedition from within. The justification for this is that established government is necessary for the existence of society and therefore its safety against violent overthrow must be secured. But an established morality is as necessary as good government to the welfare of society. Societies disintegrate from within more frequently than they are broken up by external pressures. There is disintegration when no common morality is observed and history shows that the loosening of moral bonds is often the first stage of disintegration, so that society is justified in taking the same steps to preserve its moral code as it does to preserve its government and other essential institutions. The suppression of vice is as much the law's business as the suppression of subversive activities. . . . There are no theoretical limits to the power of the State to legislate against treason and sedition, and likewise I think there can be no theoretical limits to legislation against immorality. You may argue that if a man's sins affect only himself it cannot be the concern of society. If he chooses to get drunk every night in the privacy of his own home, is any one except himself the worse for it? But suppose a quarter or a half of the population got drunk every night, what sort of society would it be? You cannot set a theoretical limit to the number of people who can get drunk before society is entitled to legislate against drunkenness. The same may be said of gambling. . . .

In what circumstances the State should exercise its power is the third of the interrogatories I have framed. But before I get to it I must raise a point which might have been brought up in any one of the three. How are the moral judgements of society to be ascertained? By leaving it until now, I can ask it in the more limited form that is now sufficient for my purpose. How is the law-maker to ascertain the moral judgements of society? It is surely not enough that they should be reached by the opinion of the majority; it would be too much to require the individual assent of every citizen. English law has evolved and regularly uses a standard which does not depend on the counting of heads. It is that of the reasonable man.[4] He is not to be confused with the rational man. He is not expected to reason about anything and his judgement may be largely a matter of feeling. It is the viewpoint of the man in the street. . . . He might also be called the right-minded man. For my purpose I should like to call him the man in the jury box, for the moral judgement of society must be something about which any twelve men or women drawn at random might after discussion be expected to be unanimous. . . .

Immorality then, for the purpose of the law, is what every right-minded person is presumed to consider to be immoral. Any immorality is capable of affecting society injuriously and in effect to a greater or lesser extent it usually does; this is what gives the law its *locus standi*[5] . . . But—and this brings me to the third question—the individual has a *locus standi* too; he cannot be expected to surrender to the judgement of society the whole conduct of his life. It is the old and familiar question of striking a balance between the rights and interests of society and those of the individual. . . .

. . . While every decision which a court of law makes when it balances the public against the private interest is an *ad hoc* decision, the cases contain statements of principle to which the court should have regard when it reaches its decision. In the same way it is possible to make general statements of principle which it may be thought the legislature should bear in mind when it is considering the enactment of laws enforcing morals.

I believe that most people would agree upon the chief of these elastic principles. There must be toleration of the maximum individual free-

[4]The notion of "the reasonable man," which permeates Anglo-American law, is better translated as "the average man" (who is assumed to be "reasonable"). EDITOR'S NOTE.

[5]That is, the right to be heard. EDITOR'S NOTE.

dom that is consistent with the integrity of society . . . Nothing should be punished by the law that does not lie beyond the limits of tolerance. It is not nearly enough to say that a majority dislike a practice; there must be a real feeling of reprobation. Those who are dissatisfied with the present law on homosexuality often say that the opponents of reform are swayed simply by disgust. If that were so it would be wrong, but I do not think one can ignore disgust if it is deeply felt and not manufactured. Its presence is a good indication that the bounds of toleration are being reached. Not everything is to be tolerated. No society can do without intolerance, indignation, and disgust; they are the forces behind the moral law, and indeed it can be argued that if they or something like them are not present, the feelings of society cannot be weighty enough to deprive the individual of freedom of choice. I suppose that there is hardly anyone nowadays who would not be disgusted by the thought of deliberate cruelty to animals. No one proposes to relegate that or any other form of sadism to the realm of private morality or to allow it to be practised in public or in private. It would be possible no doubt to point out that until a comparatively short while ago nobody thought very much of cruelty to animals and also that pity and kindliness and the unwillingness to inflict pain are virtues more generally esteemed now than they have ever been in the past. But matters of this sort are not determined by rational argument. Every moral judgement, unless it claims a divine source, is simply a feeling that no right-minded man could behave in any other way without admitting that he was doing wrong. It is the power of a common sense and not the power of reason that is behind the judgements of society. But before a society can put a practice beyond the limits of tolerance there must be a deliberate judgement that the practice is injurious to society. There is, for example, a general abhorrence of homosexuality. We should ask ourselves in the first instance whether, looking at it calmly and dispassionately, we regard it as a vice so abominable that its mere presence is an offence. If that is the genuine feeling of the society in which we live, I do not see how society can be denied the right to eradicate it. Our feeling may not be so intense as that. We may feel about it that, if confined, it is tolerable, but that if it spread it might be gravely injurious; it is in this way that most societies look upon fornication, seeing it as a natural weakness which must be kept within bounds but which cannot be rooted out. It becomes then a question of balance, the danger to society in one scale and the extent of the restriction in the other. On this sort of point the value of an investigation by such a body as the Wolfenden Committee and of its conclusions is manifest.

The limits of tolerance shift. This is supplementary to what I have been saying but of sufficient importance in itself to deserve statement as a separate principle which law-makers have to bear in mind. I suppose that moral standards do not shift; so far as they come from divine revelation they do not, and I am willing to assume that the moral judgements made by a society always remain good for that society. But the extent to which society will tolerate—I mean tolerate, not approve—departures from moral standards varies from generation to generation . . . Laws, especially those which are based on morals, are less easily moved. It follows as another good working principle that in any new matter of morals the law should be slow to act. By the next generation the swell of indignation may have abated and the law be left without the strong backing which it needs. But it is then difficult to alter the law without giving the impression that moral judgement is being weakened. This is now one of the factors that is strongly militating against my alteration to the law on homosexuality.

A third elastic principle must be advanced more tentatively. It is that as far as possible privacy should be respected . . . [W]hen all who are involved in the deed are consenting parties and the injury is done to morals, the public interest in the moral order can be balanced against the claims of privacy.

The last and the biggest thing to be remembered is that the law is concerned with the minimum and not with the maximum; there is much in the Sermon on the Mount that would be out of place in the Ten Commandments. We all recognize the gap between the moral law and the law of the land. No man is worth much who regulates his conduct with the sole object of escaping punishment, and every worthy society sets for its members standards which are above those of the law. . . .

This then is how I believe my third interrogatory should be answered—not by the formulation of hard and fast rules, but by a judgement in each case taking into account the sort of factors I have been mentioning. The line that divides the criminal law from the moral is not determinable by the application of any clear-cut principle. It is like a line that divides land and sea, a coastline of irregularities and indentations. There are gaps and promontories, such as adultery and fornication, which the law has for centuries left substantially untouched. Adultery of the sort that breaks up marriage seems to me to be just as harmful to the social fabric as homosexuality or bigamy. The only ground for putting it outside the criminal law is that a law which made it a crime would be too difficult to enforce; it is generally regarded as a human weakness not suitably punished by imprisonment. All that the law can do with fornication is act against its worst manifestations; there is a general abhorrence of the commercialization of vice, and that sentiment gives strength to the law against brothels and immoral earnings. There is no logic to be found in this. The boundary between the criminal law and the moral law is fixed by balancing in the case of each particular crime the pros and cons of legal enforcement in accordance with the sort of considerations I have been outlining. The fact that adultery, fornication, and lesbianism are untouched by the criminal law does not prove that homosexuality ought not to be touched. The error of jurisprudence in the Wolfenden Report is caused by the search for some single principle to explain the division between crime and sin. The Report finds it in the principle that the criminal law exists for the protection of individuals; on this principle fornication in private between consenting adults is outside the law and thus it becomes logically indefensible to bring homosexuality between consenting adults in private within it. But the true principle is that the law exists for the protection of society. It does not discharge its function by protecting the individual from injury, annoyance, corruption, and exploitation; the law must protect also the institutions and the community of ideas; political and moral, without which people cannot live together. Society cannot ignore the morality of the individual any more than it can his loyalty; it flourishes on both and without either it dies. . . .

. . . Society cannot live without morals. Its morals are those standards of conduct which the reasonable man approves. A rational man, who is also a good man, may have other standards. . . . [H]e may, for example, not disapprove of homosexuality or abortion. In that case he will not share in the common morality; but that should not make him deny that it is a social necessity. A rebel may be rational in thinking that he is right but he is irrational if he thinks that society can leave him free to rebel. . . .

DISCUSSION QUESTIONS

1. According to the Wolfenden Report, when should behavior be made illegal?

2. What examples does Devlin give to establish his contention that the Wolfenden Report is radically in conflict with existing British law? The legal theorist H.L.A. Hart, a critic of Devlin, claims that the cases Devlin discusses can be seen not as the law's at-

tempt to "enforce morality as such," as Devlin claims, but as paternalistic measures designed "to protect people from themselves." Is there a substantial difference between these two principles? How would you deal with the cases Devlin discusses? How would Mill deal with them?

3. Consider the following general principles for restricting an individual's behavior:

a. to prevent physical harm to others

b. to protect the property of others and to enforce contracts

c. to prevent psychic injury or offense to others

d. to protect social institutions

e. to benefit others

f. to prevent that person from making involuntary choices

g. to prevent harm to that person

h. to benefit that person

i. to prevent or punish immorality or sin

Which of these principles would you accept? How, if at all, would you attempt to limit them? Do you think that some of the principles on this list have the same practical implications?

4. How does Devlin see the connection between the existence of a society of people and the existence of a common shared morality? What do you think of Devlin's view in this regard?

5. In discussing the "Christian ideal of marriage," Devlin claims:

> . . . a non-Christian is bound by it, not because it is part of Christianity but because, rightly or wrongly, it has been adopted by the society in which he lives. It would be useless for him to stage a debate designed to prove that polygamy was theologically more correct and socially preferable; if he wants to live in the house, he must accept it as built in the way in which it is.

Critically discuss.

6. According to Devlin, even though the Wolfenden Report claims that the law can legitimately interfere with the behavior of homosexuals and prostitutes only in "special circumstances," the principles they employ to define these "special circumstances" are "so elastic as to be practically no restriction" (see p. 537). Is this true? Are the three principles Devlin provides for protecting individual freedom any less elastic in meaning? Do you prefer the Wolfenden Report's approach or Devlin's approach to the problem of weighing the interests of the individual against the interests of society? Does it make any practical difference which of the two approaches one takes? How would you approach this matter?

7. According to Devlin, how can we tell what the moral judgements of a given society are? Do you think that the utilization of Devlin's standard would establish the immorality of homosexuality and prostitution—the particular types of sexual behavior that were the concern of the Wolfenden Report?

8. Does Devlin have any way of distinguishing between a rational moral judgement and a moral prejudice? If not, is this a fundamental inadequacy of his view?

9. According to Devlin, why is society justified in utilizing the weapon of law to enforce public morality? (If you see some ambiguity in Devlin's position, point it out.) Do you agree? Why, or why not?

10. Can any plausible reason be given for making (male) homosexuality illegal, but not lesbianism and adultery, as the English law once did? How does Devlin react to this apparent discrepancy? What do you think of this matter?

11. What grounds other than the enforcement of morality can be given for making bigamy a crime, as it presently is?

12. Critically discuss the closing sentence of our excerpt from Devlin:

> A rebel may be rational in thinking that he is right but he is irrational if he thinks that society can leave him free to rebel.

63. PSYCHOLOGICAL ENGINEERING IS THE KEY TO HUMAN CONTENTMENT AND SOCIAL CONTROL

B. F. Skinner

BURRHUS FREDERIC SKINNER (1904–), professor of psychology at Harvard University since 1948, is the leading exponent of the influential twentieth-century school of psychology known as **behaviorism.** As this school of psychology sees it, the key to understanding animal (including human) behavior is in the discovery of scientific laws of learning which relate behavioral stimuli to behavioral responses (i.e., if such and such is done to an animal, then that animal will respond in such and such a way). The key to controlling behavior, behaviorists claim, is the utilization of rewards or punishments to recondition behavior (determined by the laws of learning) into desirable patterns. There is no need, behaviorists claim, to postulate hidden psychological or physical processes to account for human behavior, as Freudians, for example, do. Similarly, there is no need to refer to human intentions, reasons, beliefs, or other private states of consciousness to account for the things human beings do.

As a young man, Skinner was a pioneer in utilizing positive reinforcement (i.e., rewards for appropriate behavior) in the training of rats and pigeons. After his extensive research with animals, Skinner moved on to human beings, devising various electronic teaching devices which also utilize positive reinforcement. Skinner's work with teaching machines has had a major influence on twentieth-century educational theories and methods in the United States. He has written several books defending his behavioristic point of view. In addition, he has written two popular books, **Walden Two** (1961) and **Beyond Freedom and Dignity** (1971), which advocate the utilization of behavioral techniques on a mass social scale and criticize those who, in the name of "human freedom and dignity," oppose such techniques.

The following selection is from Skinner's **Walden Two.** (The title is taken from Thoreau's famous book **Walden**, which describes his life at his cabin on Walden Pond, near Concord, Massachusetts. At a deeper level, however, **Walden** can be read as a testimony to how human beings can live in harmony with nature.) "Walden Two" is the name Skinner assigns to an imagined society run by behavioral psychologists. In this society, positive reinforcement is utilized to condition citizens, primarily in their early years, to have the desires and motives that will lead them to behave as those in charge think is best for them and society. Through Frazier, the creator of Walden Two, Skinner argues for the desirability of such a society. Castle and Burris, the other two main characters in Skinner's novel, are professors visiting Walden Two. Castle, a philosopher, is strongly critical of the effects and theoretical underpinnings of Walden Two. Burris, a psychologist who acts as the narrator of the novel, is presented as a neutral observer trying to evaluate objectively Frazier's society. As you read this selection, you should keep various questions in mind. First, does Skinner's view of psychology seem correct? Can we control human beings as effectively as he suggests? Second, and this is the concern for moral philosophy, even if we could control human behavior, as Skinner suggests, **should** we? What, if anything, **of value** would we lose, if we did?

''Each of us,'' Frazier began, ''is engaged in a pitched battle with the rest of mankind.''

''A curious premise for a Utopia,'' said Castle. ''Even a pessimist like myself takes a more hopeful view than that.''

''You do, you do,'' said Frazier. ''But let's be realistic. Each of us has interests which conflict with the interests of everybody else. That's our original sin, and it can't be helped. Now, 'everybody else' we call 'society.' It's a powerful opponent, and it always wins. . . . Society attacks early, when the individual is helpless. It enslaves him almost before he has tasted freedom. . . .

''Considering how long society has been at it, you'd expect a better job. But the campaigns have been badly planned and the victory has never been secure. The behavior of the individual has been shaped according to revelations of 'good conduct,' never as the result of experimental study. But why not experiment? The questions are simple enough. What's the best behavior for the individual so far as the group is concerned? And how can the individual be induced to behave in that way? Why not explore these questions in a scientific spirit?

''We could do just that in Walden Two. We had already worked out a code of conduct—subject, of course, to experimental modification. The code would keep things running smoothly if everybody lived up to it. Our job was to see that everybody did. Now, you can't get people to follow a useful code by making them into so many jacks-in-the-box. You can't foresee all future circumstances, and you can't specify adequate future conduct. You don't know what will be required. Instead you have to set up certain behavioral processes which will lead the individual to design his own 'good' conduct when the time comes. We call that sort of thing 'self-control.' But don't be misled, the control always rests in the last analysis in the hands of society.

''One of our Planners, a young man named Simmons, worked with me. . . .

. . . Simmons and I began by studying the great works on morals and ethics . . .; there were scores of them. We were looking for any and every method of shaping human behavior by imparting techniques of self-control. Some techniques were obvious enough, for they had marked turning points in human history. 'Love your enemies' is an example—a psychological invention for easing the lot of an oppressed people. The severest trial of oppression is the constant rage which one suffers at the thought of the oppressor. What Jesus discovered was how to avoid these inner devastations. His technique was to *practice the opposite emotion.* If a man can succeed in 'loving his enemies' and 'taking no thought for the morrow,' he will no longer be assailed by hatred of the oppressor or rage at the loss of his freedom or possessions. He may not get his freedom or possessions back, but he's less miserable. It's a difficult lesson. It comes late in our program.''. . .

''When Simmons and I had collected our techniques of control, we had to discover how to teach them. That was more difficult. Current educational practices were of little value, and religious practices scarcely any better. Promising paradise or threatening hell-fire is, we assumed, generally admitted to be unproductive. It is based upon a fundamental fraud which, when discovered, turns the individual against society and nourishes the very thing it tries to stamp out. What Jesus offered in return for loving one's enemies was heaven *on earth,* better known as peace of mind.

''We found a few suggestions worth following in the practices of the clinical psychologist. We undertook to build a tolerance for annoying experiences. The sunshine of midday is extremely painful if you come from a dark room, but take it in easy stages and you can avoid pain altogether. The analogy can be misleading, but in much the same way it's possible to build a tolerance to painful or distasteful stimuli, or to frustration, or to situations which arouse fear, anger or rage. Society and nature throw these annoyances at the individual with no regard for the development of tolerances. Some achieve tolerances, most fail. Where would the science of immunization be if it followed a schedule of accidental dosages?

"Take the principle of 'Get thee behind me, Satan,' for example," Frazier continued. "It's a special case of self-control by altering the environment. Subclass A 3, I believe. We give each child a lollipop which has been dipped in powdered sugar so that a single touch of the tongue can be detected. We tell him he may eat the lollipop later in the day, provided it hasn't already been licked. Since the child is only three or four, it is a fairly diff—"

"Three or four!" Castle exclaimed.

"All our ethical training is completed by the age of six," said Frazier quietly. "A simple principle like putting temptation out of sight would be acquired before four. But at such an early age the problem of not licking the lollipop isn't easy. Now, what would you do, Mr. Castle, in a similar situation?"

"Put the lollipop out of sight as quickly as possible."

"Exactly. I can see you've been well trained. Or perhaps you discovered the principle for yourself. We're in favor of original inquiry wherever possible, but in this case we have a more important goal and we don't hesitate to give verbal help. First of all, the children are urged to examine their own behavior while looking at the lollipops. This helps them to recognize the need for self-control. Then the lollipops are concealed, and the children are asked to notice any gain in happiness or any reduction in tension. Then a strong distraction is arranged—say, an interesting game. Later the children are reminded of the candy and encouraged to examine their reaction. The value of the distraction is generally obvious. Well, need I go on? When the experiment is repeated a day or so later, the children all run with the lollipops to their lockers and do exactly what Mr. Castle would do—a sufficient indication of the success of our training."

"I wish to report an objective observation of my reaction to your story," said Castle, controlling his voice with great precision. "I find myself revolted by this display of sadistic tyranny."

"I don't wish to deny you the exercise of an emotion which you seem to find enjoyable," said Frazier. "So let me go on. Concealing a tempting but forbidden object is a crude solution. For one thing, it's not always feasible. We want a sort of psychological concealment—covering up the candy by paying no attention. In a later experiment the children wear their lollipops like crucifixes for a few hours." . . .

"How do you build up a tolerance to an annoying situation?" I said.

"Oh, for example, by having the children 'take' a more and more painful shock, or drink cocoa with less and less sugar in it until a bitter concoction can be savored without a bitter face."

"But jealousy or envy—you can't administer them in graded doses," I said.

"And why not? Remember, we control the social environment, too, at this age. That's why we get our ethical training in early. Take this case. A group of children arrive home after a long walk tired and hungry. They're expecting supper; they find, instead, that it's time for a lesson in self-control: they must stand for five minutes in front of steaming bowls of soup.

"The assignment is accepted like a problem in arithmetic. Any groaning or complaining is a wrong answer. Instead, the children begin at once to work upon themselves to avoid any unhappiness during the delay: One of them may make a joke of it. We encourage a sense of humor as a good way of not taking an annoyance seriously. The joke won't be much, according to adult standards—perhaps the child will simply pretend to empty the bowl of soup into his upturned mouth. Another may start a song with many verses. The rest join in at once, for they've learned that it's a good way to make time pass."

Frazier glanced uneasily at Castle, who was not to be appeased. . . .

"In a later stage we forbid all social devices. No songs, no jokes—merely silence. Each child is forced back upon his own resources—a very important step."

"I should think so," I said. "And how do you know it's successful. You might produce a lot of silently resentful children. It's certainly a dangerous stage."

"It is, and we follow each child carefully. If he hasn't picked up the necessary techniques, we start back a little. A still more advanced stage"—Frazier glanced again at Castle, who stirred uneasily—"brings me to my point. When it's time to sit down to the soup, the children count off—heads and tails. Then a coin is tossed and if it comes up heads, the 'heads' sit down and eat. The 'tails' remain standing for another five minutes."

Castle groaned.

"And you call that envy?" I asked.

"Perhaps not exactly," said Frazier. "At least there's seldom any aggression against the lucky ones. The emotion, if any, is directed against Lady Luck herself, against the toss of the coin. That, in itself, is a lesson worth learning, for it's the only direction in which emotion has a surviving chance to be useful. And resentment toward things in general, while perhaps just as silly as personal aggression, is more easily controlled. Its expression is not socially objectionable."

. . . "May you not inadvertently teach your children some of the very emotions you're trying to eliminate?" I said. "What's the effect, for example, of finding the anticipation of a warm supper suddenly thwarted? Doesn't that eventually lead to feelings of uncertainty, or even anxiety?"

"It might. We had to discover how often our lessons could be safely administered. But all our schedules are worked out experimentally. We watch for undesired consequences just as any scientist watches for disrupting factors in his experiments. . . .

"But *why?*" said Castle. "Why these deliberate unpleasantnesses—to put it mildly? I must say I think you and your friend Simmons are really very subtle sadists.". . .

. . . "[W]hat do your children get out of it?" he insisted. . . .

"If I must spell it out," Frazier began with a deep sigh, "what they get is escape from the petty emotions which eat the heart out of the unprepared. They get the satisfaction of pleasant and profitable social relations on a scale almost undreamed of in the world at large. They get immeasurably increased efficiency, because they can stick to a job without suffering the aches and pains which soon beset most of us. They get new horizons, for they are spared the emotions characteristic of frustration and failure. They get—" His eyes searched the branches of the trees. "Is that enough?" he said at last. . . .

"What alternative *had* we?" he said, as if he were in pain. "What else could we do? For four or five years we could provide a life in which no important need would go unsatisfied, a life practically free of anxiety or frustration or annoyance. What would you do? Would you let the child enjoy this paradise with no thought for the future—like an idolatrous and pampering mother? Or would you relax control of the environment and let the child meet accidental frustrations? *But what is the virtue of accident?* No, there was only one course open to us. We had to *design* a series of adversities, so that the child would develop the greatest possible self-control. Call it deliberate, if you like, and accuse us of sadism; there was no other course.". . .

Frazier turned first to Castle.

"Have you ever taught a course in ethics, Mr. Castle?" he said.

"I have taught a course in ethics every year for thirteen years," said Castle in his most precise manner.

"Then you can tell us what the Good Life consists of," said Frazier.

"Oh, no, I can't," said Castle, "not by any means. You are thirteen years too late."

Frazier was delighted.

"Then let me tell you," he said.

". . . We all know what's good, until we stop to think about it. For example, is there any doubt that health is better than sickness?". . .

"Secondly, can anyone doubt that an absolute minimum of unpleasant labor is part of the Good Life?" Frazier turned again to Castle, but he was greeted with a sullen silence. . . .

"The Good Life also means a chance to exercise talents and abilities. And we have let it be so. We have time for sports, hobbies, arts and crafts, and most important of all, the expression of that interest in the world which is *science* in the deepest sense. It may be a casual interest in current affairs or in literature or the controlled and creative efforts of the laboratory—in any case it represents the unnecessary and pleasurably selective exploration of nature.

"And we need intimate and satisfying personal contacts. We must have the best possible chance of finding congenial spirits. Our Social Manager sees to that with many ingenious devices. And we don't restrict personal relations to conform to outmoded customs. We discourage attitudes of domination and criticism. Our goal is a general tolerance and affection.

"Last of all, the Good Life means relaxation and rest. We get that in Walden Two almost as a matter of course, but not merely because we have reduced our hours of work. In the world at large the leisure class is perhaps the least relaxed. The important thing is to satisfy our needs. Then we can give up the blind struggle to 'have a good time' or 'get what we want.' We have achieved a true leisure.

"And that's all, Mr. Castle—absolutely all, I can't give you a rational justification for any of it. I can't reduce it to any principle of 'the greatest good'. This *is* the Good Life. We know it. It's a fact, not a theory. It has an experimental justification, not a rational one. As for your conflict of principles, that's an experimental question, too. We don't puzzle our little minds over the outcome of Love versus Duty. We simply arrange a world in which serious conflicts occur as seldom as possible or, with a little luck, not at all."

Castle was gazing steadily across the evening landscape. There was no sign that he was listening. Frazier was not to be refused.

"Do you agree, Professor?" he said. There was obvious contempt for the honorific title.

"I don't think you and I are interested in the same thing," said Castle.

"Well, that's what we are interested in, and I think we've turned the trick," said Frazier, obviously disappointed. "Things are going well, at least.". . .

"What's left to motivate your workers?" I said. "Take a Manager, for example. He doesn't work for money—that's out. He doesn't work for personal acclaim—that's forbidden. What's left? I suppose you'd say he works to avoid the consequences of failure. He has to keep going or he'll be held responsible for the resulting mess."

"I wouldn't say that. We don't condemn a man for poor work. After all, if we don't praise him, it would be unfair to blame him."

"You mean you would let an incompetent man continue to do a poor job?" said Castle.

"By no means. He would be given other work, and a competent man brought in. But he wouldn't be blamed."

"For heaven's sake, why not?" said Castle.

"Do you blame a man for getting sick?"

"Of course not."

"But poor work by a capable man is a form of illness.". . .

"How do you treat a man for a bad case of 'poor work'?" I asked.

"With common sense! Take him off the job.

If the boy who has charge of collecting eggs breaks too many, give him other work. And the same with a Manager. But why condemn him? Or blame him?''

''I should think you might encourage a sort of malingering,'' I said. ''Wouldn't a man be tempted to do poor work in order to get an easier job?—Oh, well. Forgive me. I see the answer to that: you have no easier jobs, of course. And he could change jobs freely anyway. I'm sorry.''

''But what if a man did poor work, or none at all, in every job you put him on?'' said Castle.

''The disease would be judged quite serious, and the man would be sent to one of our psychologists. It's more likely that he would long since have gone of his own accord. This would happen before any very critical condition developed, and a cure would be quite possible. But compare the situation in the outside world. There the man would have stuck to his job in spite of his indisposition—that is, in spite of his desire not to work or work well—because he needed the wages, or was afraid of censure, or because another job wasn't available. The condition would have become critical. I think it's that kind of ultimate violent revolt that you're thinking about. It's quite unlikely here.''

''But what would you do if it occurred?'' Castle insisted. ''Certainly you can conceive of a member refusing to work.''

''We should deal with it somehow. I don't know. You might as well ask what we should do if leprosy broke out. We'd think of something. We aren't helpless.'' . . .

''A modern, mechanized, managerial Machiavelli—that is my final estimate of you, Mr. Frazier,'' [Castle] said, with the same challenging stare.

''It must be gratifying to know that one has reached a 'final estimate,' '' said Frazier.

''An artist in power,'' Castle continued, ''whose greatest art is to conceal art. The silent despot.'' . . .

''. . . So far as I can see, you've blocked every path through which man was to struggle upward toward salvation. Intelligence, initiative—you have filled their places with a sort of degraded instinct, engineered compulsion. Walden Two is a marvel of efficient coordination—as efficient as an anthill!''

''Replacing intelligence with instinct—'' muttered Frazier. ''I had never thought of that. It's an interesting possibility. How's it done?'' It was a crude maneuver. The question was a digression, intended to spoil Castle's timing and to direct our attention to practical affairs in which Frazier was more at home.

''The behavior of your members is carefully shaped in advance by a Plan,'' said Castle, not to be taken in, ''and it's shaped to perpetuate that Plan. Intellectually Walden Two is quite as incapable of a spontaneous change of course as the life within a beehive.''

''I see what you mean,'' said Frazier distantly. But he returned to his strategy. ''And have you discovered the machinery of my power?''

''I have, indeed. We were looking in the wrong place. There's no *current* contact between you and the members of Walden Two. . . . But you were behaving as a despot when you first laid your plans—when you designed the social structure and drew up the contract between community and member, when you worked out your educational practices and your guarantees against despotism. . . .''

''I've admitted neither power nor despotism [Frazier replied]. But you're quite right in saying that I've exerted an influence and in one sense will continue to exert it forever. . . . I did plan Walden Two—not as an architect plans a building, but as a scientist plans a long-term experiment, uncertain of the conditions he will meet but knowing how he will deal with them when they arise. In a sense, Walden Two is predetermined, but not as the behavior of a beehive is determined. Intelligence, no matter how much it may be shaped and extended by our educational system, will still function as intelligence. It will be used to puzzle out solutions to problems to which a beehive would quickly succumb. What the plan does is to keep intelligence on the right track, for the good of society rather than of the intelligent individual—or for the eventual rather than the immediate good of the individual. It does this by making sure that the individual will not forget his personal stake in the welfare of society."

"But you are forestalling many possibly useful acts of intelligence which aren't encompassed by your plan. You have ruled out points of view which may be more productive. You are implying that T. E. Frazier, looking at the world from the middle of the twentieth century, understands the best course for mankind forever . . . ."

"Mr. Castle," said Frazier very earnestly, "let me ask you a question. I warn you, it will be the most terrifying question of your life. *What would you do if you found yourself in possession of an effective science of behavior?* Suppose you suddenly found it possible to control the behavior of men as you wished. What would you do?"

"That's an assumption?"

"Take it as one if you like. I take it as a fact. And apparently you accept it as a fact too. I can hardly be as despotic as you claim unless I hold the key to an extensive practical control."

"What would I do?" said Castle thoughtfully. "I think I would dump your science of behavior in the ocean."

"And deny men all the help you could otherwise give them?"

"And give them the freedom they would otherwise lose forever!"

"How could you give them freedom?"

"By refusing to control them!"

"But you would only be leaving the control in other hands."

"Whose?"

"The charlatan, the demagogue, the salesman, the ward heeler, the bully, the cheat, the educator, the priest—all who are now in possession of the techniques of behavioral engineering."

"A pretty good share of the control would remain in the hands of the individual himself."

"That's an assumption, too, and it's your only hope. It's your only possible chance to avoid the implications of a science of behavior. If man is free, then a technology of behavior is impossible. But I'm asking you to consider the other case."

"Then my answer is that your assumption is contrary to fact and any further consideration idle."

"And your accusations—?"

"—were in terms of intention, not of possible achievement."

Frazier sighed dramatically.

"It's a little late to be proving that a behavioral technology is well advanced. How can you deny it? Many of its methods and techniques are really as old as the hills. Look at their frightful misuse in the hands of the Nazis! And what about the techniques of the psychological clinic? What about education? Or religion? Or practical politics? Or advertising and salesmanship? Bring them all together and you have a sort of rule-of-thumb technology of vast power. No, Mr. Castle, the science is there for the asking. But its techniques and methods are in the wrong hands—they are used for personal aggrandizement in a competitive world or, in the case of the psychologist and educator, for futilely corrective purposes. My question is, have you the courage to take up and wield the science of behavior for the good of mankind? You answer that you would dump it in the ocean!"

"I'd want to take it out of the hands of the politicians and advertisers and salesmen, too."

"And the psychologists and educators? You see, Mr. Castle, you can't have that kind of cake. The fact is, we not only *can* control human behavior, we *must*. But who's to do it, and what's to be done?"

"So long as a trace of personal freedom survives, I'll stick to my position," said Castle. . . .

"Isn't it time we talked about freedom?" I said. "We parted a day or so ago on an agreement to let the question of freedom ring. It's time to answer, don't you think?''

''My answer is simple enough,'' said Frazier. ''I deny that freedom exists at all. I must deny it—or my program would be absurd. You can't have a science about a subject matter which hops capriciously about. Perhaps we can never *prove* that man isn't free; it's an assumption. But the increasing success of a science of behavior makes it more and more plausible.''

''On the contrary, a simple personal experience makes it untenable,'' said Castle. ''The experience of freedom. I *know* that I'm free.''

''It must be quite consoling,'' said Frazier.

''And what's more—you do, too,'' said Castle hotly. ''When you deny your own freedom for the sake of playing with a science of behavior, you're acting in plain bad faith. That's the only way I can explain it.'' He tried to recover himself and shrugged his shoulders. ''At least you'll grant that you *feel* free.''

''The 'feeling of freedom' should deceive no one,'' said Frazier. ''Give me a concrete case.''

''Well, right now,'' Castle said. He picked up a book of matches. ''I'm free to hold or drop these matches.''

''You will, of course, do one or the other,'' said Frazier. ''Linguistically or logically there seem to be two possibilities, but I submit that there's only one in fact. The determining forces may be subtle but they are inexorable. I suggest that as an orderly person you will probably hold—ah! you drop them! Well, you see, that's all part of your behavior with respect to me. You couldn't resist the temptation to prove me wrong. It was all lawful. You had no choice. The deciding factor entered rather late, and naturally you couldn't foresee the result when you first held them up. There was no strong likelihood that you would act in either direction, and so you said you were free.''

''That's entirely too glib.'' said Castle. ''It's easy to argue lawfulness after the fact. But let's see you predict what I will do in advance. Then I'll agree there's law.''

''I didn't say that behavior is always predictable, any more than the weather is always predictable. There are often too many factors to be taken into account. We can't measure them all accurately, and we couldn't perform the mathematical operations needed to make a prediction if we had the measurements. . . .

''Take a case where there's no choice, then,'' said Castle. ''Certainly a man in jail isn't free in the sense in which I am free now.''

''Good! That's an excellent start. Let us classify the kinds of determiners of human behavior. One class, as you suggest, is physical restraint—handcuffs, iron bars, forcible coercion. These are ways in which we shape human behavior according to our wishes. They're crude, and they sacrifice the affection of the controllee, but they often work. Now, what other ways are there of limiting freedom?''

Frazier had adopted a professional tone and Castle refused to answer.

''The threat of force would be one,'' I said.

''Right. And here again we shan't encourage any loyalty on the part of the controllee. He has perhaps a shade more of the feeling of freedom, since he can always 'choose to act and accept the consequences,' but he doesn't feel exactly free. He knows his behavior is being coerced. Now what else?''

I had no answer.

''Force or the threat of force—I see no other possibility,'' said Castle after a moment.

''Precisely,'' said Frazier.

''But certainly a large part of my behavior has no connection with force at all. There's my freedom!'' said Castle.

''I wasn't agreeing that there was no other possibility—merely that *you* could see no other. Not being a good behaviorist—or a good Christian, for that matter—you have no feeling for a tremendous power of a different sort.''

''What's that?''

''I shall have to be technical,'' said Frazier. ''But only for a moment. It's what the science of behavior calls 'reinforcement theory.' The things that can happen to us fall into three classes. To some things we are indifferent. Other things we like—we want them to happen, and we take steps to make them happen again. Still other things we don't like—we don't want them to happen and we take steps to get rid of them or keep them from happening again.

"*Now*," Frazier continued earnestly, "if it's in our power to create any of the situations which a person likes or to remove any situation he doesn't like, we can control his behavior. When he behaves as we want him to behave, we simply create a situation he likes, or remove one he doesn't like. As a result, the probability that he will behave that way again goes up, which is what we want. Technically it's called 'positive reinforcement.'

"The old school made the amazing mistake of supposing that the reverse was true, that by removing a situation a person likes or setting up one he doesn't like—in other words by punishing him—it was possible to *reduce* the probability that he would behave in a given way again. That simply doesn't hold. It has been established beyond question. What is emerging at this critical stage in the evolution of society is a behavioral and cultural technology based on positive reinforcement alone. We are gradually discovering—at an untold cost in human suffering—that in the long run punishment doesn't reduce the probability that an act will occur. We have been so preoccupied with the contrary that we always take 'force' to mean punishment. We don't say we're using force when we send shiploads of food into a starving country, though we're displaying quite as much *power* as if we were sending troops and guns."

"Now that we *know* how positive reinforcement works and why negative doesn't," he said at last, "we can be more deliberate, and hence more successful, in our cultural design. We can achieve a sort of control under which the controlled, though they are following a code much more scrupulously than was ever the case under the old system, nevertheless *feel free*. They are doing what they want to do, not what they are forced to do. That's the source of the tremendous power of positive reinforcement—there's no restraint and no revolt. By a careful design, we control not the final behavior, but the *inclination* to behave—the motives, the desires, the wishes.

"The curious thing is that in that case *the question of freedom never arises*. Mr. Castle was free to drop the matchbook in the sense that nothing was preventing him. If it had been securely bound to his hand he wouldn't have been free. Nor would he have been quite free if I'd covered him with a gun and threatened to shoot him if he let it fall. The question of freedom arises when there is restraint—either physical or psychological.

"But restraint is only one sort of control, and absence of restraint isn't freedom. It's not control that's lacking when one feels 'free,' but the objectionable control of force. Mr. Castle felt free to hold or drop the matches in the sense that he felt no restraint—no threat of punishment in taking either course of action. He neglected to examine his positive reasons for holding or letting go, in spite of the fact that these were more compelling in this instance than any threat of force." . . .

"The question is: Can men live in freedom and peace? And the answer is: Yes, if we can build a social structure which will satisfy the needs of everyone and in which everyone will want to observe the supporting code. But so far this has been achieved only in Walden Two. Your ruthless accusations to the contrary, Mr. Castle, this is the freest place on earth. And it is free precisely because we make no use of force or the threat of force. Every bit of our research, from the nursery through the psychological management of our adult membership, is directed toward that end—to exploit every alternative to forcible control. By skillful planning, by a wise choice of techniques we *increase* the feeling of freedom.

"It's not planning which infringes upon freedom, but planning which uses force. A sense of freedom was practically unknown in the planned society of Nazi Germany, because the planners made a fantastic use of force and the threat of force.

"No, Mr. Castle, when a science of behavior has once been achieved, there's no alternative to a planned society. We can't leave mankind to an accidental or biased control. But by using the principle of positive reinforcement—carefully avoiding force or the threat of force—we can preserve a personal sense of freedom."

DISCUSSION QUESTIONS

1. What is your general reaction to Frazier's arguments for planned behavioral conditioning as practiced in Walden II? Do you believe, as Castle does, that such a society robs people of their "free will"? Do you share Frazier's optimism that the questions behavioral scientists have to face ". . . are simple enough. What's the best behavior for the individual as far as the group is concerned? And how can the individual be induced to behave in that way?"

2. Frazier claims that "poor work by a capable man is a form of illness" and for that reason it is unreasonable to blame him for it. How does Frazier reply to the narrator's claim that such an attitude would be apt to take away one's motive to work well or even at all? What do you think?

3. Critically compare Frazier's and Castle's views of the free will-determinism issue. Do Castle and Frazier accept the same meaning of "freedom"? Indeed, does Frazier himself employ more than one definition of this concept?

4. Frazier claims that "You can't have a science about a subject matter which hops capriciously about." How do you think a libertarian would reply?

5. T.H. Huxley once wrote:

> If some great power would agree to always make me think what is true and do what is right, on condition of being turned into a sort of clock and wound up every morning before I got out of bed, I should instantly close with the offer.

Would Frazier agree with Huxley? Do you agree with him? Why, or why not?

6. Is there a conflict between Mill's view of individual freedom and the utilization of the behavioral conditioning techniques advocated by Frazier?

7. Skinner writes:

> It will be a long time before the world can dispense with heroes and hence with the cultural practice of admiring heroism, but we move in that direction whenever we act to prevent war, famine, pestilence and disaster. It will be a long time before man will never need to submit to punishing environments or engage in exhausting labor, but we move in that direction whenever we make food, shelter, clothing and labor-saving devices more readily available. We may mourn the passing of heroes but not the conditions which make for heroism. We can spare the self-made saint or sage as we spare the laundress on the river's bank struggling against fearful odds to achieve cleanliness. . . .[1]

Critically discuss.

[1]From B.F. Skinner, "Freedom and the Control of Men," *The American Scholar*, Winter 1955–56, p. 65.

64. THE COST OF HUMAN CONTENTMENT AND SOCIAL CONTROL THROUGH PSYCHOLOGICAL ENGINEERING

Aldous Huxley

ALDOUS HUXLEY (1894–1963), a grandson of Thomas Huxley (see the introduction to Selection #29), had an illustrious literary career. Educated at Oxford, England, he came to the United States in the 1930's and settled in California. After beginning his writing career with literary essays and poems, he established his fame through a series of witty and satirical novels. Among these novels is **Brave New World** (1932), which describes a futuristic totalitarian society that worships science and individual conformity. Unlike Skinner in the preceding selection, Huxley sees science not as the savior of humanity, but as its potential destroyer.

In Huxley's imagined society, babies are not brought into the world as they now are through socially uncontrolled sexual intercourse. Instead, they are created through an extra-uterine fertilization and budding process (**Bokanovsky's Process**), which is carefully controlled to produce exactly the right numbers of babies of differing genetic capacities (**alpha, beta, gamma**, and **delta** babies). Once conceived, these carefully manufactured fetuses are nurtured in a controlled man-made environment. So begins the intricate human-supervised control that permeates Huxley's imagined society. Children and adults are immunized from all diseases and, having already been genetically engineered to best fit into their particular niches in society, people are behaviorally conditioned so that they quite naturally do what their society thinks they ought to do. The euphoric drug **soma** is used to combat any depression in life and to create the most pleasurable of sensations.

In our selection from **Brave New World**, three discontented individuals who have not behaved as they should—Helmholtz Watson, Bernard Marx, and the Savage (who has not been "civilized")—are brought before Mustapha Mond, the Controller for Western Europe. The bulk of our selection consists of a conversation between Mustapha Mond and the Savage, in which the merits of Huxley's imagined society are debated.

The room into which the three were ushered was the Controller's study.

"His fordship will be down in a moment." The Gamma butler left them to themselves.

Helmholtz laughed aloud.

"It's more like a caffeine-solution party than a trial," he said, and let himself fall into the most luxurious of the pneumatic arm-chairs. "Cheer up, Bernard," he added, catching sight of his friend's green unhappy face. But Bernard would not be cheered; without answering, without even looking at Helmholtz, he went and sat down on the most uncomfortable chair in the room, carefully chosen in the obscure hope of somehow deprecating the wrath of the higher powers.

The Savage meanwhile wandered restlessly

Source: Abridged from Chapters 16 and 17 in *Brave New World* by Aldous Huxley.

round the room, peering with a vague superficial inquisitiveness at the books in the shelves, at the soundtrack rolls and the reading machine bobbins in their numbered pigeon-holes. On the table under the window lay a massive volume bound in limp black leather-surrogate, and stamped with large golden T's. He picked it up and opened it. MY LIFE AND WORK, BY OUR FORD. The book had been published at Detroit by the Society for the Propagation of Fordian Knowledge. Idly he turned the pages, read a sentence here, a paragraph there, and had just come to the conclusion that the book didn't interest him, when the door opened, and the Resident World Controller for Western Europe walked briskly into the room.

Mustapha Mond shook hands with all three of them; but it was to the Savage that he addressed himself. "So you don't much like civilization, Mr. Savage," he said.

The Savage looked at him. He had been prepared to lie, to bluster, to remain sullenly unresponsive; but, reassured by the good-humoured intelligence of the Controller's face, he decided to tell the truth, straightforwardly. "No." He shook his head.

Bernard started and looked horrified. What would the Controller think? To be labelled as the friend of a man who said that he didn't like civilization—said it openly and, of all people, to the Controller—it was terrible. "But, John," he began. A look from Mustapha Mond reduced him to an abject silence.

"Of course," the Savage went on to admit, "there are some very nice things. All that music in the air, for instance . . ."

"Sometimes a thousand twangling instruments will hum about my ears and sometimes voices."

The Savage's face lit up with a sudden pleasure. "Have you read it too?" he asked. "I thought nobody knew about that book here, in England."

"Almost nobody. I'm one of the very few. It's prohibited, you see. But as I make the laws here, I can also break them. With impunity, Mr. Marx," he added, turning to Bernard. "Which I'm afraid you *can't* do."

Bernard sank into a yet more hopeless misery.

"But why is it prohibited?" asked the Savage. In the excitement of meeting a man who had read Shakespeare he had momentarily forgotten everything else.

The Controller shrugged his shoulders. "Because it's old; that's the chief reason. We haven't any use for old things here."

"Even when they're beautiful?"

"Particularly when they're beautiful. Beauty's attractive, and we don't want people to be attracted by old things. We want them to like the new ones."

"But the new ones are so stupid and horrible. Those plays, where there's nothing but helicopters flying about and you *feel* the people kissing." . . .

"Why don't you let them see *Othello* instead?"

"I've told you; it's old. Besides, they couldn't understand it."

Yes, that was true. He remembered how Helmholtz had laughed at *Romeo and Juliet*. "Well then," he said, after a pause, "something new that's like *Othello*, and that they could understand."

"That's what we've all been wanting to write," said Helmholtz, breaking a long silence.

"And it's what you never will write," said the Controller. "Because, if it were really like *Othello* nobody could understand it, however new it might be. And if it were new, it couldn't possibly be like *Othello*."

"Why not?"

"Yes, why not?" Helmholtz repeated. He too was forgetting the unpleasant realities of the situation. Green with anxiety and apprehension, only Bernard remembered them; the others ignored him. "Why not?"

"Because our world is not the same as Othello's world. You can't make flivvers[1] without steel—and you can't make tragedies without social instability. The world's stable now. People are happy; they get what they want, and they never want what they can't get. They're well off; they're safe; they're never ill; they're not afraid of death; they're blissfully ignorant of passion and old age; they're plagued with no mothers or fathers; they've got no wives, or children, or lovers to feel strongly about; they're so conditioned that they practically can't help behaving as they ought to behave. And if anything should go wrong, there's *soma*. Which you go and chuck out of the window in the name of liberty, Mr. Savage. *Liberty!*" He laughed. "Expecting Deltas to know what liberty is! And now expecting them to understand *Othello!* My good boy!"

The Savage was silent for a little. "All the same," he insisted obstinately, "*Othello's* good, *Othello's* better than those feelies."

"Of course it is," the Controller agreed. "But that's the price we have to pay for stability. You've got to choose between happiness and what people used to call high art. We've sacrificed the high art. We have the feelies and the scent organ instead."

"But they don't mean anything."

"They mean themselves; they mean a lot of agreeable sensations to the audience."

"But they're . . . they're told by an idiot."

The Controller laughed. "You're not being very polite to your friend, Mr. Watson. One of our most distinguished Emotional Engineers . . ."

"But he's right," said Helmholtz gloomily. "Because it *is* idiotic. Writing when there's nothing to say . . ."

"Precisely. But that requires the most enormous ingenuity. You're making flivvers out of the absolute minimum of steel—works of art out of practically nothing but pure sensation."

The Savage shook his head. "It all seems to me quite horrible."

"Of course it does. Actual happiness always looks pretty squalid in comparison with the over-compensations for misery. And, of course, stability isn't nearly so spectacular as instability. And being contented has none of the glamour of a good fight against misfortune, none of the picturesqueness of a struggle with temptation, or a fatal overthrow by passion or doubt. Happiness is never grand."

"I suppose not," said the Savage after a silence. "But need it be quite so bad as those twins?" He passed his hand over his eyes as though he were trying to wipe away the remembered image of those long rows of identical midgets at the assembling tables, those queued-up twin-herds at the entrance to the Brentford monorail station. . . .

"But how useful! I see you don't like our Bokanovsky Groups; but, I assure you, they're the foundation on which everything else is built. . . .

"I was wondering," said the Savage, "why you had them at all—seeing that you can get whatever you want out of those bottles. Why don't you make everybody an Alpha Double Plus while you're about it?"

Mustapha Mond laughed. "Because we have no wish to have our throats cut," he answered. "We believe in happiness and stability. A society of Alphas couldn't fail to be unstable and miserable. Imagine a factory staffed by Alphas—that is to say by separate and unrelated individuals of good heredity and conditioned so as to be capable (within limits) of making a free choice and assuming responsibilities. Imagine it!" he repeated.

The Savage tried to imagine it, not very successfully.

"It's an absurdity. An Alpha-decanted, Alpha-conditioned man would go mad if he had to do Epsilon Semi-Moron work—go mad, or start smashing things up. Alphas can be completely socialized—but only on condition that

[1]Slang for cheap automobiles, planes, or other cheap means of transportation. EDITOR'S NOTE.

you make them do Alpha work. Only an Epsilon can be expected to make Epsilon sacrifices, for the good reason that for him they aren't sacrifices; they're the line of least resistance. His conditioning has laid down rails along which he's got to run. He can't help himself; he's foredoomed. Even after decanting, he's still inside a bottle—an invisible bottle of infantile and embryonic fixations. Each one of us, of course," the Controller meditatively continued, "goes through life inside a bottle. But if we happen to be Alphas, our bottles are, relatively speaking, enormous. We should suffer acutely if we were confined in a narrower space. You cannot pour upper-caste champagne-surrogate into lower-caste bottles. It's obvious theoretically. But it has also been proved in actual practice. The result of the Cyprus experiment was convincing."

"What was that?" asked the Savage.

Mustapha Mond smiled. "Well, you can call it an experiment in rebottling if you like. It began in A.F. 473. The Controllers had the island of Cyprus cleared of all its existing inhabitants and re-colonized with a specially prepared batch of twenty-two thousand Alphas. All agricultural and industrial equipment was handed over to them and they were left to manage their own affairs. The result exactly fulfilled all the theoretical predictions. The land wasn't properly worked; there were strikes in all the factories; the laws were set at naught, orders disobeyed; all the people detailed for a spell of low-grade work were perpetually intriguing for high-grade jobs, and all the people with high-grade jobs were counter-intriguing at all costs to stay where they were. Within six years they were having a first-class civil war. When nineteen out of the twenty-two thousand had been killed, the survivors unanimously petitioned the World Controllers to resume the government of the island. Which they did. And that was the end of the only society of Alphas that the world has ever seen."

The Savage sighed, profoundly.

"The optimum population," said Mustapha Mond, "is modelled on the iceberg—eight-ninths below the water line, one-ninth above."

"And they're happy below the water line?"

"Happier than above it. Happier than your friend here, for example." He pointed.

"In spite of that awful work?"

"Awful? *They* don't find it so. On the contrary, they like it. It's light, it's childishly simple. No strain on the mind or the muscles. Seven and a half hours of mild, unexhausting labour, and then the *soma* ration and games and unrestricted copulation and the feelies. What more can they ask for? True," he added, "they might ask for shorter hours. And of course we could give them shorter hours. Technically, it would be perfectly simple to reduce all lower-caste working hours to three or four a day. But would they be any the happier for that? No, they wouldn't. The experiment was tried, more than a century and a half ago. The whole of Ireland was put on to the four-hour day. What was the result? Unrest and a large increase in the consumption of *soma*; that was all. Those three and a half hours of extra leisure were so far from being a source of happiness, that people felt constrained to take a holiday from them. The Inventions Office is stuffed with plans for labour-saving processes. Thousands of them." Mustapha Mond made a lavish gesture. "And why don't we put them into execution? For the sake of the labourers; it would be sheer cruelty to afflict them with excessive leisure. It's the same with agriculture. We could synthesize every morsel of food, if we wanted to. But we don't. We prefer to keep a third of the population on the land. For their own sakes—because it takes *longer* to get food out of the land than out of a factory. Besides, we have our stability to think of. We don't want to change. Every change is a menace to stability. That's another reason why we're so chary of applying new inventions. Every discovery in pure science is potentially subversive; even science must sometimes be treated as a possible enemy. Yes, even science." . . .

"What?" said Helmholtz, in astonishment. "But we're always saying that science is everything. . . .

"Yes; but what sort of science?" asked Mustapha Mond sarcastically. "You've had no scientific training, so you can't judge." I was a pretty good physicist in my time. Too good—good enough to realize that all our science is just a cookery book, with an orthodox theory of cooking that nobody's allowed to question, and a list of recipes that mustn't be added to except by special permission from the head cook. I'm the head cook now. But I was an inquisitive young scullion once. I started doing a bit of cooking on my own. Unorthodox cooking, illicit cooking. A bit of real science, in fact." He was silent.

"What happened?" asked Helmholtz Watson.

The Controller sighed. "Very nearly what's going to happen to you young men. I was on the point of being sent to an island."

The words galvanized Bernard into a violent and unseemly activity. "Send *me* to an island?" He jumped up, ran across the room, and stood gesticulating in front of the Controller. "You can't send *me*. I haven't done anything. It was the others. I swear it was the others." He pointed accusingly to Helmholtz and the Savage. "Oh, please don't send me to Iceland. I promise I'll do what I ought to do. Give me another chance. Please give me another chance." The tears began to flow. "I tell you, it's their fault," he sobbed. "And not to Iceland. Oh please, your fordship, please . . ." And in a paroxysm of abjection he threw himself on his knees before the Controller. Mustapha Mond tried to make him get up; but Bernard persisted in his grovelling; the stream of words poured out inexhaustibly. In the end the Controller had to ring for his fourth secretary.

"Bring three men," he ordered, "and take Mr. Marx into a bedroom. Give him a good *soma* vaporization and then put him to bed and leave him."

The fourth secretary went out and returned with three green-uniformed twin footmen. Still shouting and sobbing, Bernard was carried out.

"One would think he was going to have his throat cut," said the Controller, as the door closed. "Whereas, if he had the smallest sense, he'd understand that his punishment is really a reward. He's being sent to an island. That's to say, he's being sent to a place where he'll meet the most interesting set of men and women to be found anywhere in the world. All the people who, for one reason or another, have got too self-consciously individual to fit into community-life. All the people who aren't satisfied with orthodoxy, who've got independent ideas of their own. Every one, in a word, who's any one. I almost envy you, Mr. Watson."

Helmholtz laughed. "Then why aren't you on an island yourself?"

"Because, finally, I preferred this," the Controller answered. "I was given the choice: to be sent to an island, where I could have got on with my pure science, or to be taken on to the Controllers' Council with the prospect of succeeding in due course to an actual Controllership. I chose this and let the science go." After a little silence, "Sometimes," he added, "I rather regret the science. Happiness is a hard master—particularly other people's happiness. A much harder master, if one isn't conditioned to accept it unquestioningly, than truth." He sighed, fell silent again, then continued in a brisker tone, "Well, duty's duty. One can't consult one's own preferences. I'm interested in truth, I like science. But truth's a menace, science is a public danger. As dangerous as it's been beneficent. It has given us the stablest equilibrium in history. . . . It's curious," he went on after a little pause, "to read what people in the time of Our Ford used to write about scientific progress. They seemed to have imagined that it could be allowed to go on indefinitely, regardless of everything else. Knowledge was the highest good, truth the supreme value; all the rest was secondary and subordinate. True, ideas were beginning to change even then. Our Ford himself did a great deal to shift the emphasis from truth and beauty to comfort and happiness. Mass production demanded the shift. Universal happiness keeps the wheels steadily turning; truth and beauty can't. And, of course, whenever the masses seized political power, then it was happiness rather than truth and beauty that mattered. Still, in spite of everything, unrestricted scientific research was still permitted. People still went on talking about truth and beauty as though they were the sovereign goods. Right up to the time of the Nine Years' War. *That* made them change their tune all right. What's the point of truth or beauty or knowledge when the anthrax bombs are popping all around you? That was when science first began to be controlled—after the Nine Years' War. People were ready to have even their appetites controlled then. Anything for a quiet life. We've gone on controlling ever since. It hasn't been very good for truth, of course. But it's been very good for happiness. One can't have something for nothing. Happiness has got to be paid for. You're paying for it, Mr. Watson—paying because you happen to be too much interested in beauty. I was too much interested in truth; I paid too."

"But *you* didn't go to an island," said the Savage, breaking a long silence.

The Controller smiled. "That's how I paid. By choosing to serve happiness. Other people's—not mine. It's lucky," he added, after a pause, "that there are such a lot of islands in the world. I don't know what we should do without them. Put you all in the lethal chamber, I suppose. By the way, Mr. Watson, would you like a tropical climate? The Marquesas, for example; or Somoa? Or something rather more bracing?"

Helmholtz rose from his pneumatic chair. "I should like a thoroughly bad climate," he answered. "I believe one would write better if the climate were bad. If there were a lot of wind and storms, for example . . ."

The Controller nodded his approbation. "I like your spirit, Mr. Watson. I like it very much indeed. As much as I officially disapprove of it." He smiled. "What about the Falkland Islands?"

"Yes, I think that will do," Helmholtz answered. "And now, if you don't mind, I'll go and see how poor Bernard's getting on."

"Art, science—you seem to have paid a fairly high price for your happiness," said the Savage, when they were alone. "Anything else?"

"Well, religion, of course," replied the Controller. "There used to be something called God—before the Nine Years' War. . . .

The Controller, meanwhile, had crossed to the other side of the room and was unlocking a large safe let into the wall between the bookshelves. The heavy door swung open. Rummaging in the darkness within, "It's a subject," he said, "that has always had a great interest for me." He pulled out a thick black volume. "You've never read this, for example."

The Savage took it. "*The Holy Bible, containing the Old and New Testaments*," he read aloud from the title-page.

"Nor this." It was a small book and had lost its cover.

"*The Imitation of Christ*."

"Nor this." He handed out another volume.

"*The Varieties of Religious Experience*. By William James."

"And I've got plenty more," Mustapha Mond continued, resuming his seat. "A whole collection of pornographic old books. God in the safe and Ford on the shelves." He pointed with a laugh to his avowed library—to the shelves of books, the racks full of reading-machine bobbins and sound-track rolls.

"But if you know about God, why don't you tell them?" asked the Savage indignantly. "Why don't you give them these books about God?"

"For the same reason as we don't give them *Othello*: they're old; they're about God hundreds of years ago. Not about God now."

"But God doesn't change."

"Men do, though." . . .

. . . we've now got youth and prosperity right up to the end [the controller continued]. What follows? Evidently, that we can be independent of God. . . . [R]eligious sentiment is superfluous. [W]hy should we go hunting for a substitute for youthful desires, when youthful desires never fail? . . . What need have we of repose when our minds and bodies continue to delight in activity? of consolation, when we have *soma?* of something immovable, when there is the social order?"

"Then you think there is no God?"

"No, I think there quite probably is one."

"Then why? . . ."

Mustapha Mond checked him. "But he manifests himself in different ways to different men. In premodern times he manifested himself as the being that's described in these books. Now . . ."

"How does he manifest himself now?" asked the Savage.

"Well, he manifests himself as an absence; as though he weren't there at all."

"That's your fault."

"Call it the fault of civilization. God isn't compatible with machinery and scientific medicine and universal happiness. You must make your choice. Our civilization has chosen machinery and medicine and happiness. That's why I have to keep these books locked up in the safe. They're smut. People would be shocked if . . ."

The Savage interrupted him. "But isn't it *natural* to feel there's a God?"

"You might as well ask if it's natural to do up one's trousers with zippers," said the Controller sarcastically. "You remind me of another of those old fellows called Bradley. He defined philosophy as the finding of bad reason for what one believes by instinct. As if one believed anything by instinct! One believes things because one has been conditioned to believe them. Finding bad reasons for what one believes for other bad reasons—that's philosophy. People believe in God because they've been conditioned to believe in God."

"But all the same," insisted the Savage, "it is natural to believe in God when you're alone—quite alone, in the night, thinking about death . . ."

"But people never are alone now," said Mustapha Mond. "We make them hate solitude; and we arrange their lives so that it's almost impossible for them ever to have it."

The Savage nodded gloomily. At Malpais he had suffered because they had shut him out from the communal activities of the pueblo, in civilized London he was suffering because he could never escape from those communal activities, never be quietly alone.

"Do you remember that bit in *King Lear?*" said the Savage at last. " 'The gods are just and of our pleasant vices make instruments to plague us; the dark and vicious place where thee he got cost him his eyes,' and Edmund answers—you remember, he's wounded, he's dying—'Thou hast spoken right; 'tis true. The wheel has come full circle; I am here.' What about that now? Doesn't there seem to be a God managing things, punishing, rewarding?"

"Well, does there?" questioned the Controller in his turn. "You can indulge in any number of pleasant vices with a freemartin and run no risks of having your eyes put out by your son's mistress. 'The wheel has come full circle; I am here.' But where would Edmund be nowadays? Sitting in a pneumatic chair, with his arm round a girl's waist, sucking away at his sex-hormone chewing-gum and looking at the feelies. The gods are just. No doubt. But their code of law is dictated, in the last resort, by the people who organize society; Providence takes its cue from men."

"Are you sure?" asked the Savage. "Are you quite sure that the Edmund in that pneumatic chair hasn't been just as heavily punished as the Edmund who's wounded and bleeding to death? The gods are just. Haven't they used his pleasant vices as an instrument to degrade him?''

''Degrade him from what position? As a happy, hard-working, goods-consuming citizen he's perfect. Of course, if you choose some other standard than ours, then perhaps you might say he was degraded. . . .

''But value dwells not in particular will,'' said the Savage. . . .

''Come, come,'' protested Mustapha Mond, ''that's going rather far, isn't it?''

''If you allowed yourselves to think of God, you wouldn't allow yourselves to be degraded by pleasant vices. You'd have a reason for bearing things patiently, for doing things with courage. I've seen it with the Indians.''

''I'm sure you have,'' said Mustapha Mond. ''But then we aren't Indians. There isn't any need for a civilized man to bear anything that's seriously unpleasant. . . .

''What about self-denial, then? If you had a God, you'd have a reason for self-denial.''

''But industrial civilization is only possible when there's no self-denial. Self-indulgence up to the very limits imposed by hygiene and economics. Otherwise the wheels stop turning.''

''You'd have a reason for chastity!'' said the Savage, blushing a little as he spoke the words.

''But chastity means passion, chastity means neurasthenia.[2] And passion and neurasthenia mean instability. And instability means the end of civilization. You can't have a lasting civilization without plenty of pleasant vices.''

''But God's the reason for everything noble and fine and heroic. If you had a God . . .''

''My dear young friend,'' said Mustapha Mond, ''civilization has absolutely no need of nobility or heroism. These things are symptoms of political inefficiency. In a properly organized society like ours, nobody has any opportunities for being noble or heroic. Conditions have got to be thoroughly unstable before the occasion can arise. Where there are wars, where there are divided allegiances, where there are temptations to be resisted, objects of love to be fought for or defended—there, obviously, nobility and heroism have some sense. But there aren't any wars nowadays. The greatest care is taken to prevent you from loving any one too much. There's no such thing as a divided allegiance; you're so conditioned that you can't help doing what you ought to do. And what you ought to do is on the whole so pleasant, so many of the natural impulses are allowed free play, that there really aren't any temptations to resist. And if ever, by some unlucky chance, anything unpleasant should somehow happen, why, there's always *soma* to give you a holiday from the facts. And there's always *soma* to calm your anger, to reconcile you to your enemies, to make you patient and long-suffering. In the past you could only accomplish these things by making a great effort and after years of hard moral training. Now, you swallow two or three half-gramme tablets, and there you are. Anybody can be virtuous now. You can carry at least half your morality about in a bottle. Christianity without tears—that's what *soma* is.''

''But the tears are necessary. Don't you remember what Othello said? 'If after every tempest came such calms, may the winds blow till they have wakened death.' There's a story one of the old Indians used to tell us, about the Girl of Mataski. The young men who wanted to marry her had to do a morning's hoeing in her garden. It seemed easy; but there were flies and mosquitoes, magic ones. Most of the young men simply couldn't stand the biting and stinging. But the one that could—he got the girl.''

''Charming! But in civilized countries,'' said the Controller, ''you can have girls without hoeing for them; and there aren't any flies or mosquitoes to sting you. We got rid of them all centuries ago.''

The Savage nodded, frowning. ''You got rid

[2]Emotional weakness. EDITOR'S NOTE.

of them. Yes, that's just like you. Getting rid of everything unpleasant instead of learning to put up with it. Whether 'tis better in the mind to suffer the slings and arrows of outrageous fortune, or to take arms against a sea of troubles and by opposing end them . . . But you don't do either. Neither suffer nor oppose. You just abolish the slings and arrows. It's too easy." . . .

. . . "Quite apart from God—though of course God would be a reason for it. Isn't there something in living dangerously?"

"There's a great deal in it," the Controller replied. "Men and women must have their adrenals stimulated from time to time."

"What?" questioned the Savage, uncomprehending.

"It's one of the conditions of perfect health. That's why we've made the V.P.S. treatments compulsory."

"V.P.S.?"

"Violent Passion Surrogate. Regularly once a month. We flood the whole system with adrenin. It's the complete physiological equivalent of fear and rage. All the tonic effects of murdering Desdemona and being murdered by Othello, without any of the inconveniences."

"But I like the inconveniences."

"We don't," said the Controller. "We prefer to do things comfortably."

"But I don't want comfort. I want God, I want poetry, I want real danger, I want freedom, I want goodness. I want sin."

"In fact," said Mustapha Mond, "you're claiming the right to be unhappy."

"All right then," said the Savage defiantly, "I'm claiming the right to be unhappy."

"Not to mention the right to grow old and ugly and impotent; the right to have syphilis and cancer; the right to have too little to eat; the right to be lousy; the right to live in constant apprehension of what may happen to-morrow; the right to catch typhoid; the right to be tortured by unspeakable pains of every kind."

There was a long silence.

"I claim them all," said the Savage at last.

Mustapha Mond shrugged his shoulders. "You're welcome," he said.

DISCUSSION QUESTION

1. Do you share the Savage's distaste for the society depicted in **Brave New World?** Why? What is your conception of an ideal society? Is such a society a realistic possibility in this world? If not, what is the best we can realistically hope for and how can it be achieved?

FURTHER READINGS

the social contract view of political obligation

Barker, Ernest, *The Social Contract*. New York: Oxford University Press, 1960. This book contains Locke's *Second Treatise of Government*, Rousseau's *The Social Contract*, Hume's "Of the Original Contract," and an introduction (38 pages) by Barker.

Gough, J.W., *John Locke's Political Philosophy*, 2nd ed. New York: Oxford University Press, 1973. This book consists of eight of Gough's clearly written and nontechnical essays on aspects of Locke's political philosophy, including its influence upon English political history.

Gough, J.W., *The Social Contract*, 2nd ed. Westport, Conn.: Greenwood Press, 1957, reprinted 1978. Gough traces the historical development of the social contract idea from its roots in ancient Greek philosophy, through its development in the Middle Ages, and in the political writings of Hobbes, Spinoza, Locke, Rousseau, Kant, and

Hegel. Gough's primary concern, however, is analytic and critical and not historical. The book is well-written, but detailed and philosophically involved.

Hobbes, Thomas, *Leviathan*, with an introduction by Herbert W. Schneider. Indianapolis: Bobbs-Merrill, 1958. This edition of *Leviathan* is modernized from the dated English in which Hobbes wrote it, making it easier to read than C.B. MacPherson's version of *Leviathan* (Gretna, La.: Pelican Classics, 1951). MacPherson's introduction is, however, considerably longer than Schneider's (154 pages vs. 7 pages).

Hume, David, "Of The Original Contract," in Ernest Barker, *The Social Contract*. New York: Oxford University Press, 1960. Hume's critique of the social contract view of political obligation. (The quotation from Hume at the beginning of this chapter is on pp. 155–56 of this book.)

Locke, John, *The Second Treatise of Government*, Introduction by Thomas P. Peardon. Indianapolis: Bobbs-Merrill, 1952. Locke's social contract defense of limited government, preceded by an introduction by Peardon (16 pages). C.B. MacPherson supplies an introduction (14 pages) in the more recent Hackett Publishing Company edition of the same work (Indianapolis: Hackett, 1968). For a longer introduction by Peter Laslett (over 100 pages), see Locke's *Two Treatises of Government* (Cambridge: Cambridge University Press, 1960; reprinted in The New American Library in 1963).

Rousseau, Jean-Jacques, *The Social Contract*. Baltimore, Md.: Penguin Books, 1968. The Penguin edition was translated from the original French by Maurice Cranston, who also wrote the introduction (34 pages). The St. Martin's Press edition of *The Social Contract* (1978), translated by Judith R. Masters, has an introduction (40 pages) by Roger D. Masters. Both translations are good.

civil disobedience

Bedau, Hugo Adam, *Civil Disobedience: Theory and Practice*. New York: Pegasus, 1968. An excellent anthology of articles expressing different viewpoints on the civil disobedience issue. The anthology was published in the late 1960's when many turned to civil disobedience in protest of the war in Vietnam or of racism. The book begins with David Thoreau's "Civil Disobedience" (1849), a defense of individual conscience over the authority of law. (The quote from Thoreau at the beginning of this chapter can be found on pp. 28–29 of this anthology.) All the other selections in the book are from twentieth-century authors. After the Thoreau selection there then follows selections on the issue of civil disobedience as a means of protesting racism or wars that are perceived to be unjust. Included in the section on civil disobedience and racism is Martin Luther King's famous "Letter from Birmingham City Jail," which defends the moral right to disobey unjust laws. The book ends with three general theoretical essays by contemporary philosophers expressing divergent views on the conditions that justify civil disobedience.

Fortas, Abe, *Concerning Dissent and Civil Disobedience*. New York: New American Library, Signet Classics, 1968. Fortas' provocative attempt to specify the conditions of justifiable disobedience, from which one of our selections was excerpted.

Lucas, J.R., *The Principles of Politics*. London: Oxford University Press, 1967. In this excellent book, which ranges over a wide range of issues in political philosophy, Lucas discusses the issue of civil disobedience in Sections 72 and 73 (pp. 319–32). (The quote from Lucas at the beginning of this chapter comes from pp. 319–20 of this work.) Lucas argues against anarchistic views, such as that presented by Robert Paul Wolff in his *Defense of Anarchism*. Those interested in the moral dilemma of choosing between the dictates of private conscience and public law would find it rewarding to compare both positions.

The Monist, Volume 54, No. 4 (October 1970). *The Monist* is a philosophical periodical published four times yearly. Each issue is devoted to a single philosophical topic. This issue consisting of seven philosophical articles is devoted to the general topic of "Legal Obligation and Civil Disobedience." The articles range over a broad area and express diverse points of view. Those interested in a critical analysis of Fortas' position in *Concerning Dissent and Civil Disobedience* will find quite valuable Alan Gewirth's article "Civil Disobedience, Law and Morality: An Examination of Justice Fortas' Doctrine."

Murphy, Jeffrie G., *Civil Disobedience and Violence*. Encino, Ca.: Wadsworth, 1971. An anthology of classical and contemporary sources on the general topic of civil disobedience, with an emphasis upon the compatibility of violence with civil disobedience. Thoreau's essay on civil disobedience is included.

Van Den Haag, Ernest, "Government, Conscience and Disobedience," in *Philosophy: A Modern Encounter*, ed. Robert Paul Wolff. Englewood Cliffs, N.J.: Prentice-Hall, 1971. (Reprinted from *Sidney Hook and the Contemporary World*, ed. Paul Kurtz, New York: John Day Company, 1968). In this sensitive essay, Van Den Haag, a distinguished conservative, clearly and forcefully captures the moral dilemma involved in choosing between the dictates of law and of individual conscience. While arguing for various general principles for resolving such dilemmas, Van Den Haag in the end concedes defeat in resolving this issue. (The quote from Van Den Haag at the beginning of this chapter comes from this work—p. 463 of the Wolff anthology.)

Wolff, Robert Paul, *In Defense of Anarchism*. New York: Harper & Row, 1970. A contemporary defense of the view that, regardless of the form of government, citizens have no moral obligation to obey laws they believe to be wrong. (The quote from Wolff at the beginning of this chapter comes from p. 18 of this work.)

Zinn, Howard, *Disobedience and Democracy: Nine Fallacies in Law and Order*. New York: Vintage Books, 1968. Zinn's heated rejoinder (a selection from which is included in our anthology) to Fortas' book *Concerning Dissent and Civil Disobedience*.

liberty and the enforcement of morals

Berger, Fred, ed., *Freedom of Expression*. Belmont, Ca.: Wadsworth Publishing Company, 1980. An anthology of selections by contemporary analytic philosophers which explore the theoretical and practical problems that arise in connection with the scope of the right to freedom of expression. Also included are selections from various legal cases that are relevant to the philosophical discussions which are included.

Berlin, Isaiah, "Two Concepts of Liberty" and "John Stuart Mill and the Ends of Life," in *Four Essays on Liberty*. New York: Oxford University Press, 1969. In the first of these well-known essays, Berlin distinguishes and discusses the concepts of *positive* and *negative freedom*. In the second, he discusses Mill's commitment to the value of individual freedom.

Brandeis, Louis, dissent in *Olmstead v. United States*, 277 U.S. 438 (1928). This 1928 Supreme Court case concerned the issue of whether or not wiretapping violates the Fourth Amendment's protection against "unreasonable searches and seizures" and/or the Fifth Amendment's protection against "self-incrimination." The majority of the court, with Chief Justice Taft writing the majority opinion, claimed that wiretapping did not violate the Constitution. Justice Holmes and Brandeis dissented. Brandeis' elegant defense of the value of individual privacy over that of more efficient crime control had a great influence on subsequent Supreme Court decisions, especially during the years of the Warren Court (1953–69), a period in which the Court often utilized a right to privacy, which it found to be implicit in the Bill of Rights as a justification for enlarging the rights of individuals. (The quote from Brandeis at the beginning of this chapter comes from Brandeis' dissent in the Olmstead case.) This dissent can be found in most casebooks on criminal or constitutional law; for example, see *Criminal Law and Its Processes,* eds. Monrad G. Paulsen and Sanford H. Kadish (Boston: Little, Brown and Company, 1962 and subsequent editions). The legal cases included and discussed in law school casebooks provide excellent source material for opposing arguments as to the scope of the individual liberties guaranteed by the Bill of Rights.

Capaldi, Nicholas, ed., *Clear and Present Danger: The Free Speech Controversy*. New York: Pegasus, 1969. In this anthology of selections concerning the free speech controversy, the views of influential political figures (e.g., Hitler, Andrei Vishinsky, and Robert Welch), as well as political theorists and philosophical analysts, are represented. Published during a period of political turmoil which was reflected in student unrest at college campuses during that period, the anthology has sections devoted to the issues of academic freedom and academic political activism.

Devlin, Patrick, *The Enforcement of Morals*. London: Oxford University Press, 1965. A collection of Devlin's essays on the general topic of morality and law. The key essay is ''Morals and the Criminal Law'' (excerpted in our anthology), which is a slightly revised version of a lecture Devlin presented in 1959 under the title of ''The Enforcement of Morals.'' In addition to this essay, of particular interest is the essay ''Mill on Liberty and Morals,'' which provides a critical analysis of Mill's position in *On Liberty*.

Hart, H.L.A., *Law, Liberty and Morality*. New York: Random House, 1963. A critique of Devlin by a famed legal philosopher in the tradition of Mill. In addition to his criticisms of Devlin's position, Hart presents his own position on the legitimate coercive powers of the state over the individual. The book is short and very readable. Highly recommended.

Skinner, B.F., *Beyond Freedom and Dignity*. New York: Bantam, 1971. An influential contemporary behavioral psychologist's widely read (hard-deterministic) criticism of the traditional picture of human beings as ''free and morally responsible.'' Continuing with the theme of his utopian novel *Walden Two*, Skinner advocates a societal commitment to behavioral engineering. Skinner presents the same view in his earlier essay ''Freedom and the Control of Men,'' *The American Scholar*, Winter 1955–56, pp. 47–65. (The quote from Skinner at the beginning of this chapter comes from this essay.)

Wasserstrom, R., ed., *Morality and the Law*. Encino, Ca.: Wadsworth, 1971. An excellent anthology of material on the question of the state's right to enforce morals. Included are excerpts from Mill's *On Liberty,* Devlin's ''Morals and the Criminal Law,'' and discussions of the issues raised by Devlin by the philosophers H.L.A. Hart, Ronald Dworkin, and A.R. Louch. In addition, there is a discussion of the justification of paternalistic laws by the philosopher Gerald Dworkin, a discussion by Louis Schwartz, a law professor, of the American Law Institute's treatment of moral offenses in its 1962 draft of its *Model Penal Code*, and excerpts from the judicial opinions in four cases involving the enforcement of morality.

Wolff, Robert Paul, *The Poverty of Liberalism*. Boston: Beacon Press, 1968. A clear and well known critique of the point of view expressed by John Stuart Mill in *On Liberty*.

INDEX